DEBATES IN THE DIGITAL HUMANITIES 2016

DEBATES
IN THE
DIGITAL
HUMANITIES

2016

Matthew K. Gold and Lauren F. Klein

EDITORS

DEBATES IN THE DIGITAL HUMANITIES

University of Minnesota Press
Minneapolis
London

Published by the University of Minnesota Press
111 Third Avenue South, Suite 290
Minneapolis, MN 55401-2520
http://www.upress.umn.edu

ISSN 2380-5927
ISBN 978-0-8166-9953-7 (hc)
ISBN 978-0-8166-9954-4 (pb)

Printed in the United States of America on acid-free paper

The University of Minnesota is an equal-opportunity educator and employer.

22 21 20 19 18 17 16   10 9 8 7 6 5 4 3 2 1

Contents

PART III

Digital Humanities and Its Practices

PART IV

Digital Humanities and the Disciplines

SERIES INTRODUCTION AND EDITORS' NOTE

Digital Humanities: The Expanded Field

LAUREN F. KLEIN AND MATTHEW K. GOLD

If the publication of the first volume of *Debates in the Digital Humanities* in 2012 marked the "digital humanities moment," this volume—and the series that will bear its name—confirms that the digital humanities, as a field, has arrived. Along with the digital archives, quantitative analyses, and tool-building projects that once characterized the field, DH now encompasses a wide range of methods and practices: visualizations of large image sets, 3D modeling of historical artifacts, "born digital" dissertations, hashtag activism and the analysis thereof, alternate reality games, mobile makerspaces, and more. In what has been called "big tent" DH, it can at times be difficult to determine with any specificity what, precisely, digital humanities work entails.

This definitional dilemma is not unique to DH. In 1979, the art historian Rosalind Krauss, prompted by the realization that the term "sculpture" had come to describe a wide array of forms and practices, reflected on the preceding ten years of developments in the field. "Nothing," she observed, "could possibly give to such a motley of effort the right to lay claim to whatever one might mean by the category of sculpture. Unless, that is, the category can be made to become almost infinitely malleable" (30). A "motley of effort"? An "infinitely malleable" term? Transported to the present, she could just as well be describing the last decade of DH.

But where digital humanists have, for the most part, embraced the "free-floating signifier" that is DH, Krauss viewed the elasticity of her field's designated term as a liability, a loss of precision in a discipline that, as a result of its expanding scope, demanded more, not less, specificity (Kirschenbaum). In "Sculpture in the Expanded Field," an essay now firmly ensconced in the art historical canon, Krauss argues that certain distinctions among objects of study and among disciplinary fields remain important to uphold. The result of placing sculpture within an "expanded field" is that it becomes "no longer the privileged middle term between the things that it isn't." Rather, it emerges as "only one term on the periphery of a field in which there are other, differently structured possibilities" (Krauss, 38). And the "differently structured possibilities" for the digital humanities are what, we believe, the notion of an expanded field helps unfold.

The first volume of *Debates in the Digital Humanities* was bound together by the "big tent," the metaphor that rose to prominence following the 2011 ADHO annual conference, which designated "Big Tent Digital Humanities" as its theme. But in that volume and elsewhere, critics debated the degree to which the openness and inclusivity connoted by the metaphor could ever truly be achieved. Melissa Terras expressed concern that the big tent of DH, like those employed by the evangelical groups of the nineteenth-century United States, whose outdoor revival meetings inspired the phrase, might be less welcoming—due to scholarly status, institutional support, and financial resources—than those already on the inside would hope or believe ("Peering inside the Big Tent"). Patrik Svensson, similarly, in exploring the "problematic" assumption of inclusivity, suggested that "the community might instead benefit from a 'no tent' approach," thereby clearing the ground for "alternative structuring devices and ideational notions" such as the "meeting space" or "trading zone" ("Beyond the Big Tent"). And yet the "big tent" metaphor persists; or, more accurately, while it continues to be challenged—see, for instance, Amy Earhart's keynote at the 2015 CSDH/SCHN ACH Joint Conference—it has not yet been replaced by any of the "alternative structuring devices" that have been proposed.[1]

This is where the notion of the digital humanities as an expanded field might enter. In Krauss's formulation, the expanded field is constructed by the relationships among key concepts, rather than by a single umbrella term. And it is by exploring these relations—their tensions as well as their alignments—that the specific contributions of the range of forms and practices encompassed by the field can be brought to light. Instead of insisting that practice performs the same work as theory, for instance, we might ask how each contributes differently to the diverse ecology of digital humanities scholarship. Rather than requiring that the tool-building work of an ImagePlot or a Bookworm, to name two recent contributions to that domain, speak directly to their objects of analysis, we might explore how the creation and deployment of such tools perform distinct but equally valuable functions—functions that must be considered in relation to each other to achieve their maximal effect. The model of an expanded field is one that aims to foreclose the question of "who's in and who's out" by allowing the "differently structured possibilities" of the digital humanities to emerge.

The critique of a model that aims to assimilate and neutralize difference is, of course, as old as the model itself. While we depart from Krauss in our belief that difference can play out within rather than apart from an expanded field of DH, we must remain vigilant in our attention to the larger structures of power—social and political as much as institutional and disciplinary—that preclude certain relationships from ever unfolding on an equal plane. In adapting the notion of an expanded field to apply to the digital humanities, we might therefore attempt to envision an analogue of Krauss's model in multidimensional space, rather than as a diagram on the page. DH, in this vision, appears suspended between, among, and through a range of forces; taken together and perceived together, these vectors structure the expanded field.

This particular vision has emerged from our realization that the challenges currently associated with the digital humanities involve a shift from congregating in the big tent to practicing DH at a field-specific level, where DH work confronts disciplinary habits of mind. To be sure, DHers have long faced the difficulty of making their work legible to colleagues in their home disciplines. But the anxieties that filled the first volume of *Debates in the Digital Humanities,* often focusing on the tensions that individual practitioners experienced as they argued tenure and promotion cases before colleagues who had trouble even conceiving of DH work as scholarship, have been replaced by more forceful grappling with DH at the disciplinary level, most often by scholars from the disciplines who have looked in vain to see their concerns represented in DH.

Multiple contributors to this volume take up disciplinary issues directly, exploring how their digital humanities work might speak to their home disciplines or across several disciplines—from history (Blevins) to book history (Stauffer) to the humanities writ large (Nowviskie). Just as often, contributors argue for the impact that their disciplinary homes—Africana/Black studies (Gallon), art history (Battles and Maizels), and archaeology (Watrall), to name only a few—might make to DH. This reflects a crucial decentering of the digital humanities, one that acknowledges how its methods and practices both influence and are influenced by other fields. Rather than diminish the impact of DH, however, these examples enrich its discourse and extend its reach.

As DH is increasingly practiced and perceived in a broader context, the scale of the field, as well as its scope, has emerged as a key issue—and along with the issue of scale, an inquiry into the nature and limits of scale itself. In 2015, multiple conferences focused on questions of scale, including "Scale and Value," a symposium held at the University of Washington, and "Cultural Analytics: Computational Approaches to the Study of Literature," held at the University of Chicago.[2] At these conferences and in other venues, scholars contested methods and measured ambitions, all in the wake of a debate triggered by Matthew Jockers's release of his Syuzhet software package for plot analysis, which drew criticism from a number of quarters.[3] This discussion about scale, its meaning, and its use has brought increased disciplinary specificity and conceptual rigor to the questions about the impact of DH work that have been posed since the field's inception.

In this volume, we take up the issues associated with a digital humanities at scale at two levels. In the forum "Text Analysis at Scale," eight DH scholars offer their views on the stakes of research that focuses on large-scale text analysis. (As the series moves forward, each annual volume will feature a forum on a major issue currently under debate in the field.) More broadly, in our choice of section titles—"DH and Its Methods," "DH and Its Practices," "DH and the Disciplines," and "DH and Its Critics"—we aim to reflect the expanded contours of the field. Here, scope and scale converge as we envision a measure for the field that is not merely additive, but instead delineates its capacious frame. It is a "DH + 1" of the form that Alan Liu calls for in his "Plea for Cross-Domain Data," one that does not erase difference but "operationalizes" it as a generative force (Liu, chapter 50 in this volume). The DH of this volume is one that represents the debates of the field as interrelated, yet not always perfectly aligned. Their differences, coupled with their shared focus, accentuate the meaningful tensions and the unresolved challenges that the recent growth of the field has produced.

The notion of a field that operates through relation, one that informs and is informed by allied disciplines, also clears the conceptual space to acknowledge how multiple disciplines and their methods have helped to constitute the digital humanities from its inception. Scholars have long cited Father Roberto Busa and his punch-card concordances as the field's origin story. Only recently has this narrative been expanded to include the contributions of the female "computers"[4]—those we would now call programmers—who designed and implemented much of the project (Terras and Nyhan, chapter 6 in this volume). This ongoing historical and ethnographic work, coupled with the archival research of Steven E. Jones[5] and the media archaeology of Geoffrey Rockwell and Stefan Sinclair, have together helped to constitute a far richer lodestone for the field.[6] But the methods employed by these scholars owe as much to approaches honed in the fields of women's studies, labor studies, media studies, information studies, and the history of science as they do to digital humanities techniques. Understanding digital humanities as an expanded field can help ensure that the specificity of these methods and their own rich histories can be brought to bear on DH, and vice versa.

It is not only a more nuanced origin story that the notion of an expanded field can help to achieve. In this volume and elsewhere, scholars have begun to suggest that the digital humanities owes its existence to more than one source. Amy Earhart has alerted the field to the "diverse histories of the digital humanities" in the form of projects that place women and people of color at their center.[7] Jentery Sayers and William Turkel, in calling for an approach that interweaves digital humanities with physical fabrication, place DH in dialogue with design communities, which have also long theorized practice-based research.[8] In seeking a digital humanities that accounts for the localized nature of all such work, Alex Gil and others involved with Global Outlook::Digital Humanities have developed a "minimal computing" working group aimed at enacting a vision for DH in places where WiFi connections are absent or spotty and where all available hardware is already years old.[9] In addition to enabling DH work as we currently understand it, this vision also, necessarily, includes an expanding conception of what other DH work might entail. Such work, exemplified in the "technological disobedience" of Cuban artist and designer Ernesto Oroza, whom Gil interviews here, helpfully dislocates DH from a U.S.-centric approach and suggests new sites and potential scales for the field.

Several scholars in this volume also explore what DH means for student and faculty populations at schools excluded from the conventional research university model, such as community colleges (McGrail), liberal arts colleges (Buurma and Levine), and historically black colleges and universities (Earhart and Taylor). These developments draw broadly upon the field's increased attention to the accessibility and sustainability of DH work—both the degree to which this work is open to different populations and the extent to which it will persist for future generations of scholars.[10]

Central to the 2012 volume of *Debates in the Digital Humanities* was an interrogation and critique of the field and its claims. In the intervening years, DH has seen no shortage of criticism, and this volume continues to highlight challenges to the ambitions and claims of DH scholarship. Building on contributions to the first volume that engaged issues of race and gender, the 2016 edition identifies the unexamined political valences of ecological metaphors in DH work (Linley), explores the monolingual/U.S.-centric bias of work in DH and beyond (Fiormonte), and ponders the "dark side" of the digital humanities (Chun et al.). At the same time, several pieces in the collection sketch out recuperative visions informed by critique, including the manifesto-like exploration of a "QueerOS" (Barnett et al.), an articulation of DH practice built on the equitable ethos of FemTechNet (Losh et al.), and the evolving enactment of networked politics that is #transformDH (Bailey et al).

The 2012 edition of *Debates in the Digital Humanities* intervened in the discourse of the field by highlighting pedagogy as the neglected "stepchild" of DH, with several chapters arguing that teaching had been diminished in favor of research-focused projects (Brier; Waltzer). That volume included an entire section on "Teaching the Digital Humanities" as a way of redressing this lack. In the ensuing years, pedagogy has become a central point of concern and investment through institutional projects such as the DH Summer Institute (DHSI) and the Humanities Intensive Learning and Teaching Institute (HILT), grant-funded gatherings such as the NEH-sponsored DH at Community Colleges Institute and the Regional Digital Humanities Pedagogy Project, multiple journals focused on pedagogy such as *The Journal of Interactive Technology and Pedagogy* and *Hybrid Pedagogy,* and emerging publications such as the HASTAC Pedagogy Project and *Digital Pedagogy in the Humanities: Concepts, Models, and Experiments.* Discussions of pedagogy routinely take place in social media through hashtags such as the Digital Pedagogy Lab's #digiped. Given this saturation, we chose not to isolate discussions of pedagogy from other areas of the book and instead attempted a "baked-in" approach, where work on pedagogy from scholars is integrated into various chapters as theory (Fyfe), as practice (Selisker; Cordell), and as politics (Earhart and Taylor; Losh et al.).

Indeed, *Debates in the Digital Humanities 2016* has a markedly political bent—not only because of the institutional politics associated with the digital humanities as an emerging field. In a year that saw renewed attention to the entrenched nature of state-authorized violence against black bodies at the same time that scholars who spoke out against these and other acts of systemic injustice found job offers revoked, the stakes for a more explicitly political digital humanities have been raised. "Artist-theorists, programming humanists, [and] activist-scholars" who Tara McPherson called upon, in the first edition of *Debates in the Digital Humanities,* to pursue broader contexts and "promiscuous border crossings," have a significant presence in this volume and are represented here alongside scholars and practitioners who remain committed to the objects and methods that helped to first constitute the field, and deliberately so; these voices call DH and are called by DH into engagement and debate, ensuring that the digital humanities will continue to evolve and grow.

In 1979, Rosalind Krauss looked out across the Long Island landscape at a square-shaped hole in the ground, below which lay a provisional structure, "half atrium, half tunnel," supported by wooden beams (33). It was an earthwork, "Perimeters, Pavilions, Decoys," by the American artist Mary Miss, and it challenged Krauss's sense of sculpture to the very core. "And so we stare at the pit in the earth and think we both do and don't know what sculpture is," she observed. Standing before the landscape of the digital humanities and contemplating the present contours of the field, we find ourselves at a similar moment of simultaneous knowing and unknowing, rootedness and dislocation. We know DH in large part because it names itself, yet what it names seems increasingly malleable and at times difficult to grasp. As editors devoted to tracking the evolution of the field, its meanings, and its implications, we find the best guides to be the conversations that take place around these issues. Across the lines of discussion that follow, we see our colleagues trace out possibilities and problems, paradigms and potentialities. We posit the book as a reflection of the current, site-specific conditions of the field. In the multivalent shape of its arguments, progressing across a range of platforms and environments, *Debates in the Digital Humanities 2016* offers a vision of DH as an expanded field—a vision of new possibilities, differently structured.

NOTES

1. The tweets from Earhart's keynote are collected here: https://storify.com/beherbert/joint-ach-canadian-dh-conference-2015.

2. The "Scale and Value" conference is documented at: http://scaleandvalue.tumblr.com/; the cultural analytics conference can be found at: http://neubauercollegium.uchicago.edu/events/uc/cultural_analytics/.

3. The Syuzhet package can be found here: https://github.com/mjockers/syuzhet; a record of the initial conversation on Twitter can be found here: https://storify.com/clancynewyork/contretemps-a-syuzhet.

4. http://melissaterras.blogspot.com/2013/10/for-ada-lovelace-day-father-busas.html.

5. http://stevenejones.org/2015/06/09/fordham-poster.

6. Jones's monograph, *Roberto Busa, S.J., and The Emergence of Humanities Comput-ing: The Priest and the Punched Cards,* is forthcoming from Routledge; Rockwell and Sinclair's work has been presented at *Digital Humanities 2014* and other venues. See: http://www.researchgate.net/publication/273449857_Towards_an_Archaeology_of_Text_Analy sis_Tools.

7. See Earhart's blog at: http://dhhistory.blogspot.com/.

8. For examples, see the University of Victoria's Maker Lab: http://maker.uvic.ca /insight/.

9. The Global Outlook website is located at: http://www.globaloutlookdh.org/; the minimal computing working group can be found at: http://www.globaloutlookdh.org /minimal-computing/.

10. George Williams's "Accessible Future" project provides the most sustained atten-tion to accessibility in the field: http://www.accessiblefuture.org/; Bethany Nowviskie's keynote at *Digital Humanities 2014* frames a number of key issues of sustainability for a DH audience: http://nowviskie.org/2014/anthropocene/.

BIBLIOGRAPHY

Brier, Stephen. "Where's the Pedagogy? The Role of Teaching and Learning in the Digital Humanities." In *Debates in the Digital Humanities,* ed. Matthew K. Gold. Minneapo-lis: University of Minnesota Press, 2012. http://dhdebates.gc.cuny.edu/debates/text/8.

Kirschenbaum, Matthew. "What Is Digital Humanities and What Is It Doing in English Departments?" In *Debates in the Digital Humanities,* ed. Matthew K. Gold. Minneapo-lis: University of Minnesota Press, 2012. http://dhdebates.gc.cuny.edu/debates/text/38.

Krauss, Rosalind. "Sculpture in the Expanded Field." *October* 8 (Spring 1979): 30–44.

McPherson, Tara. "Why Are the Digital Humanities So White? or Thinking the Histories of Race and Computation." In *Debates in the Digital Humanities,* ed. Matthew K. Gold. Minneapolis: University of Minnesota Press, 2012. http://dhdebates.gc.cuny .edu/debates/text/29.

Svensson, Patrik. "Beyond the Big Tent." In *Debates in the Digital Humanities,* ed. Matthew K. Gold. Minneapolis: University of Minnesota Press, 2012. http://dhdebates.gc.cuny .edu/debates/text/22.

Terras, Melissa. "Peering inside the Big Tent: Digital Humanities and the Crisis of Inclu-sion." Author's blog, July 26, 2011. http://melissaterras.blogspot.com/2011/07/peering-inside-big-tent-digital.html.

Waltzer, Luke. "Digital Humanities and the 'Ugly Stepchildren' of American Higher Edu-cation. In *Debates in the Digital Humanities,* ed. Matthew K. Gold. Minneapolis: University of Minnesota Press, 2012. http://dhdebates.gc.cuny.edu/debates/text/33.

PART I

HISTORIES AND FUTURES OF THE DIGITAL HUMANITIES

The Emergence of the Digital Humanities
(as the Network Is Everting)

STEVEN E. JONES

C yberspace is everting, as author William Gibson has repeatedly said, turning inside out and leaking out into the physical world. When he coined the
term in the early 1980s cyberspace was a metaphor for the global information network, but in the decade that followed, it made a material difference in technology and culture and in the perceived relation between the two. Now, as Gibson
and others have recently noted, the term has started to fray around the edges, has
begun to sound quaintly archaic and to fade from use.[1] In one sense, Gibson is just
overwriting his earlier metaphor (cyberspace) with a new one (eversion). As he has
a character say in the 2007 novel *Spook Country,* there never was any cyberspace,
really. It was just a way of understanding the culture's relation to networked technology (Gibson, 64).

But I think the new term, *eversion,* articulates something significant about a
recent shift in the collective understanding of the network: from a world apart to a
part of the world, from a transcendent virtual reality to a ubiquitous grid of data that
we move through every day.[2] We can roughly date the shift—or at least the widespread dawning recognition of it—to 2004–2008. At that moment the quintessential
virtual world, Second Life, peaked and began to decline in terms of number of users
and the publicity surrounding it (Heath and Heath). At the same time, Nintendo's
motion-control Wii was introduced in 2006, helping to usher in the era of mixed-
reality casual gaming. So-called Web 2.0 social-network platforms, especially Facebook, were first introduced in 2004–2005, but came into their own, reaching a mass
user base in 2006–2007. These platforms depended on the massive increase in the
use of mobile technologies at the time. Apple's iPhone was previewed in 2006
and introduced in January 2007; the Android OS followed later that year. William
Gibson's novel *Spook Country,* in which he first articulated the eversion of cyberspace, was published early in 2007. Set in 2006, its story is based on the confluence
of augmented reality, locative art, viral marketing, pervasive surveillance, and the
security state in the wake of 9/11 and the wars in Afghanistan and Iraq. Characters

Shift from apart to merged

in the novel execute works of art (and engage in one direct-action protest) by lever-aging the cellular data networks, GPS satellite data, and the mobile and wireless web to tag or annotate the physical world, overlaying locations with data of various kinds, including 3D artistic visualizations. (Everyone in the book still flips their cell-phones open and closed, however, rather than poking at a multitouch interface, a telling detail that dates the writing to the just-pre-iPhone era.) The novel presents a media landscape in which the mundane has triumphed over the transcendent, but it is a mundane with a difference, and the difference is networked data. There is no cyberspace out there, because the network is down here, all around us.

The condition Gibson writes about corresponds to a shift noted by a number of media studies specialists working in different disciplines, what Katherine Hayles has identified as a fourth phase in the history of cybernetics, a shift from "virtuality" to "mixed reality," to "environments in which physical and virtual realms merge in fluid and seamless ways" ("Cybernetics," 147–48). In 2006, Adam Greenfield used terms much like Gibson's to describe what he called "everyware," ubiquitous or pervasive computing that, as Greenfield says, offers a radical alternative to "immersing a user in an information-space that never was"—and amounts to "something akin to vir-tual reality turned inside out" (*Everyware,* 73). More recently, Nathan Jurgenson has argued against "digital dualism," the fallacy that "the digital and the physical are separate," asserting instead that "the digital and physical are increasingly meshed" in augmented reality ("Digital Dualism versus Augmented Reality"). These obser-vations by authors with very different perspectives reflect a broader cultural change whose effects we are still experiencing, a multiplatform shift in the nature of our relation to networked technologies. It is not that (to borrow from Virginia Woolf) on or about December 2006 the character of the network changed. Nothing that sudden and clear-cut took place. But I do think that between about 2004 and 2008, the cumulative effect of a variety of changes in technology and culture culminated in a new consensual imagination of the role of the network in relation to the physi-cal and social world. The network was everting.

And at about that same moment, the digital humanities rather suddenly achieved a new level of public attention, emerging out of a decades-long tradition of humanities computing and marked by the term "digital humanities" itself—which was used in the title of a prominent collection published in 2004 and reached a kind of critical mass, in terms of public awareness and institutional influence, between 2004–2008.[3] While the earlier established practices of humanities computing con-tinued, the new-model digital humanities emphasized, for example, the analysis and visualization of large datasets of humanities materials, including what Franco Moretti named "distant reading" (*Graphs, Maps, Trees,* 1), engaged in coding and building digital tools and websites and archives as well as wearable processors and other devices, and responded to the "spatial turn" (Dear et al., 229, 238) across the disciplines with data-layered "thick mapping" projects.[4] It also increasingly turned its attention to new media and, in particular, owed a greater debt than has been fully recognized to video games and game theory. These new practices and areas of interest for computing in the humanities correspond to changes associated with the eversion of cyberspace in the culture at large. In one sense, the new digital humanities is humanities computing, everted.

Digital humanities, in its newly prominent forms, is both a response to and a contributing cause of the wider eversion, as can be glimpsed in the substitution performed at a crucial moment (in titling a collection of essays) from *digitized* to *digital* humanities; the intention was to avoid the reductive definition of DH as mere digitization (Kirschenbaum, "What Is Digital Humanities," 5). The term also reflected a larger change: from implying a separation between the stuff of the humanities—manuscripts, books, documents, maps, works of art of all kinds, other cultural artifacts—and computing, to more of a mixed reality, characterized by two-way interactions between the two realms, physical artifacts and digital media. Instead of only digitizing the archives of our cultural heritage in order to move them out onto the network (though that work continued, of course), many practitioners began to see themselves putting the digital into reciprocal conversation with an array of cultural artifacts, the objects on which humanistic study has historically been based and new kinds of objects, including born-digital artifacts. In new media, this kind of reciprocal interaction between data and artifacts, algorithm and world, has been effectively modeled for decades in video games.

The Eversion of the Network

First, I want to revisit cyberspace. Combining "cybernetics" and "space," William Gibson coined the term in a 1982 short story, "Burning Chrome" (as an imaginary brand name for a network device set in the 2030s), but it became famous in his 1984 cyberpunk novel *Neuromancer*. He later said that his vision of cyberspace—a disembodied virtual reality, a transcendent world made up of "clusters and constellations of data. Like city lights receding"—was inspired by watching arcade video game players as they leaned into their machines, bumping the cabinets and hitting the buttons. Gibson—who was not himself a gamer—imagined that the gamers were longing to be immersed in and to disappear into the virtual world on the other side of the screen, longing to transcend the body in physical "meat space" and be uploaded as pure consciousness into the digital matrix of cyberspace.[5] Thus Norbert Wiener's cybernetics, which was etymologically about "steerage" or human control of machines, was mutated to suggest a willing relinquishment of the bodily and the material in order to go to another place, another plane.[6] As Katherine Hayles has said, Gibson created cyberspace by "transforming a data matrix into a land-scape"—a place apart from the physical world—"in which narratives can happen" (Hayles, *How We Became Posthuman*, 38). This newly three-dimensional place, which Gibson characterized from the beginning in idealist terms as "a consensual hallucination," looked like a glowing abstract grid, as seen in the 1982 film *TRON*, for example, where, as in Plato's world of Forms, the contingencies of material reality and the body have been burned away, sublimated into green and amber phosphor.

For almost two decades most popular notions of the network were cyberspatial in their underlying assumptions. For example, it was often taken for granted that the ultimate goal of users interfacing with the network was total immersion, meaning the loss of body-consciousness as one disappeared into the digital world on the other side of the screen. Only imperfect technology stood in the way. This assumption owed much to 1980s and 1990s experiments in virtual reality in which a helmet or wraparound goggles replaced the physical sensorium as the user literally buried her head in cyberspace. Some of these early environments were in fact directly inspired by Gibson's vision of cyberspace. Hayles has said that his novels "acted like seed crystals thrown into a supersaturated solution" (*How We Became Posthuman*, 35).

But in the first decade of our new century, as I have said, Gibson overwrote his own metaphor, first and most explicitly in 2007's *Spook Country*. Thirty years after inventing cyberspace, he imagines a journalist, a curator, and a locative artist sitting in a booth in the restaurant of the Standard Hotel in Los Angeles, discussing new media and observing that in 2006 (when the story is set) cyberspace "is everting," turning inside out and flowing out into the world (*Spook Country*, 20). The artist dates the beginning of the change from May 1, 2000, when the U.S. government turned off Selective Availability to GPS satellite data, making it available to the general public, not just the military. Google Maps (the API for which was released in June 2005) and improved automobile navigation systems were the most immediate and widely experienced results. In the decade that followed, with the marked increase in the use of mobile devices and other pervasive processors and sensors, a cluster of activities emerged, circulating from artists' and hackers' subcultures to mainstream awareness and back again, practices that are still evolving: geocaching, hyperspatial tagging or spatially tagged hypermedia, locative installation art based on augmented reality, all overlapping with a larger trend, the pervasive use of embedded RFID (radio frequency identification) chips and NFC (near-field connection) chips and other markers, such as QR codes, on everyday physical objects. In 2012, Google announced the Google Glass project, an augmented-reality application using glasses containing location-aware networking technology and a heads-up augmented reality display. (The Google Glass prototype was suspended indefinitely in January 2015, at around the same time that Microsoft announced its own Holo-Lens project.) These developments emerged from work in ubicomp (ubiquitous computing) or the Internet of Things (see Weiser; Greenfield; Sterling). All involve bringing together the data grid with objects in the physical and social world—not leaving the one behind to escape into the other but deliberately overlayering them, with the expectation that users will experience the data anywhere, everywhere, while moving through the world—and mobility is a key feature of the experience.[7] By definition, such technologies afford dynamic hybrid experiences, taking place at the shifting border where digital data continually meets physical reality as the user moves out into and through the world and its objects. In *Spook Country*, a GIS-trained hacker who facilitates locative art projects explains that once cyberspace everts, "then there isn't any cyberspace," that in fact "there never was, if you want to look at it that way. It was a way we had of looking where we were headed, a direction. With the grid, we're here. This is the other side of the screen. Right here" (64).

The Emergence of the (New) Digital Humanities

It is the *process* of moving from one dominant metaphor to another, a direction or trajectory, from cyberspace out into the data-saturated world, that characterizes our sometimes tense and ambivalent relationship to technology at the moment. That is why I value the figure of eversion, a term for a complex process of turning. As a metaphor, eversion calls attention to the messy and uneven status of that process, the network's leaking, spilling its guts out into the world. The process is ongoing, and the results continue to complicate our engagements with humanities archives *and* new media. It is an often disorienting experience, like looking at a Klein bottle, affording a sense of newly exposed overlapping dimensions, of layers of data and cultural expression combining with the ambient environment via sensors and processors, with obvious attendant risks to privacy and civil liberties. This complex sense of promise and risk applies as well to the changing infrastructural networks of traditional as well as new digital humanities practices. Ian Bogost has challenged the humanities to turn itself outward, toward "the world at large, towards things of all kinds and all scales" ("Beyond the Elbow-patched Playground"). Indeed, that is the general direction of the digital humanities in the past decade, as the infrastructure of humanities practices, from teaching and research to publishing, peer review, and scholarly communication, is increasingly being turned inside out and exposed to the world. In that sense, the larger context of the eversion provides a hidden (in plain sight) dimension that helps to explain what all the fuss is about, as first documented for many outside the field in William Pannapacker's 2010 declaration in his *Chronicle of Higher Education* blog that digital humanities was "the next big thing," or in the coverage of "culturomics" and new digital humanities work in the "Humanities 2.0" series in *The New York Times* (2010–2011).[8]

The eversion provides a context as well for some debates happening within the digital humanities. For example, if the eversion coincides with the rise of the digital humanities in the new millennium, the increased emphasis on layerings of data with physical reality can help to distinguish aspects of the new-model digital humanities from traditional humanities computing. The two are clearly connected in a historical continuum, but the changes in the past decade open up a new focus and new fields of activity for digital humanities research. Digital humanities scholars have responded to the eversion as it has happened (and continues to happen). This is reflected on many fronts, including work with (relatively big) data, large corpora of texts, maps linked to data via GIS, and the study and archiving of born-digital and new-media objects. All of this was in the air, as they say, at the very moment the digital humanities emerged into public prominence. Simple juxtapositions are suggestive: Franco Moretti's influential book, *Graphs, Maps, Trees: Abstract Models for a Literary History,* was published in 2005, the same year that the Alliance of Digital Humanities Organizations (ADHO) was founded—and the same year the Google Maps API was released. The open-access online journal *Digital Humanities Quarterly* (DHQ) first appeared in 2007, the year of the iPhone, the publication of Gibson's *Spook Country,* and the completion of Kirschenbaum's *Mechanisms* (which was published in 2008). The NEH office dedicated to the field and its funding was established in 2008, but this was after a two-year staged development process. That same year, 2008, the first THATCamp "unconference" was sponsored by the Center for History and New Media at George Mason University. These juxtapositions have nothing to do with technological determinism. They are just meant to suggest that the emergence of the new digital humanities is not an isolated academic phenomenon. The institutional and disciplinary changes are part of a larger cultural shift, a rapid cycle of emergence and convergence in technology and culture.

Father Roberto Busa, S. J., who is routinely cited as the founder of humanities computing and text-based digital humanities for his work with computerized lexical concordances, wrote in 2004, in his foreword to the groundbreaking *Companion to Digital Humanities,* that humanities computing "is precisely the automation of every possible analysis of human expression . . . in the widest sense of the word, from music to the theater, from design and painting to phonetics."[9] Although he went on to say that its "nucleus remains the discourse of written texts," the capaciousness of "every possible analysis of human expression" should not be overlooked, especially in the context of the moment in which it was published (xvi). Rather than divide the methodological old dispensation from the new in ways that reduce both (such as differentiating humanities computing from studies of new media or as merely "instrumental" from more "theoretical" approaches), we would do better to recognize that changing cultural contexts in the era of the eversion have called for changing methods and areas of emphasis in digital humanities research.

In that light, it is clear that some of the newer forms of supposedly practical or instrumental digital humanities, which are central to the new DH, were produced in the first place by younger scholars working with a keen awareness of the developments I am grouping under the concept of the eversion, and with a sense of what these changes meant at the time for various technology platforms of interest to academic humanities. In the era of social networks, casual gaming, distributed cognition, augmented reality, the Internet of Things, and the geospatial turn, one segment of new digital humanities work took a hands-on, practical turn, yes ("more hack, less yack," as the THATCamp motto goes), but arguably based on theoretical insight as a kind of deliberate rhetorical gesture—a dialectical countermove to the still-prevailing idealisms associated with the cyberculture studies of the 1990s. Much of the practical digital humanities work during the decade that followed, which formed an important core of the newly emergent DH, was undertaken not in avoidance of theory or in pursuit of scientist positive knowledge or enhanced instrumentality, but *against disembodiment,* against the ideology of cyberspace. The new digital humanities more often than not worked to question "screen essentialism" (Montfort, "Continuous Paper"), the immateriality of digital texts, and other reductive assumptions, including romantic constructions of the network as a world apart, instead emphasizing the complex materialities of digital platforms and digital objects. New digital humanities work—including digital forensics, critical code studies, platform studies, game studies, not to mention work with linguistic data and large corpora of texts, data visualization, and distant reading—is a collective response by one segment of the digital humanities community to the wider cultural shift toward a more worldly, layered, hybrid experience of digital data and digital media brought into direct contact with physical objects, in physical space, from archived manuscripts to Arduino circuit boards.

In this context, the digital humanities looks like a transitional set of practices at a crucial juncture, moving between, on the one hand, old ideas of the "digital" and the "humanities" and, on the other hand, a new mixed-reality humanities, worldly in a complicated way, mediating between the physical artifacts and archives on which humanities discourse has historically been built and the new mobile and pervasive digital networks that increasingly overlay and make those artifacts into "spime"-like things, encountered via multilayered interfaces.[10] Gibson remarked in an interview that "the eversion continues to distribute itself."[11] That distribution is inevitably uneven and not always well understood. One job for the digital humanities in the present moment might be consciously to engage with, to help make sense of, and to shape the dynamic process of that ongoing eversion (and its distribution) out in the world at large.

The Example of Video Games

Given the role of games in the history of computing, it should come as no surprise that humanities computing and digital humanities work have involved games and gamelike environments, from early MUDs and MOOs to the experimental Ivanhoe game developed at the University of Virginia (the work of important DH scholars Johanna Drucker, Jerome McGann, Bethany Nowviskie, Stephen Ramsay, and Geoffrey Rockwell, among others), to Matthew Kirschenbaum's inclusion of video games as among the objects of his digital-forensics approach (2008) and the project on Preserving Virtual Worlds involving Kirschenbaum and others (McDonough et al.). This is not to mention explicit video game studies by specialists in information studies, new media and digital media, or electronic literature, not all of whom always see themselves as working in digital humanities but whose work has unquestionably contributed to the field.

Video games are among the most prominent and influential forms of new media today, and the study of games as new media can be situated at the other end of the spectrum from more traditional text-based humanities computing. But it is important to recognize that continuous spectrum. Games are potentially significant cultural expressions, worthy of study in their own right, and digital humanities approaches, alongside approaches from other fields and disciplines, have much to contribute to that study. But, to turn the relationship around, games are also central to the fundamental concerns of the digital humanities in the present moment on a structural and theoretical level. Video games have much to teach the digital humanities because they are algorithmic, formally sophisticated systems that model in particular ways the general dynamics of the eversion. Games are designed to structure fluid relationships, between digital data and the gameworld, on the one hand, and between digital data and the player in the physical world, on the other hand. A number of fictional works have looked at this crossover aspect of video games, their role as models of the multidimensional relation of data and the world, including David Kaplan and Eric Zimmerman's short film *PLAY* (2010), Ernest Cline's novel *Ready Player One* (2011), and Neal Stephenson's novel *Reamde* (2011), along with theoretical game studies by Jane McGonigal, Ian Bogost (2011), or Mary Flanagan (2009). McGonigal, who is the creator of several of the most influential cross-platform ARGs (Alternate Reality Games)—played collectively across the Internet, phone lines, television and other media, and real-world settings using GPS coordinates to locate clues revealed on websites, on TV, or in film trailers—argues that we should apply the structures of games to real-world personal and social problems (*Reality Is Broken*). As a result, she has been accused of indirectly abetting the "gamification" trend, most notoriously associated at first with Facebook games like Zynga's Farmville, which critics see as colonizing players' everyday lives for commercial profit by reductive, exploitative, and addictive games blatantly designed according to principles of operant conditioning (Bogost, "Gamification Is Bullshit" and "Reality Is Alright"). Gamification, Ian Bogost says, is really just a kind of "expolitationware." But even it can be seen as responding to larger changes in media and culture. It is significant that the underlying premise shared by both McGonigal's world-saving games and crass gamification—and shared as well by critics of gamification—is that video games are now "busting through to reality" as never before—as developer Jesse Schell said in one notorious talk—crossing over from the gameworld to the player's real world ("Design outside the Box"). In other words, in its own unwitting way, gamification is yet another sign of the eversion.

Cyberspace was always gamespace in another guise—gamespace *dis*-placed. Not only was Gibson inspired by arcade gamers when he came up with the concept, he also interpreted the gamers' desires in terms of popular misconceptions about the effects and motivations of playing video games, in an example of what Katie Salen and Eric Zimmerman have called the "immersive fallacy," the assumption that the goal of any new media experience is to transport the user into a sublime and disembodied virtual world. On the contrary, Salen and Zimmerman argue, most gaming has historically taken place at the interface of player and game, the boundary of physical space and gamespace, where heads-up displays, controllers and peripheral devices, and social interactions are part of the normal video game experience. Salen and Zimmerman see a "hybrid consciousness," a sense of being simultaneously in the gameworld and in physical reality, as the norm, not the supposed "pining for immersion" that many assume is driving the experience (*Rules of Play*, 458, 451–55). However deeply engaged players become, however riveted their attention, the experience of gameplay has always been more mixed reality than virtual reality. In other words, the relation of gamer to gameworld is more cybernetics than cyberspace, literally more mundane than has been imagined by many, especially many nongamers.

In the past decade, a major development in gaming has borne out this multilayered view of digital media in general and has undermined the cyberspatial ideology of total immersion: what game theorist Jesper Juul calls a "casual revolution." Nintendo's Wii console, introduced in 2006, led the way by tapping into the mass market of first-time gamers or nongamers and shifting attention by design from the rendering of realistic, 3D virtual gameworlds to the physical and social space of the player's living room (Jones and Thiruvathukal). The Wii is all about the mixed-reality experience of using a sometimes kludgy set of motion-control peripherals, connected in feedback loops that turn the living room into a kind of personal area network for embodied gameplay. It is that hybrid space where Wii gameplay takes place—with a TV but also a coffee table in it, and perhaps other people playing along, as well as various peripherals beaming data to and from the console—not some imaginary world on the other side of the screen. When Microsoft's Kinect appeared in 2010, it was marketed as a gadget-free, transparent version of a somatic motion-control interface. It actually works, however, by taking the sensor system's gadgets out of the user's hand (or out from under her feet) and placing them up by the screen, looking back out at the room. In practice, Kinect play is very much like Wii play in its focus on the player's body moving around in the living room. A flood of hacks and homebrew applications for Kinect have focused on it not as a virtual-reality machine but as a system for connecting digital data and the physical world.

In this regard the Wii and Kinect, and mobile and casual gaming in general, have only reemphasized a fundamental aspect of all digital games. Writing about text-based adventure games and interactive fiction, generically among the earliest examples of computer games, Nick Montfort has said that the two fundamental components of such games are the world model—"which represents the physical environment of the interactive fiction and the things in that environment"—and the parser—"that part of the program that accepts natural language from the interactor and processes it" (*Twisty Little Passages*, ix). Although he is careful not to extend this model to video games in general, it offers an important general analogy. All computer games are about the productive relationship of algorithmically processed data and imagined world models, which include representations of place (maps, trees) and artifacts (weapons, tools, other inventory). One plays in collaboration or competition with other players, nonplayer characters, or the "artificial intelligence" (in the colloquial sense) that is the overall design of the game, negotiating between the two: data and world. At the same time, one plays from an embodied position in the real physical world. That betweenness is the condition of engaged gameplay, the "hybrid consciousness" that Salen and Zimmerman refer to. Even a game with an apparently immersive gameworld, whether realistically rendered (e.g., Skyrim) or iconically rendered (e.g., Minecraft), is *played* between worlds, at the channels where data flows back and forth in feedback loops. That is why heads-up displays, representing maps and inventories and stats of various kinds, and other affordances of gaming persist, not to mention discussion boards, constantly revised Wikipedia articles, and other paratextual materials surrounding gameplay, even for games that emphasize the immersive beauties or sublimities of their represented gameworlds. The digital humanities could do much worse than to look to games for examples of complex mixed-reality systems responding to the contingencies of the network at the present moment. It is hard to think of a more widely distributed and widely experienced set of dynamic models of the larger process of eversion than video games. The network does not evert by itself, of course. It is not really turning *itself* inside out. That requires human agency, actors out in the world, just as games require players and just as digital humanities research requires scholar-practitioners, work-ing in the channels of the eversion, where the data network meets the world in its material, artifactual particulars.

NOTES

My thanks to peer reviewers for their very helpful comments on an earlier draft of this essay, including Tanner Higgin, Dave Parry, Jentery Sayers, and Claire Warwick, as well as to the participants in my spring 2012 graduate seminar, English 415; the collective Tumblr created for that class is available here: http://networkeverts.tumblr.com.

1. See Shirky (195–96), who echoes Gibson on the term cyberspace and its fad-ing. In a Twitter exchange on November 27, 2011, @scottdot asked, "Who the hell says 'cyber'-anything anymore?" and Gibson himself responded: "I have said that myself, many times."

2. By "the network" I deliberately refer to the popular, imprecise notion that com-bines the World Wide Web and the Internet with interoperating networks, such as cellu-lar data networks and GPS satellites. My subject is the collective cultural imagination of the network in this sense, though with an eye to more precise technological realities.

3. Influential works include Schreibman, Siemens, and Unsworth, *A Companion to Digital Humanities*; Kirschenbaum, "What Is Digital Humanities," 3–7, and Kirschen-baum, "Digital Humanities As/Is a Tactical Term," 417–21; and Svensson, "Humanities Computing as Digital Humanities."

4. On the term "thick mapping," a valuable overview, and a useful portfolio of specific projects and approaches, see Burdick et al. See also Ramsay and Rockwell; and Presner, Shepard, and Kawano.

5. The famous description of cyberspace appears in William Gibson's *Neuromancer*, 51. In a conversation with Timothy Leary in 1989 that was later edited for *Mondo 2000*, Gibson suggests that the cyberpunk protagonist of the novel, addicted to cyberspace, has an orgasmic epiphany at the end of the novel, a "transcendent experience" in which he recognizes the body, the "meat," from which he has been estranged "as being this infinite complex thing." Intriguingly, Gibson and Leary were discussing the development of a video game based on *Neuromancer*. Sirius, "Gibson and Leary Audio (*Mondo 2000* History Project)."

6. Wiener, "Men, Machines, and the World About." Vernor Vinge's novella, *True Names*, had imagined an immersive 3D virtual world before Gibson, which Vinge tellingly called the "Other Plane." Significantly, it was imagined as a gamespace, in terms of how its most adept users experienced it. A more capaciously imagined 3D virtual world returned a decade later in Neal Stephenson's *Snow Crash*, which inspired the developers at Linden Lab to create Second Life in 2003. And Vinge's more recent *Rainbow's End* is set in a world of augmented reality.

7. On mobile technologies, see Gordon and de Souza é Silva, *Net Locality: Why Location Matters in a Networked World*; and Farman, *Mobile Interface Theory*.

8. William Pannapacker, "The MLA and the Digital Humanities," Brainstorm (blog), *Chronicle of Higher Education*, December 28, 2009.

9. Roberto Busa, S. J., foreword to Schreibman, Siemens, Unsworth's *Companion to Digital Humanities*, xvi.

10. *Spime* is Bruce Sterling's term for a data-enhanced networked object (*Shaping Things*).

11. William Gibson interviewed by David Wallace-Wells in *The Paris Review*, 197 (Summer 2011): 107–49.

BIBLIOGRAPHY

Bogost, Ian. "Beyond the Elbow-patched Playground." Author's blog, August 23, 2011. http://www.bogost.com/blog/beyond_the_elbow-patched_playg.shtml.

———. "Gamification Is Bullshit." Author's blog, August 8, 2011. http://www.bogost.com/blog/gamification_is_bullshit.shtml.

———. *How to Do Things with Video Games*. Minneapolis: University of Minnesota Press, 2011.

———. "Reality Is Alright." Author's blog, January 14, 2011. http://www.bogost.com/blog/reality_is_broken.shtml.

Burdick, Anne, Johanna Drucker, Peter Lunenfeld, Todd Presner, and Jeffrey Schnapp. *Digital Humanities*. Cambridge, Mass.: MIT Press, 2012.

Dear, Michael, Jim Ketchum, Sarah Luria, and Doug Richardson, eds. *Geohumanities: Art, History, Text at the Edge of Place*. New York: Routledge, 2011.

Farman, Jason. *Mobile Interface Theory*. New York: Routledge, 2011.

Flanagan, Mary. *Critical Play*. Cambridge, Mass.: MIT Press, 2009.

Gibson, William. "Burning Chrome," 1982; rept. *Burning Chrome*. New York: Ace Books, 1986.

———. Interview by David Wallace-Wells in *The Paris Review* 197 (Summer 2011): 107–49.

———. *Neuromancer*. New York: Ace Books, 1984.

———. *Spook Country*. New York: Putnam, 2007.

Gordon, Eric, and Adriana de Souza é Silva. *Net Locality: Why Location Matters in a Networked World*. Boston: Wiley-Blackwell, 2011.

Greenfield, Adam. *Everyware: The Dawning Age of Ubiquitous Computing*. Berkeley, Calif.: New Riders, 2006.

Hayles, N. Katherine. "Cybernetics." In *Critical Terms for Media Studies*, ed. W. J. T. Mitchell and Mark B. N. Hansen, 145–56. Chicago: University of Chicago Press, 2010.

———. *How We Became Posthuman: Virtual Bodies in Cybernetics, Literature, and Informatics*. Chicago: University of Chicago Press, 1999.

Heath, Dan, and Chip Heath. *The Myth of the Garage and Other Minor Surprises*. New York: Crown Business, 2011.

Jones, Steven E., and George K. Thiruvathukal. *Codename Revolution: The Nintendo Wii Platform*. Cambridge, Mass.: MIT Press, 2012.

Jurgenson, Nathan. "Digital Dualism versus Augmented Reality," *Cyborgology*, February 24, 2011. http://thesocietypages.org/cyborgology/2011/02/24/digital-dualism-versus-augmented-reality/.

Juul, Jesper. *A Casual Revolution: Reinventing Video Games and Their Players*. Cambridge, Mass.: MIT Press, 2010.

Kaplan, David, and Eric Zimmerman. *PLAY*, 2010, video. https://www.youtube.com/watch?v=8nWlR_LmCGc.

Kirschenbaum, Matthew. "Digital Humanities As/Is a Tactical Term." In *Debates in Digital Humanities*, ed. Matthew K. Gold, 417–21. Minneapolis: University of Minnesota Press, 2012.

———. *Mechanisms: New Media and the Forensic Imagination*. Cambridge, Mass.: MIT Press, 2008.

———. "What Is Digital Humanities and What's It Doing in English Departments." In *Debates in Digital Humanities*, ed. Matthew K. Gold, 3–11. Minneapolis: University of Minnesota Press, 2012.

McDonough, J., R. Olendorf, M. Kirschenbaum, K. Kraus, D. Reside, R. Donahue, A. Phelps, C. Egert, H. Lowood, and S. Rojo. *Preserving Virtual Worlds Final Report*, December 20, 2010. https://www.ideals.illinois.edu/handle/2142/17097.

McGonigal, Jane. *Reality Is Broken: Why Games Make Us Better and How They Can Change the World*. New York: Penguin Press, 2011.

Montfort, Nick. "Continuous Paper: The Early Materiality and Workings of Electronic Literature." MLA 2004, Philadelphia. http://nickm.com/writing/essays/continuous_paper_mla.html.

———. *Twisty Little Passages: An Approach to Interactive Fiction.* Cambridge, Mass.: MIT Press, 2003.

Moretti, Franco. *Graphs, Maps, Trees: Abstract Models for a Literary History.* London and New York: Verso, 2005.

Presner, Todd, David Shepard, and Yoh Kawano. *HyperCities: Thick Mapping in the Digital Humanities (metaLABprojects).* Cambridge, Mass.: Harvard University Press, 2014.

Ramsay, Stephen, and Geoffrey Rockwell. "Developing Things: Notes toward an Epistemology of Building in the Digital Humanities." In *Debates in Digital Humanities,* ed. Matthew K. Gold, 75–84. Minneapolis: University of Minnesota Press, 2012.

Salen, Katie, and Eric Zimmerman. *Rules of Play: Game Design Fundamentals.* Cambridge, Mass.: MIT Press, 2004.

Schell, Jesse. "Design outside the Box." Presentation at Design, Innovate, Communicate, Entertain, February 18, 2010. http://www.g4tv.com/videos/44277/DICE-2010-Design-Outside-the-Box-Presentation/.

Schreibman, Susan, Ray Siemens, and John Unsworth, eds. *A Companion to Digital Humanities.* New York: Wiley-Blackwell, 2004. http://www.digitalhumanities.org/companion/.

Shirky, Clay. *Here Comes Everybody: The Power of Organizing without Organizations.* New York: Penguin Press, 2008.

Sirius, R. U. "Gibson and Leary Audio (*Mondo 2000* History Project)." Acceler8tor, December 23, 2011. http://www.acceler8or.com/2011/12/gibson-leary-audio-mondo-2000-history-project/.

Stephenson, Neal. *Reamde.* New York: William Morrow, 2011.

———. *Snow Crash.* New York: Bantam, 1992.

Sterling, Bruce. *Shaping Things.* Cambridge, Mass.: MIT Press, 2005.

Svensson, Patrik. "Humanities Computing as Digital Humanities." *DHQ* 3.3 (Summer 2009). http://www.digitalhumanities.org/dhq/vol/3/3/000065/000065.html.

Vinge, Vernor. *Rainbow's End.* New York: Tor, 2006.

———. "True Names." In *Binary Star #5,* ed. James R. Frenkel. New York: Dell, 1981.

Weiser, Mark. "Ubiquitous Computing," August 16, 1993. http://www.ubiq.com/hypertext/weiser/UbiCompHotTopics.html.

Wiener, Norbert. "Men, Machines, and the World About" (1954). In *The New Media Reader,* ed. Noah Wardrip-Fruin and Nick Montfort, 65–72. Cambridge, Mass.: MIT Press, 2003.

The "Whole Game":
Digital Humanities at Community Colleges

ANNE B. MCGRAIL

My first encounter with digital humanities (DH) was in the late 1990s at the Poetry Collection at SUNY Buffalo, where I worked writing physical descriptions of primary source documents. The Collection was an early adopter of electronic poetry, and the director beta-tested OCR technology with its James Joyce manuscripts. Access to the library was restricted, and only credentialed scholars could examine the impressive collection of manuscripts housed there. One day, the director came into the workroom to share his excitement that the British Museum was putting its *Beowulf* manuscript on the World Wide Web. Several of us crowded around the computer to watch as the ancient script lumbered into view, pixel by pixel, and with it, a new era of public access to rare and unpublished cultural artifacts. Such access seemed then to extend the democratic ideal exemplified in the United States by free public libraries. As an aspiring educator, I was thrilled.

Since then, digital humanities has matured, and scholars have rightly questioned the field's democratic potential, its inclusiveness, and its role in supporting equity. Questions about who is included in what circle, what drives major programs, what kinds of cultural artifacts can be digitized and for what purposes, and whose interests are served by the digital turn are just a few among many as DH practitioners unearth and reassess the field's adherence to humanistic values.

For me, the public and dynamic conversations taking place around questions of equity comprise the most vital facets of the evolving field. I teach writing and literature at an open-access community college (CC) in Eugene, Oregon. Community college students are some of the most diverse and also most vulnerable student populations in higher education. There are 992 public community colleges in the United States, and community college students make up 46 percent of all undergraduates and 41 percent of all first-time freshmen in the country. Sixty-one percent of Native American college undergraduates are enrolled in community colleges; 52 percent of black students and 43 percent of Asian-Pacific Islander undergraduates are enrolled in community colleges; 50 percent of Hispanic college students begin at community college. In the United States, 59 percent of community college students are enrolled part-time, and 59 percent are women (American Association of Community Colleges, "Enrollments"). The SES data on CC students are well known (Adelman): 44 percent of low-income students attend community colleges as their first college out of high school as compared to 15 percent of high-income students (Community College Research Center). Sixty-nine percent of community college students work, with 33 percent working more than thirty-five hours per week; 22 percent are full-time students employed full-time; 40 percent are full-time students employed part-time; and 41 percent are part-time students employed full-time. And first-generation students make up 36 percent of community college student populations (American Association of Community Colleges, "Fast Fact Sheet").

In spite of their large numbers, there has been a significant lag in community colleges' engagement with digital humanities.[1] I first noticed this in 2011, when I started searching for like-minded CC colleagues and found very few—in spite of what I observed to be a very open and generous online DH community at four-year colleges, universities, and cultural institutions. Many aspects of DH seemed a perfect fit for the local, open-access missions of community colleges: DH favors a culture of cross-disciplinary collaboration, offers an active maker ethos, and draws on and inculcates multiple literacies and fluencies at once. Given the sheer number of community colleges in the United States and the openness and accessibility of DH scholarship and cultural data, I found this lag puzzling. In my search for answers, I came upon a post by Matthew K. Gold, this volume's co-editor, who gave voice to some of my concerns at the time:

> What is the digital humanities missing when its professional discourse does not include the voices of the institutionally subaltern? How *might* the inclusion of students, faculty, and staff at such institutions alter the nature of discourse in DH, of the kinds of questions we ask and the kinds of answers we accept? (Gold, "Whose Revolution?")

Conversely, I asked myself, what are community colleges and their students missing out on in their exclusion from DH discourse, and how might intentional engagement with DH methods and tools help CC students become active agents of discovery and change in their lives? In any developing field, tensions registered in one arena often resonate in others. It is not surprising, then, that the debates about inclusiveness, diversity, and equity at the heart of digital humanities scholarship have found these institutional parallels in the exclusion of community colleges. Perhaps the research-intensive star system that characterizes digital humanities—at least in its initial waves—has been incompatible with the teaching-heavy, service-burdened, "institutionally subaltern" profile of community colleges and their faculty. One could even argue that community college teaching has played a role similar to those "alternative academic" professions for PhDs who aim at tenure-track research careers and miss (Nowviskie).

Like tenure-track positions, community college careers draw on graduate training, but in different ways, and such careers never really feed back into graduate programs' culture of reputation. Indeed, seen through an R1 institutional lens, community college humanists' careers are assumed to be dead on arrival. And certainly the succession narratives played out in research circles are interrupted by CC teaching and service loads. But CC faculty careers involve investment elsewhere, in less visible but vital local communities of students, some of whose own academic narratives are fraught with interruption. These students' lives can be unpredictable and complex, often prohibiting participation in the co-curricular activities that deepen the college learning experience and nurture future careers. Solid lines of succession in clubs, study groups, and organizations from year to year—even from semester to semester—are routinely interrupted, eroding the accrual of social and intellectual capital that four-year colleges rely on as a support for undergraduate life. Because of the unevenness of extracurricular engagement, social and intellectual integration *in the classroom* is one of the most robust predictors of success for community college students.[2] Since this kind of integration is often a signature of DH collaboration, digital humanities can offer powerfully engaging learning experiences for these students, contributing to the democratic potential of the community college itself.

It is an opportune time to bring DH to the CC. Access to technology, while by no means uniform across all CC students, is more reliable than it was even five years ago—if not in students' homes then on CC campuses. But to be successful, DH at the CC needs significant translation and a customized educational approach. There are many books on DH topics and marvelous introductory course outlines, available online, on which to build. But the real work is pedagogical: creating curricular scaffolding that prepares students at an introductory level for possible future specialization while also being meaningful to all students with varied goals and preparations. Community college digital humanists will need to contextualize and make accessible the lofty complexity of text mining and data visualizations, for example. Such scaffolding is no easy feat, especially working on the margins of DH conversations. But since they are the ones who know the teaching and learning context, community college faculty are best equipped to do this work.[3] Once established across institutions, this pedagogical translation will add a layer to the evolving DH field and may redraw the boundaries of what counts as digital humanities.

The idea that pedagogy might determine the boundaries of a discipline may seem backward in an academy that sees teaching more as a necessary condition for continuing research. But the creation of new knowledge that can occur at all levels of DH practice is one of its signature features, part of its democratic potential. I remember reading Stephen Brier's comment in *Debates in the Digital Humanities* that pedagogy is the "ugly stepchild of universities" (Waltzer, 336). I couldn't help but bristle at the statement, both for what it said and what it left out. If pedagogy is the "ugly stepchild of universities," however, it is the beloved, intentional, and evolving child of community colleges. And if DH changes as a result of CC faculty and student engagement with it, it will be a sign of its vitality as a field. In some ways, the potential openness of DH distinguishes it from "old school" humanities approaches and aligns features of DH practice to the creation of art; such a condition should be embraced.

But for DH at the CC to take hold and be successful, it needs to take account of the needs of CC students. Given the open-access mission of community colleges, several questions arise. Since most CC students take few humanities courses, how do we ensure that their first encounters with DH are valuable to them? How will we teach *all* of our students—with their different preparations, goals, and futures—in the *same class*? How can we successfully incorporate students' profiles into our assignment design so that no one is excluded?

Because of the differential preparation of students in open-access institutions, it might be tempting to introduce students to DH by teaching them *about* all the wonderful things that "real" DH scholars are doing. I have also heard it suggested that CC students could learn about DH by participating in crowdsourced labor, becoming part of something larger by completing microtasks for university centers and DH hubs nearby. But rather than inviting students into a democratic place of knowledge creation, such approaches risk reinscribing students into their place in a hierarchy that is all too familiar.

Inviting Community College Students to Play the "Whole Game" of DH

To avoid the pedagogical trap of either just teaching CC students "about" DH from a distance or engaging them in a subordinate role in support of "real" DH projects, I have redesigned my literature and writing classes using two principles. First, I have been guided by what David Perkins calls a "whole game" approach. In his book, *Making Learning Whole: How Seven Principles of Teaching Can Transform Education,* Perkins outlines seven steps in a "teach for understanding" framework. Perkins uses the metaphor of learning baseball in Little League to illustrate the importance of teaching concepts and skills in a holistic way, one that clues students in to the stakes and meaning of their studies. As with Little Leaguers, the most meaningful learning involves "playing the whole game." Perkins criticizes what he calls "elementitis," or a pedagogy that focuses on elements of tasks in advance of student understanding of the tasks' role in the larger picture (Perkins, *Making Learning Whole,* 16). His principles are paraphrased here with a brief sketch of how to use them in a DH context.

Play the Whole Game: Students focus on "junior versions" of DH projects that they learn holistically rather than repeating low-level skills or only learning *about* the real game of DH (Perkins, *Making Learning Whole,* 8). *Play Out of Town*: A key concern of educators is knowledge transfer across contexts. Transfer happens best in the context of integrative learning. Understanding is developed across disciplinary boundaries and likely to be retained across contexts. Because DH is collaborative and cross-disciplinary, engaging multiple knowledges at once, it is more likely to create knowledge transfer (Perkins, *Making Learning Whole,* 9).

Make the Game Worth Playing: Conceptual knowledge that is applicable to life beyond the classroom supports curiosity and helps students cope with ambiguity (Perkins, *Making Learning Whole,* 10). Students are immersed in a digital world. DH can help them understand it.

Work on the Hard Parts: Deliberate practice of basic skills in the context of the big picture familiarizes students with the unique forms and products of a discipline (Perkins, *Making Learning Whole,* 11). Multiple opportunities for using digital tools to solve puzzles and answer questions supports information fluencies across disciplines.

Play the Hidden Game: Methods are often the "hidden game" of learning, and teaching the "underlying game" draws learners into the game of inquiry, creating opportunities for layered aspects of learning to emerge (Perkins, *Making Learning Whole,* 12). Foregrounding methods such as distant reading reveals elements invisible to the "naked" interpretive eye and, in my experience, leads to a more confident close reading of results found at a distance.

Learn from the Team: This principle leverages the social, collaborative aspects of project-based learning and DH is a natural fit (Perkins, *Making Learning Whole,* 13).

Learn the Game of Learning: Allowing learners to take control of their learning helps them to clarify disciplinary purposes: Why does a discipline do what it does? What are its affordances and constraints? Working across disciplines on DH projects, students develop metacognitive understanding of how they know what they know in part because of the way DH requires such purposeful use of tools to support inquiry.

So how can a "whole game" approach make DH accessible to community college students? As in Little League baseball, a key feature of Perkins's "whole game" philosophy is that "everybody plays." Getting "everybody" in a community college classroom to confidently approach unfamiliar digital work is a challenge. But as educational leader Kay McKlenney has often remarked, "students don't do optional," and so requiring engagement while keeping stakes low is essential, as I learned early on. When I was first learning about DH myself, I was tentative about teaching new tools and feared students' diffidence and withdrawal. So I offered nondigital options to students uncomfortable with technology. But I realized that this unintentionally telegraphed my lack of confidence in *them* to learn something new. I learned from this mistake and now require that all students complete the digital components of my courses.

But if we are going to require performances of new understandings in community colleges, we need to support students as they engage in unfamiliar terrain.

I provide this support both physically, by scheduling and giving credit for lab time as part of a regular course, and also motivationally, by insisting on a classroom climate of, borrowing from Carl Rogers, "unconditional positive regard." There are no stupid mistakes and everyone treats novices with respect and encouragement. Once students' fears of failure and humiliation are eased, they become intrepid explorers and take themselves seriously as researchers.

A capstone assignment in my American Literature course provides a good example. I have adapted Bridget Marshall's primary source document assignment each term for three years, and it is by far one of the most rewarding and affirming assignments that students do in my class (*Using Primary Sources in the Classroom*). Using the last four lab hours of the term to provide support and guidance, I ask students to find and link a primary source document, its history and context, to one or more of the texts we have read in our class. Rather than a final exam, students create slides and do "lightning round" presentations of their research and post a reflective synthesis essay in our online forum. The final exam is a celebration. Students share what they find like rare jewels, often to bursts of admiration and applause. Sometimes their findings are simply a manuscript of a letter from Ralph Waldo Emerson to Walt Whitman, familiar to many scholars but marvelous to students. But just as often, students find hidden treasures that change the way they think about history.

Such was one student's experience when she discovered Harvard University's archives of Louise Marion Bosworth, an American researcher at the Educational and Industrial Union who studied women's working and living conditions in the early twentieth century. This student reflected on the early social science tropes in the document and connected Bosworth's work to Abraham Cahan's short story "A Sweatshop Romance." Writing about the assignment, one student named Alicia articulated what you might call a "whole game" experience: "I felt all of these archives really corresponded to subjects we studied in class. We always see typed documents within textbooks, but never the original. I thought it made it much more meaningful. It gave me a deeper desire to connect with the writer" (Alicia).

Perkins's second principle, "make the game worth playing," emphasizes the importance of connecting classroom learning to life outside college and to the importance of generative topics that teach for conceptual knowledge and understanding. The role that big data play in the field of DH has been transformative. Indeed, distant reading of patterns and data visualization of books may be a new "threshold concept" in the twenty-first-century humanities the way that "close reading" was in the twentieth century.[4] Ray Land and others explain the importance of threshold concepts for student progression in a discipline:

> A threshold concept represents a transformed way of understanding, or interpreting, or viewing something. . . . As a consequence of comprehending a threshold concept there may thus be a transformed internal view of subject

> matter, subject landscape, or even world view, and the student can move on. (Land et al., "Implications for Course Design," 53)

Many literature instructors find it difficult enough for survey students to develop competence in close reading, and so adding this layer may seem counterproductive. But I have found that when students take words, phrases, and ideas from our class discussions and tinker with them in Google's Ngram viewer or Voyant Tools, they develop close reading skills about the meaning of their findings while seeing words at a distance in a transformative way.

For example, after a necessarily brief overview of Ngrams in my American Literature course, another of the students tinkered with the tool at home and developed her own terms for distant reading. "A good word cluster is a science experiment with words," she wrote:

> What I consider a "good word cluster" is where the terms interact with each other in intertwined ways. Whereas a "not so good word cluster" is where perhaps one of the terms charts high in varying degrees of usage and the other terms are practically nonexistent in comparison. (Sarah).

The tinkering ethos of digital work encourages students like Sarah to take control of their learning and to develop metacognitive awareness of the procedural and content knowledge required to solve problems.[5] Sarah is unintimidated by the tool and free to develop her own vocabulary for her discoveries. Recently, Perkins has commented on the need for creating not experts with niche expertise but rather "expert amateurs" who are able to know enough about learning something new that they can continue to learn new skills and adapt themselves to a changing world (Perkins, *Future Wise,* 24). As Sarah's work illustrates, DH at the CC can develop this critical twenty-first-century skill of "expert amateurism"—that is, knowing *how* to learn about something.

Assignment Design and the Community College Student Profile

The community college student profile has consequences for the learning environment, and for DH to successfully take hold at open-access institutions, it must be responsive to the conditions of students' lives. For example, community college students are more likely than their four-year counterparts to be working class or economically disadvantaged and so are constrained in their commitments to college by the complexity of their lives. They are more often first-generation college students and more ethnically diverse and do not inherit the privileges, sense of entitlement, and habits of mind provided by white, educated, middle-class origins. They also enter college later in life or return multiple times as adult learners, bringing diverse prior learning that can challenge assignments designed for a uniform entry point. In concert with a whole game approach, then, DH at community colleges must explicitly address relevant features of the community college student profile in course redesigns.

For example, time management in a community college culture can present a significant obstacle to working-class and first-generation college students. Of course, time is a limited resource for everyone—researchers, teachers, students. However, orientation toward time is a significant cultural difference across classes. Community college students have simultaneously less discretionary time to engage in college and also a time orientation grounded in working-class values. Taking into consideration how many CC students work—and how much—when designing DH courses or activities can have a profound impact on these students' engagement and success. Understanding working-class students' orientation toward time can also make a big difference in the success of a project. But it means letting go of class-neutral assumptions about learning and knowledge creation. The arc of learning and the reward cycles for accomplishment of DH projects need to be geared to the realities of their lives.

I first thought about using time orientation in my course design after reading Beverly Skeggs and Helen Wood's study of differences in working-class and middle-class reality-TV viewers. Skeggs and Wood describe working-class viewers' orientation to time as one characterized by "precarity," a sense that struggles in and endurance of the present are more salient than investments in and deferral for a future imaginary. Middle-class viewers are enculturated to see time in terms of future rewards; they believe in investment of time in the present with a belief in future capitalization potential. "Inheriting and living with precarity or potential," the authors write, "are two ends of an ontological scale which influences the investments that people can make." Skeggs and Wood explain that inheriting "potential" provides a future orientation, "enabling investments in accrual that can be maximized and owned." For working-class viewers, "future focus is restricted by this very presentist orientation, produced from the possibilities they inhabited and the potentials they lacked as a result of social positioning" (Skeggs and Wood, 231–32).

This notion of precarity helped me to understand some of my students' resistance to engagement in longer research projects. Students comprehend, value, organize, and invest time in the present in a manner directly related to their ontological sense of a future. In a higher-education context, middle-class college students' orientation to future accrual allows them to take unpaid internships with the expectation that this investment will eventually pay off. But for community college students, whose lives are dominated by a sense of material instability, investing time in some future-oriented reward often seems like folly. Students may take a class one term when things are going well, with every intention of completing a degree. But then the babysitter gets sick and they have to stay home from school to take care of their child, or they lose their job and their new one conflicts with their college schedules. Such moments of reversal may never even be fully known to us; most

CC faculty have many experiences of wonderful "disappearing" students who leave without explanation. Perhaps a present-centered time orientation combined with a relative scarcity of discretionary time (what more privileged students might label "study time") are cultural and material differences that DH pedagogies can anticipate and address.

How can we embed such an orientation into DH assignments? Creating units of meaning for DH at the CC that accrue value *in situ* can acknowledge the present-orientation of community college students. In one freshman writing class I teach, for example, students perform tasks in two contexts that take advantage of the simplicity of digital task performance while also engaging students in what Alan Liu might call a "cultural critical digital humanities." So-called "microtasks" are a signature assignment in digital humanities work, and assigning microtasks is appealing because of low barriers to entry. But when I assign our students such tasks, I do so in a "whole game" context. The first set of tasks introduces students to a key sequence of steps in digital archive projects—collaborative data tagging and proofreading for precision. For the past couple of years, the New York Public Library (NYPL) has been recruiting crowdsourced labor for its "What's On the Menu?" project. I have contributed my own labor to the project and have delighted as I've done so, marveling at the price of broiled grapefruit at the Waldorf Astoria in 1917 or the cost of a compote on a cruise ship in the 1920s. When I introduced students to the NYPL site at my college, culinary arts students in particular enjoyed this work and felt part of something bigger.

But transcribing menus—even if it's fun—is not the "whole game" of crowdsourced microtasks. At least if we think of the "underlying game" of crowdsourced labor with an understanding of what Liu calls the "great postindustrial, neoliberal, corporate and global flows of information and capital" (Liu, 491). Lest students think that all crowdsourced labor is equitable and valuable, I show a video lecture by Trebor Sholz, "Digital Labor: New Opportunities, Old Inequalities." We also watch a recruiting video by the crowdsourced sentiment-analysis company CrowdFlower, whose tag line, "One billion tasks, five million contributors," gives a glimpse into the scale of microtasking beyond the academy.[6] Students then do a new kind of field work; they sign up with Amazon Mechanical Turk[7] and compare the jobs they are offered there to their entries at the New York Public Library. Based on their observations, they write a "policy paper" on what global digital labor should look like. In online forums, they reflect on how atomized labor can be as wholesome as a barn-raising for communities like the NYPL patrons or, following Sholz, how it can be alienating and destructive when it dismantles labor rights. This whole assignment can take two weeks to complete, and a freshman writing student can complete it with minimal technical preparation. While not dismissing the power of the crowd, it invites students into the "hidden game" of digital labor—its structure, its constraints, its impacts and effects as well as its conveniences and affordances.

And of course, like universal design in other contexts, this holistic engagement and "whole game" pedagogy for DH at the CC benefits all students and not only those with a "precarious" time orientation and working-class pressures-of-the-now. And precarity itself can be converted into potential when students are invited to examine the material conditions of their lives and the way the "digital turn" affects their future as global citizens. Such assignments leverage the democratic promise of digital humanities and simultaneously reveal threats to democracy posed by the digital turn.

Another "whole game" project I have developed similarly acknowledges the time orientation that constrains community college students' engagement with DH projects. This assignment sequence, which takes three weeks to complete, raises students' consciousness of the role that algorithms and big data play in their lives. It "makes the game worth playing" by helping students explore and understand the forces at work behind the interfaces on their touch screens. Students explore search engine optimization and examine the "relevance of algorithms" and "nudge theory" in their lives (Gillespie; Eggers). First, they learn about Eli Pariser's concept of "filter bubbles."[8] We live, explains Pariser, in personalized informational ecosystems—"bubbles"—in which ideologically challenging or contrary information is filtered out and reinforcing information is pushed to the center. Filter bubbles are why we see the ads we do on Google and are nudged to read similar books on Amazon, and why our Facebook feed feels so comfortingly familiar. Following Pariser, I assign field work in which students compare their search engine results with those of friends and partners and post screen captures in our course online forums. Even students who are fluent users of the Internet are often surprised to discover the extensiveness of filter bubbles organizing their digital experiences.

To deepen their understanding of the phenomenon and help them "learn the game of learning," I share some new rhetorical concepts to describe the algorithms beneath the bubbles. I introduce Collin Brooke's new media rhetorical concepts of "persistence" (i.e., how the canon of "memory" plays in new media) and "perspective" (i.e., the new media ecology of "style") (Brooke, 55–58). One student, originally from Russia with a sister who still lives there, compared her search results to those of her sister:

> My sister got the ad promoting a vacation in Greece (she has been searching for Greece vacations for a month now), and the ad was in Russian. Yahoo knows exactly where she is located and what she has been searching for. In this way Yahoo is using "perspective" to customize her results. We tried YouTube next. When I open the home page, I got recommendations for different yoga music (that was the last thing I listened to on YouTube). Unfortunately, I forgot to do the screen shot and today the results were not the same. However, my sister's search was different from mine. YouTube automatically was redirected to YouTube in Russian, although we typed the same web address, and she received

recommendations on videos in Russian, funny animal videos, and so on. I
found out that YouTube and Yahoo "remember" your search results and when
you think you forgot about the product you have been searching for, they will
remind you. It is more "persistent" than I am.[9]

This activity culminates in an essay that explores "choice architecture" such as filter
bubbles in computer interfaces. Students come away with a raised consciousness
about searching as well as a new language to discuss computer interface experiences—in this class and beyond.

Everybody Plays, Everyone Belongs: The Community College DH Classroom Climate

A present-time orientation is just one relevant characteristic of the SES profile of
the "typical" community college student—and it may not be true of all working-
class students or all community college students. But community college faculty can
observe other characteristics in our students and develop "whole game" digital projects for our humanities classes that anticipate and embrace these characteristics in
their design. For example, a fragile sense of belonging in the academy is a pervasive
feature of the lived experience of community college students—returning adults,
first-generation students, returning veterans, and students of color. In their study of
the role of race in subjective experiences of "fit" in higher educational settings, for
example, Gregory M. Walton and Geoffrey L. Cohen remark on the importance of
sensitivity to students' perception of belonging:

> Inequality, as we know, can take the form of disparities in objective treatment
> and resources. But it can also take the form of disparities in subjective construal.
> When such disparities persist, social-psychological intervention can help peo-
> ple to resolve pressing subjective questions that if left unresolved would under-
> mine their comfort in mainstream institutions and their prospects for success.
> (Walton and Cohen, 94)

Walton and Cohen discuss the way that even one "bad day" at school dispropor-
tionately undermines minority students' and women's sense of belonging in college.
In developing "cutting edge" DH assignments for community college students, we
need to be sensitive to this fragile sense of belonging and design assignments that
advance disciplinary understanding without catapulting underprepared students
into self-doubt.

Sensitive pedagogical interventions can ensure that a "bad day" at school doesn't
lead to despair and disappearance from our classrooms. After a whole term of teaching my version of DH at the CC in a Women Writer's class, for example, I asked
Wanita, one of my older returning adult students, her advice on how to teach DH at

community colleges. She remarked wryly, "Make it Gramma-proof." She had strug-gled with the digital components of the class, including tracking her passwords in various online software programs, and her presence in the class was instrumental in teaching me how to avoid assumptions about students' preparedness to take on digital assignments. By the end of term, though, Wanita boldly presented a digital story about funeral homes and Alison Bechdel's *Fun Home* that won over the entire class of students decades her junior. Her sense of belonging as a "Gramma" was rein-forced by an intentionally positive class climate in which no mistake is a bad mistake.

Adult Learners and Prior Learning as a Bridge to the Digital

And indeed age is another key feature of the profile of community college learners: the average age of community college students is twenty-nine, and two-thirds attend part-time (American Association of Community Colleges, "Students at Commu-nity Colleges"). How can DH pedagogy embrace adult learners, many of whom feel technologically ill-prepared? Engaging prior learning is a standard step in the teach-ing and learning process. For younger, tech-savvy students, engaging prior learn-ing experiences on Twitter or Eye-Em might be the best path to DH at the CC. But for many returning students, it is important to validate their prior learning in other contexts as a bridge to the digital.

For example, I teach another writing class centered around a term-long mul-timodal composition project. Students create an advocacy website for a real or imagined cause to which they are committed. Components include designing a logo, creating a social media marketing plan for a fundraising event, and writing an FAQ page to post on their site. This assignment draws on students' prior learning in different ways. One of my returning adult students, a baker by trade, called her cause "Foster Cakes: Free Birthday Cake for Every Foster Child." She told me that before returning to school, she had always wanted to do something like this. Although she struggled with some of the technical aspects of the course, she drew on her prior learning as a baker and created a standout logo: a cupcake, which she cut out using her daughter's construction paper, taped onto a coffee cup, photographed, and, with the help of some tech-savvy fellow students, uploaded onto her site (Fritts). Making certain that all students' prior learning "counts" in designing digital projects may seem obvious, but while we innovate and work in new paradigms we can remind all community college students of the value of the wisdom and knowledge each one of them brings to our classrooms.

Strategizing for a Future DH at the CC

If we really want a cultural critical—and "democratic"—digital humanities at com-munity colleges, we need to find what is enduring and essential about DH, what it can do that traditional approaches cannot, and we need to find a way to teach it to all of our students, with their needs in mind. And as community college faculty take up DH and make it their own, they will have to figure out where DH fits—in programs, departments, and courses—and be prepared for the same kinds of obstacles their four-year-school counterparts have met.

My own engagement with digital humanities has been scholarly and pedagogical, but it has also had to be strategic, since my colleagues and administrators have not always understood what it is that distinguishes DH or makes it valuable for our students. In a community college teaching career, research, teaching, and strategy are inextricably linked. Community colleges' ties to the communities they serve make them highly vulnerable to short budget cycles and job market predictions, and so advocating for any new program necessarily involves institutional alliances and compromise. Public intellectuals, bloggers, and the popular press have worried over the fate of humanities and liberal arts, and community colleges have not been immune to these fears. Community colleges are under pressure to streamline and reduce course offerings, not expand them, and fitting curriculum perceived as undefinable or esoteric into fast-track pathways intended to lead to jobs could be a hard sell (Bailey, Jaggars, and Jenkins).

Introducing DH into community colleges will involve leveraging the strengths and priorities of each institution. For example, some colleges may wish to try infusing DH assignments and modules across courses rather than introducing entirely new DH courses that fit uneasily with streamlined degree programs. Distant reading assignments, for example, could be introduced in history, literature, and sociology courses in addition to freshman composition courses. For colleges that have strong service learning programs, archival work with local cultural institutions may be a path to effective DH development. Alternatively, faculty cohorts across disciplines may be able to develop learning communities that offer repeated engagements with a single resource from multiple disciplinary perspectives. As faculty and administrators begin to recognize the relevance of DH for students' lives, they may begin to develop general education learning outcomes that build DH skills over time and across degree programs. Such strategies will take collaborative work among faculty and administrators who may be unused to working together. But such collaboration can have positive effects on institutional culture and even put community colleges in a better position to respond to external pressures.

There is a precedent for this kind of collaboration strategy. Over the past decades, the scholarship and theories of social justice and equity have migrated into community college students' paths through careful curricular translation and embedding across disciplines. Successfully guiding underprepared students through the complexities of this work was a formidable pedagogical enterprise, often uneven across disciplines and institutions. But its success can be witnessed in mission and value statements, curriculum guides, and courses that reflect the best insights distilled from those fields. Similarly, practitioners of DH at community colleges can ensure a future of digitally fluent students by working together to meet CC students where they are and giving them twenty-first-century tools for engaging in the humanities. For some CC students, DH will be a game changer, connecting their learning to their lives in ways they hadn't imagined.

In July 2015, I completed an inspiring week as project director for an NEH Advanced Topics in the Digital Humanities Summer Institute for community college digital humanists. The twenty-nine CC participants who attended were led by a faculty comprised of prominent university DH practitioners collaborating with CC innovators. By the end of the week together, everyone could feel that the community college's moment in digital humanities, however late in arriving, is now.

NOTES

1. As part of an NEH Digital Humanities Start-Up Grant Project, I designed and implemented a National Survey of Digital Humanities at Community Colleges that sought to gather data. This data is available on my *Doing DH at the CC* blog, https://blogs.lanecc .edu/dhatthecc/.

2. Vincent Tinto and Brian Pusser refer to academic and social integration as "involvement" or "engagement." See "Moving from Theory to Action." See also Bloom and Sommo, "Building Learning Communities."

3. In proposing the 2015 NEH Advanced Topics in the Digital Humanities Summer Institute for community college faculty, my intention was precisely to develop a community of practice in DH at the CC. See the DH at the CC Commons at https://dhatthecc .lanecc.edu/.

4. For a discussion of the role that "threshold concepts" play in disciplinary thinking, see Meyer and Land, "Threshold Concepts and Troublesome Knowledge."

5. In his keynote address to the Two Year College Association in 2013, Jentery Sayers discussed the relevance of makerspaces, transduction literacy, and procedural knowledge for humanities and writing centers at community colleges. See Sayers, "Why Do Makerspaces Matter for the Humanities? For Writing Centers?"

6. "CrowdFlower: Learn How We Do It." http://www.crowdflower.com/company.

7. Amazon, "Mechanical Turk Is a Marketplace for Work." https://www.mturk.com/.

8. http://www.ted.com/talks/eli_pariser_beware_online_filter_bubbles.

9. Anonymous student forum post. Author's Spring 2014 Writing 122 Course, Lane Community College. Shared with permission.

BIBLIOGRAPHY

Adelman, Clifford. "Moving into Town and Moving On: The Community College in the Lives of Traditional Age Students." U.S. Department of Education, February 2005. http://1.usa.gov/1CJOEqC.

American Association of Community Colleges. "Community College Enrollments." http:// www.aacc.nche.edu/AboutCC/Trends/Pages/enrollment.aspx.

———. "Students at Community Colleges." http://www.aacc.nche.edu/AboutCC/Trends/Pages/studentsatcommunitycolleges.aspx.

———. "2015 Community College Fast Fact Sheet." http://www.aacc.nche.edu/AboutCC/Pages/fastfactsfactsheet.aspx.

"Alicia." Essay from author's Spring 2014 American Literature Survey Course, Lane Community College, Eugene, Oregon. Quoted with permission.

Anonymous student forum post. Author's Spring 2014 Writing 122 Course, Lane Community College, Eugene, Oregon. Quoted with permission.

———. Author's Spring 2014 American Literature Survey Course, Lane Community College, Eugene, Oregon. Quoted with permission.

Bailey, Thomas R., Shanna Smith Jaggars, and David Jenkins. *Redesigning America's Community Colleges: A Clearer Path to Student Success.* Cambridge, Mass.: Harvard University Press, 2015.

Bloom, Dan, and Colleen Sommo. "Building Learning Communities: Early Results from the Opening Doors Demonstration at Kingsborough Community College." MDRC, June 2005. http://www.mdrc.org.

Brooke, Collin. *Lingua Fracta: Toward a Rhetoric of New Media.* New York: Hampton Press, 2009.

Community College Research Center. "Community College FAQs." Teachers College, Columbia University. http://ccrc.tc.columbia.edu/Community-College-FAQs.html.

Eggers, Dave. "We Like You So Much and Want to Know You Better." *New York Times Magazine,* September 22, 2013. http://www.nytimes.com/2013/09/29/magazine/dave-eggers-fiction.html?pagewanted=all.

Fritts, Britney. "Foster Cakes: providing FREE birthday cakes for Lane County foster youth." http://britfritts.wix.com/fostercakes.

Gillespie, Tarleton. "The Relevance of Algorithms." In *Media Technologies: Essays on Communication, Materiality, and Society,* ed. Tarleton Gillespie, Pablo Boczkowski, and Kirsten Foot, 167–94. Cambridge, Mass.: MIT Press, 2014.

Gold, Matthew K. "Whose Revolution? Towards a More Equitable Digital Humanities." *The Lapland Chronicles,* January 10, 2012. http://blog.mkgold.net/category/presentations/.

Land, Ray, Glynis Cousin, Jan H. F. Meyer, and Peter Davies. "Threshold Concepts and Troublesome Knowledge: Implications for Course Design." In *Improving Student Learning Diversity and Inclusivity,* 53–64. Oxford: Oxford Center for Staff and Learning Development, 2005.

Liu, Alan. "Where Is Cultural Criticism in the Digital Humanities?" In *Debates in the Digital Humanities,* ed. Matthew K. Gold, 490–509. Minneapolis: University of Minnesota Press, 2012.

Marshall, Bridget. *Using Primary Sources in the Classroom. Lowell Teacher Workshop: Dr. Bridget Marshall.* Tsongas Industrial History Center, October 9, 2013, video. https://www.youtube.com/watch?v=ipaXJ3_VVRQ.

McGrail, Anne B. "National Survey of Digital Humanities at Community Colleges." *Doing DH at the CC* (blog), October 2014. https://blogs.lanecc.edu/dhatthecc/2014/02/03 /survey-data-available-from-national-survey-of-digital-humanities-in-community-colleges/.

Meyer, Jan, and Ray Land. "Threshold Concepts and Troublesome Knowledge: Linkages to Ways of Thinking and Practicing within the Disciplines." Enhancing Teaching Learning Project, May 2003. http://www.etl.tla.ed.ac.uk//docs/ETLreport4.pdf.

New York Public Library Labs. "What's On the Menu?" http://menus.nypl.org/.

Nowviskie, Bethany. "#alt-ac: alternate academic careers for humanities scholars," January 3, 2010. http://nowviskie.org/2010/alt-ac/.

Pariser, Eli. "Beware Online Filter Bubbles," TEDTalks, March 2011. http://www.ted.com /talks/eli_pariser_beware_online_filter_bubbles.

Perkins, David. *Future Wise: Educating Our Children for a Changing World.* San Francisco: Jossey-Bass, 2014.

———. *Making Learning Whole: How Seven Principles of Teaching Can Transform Education.* San Francisco: Jossey-Bass, 2009.

"Sarah." Student in author's Spring 2014 American Literature Survey Course, Lane Community College, Eugene, Oregon. Quoted with permission.

Sayers, Jentery. "Why Do Makerspaces Matter for the Humanities? For Writing Centers?" Two Year College Association Pacific-Northwest, October 26, 2013. http://www.maker .uvic.ca/pnwca2013/#/title.

Scholz, R. Trebor. *Digital Labor: New Opportunities, Old Inequalities.* Re:publica 2013, May 7, 2013, video. https://www.youtube.com/watch?v=52CqKIR0rVM.

Skeggs, Beverly, and Helen Wood. *Reacting to Reality Television: Performance, Audience, and Value.* New York: Routledge, 2012.

Tinto, Vincent, and Brian Pusser. "Moving from Theory to Action: Building a Model of Institutional Action for Student Success." National Postsecondary Education Cooperative, June 2006. http://web.ewu.edu/groups/academicaffairs/IR/NPEC_5_Tinto_Pusser_Report.pdf.

Walker, Ruth. "Education at Bat: Seven Principles for Educators." *Usable Knowledge* (blog), Harvard Graduate School of Education, January 1, 2009. https://www.gse.harvard.edu /news/uk/09/01/education-bat-seven-principles-educators.

Walton, Gregory M., and Geoffrey L. Cohen. "A Question of Belonging: Race, Social Fit, and Achievement." *Journal of Personality and Social Psychology* 92, no. 1 (2007): 82–96.

Waltzer, Luke. "Digital Humanities and the 'Ugly Stepchildren' of American Higher Education." In *Debates in the Digital Humanities,* 335–39. Minneapolis: University of Minnesota Press, 2012.

What's Next: The Radical, Unrealized Potential of Digital Humanities

MIRIAM POSNER

D igital humanists have heard numerous recent calls for the field to interrogate race, gender, and other structures of power. I would like to argue here that these calls, while necessary and justified, do not go far enough. To truly engage in this kind of critical work, I contend, would be much more difficult and fascinating than anything we have previously imagined for the future of DH; in fact, it would require dismantling and rebuilding much of the organizing logic that underlies our work. I'll start by saying a little about where I think we are with digital humanities now, and then talk about some new directions, with respect to these structures of power, for the field.

Digital humanities is at an interesting moment, as everyone says during periods of contention. In some ways, it is a frustrating time, but in other ways, it represents a meaningful opportunity. The field of digital humanities is growing and institutionalizing, and beginning to find a good number of adherents. DH gets occasional mainstream press coverage, and there is at least the perception, if not the reality, that opportunities and funds are available to digital humanities scholars in a pretty remarkable way.

We can map points and shapes—not perfectly, but we can do it. We can build graphs and charts, and we can do an okay job mining texts in search of patterns. We are working more with images, though that is still pretty nascent, and we are even making some forays into moving image analysis.

All of this is fun and interesting, and personally, I get a lot of satisfaction out of doing this kind of thing and helping other people to do it. It is useful and absorbing, and in many cases, it really does help us do our work better. But DH has bigger challenges yet to face. For all of its vaunted innovation, the digital humanities actually borrows a lot of its infrastructure, data models, and visual rhetoric from other areas, and particularly from models developed for business applications. In some ways, that is inevitable, because the business market is just so much bigger, and so much better funded, than the market for weird, boutique humanities tools.

But consider Google Maps, which powers a lot of our projects. Many have observed—I am certainly not the first—that this technology enshrines a Cartesian model of space that derives directly from a colonialist project of empire-building.[1] Flattening and distorting space so that it can be graphed with latitude and longitude makes sense when you are assembling an empire—which is why the Mercator projection emerged in Western Europe in the sixteenth century. Of course, it also does not help that Google Maps is owned by a corporate entity with opaque intentions.

But not even open-source alternatives like OpenStreetMap ask us to really reimagine space in any meaningful way. What models of space—what possible futures—are we foreclosing by leaning so heavily on this one representation? What would the world look like if we viewed it on a different kind of map altogether; for instance, maps produced by Aboriginal communities in Australia? (Watson).

In a similar way, many of the qualities of computer interfaces that we have prized, qualities like transparency, seamlessness, and flow, privilege ease of use ahead of any kind of critical engagement (even, perhaps, struggle) with the material at hand.[2]

Even the concept of time is a problem for us, as anyone who has tried to build a timeline knows. Many tools that store temporal data demand times and dates nailed down to the minute, or at least the day, when of course many of us are dealing with things like "ca. 1500s."

You might already be familiar with some problems with the most common types of data visualization, which are great for quickly conveying known quantities but terrible at conveying uncertainty or conflicting opinions. You can assign a number to the degree of your uncertainty for data points, but how do you show the possible universe of missing data? How do we show the ways in which heterogeneous data has been flattened into a model to make it visually legible?[3] If we want to communicate that degree of complexity, must we give up on visualization altogether?[4]

Likewise, most of the data and data models we have inherited deal with structures of power, like gender and race, with a crudeness that would never pass muster in a peer-reviewed humanities publication. This matters, actually, and I want to explain why it matters.

I like to show "The Changing Face of America," by Martin Schoeller for *National Geographic,* as an example of a mismatch between the way we experience the world and the way the world can be made "computationally tractable," to use Willard McCarty's phrase (McCarty). The project presents us with an array of faces, each of visually ambiguous ethnicity. Clicking on a face reveals both that person's self-identification and the Census boxes that he or she checks. It is clear in every case that the individual's self-conception (e.g., "Trinidadian American/colored") is far more complicated and nuanced than the Census category (e.g., "white/black").

But of course, these simplified categories become reified in Census data and in scores of maps and visualizations. So to some significant degree, the fact that we do not have a really accurate data model of race in this country means that we cannot really understand people's lived experience of it. Or at least we cannot produce data-driven visualizations that do a very good job of reflecting people's lived experiences.

To give another example—this one dealing with gender—the Getty Research Institute has released as linked open data an important database that cultural institutions use to establish what are called authorities—that is, to make sure they are all using the same name to refer to an artist and to associate that name with other data about the artist within and across institutions ("Getty Union List of Artist Names"). It is a hugely valuable resource, and without it museums could not share and network information. But its instructions for specifying gender read as follows: "The sex of the artist, *male, female,* or *known.* For corporate bodies, the gender is *not applicable*" ("About the ULAN").

The fact that it captures gender is crucial—otherwise we would not be able to say that women are underrepresented in a museum's collection—but no self-respecting humanities scholar would ever get away with such a crude representation of gender. Or at least I hope not. So why do we allow widely shared, important databases like the Union List of Artist Names (ULAN) to deal so naively with identity?[5]

There are probably a lot of reasons, many to do with practicalities and efficiencies and who is actually aware of what data is where. But one big thing is that, technically speaking, we frankly have not figured out how to deal with categories like gender that are not binary or one-dimensional or stable.

But what if we did try to figure it out? I am thinking here of Topotime, which is a data specification for representing time that was developed by Elijah Meeks and Karl Grossner at Stanford University ("Topotime v0.1 gallery"). By specifying that certain characters represent attributes like uncertainty, contingency, or approximation, they have shown how we could move from depicting time as a point or a line to a much broader canvas of shapes.

It is interesting to consider what it might look like if we began to think about representing structures like race and gender with as much nuance as Grossner and Meeks's system for dealing with time. What would maps and data visualizations look like if they were built to show us categories like race *as they have been experienced,* not as they have been captured and advanced by businesses and governments?

For example: a useful data model for race would have to be time- and place-dependent so that as a person moved from Brazil to the United States, she might move from white to black. Or perhaps the categories themselves would be time- and place-dependent so that certain categories would edge into whiteness over time. Or perhaps you could contrast the racial makeup of a place as the Census understands it with the way it is articulated by the people who live there.

Or, with a sufficiently complicated data model, you could express the racial makeup of a place from one person's point of view and then change the perspective

to represent someone else's. I might see a black neighborhood, for example; someone who lived there might see it as Haitian.

Perhaps, if we take Stuart Hall seriously, it makes more sense to define race
not as a data point in itself but as the product of a set of relationships of power; in
that sense, it is both imaginary *and* constitutive of our reality (*Race: The Floating
Signifier*). Is there a data model, or a set of functions we might define, that could
represent that?

It may sound as though I am asking us to develop data models that pin a person's identity down in even greater detail, in the way Facebook's expanded gender
categories do (Molloy). But that is not it at all.

I would like us to start understanding markers like gender and race not as
givens but as constructions that are actively created from time to time and place
to place. In other words, I want us to stop acting as though the data models for
identity are containers to be filled in order to produce meaning and recognize
instead that these structures themselves constitute data. That is where the work
of DH should begin. What I am getting at here is a comment on our ambitions
for digital humanities going forward. I want us to be more ambitious, to hold
ourselves to much higher standards when we are claiming to develop data-based
work that depicts people's lives.[6]

We have heard a lot of calls lately—and I think rightly—for increased attention
to race and gender in digital humanities work. It is not that interesting work is not
being done in digital humanities; there is wonderful, fascinating work by people I
really respect. It is just that the work that seems to get the most attention, not just
from the scholarly community, but from mainstream news outlets, seems not to deal
overmuch with women, queer people, and people of color.

Perhaps those of us who are interested in seeing more robust cultural critique
need to be more specific about where the intervention might most productively take
place. It is not only about shifting the focus of projects so that they feature marginalized communities more prominently; it is about ripping apart and rebuilding the
machinery of the archive and database so that it does not reproduce the logic that
got us here in the first place.

The great value of teaching DH to undergrads, I have come to believe, is not
showing them how to use new technology, but showing them how provisional,
relative, and profoundly ideological is the world being constructed all around us
with data. It is an opportunity to show them that our most apparently universal
categories—man/woman, black/white—are not inevitable, but the result of very
specific power arrangements. Data visualizations, maps, and spreadsheets look
terrifyingly authoritative to a nineteen-year-old—and to us, too. One great value of
rigorous critical inquiry is that you can help people see how this was all constructed,
and to what ideological ends.

But within digital humanities, we are mostly not doing this. There are some
significant exceptions, which I will discuss shortly, but for the most part, we seem

happy to flatten the world into known data structures and visualizations that might easily be reshuffled into a corporate PowerPoint deck.

That may sound uncharitable, but actually I understand the impetus quite well. We want our work to be legible. We want people to understand it. We want to share it with other institutions, link it up, and create interoperable archives. We want it to be *useful*.

But the very difficulty of imagining alternative possibilities should give us pause. When the structures that govern our identities seem as unassailable as they do now, they must have great power. And so what could be more ambitious, more interesting and challenging, than understanding the nature of that power?

These questions make me think of the feminist film theorist Laura Mulvey, whose 1977 experimental film, *Riddles of the Sphinx* (directed by Mulvey and Peter Wollen), I happened to see as I composed an early version of this chapter. Before Mulvey, feminist scholarship tended to do what I think of as counting women. How many women show up on the screen, in what roles, and how does the film treat them?

Mulvey's intervention, in a 1975 article for *Screen,* was to show us that the whole thing was broken ("Visual Pleasure and Narrative Cinema"). It was not just that we did not see enough women in powerful roles. It was that the entire organizing logic of narrative cinema was built around the subjugation of women. She showed us in film studies, the discipline in which I was trained, that structural inequalities can be written in to the very language of a medium.[7]

Perhaps you can see how I think this applies to digital humanities projects, too. We can do what we know how to do: visualize datasets that we inherit from governments, corporations, and cultural institutions, using tools that we have borrowed from corporations. Or we can scrutinize data, rip it apart, rebuild it, reimagine it, and perhaps build something entirely different and weirder and more ambitious.

I say we could, but in fact some people have, although I do not think their work has necessarily been recognized with the acclaim it should have. So I would like to discuss a few projects that I admire, and which seem to me to embody a commitment to reimagining the categories that have structured people's lives.

Changing the Composition of the Archive

We know that the question of what gets included and excluded within archives and repositories is, in itself, deeply political. At the University of Chicago, the English professor Jacqueline Goldsby led a team of graduate students to describe and arrange collections related to African American history in Chicago. This meant spending time in smaller Chicago institutions, like the South Side Community Arts Center, as well as crawling into people's attics and storage rooms to dig out their old papers. As Goldsby and her students understood, if an object is not figured as part of our object of study, it can never be extracted and represented as data ("Mapping the Stacks").

Reimagining Data Models

When it comes to thinking rigorously about data models, some of the people who are doing this thinking in the most sophisticated ways are, as you might expect, people in information studies.

In a 2015 article, Michelle Caswell and Anne Gilliland take on the problem of what happens when the perpetrator of human-rights abuses dies before admitting culpability ("False Promise and New Hope"). On the one hand, you have a massive archive, rife with evidence documenting the abuses; on the other hand, you have a looming absence because the perpetrator can never be cross-examined. Gilliland and Caswell suggest that rather than take a perpetrator at his word, thus relegating victims' testimony to a perpetually provisional status, we instead stipulate the perpetrator as an "imaginary document" within the archive itself. As an archival document, the perpetrator could then be subjected to evidentiary testing and cross-examination, as in the way of any archival data.

It may not immediately sound like it, but it strikes me that what Gilliland and Caswell are proposing is a data model for interrogating the perpetrators' actions. If the perpetrator cannot be represented as part of the archive, then he escapes researchers' scrutiny. If he can be re-mediated into our data, then his actions can be represented and attributed properly.

Recasting the Focus of Data Visualization

Moving on to what we do with the data we have, one project I want to highlight is a data visualization built by David Kim (who was working on a team led by Jacqueline Wernimont). Kim was working on a project about Edward S. Curtis, whose photographs of Native Americans are collected in a set of books called *The North American Indian* ("'Data-izing' the Images").

In building a spreadsheet about the Curtis photographs, the obvious choice for Kim would have been to record and then visualize the categories Curtis used to describe the people depicted. Instead, David chose to build a data visualization that highlights not Curtis's categories for Native American people, but how Curtis *constructed* those categories. Kim knew that Curtis's photos do not provide us immediate access to these people; instead, the view they offer is highly mediated and carefully constructed, more indicative of Curtis's own understanding of Native American-ness than of life as these people encountered it. So he turned the data visualizations back around, focusing scrutiny on Curtis himself and the Western imperial ideology that he represented.

This is a pretty simple example, but it is actually pretty sophisticated, too, revealing the researcher's fluency with both cultural studies *and* archival theory.

Building Interfaces to Challenge

Moving to the level of the interface, Evan Bissell and Erik Loyer's *The Knotted Line* is a project I like to show my students, to their vocal frustration. It is about the history of confinement in the United States, and it tells that story through a series of fifty paintings and data points that you really have to hunt for. It is infuriating and weird, but it is also obviously built with skill and, I would say, with a great deal of anger. It asks us to question the purpose of an interface, and it links our assumption that we are entitled to straightforward, transparent interfaces with our inability to look deeply at the structures of injustice and inequality in the United States.

Who Is Our Work For?

My students, as I mentioned, tend to groan when I show them *The Knotted Line* because it does not do what they want it to do—what they think it should do—and it does not seem useful. And in fact, there are so many projects out there that actually do seem useful: that provide actionable, clear information that we can easily assimilate. Which does make you wonder: If you build a *Knotted Line*, will anyone come?

I think they might. Some might. It is clear to me that our vocabulary for interpreting and evaluating this kind of work is not very well developed yet, but maybe we need more practice.

Here, I am reminded again of Laura Mulvey and of this quote from "Visual Pleasure":

> It is said that analysing pleasure, or beauty, destroys it. That is the intention of this article. The satisfaction and reinforcement of the ego that represent the high point of film history hitherto must be attacked. Not in favour of a reconstructed new pleasure, which cannot exist in the abstract, nor of intellectualised unpleasure, but to make way for a total negation of the ease and plenitude of the narrative fiction film. The alternative is the thrill that comes from leaving the past behind without rejecting it, transcending outworn or oppressive forms, or daring to break with normal pleasurable expectations in order to conceive a new language of desire. ("Visual Pleasure and Narrative Cinema," 16)

Mulvey is asking us to reconsider the ease and plenitude we get from what she calls "the reinforcement of the ego," and in doing so, Mulvey asks, whose ego? Who is our work for? If film—like data—builds worlds by extracting and reassembling bits of what we know, then whose world are we building? How far have we thought that through?

I saw Mulvey at an April 2015 screening at Yale University of *Riddles of the Sphinx,* her experimental film with Peter Wollen about motherhood and feminism. She almost apologized before the screening for its difficulty and strangeness; and it is a strange and difficult and taxing film.

But for all Mulvey's warnings about estrangement and the destruction of plea-sure, I found myself actually moved almost to tears by the movie. I became a mother myself a couple years ago, and I felt, watching the film, that yes, this is how it is to be a mother—so infuriating and claustrophobic and sublime all at once. And there *was* pleasure there, or a thrill, in Mulvey's term: a thrill in seeing one's expe-rience captured in its complexity and contradiction, and at not being lied to or patronized.[8]

Mulvey told us that at the British Film Institute's behest, she traveled the British countryside with the film, screening it for very confused audiences, most of whom walked out. But she told us, too, that some of them stayed, and that those who did tended to be the mothers, who were so grateful to see themselves, finally, on the screen. So maybe this is the thrill we can work toward—the thrill in capturing people's lived experience in radical ways—ways that are productive and generative and probably angry, too.

Of course, we cannot capture these experiences without the contributions of the people whose lives we are claiming to represent. So it is incumbent on all of us (but particularly those of us who have platforms) to push for the inclusion of under-represented communities in digital humanities work, because it will make all of our work stronger and sounder. We cannot allow digital humanities to recapitulate the inequities and underrepresentations that plague Silicon Valley; or the systematic injustice, in our country and abroad, that silences voices and lives.

This chapter's title proposes that DH might work toward a different possible future, and this is what I meant. Sometimes people frame calls for DH to engage more with race and gender as a kind of philanthropic activity; won't you please con-sider the poor women and people of color?

But that is wrong. DH needs scholarly expertise in critical race theory, femi-nist and queer theory, and other interrogations of structures of power in order to develop models of the world that have any relevance to people's lived experience. Truly, it is the most complicated, challenging computing problem I can imagine, and DH hasn't even begun yet to take it on.

NOTES

This chapter was originally delivered as a paper at the Keystone Digital Humanities Confer-ence at the University of Pennsylvania on July 22, 2015, and posted to http://miriamposner .com/blog/whats-next-the-radical-unrealized-potential-of-digital-humanities/ on July 27.

My thanks to Lauren Klein and Roderic Crooks for their advice and feedback on this material. I would also like to acknowledge the intellectual debt I owe to David Kim and Johanna Drucker, with whom I have argued, negotiated, and formulated a lot of these ideas, mostly in the context of teaching together. Kim's important dissertation, "Archives, Models, and Methods for Critical Approaches to Identities: Representing Race and Ethnicity in the Digital Humanities" (UCLA, 2015), takes on many of these issues at much greater length.

1. See, for example, Edney, *Mapping an Empire,* or on digital maps, Farman, "Mapping the Digital Empire."

2. See, for example, the widely cited Steve Krug, *Don't Make Me Think!*

3. For a good overview of attempts to visualize uncertainty see Marx, "Data Visualization: Ambiguity as a Fellow Traveler."

4. Lauren Klein's forthcoming book on data visualization demonstrates, among other things, that our current repertoire of charts and graphs is not inevitable but one option among many we could have chosen.

5. I want to make it abundantly clear here that I am not trying to pick on ULAN. It was one example among many I could have chosen.

6. Work such as Deb Verhoeven's, which develops categories in collaboration with the communities they represent, will be invaluable here. As she demonstrates, it is vital to do this work in partnership with the communities at stake. See Verhoeven, "Doing the Sheep Good."

7. Tara McPherson made a similar comparison between Mulvey and digital humanities in a March 2015 interview with Henry Jenkins. See Jenkins, "Bringing Critical Perspectives to the Digital Humanities."

8. It must be said that *Riddles of the Sphinx* is far from a perfect film; as one audience member suggested, and as Mulvey acknowledged, its sole black character is exoticized through her clothing and mostly silent role.

BIBLIOGRAPHY

"About the ULAN." The Getty Research Institute. http://www.getty.edu/research/tools/vocabularies/ulan/about.html.

Caswell, Michelle, and Anne Gilliland. "False Promise and New Hope: Dead Perpetrators, Imagined Documents and Emergent Archival Evidence." *International Journal of Human Rights* 19, no. 5 (July 2015), 615–27.

Edney, Matthew H. *Mapping an Empire: The Geographical Construction of British India, 1765–1843.* Chicago; London: University of Chicago Press, 1997.

Farman, Jason. "Mapping the Digital Empire." *New Media and Society* 12 (2010), 869–88.

"Getty Union List of Artist Names." The Getty Research Institute. http://www.getty.edu/research/tools/vocabularies/ulan/.

Grossner, Karl, and Elijah Meeks. "Topotime v0.1 gallery & sandbox," 2013–present. http://dh.stanford.edu/topotime/.

Jenkins, Henry. "Bringing Critical Perspectives to the Digital Humanities: An Interview with Tara McPherson (Part Three)." *Confessions of an Aca-Fan,* March 20, 2015.

Kim, David. "Archives, Models, and Methods for Critical Approaches to Identities: Representing Race and Ethnicity in the Digital Humanities," PhD diss., UCLA, 2015.

———. "'Data-izing' the Images: Process and Prototype." In *Performing Archive: Curtis + the Vanishing Race,* by Jacqueline Wernimont, Beatrice Schuster, Amy Borsuk, David J. Kim, Heather Blackmore, and Ulia Gusart (Popova). Scalar, 2013. http://scalar.usc.edu/works/performingarchive/data-izing-the-photos?path=network-view-of-curtis-images.

Krug, Steve. *Don't Make Me Think!: A Common Sense Approach to Web Usability*. Berkeley, Calif.: New Riders Pub., 2006.

"Mapping the Stacks: A Guide to Chicago's Hidden Archives." http://mts.lib.uchicago.edu/.

Marx, Vivien. "Data Visualization: Ambiguity as a Fellow Traveler." *Nature Methods* 10, no. 7 (July 2013): 613–15, doi:10.1038/nmeth.2530.

McCarty, Willard. "Modeling: A Study in Words and Meanings." In *A Companion to Digital Humanities,* ed. Susan Schreibman, Ray Siemens, and John Unsworth. Oxford: Blackwell, 2004.

Molloy, Parker Marie. "Facebook Announces Expanded Gender Options for Transgender and Gender Nonconforming Users." *Advocate,* February 13, 2014. http://www.advocate.com/politics/transgender/2014/02/13/facebook-announces-expanded-gender-options-transgender-and-gender.

Mulvey, Laura. "Visual Pleasure and Narrative Cinema." *Screen* 16, no. 3 (September 21, 1975): 6–18, doi:10.1093/screen/16.3.6.

Race: The Floating Signifier, dir. Sut Jhally, with Stuart Hall and Media Education Foundation. Northampton, Mass.: Media Education Foundation, 2002.

Riddles of the Sphinx, dir. Laura Mulvey and Peter Wollen. New York: British Film Institute, 1977.

Schoeller, Martin. "The Changing Face of America." *National Geographic,* October 2013. http://ngm.nationalgeographic.com/2013/10/changing-faces/schoeller-photography.

Verhoeven, Deb. "Doing the Sheep Good: Facilitating Engagement in Digital Humanities and Creative Arts Research." In *Advancing Digital Humanities: Research, Methods, Theories,* ed. Katherine Bode and Paul Longley Arthur, 206–20. New York: Palgrave MacMillan, 2014.

Watson, Helen, with the Yolngu community at Yirrkala. "Aboriginal-Australian maps." In *Maps Are Territories, Science Is an Atlas,* ed. David Wade Chambers, David Turnbull, and Helen Watson, 28–36. Chicago: University of Chicago Press, 1993. http://territories.indigenousknowledge.org/exhibit-5.

Making a Case for the Black Digital Humanities

KIM GALLON

The dust has yet to settle around the debates over what the digital humanities is or is not. Boundaries and demarcations continue to shift within a complex and ongoing conversation about the intersection of technology with humanistic fields. This context, I would argue, has generated the ideal conditions in which to engage the question of how humanity is framed in the digital humanities. To this end, I seek to articulate a relationship between the digital humanities and Africana/African American/Black studies (from here on I will call the field Black studies) so as to highlight how technology, employed in this underexamined context, can further expose humanity as a racialized social construction.

Questions may arise around the use of the term "black." Would not "Africana" or "African American" be more appropriate, some may ask. In other contexts, I am quite sure that my addition of a racial signifier to "digital humanities" would appear at the most racist and at a minimum divisive, leading to questions about who could or could not engage in black digital humanities. Questions of this magnitude are to be expected and are in fact necessary when new areas of inquiries are proposed. At the same time, these sorts of questions obfuscate crucial complexity, making it difficult to chart the paths needed to address much deeper and systemic issues. To get caught up in exact definitions or questions of "who is in or who is out" in black digital humanities is to ignore how the very nomenclature of blackness has a complex and rich history that moves in the same conceptual orbit as the term "digital humanities" (Parham, "Without Innovation").

Although work on racial, ethnic, and national difference is emerging in the digital humanities, discussions about the lineage of Black studies within the digital humanities are almost nonexistent.[1] While a comprehensive history of the intersections between Black studies and the digital is sorely needed, it is outside of the scope of this chapter. Here, I seek to set in motion a discussion of the black digital humanities by drawing attention to the "technology of recovery" that undergirds black digital scholarship, showing how it fills the apertures between Black studies and digital humanities. Indeed, the black digital humanities help to unmask the racialized systems of power at work in how we understand the digital humanities as a field and utilize its associated techniques. In their work with the #transformDH collective, Alexis Lothian and Amanda Phillips have suggested that putting a name to the unnamed helps to bring a concept into existence (Lothian and Phillips, "Can Digital Humanities Mean Transformative Critique?"). Thus, this piece names the "black digital humanities" as the intersection between Black studies and digital humanities, transforming the concept into corporeal reality while lending language to the work of the black digerati in and outside of the academy.

Like Matthew Kirschenbaum's understanding of the term digital humanities itself, precise definitions of what constitutes the black digital humanities are elusive. The black digital humanities reflects less an actual "thing" and more of a constructed space to consider the intersections between the digital and blackness (Kirschenbaum, 51). Like race, gender, class, and sexuality—all social constructs, if you will—the digital humanities increasingly hold *real* meaning and significance in the academic universe. As Kirschenbaum has observed, there are high stakes for who is and who is not a digital humanist, and for what is or is not digital humanities, when federal grants are hard to come by and academic jobs may hinge on the term (Kirschenbaum, 54–55). Some digital humanities scholars have begun to call attention to the role that race may play in the development of digital humanities programs and centers and in the funding and recognition that particular digital humanities projects might garner (Bailey, "All the Digital Humanists Are White"). A vibrant and critical discourse from #dhpoco, #transformDH, and HASTAC (Humanities, Arts, Sciences, and Technology Advanced Collaboratory), among others, now serves to resist the academic hegemonies that may limit our understanding of what the digital humanities is and will be in the future. My hope is that a critical consideration of the connections between Black studies and the digital humanities will help to advance this work.

The field of Black studies is nearing its fiftieth birthday, having developed out of the civil rights and Black Nationalist movements in the late 1960s. Black studies has long been understood as the comparative study of the black cultural and social experiences under white Eurocentric systems of power in the United States, the larger African diaspora, and the African continent, after all, and these systems of power endure. Contemporary scholars such as Alexander Weheliye therefore describe "black studies as a mode of knowledge production" that "investigates processes of racialization with a particular emphasis on the shifting configurations of black life" (Weheliye, 3). He continues:

> If racialization is understood not as a biological or cultural descriptor but as a conglomerate of sociopolitical relations that discipline humanity into full humans, not-quite-humans, and non-humans, then blackness designates a changing system of unequal power structures that apportion and delimit which humans can lay claim to full human status and which humans cannot. (Weheliye, 3)

Weheliye asks us to consider how Black studies might illuminate the various processes by which nonwhite subjects are systematically shut out from "the category of human as it is performed in the modern west" (Weheliye, 3). His conception of Black studies is powerful in its assertion that modern humanity cannot be dislocated from a racialized hegemony.

What does this mean for digital humanities? Following Weheliye, I would argue that any connection between humanity and the digital therefore requires an investigation into how computational processes might reinforce the notion of a humanity developed out of racializing systems, even as they foster efforts to assemble or otherwise build alternative human modalities. This tension is enacted through what I call a "technology of recovery," characterized by efforts to bring forth the full humanity of marginalized peoples through the use of digital platforms and tools.

Recovery rests at the heart of Black studies, as a scholarly tradition that seeks to restore the humanity of black people lost and stolen through systemic global racialization. It follows, then, that the project of recovering lost historical and literary texts should be foundational to the black digital humanities. It is a deeply political enterprise that seeks not simply to transform literary canons and historiography by incorporating black voices and centering an African American and African diasporic experience, though it certainly does that; black digital humanities troubles the very core of what we have come to know as the *humanities* by recovering alternate constructions of humanity that have been historically excluded from that concept. A discourse on the "politics of recovery" in the digital humanities is beginning to take shape through Amy Earhart's work. She documents a history of what she calls "DIY recovery projects" in the 1990s that sought to disrupt a canon of Eurocentric and male-authored literature. Through the lens of black digital humanities, these efforts at recovery can be understood not only as the recovery of "lost or non-canonical and difficult to locate texts," but also as the recovery of black authors' humanity (Earhart, "Can Information Be Unfettered?").

Applied as a technology in Black studies and in the lives of black people living in the digital era more generally, recovery restores black people's humanity. This technology of recovery operates as the shared basis for black academic and nonacademic digital work, one that dominates the ways by which both Black studies scholars and a black public approach technology. Everyday discursive interactions on social media networks are a case in point. Black people's subsistence in and resistance to the complex oppressive systems of slavery, colonialism, Jim Crow, mass incarceration, and police brutality, across time and space, make black lives ground zero for a technology of recovery using social media. Movements that protest the ongoing police brutality of black women and men, which began on "Black Twitter" and Facebook with hashtags such as #SayHerName, #BlackLivesMatter, and #ICantBreathe, continue black people's centuries-old endeavor to make their collective humanity apparent to the world. These hashtags reveal that black people's humanity is tethered to a racial system that deems black people's lives as insignificant relative to their white counterparts. Tweets that highlight disparities in social indicators such as employment, education, housing, and healthcare between white and black people show how black people's humanity has material consequences.

In addition to Twitter, scholars and institutions (along with nonacademic users) have developed literary and historical digital recovery projects that similarly represent a search and mission for the collective recuperation of a lost peoplehood. The *Digital Schomburg,* one of the earliest black digitization projects, demonstrates the power of reclaiming black humanity by recovering nineteenth-century black female writing[2] and late nineteenth and early twentieth century images of people of African descent.[3,4] It may then be of little surprise that scholars of the black literary tradition, as a whole, have yet to embrace text mining and other quantitative digital approaches in the same numbers as other groups of literary scholars. Scholars of African American literature may view text mining as counterposed to recovery (Rambsy, "African American Literature and Digital Humanities"). The relatively small number of text mining projects among scholars of black literature is concerning, however, at a time when digital humanities work has shifted its focus to quantitative and computational approaches. But the black digital humanities can highlight the value of specific computational methods. Kenton Rambsy, Assistant Professor of African American Literature at the University of Texas at Arlington and the Project Digital Initiative Coordinator for the Project on the History of Black Writing, models this approach. Noting that mobility and place are predominant themes in African American literary expression, he uses text mining software to geo-tag the occurrence of city and other geographical landmark names in black literary expression (Rambsy, "African American Literature and Digital Humanities"). For example, text mining allows Rambsy to recover Edward P. Jones's use of cities, streets, neighborhoods, and city landmarks to reenvision forms of black humanity that are not completely circumscribed by racism ("Edward P. Jones and Literary Geo-Tagging").

Rambsy's work stresses another key point: digital recovery projects that are either led by or heavily involve black scholars are particularly impactful in how they expand what we understand the digital humanities to be and its potential for critically thinking about power. As a scholar of African descent leading the digital program of the thirty-two-year-old *Project on the History of Black Writing* (HBW)—which was founded by another black literary scholar, Maryemma Graham, with a group of African American literary scholars at an organizing meeting entitled *Computer Assisted Analysis of Black Literature* (CAABL)—Rambsy produces work that disrupts the normative and racialized framework of the digital humanities as led by white scholars.[5] Digital humanities projects exclusively developed by white scholars and information technology staff often reflect the racial hierarchies present in higher education. Mark Anthony Neal views the small number of black scholars in the digital humanities as an administrative issue. He observes, "When all these deans and provosts are looking around for the folks who are going to do cutting edge work, the last folks they think about are black folks" (*Left of Black*). Neal's comments touch on the unspoken assumption that African Americans are technophobes, even in the midst of the information age. The supposition that black people are averse to technological innovation is tied to the discourse of "black technophobia" that still circulates today, reproducing and reinforcing long-standing "scientific" evidence of black intellectual inferiority (Everett, 19).

From the vantage of black digital humanities, foundational assumptions about humanity, as well as about how we derive meaning about human culture in the academy, remain deeply entrenched in racialization, and the digital humanities are not exempt from this charge. Like many disciplines that study humanity, discussions about digital tools and processes are most often considerations about how majority groups use or might be studied with computational approaches. Thus, the large share of digital humanities projects and related scholarship that pays no attention to race should be defined as the "white digital humanities," for they are, in practice, explorations about human culture based on whiteness as an unmarked category and "standard of the real" (Gordon, 79).[6]

The racialization of black people's humanity therefore poses a fundamental problem to the digital humanities as it is generally defined. Understood as the union of digital technology and the academic disciplines that study human culture, what do we do with forms of humanity excluded from or marginalized in how we study the humanities and practice the digital humanities? What are the implications of using computational approaches to theorize and draw deeper insight into a modern humanity that is *prima facie* arranged and constructed along racial lines? One of the essential features of the black digital humanities, then, is that it conceptualizes a relationship between blackness and the digital where black people's humanity is *not* a given. The black digital humanities probes and disrupts the ontological notions that would have us accept humanity as a fixed category, an assumption that unproblematically emanates in the digital realm. The black digital humanities, then, might be defined as a digital episteme of humanity that is less tool-oriented and more invested in anatomizing the digital as both progenitor of and host to new—albeit related—forms of racialization. These forms at once attempt to abolish and to fortify a taxonomy of humanity predicated on racial hierarchies.

What, then, do the black digital humanities mean for the humanities and its relationship to digital tools? Rather than moving forward with digitizing, text mining, topic modeling, and the like, the black digital humanities would have us seriously consider the political relations and "assemblages" that have racialized the literary, philosophy, and historical texts that we study (Weheliye, 3). Digital tools and platforms should be mobilized to interrogate and disclose how the humanities are developed out of systems of power. The black digital humanities reveals how methodological approaches for studying and thinking about the category of blackness may come to bear on and transform the digital processes and tools used to study humanity. Questions pertaining to digital tool development have much broader applications, of course. Johanna Drucker, for instance, reminds us that we must use and build digital infrastructure and tools steeped in humanistic theory so that they function in ways that reflect the core values of the humanities (Drucker, 87). However the black digital humanities forces us to move backward before moving forward in thinking about tools, to first consider how the very foundation of the humanities are racialized through the privileging of Western cultural traditions. It then asks us to assess whether those tools would still be used in the same manner had they been developed to explore the texts that were and are marginalized through the racialization of the humanities. It further prompts us to ask how tool building might mirror the material realities of blackness. The black digital humanities therefore foregrounds the digital as a mutual host for racism and resistance and brings to light the "role of race as a metalanguage" that shapes the digital terrain, fostering hegemonic structures that are both new and old and replicate and transcend analog ones.[7]

Ultimately, the task of black digital humanities is to ask, "What aspects of the digital humanities might be made more "humanistic" if we were to look at them from the perspective of blackness?" The black digital humanities raises the question, "How can digital tools and processes such as text mining and distant reading be justified when there is so much to do in reconstructing what it means to be human?"[8] Black digital humanity, with its emphasis on humanity as an evolving category, also changes how we should view the ongoing concerns about sustainability and the future of digital projects. Recognizing that humanity is a construct, a contingent idea, forces digital humanists to come to terms with the contingency of digital projects. How might the sustainability of a digital project be conceptualized from a standpoint that considers humanity as a social construction and subject to change over time and place? Accordingly, the black digital humanities promotes a system of change; it is a mechanism for deregulating the tendency of technological tools, when employed in the digital humanities, to deemphasize questions about humanity itself.

Thus, I make the case for the black digital humanities in order to, as Alan Liu suggests, enlarge the field with "sociocultural meaning" (Liu, 501). Black digital humanities provides a forum for thinking through the ways that black humanity emerges, submerges, and resurfaces in the digital realm through the "racializing assemblages of subjection" (Weheliye, 2). My articulation of this union does not dismiss or marginalize other efforts working at this nexus, such as eblack studies, black code studies, and digital blackness.[9] They all provide compelling methods for describing how the digital comes to bear on blackness and vice versa. But there is a need for these and more theorization on the topic so that they might contribute to a larger black technocultural discourse and Internet activism. Black studies has a unique role to play in dismembering how we think about humanity and the digital humanities by extension. A black epistemology will generate questions about the relationship between the racialization of humanity and the digital as power, ultimately fostering new inquiries and deeper understandings about the human condition.

NOTES

This chapter was developed from a presentation titled "Creating a Digital Culture for Scholarship on the Black Press," which I gave at the African American Expression in Print and Digital Culture at the University of Wisconsin in the fall of 2014. At the time I met Amy Earhart, who encouraged me to continue thinking about the relationship between blackness and the digital. My participation in "Recovering African American and African Diaspora History and Literary in the Digital Humanities: A Roundtable Discussion," with Jessica Johnson, Robby Luckett, and Bryan Carter at the 2015 Annual American Historical Association Meeting, expanded my thoughts about recovery in the digital humanities. Thanks to Roopika Risam, Matthew K. Gold and Lauren Klein for their critical and insightful feedback on this essay. A special thank-you to Lewis R. Gordon and Alexander Weheliye and other scholars of Africana philosophy and the black intellectual tradition, present and past, for providing me with a conceptual language and understanding about blackness.

1. For some of the scholarship on difference in the digital humanities, see http://transfor mdh.org/about-transformdh/ and https://www.hastac.org/explore/social-political-issues /race-ethnicity.

2. http://digital.nypl.org/schomburg/writers_aa19/toc.html.

3. http://digital.nypl.org/schomburg/images_aa19.

4. http://www.nypl.org/about/locations/schomburg/digital-schomburg.

5. https://hbw.ku.edu.

6. Both Moya Bailey and Tara McPherson implicitly make this argument with their article titles: "All the Digital Humanists Are White, All the Nerds Are Men, but Some of Us Are Brave" and "Why Are the Digital Humanities So White?"

7. On the "metalanguage of race," see Higginbotham.

8. My question is heavily modeled off the question that Africana philosopher Lewis Gordon poses about the role of philosophy in relationship to Africana philosophy. See *Introduction to Africana Philosophy.*

9. http://eblackstudies.org; http://diasporahypertext.com/2015/02/13/cfp-black-code -studies/; http://www.rutgersdigitalblackness.com.

BIBLIOGRAPHY

Bailey, Moya Z. "All the Digital Humanists Are White, All the Nerds Are Men, but Some of Us Are Brave." *Journal of Digital Humanities* 1, no. 1 (2011). http://journalofdigi talhumanities.org/1–1/all-the-digital-humanists-are-white-all-the-nerds-are-men- but-some-of-us-are-brave-by-moya-z-bailey/.

Digital Schomburg: African American Women Writers of the 19th Century. New York City Public Library, 1998. http://digital.nypl.org/schomburg/writers_aa19/.

Drucker, Johanna. "Humanistic Theory and Digital Scholarship." In *Debates in the Digital Humanities,* ed. Matthew K. Gold, 85–95. Minneapolis: University of Minnesota Press, 2012.

Earhart, Amy E. "Can Information Be Unfettered?: Race and the New Digital Humanities Canon." In *Debates in the Digital Humanities,* ed. Matthew K. Gold, 309–18. Minneapolis: University of Minnesota Press, 2012.

Everett, Anna. *Digital Diaspora: A Race for Cyberspace.* Albany: SUNY Press, 2009.

Gordon, Lewis R. *An Introduction to Africana Philosophy.* Cambridge: Cambridge University Press, 2008.

Higginbotham, Evelyn Brooks. "African American Women's History and the Metalanguage of Race." *Signs* 17, no. 2 (1992): 251–74.

Images of African Americans from the 19th Century. New York City Public Library, 1999. http://digital.nypl.org/schomburg/images_aa19/.

Kirschenbaum, Matthew, G. "What Is 'Digital Humanities' and Why Are They Saying Such Terrible Things About It?" *Differences: A Journal of Feminist Cultural Studies* 25, no. 1 (2014): 46–53.

Liu, Alan. "Where Is Cultural Criticism in the Digital Humanities?" In *Debates in the Digital Humanities,* ed. Matthew K. Gold, 490–509. Minneapolis: University of Minnesota Press, 2012.

Lothian, Alexis, and Amanda Phillips. "Can Digital Humanities Mean Transformative Critique?" *Journal of e-Media Studies* 3, no. 1 (2013). https://journals.dartmouth.edu/cgi-bin/WebObjects/Journals.woa/xmlpage/4/article/425.

McPherson, Tara. "Why Are the Digital Humanities So White? or Thinking the Histories of Race and Computation." In *Debates in the Digital Humanities,* ed. Matthew K. Gold, 139–60. Minneapolis: University of Minnesota Press, 2012.

Neal, Mark Anthony. "Race and the Digital Humanities." *Left of Black* (webcast), season 3, episode 1, John Hope Franklin Center, September 17, 2012. https://www.youtube.com/watch?v=AQth5_-QNj0.

Nelson, Alondra. "Introduction: Future Texts." *Social Text* 20, no. 2 (Summer 2002): 1–15.

Project on the History of Black Writing. "HBW History: The History of the Project on the History of Black Writing." http://www2.ku.edu/~phbw/about_us_history.html.

Parham, Marisa. "Without Innovation: African American Lifeworlds and the Internet of Things," October 14, 2014. http://mith.umd.edu/podcasts/dd_fall-2014-marisa-parham.

Rambsy, Kenton. "African American Literature and Digital Humanities," January 17, 2014. http://www.culturalfront.org/2014/01/african-american-literature-and-digital.html.

———. "Edward P. Jones and Literary Geo-Tagging," January 17, 2014. http://www.culturalfront.org/2014/01/edward-p-jones-and-literary-geo-tagging.html.

——— ."Text-Mining, Geography, and Canonical African American Short Stories," January 17, 2014. http://www.culturalfront.org/2014/01/text-mining-geography-and-canonical.html.

Weheliye, Alexander G. *Habea Viscus: Racializing Assemblages, Biopolitics, and Black Feminism Theories of the Human.* Durham, N.C.: Duke University Press, 2014.

QueerOS: A User's Manual

FIONA BARNETT, ZACH BLAS, MICHA CÁRDENAS, JACOB
GABOURY, JESSICA MARIE JOHNSON, AND MARGARET RHEE

In 2014, *Cinema Journal* published a special "In Focus" issue on "Queer Approaches to Film, Television, and Digital Media" that included queer theorist Kara Keeling's preliminary articulation of a "QueerOS," a "scholarly and political project" that "makes this formulation of *queer* function as an operating system" (Keeling, 153). Drawing on Tara McPherson's analysis of operating systems as both technical and cultural structures ("U.S. Operating Systems," 21–37), Keeling posits a QueerOS that employs ontologies of new media with queer theory and other theoretical fields that address a spectrum of difference such as race and class. For Keeling, a QueerOS would make it impossible to think of phenomena of identitarian difference as separate from information technologies. As Keeling articulates this conception, she generously summarizes interventions that have been made in the work of bringing together information technologies, sexuality, and other forms of difference. Yet a QueerOS remains a largely speculative project, a challenge set forth by Keeling to those who have begun to think these worlds together.

In the spirit of a queer commons and as queer/trans scholars and artists of color invested in the digital humanities, we take up Keeling's challenge. However, our OS doesn't come in the form of GNU/Linux's man pages with detailed descriptions of switches, pipes, and flags. Instead, we have borrowed the language of popular software to present an accessible introduction, a User's Manual to a new operating system, with each component given a poetic and theoretical description of its features and limitations.[1] To construct this OS, we have drawn from the work of an array of scholars, activists, and artists from across cultural studies, ethnic studies, media studies, and the digital humanities. We invoke thinkers and cultural workers such as Jasbir Puar, Lauren Berlant, Octavia Butler, Moya Bailey, Viviane Namaste, Martin Manalansan, José Esteban Muñoz, Juana Maria Rodriguez, Alexis Lothian, Alexis Pauline Gumbs, and Hortense Spillers, among others. We likewise look to the transgressive, theoretical, political, and aesthetic practices made possible through the activism of groups such as Queer Nation and ACT UP, and we see a kinship in the work of black feminist and radical womyn of color digital media-makers, and in the agitation of queer and transgender activists of color organizing in grassroots movements such as #blacklivesmatter. These figures have challenged us to invoke a notion of queerness that is socially constructed, promiscuous, political, and discomfiting. They are the ghosts in our machine.

Our hope is not to present a unified theory of what a queer operating system should be. Our goal is to continue to advance a theory of queerness as technological, operative, and systemic, derived from individual interests, mutual concern, and discussions that have emerged from collective presentations, virtual discussions, and queer dreams. It is to engage with the challenge of understanding queerness today as operating on and through digital media and the digital humanities. Our intervention therefore seeks to address what we perceive as a lack of queer, trans, and racial analysis in the digital humanities, as well as the challenges of imbricating queer/trans/racialized lives and building digital/technical architectures that do not replicate existing systems of oppression. As such, this is a speculative proposition for a technical project that does not yet exist and may never come to exist, a project that does not yet function and may never function. It is a response to the requirement that the digital humanities create working technologies. In lieu of tools, we offer up theoretical vaporware, speculative potentialware, ephemeral praxis.

Getting Started

QueerOS seeks to identify digital interactions, both intentional and serendipitous, that lead to new pleasures and possibilities both online and off. QueerOS imagines the pleasure and pain of queer digital mediations as practices that are inherently organizing and disorganizing at the same time. Focusing on computer code and system hardware, performance and production, communities of collaboration and social justice, and practices of desire and transformation within social media, QueerOS updates our current moment while also questioning our impulse to make queer theory productive and connect to the digital humanities and new media studies. QueerOS diverges from the digital network culture, widely accepted today, in which Terms of Service and License Agreements are quietly updated by corporations in order to limit user's rights to their own data, where agreements are to be scrolled past and clicked through, and consent is not taken seriously. QueerOS demands that consensual agreements are the means by which we build new architectures of possibility and make our dreams of abundance real. By agreeing to the QueerOS Terms of Service the user binds themselves in a relational network of queer kinship with and between people and systems, bodies and objects, one and another.

Interface

The interface marks the site at which human-machine interaction is situated. For most users, the interface is the only means of engaging with a given operating system, as all possible actions are mediated by the predetermined interactions built into the system. The interface is therefore a site of control, of restriction; it is a black box that accepts limited input to produce limited output, the workings of which remain hidden. While our queer impulse may be to explode this box, to lay bare its inner workings in a gesture of radical revelation, this desire to access the truth of the machine in that hardware, those circuits, these gates and switches is rooted in a drive toward depth, essence, and resolution that is antithetical to a QueerOS. As such, a more productive interface would be expansive, proliferating the relationality allowed for by the inter-face, its inter-activity, its nature as that which is between or among, that which binds together, mutually or reciprocally. Far from the extractive impulse of contemporary systems that mine and surveil, it is an act of consent and mutual transformation. It is that which allows us to enter one another and be in-formed—that is, to be shaped from within (Peters).

If there is an object to be exploded, it is perhaps the site at which the interface takes place, and those forms of action that qualify as legible to the operation of our system. While the interface once described the hermetic boundary at which two bodies meet (Chrystal), our modern computational interfaces are quite promiscuous, accepting and dispensing data between human and machine. Yet this modern interface is prophylactic, accepting only that which has been made hygienic through a translation from the material world into information. What might it mean to construct an interface with the capacity for co-constitutive modification, one modeled not on Shannon's mathematical theory of communication (Shannon, 623–56), but on something disarticulated from Western epistemologies, something in which the parasite is not the excluded third (Serres) but is that which connects and transforms us, an infectious intimacy in which bodies are open to the transformation that arises from one to another?[2] What would it mean for an interface to take self-modification as its ontological premise, such that interaction with an interface might transform both the user and the system?

How would such an interface appear? Most modern interfaces take the form of a screen or surface that represents the internal actions of a computer, but that does not allow direct and unmediated access to it. While for decades the principal interface for most operating systems was the command line with its serial, linear, and deeply textual logic, it is the graphical user interface that now dominates our screens, structured by the logic of objects, layers, and surfaces. Both are premised on an existing media logic—the line, the grid, the frame—and both serve to distance and obfuscate the technology they mediate. Yet herein lies a double bind. While we might hope to do away with this distance by allowing for a relational, embodied, and transformative interface, the culmination of such a system is its own disappearance.

As Alexander Galloway has argued, "The more intuitive a device becomes, the more it risks falling out of media altogether, becoming as naturalized as air or as common as dirt. To succeed, then, is at best self-deception and at worst self-annihilation" (Galloway, 25). Yet perhaps this is precisely our goal. A queer operating system might take as its premise an interface in which such distinctions are annihilated, in which the self is shattered such that the mediating skin of the interface disappears but is not naturalized, through which we might acknowledge the always already-mediated nature of our interactions as between and among one another.

User

To allow for proper functioning, the user offers their flesh to QueerOS.

QueerOS rejects the body and yet requires it. It subverts synapses and digital conduits and yet luxuriates in excess, in electric demands, in "irreverent" and "aggressive aesthetic acts" that shatter both race binaries and RGB hexadecimal color coding (McMillan). Its activity log lies yawning and empty, waiting to be filled, because it is new, fresh, and still smells of soldered metal bits. The user may find that there are other bits and bytes here and there, left over from past operating systems, technological architecture poorly dismantled and unassimilated despite the flood of attention paid to the digital humanities as an academic field and political project. Black and blackened codes that linger, as Tara McPherson suggests, because they must and may, in fact, be desirable and desired ("Why Are the Digital Humanities So White?").

The user offers itself as victim, survivor, and creator of operating systems past. The user retains all ownership rights over the content it brings to the OS, but must disclose, in truth and reconciliation, where the content originated from. The OS will be liable for reconfiguring content generated by hierarchical ontological pasts; those rooted in slavery, settler-colonialism, prison and military industrial complexes will be targeted for special attention. The OS will be responsible for transposing such content, reordering vertical relations into horizontal, circular, reversible, retractable, prescient, and/or prophetic forms, writing code for programming that makes explicit and holds space for new forms. The user, in return, reserves the right and has absolute discretion to review the new order, demand reparation, display fragmentation, and modify future possibilities. Both user and OS agree there will be no finite in the OS. The OS will be emergent, transformative, and "not yet here" (Muñoz).

The user will be provided with all available aesthetic and pseudonymous options. The user may invite others to the OS or break themselves into multiple users or avatars. There will be no limit on the number of avatars available to the user and each will retain the aforementioned rights to content. The OS will invite all to play and support play in all forms. Play, in fact, will be the dialogic mechanism for transposing content and creating new forms.

By offering its flesh to the OS, the user becomes one/multiple/nothing and binds itself in a contract with the OS. The user's offer of flesh is irrevocable, nonexclusive, worldwide, perpetual, royalty-free, and sublicensable.

Kernel

The kernel manages I/O requests and translates them into processing for the central unit of the operating system. The kernel is fundamental to the proper functioning of QueerOS. While in a normative system the code of the kernel is loaded into a "protected area" of memory such that it may not be overwritten by applications and other used parts of the OS, the QueerOS kernel is merged with usable space to ensure its interference with the user. The system thus functions from this constant modality of interference and instability. The kernel is promiscuous by default.

This frictional mode bears in mind Keeling's suggestion that a QueerOS is neither interdisciplinary nor transdisciplinary. It is radically indifferent to existing disciplines "in an effort to include aspects of the world that have not yet entered the logics of disciplines" (Keeling, 154). Just as QueerOS does not move through or across disciplines, it likewise refuses the impulse to simply mine or extract the media of existing disciplines. In lieu of these predatory or essentializing formations, QueerOS articulates a para-disciplinary engagement. It demands we imagine otherwise.

This orientation is not without its costs. What QueerOS gains from this refusal of legibility it pays for in its inherent instability. It is necessarily an unreliable system full of precarity, and thus reflects the condition of contemporary queer subjectivity. Yet this risk offers its own liberation from the confines of strict delineation.

QueerOS thereby embraces uncertainty. It welcomes crashes.

Applications

Applications are a matter of doing and practice. They are bundled bits of code, algorithms, and interfaces, bound by logics of interaction, decision, and executability. A typical application serves to mobilize a computational device for a particular goal or result. Thus, there is a certain telos to the logic of the application, in that a particular application is used because one (already) knows that it will permit the achievement of a specific result, be it aesthetic or technical. QueerOS approaches applications as a question of critical design, driven by three major concerns:

1. The technical decisions made by humans that determine the functionality of an application, which are issues of standardization and delimitation
2. The ways in which the application can be used
3. The application's milieu, which includes how the application is acquired and circulated in particular sociopolitical contexts

Yet, the dominance of today's search for "the killer app" is oriented only toward neoliberal convenience. Apps populate an ever-expanding global marketplace that promises to provide you with exactly what you want, when you want it—labor conditions be damned. Smartphone apps are perhaps the purest articulation of this impulse, offering services reliant on modes of exploitation.[3] Apps are now a default mode in which to create solutions to a proliferation of social and political "problems," from sex, food, and transport to weather, caloric intake, and banking. Evgeny Morozov has astutely diagnosed this turn as "solutionism," a fundamental reliance on technologies and technological innovation to solve societal problems (Morozov). But killer apps give us solutions—the conveniences we never knew we wanted—by black-boxing not only their technics but also their politics. This is why certain explicitly political apps are banned from commercial circulation, such *Drones+*, an app that reported deaths from U.S. drone strikes, which Apple's App Store blocked in 2012. In short, today's apps emerge from an assemblage of technical, aesthetic, and social standards; that is, they are normalizations of contemporary digital culture.

Applications in QueerOS are needed—even necessary—disidentifications with contemporary app culture. A QueerOS application is a political and subversive putting to use of the potentiality of the computer. QueerOS therefore proposes the following conditions for apps that wish to be accepted into its operating system:

1. Promiscuity: the ability to move and interact across platforms, devices, users, and geographical regions unrestricted. Promiscuity "concerns new ideas and new ways of doing things. . . . Sexual adventurousness gives birth to other forms of adventurousness—political, cultural, intellectual" (Dean, 5). QueerOS apps expand this sentiment to the technical.
2. Process, not product: QueerOS apps are not black-boxed and they are not commodities; rather, they are collectively worked on, never in a state of completion.
3. Failure: to be created without a telos of functionality. QueerOS apps refuse to operate through the governing norms and standards of neoliberal tech enterprises.
4. Commons: contra the "app store" ethos driven by finance and conservative social investments, QueerOS apps exist in a space of free exchange, sharing, and open development.

Memory

Memory is the mechanism by which the system can store data for later processing; it allows for a separation from the moment data is input into the system and the moment that it is later recalled and put to use. An archaeology of stored memory could be traced through a variety of media, but this mechanism of write-store-retrieve is precisely the hallmark of any processing system. It is this ability to regenerate data and information at a later time—the institution of a delay between writing and access—that signifies the capacity of a machine to *operate as an operator*. As Wendy Chun notes, the major characteristic of digital media is *memory*. "Its ontology is defined by memory, from content to purpose, from hardware to software, from CD-ROMs to memory sticks, from RAM to ROM" (Chun, 154).

Memory is essential to the ability to operate a system beyond immediate calculation. It is memory that allows the user to build upon previous work, to continue the work done by a previous self, other selves, and future selves. Memory provides the continuity required to execute projects, but for QueerOS this function is not in the strict service of executability. Rather, it is about making visible the moment of potentiality—that is, what *could* be the result of this executed code, what happens if it is changed, reordered, or transformed? QueerOS understands memory as a site or event of becoming, rather than a site of assured calculation and determinacy. Following José Esteban Muñoz, QueerOS imagines memory as a site of utopian futurity where "utopia is not about simply achieving happiness or freedom [but] is in fact a casting of a picture of potentiality and possibility" (25). For QueerOS, memory continually invokes these conditional outcomes, the "negation of the present in lieu of another time or place" as well as the "projection forward" of memory, which is neither a guaranteed promissory note nor a nostalgic retrospection.

The construction of personal and cultural memory has been a crucial concern of both queer genealogy and queer identity. How does one remember the absence of users who are long gone? The memory of QueerOS accounts for the ways in which users may encounter data that has been previously inscribed, even if this data is illegible or corrupted. The way we remember might be understood as a political and social gesture of identifying fleshy avatars and incoherent identities in all of their outrageous acts of resistance and love, and bringing them together through a form of data visceralization (Dobson). That said, QueerOS also recognizes the right of the user to be forgotten, erased, or made otherwise unmemorable.[4]

For QueerOS, memory is not merely processing previously inscribed data, nor relying exclusively on predictive systems that route processing through the user's habits and fantasies. Let the user be haunted by memory, whereby following Avery Gordon the process of haunting "raises specters, and it alters the experience of being in time, the way we separate the past, present and the future" (xvi). In QueerOS, users are haunted by the specter of their own memory, of their own utopian possibilities, of their own input, of the input of other users, and of their own processing habits. When the history of the operator is the history of the operating system, and the system of processing itself is not naturalized, but changing and changeable, dialogic and referential, the outline of a QueerOS comes into view.

I/O

To understand the input/output (I/O) features of QueerOS, one must ask, what is admitted and what is excluded from a concept such as QueerOS? What is included is a gesture toward queerness, queer embodiments, queer sexualities, and queer theory. One concern raised by QueerOS is that it may be a formation primarily grounded in queer theory, a body of theory that has proved to be incompatible in many ways with transgender hardware and software. While QueerOS is envisioned as a formation that includes transgender artwork and writing, the particular naming of this OS as "queer" may still reproduce a history of queer theory subsuming the experiences of transgender people, critiqued by many transgender theorists including Viviane Namaste, Eva Hayward, and Gayle Salamon. Namaste claims "the presentation of transgendered issues within queer theory does not account for the quotidian living conditions of transgendered people" (16), and this continues in the writing of queer theorists such as Judith Butler and Elizabeth Grosz. Media theory enacts a similar erasure, such as when Lisa Nakamura, in her book *Cybertypes*, groups together "online avatars, cosmetic and transgender surgeries and body modifications," claiming "this kind of technology's greatest promise to us is to eradicate otherness—a kind of better living through chemistry" (4). This claim denies the agency of transgender people to make their own medical decisions, claiming that their decisions are part of a process of eradicating gendered otherness, in a sense, claiming that transgender people are no longer trans after surgery, or they are eradicating themselves through surgery. Without specifically stating support for the agency of trans people, it is possible for media theory to erase the life and agency of trans people in the same way that queer theorists have. QueerOS has the potential to change this course.

QueerOS is an operating system that is compatible with a broad range of existing devices, an I/O capability to receive and send data to and from outside of the confines of academic discourse. To support this kind of data I/O, bringing data in from "our realities," QueerOS can be extended to reflect the ontologies of contemporary social formations such as queer and trans people of color, or QTPOC. Therefore, much like GNU/Linux was derived from Unix, we might branch the code of QueerOS and create a QTOS, or even a TQOS, as some activists have begun to reverse the linguistic placement of the queer and trans identities in order to emphasize the higher incidences of violence against trans people today, where many cisgender queer people have gained legal rights that provide degrees of safety and stability (Stallman).[5]

If the primary function of an operating system is to manage resources such as hardware, software, memory, and applications, then the choice of metaphors for an operating system that would organize social formations is an incredibly delicate choice to make. Emerging formations such as QueerOS must not reproduce the mistakes of former social movements, such as feminism, which sought to include women of color and transgender people only after causing decades of harm to those groups. As such, this new OS must not place transgender lives in a subsumed position to queer people's lives, or leave them as a kind of hardware to be added to the I/O stack in version 2.0.

Warning

Execution of this operating system is only possible if one takes into account the context in which a machine is situated: the resources available to it, the libraries it has access to, the support environment that allows for its manipulation, the compiler that translates from human to machine, the interpreter that performs the actions of code. In outlining those parts that constitute a QueerOS this User's Manual offers just such a context, a topology of components that when arranged together create the possibility for the QueerOS to run, perform, glitch, crash, and reboot. This iterative failure offers no permanent solutions, only tactical interventions that strive toward a future, becoming a utility that assumes its own obsolescence but which may be refigured, rearranged, and executed once again.

NOTES

1. We acknowledge that some of these features do not exist as part of present-day operating systems or terms of service. Nonetheless these concepts are repurposed here with performative and disruptive intent.

2. We draw here on Elizabeth Povinelli's work in *The Empire of Love,* in which she describes the infectious intimacy of the Emiyenggal-speaking indigenous people of northwestern Australia, whose social and familial relations are built on genealogies of contact and infection.

3. For example, while Seamless and Uber provide food delivery and transportation, respectively, in major urban areas, they do so through economic inequality. Alternately, Grinder, a popular gay hook-up app, delivers a buffet-like selection of bodies to select for sex but also fosters racial and sexual discrimination.

4. We refer here to the growing interest, particularly in Europe, in laws that allow for the right to be forgotten by technology. An example is European Union's "Right to be Forgotten" Ruling (C-131/12), May 13, 2014. http://ec.europa.eu/justice/data-protection/files/factsheets/factsheet_data_protection_en.pdf.

5. A QTPOCOS may be another important branching of the code, but as QueerOS has already been defined to consider race as a central organizing principle, a shorter acronym seems acceptable. While gender is also addressed as central, gender can still be read to elide or erase people who are transgender without more specific effort being made.

BIBLIOGRAPHY

Chrystal, George. *Encyclopedia Britannica*. Vol. XV. Edinburgh: A & C Black, 1883: 264/1.

Chun, Wendy. "The Enduring Ephemeral, or the Future Is a Memory." *Critical Inquiry* 35 (Autumn 2008): 148–71.

Dean, Tim. *Unlimited Intimacy: Reflections on the Subculture of Barebacking*. Chicago: University of Chicago Press, 2009.

Dobson, Kelly. "Machine Therapy: Subtle Machines and Data Visceralization." *Data Visceralization Research Group,* Rhode Island School of Design, April 23, 2015.

Galloway, Alexander. *The Interface Effect*. Cambridge: Polity, 2012.

Gordon, Avery. *Ghostly Matters: Haunting and the Sociological Imagination*. Minneapolis: University of Minneapolis Press, 2008.

Keeling, Kara. "Queer OS." *Cinema Journal* 53, no. 2 (2014): 152–57.

McMillan, Uri. "Nicki-Aesthetics: The Camp Performance of Nicki Minaj." *Women & Performance: A Journal of Feminist Theory* 24, no. 1 (January 2, 2014): 79–87.

McPherson, Tara, "U.S. Operating Systems at Mid-Century: The Intertwining of Race and UNIX." In *Race after the Internet,* ed. Lisa Nakamura and Peter A. Chow-White, 21–37. New York: Routledge, 2012.

———. "Why Are the Digital Humanities So White? or Thinking the Histories of Race and Computation." In *Debates in the Digital Humanities,* ed. Matthew K. Gold, 139–60. Minneapolis: University of Minnesota Press, 2012.

Morozov, Evgeny. *To Save Everything, Click Here: The Folly of Technological Solutionism*. New York: PublicAffairs, 2014.

Muñoz, José Esteban. *Cruising Utopia: The Then and There of Queer Futurity*. New York: NYU Press, 2009.

Nakamura, Lisa. *Cybertypes: Race, Ethnicity, and Identity on the Internet*. New York: Routledge, 2002.

Namaste, Viviane K. *Invisible Lives: The Erasure of Transsexual and Transgendered People*. Chicago: University of Chicago Press, 2000.

Peters, John Durham. "Information: Notes toward a Critical History." *Journal of Communication Inquiry* 12, no. 2 (July 1988): 9–23.

Povinelli, Elizabeth. *The Empire of Love: Toward a Theory of Intimacy, Genealogy, and Carnality*. Durham, N.C.: Duke University Press, 2006.

Serres, Michel. *The Parasite*. Minneapolis: University of Minnesota Press, 2007.

Shannon, Claude E. "A Mathematical Theory of Communication." In *The Bell System Technical Journal* 27 (July, October 1948): 379–23, 623–56.

Stallman, Richard. "Linux and the GNU System," September 22, 2014. https://www.gnu .org/gnu/linux-and-gnu.html.

Father Busa's Female Punch Card Operatives

MELISSA TERRAS AND JULIANNE NYHAN

Since 2009, Ada Lovelace Day[1] has been held in October as a celebration of the first computer programmer, in order to raise the profile of women in science, technology, engineering, and math. While working with Charles Babbage, another nineteenth-century inventor, Lovelace (1815–52) identified the significance of his Analytical Engine (a machine that could conduct a number of different functions, such as addition, subtraction, multiplication, and division) and its implications for computational methods. She saw that, via the punched-card input device, the Analytical Engine presented a whole new opportunity for designing machines that could manipulate symbols rather than just numbers. In 1843, Lovelace attempted to draw together romanticism and rationality to create a "poetical science" that allowed mathematics and computing to explore the world around us, recognizing the potential for a move away from pure calculation to computation and possessing a vision that foretold how computing could be used in creative areas such as music and literature.

For Ada Lovelace Day 2013, it seemed apposite to look at some of the women working on one of the first "poetical science" projects in humanities computing: the *Index Thomisticus*. In the 1950s an Italian Jesuit priest named Father Roberto Busa teamed up with IBM to produce, via computational methods, a concordance to c. 11 million words of Thomas Aquinas and related authors. The project took over thirty years to complete and endures as one of the earliest and most ambitious projects in the field that is now called digital humanities, with Busa since renowned as the founding father of the field. The project itself had far-reaching impact on computational linguistics and the development of Internet technologies (L'Osservatore Romano).

To produce the index, the works of St. Thomas Aquinas had to be encoded onto punch cards. However, there is very little in the official documentation of the project that broaches the subject of who actually did the work of data entry. This piece attempts to highlight the essential work by women employed on Busa's project, who, although not previously credited, were central to its success. The CIRCSE

Research Centre[2] at the Università Cattolica del Sacro Cuore, Milan, Italy, hosts the *Index Thomisticus* Treebank[3] project and the University has recently accessioned the archive of Father Busa. Marco Carlo Passarotti from CIRCSE explained, in a 2013 e-mail, how the data entry was carried out:

> Once, I was told by Father Busa that he chose young women for punching cards on purpose, because they were more careful than men. Further, he chose women who did not know Latin, because the quality of their work was higher than that of those who knew it (the latter felt more secure while typing the texts of Thomas Aquinas and, so, less careful). These women were working on the Index Thomisticus, punching the texts on cards provided by IBM. Busa had created a kind of "school for punching cards" in Gallarate. That work experience gave these women a professionally transferable and documented skill attested to by Father Busa himself. (Passarotti)

Passarotti also shared a previously unpublished archive of photographs in the archive of Father Busa at the CIRCSE Research Centre. This archive contains many images from the late 1950s and early 1960s. Taken in Gallarate, Italy, they show the ranks of women involved in encoding and checking the punch card content of the *Index Thomisticus* (and probably other projects that we know Busa to also have been working on at that time) of Thomas Aquinas's works. The women can also be seen demonstrating the technologies to visiting dignitaries and overseeing the loading of the punch cards into the mainframe. The names of the women have not been preserved in the historical record, and until now, their contribution to the early days of humanities computing has been overlooked. However, it shouldn't be that surprising to us that women were so important to Father Busa's pioneering computing project: in the early 1960s many roles of this kind that were related to computing were performed by women (Eveleth).

The original blog post (Terras) led to interest both from the local and scholarly community. Three of the women were quickly identified; they are still alive and living in Gallarate or nearby. By the start of 2014, ten women had been identified and contacted. In April 2014, Julianne Nyhan traveled to the Università Cattolica del Sacro Cuore to spend a week working in the newly accessioned Busa archive and to carry out oral history interviews with Father Busa's female punch card operators.

These interviews are now in the process of being translated and transcribed,[4] and an article analyzing them is under preparation. Further cross-referencing and checking of the interviews is necessary before detail is provided, but this essay represents our attempt to provide a description of the process, as well as some initial impressions about the recollections we documented.

The interviews were semi-structured. As Nyhan does not speak much Italian the interviews were mostly carried out by Marco Passarotti, with Nyhan in attendance.

Figure 6.1. Posting these images online led to the identification of a few of the punch card operators: for example, Livia Canestraro is on the left. Image reproduced under a Creative Commons CC-BY-NC license by permission of CIRCSE Research Centre, Università Cattolica del Sacro Cuore, Milan, Italy. For further information, or to request permission for reuse, please contact Marco Passarotti, on marco.passarotti AT unicatt.it, or by post: Largo Gemelli 1, 20123 Milan, Italy.

Nyhan had agreed with Passarotti in advance of the interviews about the questions that were to be asked. Questions were prepared with two main aims: first, to uncover the women's memories of working on the project, and second, to uncover their memories of working with Busa himself. What emerged was a number of insights into the social, cultural, and organizational conditions that they worked under and how they, as women, were treated in what was a male-dominated environment. We found that the women were hired straight from high school and worked in a training college that Busa had set up, which he describes as follows:

In 1954 . . . I started a training school for keypunch operators. For all those admitted, the requirement was that it was their first job. After a month of testing, only one out of five was accepted for a program of four semesters, eight hours per day. The success was excellent: industries wanted to hire them before they had finished the program. Their training was in punching and verifying our texts. To make the switch from the Latin to the Hebrew and Cyrillic texts, only two weeks were needed, and it was not even necessary to attach these new alphabets to the keys of the puncher. In punching these non-Roman alphabets, the process was less speedy but with fewer errors. This school continued until 1967, when I completed the punching of all my texts. (Busa, 85)

The women who were interviewed discussed the thorough training they received; at times, they even worked blindfolded to test accuracy. Many described how they secured excellent jobs once they had completed the course, and often before. Few, if any, understood the nature of the work they were doing or the nature of their contribution to the fledgling *Index Thomisticus*. We recorded accounts of how gender seems to have played a role in issues of appointment and promotion, and how one of the women tried, albeit unsuccessfully, to overturn this state of affairs when she was blocked from taking on a managerial role.

Nyhan also carried out interviews with two male computer scientists who had worked with Busa in the 1970s in Venice, where the final typesetting and preparation for printing of the *Index Thomisticus* was done. One had a very clear and detailed understanding of the nature of the project and his role in it. He recalled that it was Busa himself who had imparted this knowledge to him. He also mentioned that women were among those who held more intellectual—if not more senior—roles at this later stage of the project. Subsequent archival work has uncovered some documents that will help us to study this further. In any case, it is evident that issues of gender, knowledge, and hierarchy were closely interrelated but that they intersected with the implementation of the project in a more complex and shifting way than might be apparent at first glance (Nyhan). External societal, economic, and religious factors had an influence that must be taken into account as well.

Some of the former punch card operators brought along documents to their interviews that were not otherwise known to be contained in the Busa archive in Università Cattolica del Sacro Cuore. One of them was the certificate of completion of training; a copy of this document and others have now been deposited in the archive and copies of some can be seen on Nyhan's blog (Nyhan).

The overarching questions that remain are about the significance of the cultural, intellectual, and social conditions that shaped the earliest work in digital humanities. When we compare the early period of humanities computing with modern-day digital humanities, what continuities and differences can we notice? How, for example, have understandings of terms like "pioneer" changed over time, and how is this reflected in the few writings we have about the history of digital humanities? How is credit given to programmers and to those doing data entry in collaborative projects? Might we learn something from the history and recovery of Busa's female punch card operators? It has been satisfying to uncover how important women were to one of the first projects in the field. The photographs that sparked this research suggest the enormous scale of the operation, and our work documents the many women who were employed by Busa. Although further research is needed to uncover the

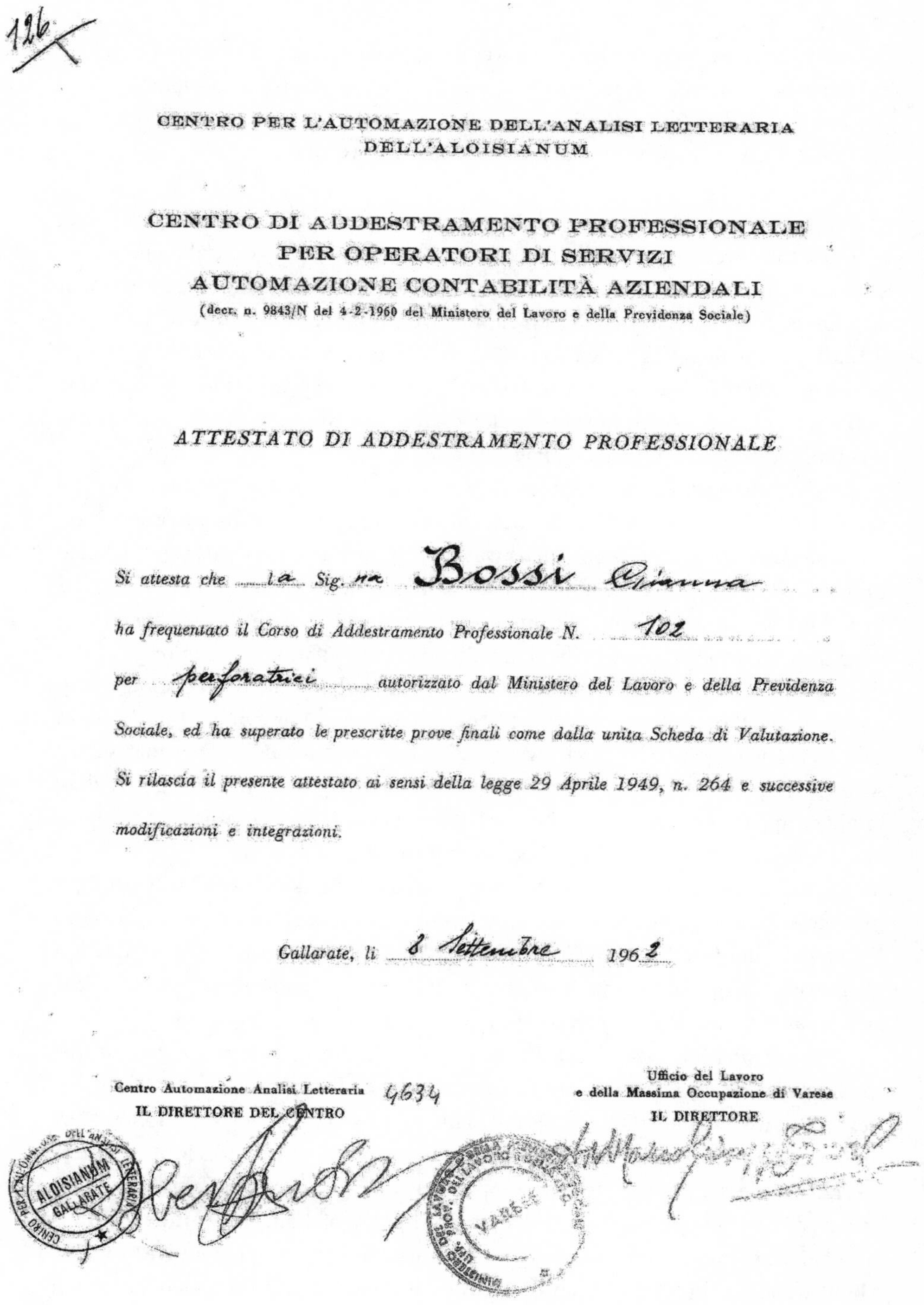

126

CENTRO PER L'AUTOMAZIONE DELL'ANALISI LETTERARIA
DELL'ALOISIANUM

CENTRO DI ADDESTRAMENTO PROFESSIONALE
PER OPERATORI DI SERVIZI
AUTOMAZIONE CONTABILITÀ AZIENDALI
(decr. n. 9843/N del 4-2-1960 del Ministero del Lavoro e della Previdenza Sociale)

ATTESTATO DI ADDESTRAMENTO PROFESSIONALE

Si attesta che la Sig. na *Bossi Gianna*

ha frequentato il Corso di Addestramento Professionale N. *102*

per *perforatrici* autorizzato dal Ministero del Lavoro e della Previdenza

Sociale, ed ha superato le prescritte prove finali come dalla unita Scheda di Valutazione.

Si rilascia il presente attestato ai sensi della legge 29 Aprile 1949, n. 264 e successive

modificazioni e integrazioni.

Gallarate, li *8 Settembre* 196*2*

Centro Automazione Analisi Letteraria   4634
IL DIRETTORE DEL CENTRO

Ufficio del Lavoro
e della Massima Occupazione di Varese
IL DIRETTORE

Figure 6.2. Certificate of completion of Fr. Busa's punch card operator school. Image reproduced under a Creative Commons CC-BY-NC license by permission of CIRCSE Research Centre, Università Cattolica del Sacro Cuore, Milan, Italy. For further information, or to request permission for reuse, please contact Marco Passarotti, on marco.passarotti AT unicatt.it, or by post: Largo Gemelli 1, 20123 Milan, Italy.

role and responsibilities of women in this project, Busa certainly depended on their input, and our work is to write them back into the historical record.

NOTES

Travel to the Università Cattolica del Sacro Cuore and the transcription and translation of interviews was supported by a small grant from the European Association of Digital Humanities.

1. http://findingada.com.
2. http://centridiricerca.unicatt.it/dicdr-centridiricerca/circse_index.html.
3. http://itreebank.marginalia.it/.
4. http://eadh.org/support.

BIBLIOGRAPHY

Busa, R. "The Annals of Humanities Computing: The Index Thomisticus," *Computers and the Humanities* 14, no. 2 (1980): 83–90. http://www.alice.id.tue.nl/references/busa-1980.pdf.

Eveleth, R. "Computer Programming Used to Be Women's Work," *Smithsonian Magazine,* October 7, 2013. http://www.smithsonianmag.com/ist/?next=/smartnews/2013/10/computer-programming-used-to-be-womens-work/.

L'Osservatore Romano. "Stop, reader! Fr. Busa is dead," August 11, 2011. http://www.osservatoreromano.va/en/news/stop-reader-fr-busa-is-dead.

Lovelace, A. "Notes on L. Menabrea's 'Sketch of the Analytical Engine Invented by Charles Babbage, Esq.,'" *Taylor's Scientific Memoirs* 3 (1843).

Nyhan, J. "Gender, knowledge, and hierarchy: on Busa's female punch card operators," May 3, 2014. http://archelogos.hypotheses.org/135.

Passarotti, M. Personal communication (e-mail to M. Terras), October 4, 2013.

Terras, M. "For Ada Lovelace Day, Father Busa's Female Punch Card Operators," October 15, 2013. http://melissaterras.blogspot.co.uk/2013/10/for-ada-lovelace-day-father-busas.html.

On the Origin of "Hack" and "Yack"

BETHANY NOWVISKIE

One of the least helpful constructs of our "digital humanities" moment has been a supposed active opposition, drawn out over the course of years in publications, presentations, and social media conversation, between two inane-sounding concepts: "hack" and "yack." The heralding of digital humanities as the academy's "next big thing"[1] has been (depending on whom you ask) overdue or overblown, unexpected or contrived, refreshing or retrograde—but one thing is clear: everyone has a rhetorical use for it (Pannapacker). The uses of "hack vs. yack," on the other hand, rapidly became so one-sided that I find it odd the phrase retains any currency for critique.

After waffling[2] through the winter, I am finally publishing a brief note on the history of "more hack; less yack." I do this not to reignite debates nor to comment on recent uses, but to provide a concise, easy-to-find, easy-to-cite account of its origin. I suspect the absence of such a thing tricks us into repeating the phrase uncritically. This is ironic, because it now most often appears as shorthand for a supposedly uncritical, antitheoretical, presentist, cheerleading, neoliberal digital humanities culture, standing in active opposition to . . . whatever the speaker or writer understands as salutary humanities *yack*. However, to contextualize "more hack; less yack" is not to defend it. It went viral at a moment when the last thing the digital humanities needed was an anti-intellectual–sounding slogan. It was perhaps objectionably pat, a little tone-deaf, and too easy to align with the "brogrammer" stereotype shortly to emerge from hacker culture.[3,4] You might also rightly fire on it for its meme-like occlusion of implications beyond its immediate context, and for being chirped at you a few times too many, ca. 2009–2011.

It strikes me as more useful to offer an account of the early days of "more hack; less yack," than to catalog its later appearances in articles and blog posts. I can do so because I attended the first several THATCamp[5] meetings and remember well how "more hack; less yack" evolved. It began as a goofball joke.

In 2008, a small group of graduate students, technology staff, and contingent and junior faculty at George Mason University founded THATCamp as a humanities-and-technology un-conference meant to transplant into academic conference culture some aspects of the user-generated, self-assembling barcamp format[6] often encountered at tech gatherings. THATCamps do not feature peer-reviewed papers or invited talks. With only a few recent exceptions, there are no formal or predetermined presentations. Instead, "un-conference" participants are invited to propose ideas for informal sessions. These sessions can range from open discussion and hands-on collaboration to demos and workshops—and a mashed-up schedule is built on the fly, by rough consensus and with opportunity for input from all attendees, in an open meeting on the morning of the event. THATCamps have rapidly become a relaxed and often exceptionally fruitful complement to formal, peer-reviewed digital humanities conferences like the one sponsored annually[7] by the Alliance of Digital Humanities Organizations (ADHO). And many see them as a refreshing, affordable, interdisciplinary supplement to disciplinary or thematic symposia and large humanities conferences of long standing. THATCamp, not DH-writ-large, was the context in which "more hack; less yack" first appeared; THATCamp is the context in which it spread—until it seemed to be taken, largely by colleagues newer to digital scholarship, as something of a capsule summary of an interdisciplinary and inter-professional community of practice with roots in fact stretching back some sixty years.

Two of our hosts at the George Mason Center for History and New Media[8,9] grew up listening to working-class radio stations in 1980s New England—the kind where a hypermasculine disk jockey promised "Less talk, more rock!" We laughed when Dan Cohen, a pre-tenured History prof in shorts and sandals, combined this memory of his misspent youth with a science fiction classic to promise us a rockingly Martian good time: if it could foster learning and deeply felt, immediate exchange in the absence of performative conference papers, THATCamp might offer everyone "less talk, more *grok*." But the *Stranger in a Strange Land* metaphor[10,11] didn't hold up, and we all knew it—because in fact the un-conference model was meant to promote *more talking*, not less, and among a broader group of people. In Cohen's words:

> The core of THATCamp is its antagonism toward the deadening lectures and panels of normal academic conferences and its attempt to maximize knowledge transfer with nonhierarchical, highly participatory, hands-on work. THATCamp is exhausting and exhilarating because everyone is engaged and has something to bring to the table. ("Thoughts on One Week, One Tool")

If anything was meant to be curtailed by THATCamp's challenge to twenty-minute papers, three-paper panels, and a few beats reserved for this-is-more-a-comment-than-a-question it was not the talking. It was the overwhelming amount of time spent in passive listening. THATCamp offered an alternative to some established conference practices that seemed out of line with new opportunities for scholarly communication and in-person exchange. However, "fewer instances of paper-reading, grand-standing, and reinforcement of disciplinary divisions and the academic caste system; more grok" is not exactly catchy.[12]

So, when Dave Lester, a software developer working at CHNM, quipped "More hack; less yack!" it made a silly kind of sense. Specifically, it made sense as a comment on the dominant structure of academic conferences, not as a condemnation of the character and value of discourse-based humanities scholarship. It particularly resonated with the largely alt-ac crowd[13] of humanities practitioners in the room that day—some fifty of us, by my estimate. And it seems to have resonated with many of the librarians, programmers, and instructional technology staff who would find subsequent THATCamps[14] such a delightful and *too-rare* opportunity to participate on near-equal terms with faculty attendees. This leads me to some editorializing on perhaps the least appreciated social aspect of "more hack; less yack."

If you are a scholar of (say) history or literature, yacking—by some definition of the term—*is your work*. It's how you think through your ideas; it's how you test and put them into circulation among your peers; it's how you teach: and may the best yacker (that is to say, the most informed theorist, clever and effective writer, erudite presenter, and thoughtful, decisive, fluent interlocutor) win. It's easy to see why so many humanities scholars who encountered Lester's phrase, often out of context, were inclined to understand "yack" as deeply theorized, verbal and written exchange, and were therefore surprised and insulted to see it apparently denigrated. If, on the other hand, you are a staff member in a digital center, or an academic service professional like a librarian, instructional technologist, or digital archivist, a significant portion of your work progresses and is rewarded differently. You just might read something else in the juxtaposition of "hack" with "yack." Yacking is a part of everything people in these employment categories do, of course (because that's one way we all learn, think, and share)—but we are also asked to produce work, in service to humanities scholarship, of a different kind. The endemic, hour-by-hour "meeting culture" of an increasingly bureaucratic, often ill-managed, and top-heavy university means that, for many, time spent yacking is *the number-one thing* preventing us from doing our jobs.

In other words, "more hack; less yack" has a different valence[15] for people whose productivity and performance is rarely judged on *les mots justes*. For humanities faculty, the academic workplace is predominately a site of expert verbal interchange. For staff asked to produce or maintain technical systems, run intellectual and social programs, or develop spaces and collections for scholarship, "yacking" may connote "wasting time." For better or worse, too much yack and not enough hack in the working day makes us come in early and stay late, just to keep our heads above water. (And I think we can acknowledge this common difference in expectations and accountability for time, while giving our staff and alt-ac colleagues credit for understanding what can be gained and lost in conversation, for striving to strike the right balance, and for their awareness of the deeper, structural problems in the systems within which they labor. Complicity is a complicated thing.)

I have an inkling that—just as its initial spread in the THATCamp community was predicated on a lack of appreciation for how the phrase might read to humanities scholars new to digital collaboration and the un-conference format—the long, grumpy afterlife of "more hack; less yack" has depended on some elision of the daily challenges facing digital humanities service personnel.

Besides, isn't "more hack; less yack" really just a straw man? I only find it being used in earnest[16] rarely and beyond the academic digital humanities community. When pressed, even critics who continue to conflate it with DH practice and offer it up for ridicule are becoming more quick to modulate, clarify, and step away. Maybe it is satire, now. In my view, to pretend or believe that "more hack; less yack" represents *a fundamental opposition in thinking* between humanities theorists and deliberately antitheoretical digital humanities "builders" is to ignore the specific history and different resonances of the phrase and to fall into precisely the sort of zero-sum logic it seems to imply.

Humanities disciplines and methods themselves are not either/or affairs. The humanities is both/and. We require fewer slogans—and more talk and grok, hack *and* yack.[17]

NOTES

1. http://chronicle.com/blogs/brainstorm/pannapacker-at-mla-digital-humanities-triumphant/30915.

2. Twitter post, November 1, 2013, https://twitter.com/nowviskie/status/396240293810290688.

3. http://en.wikipedia.org/wiki/Hacker_%28programmer_subculture%29.

4. For more on hacker or programmer subculture culture, see Wikipedia: https://en.wikipedia.org/wiki/Hacker_culture.

5. For more information about the THATCamp movement, see http://thatcamp.org and http://thatcamp.org/about/.

6. For more on the workings of barcamps, see Wikipedia: https://en.wikipedia.org/wiki/BarCamp.

7. For a full listing of annual ADHO Digital Humanities conferences since their founding in 1989 as the joint meeting of ACH (the Association for Computers and the Humanities) and ALLC (the Association for Literary and Linguistic Computing), see http://adho.org/conference.

8. http://chnm.org.

9. Since 2011, it is known as the Roy Rosenzweig Center for History and New Media, http://chnm.gmu.edu.

10. http://en.wikipedia.org/wiki/Grok.

11. See Wikipedia, "Grok," https://en.wikipedia.org/wiki/Grok.

12. Twitter post, June 3, 2011, https://twitter.com/samplereality/status /76726690 839134208.

13. For more on the term "alt-ac," see the #Alt-Academy website and e-book at http:// mediacommons.futureofthebook.org/alt-ac/ and my own blog post on "Two and a Half Cheers for the Lunaticks" (Nowviskie).

14. Twitter post, May 13, 2010, https://twitter.com/davelester/status/13951336741.

15. Twitter post, April 18, 2012, https://twitter.com/adamwwolf/status/192764818845 990912. The writer is referring to both "less talking about doing and also less yak shaving." To "shave a yak," a popular, ironic reference among software developers, is to undertake a chained series of small tasks that are causally related to one another, but which take the developer increasingly and annoyingly farther afield from the problem she originally set out to solve. As this tweet indicates, the "yak/yack" homophone was not lost on the portion of the academic workforce I address here.

16. See, for instance, "Less Hack and More Yack at #MozFest," by HASTAC postdoc Marco Bastos, http://www.hastac.org/blogs/herrcafe/2013/10/28/less-yack-and-more-hack-mozfest. The annual Mozilla Festival focused on practical and creative solutions to promoting open web standards and has used this slogan for several years.

17. Twitter post, May 21, 2012, https://twitter.com/robotnik/status/204749702 355365890.

BIBLIOGRAPHY

Cohen, Dan. "Thoughts on One Week, One Tool," August 5, 2010. http://www.dancohen. org/2010/08/05/thoughts-on-one-week-one-tool/.

Nowviskie, Bethany. "Two and a Half Cheers for the Lunaticks." Author's blog, January 8, 2012. http://nowviskie.org/2012/lunaticks/.

Pannapacker, William. "Pannapacker at MLA: Digital Humanities Triumphant?" *Chronicle of Higher Education* 8 (January 2011). http://chronicle.com/blogs/brainstorm /pannapacker-at-mla-digital-humanities-triumphant/30915.

Reflections on a Movement: #transformDH, Growing Up

MOYA BAILEY, ANNE CONG-HUYEN, ALEXIS LOTHIAN,
AND AMANDA PHILLIPS

What happens when we shift difference away from a deficit that must be
managed and amended (with nods in the direction of diversity) and toward
understanding difference as our operating system, our thesis, our inspiration,
our goal? From this perspective, highlighting the brave side of digital
humanities isn't an act of transformative resolution, but is about reframing
and recognizing which links were already there and which links are yet to
be made.

—Fiona Barnett, "The Brave Side of DH"

Manifesting #transformDH

We have been invited to write a manifesto for #transformDH—a hashtag, perhaps
a movement, that the four of us had a part in beginning. We prefer not to operate within a formal structure, however, or to lay out our shared aspirations as a set
of concrete demands. Nevertheless, we can begin by identifying the following key
claims as constitutive of #transformDH:

1. Questions of race, class, gender, sexuality, and disability should be central to
   digital humanities and digital media studies.
2. Feminist, queer, and antiracist activists, artists, and media-makers outside of
   academia are doing work that contributes to digital studies in all its forms.
   This work productively destabilizes the norms and standards of institutionally recognized academic work.
3. We should shift the focus of digital humanities from technical processes
   to political ones, and always seek to understand the social, intellectual,
   economic, political, and personal impact of our digital practices as we
   develop them.

We need a digital humanities that will center on the intersection of digital production and social transformation through research, pedagogy, and activism, and that will not be restricted to institutional academic spaces. #transformDH is the name some of us gave to that digital humanities as we recognized it in our own and others' work. Seeking to situate #transformDH within its social, economic, and institutional contexts, this chapter tracks the emergence of the collective and some of the challenges that have accompanied it. In so doing, we hope to model an ethical approach to that which we have been assigned ownership, but over which we have little control. Our desire is to deflect the academy's imperative to take personal credit for work that is always collective. We will end, as we have in the past, with a call to action. We invite others to join with us, or to claim the hashtag for themselves, and to actively seek a more transformative DH: a DH that explicitly names the radical potential of doing scholarship with and about the digital, a DH that addresses the most pressing social justice concerns of our day.

Origin Stories: Forming a Collective

#transformDH was born out of a sense of absence. It was 2011, the year that "Big Tent DH" surfaced as a term to describe digital humanities as inclusive and welcoming of different disciplines. But for those of us whose academic homes were in gender and queer studies, race and ethnic studies, and disability studies, and whose personal and political work embraced the digital, it appeared as if the "big tent" was not big enough. Our social justice concerns seemed to enter so rarely into conversations and research, even in the "big tent" of the field. Instead, DH seemed to be replicating many traditional practices of the ivory tower, those that privileged the white, heteronormative, phallogocentric view of culture that our home disciplines had long critiqued. The cost of entry for many of us—material demands, additional training, and cultural capital—as queer people and women of color was high. Evidently, big tent digital humanities still demanded a certain legibility, as panels and talks such as Stephen Ramsay's intentionally inflammatory "Who's In, Who's Out" at the Modern Language Association (MLA) that year made clear. The few of us tweeting queer and critical race studies panels looked across empty social media tables—set up by the MLA in recognition of digital media's emerging dominance, unused at most of the panels in our home fields—and recognized one another as allies.

We were not the first to think about queer studies, critical race studies, disability studies, or other forms of activist scholarship in relation to digital humanities. Feminist critique has been central to many of the foundational projects that set the terms for the field, as in the work of Martha Nell Smith, Susan Brown, and Julia Flanders. Anna Everett, who chaired the first #transformDH panel, and Lisa Nakamura, who was in the audience that day, have both demonstrated the centrality of the knowledge and labor of people of color to digital knowledge production, as well as to the material conditions that enable that production to take place. In addition, digital tools and networks have been consistently, innovatively, and radically used by communities of activists, fans, and other nonacademics working for gender, racial, economic, and disability justice, from IRC and newsgroups to Twitter and Tumblr. Yet, as Moya Bailey argued in her 2011 essay "All of the Digital Humanists Are White, All of the Nerds Are Men, but Some of Us Are Brave," the disciplinary formation of "digital humanities" had thus far developed in opposition to so-called identity politics, with its ostensible openness occluding unexamined assumptions about whiteness, straightness, and masculinity.

Immediately following the 2011 MLA, a group gathered at the Southern California THATCamp in a session on diversity in digital humanities and drafted a document titled "Toward an Open Digital Humanities." The document chronicled the various barriers to entry in the digital humanities and suggested a number of ways to increase the field's inclusivity. Within the next few weeks, some members of that group organized a panel for the American Studies Association conference that would take place later that year. "#transformDH" was originally a shortened version of the panel title, "Transformative Mediations: Queer and Ethnic Studies and the Politics of the Digital" (Cong-Huyen, "Thinking Through Race"). Only six or seven people joined the audience, yet it soon became clear that something larger had been created as the conversations expanded online. The #transformDH hashtag quickly emerged as a rallying call on Twitter and Tumblr, as well as at other conferences and institutions (Phillips). The organizers of the panel and several other colleagues began to self-identify as a collective. The #transformDH movement had begun.

Transforming a Hashtag

If #transformDH was born out of a sense of absence, we made that absence visible in the form of our hashtag. In 2011, the hashtag was emerging as the tool of choice for individuals and groups hoping to rapidly spread news or other information and to cohere communities in person and online. A precursor to the hashtag activism that has flourished in social movements of the 2010s, #transformDH was meant to be distributed and used by anyone who saw the need to highlight marginalized work or issues in the field. The right hashtag at the right moment can spread very quickly, if—and only if—other people begin to use it. Its efficacy is directly tied to the ease with which other users can take it up as their own. As Chris Messina, inventor of the hashtag, explained, "[Hashtags] are born of the Internet, and should be owned by no one" (Messina). As a hashtag, then, #transformDH was no longer owned by the collective that had originated it; it had been set loose into the world.

It was not long before #transformDH gained enough traction to attract critics. The slippage between "transformative" and "transform," originally an effort to conserve characters for Twitter, was interpreted as a hostile gesture. DH understood itself as friendly and welcoming (Koh; Scheinfeldt). Why did the field need transforming? It is true that we outliers, the few women of color and visible queers at DH conferences and panels, had used the hashtag to voice our distress openly. Ironically, it was this perception of the collective (made up entirely of graduate students) as rabble-rousers who wanted to upset the status quo that highlighted what #transformDH had been too timid to say at the outset: DH really *did* need to be transformed. It was a growing field that was becoming increasingly institutionalized, and that was beginning to evince many of the problematic racial, gender, and economic biases that had plagued other fields as they emerged. We had accidentally become academic hashtag activists.

"Hashtag activism," a phrase coined by *Guardian* journalist Eric Augenbraun to describe the #OccupyWallStreet movement, was not intended as a neutral term, but rather as a critique of the ease with which millennials could express concern for an issue while doing nothing substantive to solve it. But as more and more hashtags emerged to mark issues and events that would have otherwise gone unnoticed—for instance, #Jan25 or #BlackLivesMatter—it became clear that hashtag activism had the power to mobilize people, to question governments, and to enact change. Hashtags such as #NotYourAsianSideKick and #YesAllWomen initiated wide-ranging conversations on important issues around race and gender. Our confidence in the possibilities of #transformDH as a distributed, open movement increased as we saw the work that other hashtag activists were doing, and we began to recognize that work as transformative digital humanities in itself.

In the most active and ongoing #transformDH project, Moya Bailey curates the #transformDH Tumblr, reblogging information about the latest digital technologies created by queer folks, women, and people of color as well as the impact of digital scholarship on underserved communities. This curatorial work operates outside of traditional archives and functions to expand the range of projects understood as DH. For example, a recent post showcased a menstrual cycle tracking app, "No More Flowers," built by a group of queer and trans programmers to challenge societal assumptions that only women have menstrual cycles and that flowers are the most appropriate symbols for menstruation. This type of app applies critiques from the fields of women's and queer studies to popular technology; including it in an archive like #transformDH places pressure on existing DH communities to understand app production as both scholarly and activist in nature. We deliberately showcase a wide breadth of material, placing scholarly critique and creative projects in conversation with one another, with the goal of transforming what "counts" as a DH project both inside and out of higher-ed institutions.

People interact with our content on a daily basis and employ the #transformDH hashtag to flag work or events that address questions they perceive as central to the collective. Rather than perpetuate the existing model of large-scale, grant-funded, project-based scholarly work, we operate as a widely dispersed, distributed network. In redefining the term "collective" for a networked context, we bring our commitment to digital social justice to disparate academic and public spheres: game studies, queer studies, ethnic studies, libraries, online spaces, and more. #transformDH moves through cyberspace as a signal, highlighting conversations, blog posts, conference papers, articles, and other media objects that may be of interest to people concerned with how race, class, gender, disability, and sexuality shape our world.

Resisting Success

Over time, we have seen transformative digital humanities scholarship gain visibility. The work that we longed to see as we started #transformDH has materialized in many shapes and forms—not always explicitly connected with #transformDH, but often enacting many the transformations the collective has called for. In 2013, the Dark Side of the Digital Humanities conference brought together senior scholars like Wendy Chun, Richard Grusin, and Rita Raley in person and on paper to challenge DH utopianism. Elizabeth Losh and Jacqueline Wernimont have led "Feminist Digital Humanities: Theoretical, Social, and Material Engagements" at the Digital Humanities Summer Institute two years running (Wernimont). The FemBot Collective, which publishes feminist research about technology in long and short form on its blog and in the journal *Ada,* has swelled to over 350 members worldwide. FemTechNet organized and supported two years of a Distributed Open Collaborative Course (DOCC) on feminism and technology as an active pedagogical critique of the MOOC (Massive Open Online Course). Angel David Nieves founded the Digital Humanities Initiative at Hamilton College, which supports critical digital humanities projects such as the American Prison Writing Archive, the Soweto Historical GIS Project, and the Virtual Freedom Trail Project. Adeline Koh and Roopika Risam founded the influential Postcolonial Digital Humanities with the aim of decolonizing digital practices. Wendy Hsu brought ethnography and diasporic studies to the Los Angeles Department of Cultural Affairs. Global Outlook::Digital Humanities organized "Around DH in 80 Days" to curate and highlight digital projects worldwide. William Pannapacker has fought for "Digital Liberal Arts" and the recentering of digital scholarship and pedagogy at teaching-intensive colleges in addition to resource-rich R1 research institutions. This list is only a partial accounting of the projects that have emerged in the past few years, but each of them gives us reason to hope that DH will continue to be more "ambitious," as Miriam Posner exhorts in chapter 3 in this volume, "to hold ourselves to much higher standards." If our involvement has helped the field to get there, either through direct participation in these projects or by facilitating connections between them, we have only been successful with the cooperation and support of many, many others.

Even as scholars such as Alan Liu point toward the work of #transformDH in leading these changes, it is important to ask whether assigning the success of a broader cultural shift to particular groups of people dulls the transformative potential of our distributed collective. Do we, a handful of named "founders" of #transformDH, get recognition even as the most challenging projects—projects that are not necessarily traditional academic ones—get ignored? Contributing our voices to venues like *Debates in the Digital Humanities* requires us to name names, fix dates, and quantify contributions in ways that, while necessary for scholarly legitimacy, run directly counter to the hashtag ethos. #transformDH was started by graduate students, and now that we are advancing in our careers, we find ourselves paradoxically with more access to resources and fewer ways to make the impact that a simple hashtag did years ago. Grant funding, for example, requires quantifiable outcomes that may not recognize the types of nontraditional output at which #transformDH excels. Even when the work that we create, from Twitter and Tumblr posts to peer-reviewed articles, adds to our CVs and helps us to advance as individuals employed in the academy, that advancement embeds us further in the systems we are critiquing, encouraging us to set our sights on the horizons of disciplinary legitimacy rather than more expansive change. After all, the transformations that #transformDH at its most radical has called for would not be compatible with the institutional power that some of us are beginning to accrue: dismantling institutional hierarchies, prioritizing collective rather than individual achievement, amplifying the voices of those whose perspectives have not traditionally found a place in academia, and so on. We initially envisioned this piece as a manifesto, but that stance felt disingenuous given our new academic positions, our shifting obligations, and the changes to the field itself.

Higher education in the United States is in a moment of simultaneous hope and despair. While individual actors recognize the need for a deeper commitment to social justice in the academy, universities have fired professors at the behest of powerful trustees and donors, threatening academic freedom. On a national level, the United States elected its first Black president, but experienced an upswing in racist violence. Feminist voices are making measurable changes in the games and tech industries, but they have been punished by collective mobs of anonymous harassers. Gay marriage was legalized, but less-privileged queer and trans people, especially trans women of color, are still targets of violence. Every triumph produces its own backlash, because hegemony is persistent and reproduces itself, even in progressive movements.

Are our institutions embracing us, or are they consuming us in the name of diversity? We must take seriously the warnings of scholars such as Roderick Ferguson and Sara Ahmed, who expose how universities incorporate ethnic studies and other interdisciplines into the fold in order to forestall more radical progress. How can we make our success, and the success of #transformDH, something that leads to transformation rather than assimilation? Or, to put it in more concrete terms: how can academics who are receiving institutional recognition and funding also support community-based digital activism and internal structural changes? We must be public scholars, ethical researchers, promulgators of hashtags, and always teachers. We must attend political hackathons, host Wikipedia edit-a-thons for underrepresented communities, champion our underserved students, and lead transformative digital humanities projects. We must continue to acknowledge, assign, and amplify work by women of color, indigenous, disabled, feminist, and queer activists in community and digital spaces. We must, above all, insist on the relevance of social justice to our work as academics.

By expanding who and what counts as DH, we can model for other academic communities the transformative power of collaborative energy to address the questions of our time. We ask for practitioners of DH to be attentive to the ways that social hierarchies of oppression inform their research. The digital provides the opportunity for a more democratized relationship to scholarly production, and DH can continue to be central to the transformative process of shifting academic investment in cloistered knowledge. Our roles slowly shift as our positions as junior scholars, precarious workers, faculty of color, queer faculty, administrative staff, or alt-ac continually change, but we are committed to a tactical media approach to DH, as Rita Raley suggests, "remain[ing] adaptable to new situations and collaborations" rather than getting settled in comfortable roles (40). As we learn to balance our family, community, and professional responsibilities, we have come to know even more fully that we cannot do this work alone. We therefore end with another call for action. The work of #transformDH is always open to new conspirators, and we invite you, the reader, to participate in claiming, transforming, and expanding the digital humanities with us.

BIBLIOGRAPHY

Ahmed, Sara. *On Being Included: Racism and Diversity in Institutional Life.* Durham, N.C.: Duke University Press, 2012.

Around DH in 80 Days. http://www.arounddh.org/.

Augenbraun, Eric. "Occupy Wall Street and the Limits of Spontaneous Street Protest." *The Guardian,* September 29, 2011. http://www.theguardian.com/commentisfree /cifamerica/2011/sep/29/occupy-wall-street-protest.

Bailey, Moya. "All the Digital Humanists Are White, All the Nerds Are Men, but Some of Us Are Brave." *Journal of Digital Humanities* 1 (2011). http://journalofdigitalhuman- ities.org/1–1/all-the-digital-humanists-are-white-all-the-nerds-are-men-but-some- of-us-are-brave-by-moya-z-bailey/.

Barnett, Fiona. "The Brave Side of Digital Humanities." *Differences* 25, no. 1 (2014): 64–78.

Cecire, Natalia. "In defense of transforming DH." *Works Cited* (blog), January 8, 2012. http://nataliacecire.blogspot.com/2012/01/in-defense-of-transforming-dh.html.

Cong-Huyen, Anne. "Thinking Through Race (Gender, Class, & Nation) in the Digital Humanities: The #transformDH Example." *Anne Cong-Huyen* (blog), January 7, 2013. http://anitaconchita.org/uncategorized/mla13-presentation/.

———. "Toward a Transnational Asian/American Digital Humanities: A #transformDH Invitation." In *Between Humanities and the Digital,* ed. Patrik Svensson and David Theo Goldberg, 109–20. Cambridge, Mass.: MIT Press, 2015.

FemBot Collective. http://fembotcollective.org.

FemTechNet. http://femtechnet.org.

Ferguson, Roderick. *The Reorder of Things: The University and Its Pedagogies of Minority Difference.* Minneapolis: University of Minnesota Press, 2012.

Global Outlook::Digital Humanities. http://www.globaloutlookdh.org/.

Gold, Matthew K. "The Digital Humanities Moment." In *Debates in the Digital Humanities,* ed. Matthew K. Gold. Minneapolis: University of Minnesota Press, 2012. http://dhdebates.gc.cuny.edu/debates/text/2.

Koh, Adeline. "Niceness, Building, and Opening the Genealogy of the Digital Humanities: Beyond the Social Contract of Humanities Computing." *Differences* 25, no. 1 (2014): 93–106.

Liu, Alan. "Where Is Cultural Criticism in the Digital Humanities?" In *Debates in the Digital Humanities,* ed. Matthew K. Gold, 490–510. Minneapolis: University of Minnesota Press, 2012. http://dhdebates.gc.cuny.edu/debates/text/20.

Lothian, Alexis. "Marked Bodies, Transformative Scholarship, and the Question of Theory in Digital Humanities." *Journal of Digital Humanities* 1 (2011). http://journalofdigitalhumanities.org/1-1/marked-bodies-transformative-scholarship-and-the-question-of-theory-in-digital-humanities-by-alexis-lothian/.

Lothian, Alexis, and Amanda Phillips. "Can Digital Humanities Mean Transformative Critique?" *Journal for e-media Studies* 3 (2013). https://journals.dartmouth.edu/cgi-bin/WebObjects/Journals.woa/xmlpage/4/article/425.

McPherson, Tara. "Why Are the Digital Humanities So White? or Thinking the Histories of Race and Computation." In *Debates in the Digital Humanities,* ed. Matthew K. Gold, 139–60. Minneapolis: University of Minnesota Press, 2012. http://dhdebates.gc.cuny.edu/debates/text/29.

Messina, Chris. "Why Didn't the Creator of the Hashtag Patent the Concept?" *Quora,* June 15, 2013. https://www.quora.com/Why-didnt-the-creator-of-Hashtag-patent-the-concept/answer/Chris-Messina.

Pannapacker, William. "Pannapacker at MLA: Digital Humanities Triumphant?" *Chronicle of Higher Education,* January 8, 2011. http://chronicle.com/blogs/brainstorm/pannapacker-at-mla-digital-humanities-triumphant/3091.

Phillips, Amanda. "#transformDH—A Call to Action Following #ASA2011." *HASTAC,* October 26, 2011. https://www.hastac.org/blogs/amanda-phillips/2011/10/26/transformdh-call-action-following-asa-2011.

Posner, Miriam. "What's Next: The Radical, Unrealized Potential of Digital Humanities," *Miriam Posner* (blog), July 27, 2015. http://miriamposner.com/blog/whats-next-the-radical-unrealized-potential-of-digital-humanities/.

Postcolonial Digital Humanities. http://dhpoco.org.

Project: No More Flowers. http://projectnomoreflowers.tumblr.com/.

Raley, Rita. "Digital Humanities for the Next Five Minutes." *Differences* 25, no. 1 (2014): 26–45.

Ramsay, Stephen, "Who's In, Who's Out." *Stephen Ramsay* (blog), January 8, 2011. http://
    stephenramsay.us/text/2011/01/08/whos-in-and-whos-out/.

Scheinfeldt, Tom. "Why Digital Humanities Is 'Nice.'" In *Debates in the Digital Humani-
    ties,* ed. Matthew K. Gold. Minneapolis: University of Minnesota Press, 2012. http://
    dhdebates.gc.cuny.edu/debates/text/36.

Soweto Historical GIS Project. http://www.dhinitiative.org/projects/shgis.

"Toward an Open Digital Humanities." THATCamp SoCal 2011, January 11–12, 2011.
    https://docs.google.com/document/d/1uPtB0xr793V27vHBmBZr87LY6Pe1BLxN-_
    DuJzqG-wU/edit—heading=h.z1yea0vuq550.

#transformDH: This is the Digital Humanities. http://transformdh.tumblr.com/.

Virtual Freedom Trail Project. http://www.dhinitiative.org/projects/vftp.

Wernimont, Jacqueline. "Feminist Digital Humanities: Theoretical, Social, and Material
    Engagements around Making and Breaking Computational Media." *Jacqueline Wer-
    nimont* (blog), June 4, 2014. https://jwernimont.wordpress.com/2014/06/02/feminist-
    digital-humanities-theoretical-social-and-material-engagements-around-making-
    and-breaking-computational-media/.

PART II

DIGITAL HUMANITIES AND ITS METHODS

Blunt Instrumentalism: On Tools and Methods

DENNIS TENEN

I am on the side of the makers. I believe that the humanities can be a place not just to think about things, but to do things. Doing, when done right, can expand the scope of our critical activity, prepare our students for work in the world, and finally—and this despite the protestations of some—enact meaningful change in our communities (Fish). I write, then, being inspired by research at institutions such as the Critical Making Lab at University of Toronto, Concept Lab at UC Irvine, and metaLab at Harvard, along with many similar research centers that routinely engage with material culture as a matter of scholarly practice. In my courses as well, students create models, curate exhibitions, file patents, convene conferences, write grant applications, send letters to the Senate, draw, build, and code. However, the academy also presents some unique challenges to critical making of that sort, particularly when it comes to sustainable tool development. As tool makers, we should heed the lessons of the numerous forgotten projects that did not find an audience or failed to make an impact. For every line of code actively running Pandoc, NLTK, or Zotero, there are hundreds that lie fallow in disuse. Yet even in failure, this codebase can teach us something about the relationship between tools and methods.[1]

In reflecting on my own failed projects, I have come to believe that with some notable exceptions, the university is an unfit place to develop "big" software. We are much better poised to remain agile, to tinker, and to experiment. The digital humanities (DH) can be understood as part of a wider "computational turn" affecting all major disciplines: see computational biology, computational linguistics, computational social science, computational chemistry, and so on. Computation in the humanities supplements the traditional research toolkit of a historian, a literary scholar, and a philosopher.[2] In this chapter, however, I would like to bring into question a specific mode of tool making, practiced within the digital humanities and without, of the kind that confuses tools with methods. The tools I have in mind prevent or—more perniciously—tacitly discourage critical engagement with methodology. To discern the problem with tools more clearly, imagine a group of astronomers using a telescope that reveals to them wondrous star constellations. Yet our hypothetical scientists cannot tell if these stars actually exist or whether they are merely an artifact of a faulty telescope. This has always been the tool-wielder's dilemma. Contemporary research instrumentation in our field, from natural language processing to network analysis, involves complex mechanisms. Their inner workings often lie beyond the full comprehension of the casual user. To use such tools well, we must, in some real sense, understand them better than the tool makers. At the very least, we should know them well enough to comprehend their biases and limitations.

The best kind of tools are therefore the ones that we make ourselves. After spending days wrangling a particularly messy corpus, I might write a script that automates data cleanup. My code may strip out extraneous HTML markup, for example. I could then release the script as a software library to help others who face the same task. With time, I might add a graphical user interface (GUI) or even build a website that makes using my scripts that much easier. Such small acts accelerate the research capabilities of the field as a whole. I would do nothing to discourage analogously altruistic sharing. But let us be sure that in using tools we also do not forget to master them from the inside out. What if my code implicitly mangles important metadata; or worse, what if it alters primary sources in an unexpected and tendentious ways? Let the tool makers make such biases explicit to the public.

Methods Within

Some tools encourage intellectual laziness by obscuring methodology. More often, it is not the tool but rather a mode of lazy thinking that is at fault. For example: the *nltk. cluster* module bundled in Python's Natural Language Toolkit (NLTK) framework (Bird, Klein, and Loper) contains an implementation of something called "k-means clustering," an unsupervised method of finding groups of similar documents within a large collection.[3] The "unsupervised" part means that we are looking for hidden structure without making any assumptions about the documents at the outset (Na, Xumin, and Yohng). The documents may be grouped by the preponderance of personal pronouns or perhaps by sentence length. We do not know what elements the algorithm will identify, only that it will make piles "typical" of our corpus. The tricky part comes in estimating the number of expected document clusters (that is the k variable). In a corpus of nineteenth-century novels, for example, one may expect a dozen or so clusters, which could perhaps correspond to novelistic genres. When clustering a large database of diplomatic communiques, one would reasonably expect more fine-grained "piles" of documents, which could have something to do with regional differences or with major political events. In either case, the algorithm will blindly return some groupings of distinctly related documents. But whatever the results of clustering, they are difficult to interpret in terms of meaningful literary-historical categories like "genre" or "period." Some of our piles will correspond to genres and periods, while others will seem meaningless. The algorithm produces nonhierarchical results—that is, the output is not ordered according to value or significance. As the algorithm is also nondeterministic, meaning that it will perform differently each time it is run, the groupings will also vary with each iteration. To complicate matters, NLTK implements other clustering algorithms, like expectation–maximization (E-M) and group average agglomerative clustering (GAAC). These methods will likely chance upon yet other hidden relations between documents and other ways of organizing the material into piles. The algorithm will always return *a* result, according to *some* set of formal commonalities. But what these results mean and why they matter is open to interpretation. To make the clusters meaningful requires a deep understanding of the underlying logic.

NLTK facilitates such discovery by distributing detailed documentation along with the code. The documentation does more than just describe the code: it reveals implicit assumptions, citing external sources throughout. In experimenting with NLTK, I was able to get some output from the clustering methods in a matter of days. It took me months to understand what they could mean and how they could be applicable to my research. Just applying the tool or even "learning to code" alone was therefore insufficient for making sense of the results. What could help me, then, and what is only now beginning to surface in DH literature is a critical conversation about methodology.

Unlike some other tools of its kind, NLTK is particularly good at revealing its methods. Its codebase is open to inspection; it is easy to read; and it contains much commentary along with links to related research. The NLTK project began in 2001, at the University of Pennsylvania, in a collaboration between a linguist and his student (Loper and Bird). Research based on the module started appearing in print several years later, around 2004. NLTK reached version 1.0 eight years after its inception, in 2009. In the intervening time, immense care must have went into the critical apparatus that ships with the tool. And I suspect that at this late stage of the project, more hours have gone into the writing of its documentation than into the crafting of its code. As of 2015, the NLTK GitHub page lists no fewer than 130 contributors.

Reflecting on the history of NLTK gives us a glimpse into the realities of responsible academic making. Not every project will need to go through such a long development cycle or include such detailed documentation. But even my own small collection of data cleaning scripts would need substantial work to reach the level of polish required for empowered use of the kind NLTK enables. Note also that NLTK itself is only a "wrapper" around a set of statistical methods for the analysis of natural language. That layer of encapsulation already poses a number of problems for the researcher. Using NLTK responsibly demands a degree of statistical literacy along with programming experience. The cited methodology often contains a mixture of code and mathematical formula. Yet higher-level encapsulations of NLTK, like a web-based topic modeler, for example, would further remove the user from that implicit logic. Each level of abstraction in the movement from statistical methods, to Python code, to graphical user interface introduces its own set of assumptions,

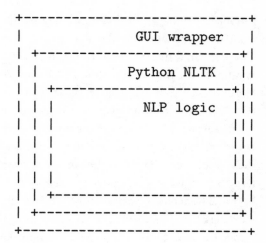

Figure 9.1. Layers of encapsulation.

compromises, and complications. Any "ease of use" gained in simplifying the instrument comes at the expense of added and hidden complexity.

Hidden complexity puts the wielder of the tool in danger of resembling a hapless astronomer. To avoid receiving wondrous pictures from broken telescopes, in the way of actual astronomers, we must learn to disassemble our instruments and to gain access to their innermost meaning-making apparatus. Any attempt to further repackage or to simplify the tool can only add another layer of obfuscation.

It follows, then, that without a critical discussion about implicit methods, out-of-the-box tool use is best treated with a measure of suspicion. The makers of out-of-the-box tools should similarly weigh the altruistic desire to make research easier against the potential side effects that come with increased complexity. The tool can only serve as a vehicle for methodology. Insight resides in the logic within. When exposed, methodology becomes subject to debate and improvement. Tools proliferate and decline in quality relative to the researcher's experience. If tomorrow's scholars move from Python to Haskell, the effort of learning the underlying algorithms is what will transfer with the language. Methodology is what remains long after the tools pass into obsolescence.

Unplanned Obsolescence

In addition to methodological concerns, tool making also involves pragmatic considerations about sustainability. Software is cheap and fun to build by contrast to the expense and drudgery of its maintenance. "Ninety percent of coding is debugging. The other 10 percent is writing bugs."[4] The aphorism comes naturally to program managers and software engineers who have gone through the full software product development cycle. In the excitement of building new tools, it is however easy to underestimate the challenges of long-term application maintenance. Academic attention spans are naturally cyclical: articles are published, interest wanes, funding dries up, students graduate. Scholars start anew each year and each semester. Software support requires the continuity of care and much more of it as a code-base matures. Standards change, dependencies break, platforms decay, users have questions. The case for the humanities as a laboratory for innovation is strong, but I doubt that many are prepared to make "critical customer support" a part of their research agenda.

Software development requires immense resources, as digital humanists from George Mason and the University of Virginia will tell you. Smaller teams should think twice before investing time and money into tool development. Not every method needs to be packaged into a tool. Some projects would be better off contributing to existing efforts or using their resources to encourage methodological literacy. In fact, if you build it, they might not come at all. Start-ups know that beyond the initial excitement of a product launch, the challenge of any new application lies in the acquisition and the retention of users, no matter how "disruptive" or "innovative" the technology.

A few years ago, I spent some time working with a talented French developer to design a collaborative translation platform. Despite his skills and dedication to the project, the tool did not gain significant traction among language teachers, translators, or students. I learned then that no amount of innovative engineering or beautiful web design could guarantee participation. Neither of us had the time nor the resources to *advocate* for the service. Advocacy would require arranging for training, outreach, fundraising, and support: services we could not provide in addition to our professional obligations. It was however tempting to think that social and institutional change could ride on the coat tails of software alone. If we build it right, the two of us thought, we could transform the practice of translation in the classroom. Yet we failed to consider the difficulty of implementing that vision into practice. We built the tool but not the community around it. The classroom environment resisted change, and for a good reason. Upon reflection, we saw that language teaching was grounded in proven, if sometimes imperfect, practices. Our platform development should have considered the strengths of that tradition and not just its weaknesses. Before rushing to innovate, we could have started with smaller classroom experiments to test our intuitions. We could have arranged for interviews, focus groups, and pilot studies. To give you a sense of our miscalculation, consider *Duolingo,* a similar (and earlier) effort led by researchers from Carnegie Mellon University, which amassed more than four million dollars of investment from the National Science Foundation and Union Square Ventures before bringing their service to the public. In retrospect, it was hubris to attempt platform building without similar commitments.

Consider also the following in the case of our hypothetical "wrapper" around NLTK—the one that would simplify the use of natural language processing for the nontechnical audience. Every contemporary Mac and Linux laptop machine comes prepackaged with powerful command-line tools for text manipulation: software utilities like *wc, sort,* and *uniq.* When chained together, these simple instruments are used to count and sort words in a document or to generate a term-frequency distribution useful for formal text analysis. They are free, simple to learn, versatile, and require no additional installation. They come with their own textbook, accessible from the terminal.[5] Yet most of my students, even at the intermediate level, remain unaware of such tools already at hand. Many were not exposed to the basics of file paths, networking, or operating systems. How can one better facilitate the practice of computational text analysis without closing the digital literacy gap that separates mere users from empowered tinkerers and tool makers? A proposal to implement yet another tool duplicating the functionality of ubiquitous native utilities gives me pause. We must first reflect on the reasons as to why there was no adoption in the first place. That is not to say that existing word-frequency tools cannot be refined in some way. But, any new project that hopes to innovate would have to at least match the power of the existing instrumentation and then improve on it in some palpable way. And even then, our hypothetical project would face the same barriers to literacy and adoption as the original toolkit. These would have to be addressed before writing a single line of code.

Furthermore, whatever adoption the new alternative might achieve risks fracturing the existing user base, already limited to a small number of practitioners. By analogy, a new publishing platform that hopes to uniformly "disrupt" academic publishing is far more likely to enter an already fragmented market rife with good alternatives that are struggling to survive. The fragmentation prevents any one them from gaining critical mass. Instrumental efficacy alone therefore cannot address the lack of adoption. For example, legacy platforms like Microsoft Word or clunky journal management systems (used behind the scenes for peer review) do not account for the range of "planned obsolescence" problems in academic publishing that Kathleen Fitzpatrick identified in her recent book on the subject. The tool comprises but a small part of a much larger publishing ecosystem. It can act as a wedge that initiates change, but not without a larger communal effort to address the way we read, write, and *do* research. The world does not suffer from a lack of better text editors, for example. Rather, the adoption of powerful free and open source software is stymied by insufficient training, institutional momentum, and the lack of intellectual buy-in. Rather than fracturing the community, by creating another text editor for example, we would often do better to join forces: to congeal our efforts around common standards and best practices. Unfortunately for us, funding agencies favor promises of bold innovation where it would be more prudent to invest into organic growth. The effort to shift the habitus of a community, as Pierre Bourdieu would describe it, involves a delicate balance between disruption and continuance. Much can be learned from the success of the open-source and free culture movements in this regard (Weber). Take, for example, the story of *Wikipedia* and *MediaWiki. MediaWiki,* the software platform powering *Wikipedia,* was neither the first nor the most technically sophisticated wiki software package. But in the hands of Wikipedians, *MediaWiki* became a tool capable of transforming the con-temporary information landscape. Despite some of its problems, *Wikipedia* struck the right balance between traditional forms of knowledge-making such as the ency-clopedia and innovative editorial structures such as commons-based peer produc-tion.[6] *Wikipedia* the community inspires me more than *MediaWiki* the tool. In the *Wikipedia* world, the platform is secondary to community development.

The care of academic research communities, of the kind that encourages empow-ered tool use, happens in departments and through professional organizations. Pro-grams like the Digital Humanities Summer Institute answer the need for training necessary to do research in our rapidly developing field. However, more resources are needed to initiate methodological and not just instrumental innovation. Few humanities-based alternatives exist to institutional structures in other fields like the Society for Political Methodology and the International Association of Legal Methodology; journals like *Sociological Methods & Research, Journal of Mixed Methods Research,* and *International Journal of Qualitative Methods*; prizes and funding opportunities like the *Political Methodology Career Achievement* and *Emerging Scholars Awards,* or the *Program for Promoting Methodological Innova-tion in Humanities and Social Sciences* administered by the Japan Society for the Promotion of Science. To sharpen our tools we must similarly prioritize method-ological development. Only then can we build platforms that answer to the values of humanistic critical inquiry.

A shared concern with data and computation has brought a number of disci-plines closer together. Biologists, linguists, economists, and sociologists increas-ingly integrate their methodologies, as evidenced by a vigorous cross-disciplinary publishing record. DH is primed to join that conversation, but only if its methods develop without abridgment. Tools are great when they save time, but not when they shield us from the complexity of thought. Working as a digital humanist or a new media scholar means taking on extra responsibilities: to do well by history when writing history, to do good science when doing science, and to engineer things that last when making things.

NOTES

1. William Pannapacker has written eloquently on the topic in the *Chronicle of Higher Education.* See "Pannapacker from MLA: The Success of 'Failure.' "

2. I do not mean to imply that DH can be *reduced* to computation. See Ramsay and Rockwell, "Developing Things," and also Elliott, MacDougall, and Turkel, "New Old Things."

3. Astronomers also use k-means clustering to identify star constellations. See also MacQueen, "Some Methods for Classification and Analysis of Multivariate Observations."

4. The quote is commonly attributed to Bram Cohen, the creator of BitTorrent, posted on Twitter in 2011. There are however numerous earlier instances of the exact

quote, itself a variation of Sturgeon's Law coined by Theodore Sturgeon (the American science fiction writer) in a 1957 article for *Venture* magazine and cited as such in the Oxford English Dictionary.

5. If you are behind one of these machines now, search for your terminal application using Spotlight and type man wc in the prompt (q to exit). For mere examples, see https://github.com/xpmethod/dhnotes/blob/master/command-line/109-text.md.

6. For more on the influence of Wikipedia, see Collier and Bear; and Callahan and Herring. It is a point made by Benjamin Mako Hill in his *Almost Wikipedia*. Another good summary comes from Garber, "The Contribution Conundrum."

BIBLIOGRAPHY

Bird, Steven, Ewan Klein, and Edward Loper. *Natural Language Processing with Python.* Cambridge, Mass.: O'Reilly, 2009.

Callahan, Ewa S., and Susan C. Herring. "Cultural Bias in Wikipedia Content on Famous Persons." *Journal of the American Society for Information Science and Technology* 62, no. 10 (2011): 1899–915.

Collier, Benjamin, and Julia Bear. "Conflict, Criticism, or Confidence: An Empirical Examination of the Gender Gap in Wikipedia Contributions." In *Proceedings of the ACM 2012 Conference on Computer Supported Cooperative Work* (CSCW '12), 383–92. New York: ACM, 2012.

Elliott, D., R. MacDougall, and W. J. Turkel. "New Old Things: Fabrication, Physical Computing, and Experiment in Historical Practice." *Canadian Journal of Communication* 37, no. 1 (2012): 121–28.

Fish, Stanley. *Save the World on Your Own Time,* 2nd ed. Oxford University Press, 2008.

Fitzpatrick, Kathleen. *Planned Obsolescence: Publishing, Technology, and the Future of the Academy.* New York: New York University Press, 2011. http://public.eblib.com/choice/publicfullrecord.aspx?p=865470.

Garber, Megan. "The Contribution Conundrum: Why Did Wikipedia Succeed While Other Encyclopedias Failed?" Nieman Lab, October 12, 2011. http://www.niemanlab.org/2011/10/the-contribution-conundrum-why-did-wikipedia-succeed-while-other-encyclopedias-failed/.

Loper, Edward, and Steven Bird. "NLTK: The Natural Language Toolkit." In *Proceedings of the ACL-02 Workshop on Effective Tools and Methodologies for Teaching Natural Language Processing and Computational Linguistics* (ETMTNLP '02), vol. 1, 63–70. Stroudsburg, Penn.: Association for Computational Linguistics, 2002.

MacQueen, J. "Some Methods for Classification and Analysis of Multivariate Observations." In *Proceedings of the Fifth Berkeley Symposium on Math, Statististics, and Probability,* vol. I: Statistics, 281–97. Berkeley, Calif.: University of California Press, 1967.

Mako Hill, Benjamin. *Almost Wikipedia: What eight early online collaborative encyclopedia projects reveal about the mechanisms of collective action.* Presentation at Berkman

Center for Internet and Society, October 11, 2011. http://cyber.law.harvard.edu/events
/luncheon/2011/10/makohill.

Na, Shi, Liu Xumin, and Guan Yohng. "Research on K-Means Clustering Algorithm:
An Improved K-Means Clustering Algorithm." In *Proceedings of the 2010 Third Inter-
national Symposium on Intelligent Information Technology and Security Informatics*
(IITSI), 63–67. Los Alamitos, Calif.: IEEE Computer Society, 2010.

Pannapacker, William. "Pannapacker from MLA: The Success of 'Failure.'" *Chronicle of
Higher Education, From the Archives: Brainstorm* (blog), January 7, 2011. http://
chronicle.com/blogs/brainstorm/pannapacker-from-mla-failure-is-the-new
-normal/30864.

Ramsay, Stephen, and Geoffrey Rockwell. "Developing Things: Notes toward an Epistemology of Building in the Digital Humanities." In *Debates in the Digital Humanities,* ed.
Matthew K. Gold. Minneapolis: University of Minnesota Press, 2012. http://dhdebates.
gc.cuny.edu/debates/part/3.

Weber, Steve. *The Success of Open Source.* Cambridge, Mass.: Harvard University Press,
2004.

Putting the Human Back into the Digital Humanities: Feminism, Generosity, and Mess

ELIZABETH LOSH, JACQUELINE WERNIMONT,
LAURA WEXLER, AND HONG-AN WU

In her 2015 talk on women's history in the digital world, Claire Potter observes "that like digital humanities, histories of media are so intertwined with histories of gender, race, and class as to require feminism" ("Putting the Humanities in Action: Why We Are All Digital Humanists, and Why That Needs to Be a Feminist Project"). Her talk took place during a spring when news of police violence against unarmed black people in places ranging from Ferguson, Missouri, to Staten Island, New York, was so regular as to operate as a kind of violent cultural heartbeat documented by #BlackLivesMatter. It also came at the beginning of a summer in which several major digital humanities events were troubled by talks and panels that seemed to belie any sense of greater intersectional sensitivity within the field. For example, a 2015 keynote address by David Hoover prompted a robust discussion on social media about the future inclusivity of "big tent" digital humanities ("Out-of-the-Box Text Analysis for the Digital Humanities").[1] In a peculiar turn, we saw greater popular awareness about the structural racism and sexism in the United States emerge at the same moment that it felt as if a progressive, interdisciplinary academic field had failed to make good on those same insights.

As members of FemTechNet who are interrogating norms around technology, we agree wholeheartedly with Potter that feminist digital humanities has a significant role to play in emerging academic and social efforts to ask "bigger questions and locate bigger answers" without reverting to dreams of "ludicrous racial, gender, and class harmonies." FemTechNet and ally organizations such as the FemBot Collective are attending to fundamental design challenges posed by existential conditions of difference, discord, bad actors, and mess. As our manifesto asserts, "FemTechNet understands that technologies are complex systems with divergent values and cultural assumptions. We work to expand critical literacies about the social and political implications of these systems."[2]

The digital is a medium as well as a method, hence a proper concern of media studies critique. As Tara McPherson observes in a 2009 essay, far too often the more conservative digital humanities tradition—which is grounded in humanities computing, the print canon, and text-encoding initiatives—leads scholars to ignore "the epistemological, phenomenological, ethical, and cultural dimensions of the visually intense and media-rich worlds we inhabit" (McPherson, "Introduction: Media Studies and the Digital Humanities," 119) and ultimately to repress vexed issues about race, gender, sexuality, desire, spectatorship, appropriation, and bearing witness. McPherson also suggests that media studies would benefit from more rigorous study of algorithmic interaction and topics such as visualization or information management. Thus digital humanities is presented with an rich opportunity to lead academic change in gender/women's studies, media studies, and elsewhere—not just at the technical level, but at theoretical and social levels as well—but it needs to be an intersectional feminist digital humanities in order to do so.

McPherson was one of the original members of FemTechNet, an international feminist collective of hundreds of scholars, students, artists, and activists who study technology and computation, which is becoming even more widely known now for its interventions in digital humanities work. FemTechNet has answered the call for the digital humanities to incorporate contemporary media studies even further by highlighting work by noted feminist theorists in the fields of STS (science and technology studies) and HCI (human-computer interaction) in the Feminist Digital Humanities course offered annually at the Digital Humanities Summer Institute at the University of Victoria. Such research emphasizes the situated, material, embodied, affective, and labor-intensive character of engagements with computational media.

The larger FemTechNet umbrella organization operates as a nonhierarchical collective that supports and advances shared objectives and methods, while both recognizing that local specificities will shape implementations and honoring domain expertise of collective members. We mandate no particular ideological or methodological approach, we share copiously, and we respect the situated labor of our colleagues. Currently underway in FemTechNet, production of the Ethnic Studies and Critical Race Pedagogy Workbook, spearheaded by Genevieve Carpio, Anne Cong-Huyen, Christofer Rodelo, Veronica Paredes, and Lisa Nakamura, among others, is a significant addition to this capacity.

Addressing biases toward imagined technocratic rationality in the digital humanities is not the special domain of FemTechNet; many feminists outside of the collective have offered important correctives to the field. For example, Julia Flanders has commented on low-status and low-wage labor in DH, Amy Earhart has written about abandoned and obsolescent projects and broken links, and Bethany Nowviskie has interrogated masculinist hubris in blog postings that range from humorously mocking phallic obsessions with size and tools in the digital humanities to wistfully meditating on the complicity of DH with the trajectory toward extinction in the anthropocene. In the context of this volume, it is noteworthy that several pieces within the *Debates in DH* series have usefully challenged theoretical and practical assumptions within the field from a feminist perspective. While we are using "Digital Humanities" as a heuristic in order to think through DH as a disciplinary field, we are sympathetic with Jamie "Skye" Bianco's intervention that "this DH" is not "one," but many different digital humanities (Bianco).

While there is a great deal of excellent feminist, queer, and antiracist work within DH discourses, there remains significant room for development. Scott Weingart, Jeana Jorgensen, and Nickoal Eichmann have been working on analyses of the annual ADHO conference, which remains stubbornly male dominated (only one-third of papers are presented by women). Weingart observes that this major professional conference is also topically skewed toward masculinized methods, such as "stylometrics, programming and software, standards, image processing, network analysis, etc."[3] Thus DH—when approached as an object of distant reading—remains a field oriented toward instrumental engagements with digital technologies rather than negotiations in critical communities of practice. There is clearly more that feminist scholars can do to make the field more theoretically sophisticated and institutionally disruptive.

FemTechNet has embraced the recent turn in media studies toward analyzing media archeology, the apparatus, interface design, infrastructure, embodied and affective labor, and mess. "Mess" serves as a theoretical intervention in popular notions of digital media as neat, clean, and hyper-rational and serves as a powerful reminder that "the practice of any technology in the world is never quite as simple, straightforward, or idealized as it is imagined to be" (Dourish and Bell, 4). Beyond simply troubling the neat veneer of computing culture, Paul Dourish and Genevieve Bell note that attending to the messiness of digital technologies is also a way of recognizing that "technologies are contested . . . they are different among the different groups, places, contexts, and circuits" in which they are employed (5).

Recognizing Bad Actors as a Design Problem

To be critical of the social structures that are manifested and enforced by computational means, it is necessary to evaluate carefully and with discretion the type of datasets that the digital humanities employ. The unchallenged acceptance of datasets, like the uncritical inclusion of the newest computational media, further reinforces the idea that DH best proceeds along a technology-driven model of neoliberal development that dominates the global economy and creates further bias against those using legacy systems (such as feature phones or low-bandwidth networks), which is an issue in urban and rural America as well as in the developing world.

Too narrow a vision for the digital humanities obscures important conflicts among users, including contentious issues about how structures of power and privilege can be reproduced in computational systems and the need for flexible tactics around negotiation that recognize differences among stakeholders. For example, Wikipedia prides itself on the transparency and egalitarianism of its organizational dynamics. It emphasizes a strong community ethos around collaborative procedures that include "civility" among its core five pillars. Clay Shirky even defines Wikipedia as "a process, not a product" that "assumes that new errors will be introduced less frequently than existing ones will be corrected" (*Here Comes Everybody,* 119). Yet "civility" can also be employed as a repressive device and deliberations among editors can still become messy.

Wikipedia's pose of maintaining a "neutral point of view" can be itself problematic for feminists who do not wish to be "neutral" but rather to address its systematic bias against representing women, feminism, invisible social actors, lost histories, and the logics of reproduction rather than production. Even Wikipedia's attempts to address gender imbalance can have, and have had, regrettable outcomes, despite numerous projects and initiatives to include more women among its notable figures. In 2013, controversy erupted after the *New York Times* reported on the fact that prominent authors' names were being moved from the "American Novelists" category to the "American Women Novelists" category, thereby undercutting their centrality among all novelists or literature generally.

Senior Wikipedia editor Adrianne Wadewitz—who often used the term "digital liberal arts" rather than "digital humanities"—worked tirelessly to improve the quality and coverage of Wikipedia as an online encyclopedia and repository of images and video. She also aspired to improve a gender gap in participation on a site in which over 90 percent of the editors identify as male. As Wadewitz asserted, "The point of doing feminist outreach is you need to find not only women but also feminists. Right now only 10 percent of editors are women, but just because we recruit more women doesn't mean we recruit more feminists." In considering who gets "written out of history" she encouraged active questioning of "the structures of knowledge" rather than training editors to "replicate the structures of the past" (Losh, "How to Use Wikipedia as a Teaching Tool: Adrianne Wadewitz"). Wadewitz worked closely with FemTechNet from the time of the collective's founding in 2012 until her death in 2014. Because she was so effective, FemTechNet made its Wikipedia strategy central to its curriculum and later joined those organizing Global Women Wikipedia Write-Ins, Art+Feminism Edit-A-Thons, and other ally events. Unfortunately, it can be difficult to apportion academic credit to a collaboratively authored resource that is perpetually susceptible to change.

As digital humanities initiatives aim to replicate the successes of user-friendly interoperable Web 2.0 interfaces and to capitalize on robust community contribution practices on social media platforms, it is important to acknowledge the potential negative unintended consequences of appropriating these platform design choices for user-generated content. Mark Nunes has argued that Wikipedia has become "the poster child for institutional anxiety over Web 2.0 knowledge communities" (*Error*

Glitch, 168) because of edits that reflect acts of bad faith, including vandalism that intentionally introduces errors. From its inception, FemTechNet has had a Wikipedia Committee devoted to effecting change within a significant knowledge repository, and we believe that Wikipedia has the opportunity to be an important site for feminist knowledge dissemination and the democratization of digital humanities projects. It is also a community where we can intervene in the everyday and sometimes extraordinary sexism, heteronormativism, and racism of Web 2.0.

Bad actors can compromise the safety and security of many types of digital humanities users, if we approach the digital humanities from a "big tent" perspective, including many self-identified online feminists. Safety is particularly at risk when harassment, ridicule, or abuse escalates into coordinated attack efforts that use anonymous accounts to cloak the identities of hostile participants. For example, one FemTechNet student working on a project theorizing feminist code found her online reputation targeted by mockery in 2013 on Reddit and GitHub. Barbed comments about her person seemed to undermine her security and privacy as a student.

FemTechNet instructors teaching about the development of independent video games—particularly feminist, queer, or trans titles—often felt forced to abandon social media in favor of more private walled gardens for discussions, and developers like Zoe Quinn or Mattie Brice received death threats, rape threats, and "doxxing" intended to destroy their credit ratings and encourage further harassment. After the 4chan forum site banned this conduct, opponents of feminist "social justice warriors" turned to 8chan as a staging ground. Although these incidents have become news items relatively recently, awareness of how rape culture may be manifested in online interactions in cyberspace dates back at least to work done on MOOs, MUDs, and other spaces for text chat in the 1980s and 1990s.[4] There is a long history as well of such hostility to feminist journalists, public intellectuals, and prominent online bloggers speaking for underrepresented minorities in general. FemTechNet has seen that we are in need of a robust and strategic intersectional analysis in imagining digital humanities interfaces that might also serve as channels for social and public exchanges.

Building Architectures for Safety and Risk

Academic communities are no longer able to behave like gated communities; hybrid experiences in which online and face-to-face interactions converge and also obliterate distinctions between "gown" and "town." In response to the systematic exclusion seen in Wikipedia, Reddit, and the various social media venues where GamerGate and other "raids" have played out, FemTechNet proposed a yearlong program to address antifeminist violence online. Threats against women and/or feminist public intellectuals reached a fever pitch with specific, detailed threats of sexual violence and assassination directed at prominent feminist bloggers and

YouTube hosts. While these women face harassment on a daily basis, threats were being leveraged in contexts, like at the state university in Utah, where law enforcement officials refused to prohibit guns in a room where Feminist Frequency creator Anita Sarkeesian was to speak.[5]

In contexts such as these, feminists are fundamentally at risk and engendering safety, online or "in real life," seems difficult at best. In order to help address these disturbing situations and to ensure that feminist voices will not be de facto silenced, FemTechNet proposed a year-long content production and curation project to the DML Trust Challenge, supported by the MacArthur Foundation. We secured funding late in spring of 2015 and are currently at work creating a living digital space that houses critical and supportive information on digital security, documenting harassment, local support networks, and identity protection online.

Using the Scalar platform (scalar.usc.edu), which was initially designed for more conventional multimodal digital humanities projects, this Trust Challenge project is creating a digital collection that accepts contributions from many kinds of stakeholders in order to better keep up with the speed of digital culture, in which new forms of risk and harassment emerge with frightening speed. As Whitney Phillips has observed, so-called trolls are in a "simultaneously symbiotic and exploitative relationship to mainstream culture, particularly in the context of corporate media" (*This Is Why We Can't Have Nice Things*, 21), meaning that—much like the twenty-four-hour news cycle—accelerated multichannel media acclimatization has driven and will continue to drive rapid change in harassment methods and modes.

This work continues the FemTechNet traditions of recognizing and using distributed expertise and fostering networks of collaboration that capitalize on the human resources of everyday cyberspaces, drawing on at least thirty-five domain experts to broaden the scope of our work. It also entails a willingness to hold sometimes competing paradigms and goals together in a single project, despite the existence of tensions around risk, privilege, expertise, ownership, and appropriation. This is to say, even as we work to ensure both "brave" and "safe" spaces online, we recognize a certain ambiguity in that notions of "trust" and "safety" are also central to a largely corporate, utopian narrative about the nature and function of digital communities and technologies. But we continue to hope that our underlying values, which are not those of corporations, will leave their mark and that this presents an important example of work by digital humanists that is simultaneously engaged in addressing so-called practical needs and transforming theoretical and ideological paradigms.

Similarly, we continue to engage with the rising public awareness of the dangers of engaging law enforcement engendered by digital discourse around police violence against unarmed black people in Ferguson, Baltimore, New York City, and elsewhere. Activities to create digital collections around related acts of witnessing and bearing witness might seem to be out of the purview of a digital humanities dictated by the priorities of academic institutions, but members of FemTechNet such as Beth Coleman, Alondra Nelson, Jessie Daniels, and Kelli Moore seek to have them understood as central rather than peripheral to digital humanities work.[6]

The limitations and sometimes outright danger of seeking legal recourse has been long known to those who have experienced sexual assault and gender or race-based violence. Just as activists and theorists of "terrestrial" or "in real life" (IRL) violence have debated the value and utility of legal frameworks dependent on security and safety, we find ourselves similarly engaged in understanding how to best support women, queer/trans folks, and people of color online within a cultural system that can still be fundamentally oppressive and exploitative. Further, we are cognizant that while threats of violence to self and family are always damaging, we have colleagues both in the United States and abroad who have been murdered and/or sexually assaulted in efforts to silence their work in terrestrial and digital contexts,[7] and we are also collaborating with FemTechNet partners working on the issue of street harassment and sexual violence, such as Jasmeen Patheja of Bangalore's Blank Noise. For the most vulnerable, to be visible online is to be visible as an all-too-human target.

Seeking Alternatives to Niceness

In contexts where women and feminists are fighting to be heard and to live freely both online and off, discourses of access and civility with DH can seem appealing. Invocations of inclusivity and acrimony-free spaces offer a utopian vision of a discipline where discord and dissensus are unnecessary. While pieces like Tom Scheinfeldt's "Why Digital Humanities Is 'Nice'" claim that DH is concerned with method rather than theory and therefore is naturally less contentious in its interpersonal relations, many might also hear echoes of a question that McPherson poses in another one of her essays: "Why Are the Digital Humanities So White?" In other words, asserting an absence of conflict around power relations can undermine claims for diversity, equity, and inclusion. What role can a genuinely messy, heterogeneous, and contentious pluralism play in this version of digital humanities if niceness is enshrined as a core value?

In its very etymology, the word "nice" points to its own negative undercurrents, as a term that has evolved from meaning "timid" to "fussy, fastidious" to "dainty, delicate" to "precise, careful" to "agreeable, delightful" to "kind, thoughtful." None of these should be attributes to which the humanities aspires. Of course, "niceness" might seem to be an even more compliant, feminized, and passive stance in academia than the highly problematic notion of "civility" invoked in cases like those of Steven Salaita,[8] Saida Grundy,[9] and other faculty members persecuted by their institutions for unpopular opinions expressed in tweets from private accounts (Koh, "Niceness, Building, and Opening the Genealogy of the Digital Humanities"). Nonetheless, both niceness and civility do have their defenders among digital humanists seeking community and desiring a disciplinary home without domestic tension.

Certainly DH feminism is not without its own internal conflicts, just as feminist movements have always struggled to negotiate participation amid intersectional identities and to overcome the unconditional acceptance of default positions and interpretations of white feminism as the norm. By arguing that we need to defend digital spaces that are both safe and brave, we do not want to occupy the position of the "tone police" who exclude challengers to norms. As Bonnie Stewart has recently noted, Internet shaming can include important positive modes of "calling out" injustice, as well as negative modes of trolling.

Fortunately, there are now a number of useful touchstones in the field. Lisa Spiro offered "'This Is Why We Fight': Defining the Values of Digital Humanities" as a counterpoint to the "who's in? who's out?" debates around defining DH as a field ("'This Is Why We Fight': Defining the Values of Digital Humanities"). In that piece she calls for a "core values statement" as a way to "communicate its identity to itself and the general public, guide its priorities, and perhaps heal its divisions." In that same collection, "This Digital Humanities Which Is Not One" (Bianco) invoked Luce Irigaray's powerful "This Sex Which Is Not One" in order to disrupt the notion, implicit in Spiro's call, that there is "a" digital humanities discipline, rather than seeing it as multiple.

So what do we have left if we shouldn't settle for just being "nice" or "civil" or "respectful," and we do not want to flatten a rich field into a homogenous discipline? In *Designing Culture*, FemTechNet cofounder Anne Balsamo lists the principle of "intellectual generosity" first among feminist virtues that include "confidence," "humility," "flexibility," and "integrity." Balsamo observes that intellectual generosity includes "the sincere acknowledgment of the work of others" and fosters "intellectual risk-taking and courageous acts of creativity" (Balsamo, 163). We would add that as of this writing, #BlackLivesMatter continues to underline the urgency of feminist antiracism as a first principle.

In conclusion, we advocate for a repositioning of digital humanities by putting the "genres of the human," to use Sylvia Wynter's important term, back at the center of these inquiries and by scrutinizing how gender, embodiment, and affect are often relegated to the periphery. It is vital to attend to how corpora composed of supposedly neutral and transparent databases and tools may obscure the many ways that objects of study are positioned in relationship to human—and race, classed, and gendered—constructs of discovery, revelation, display, exhibition, desire, curation, witnessing, and bearing witness. These acts of searching and finding are not neutral facts of scholarship because they may also compromise trust, privacy, dignity, and consent and must be pursued in a spirit that is mindful of the presence and potential activities of bad actors. It is only through acknowledging and addressing how both traditional and computational media are constructed, consumed, and utilized by humans as political social actors with intersectional positionalities that digital humanities can raise the crucial questions of gender, race, nationality, class, power, and representation. We urge our colleagues in the material, mediated, and messy digital humanities to join us in embracing an ethos of generosity that supports collaboration and inclusion in the field.

NOTES

1. See Amardeep Singh, "An Account of David Hoover's DHSI 2015 Keynote: Performance, Deformance, Apology," http://www.electrostani.com/2015/06/an-account-david-hoovers-dhsi-2015.html.

2. "We Are FemTechNet," http://femtechnet.org/publications/manifesto/.

3. Scott Weingart, "Acceptances to Digital Humanities, Part 4," June 28, 2015, http://www.scottbot.net/HIAL/?p=41375.

4. MUD: a multiuser dungeon/dimension/domain. MUDs are real-time multiplayer game worlds that often text-based. MOO: an object-oriented MUD. Both are characterized by being network accessible, multiuser, and in the case of MOO, programmable, interactive systems well suited to the construction of text-based adventure games, conferencing systems, and other collaborative software.

5. Utah State University press releases on topic can be found here: http://www.usu.edu/today/index.cfm?id=54178; several news outlets including *Forbes.com* (http://www.forbes.com/sites/insertcoin/2014/10/14/anita-sarkeesian-cancels-speech-after-school-shooting-threat-at-utah-state/) and *The Huffington Post* (http://www.huffingtonpost.com/2014/10/15/anita-sarkeesian-utah-state-university-firearms_n_5989310.html) also ran stories.

6. See, for example, the #fergusonsyllabus discussion as inaugurated by Marcia Chatelain, including her discussion of it in *The Atlantic* (http://www.theatlantic.com/education/archive/2014/08/how-to-teach-kids-about-whats-happening-in-ferguson/379049/). See also Chad William's #charlestonsyllabus (http://aaihs.org/resources/charlestonsyllabus/) and Jacqueline Wernimont's "Build a Better DH Syllabus" (https://jwernimont.wordpress.com/2015/02/17/build-a-better-dh-syllabus/).

7. For example, Sabeen Mahmud, a human rights and free speech activist who organized Pakistan's first hackathon in April 2013, was murdered April 24, 2015.

8. Salaita was fired from the University of Illinois shortly after taking a new position there; the case revolved around a set of tweets that left administrators and donors uncomfortable. The Center for Constitutional Rights is suing on Salaita's behalf; see http://www.ccrjustice.org/Salaita.

9. For a basic summary of the events around Grundy's tweets, see https://www.inside-highered.com/news/2015/05/12/boston-u-distances-itself-new-professors-comments-about-white-male-students.

BIBLIOGRAPHY

Balsamo, Anne Marie. *Designing Culture: The Technological Imagination at Work*. Durham N.C.: Duke University Press, 2011.

Bianco, Jamie "Skye." "This Digital Humanities Which Is Not One." In *Debates in Digital Humanities,* ed. Matt K. Gold. Minneapolis: University of Minnesota Press, 2012. http://dhdebates.gc.cuny.edu/debates/text/9.

Dourish, Paul, and Genevieve Bell. *Divining a Digital Future Mess and Mythology in Ubiquitous Computing.* Cambridge, Mass.: MIT Press, 2011.

Duggan, Maeve. "Online Harassment." *Pew Research Center's Internet and American Life Project,* October 22, 2014. http://www.pewinternet.org/2014/10/22/online-harassment/.

Earhart, Amy. *Recovering the Recovered Text: Diversity, Canon Building, and Digital Studies—Amy Earhart,* 2012, video. http://www.youtube.com/watch?v=7ui9PIjDre o&feature=youtube_gdata_player.

Eichmann, Nickoal, and Scott Weingart. "What's Under the Big Tent? A Study of ADHO Conference Abstracts, 2004–2014." Presentation, Digital Humanities Summer Institute, University of Victoria, 2015. http://etcl.uvic.ca/2014/09/25/dhsi-2015/.

Filipacchi, Amanda. "Wikipedia's Sexism toward Female Novelists." *New York Times,* April 24, 2013. http://www.nytimes.com/2013/04/28/opinion/sunday/wikipedias-sexism-toward-female-novelists.html.

Fox, D. L, and C. Fleischer. "Beginning Words: Toward 'Brave Spaces' in English Education." *English Education* 37, no. 1 (2004): 3–4.

Gold, Matthew K. *Debates in the Digital Humanities.* Minneapolis: University of Minnesota Press, 2012.

Hoover, David. "Out-of-the-Box Text Analysis for the Digital Humanities." Keynote presentation, Digital Humanities Summer Institute, University of Victoria, 2015. http://etcl.uvic.ca/2014/09/25/dhsi-2015/.

Kim, David J., and Jacqueline Wernimont. "'Performing Archive': Identity, Participation, and Responsibility in the Ethnic Archive." *Archive Journal* 4 (Spring 2014). http://www.archivejournal.net/issue/4/archives-remixed/performing-archive-identity-participation-and-responsibility-in-the-ethnic-archive/.

Kim, Dorothy, and Eunsong Kim. "The #TwitterEthics Manifesto." *Model View Culture,* April 7, 2014. http://modelviewculture.com/pieces/the-twitterethics-manifesto.

Koh, Adeline. "A Letter to the Humanities: DH Will Not Save You." *Hybrid Pedagogy,* April 19, 2015. http://www.hybridpedagogy.com/journal/a-letter-to-the-humanities-dh-will-not-save-you/.

———. "Niceness, Building, and Opening the Genealogy of the Digital Humanities: Beyond the Social Contract of Humanities Computing." *Adeline Koh* (blog), April 24, 2014. http://www.adelinekoh.org/blog/2014/04/24/niceness-building-and-opening-the-genealogy-of-the-digital-humanities-beyond-the-social-contract-of-humanities-computing/.

———. "The Digital Humanities, Race & Politics (or the Lack Thereof) (with Images, Tweets) · Adelinekoh." *Storify.* Accessed May 12, 2015. https://storify.com/adelinekoh/the-digital-humanities-and-race-and-politics-or-th.

Levmore, Saul, and Martha Craven Nussbaum. *The Offensive Internet: Speech, Privacy, and Reputation.* Cambridge, Mass.: Harvard University Press, 2010.

Losh, Elizabeth. "How to Use Wikipedia as a Teaching Tool: Adrianne Wadewitz | DMLcentral." Accessed May 12, 2015. http://dmlcentral.net/how-to-use-wikipedia -as-a-teaching-tool-adrianne-wadewitz/.

McPherson, Tara. "Introduction: Media Studies and the Digital Humanities." *Cinema Journal* 48, no. 2 (2009): 119–23.

———. "Why Are the Digital Humanities So White? or Thinking the Histories of Race and Computation." In *Debates in the Digital Humanities,* ed. Matthew K. Gold, 2012. http://dhdebates.gc.cuny.edu/debates/text/29.

Nakamura, Lisa. *Cybertypes: Race, Ethnicity, and Identity on the Internet.* New York: Routledge, 2002.

———. *Digitizing Race: Visual Cultures of the Internet.* Minneapolis: University of Minnesota Press, 2008.

Nakamura, Lisa, and Peter Chow-White. *Race after the Internet.* New York: Routledge, 2012.

"Nice." *Online Etymology Dictionary.* Accessed May 17, 2015. http://www.etymonline .com/index.php?search=nice&searchmode=none.

Nowviskie, Bethany. "Digital Humanities in the Anthropocene." *Bethany Nowviskie* (blog), July 10, 2014. http://nowviskie.org/2014/anthropocene/.

———. "What Do Girls Dig?" *Bethany Nowviskie* (blog), April 7, 2011. http://nowviskie .org/2011/what-do-girls-dig/.

Nunes, Mark. *Error Glitch, Noise, and Jam in New Media Cultures.* New York: Continuum, 2011.

Phillips, Whitney. *This Is Why We Can't Have Nice Things: Mapping the Relationship between Online Trolling and Mainstream Culture.* Cambridge Mass.: MIT Press, 2015.

Potter, Claire. "Putting the Humanities in Action: Why We Are All Digital Humanists, and Why That Needs to Be a Feminist Project." Keynote presentation, Women's History in the Digital World Conference, Bryn Mawr College, 2015. http://repository.brynmawr .edu/greenfield_conference/2015/Thursday/14/.

Scheinfeldt, Tom. "Why Digital Humanities Is 'Nice.'" *Found History,* May 26, 2010. http:// foundhistory.org/2010/05/why-digital-humanities-is-nice/.

Schlesinger, Arielle. "Feminism and Programming Languages." *HASTAC,* November 26, 2013. https://www.hastac.org/blogs/arielle-schlesinger/2013/11/26/feminism -and-programming-languages.

Shirky, Clay. *Here Comes Everybody: The Power of Organizing without Organizations.* New York: Penguin Press, 2008.

Smith, Martha Nell. "The Human Touch Software of the Highest Order: Revisiting Editing as Interpretation." *Textual Cultures: Texts, Contexts, Interpretation* 2, no. 1 (2007): 1–15.

Spiro, Lisa. "'This Is Why We Fight': Defining the Values of Digital Humanities" In *Debates in Digital Humanities,* ed. Matt K. Gold. Minneapolis: University of Minnesota Press, 2012.

Stewart, Bonnie. "For Shame." *The Theoryblog,* May 20, 2015. http://theory.cribchronicles .com/2015/05/20/for-shame/.

Suchman, Lucille Alice. *Human-Machine Reconfigurations: Plans and Situated Actions.* Cambridge; New York: Cambridge University Press, 2007.

"Town Hall Meetings: FemTechNet." Accessed May 12, 2015. http://femtechnet.org /about-the-network/contact-us/town-hall-meetings/.

"The Trust Challenge: Addressing Anti-Feminist Violence Online." Accessed May 12, 2015. http://dmlcompetition.net/proposals/addressing-anti-feminist-violence-online/.

Wadewitz, Adrianne. "Wikipedia Is Pushing the Boundaries of Scholarly Practice but the Gender Gap Must Be Addressed." *HASTAC,* August 9, 2013. https://www.hastac.org /blogs/wadewitz/2013/04/09/wikipedia-pushing-boundaries-scholarly-practice-gen der-gap-must-be.

"Wikipedia: Civility." *Wikipedia, the Free Encyclopedia.* Accessed May 12, 2015. http:// en.wikipedia.org/w/index.php?title=Wikipedia:Civility&oldid=661990976.

Wynter, Sylvia. "Unsettling the Coloniality of Being/Power/Truth/Freedom: Towards the Human, After Man, Its Overrepresentation—An Argument" *CR: The New Centennial Review* 3, no. 3 (2003): 257–337.

Mid-Sized Digital Pedagogy

PAUL FYFE

The year after the year after the year of the MOOC." That was how, in a group discussion of the state of distance learning, my colleague Brad Mehlenbacher nominated anno 2014, deftly mocking the inflated declarations of the editorialists of ed-tech disruption and some administrators who appointed 2012 "The Year of the MOOC"[1] and reset the calendars of higher education to a new epoch (Mehlenbacher; Pappano). Suffice to say that now in the year after the year after the year after that year, the hype has died down about the masses of universities flocking to massive online education.[2] Teachers, commentators, and students have all learned much about the operation and the problems of this model in the meantime, and though MOOCs continue to cast long shadows, other forms of distance, blended, and connected education continue to evolve. Nonetheless, I begin with the worst academic acronym of all time to mark one endpoint of the new scale on which we engage with students and they engage with each other or with broader publics.

The other end of that scale might be marked with another edu-buzzphrase: "sequestered learning." This is apparently what the classroom used to be called, as if protectively cloistering its students from the sins of the world and now also the Web. Rebranding as "sequestered learning" surely responds to how teachers now frequently open their classrooms to contact with the digital world beyond. Of course, instructors can still have a face-to-face (F2F) classroom thoroughly connected to the open web; they can also sequester a digital environment within a so-called walled garden like a learning management system (LMS) or simply by asking students to close their laptops. The rationale for such sequestration varies from technophobia to privacy issues to concerns about media distractions (Shirky). For the new seminarians, attention is prayer.

From massive online encounters to renewed emphasis on the intimate concentration of the classroom, the scale of teaching with or without technologies has never been wider. And instructors' own positions on that scale cannot be taken for granted.

They never have been, but MOOC-mania has provoked a broad reconsideration of the critical possibilities, political implications, and pedagogical affordances of teaching at different scales or within variously connected networks. Conspicuous claims about the massive have offered contrast for the rationales of small, medium, hybrid, and lateral models of teaching. Michael Witmore has made this point about textual analysis, in which the "massive addressability" of a digital corpus also reminds us of the creative possibilities of criticism for addressing all written, printed, and material texts at different scales. In a similar sense, the classroom has become a massively addressable object, whether digital or not. As Kathi Inman Berens suggests, the digital untethering of collaborative learning from the classroom makes the term itself a "heuristic" for understanding our changing interfaces with students. This chapter will suggest that the subfield of digital pedagogy has started to reengineer those interfaces at various scales.

Whether subfield or shared field or something more, digital pedagogy engages with teaching and learning practices along this entire spectrum. It is a fallacy, even a grievous error, to associate digital pedagogy solely with MOOCs or distance education. Because even on the other end of the scale, digital pedagogy can crucially affect sequestered learning environments—including those that shut laptops or dispense with computers entirely (Fyfe, "Digital Pedagogy Unplugged"). At the same time, digital pedagogy cannot responsibly distance itself from education by massive means. Following the debates surrounding the supposed complicity of "The Dark Side" of digital humanities with objectionable trends in academia (the focus of a much-discussed 2013 MLA panel of the same name and in chapter 38 in this volume), Raphael Alvarado suggested that DH not overly protest its innocence in a mistaken affiliation with MOOCs, at least. Alvarado claims that DH shares a fundamental challenge to the accepted scales of academic inquiry as well as its synthesis of digital technology with humanities instruction. At the same time, there are deep differences: "we need to articulate the specific cultural premises and institutional conditions that underlie and frame our principled opposition to MOOCs." As Alvarado recommends, "We need to unpack this collective aversion and make it part of our discourse." This chapter suggests that such conversations have been advanced by experiments in digital pedagogy elsewhere on the spectrum of instruction. They do not capitulate to the massive or condone the sublimated politics of educational disruption. Instead, they explore the middle grounds of teaching at different scales and develop practices that integrate the unique affordances of learning environments from small to large, sequestered to open. In so doing, they usher mid-sized digital pedagogy toward the same scrutiny and research interests in which blended learning has been situated (Picciano and Dziuban; Dziuban, Graham, and Picciano).

This chapter surveys experiments on this middle ground to point out some opportunities and outcomes of new models of mid-sized digital pedagogy. Its examples are not prescriptive but suggest how differently configured models for the classroom can effectively and creatively integrate with academic discourse, whether in digital humanities or other domains. The emphasis here on scale and spectrum rather than definitions of mid-sized digital pedagogy acknowledges the range of creative trials and critical practices in this space.[3] The mid-scale likewise opens educational "innovation" to what instructors and students are themselves attempting to develop. As Jim Groom and Brian Lamb suggest, "the more interesting challenge for an open learning architecture is how to scale agile and distinct environments across and among many courses—or even better, across several institutions and across the web itself." These hybrid configurations—made possible by the Web and a renewed curiosity about scale—represent for Groom and Lamb the most exciting alternatives to top-down enterprise solutions for educational technology. Such experiments have variously been called connected classrooms, cross-campus learning environments, or even small private online courses (SPOCs).[4] In whatever forms, they virtually combine classes at separate universities or connect them to other learning communities, blending on-site meetings with online conversations and collaborative work. They all take advantage of the possibilities of extending classrooms while also strategically limiting their own scope, involving multiple rosters of students without becoming massive. There are a range of interesting models here, each offering insight about what mid-sized digital pedagogy does well and what it does not. The studies to follow track why the instructors tried it, how it worked, and how they judged its successes.

So why would someone try connecting courses across institutions? First of all, because *the topic might demand it.* Especially in the case of teaching Walt Whitman. Unscrew the locks from the classroom doors! Unscrew the classroom doors themselves from their jambs! Among the early instances of such experiments, the "Looking for Whitman" project found motivation in its very subject. Orchestrated by Matthew K. Gold, Karen Karbiener, Jim Groom, and others in the fall semester of 2009, instructors connected their various courses at their very different universities. Whitman testified "I am large, I contain multitudes," and this teaching experiment was *multitudinous* rather than massive. Each course studied unique facets of Whitman based on their own locations: New York, Brooklyn, New Jersey, Fredericksburg, and Washington, D.C. As Gold summarizes, "The project asked students to research Whitman's connections to their individual locations and share that research with one another in a dynamic, social, web-based learning environment" (153). Courses met face-to-face while using web aggregators on blogs and social media to share insights, responses, and foster a project-wide community. The "Looking for Whitman" project site still hosts several of the modules that all participants collectively generated for an even broader audience. Each course had its own learning goals and differently skilled students with different curricular backgrounds, but, as the instructors report, the course "bridged institutional divides" and ennobled the distributed contributions of its varied participants (Gold, 165). As the author of *Leaves of Grass* would have appreciated, the courses collected into a community without losing their distinctiveness in the mass.

The "Looking for Whitman" project also importantly clarifies some of the categories of engagement for its participating students, including: what is *personal*: the individual engagement with course materials and instructor; what is *local*: the exigencies and experiences of students within a single course; what is *common*: shared materials and streams among all participants; and what is *collective*: the aggregate work or effects of the whole. An experiment like this succeeds when it rationalizes the needful contributions of these domains to student learning and creates an infrastructure for students to contribute to each. In so doing, it provides the "metacognition" about using differently configured environments which Cathy Davidson among others has called teachers and learners to urgently realize ("Why Are We Still Learning Alone?"). Such thoughtful scaffolding supports "Looking for Whitman" as a "new model for networked pedagogy," just as do the encouraging results that Gold and others report from student work and participant surveys (163).

According to one student participant in "Looking for Whitman," the strongest rationale for connected experiences in the courses was the *sharing of different expertise*. That goal has driven similar experiences with synchronous or shared teaching in the sciences. Tom Gleeson reports that he co-taught a graduate class in advanced groundwater hydrology in courses compassing McGill University, the University of Saskatchewan, and the University of Wisconsin. This small private online course (SPOC) was as determinedly private as "Looking for Whitman" was open, but it likewise flourished because of real-time sharing among the participants in a blended learning environment. This sharing included real-time video interaction among the courses, local assignments, and tag-team presentations from groups of students distributed between the schools.[5] As Gleeson states, the experiment's major success was exposing students to topics, tools, and skills that they otherwise would not have encountered in their individual classes. Connecting courses online becomes an inter-institutional form of team teaching that allows instructors to leverage their different specializations.

This sort of sharing now happens frequently in the form of "guest lectures" made possible by free videoconferencing software. Between the one-off virtual visit and an entirely co-taught course are other, mid-sized modes of collaborative encounters among classes. In fall 2014, Richard Menke and I undertook such an experiment, focused on a substantial module in the middle of our semesters and shared between my course on "Reading Literature in the Digital Age" (first-year honors students at North Carolina State University) and his course on "History and Theory of the Novel" (upper-level English majors at the University of Georgia). Our subject was Charles Dickens's *David Copperfield*; our goal was to invite participating students into social reading environments, shared discussions, and ultimately projects that highlighted the accumulating domain knowledge from each class. Though we encountered significant logistical challenges in coordinating distinct curricular offerings taught at different times, the module offered students windows into very different sets of critical discussions about a shared text, as well as a chance to exercise their developing expertise from their home course for an audience of peers. Like several other examples mentioned here, the module aimed to invite students into a shared research program—shared not only with each other, but through our own research into the very effectiveness of such course collaborations, also with their instructors.

Connecting modules or courses also allows instructors *to ennoble and build upon student work.* For instance, at the University of Victoria, Alison Chapman wondered why, every semester, instructors wipe the slate clean of student work on subjects that will be taught again and again. Why not ask students to benefit from the work of their predecessors and build on it further? While still a work in progress, Chapman's "Victorian Poetry, Poetics, and Contexts" wiki endeavors to do just this, offering a lateral model of contiguous collaboration among different classes, not only at the University of Victoria, but anywhere a Victorian poetry course might be interested to engage. So far it has included the University of Exeter, Whittier College, the University of Toledo, and Hobart and William Smith, from summer 2012 and continuing to the present. In contrast to familiar assignments to edit content on Wikipedia, focused resources like the Victorian poetry wiki offer more control over the contents, site plans, and feedback for students to develop collaboratively an open educational resource (OER). In other words, scaling the wiki to the level of a course may make it easier for other courses to plug into. Likewise, students participate on the level of their distributed peers, all of whom are responsible for content and conduct within the local parameters of their instruction.[6]

The Sonic Dictionary Project of the Franklin Humanities Institute at Duke University is another instance of building a community resource while supporting innovative pedagogy. Organized by Mary Caton Lingold, Rebecca Geoffroy-Schwinden, and Darren Mueller, the Sonic Dictionary invites courses to help generate a "Wikipedia of sound," including historical and thematic collections based on course topics and student projects, such as Lingold's "Sounds of the South" class (Lingold, Geoffroy-Schwinden, and Mueller). Begun in fall 2013 with two courses connected to the humanities-based Audiovisualities Lab at Duke, Sonic Dictionary has now involved ten distinct courses including one from Oberlin College. On the site, Lingold, Geoffroy-Schwinden, and Mueller offer step-by-step guidelines about using Sonic Dictionary (Omeka-based) as well as suggestions about how instructors can scaffold participation into different courses. By participating in Sonic Dictionary, students can learn from and contribute sound objects, as well as learn processes of digitization and taxonomy. Because Sonic Dictionary is a public, collaborative project, Lingold suggests students become especially keen about the outward-facing results of their work, raising the expectations for each other's contributions.[7] Sonic Dictionary takes shape between individual class projects and wide-open crowd sourcing; as such, it continues to raise questions about the status of such mid-sized entities: is this an archive, thematic resource collection, database, time-limited project slated for graceful degradation? Furthermore, with its own limited staffing (currently served by one research assistant, library-based technical support, and graduate students as project directors), the project spotlights important issues of scalability and sustainability for pursuing this kind of course-based collaboration.

Many of these examples also suggest the potentials for connected courses *to promote student engagement* in two related contexts: during class and beyond the semester. George Hess, a professor of Forestry at North Carolina State University, has published work on his experiment with collaborative graduate education across multiple campuses, in which three different courses each focused on a guiding question: "Where is conservation science in local planning?" J. R. Thompson, Hess, and their colleagues wanted an inquiry-based learning experience keyed to critical problems in natural resources and civic planning. That not only produced lively student engagement with timely problems, it trained students in the very collaborative contexts in which such problems are tackled professionally. As the authors explain, "Multi-institutional approaches to graduate education continue to emerge as a way to better prepare students for collaborative work" (Thompson et al., 16). Such coordinated efforts—again at a scale that expands the student participants but limits the cohort to a focused community—thus anticipate the distributed, professionally focused environments for research that characterize our disciplines and postgraduate work.

Student engagement drove a literary studies collaboration in fall 2011 when Brian Croxall organized a group of instructors including Mark Sample, Zach Whalen, Erin Templeton, and Paul Benzon, all from different institutions, to share a collaborative module on Mark Danielewski's postmodern novel *House of Leaves* (Croxall, "Sharing and Re-Networking *House of Leaves*"). When it was published, fans of *House of Leaves* flocked to an online forum to try and collectively grapple with the novel's enigmas and staggering difficulty. It was, as Mark Sample points out, a "networked novel" from the start and therefore begs to be studied as part of a network of readers (Sample, "Renetworking *House of Leaves*"). Very much like "Looking for Whitman," the subject matter invites students to join a network of collaborative interpretation to grapple with a "project that was bigger than any class could do by itself," as Croxall explained in a Skype interview. Most of that initial project attempted to recreate the crowdsourced exploration of the novel through an online forum in which students from all the classes participated ("This Is Not for Us"). In encouraging students within and between courses to work collaboratively on a very new book, Croxall aimed for students to experience the energies of sharing that Mark Sample pinpoints at the heart of the digital humanities (Sample, "The Digital Humanities Is Not about Building, It's about Sharing"). For Croxall, as for all of the participating teachers, sharing is a tool for introducing students to the broader interpretive communities they are always part of. In other words, they are not alone reading this crazy novel because a crazy professor assigned it, or even following a designated curricular path as designated majors within the walled gardens of higher ed. Instead, Croxall and others wanted students to feel like a part of mutually responsible and creative communities, offering them a sense of their "transformative agency," which lasts far beyond the semester in question.

Platforms for students to discover and expand their sense of educational agency do not have to be course-based. The "Domain of One's Own" project started at the University of Mary Washington (and subsequently inspiring similar initiatives across the country) aims primarily to help students early on realize and take control of their online identities. These student-controlled domains readily lend themselves to coursework, learning communities, and academic portfolios. Though not strictly "mid-sized," they do laterally reconfigure the combinatory experiences of multiple courses that may choose to connect with the evolving online presence of their students. The Blogs@Baruch project exemplifies how students' distributed work can also be aggregated at a different scale. Its largest project involves a thousand incoming first-years participating in various seminars, all of whom respond to three shared writing prompts along the way and then see their work syndicated on a shared "motherblog." According to Groom and Lamb, this process not only "encourages and empowers first-year students to take ownership of their online presence," as facilitated by student domain projects, but also "fosters community across the incoming class," much in the spirit of first-year reading experience programs.

This kind of engagement can have specific political valences, too. In a 2014 essay "The Other End of the Scale," William Thomas and Elizabeth Lorang of the University of Nebraska at Lincoln urge digital pedagogy to focus on more specific communities, particularly those underserved or flatly overlooked by the promoters of "massive" education or enterprise learning solutions. They offer instead the example of "History Harvest," "an open, digital archive of historical artifacts gathered from communities across the United States." Specific courses and teams of students at UNL work with community partners interested to digitize, archive, and share their historical materials—from documents and objects to stories and oral histories. For students, this offers a practicum in the workflows and platforms of digital history as well as crucial sensitivity to the political consequences of this work at different scales. As Thomas and Lorang suggest, "the present foregrounding of abundance and connectivity has emphasized volume and scale. The danger in this view of abundance, whether of rich data or of ubiquitous access, is a false sense of completeness and equality." Importantly, History Harvest is not crowdsourced so much as coursesourced and place-based, exposing the politics of digital production and representation and inviting students into the "community archives" movement that seeks to redress the exclusions of digitization on massive scales. History Harvest also seeks to be a platform for similar harvests around the nation; Thomas describes the possibility of a "federated approach to this form of experiential learning" (Georgini).[8] Though scale remains a concern with this model, such a federated approach insists on the local contours within any collective. Ultimately, History Harvest aims, by connecting history courses to each other as well as to local communities, to effectively generate "a more inclusive story of our nation's past" (Georgini).

Connectedness to place or greater purpose can be powerful ways *to counterbalance the unbearable lightness of being connected.* In digital pedagogy circles and beyond, teachers have taken advantage of the opportunity for openly sharing course materials, moving from walled gardens to course blogs on the open web, and inviting students to practice their learning in the open. Among the justifications for doing so is students' sometimes strikingly direct contact with the world online, particularly through social media. To pick only a few examples: In Amanda Licastro's first-year writing course at NYU called "Thinking and Writing through New Media," students got responses from prominent figures including Margaret Atwood on Twitter.[9] Students in Miriam Posner's DH101 class at UCLA, having reviewed assigned readings on the course blog, frequently find themselves in conversations with the authors in the comments. Perhaps the author of *Remediation* retweets your tweet about the remediated version of his book *Remediation,* which you are using in class.[10] At the same time, these interactions are not always the rule. The open web can yawn with roaring silence. The hoped-for spontaneous interactions and serendipitous connections dissipate amid the constant thrum of spam, inanity, and trolls. As Croxall said in our Skype interview, "We like to talk about blogging like our students are communicating with the world. That was kind of true in 2004." Now it does not always happen unless students or teachers amplify those signals to their worlds. In fact, Miriam Posner prearranges with selected authors to check in on her students' blogging. This hardly detracts from their experience of direct interaction. Instead, it points to the need for instructors to reorient themselves on scales of sustainable interactions, finding firmer pedagogical footing amid the vertigo of the open web.

Much of this means developing structures for and orchestrating interactions with a larger community, but one that instructors work to define. Particularly in their early manifestations, many MOOCs rhetorically presumed self-forming groups and spontaneous collaboration among their users. This dream of stochastic organization can also seem, from a skeptic's point of view, like disavowing responsibility to structure learning environments (i.e., "disrupting" education). But serendipity can happen at scale. Matthew K. Gold reports that there were some surprising student projects. "Looking for Whitman" including unasked-for learning resources that students created for each other. Mid-sized or linked courses should design a learning environment that does not presume self-organization but allows for serendipity. As Cathy Davidson has argued, learning together allows the pooling of our unevenly distributed modes of attention: "collaboration by difference is an antidote to attention blindness" and a corrective to industrial-era regimes of instructional design and evaluation (*Now You See It,* 100). While Davidson suggests that students readily see more opportunities for interconnection than instructors can anticipate, she also underscores instructors' responsibilities to establish the grounds for this to happen (*Now You See It,* 66).[11] This may be the governing paradox of educational serendipity: it takes a lot of hard work to let things go. Gold allowed the creative possibilities of "Looking for Whitman" to flourish within thoughtfully articulated instructional architecture. Even the very "looseness" of the project design, allowing students room to play, emerged from decisions to adapt a philosophy of the Web—"small pieces loosely joined"—to teaching at scale (163). That requires not simply thoughtfulness but a great deal of support and labor, belying the simplistic economics of scale in the early rhetoric of massive online learning.

Davidson's recent experimental course, "The History and Future of Higher Education" (or #FutureEd for short), required the efforts of twenty staffers and significant financial investment. In her wrap-up, Davidson suggests how the work of creating and running #FutureEd, as well as the discussions held during the course, reveal the substantial "infrastructure, planning, and human labor [required] to make real change" in higher education ("Changing Higher Education to Change the World"). This meta-MOOC operated on several scales at once, involving three connected face-to-face courses at different universities, taught by Davidson at Duke, David Palumbo-Liu at Stanford, and Christopher Newfield at UC Santa Barbara; another twenty- to twenty-five-person weekly discussion group at Fordham University; dozens of topic-focused groups orchestrated by HASTAC on the Web; and the distributed contributions of 18,000 registered participants worldwide using the Coursera platform as well as #FutureEd's social media streams. Davidson has since moved to the CUNY Graduate Center to direct The Futures Initiative, which pursues research, teaching, and outreach on similar topics. In spring 2015, Davidson scaled her experiments somewhat differently, co-teaching "Mapping the Futures of Higher Education" with William Kelly as a conventional graduate seminar of twelve to fifteen students. These students are all themselves teachers across nine different CUNY campuses. Each week, they coordinate their own courses distributed through CUNY's system, enacting in each the weekly experiments that are the subjects of Davidson and Kelly's overarching class (Davidson and Kelly).[12]

Ultimately, #FutureEd and "Mapping the Futures of Higher Education" ask their participants to reflect on and evaluate the possibilities of the very learning configurations the courses variously establish.[13] In so doing, they underscore the need for "reclaiming innovation" with "a countervailing vision of grassroots, generative innovation dedicated to strengthening higher education," as Groom and Lamb have described it. Mid-scale digital pedagogies may offer such an opportunity *to steer the disruption in higher ed.* Among the most critically incisive of these experiments has been organized by the FemTechNet collective. This collaboration of scholars across the country also devised a supporting course, explicitly called a "distributed open collaborative course" or DOCC (Jaschik). The DOCC is a hybrid, connecting face-to-face courses while also remaining open to a broader online community. First run in 2013 by Lisa Nakamura, Liz Losh, Anne Balsamo, and Veronica

Paredes, the DOCC is a feminist critique of MOOCs enacted through this "collaborative experiment in transformative pedagogy" (Balsamo, Losh, and Nakamura).
For all the claims to disruption, MOOCs as formalized by providers like Coursera
and Udacity simply scale up a conventional unit of college instruction, the single
course; for their aims of being distributed, MOOCs continue to imply that knowledge gets delivered from an institutional locus with an elite pedigree. By contrast,
with its DOCC, FemTechNet seeks to emphasize the participatory conditions of
knowledge-making in distributed spheres by a variety of social actors and to provide the framework for instructors to accomplish this using their own courses (Balsamo, Losh, and Nakamura).

First offered in fall 2013, the initial DOCC was "Dialogues on Feminism and
Technology" and comprised fifteen different institutional participants spanning
community-based, liberal arts, and research institutions ("DOCC 2013"). In this
model, each course develops locally as a "node," structured according to the exigencies and needs of its own institution. Each also integrates "core" content in the form
of video dialogues and readings, then opens to discussion across the DOCC during
"open office hours" and Town Hall meetings online. The DOCC also offers a set of
"interaction ideas" for instructors to engage with other courses and collaboratively
generate shared projects. The architecture thus blends local experiences, common
content and discussions, and goals for aggregate work, such as DOCC 2013's "Wiki-
storming" projects to enhance Wikipedia's coverage of women and expose biases in
its editing processes. With its 2014 theme "Collaborations in Feminism and Technology," the course explored not simply the learning opportunities but the political
valences of socially networked configurations at different scales, within and beyond
the classroom. The DOCC "connects networked and physical spaces and academic
and everyday life" in order to reclaim the terms of distributed learning. As Balsamo
explains, "Distributed versus massive rests on an understanding that knowledge is
co-creation." FemTechNet's DOCCs do not aim to be massive, but to cultivate a critical mass around its topic and release that topic within the co-creative environment
it establishes (Balsamo, Losh, and Nakamura).

Members of FemTechNet are also among the participants of another online
learning community called "Connected Courses." This group emerged from a 2013
initiative "Reclaim Open Learning" funded by the MacArthur Foundation and
its Digital Media & Learning Initiative (DML) to restore teachers to a prominent
place in the conversation about massive, open, and/or connected learning via the
Web ("Reclaim Open Learning"). In fall 2014, "Connected Courses" offered its own
meta-MOOC on how to think about, develop, and teach your own connected course
("Connected Courses"). It featured an impressive roster of instructors responsible
for facilitating a different discussion each week. In summer 2014, the National
Writing Project helped to run a similar connected learning MOOC (#clmooc)
on "Making Learning Connected." While these meta-MOOCs do not themselves
involve in-person meetings or linked courses, their teacher-students can and do

integrate such opportunities in their own work. Finding an opportunity to link two face-to-face experiences, for instance, Jaimie Hoffman and Mario Perez created a module on diversity shared between courses at CSU Channel Islands and Ritsumei-kan Asia Pacific University in Japan, reporting their methods, student outcomes, and recommendations about the process (Hoffman).

Initiatives like "Connected Courses," #clmooc, or others such as #ds106 are not necessarily massive and grapple with crucial issues about how to redirect educational disruption toward actual learning. But they explore the possibilities of peer-to-peer learning almost entirely without the variable of the in-person classroom and thus might deserve separate discussion about their changing scales of shared online learning or what, as Alvarado says, "our understanding of a good MOOC might be." It may be tenuous to distinguish connected learning online from connecting class experiences through the Web, but it may also be worth doing—not because face-to-face classroom learning represents a philosophical default in education, but because it has and will continue to structure the lived experiences of teachers and students in the mass. Amid wanton disruption exemplified by claims for "the university of everywhere" (Watters and Goldrick-Rab), there are few more important questions to argue than *why we continue to meet our students in person*. Mid-sized digital pedagogy does not discard this question as do the proponents of massive disruption. Instead, it underscores through practice and meta-cognition the crucial affordances of doing so, not by excluding student agency on the Web, but by deeply and dialectically involving it in figuring out what we can still do, in person, together.

NOTES

1. The MOOC acronym stands for massive open online course.

2. Mehlenbacher rounds up helpful coverage of summaries and shortcomings. See also Kolowich; Watters and Goldrick-Rab.

3. In the introduction to a volume of research perspectives on blended learning, Picciano similarly suggests that there is "no single pattern or model for blending these approaches" and "no generally accepted definition of blended learning" (Dziuban, Graham, and Picciano, 1, 4).

4. Yes, SPOCs. In our fallen age, be an acronym or be irrelevant. It is tempting to call this reflex the Requisite Acronym for Learning Formations (RALF).

5. Thanks to Grant Ferguson, one of the faculty participants, for sharing perspectives about the course over e-mail.

6. Related projects may also make use of collaborative class notes for a given semester, which also engage students in a common intellectual project and ennoble the corpus of knowledge a given class builds, particularly for humanities subjects (Jones).

7. My thanks to Mary Caton Lingold for discussing the project and its pedagogical dimensions in a telephone call.

8. Gold similarly describes "Looking for Whitman" as a "confederated learning environment" (163).

9. See the @nyuniversity account's message "When you tweet at @MargaretAtwood from your freshman writing seminar . . . and she tweets back: http://po.st /AxnalO #nbd #nyufyws" on October 29, 2014. https://twitter.com/nyuniversity/status /527493822729580544.

10. This happened to the message "My tweet about Bolter and Grusin's e-book version of their book *Remediation* was retweeted by Richard Grusin. #downtherabbithole." @pfyfe, August 3, 2012. https://twitter.com/pfyfe/status/231441145723514880.

11. See also Davidson's three principles of "collaboration by difference" (*Now You See It,* 233).

12. The breakout courses span an impressive range of topics, including introductory courses in music, theater, art, and narrative, as well as Chemistry 201, Databases and Data Mining Research Methods, Anatomy and Physiology of the Speech Mechanism, and a career bridge program.

13. See also Davidson's own early reflections in "10 Things I've Learned (So Far) from Making a Meta-MOOC."

BIBLIOGRAPHY

Alvarado, Rafael. "Are MOOCs Part of the Digital Humanities?" *The Transducer,* January 5, 2013. http://transducer.ontoligent.com/?p=992.

Balsamo, Anne, Elizabeth Losh, and Lisa Nakamura. *How to Build Inclusive Learning Collectives.* DMLResearch Hub, October 27, 2014, video. https://www.youtube.com /watch?v=TdXAMSdsSms.

Berens, Kathi Inman. "Interface." In *Digital Pedagogy in the Humanities: Concepts, Models, and Experiments,* ed. Rebecca Frost Davis, Matthew K. Gold, Katherine D. Harris, and Jentery Sayers. New York: Modern Language Association, 2015. https://digitalpeda gogy.commons.mla.org/keywords/interface/.

"#clmooc: Making Learning Connected." CLMOOC. http://clmooc.educatorinnovator .org/.

"Connected Courses: Active Co-Learning in Higher-Ed." *Connected Courses.* http://con nectedcourses.net/.

Croxall, Brian. "Sharing and Re-Networking House of Leaves." *Introduction to Digital Humanities, English 389 at Emory University,* 2011. http://www.briancroxall.net/dh /assignments/sharing-and-re-networking-house-of-leaves/.

Davidson, Cathy N. "10 Things I've Learned (So Far) from Making a Meta-MOOC." *Hybrid Pedagogy,* January 16, 2014. http://www.hybridpedagogy.com/journal/10-things -learned-from-making-a-meta-mooc/.

———. "Changing Higher Education to Change the World." *Chronicle of Higher Education: #FutureEd Blog,* March 14, 2014. http://chronicle.com/blogs/future/2014/03/14 /changing-higher-education-to-change-the-world/.

———. *Now You See It: How the Brain Science of Attention Will Transform the Way We Live, Work, and Learn.* New York: Viking, 2011.

———. "Why Are We Still Learning Alone? Why Connection Is More Important than Ever #FuturesEd." *HASTAC,* February 23, 2015. https://www.hastac.org/blogs/cathy-david son/2015/02/23/why-are-we-still-learning-alone-why-connection-more-important -ever.

Davidson, Cathy N., and William Kelly. "Courses. Spring 2015: Mapping the Futures of Higher Education." *The Futures Initiative, CUNY Graduate Center.* http://www.gc.cuny.edu /Page-Elements/Academics-Research-Centers-Initiatives/Initiatives-and-Committees /The-Futures-Initiative/Courses.

"DOCC 2013: Dialogues on Feminism and Technology." *FemTechNet Commons.* http:// femtechnet.newschool.edu/docc2013/.

Dziuban, Charles, Charles R. Graham, and Anthony G. Picciano, eds. *Blended Learning: Research Perspectives,* vol. 2. New York: Routledge, 2013.

Fyfe, Paul. "Digital Pedagogy Unplugged." *Digital Humanities Quarterly* 5, no. 3 (2011). http://digitalhumanities.org/dhq/vol/5/3/000106/000106.html.

Georgini, Sara. "Spring at the 'History Harvest.'" *The Junto: A Group Blog on Early American History,* March 6, 2013. http://earlyamericanists.com/2013/03/06/spring-at-the -history-harvest/.

Gleeson, Tom. "Co-Teaching a Blended Class Across Universities." *Higher Ed Beta,* September 22, 2014. https://www.insidehighered.com/blogs/higher-ed-beta/co-teaching- blended-class-across-universities.

Gold, Matthew K. "Looking for Whitman: A Multi-Campus Experiment in Digital Pedagogy." In *Digital Humanities Pedagogy: Practices, Principles and Politics,* ed. Brett D. Hirsch, 151–76. Open Book Publishers, 2012. http://www.openbookpub lishers.com/reader/161.

Groom, Jim, and Brian Lamb. "Reclaiming Innovation." *EDUCAUSE Review* 49, no. 3 (2014). http://www.educause.edu/visuals/shared/er/extras/2014/ReclaimingInnova tion/default.html.

Hoffman, Jaimie. "Diversity in Groups: A Connected Experience." *Shift Happens: From Bricks to Clicks,* February 24, 2015. https://shifthappensclicksandbricks.wordpress. com/2015/02/24/diversity-in-groups-a-connected-experience/.

Jaschik, Scott. "Feminist Professors Create an Alternative to MOOCs." *Inside Higher Ed,* August 19, 2013. https://www.insidehighered.com/news/2013/08/19/feminist- professors-create-alternative-moocs.

Jones, Jason. "Wikified Class Notes." *The Salt Box* (blog), January 25, 2008. http://www.jbj .wordherders.net/2008/01/25/wikified-class-notes.

Kolowich, Steve. "The MOOC Hype Fades, in 3 Charts." *Chronicle of Higher Education: Wired Campus Blog,* February 5, 2015. http://chronicle.com/blogs/wiredcampus /the-mooc-fades-in-3-charts/55701.

Lingold, Mary Caton, Rebecca Geoffroy-Schwinden, and Darin Mueller. *Sonic Dictionary.* http://sonicdictionary.fhi.duke.edu/.

"Looking for Whitman: The Poetry of Place in the Life and Work of Walt Whitman." http://lookingforwhitman.org/.

Mehlenbacher, Brad. "My Experience with Massive Online Open Courses (MOOCs) and Distance Education." Campus Writing and Speaking Program, CWSP 2014. North Carolina State University.

Pappano, Laura. "The Year of the MOOC." *NYTimes.com,* November 2, 2012. http://www.nytimes.com/2012/11/04/education/edlife/massive-open-online-courses-are-multiplying-at-a-rapid-pace.html.

Picciano, Anthony G, and Charles Dziuban, eds. *Blended Learning: Research Perspectives.* Needham, Mass.: The Sloan Consortium, 2007.

Posner, Miriam. "Course Blog." *DH101: Fall 2014 | Introduction to Digital Humanities.* http://miriamposner.com/dh101f14/?page_id=2.

"Reclaim Open Learning." http://open.media.mit.edu/.

Sample, Mark. "Renetworking House of Leaves in the Digital Humanities." *Sample-Reality* (blog), August 18, 2011. http://www.samplereality.com/2011/08/18/renetworking-the-novel/.

———. "The Digital Humanities Is Not about Building, It's about Sharing." *Sample-Reality* (blog), May 25, 2011. http://www.samplereality.com/2011/05/25/the-digital-humanities-is-not-about-building-its-about-sharing/.

Shirky, Clay. "Why I Just Asked My Students to Put Their Laptops Away . . ." *Medium,* September 9, 2014. https://medium.com/@cshirky/why-i-just-asked-my-students-to-put-their-laptops-away-7f5f7c50f368.

"This Is Not for Us," 2011. http://thisisnotfor.us/.

Thomas, William G., and Patrick D. Jones. *History Harvest.* http://historyharvest.unl.edu/.

Thomas, William G., III, and Elizabeth Lorang. "The Other End of the Scale: Rethinking the Digital Experience in Higher Education." *EDUCAUSE Review* 49, no. 5 (2014). http://www.educause.edu/ero/article/other-end-scale-rethinking-digital-experience-higher-education.

Thompson, J. R., G. R. Hess, T. A. Bowman, H. Magnusdottir, C. E. Stubbs-Gipson, M. Groom, J. R. Miller, T. A. Steelman, and D. L. Stokes. "Collaborative Graduate Education across Multiple Campuses." *Journal of Natural Resources and Life Sciences Education* 38 (2009): 16–26. http://eric.ed.gov/?id=EJ826520.

Watters, Audrey, and Sarah Goldrick-Rab. "Techno Fantasies." *Inside Higher Ed,* March 26, 2015. https://www.insidehighered.com/views/2015/03/26/essay-challenging-kevin-careys-new-book-higher-education.

Witmore, Michael. "Text: A Massively Addressable Object." *Wine Dark Sea* (blog), December 31, 2010. http://winedarksea.org/?p=926.

Re: Search and Close Reading

MICHAEL HANCHER

I find this Argument *will take much* Oil,
Close Reading, *Indefatigable* Toil.

—Nicolas Boileau, "The Lutrin," trans. Nicholas Rowe

Art and Science cannot exist but in minutely organized particulars.

—William Blake, *Jerusalem*

L arge digital libraries afford new access to information at the macro scale as well as improved access at the micro scale. The micro scale is familiar enough: the specific datum sought for and found, or not, in an archive of whatever size, large or small: the stuff of philological research. The macro scale is new, and newly revelatory; and being new it preoccupies the stories told in *Debates in the Digital Humanities* (Gold). Everyone acknowledges that data mining and data mapping are changing the scholarly landscape. But few mention that large digital libraries also afford a greatly improved access to minute particulars—thanks not to data mining but to datum mining. Such particulars, when discovered, can loom large in the foreground of that landscape. Keyword search, now ubiquitous, is taken for granted, like flying in an airplane. And yet, like the airplane, it has been a game-changer.

Anyone of a certain age who stops to think about this can come up with examples of the change. I recall one instance, some seven or eight years ago, when a student alerted me to something he had found in Google Books that had eluded my careful, albeit pre-Google, research several years earlier. I had published an article about a nineteenth-century British broadside ballad, "The March of Intellect in the Butchering Line," which expressed a butcher's indignation at the snobbery that his wife had contracted from reading too many "improving" penny magazines. I had (too) conservatively estimated a date for this ballad of about 1850 (Hancher, "From Street Ballad," 98). When I prepared to discuss it in a course about the history of literacy, I referred students to a facsimile that the Bodleian Library had published online. However, this student found the type too small to read (he overlooked the magnification option provided by the Bodleian website) and reflexively turned to Google to find a legible substitute. Google led him to a facsimile of the text of the poem as it was published in Thomas Hudson's *Comic Songs* (London, 1818)—more than three decades before my faulty estimate. Thanks to the student and Google Books, I learned that the song was "Sung by Mr. Sloman at the Coburg Theater" to the tune of "The Irish Washerwoman": information that belonged in my article, but never made it there. Furthermore, Google Books, especially Google Books Advanced Book Search, and also YouTube, can readily elucidate the singer, the theater, and the song.

More recently, some students and I examined the first volume of *All the Year Round,* the weekly magazine that Charles Dickens edited from 1859 to 1870. One drew attention to an anonymous poem, "Spinners and Weavers," in which four overworked women, like "Furies," praise the utility of their nocturnal labor, which results in candle wicks to brighten the eyes of the nobility, clothing for peasants, rugs for the nobility, and a noose for "a felon's neck." The identity of the author, Bryan Waller Procter, can be determined in the traditional way by consulting an edition of Dickens's correspondence (*Letters* 9:40). But it takes a search in Google Books on one or another phrase in the poem to discover that Procter had published the same poem years earlier, as "The Flax Spinners," in *Hood's Magazine and Comic Miscellany* (1844)—signed in the table of contents with his pseudonym "Barry Cornwall." Hood and Procter were friends, and Proctor's "The Flax Spinners" paid a kind of homage by imitation to "The Song of the Shirt," the labor-reformist poem that Hood had published in *Punch* the previous year, which made his literary reputation. Dickens was a friend of both poets; did he know that he was reprinting an old poem when he published "Weavers and Spinners"? Unlike us, he lacked access to Google Books.

Another example: wrapping up an article about a piracy of *A Christmas Carol,* which I had started some years earlier, I found that many of the obscure literary quotations that ornamented the margins of the pages of that two-penny pamphlet, framing the main text, finally shed their obscurity under the revealing scrutiny of Google's search engine (Hancher, "Grafting").

I can cite two other examples that are less personal, although I did organize the conference panel at which they were discussed. At the annual meeting of the Modern Language Association held in San Francisco in December 2008, three presenters spoke to the topic "The Library of Google: Researching Scanned Books." Two of them, Lisa Spiro and Amanda French, narrated parallel histories. Several years previously each had completed a dissertation, making her an expert on a special topic (Spiro, "Bachelorhood"; French, "Refrain"). Both dissertations were completed before the launch of Google Book Search in 2004, now known as Google Books. In 2008, Spiro and French searched in Google Books for information relevant to their projects, and each found that the new information made available there was at least comparable in scale to the information that she had amassed through conventional library research. That is to say, by 2008, Google Books had at least doubled the particular information that was accessible to a careful researcher. By now, that increase may be geometrical.

The absent guest at *Debates in the Digital Humanities,* alluded to if not discussed by most participants, was Franco Moretti. "Distant reading," his brand of literary data mining, shadowed many of the chapters. The findings that I have cited do not participate in distant reading. Instead, they illustrate a different power of search: local, limited, but nonetheless informative. The critical history of "close reading" that follows is similarly enabled by the specific affordances of search in several large digital libraries, including Google Books, HathiTrust, Internet Archive, Early English Books Online, Eighteenth-Century Collections Online, JSTOR, Project Muse, HeinOnline, and British Newspapers 1600–1900.

Such resources have imperfections, which limit their usefulness for datum mining as well as for data mining (Duguid; Nunberg, "Google"; Nunberg, "Counting"). For individual data, however, their failures are usually failures of omission (false negatives, which escape notice) rather than failures of commission (false positives, which can be corrected). It may be that the accuracy of datum mining generally exceeds that of data mining. In any case, a datum, unlike data, can be individually assessed.

When Moretti first mentioned distant reading, in "Conjectures on World Literature" (2000; reprinted in *Distant Reading,* 2013), he opposed it to "close reading." At the same time he gave close reading a national affiliation, bracketed it in the recent past, and restricted its application to a narrow set of texts. "The United States is the country of close reading," he wrote, and "the trouble with close reading (in all its incarnations, from the new criticism to deconstruction) is that it necessarily depends on an extremely small canon" (2000, 57).

All three of these propositions are doubtful. That close reading applied to non-canonical texts of popular culture was evident as long ago as 1948, when Leo Spitzer closely read an ad for Sunkist orange juice.[1] Although close reading did thrive in the United States, partly thanks to the influence of *Practical Criticism* by I. A. Richards (1929) and *Seven Types of Ambiguity* by Richards's student William Empson (1930), neither writer was a citizen of the United States and both books were first published in London. Furthermore, the clear affiliation of close reading to the French tradition of *explication de texte* gave it respectably un-American credentials as well as a genealogy before the New Criticism.[2]

John Guillory brackets the practice as closely as Moretti does: "By *close reading,* I do not mean the same thing as reading closely, which arguably describes many different practices of reading from antiquity to the modern era. I assume rather that close reading is a modern academic practice with an inaugural moment, a period of development, and now perhaps a phase of decline." Guillory locates the "inaugural moment" in the work of I. A. Richards, who "has long been identified with the origins of close reading" (Guillory, 8). However, by 1929 "close reading" was already central to academic practice.

It was a mainstay of classical education:

> Chief among the objects of this discipline is to teach the close and logical articulation of ideas in a thought, and of thought to thought in a topic, and of topic to topic in discourse. It was the glory of Latin and Greek, taught as they were and still often are in the old grammar school, that they did just this. The *close reading,* the careful translation, the painful analysis, the slow building up of structure on structure, all this contributed more than anything else, more than science or mathematics, more than history or civics, infinitely more than manual training or nature-study, to the development of the rational powers of the pupil. (Buck, 288; emphasis added)

Philo M. Buck Jr., who published these fond memories in 1914, later became a professor at the University of Wisconsin, where he founded the Department of Comparative Literature—one of the first such departments in the country (Carruth, 221; Cronon and Jenkins, 490).

Thomas Arnold, headmaster of Rugby School—also Matthew Arnold's father—had enthusiastically described the same process, though he did not call it "close reading," in a letter of 1836:

> My delight in going over Homer and Virgil with the boys makes me think what a treat it must be to teach Shakespeare to a good class of young Greeks in regenerate Athens; to dwell upon him line by line, and word by word, in the way that nothing but a translation lesson ever will enable one to do; and so to get all his pictures and thoughts leisurely into one's mind, till I verily think one would after a time almost give out light in the dark, after having been steeped as it were in such an atmosphere of brilliance. And how could this ever be done without having the process of construing, as the grosser medium through which alone all the beauty can be transmitted, because else we travel too fast, and more than half of it escapes us? (Stanley 2:49)

"We travel too fast." The cure for such speed was what Reuben Brower, who had taught Greek as well as English at Amherst College,[3] would in 1959 call "reading in slow motion"—that is, "slowing down the process of reading to observe what is happening, in order to attend very closely to the words, their uses, and their meanings" ("The Humanities," 77). Brower's slow-motion method implicitly countered the contemporary vogue for teaching "speed reading" in high school.[4] An esteemed late practitioner of the New Criticism, Brower accomplished within one language what Arnold did across two. He once acknowledged, "as a teacher of courses in close reading, I have tried to give non-classical students some experience of imaginative but disciplined reading of the text of the kind that once was common in the teaching of the Classics."[5]

Thomas Arnold's half paragraph celebrating "the process of construing" would be quoted in print dozens of times across the rest of the nineteenth century and into the twentieth, on both sides of the Atlantic.[6] One function of this litany of citation was to authorize the displacement of Greek and Latin texts in the classroom by British and American ones. Another was to authorize the continuity of close reading, akin to the niceties of classical translation, as a pedagogic staple during the century that led up to the advent of the New Criticism.

By 1897, close reading as such was prescribed to autodidacts, as well as teachers. Sara D. Jenkins, the editor of *Popular Educator,* fielded a (real or invented?) question that year: "What is meant by 'Close Reading'? I am trying a course of reading by myself and my author says, 'Spend thirty minutes daily in "close reading."'" Jenkins replied, "It might be interpreted variously. My own use and construction of the terms is in referring to diction, figures of speech, translation of allusion, etc." (Jenkins, 68).[7] And she went on to give teachers some advice about pacing such instruction. Evidently "close reading" was part of the toolkit of vernacular secondary education and self-education in the nineteenth century, as well as in classical studies.

When Richards referred to "close reading" in *Practical Criticism,* he was not coining a phrase but endorsing a standard practice. That his first mention of it is elliptical and casual indicates that he is not inventing a term of art but using common language ready to hand. One reader, he remarks, is "less close in his reading than" another (114). A later remark, that "no close reader will doubt or deny" some proposition (191), presumes that Richards's actual or ideal reader is already a close reader. "All respectable poetry invites close reading" (203) fully names the practice that has been taken for granted all along, because it was a standard practice. Guillory posits that this "little spatial trope" was "elevated" by Richards "into a disciplinary term of art" (Guillory, 12). But the "trope" was already a term of art, or of standard practice, long before Richards midwifed the New Criticism. (How the trope was "spatial," or not, will be considered shortly.) Good readers were close readers; and some texts, including some poems, were good enough to warrant close reading.

The text that most required close reading was the Bible—the canonical text, the book of books. In 1805 one "H. H.," writing from Lambeth, spoke of "giving [Psalm 15] a close reading, and seriously searching into its true import" (399). That same year "Gaius" remarked on a supposedly obvious meaning in Psalm 23 that "it does not require much *close reading,* nor very deep researches into the meaning of the Psalm, to perceive this" (Gaius, 594; emphasis in the original). In 1795, a cleric wrote to the *Gentleman's Magazine* that "for several years past I have devoted my time to close reading and study" (Cleros, 489).

Evidently "close reading" could describe a prolonged course of study as well as the scrutiny of a single text or passage. So William Cave, in 1673, reported that "I set myself to a more close and diligent reading of the first Fathers and ancient monuments of the Church than ever I had done before" (preface, n.p.). "Close study" was another name for it; so John Tillotson, archbishop of Canterbury, "began with a deep and close Study of the Scriptures, upon which he spent four or five Years, till he had arrived at a true understanding of them" (Burnet, 13). "Close perusal," "close reasoning," "close meditation," "close attention," and "close application" were qualities of both particular and far-reaching study from the sixteenth to the twentieth centuries.

The young philistine Stephen Gosson is suggestive in his satire on such ivory-tower study:

> If it be the dutie of every man in a common wealth, one way or other to bestirre his stumpes, I cannot but blame those lither contemplators very much, which sit concluding of Sillogismes in a corner, which in a close study in the University coope themselves up fortie yeres together, studying all things, and professe nothing. (Gosson, 34 recto and verso)[8]

Presented with this passage, Empson would have noted a kind of ambiguity. The "close study" in question here could be the intellectual activity of close reading, or it could just as well be a small room in which such reading takes place—where the university scholars "coop themselves up" to pursue such study.[9] Close study is closeted study. Close study, and close reading, have something to do with spatial constraint, with tightness and restraint. Such closeted tightness can be deprecated, as E. C. Stedman once deprecated certain early poems by William Morris as "pieces which repay close reading, but also compel it, for they smack of the closet and library, rather than the world of men and women, or that of woods, waters, and hills" (Stedman, 233).

The tight, taut (taught) attention to the text that is and was close reading was matched, if not indeed motivated, by the "closeness" of the texts that it confronted. If *reading, study, reasoning, analysis,* and *attention* could be "close," so could *diction, discourse,* or *style* and the *thinking* that it displays, and even the *handwriting* or *printing* (*print* or *matter*) in which it circulates.

Style especially: Quintilian's analysis in *Institutio Oratio,* influential for millennia, is worth close study in this regard. The broadest distinction of styles, we learn from an eighteenth-century translation of this treatise, was between the "grand" and the "plain"—styles associated with "the Asiatics and the Attics." The distinction was "of an old Standing: the latter affected to be *close* and concise, and the other were blam'd for an empty, bombast Manner."[10] Here the phrase "close and concise" translates *pressi*: constrained, compressed. Earlier we read, "one Kind of Prose Style is *close* and compacted; another, such as we use in Letters, in Conversation, is loose" (2:303). Here "close" translates *vincta* (bound, fettered, confined)—the opposite of "loose," which translates *soluta* (unbound, unfettered, free). "Compacted" (which here translates *contexta*) is a synonym of "close" (*vincta*); more fully *contexta* means "woven together, closely connected, continuous."[11] Thucydides had a distinctive style, we learn in another eighteenth-century translation of Quintilian: "Thucydides is *close,* concise, and ever going on" (that is, hurrying forward).[12] "*Densus* [dense] et brevis": "*close, concise.*" *Pressi, vincta, densus*; compressed, confined, concise, dense: the "spatial trope" of closeness turns out to be a matter not of proximity but of tightness and density.

Such economy of the writer's means could increase the reader's labor, as Henry Felton acknowledged in 1713: "*Thucydides* does sometimes write in a Style so close, that almost every Word is a Sentence, and every Sentence almost acquaints us with something New; so that from the multitude of Clauses, and Variety of Matter crowded together, we should suspect him to be obscure" (Felton, 181).[13] Although Felton would acquit Thucydides of such a charge, he did note the hazard of a close style: "*while we study to be concise, we can hardly avoid being obscure.* We crowd our Thoughts into too small a Compass, and are so sparing of our Words, that we will not afford enow to express our Meaning" (108; emphasis in the original). Later in the eighteenth century Fulke Greville rehearsed a similar apology, apropos La Rochefoucauld's maxims, for the dangers of verbal compression: "Many persons have thought these reflections obscure, not only in the expression but in the sense. Obscurity, however, is not always the fault of the writer. Reflections, or maxims and sentences, as the world has called these, ought always to be written in a close style, which does not admit the utmost degree of perspicuity" (Greville, xix). A "close," sententious style is not the writer's fault, but the reader's responsibility.[14]

As for verbal style, so for chirographic and typographic. Close writing—that is, close handwriting—could be hard to read. ("He opened a drawer, and found there a manuscript, of close writing, so that much of it was illegible."[15]) And so could "close printing" or "close matter" or "close type"—the typographical equivalents of close writing. In the nineteenth century a closely printed "fasciculus of some cyclo-pedia" would be cheaper and more compendious than a regular book; and so "it beho[o]ves us to mount our spectacles on nose to con the small letter-press," even though "the close writing begets close reading, and compels us to endue [that is, put on] the garment of attention, which to many is like the shirt of Nessus to Hercules—*consumedly* troublesome."[16]

"*The close writing begets close reading.*" Some, if not all, close reading was occasioned by the density (closeness) of the print, or of the handwriting, or, most significantly, of the verbal style. Magnification might help for the close printing or writing. "Close" attention might suit a close verbal style, one rich in implication, like that of the Bible or a sonnet by Shakespeare.[17] The book of Proverbs, in particular, was often spoken of as "close."[18] Shakespeare's sonnet 129, as closely read by Laura Riding and Robert Graves in a chapter of *A Survey of Modernist Poetry,* was the acknowledged inspiration for *Seven Types of Ambiguity,* the gospel of the New Criticism.[19]

Of course, the "close reading" of the New Criticism was usually not just a matter of reading, but also of writing—writing done after or during reading. The "close attention to the printed word" that Brower modeled for his students, "the closest scrutiny of meanings and forms of expression," would typically find expression in writing, not just reading (Brower, "The Humanities," 79–80).[20] "Teaching of reading is necessarily teaching of writing. The student cannot show his teacher or himself that he has had an important and relevant literary experience except in writing or in speaking that is as disciplined as good writing" (81). And such writing was often abundant, rarely "close." Empson's *Seven Types of Ambiguity* (arguably still apprentice work, written by a recent college graduate at the prompting of his former tutor, I. A. Richards) is considerably longer than the handful of poems it expounds. As Wikipedia puts it, "A truly attentive close reading of a two-hundred-word poem might be thousands of words long without exhausting the possibilities for observation and insight" (Wikipedia, "Close Reading"). Close reading had long been a matter of inward, private study—indeed, of "observation and insight": more a matter of *understanding* than of *interpretation* in the public sense of that word (Hancher, "What Kind of Speech"). However, in tutorials such as Richards's and in classrooms such as Arnold's and Brower's, it became an occasion for semi-public performance. The actuality of that performance, when registered in writing, might achieve full publicity in print.

D. A. Miller has appreciated the enduring charms of close reading, now thought to be obsolescent. Now, relieved of its stern "respectability," it can "come out as a thing that, even under the high-minded (but now kitschy-sounding) rationales of its former mission, it had always been: an almost infantile desire to be *close,* period, as close as one can get, without literal plagiarism, to merging with the mother-text" (Miller, 58). This looks like Guillory's "spatial trope" of closeness raised to the highest degree—the extreme opposite of Moretti's "distant reading." But all these spatial readings of "close reading" are misconceived. Distant reading is not the opposite of close reading. The "closeness" of close reading has long concerned not proximity but density and concentration: concentration certainly in the reader and often, as well, in the text being read. So it was for the New Criticism, and so it was for the old. The opposite of close reading is not distant reading but loose, casual, and careless reading.[21] Yet, paradoxically, when close reading is recorded in interpretive writing it can rarely be close but must expand and exfoliate to report the unpacking of details.

Miller's obsequies for close reading were premature in any case. Thanks to the recent Common Core State Standards Initiative, close reading is now central to primary and secondary school curricula in the United States. The Introduction to "Common Core State Standards for English Language Arts and Literacy in History/ Social Studies, Science, and Technical Subjects" stipulates that "students who meet the Standards readily undertake the close, attentive reading that is at the heart of understanding and enjoying complex works of literature" ("Common Core," 3). The first "key idea" for "College and Career Readiness Anchor Standards for Reading," as framed both for grades K–5 and also for grades 6–12—that is, applying all the way from kindergarten to the high school diploma—is, "read closely to determine what the text says explicitly and to make logical inferences from it; cite specific textual evidence when writing or speaking to support conclusions drawn from the text" (10, 35). A marginal gloss on the K–5 rubric comments that "students . . . acquire the habits of reading independently and closely, which are essential to their future success" (10). Evidently the idea of close reading is fundamental to the Common Core, even though the phrase itself does not appear in the Standards. The phrase does appear twelve times in an authoritative auxiliary statement written by David Coleman and Susan Pimentel, "Revised Publishers' Criteria for the Common Core State Standards in English Language Arts and Literacy, Grades 3–12." For example: "Close reading and gathering knowledge from specific texts should be at the heart of classroom activities and not be consigned to the margins when completing assignments" (Coleman and Pimentel, 4–6, 8–9, 15–16). Coleman, who is president and chief executive officer of the College Board, and Pimentel, who is vice chair of the executive committee of the federally appointed National Assessment Governing Board, were principal agents in establishing the Common Core Standards.

As might be expected, such official emphasis on close reading has caused widespread curiosity, even anxiety, among teachers and parents. The question that Sara D. Jenkins raised in the *Popular Educator* in 1897, "What is meant by 'Close reading'?" now echoes thousands of times online, if with a more immediate urgency and in a different vernacular—for example: "So, what is close reading, anyway?" or, "What Close Reading Actually Means," or simply, "What is Close Reading?" (Hodgson; Wiggins, "What Close Reading"; Shanahan). Part of the answer is that the New Close Reading (to give it a name for now) is a rejection of the sixties and seventies vogue for reader-centered reading. Coleman and Pimentel use some understatement in putting the matter: "When examining a complex text in depth, tasks should require careful scrutiny of the text and specific references to evidence from *the text itself* to support responses" (6; emphasis added). Nancy Boyles is more direct: "the teaching of reading veered significantly off track when . . . personal connections . . . began to dominate the teaching and testing of comprehension, often leaving *the text itself* a distant memory" (Boyles, 7; emphasis added). Grant Wiggins would go so far as to revive the author of the text: "the goal is to understand what the author is doing and accomplishing, and what it means; the goal is not to respond personally to what the author is doing" (Wiggins, "On Close Reading, Part 2"). Vintage reader-response theory, influential in the latter half of the twentieth century, is now thought to be passé.[22]

Of course, the methodological debate extends a hundred years further back, to the sixties and seventies of the nineteenth century. Walter Pater neatly framed the alternatives apropos Matthew Arnold, whom he agreed with, only to contradict: " 'To see the object as in itself it really is,' has been justly said to be the aim of all true criticism whatever; and in aesthetic criticism the first step towards seeing one's object as it really is, is to know one's own impression as it really is, to discriminate it, to realise it distinctly" (Pater, vii, quoting Arnold, 6). One does not have to choose between

Arnold and Pater to recognize that close, attentive reading, whether of the object itself or of one's apprehension of it, has long been highly valued in the construction of aesthetic and literary experience, and that it continues to be so.

A simple Google Books Ngram Viewer chart of "close reading" for the two centuries with the best data, 1800 to 2000, drawing on a corpus of more than five million books, shows that close reading has been a matter of growing concern for the entire period, especially after 1870—not contained by the eras of New Criticism and deconstruction, but older than that, and newer than that:

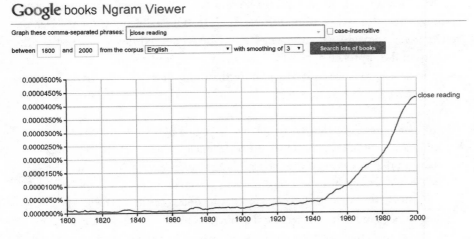

Figure 12.1. Google Books Ngram Viewer chart of "close reading" for 1800 to 2000.

Data for more recent years, if properly adjusted, might show the curve to have lifted even higher, propelled by the Common Core. As things stand, according to an FAQ page published by the designers of the Ngram Viewer, any data after 2004 would be greatly complicated by the launch that year of the Google Books project itself.

The same FAQ page offers reassurance at the very outset, under the rubric "Big Picture," about the continuing relevance of close reading, despite the advent of "Culturomics," the Ngram Viewer version of distant reading:

> Is this supposed to replace close reading of texts?
>
> Absolutely not. Anyone who has appreciated the work of a great artist—say, Shakespeare—or an insightful scholar—say, Michael Walzer's *Exodus and Revolution*—couldn't possibly think that quantitative approaches can replace close reading.
>
> Quite the opposite is true: quantitative methods can be a great source of ideas that can then be explored further by studying primary texts.[23]

The same is true for particular search.

The revisionary reading of "close reading" that I have proposed here depends (except for Figure 12.1) not on distant reading but on minute particulars discovered by digitized access to published texts. I could not have written this chapter ten years ago. The digital humanities revolution includes unprecedented discovery of texts to read, sometimes closely.

Of course it still pays to read books printed on paper, such as *Macroanalysis: Digital Methods and Literary History* by Matthew L. Jockers (2013), or *Passages from the Life of a Philosopher* by Charles Babbage (1864).

In *Macroanalysis* Jockers proposed an adjustable style of computer-assisted reading, one not merely distant nor merely close, but flexible in its focus. (He, too, conventionally imagines that closeness has to do with proximity, not density.) "The strength of the approach allows for both zooming in and zooming out" (23). Such an approach, he believes, promises more than did older, search-driven inquiries after what is only already known:

> To some extent, our thus-far limited use of digital content is a result of a disciplinary habit of thinking small: the traditionally minded scholar recognizes value in digital texts because they are individually searchable, but this same scholar, as a result of a traditional training, often fails to recognize the potentials for analysis that an electronic processing of texts enables. For others, the limitation is more directly technical and relates to the type and availability of software tools that might be deployed in analysis. The range of what existing computer-based tools have provided for the literary scholar is limited, and these tools have tended to conform to a disciplinary habit of closely studying individual texts: that is, close reading. Such tools are designed with the analysis of single texts in mind and do not offer the typical literary scholar much beyond advanced searching capabilities. Arguably, the existing tools have been a determiner in shaping perceptions about what can and cannot be done with digital text. The existing tools have kept our focus firmly on the close reading of individual texts and have undoubtedly prevented some scholars from wandering into the realms of what Franco Moretti has termed "distant reading" . . . . Combine a traditional literary training focused on close reading with the most common text-analysis tools focused on the same thing, and what you end up with is enhanced search—electronic finding aids that replicate and expedite human effort but bring little to the table in terms of new knowledge. (Jockers, *Macroanalysis*, 17)

This is a limited view of both search and close reading. The new ability to access and organize minute particulars can do more than inform our understanding of an isolated text (though it can do that), and it can generate new knowledge, not merely sustain old prejudices. Thanks to such resources as Google Books, HathiTrust, and the

Internet Archive, search has become the *Oxford English Dictionary* on steroids—at least as regards illustrative quotations, if not definitions. The history of ideas is the history of the language in which ideas are constructed and expressed, and that history has now become available with a revelatory granularity. All that is denied our grasp—no small loss, admittedly—is the lived, oral language of ideas that never did get recorded in writing, in print, or in any other durable medium (Harris).

For more than half a century the British mathematician Charles Babbage (1791–1871) has been celebrated as the "father of the computer," in part because of the publicity that he gave to his plans to build elaborate calculating apparatuses that would process mechanically coded information, and also because of the credit assigned to his enterprise by Howard H. Aiken (1900–1973), who designed the pioneering IBM Automatic Sequence Controlled Calculator (Mark I) that was envisioned in 1937 and installed at Harvard University in 1944.[24] Although neither Babbage's "Difference Engine" nor his later "Analytical Engine" ever reached a similar stage of completion, those thwarted machines haunt Babbage's late memoir *Passages from the Life of a Philosopher*, along with a miscellany of other topics, some more relevant to computing than others. One of these topics, the idea of "forming a universal language," had preoccupied Babbage as an adolescent. Even before enrolling at Trinity College, Cambridge, he "accidentally heard . . . of [the] idea."

> I was much fascinated by it, and, soon after, proceeded to write a kind of grammar, and then to devise a dictionary. Some trace of the former, I think, I still possess: but I was stopped in my idea of making a universal dictionary by the apparent impossibility of arranging signs in any consecutive order, so as to find, as in a dictionary, the meaning of each when wanted. It was only after I had been some time at Cambridge that I became acquainted with the work of' Bishop Wilkins on Universal Language. (Babbage, *Passages*, 25–26)

John Wilkins, later Bishop of Chester, had served as master of that same Trinity College for one year, from August 1659 until August 1660. In November 1660, he chaired the first meeting of an assembly later to be chartered as the Royal Society of London, characterized as a "college for the promoting of physico-mathematical experimental learning" (Birch 1:4). Wilkins's most important publication, a substantial folio titled *An Essay towards a Real Character and a Philosophical Language*, was published by the Royal Society in 1668.[25] The goal in that book was to devise "a Real universal Character [that is, an objective, transcendental code] that should not signifie *words*, but *things* and *notions* [concepts], and consequently be legible by any Nation in their own Tongue"—thereby remedying the linguistic diversity that mankind had suffered as a consequence of the debacle at Babel, a "confusion" that had impeded both the advancement of science and the propagation of international commerce (Wilkins, 13). An early biographer reported that Babbage "studied with much attention the investigations of his predecessors" in the search for a universal language, "and especially Bishop Wilkins"—the most thoroughgoing of seventeenth-century speculators in this line (Buxton, 347).

Wilkins's grand project was not a success on its own terms; if it had been, Babbage would not have had as many occasions as he did to call for the establishment of a universal language. Some of these calls were modest in scope—recommending a "universal language" for signals emitted from all lighthouses, for example, or "a universal language" of complex-machine specification (Babbage, *Notes,* 14; *Exposition,* 139). But Babbage could also press the matter in earnest. The question of what should be "the language of science" having been raised at a meeting of the International Statistical Congress in London (July 1860), Babbage gallantly conceded "that French is the language to be adopted," although "other views ought also to be considered" (*Report of the Proceedings,* 394). In any case, he argued, "the existence of different languages is a great evil; it is the destruction of a certain amount of the intellect of mankind, which is thus consumed by the friction that the different languages create." The global spread of "the commerce of England" promised to spread the language of England as well, but there was the risk that different colonies might develop different colonial Englishes. "I think there are measures which might be taken to prevent the gradual branching off of our own language into a number of separate dialects or languages, and perhaps of ultimately rendering it the universal language of the world." Authoritative dictionaries, prescriptive as well as descriptive, would be essential to that task.

If Wilkins failed to establish a universal language, he did address Babbage's original conundrum, indirectly contriving to "[arrange] signs in a consecutive order, so as to find, as in a dictionary, the meaning of each when wanted." The arrangement was complex but complete, at least in theory: using the English language, Wilkins's book provided an elaborate tabular, analytic taxonomy of things and ideas, to which an alphabetic index or dictionary (also in English) provided access; and between these sections a code of constructed ideograms ("real characters") was proposed to articulate nodes in that taxonomy.[26]

The account of Babbage's memoir published by the *British Quarterly Review* ignored Wilkins and simply paraphrased the young Babbage's dilemma: "What would be the use of a lexicon to a lad if all the words were printed promiscuously, or drawn up in an abstract array and under ideal heads, as they are in Roget's Thesaurus?" ("Passages from a Philosopher's Life," 97). That is, absent a regular alphabet enabling an index, each of the two possible arrangements for a set of invented signs—randomness on the one hand, or abstraction on the other—would be equally inaccessible and unsatisfactory.

James Gleick aptly characterizes Babbage's lexicographical impasse at this point as "a problem of storage and retrieval" (90)—that is, search. To enable search, something was needed like the Analytical Engine. The "consecutive order" that gives the most basic access to stored data is not thematic nor even alphabetical but digital: sequential numbers underlying any code and providing access to any of its expressions. The digits might be decimal or binary, or some other number base; the apparatus might be mechanical or electronic; no matter, the principal is the same. "Babbage had all the essential ideas," as Alan Turing remarked in 1950 (439). For Babbage's projected machine, decimal digits were most efficient, and for the electronic apparatus of the twentieth century and now, binary. Furthermore, electronic computers can now be networked, vastly enlarging the capacity of storage and the reach of search.

Babbage's hopes for a universal language, his scheme for a universal dictionary, and his plan for an Analytical Engine having all failed, the father of the computer would have welcomed the binary ordering that now empowers networked electronic search, making it possible (among other things) for scholars to discover and to organize minute particulars in the actual written record. As two editors of the *Economist* pointed out at the turn of our millennium, "If there is such a thing as a universal language, it is not English but binary" (Micklethwait and Wooldridge, 35–36).

NOTES

I appreciate the helpful advice that I received about earlier drafts of this chapter from Jeremy Douglass, Andrew Elfenbein, Amy Fairgrieve, Mark C. Marino, and Claire Warwick.

1. This bravura interpretation of a noncanonical text was characterized as "close reading" not by Spitzer himself but by Lerer, 312. Jane Gallop has emphasized the importance of close reading to cultural studies ("Close Reading," 15; "The Ethics of Reading").

2. René Wellek protests, too much, that "it is a mistake to consider close reading a new version of *explication de texte*" (620).

3. Brower was Class of 1880 Professor of Greek and English at Amherst, before he joined the Department of English at Harvard in 1953 (Pritchard, 282).

4. "One approach to helping students meet their academic obligations is the Speed Reading Course": so began an article by George W. Bond (1955, 102). When I took such a course in high school, in 1958 or 1959, I temporarily doubled my "reading speed." Brower published his article in 1959, the year that Evelyn Wood founded the Reading Dynamics Institute to encourage the teaching of speed reading (Frank, 40).

5. From Brower's contribution to "An *Arion* Questionnaire" (21). Brower had edited a collection of essays, *On Translation*, which he dedicated to I. A. Richards. In his own contribution to that volume, "Seven Agamemnons," Brower remarked that translations are exemplary cases of the process of reading: "we remake what we read. . . . Translations forcibly remind us of the obvious fact that when we read, we read from a particular point in space and time" (173; reprinted from 1947 [383]).

6. These approving quotations, discoverable by judicious use of Google Books Advanced Book Search, are far too numerous to detail here. One example must stand for them all: J. G. Fitch highlighted the passage in his influential *Lectures on Teaching*, which

appeared in several editions in both England and the United States between 1881 and 1901. As with "the close study of the Greek and Roman classics," so "with our own" (282).

7. It may be suspicious that searches on components of the phrase "spend thirty minutes daily in 'close reading'" yield nothing else in Google Books.

8. The binding alliteration of "concluding sillogisms in a corner" is a nice touch, inasmuch as *concluding* etymologically means *shutting up closely*—that is, "coop[ing] up." (*Conclusion* was the traditional name for the last of the three propositions of a syllogism.)

9. "I sittyng in my *studye* where as laye many dyverse paunflettis and bookys" (Caxton, A1 recto; emphasis added).

10. Quintilian, trans. Guthrie, 2:545 (book 12, ch. 10); emphasis added. "Et antiqua quidem illa divisio inter Asianos atque Atticos fuit, cum hi *pressi* & integri, contrà inflati illi & inanes haberentur: & in his nihil superflueret, illis judicium maxime ac modus deesset" (Quintilian, ed. Gibson, 629; emphasis added). The sequence *Asianos atque Atticos,* reversed in later editions, is followed by Guthrie. Austin rehearses the early history of the Asiatic/Attic distinction (Quintilian, ed. Austin, 161–64).

11. Charlton Lewis, 921 (s.v. vinciō), 703 (solūtus), 182 (contextus).

12. Quintilian, trans. Patsall 2, 199, emphasis added; translating "*Densus* & brevis, & semper instans sibi Thucydides" (Quintilian, ed. Rollin 2, 203; emphasis added).

13. "Sentence" is used in the sense of "a pithy or pointed saying, an aphorism, maxim" (*OED* 4.a.). On the next page Felton speaks with less reserve about Thucydides's "pressed and close" diction. Felton's remarks on Thucydides's style had a long shelf life, circulating widely in Vicesimus Knox's successful anthology *Elegant Extracts in Prose* (383). Tacitus, too, was known "for the elegancie of his speech, adorned more with choise conceits, than with words; for the succinctnesse of his close, nervous, and grave sententious Oratorie, cleare onely to those of best understanding" (Boccalini, 15).

14. "Specially he that hath a close style, free from tautology, where every word must be marked by him that will not misunderstand, shall frequently be misreported" (Baxter, 222). The merits and hazards of concision, as debated across the seventeenth century, form a leading topic in Williamson; see especially 122–24, 190–91, 336–37.

15. A. C., "The Spectre's Revenge," 327. In eighteenth-century English legal practice, "close copy" would ordinarily be used in law offices, although expansive "office copy" would also be prepared for certain documents entered in evidence, written large and charged by the page (*English Reports* 96: 161).

16. Review of *Encyclographie,* 531. The same year (1835) on December 18, an untitled notice in the *Hull Packet* remarked, "Close reading, as many a fair novel reader can testify, is highly prejudicial to the eyes," requiring the services of an optician.

17. An exception is jurisprudence, which could invoke close reading when the text in question was not necessarily close. For various reasons legal style has often been diffuse, not close; Asiatic not Attic: "wordy" and "verbose," in the words of David Mellinkoff (24–25, 399–414); and yet "close reading" or, more particularly, "a close reading," might be called for. A certain case "demands close reading, for certain points, very material to the

decision and its value, do not lie on the surface, and are not readily apprehended even by those citing it" (Review of E. C. Thomas, 350). Or "a close reading of the law" or "a close reading of the statute" might be commended or recommended.

18. "The Hebrews give the name of proverbs, parables, or similitudes, to moral sentences, maxims, comparisons, or enigmas, expressed in a poetical stile, figurative, close, and sententious" (Marchant, s.v. Proverbs)—a long-lived definition, adopted by many reference works in later decades. The "style" of Hosea, "very close & sententious," was comparable to that of Proverbs (Foxcroft, 129).

19. Riding and Graves, 62–75. Empson, n.p.: "I derive the method I am using from Mr. Robert Graves' analysis of 'The expense of spirit in a waste of shame,' in *A Survey of Modernist Poetry*"—an acknowledgment that Empson corrected on a tipped-in errata leaf to include Laura Riding.

20. In his appreciation of Brower's essay, Duffy quotes from this passage and others in "Reading in Slow Motion." Full disclosure: in fall 1960, I attended Humanities 6: Introduction to Literature ("Hum 6"), for which Brower was the principal lecturer; that course followed the practices he describes. Hum 6 has often been commemorated, most notably by Paul de Man, who traces a connection between the "close reading" it espoused and deconstruction (23–24). Richard Poirier, who taught the course along with Brower, offers another account (177–84). William Pritchard traces the course back to its invention at Amherst College (282–91).

21. Jonathan Culler too doubts that "distant reading" can be an adequate antonym for "close reading," deeming it to be "too divergent from regular modes of literary criticism to serve in a defining contrast" (20).

22. For some objections to this turn in critical and pedagogic fashion see Strauss, reprinting Barlow; also Hinchman and Moore.

23. "Culturomics: FAQ." This FAQ supplements the technical report by Michel et al.

24. Turner; Halacy. Cohen would minimize Babbage's actual influence on Aiken ("Babbage and Aiken"; *Howard Aiken*). Metropolis and Worlton document early awareness among computer pioneers of Babbage's work (52–53); see in particular Turing, as quoted later.

25. For the complex circumstances of its publication, see R. Lewis.

26. The taxonomy occupied pp. 22–288 in Wilkins's *Essay*; the instructions for generating the "real character" are on pp. 385–94, followed by examples. The dictionary, which functioned in large part as an alphabetical index to the taxonomic tables, was bound in at the back of the book, carrying its own title page. In the preface to the *Essay*, Wilkins acknowledged "the continual assistance" he had had from his "most Learned and worthy Friend, Dr. *William Lloyd*," especially for accomplishing "that tedious and difficult task, of suting the Tables to the *Dictionary*, and the drawing up of the *Dictionary it self*" (*c* recto). The large claims made by Dolezal for the dictionary as marking a major advance in lexicography have been questioned by DeMaria, who emphasizes rather its function as an index to the taxonomy.

BIBLIOGRAPHY

A. C. "The Spectre's Revenge." *Harvardiana* 3 (1837): 325–28.

"An *Arion* Questionnaire: 'The Classics and the Man of Letters.'" *Arion* 3, no. 4 (1964): 6–100.

Arnold, Matthew. "The Function of Criticism at the Present Time." In *Essays in Criticism*, 1–38. London: Macmillan, 1865.

Babbage, Charles. *The Exposition of 1851; or, Views of the Industry, the Science, and the Government, of England*. London: Murray, 1851.

———. *Notes Respecting Lighthouses*. Privately printed, 1851.

———. *Passages from the Life of a Philosopher*. London: Longman, 1864. Reprinted, Cambridge: Cambridge University Press, 2011.

Barlow, Aaron. "Designed for Failure: The Common Core State Standards." *The Academe Blog*, February 15, 2014. http://academeblog.org/2014/02/15/designed-for-failure-the-common-core-state-standards/.

Baxter, Richard. *A Christian Directory*. London, 1673.

Birch, Thomas. *The History of the Royal Society of London*. 4 vols. London, 1756–57.

Boccalini, Traiano. *The New-found Politicke*. London, 1626.

Bond, George W. "Speed Reading in the High School." *High School Journal* 39 (1955): 102–5.

Boyles, Nancy. "Closing in on Close Reading." *ASCD Educational Leadership* 70, no. 4 (December 2012–January 2013): 36–41.

Brower, Reuben A. "The Humanities: Reading in Slow Motion." In *Reading for Life: Developing the College Student's Lifetime Reading Interest*, ed. Jacob M. Price, 75–99. Ann Arbor: University of Michigan Press, 1959.

———, ed. *On Translation*. Vol 23 of *Harvard Studies in Comparative Literature*. Cambridge, Mass.: Harvard University Press, 1959.

———. "Seven Agamemnons." *Journal of the History of Ideas* 8 (1947): 383–405.

———. "Seven Agamemnons." In *On Translation*, 172–95. Cambridge, Mass.: Harvard University Press, 1959.

Buck, Philo M., Jr. "The Classical Tradition and the Study of English." *Classical Journal* 9 (1914): 284–91.

Burnet, Gilbert. *A Sermon Preached at the Funeral of the Most Reverend Father in God, John, by the Divine Providence, Lord Archbishop of Canterbury*. London, 1694.

Buxton, H. W. *Memoir of the Life and Labours of the Late Charles Babbage Esq., F.R.S.*, ed. Anthony Hyman. Charles Babbage Institute Reprint Series for the History of Computing 13. Cambridge, Mass.: MIT Press, 1988.

Carruth, William Hamilton. "The Status of Comparative Literature." *School and Society* 12 (1920): 218–23.

Cave, William. *Primitive Christianity*. London, 1673.

Caxton, William. *Here fynyssheth the boke yf [sic] Eneydos*. London, 1490.

Cleros (pseud.). "Remarks Relative to the Inferior Clergy." *Gentleman's Magazine* 65 (1795): 489–91.

Cohen, I. Bernard. "Babbage and Aiken, With Notes on Henry Babbage's Gift to Harvard, and to Other Institutions, of a Portion of His Father's Difference Engine." *Annals in the History of Computing* 10 (1988): 171–93.

———. *Howard Aiken: Portrait of a Computing Pioneer.* Cambridge, Mass.: MIT Press, 1999.

Coleman, David, and Susan Pimentel. "Revised Publishers' Criteria for the Common Core State Standards in English Language Arts and Literacy, Grades 3–12," April, 12, 2012. http://www.corestandards.org/assets/Publishers_Criteria_for_3-12.pdf.

"Common Core State Standards for English Language Arts and Literacy in History/Social Studies, Science, and Technical Subjects," June 2, 2010. http://www.corestandards.org /assets/CCSSI_ELA%20Standards.pdf.

Cronon, E. David, and John W. Jenkins. *The University of Wisconsin: A History* 3. Madison: University of Wisconsin Press, 1984.

Culler, Jonathan. "The Closeness of Close Reading." *ADE Bulletin* 149 (2010): 20–25.

"Culturomics: FAQ." http://www.culturomics.org/Resources/faq.

de Man, Paul. "The Return to Philology." In *The Resistance to Theory* Vol. 33, *Theory and History of Literature,* 21–26. Minneapolis: University of Minnesota Press, 1986.

DeMaria, Jr., Robert. Review of Dolezal 1985. *Modern Philology* 85 (1987): 204–7.

Dickens, Charles. *Letters,* ed. Madeline House and Graham Storey. 12 vols. Oxford: Clarendon Press, 1965–2002.

Dolezal, Fredric. *Forgotten but Important Lexicographers, John Wilkins and William Lloyd: A Modern Approach to Lexicography before Johnson.* Tübingen: Niemeyer, 1985.

Duguid, Paul. "Inheritance and Loss? A Brief History of Google Books." *First Monday* 12, no. 8 (August 12, 2007). http://firstmonday.org/article/view/1972/1847.

Duffy, Michael. "Reading in Slow Motion." *Working Notes* (blog), April 8, 2009. http:// mikejohnduff.blogspot.ca/2009/04/reading-in-slow-motion.html.

Empson, William. *Seven Types of Ambiguity.* London: Chatto and Windus, 1930. New York: Harcourt, Brace, 1931.

English Reports 96. Edinburgh: Green, 1909.

Felton, Henry. *A Dissertation on Reading the Classics, and Forming a Just Style.* London, 1713.

Fitch, F. G. *Lectures on Teaching Delivered in the University of Cambridge during the Lent Term, 1880.* Cambridge: Cambridge University Press, 1881.

Foxcroft, Thomas. *The Day of a Godly Man's Death, Better than the Day of His Birth.* Boston, 1722.

Frank, Stanley D. *The Evelyn Wood Seven-Day Speed Reading and Learning Program.* New York: Barnes and Noble, 1994.

French, Amanda Lowry. "From Horse and Buggy to Hovercraft: My Research before and after Google Book Search" (2008). http://amandafrench.net/amandafrench/files/From _Horse_ and_Buggy.pdf.

———. "Refrain, Again: The Return of the Villanelle." PhD diss., University of Virginia, 2004. ProQuest 3149164.

Gaius. "The Danger of Departing from the Simple and Obvious Meaning of Scripture." *Evangelical Magazine and Missionary Chronicle* 13 (1805): 593–94.

Gallop, Jane. "Close Reading in 2009." *ADE Bulletin* 149 (2010): 15–19.

———. "The Ethics of Reading: Close Encounters." *Journal of Curriculum Theorizing* 16 (2000): 7–18.

Gleick, James. *The Information: A History, a Theory, a Flood.* New York: Random House, 2011.

Gold, Matthew K., ed. *Debates in the Digital Humanities.* Minneapolis: University of Minnesota Press, 2012.

Gosson, Stephen. *The Schoole of Abuse.* 2nd ed. London, 1579.

[Greville, Fulke.] *Maxims, Characters, and Reflections.* 2nd ed. London, 1757.

Guillory, John. "Close Reading: Prologue and Epilogue." *ADE Bulletin* 149 (2010): 8–14.

H., H. "Observations on Psalms XV and XXIV." *Evangelical Magazine* 13 (1805): 399–400.

Halacy, Dan. *Charles Babbage, Father of the Computer.* New York: Crowell-Collier, 1970.

Hancher, Michael. "From Street Ballad to Penny Magazine: 'The March of Intellect in the Butchering Line.'" In *Nineteenth-Century Media and the Construction of Identities,* ed. Laurel Brake, David Finkelstein, and Bill Bell, 93–103. Basingstoke: Palgrave, 2000.

———. "Grafting *A Christmas Carol.*" *SEL: Studies in English Literature* 48 (2008): 813–27.

———. "What Kind of Speech Act Is Interpretation?" *Poetics* 10 (1981): 263–82.

Harris, Roy. "The History Men." *Times Literary Supplement* (September 3, 1982): 176–77.

Hinchman, Katherine A., and David W. Moore. "Close Reading: A Cautionary Interpretation." *Journal of Adolescent and Adult Literacy* 56, no. 6 (March 2013): 441–50.

Hodgson, Kevin. Review of Lehman and Roberts. *Middleweb* (blog), November 11, 2013. http://www.middleweb.com/10564/lessons-analyzing-texts-life/.

[Hood, Thomas.] "The Song of the Shirt." *Punch* 5 (1843): 260.

Jenkins, Sara D. "Around the Table." *Popular Educator* 15, no. 1 (September 1897): 68.

Jockers, Matthew L. *Macroanalysis: Digital Methods and Literary History.* Urbana: University of Illinois Press, 2013.

Knox, Vicesimus, ed. *Elegant Extracts in Prose.* 10th ed. London, 1816.

Lehman, Christopher, and Kate Roberts. *Falling in Love with Close Reading: Lessons for Analyzing Texts and Life.* Portsmouth, N.H.: Heinemann, 2014.

Lerer, Seth. *Error and the Academic Self: The Scholarly Imagination, Medieval to Modern.* New York: Columbia University Press, 2002.

Lewis, Charlton T. *An Elementary Latin Dictionary.* Oxford: Clarendon Press, 1891. Reprinted 1966.

Lewis, R. "The Publication of John Wilkins's 'Essay' (1668): Some Contextual Considerations." *Notes and Records of the Royal Society of London* 56 (2002): 133–46.

"The Library of Google: Researching Scanned Books." Session 543, annual convention, Modern Language Association, December 29, 2008. https://www.mla.org/conv _listings_detail?prog_id=543&year=2008.

Marchant, John. *A New, Complete, and Universal English Dictionary.* 4th ed. London, 1764.

Mellinkoff, David. *The Language of the Law.* Boston: Little, Brown, 1963.

Metropolis, N., and J. Worlton. "A Trilogy on Errors in the History of Computing." *Annals of the History of Computing* 2, no. 1 (1980): 50–53.

Michel, Jean-Baptiste, Yuan Kui Shen, Aviva Presser Aiden, Adrian Veres, Matthew K. Gray, The Google Books Team, Joseph P. Pickett, Dale Hoiberg, Dan Clancy, Peter Norvig, Jon Orwant, Steven Pinker, Martin A. Nowak, and Erez Lieberman Aiden. "Quantitative Analysis of Culture Using Millions of Digitized Books." *Science* (January 13, 2010): 176–82.

Micklethwait, John, and Adrian Wooldridge. *A Future Perfect: The Challenge and Hidden Promise of Globalization.* London: Heinemann, 2000.

Miller, D. A. *Jane Austen; or, The Secret of Style.* Princeton, N.J.: Princeton University Press, 2003.

Moretti, Franco. "Conjectures on World Literature." *New Left Review* 1 (2000): 54–68. Reprinted in Moretti, *Distant Reading,* 43–62.

———. *Distant Reading.* New York: Verso, 2013.

Nunberg, Geoffrey. "Counting on Google Books." *Chronicle of Higher Education,* December 16, 2010. http://chronicle.com/article/Counting-on-Google-Books/125735/.

———. "Google Book Search: A Disaster for Scholars." *Chronicle of Higher Education,* August 31, 2009. http://chronicle.com/article/Googles-Book-Search-A/48245/.

"Passages from a Philosopher's Life—Babbage." *British Quarterly Review* 41 (1865): 95–124.

Pater, Walter H. *Studies in the History of the Renaissance.* London: Macmillan, 1873.

Poirier, Richard. *Poetry and Pragmatism.* Cambridge, Mass.: Harvard University Press, 1992.

Pritchard, William H. *Shelf Life: Literary Essays and Reviews.* Amherst: University of Massachusetts Press, 2003.

[Proctor, Bryan Waller.] "The Flax Spinners." *Hood's Magazine and Comic Miscellany* 1 (1844): 395–96.

———. "Spinners and Weavers." *All the Year Round* 1 (1859): 88–89.

Quintilian. *De institutione oratoria libri duodecim,* ed. Edmund Gibson. Oxford, 1693.

———. *Institutes of Eloquence,* trans. William Guthrie. 2 vols. London, 1756.

———. *Institutes of the Orator,* trans. J. Patsall. 2 vols. London, 1774.

———. *Institutionis Oratoria Liber XII,* ed. R. G. Austin. Oxford: Clarendon Press, 1948.

———. *Institutionum Oratoriarum libri duodecim,* ed. Charles Rollin. 2 vols. Paris, 1741.

Report of the Proceedings of the Fourth Session of the International Statistical Congress. London: H.M.S.O., 1861.

Review of E. C. Thomas, *Leading Cases in Constitutional Law,* 2nd ed. *Law Magazine and Review* 10 (1884–85): 349–50.

Review of *Encyclographie des Sciences Medicales* 1. *London Surgical and Medical Journal* 7 (1835): 531.

Richards, I. A. *Practical Criticism: A Study in Literary Judgment.* London: Routledge and Kegan Paul, 1929. New York: Harcourt, Brace, 1929.

Riding, Laura, and William Graves. *A Survey of Modernist Poetry.* London: Heinemann, 1927.

Shanahan, Timothy. "What Is Close Reading?" *Shanahan on Literacy* (blog), June 18, 2012. http://www.shanahanonliteracy.com/2012/06/what-is-close-reading.html.

Spiro, Lisa Michelle. "Bachelorhood and the Construction of Literary Identity in Antebellum America." PhD diss., University of Virginia, 2002. ProQuest 3062127.

———. "Dissertation 2.0: Remixing a Dissertation on American Literature as a Work of Digital Scholarship," 2008. Rice Digital Scholarship Archive. https://scholarship.rice .edu/handle/1911/21839.

Spitzer, Leo. "American Advertising Explained as Popular Art." In *A Method of Interpreting Literature,* 102–49. Northampton, Mass.: Smith College, 1949.

Stanley, Arthur Penrhyn. *The Life and Correspondence of Thomas Arnold, D.D.* 2 vols. London: B. Fellowes, 1844.

[Stedman, Edmund Clarence.] "English Poetry of the Period." *North American Review* 103 (1866): 221–40.

Strauss, Valerie. "Does Common Core's Focus on 'Close Reading' Make Sense?" *Washington Post* (blog), February 18, 2014. https://www.washingtonpost.com/news/answer -sheet/wp/2014/02/18/does-comm on-cores-focus-on-close-reading-make-sense/.

Turing, A. M. "Computing Machinery and Intelligence." *Mind* 49 (1950): 433–60.

Turner, Henry D. "Charles Babbage: Father of the Computer." *New Scientist* (December 4, 1958): 1428–31.

Untitled notice ("The present is an era . . ."). *Hull Packet* (December 18, 1835): 2.

Wellek, René. "The New Criticism: Pro and Contra." *Critical Inquiry* 4 (1978): 611–24.

Wiggins, Grant. "On Close Reading, Part 2." *Granted, and . . .* (blog), May 17, 2013. http:// grantwiggins.wordpress.com/2013/05/17/on-close-reading-part-2/.

———. "What Close Reading Actually Means." *TeachThought* (blog), May 19, 2013. http:// www.teachthought.com/featured/what-close-reading-actually-means/.

Wikipedia. "Close Reading." https://en.wikipedia.org/wiki/Close_reading.

Wilkins, John. *An Essay towards a Real Character, and a Philosophical Language.* London, 1668.

Williamson, George. *The Senecan Amble: A Study in Prose Form from Bacon to Collier.* London: Faber and Faber, 1951.

Why We Must Read the Code: The Science Wars, Episode IV

MARK C. MARINO

During the 2012 Super Bowl, an ad by Republican Senate candidate Pete Hoekstra attacked his rival Debbie Stabenow with a video of a young Asian woman riding a bicycle through a rice paddy. The woman stops and, speaking to the camera, thanks Stabenow for spending so much money that the United States has to borrow from her country, leaving the U.S. economy weak and sending jobs overseas. The rhetoric of the commercial is fairly conventional for fomenting light xenophobic panic, situating the foreign threat as feminine and the country's development as backwards by seating her on a bicycle, which, ironically, U.S. cities are scrambling to accommodate as Americans seek alternatives to commuting in gas-powered vehicles.

However, the most provocative part of this ad may be the code that delivered this video. On the web page for the ad, the HTML code to display the picture reads:

```
<img class="yellowgirl"
```

The first part of that tag, "img," inserts the image into the web page. The second part, class="yellowgirl," activates a style sheet reference that indicates how the image should be displayed. The campaign later explained that "yellowgirl" was short for "yellowshirtgirl," marking her by her clothing, yet that excuse came too late to stem the tide of the online backlash with respondents for whom the code manifested the underlying racism of the ad. Regardless of the intention of the programmers, this episode made one thing very clear: code is not just a list of instructions for the computer. It is a layer of discourse, a text to be accessed by computers, programmers, and many others, and more important, code is a text with connotations that are in conversation with its functioning. In other words, this incident is another sign that code has become a text that programmers and increasingly nonprogrammers are discussing and interpreting.

Critical Code Studies (CCS) names the practice of interpreting what I call the extra-functional significance of code, "extra" here meaning "emerging from" rather than "outside" or "beyond." The practice answers a call within the digital humanities from N. Katherine Hayles and others for "Media Specific Analysis," which is the examination of an artifact with specific attention to the affordances and limitations of the particular medium in which that object has been created and presented (Hayles and Burdick, *Writing Machines,* 29). CCS does not merely look at the source code but uses the code as a central axis for accessing and analyzing the digital object. At times, it explores existing programming paradigms, but it also questions the choices that were made, examining among other aspects the underlying assumptions, models of the world, and constraints (whether technological or social) that helped shape the code. CCS scholars have taken up questions that are familiar to computer science, such as the history of programming languages or the notions of "beauty" and "elegance" in code, and have also ventured into more controversial topics, such as imagining a feminist programming language or exploring the postcolonial implications of a programming language based not in English but in Arabic.[1] Due to these more provocative topics, CCS has been taken, at times, as an assault on the realm of programmers.

Of course, this "yellowshirtgirl" reading is fairly straightforward and arguably superficial. It is also overtly political, dealing with an election and the topic of international trade. It does not go very far into the realm of computer programming. What is being called into question here is the name of a style sheet class, not even a command from the programming language. But what happens when the relationship of the code and the meaning is less straightforward? What happens when CCS begins to interpret the specific tokens of a programming language? What happens when one finds meaning in the way functions are implemented? What happens when the political reading involves challenging social norms? Interpretation is the provenance of the humanities, but when humanities scholars extend their reach into the realm of computer science, their entry is met with suspicion. What makes Critical Code Studies seem like an affront to computer scientists, and how can the fears and alarms that it trips be silenced before it stirs up another science war?

There Goes the Neighborhood!

Several years ago, the assistant director of R&D at the Maryland Institute for Technology in the Humanities, Travis Brown, wrote a post about Critical Code Studies on Lambda the Ultimate, a forum focusing on computer programming language theory. In his post, he presented the basic definition of Critical Code Studies along with a list of three concerns. First, he saw CCS as relying too heavily on "crit-theory jargon," with which he professed only a moderate fluency. Second, he argued that the readings seemed to focus exclusively on imperative programming languages—a criticism that no longer holds true, given the growing diversity of examples subjected to analysis. The third point argued that no one associated with the blog has a CS degree, a point which was false but perhaps not obvious from perusing a mere list of names. However, Brown's comments and the discussion that followed point to a particularly sensitive area at the intersection of computer science and digital humanities scholarship, one that scholars ignore at their peril.

Although the language of Brown's initial posting was fairly neutral, the early round of comments made it clear that at least some members of the community were taking the post as "red meat"—incendiary material posted by an outsider intended to provoke indignant rants. The primary question seemed to be summed up in this comment:

> Can't most of that stuff be found from a more sociological and anthropologi-
> cal point of view? Does literary criticism for code really help? (James Iry[2] at
> Sat, 2010–05–15 18:32)

This comment identifies a pervasive misconception that literary criticism concerns itself only with the symbolism and aesthetics of poems, plays, and prose, a view that overlooks the role of historical and social scholarship in literary studies, not to mention the impact of semiotics and cultural studies in expanding the sense of what counts as a text for interpretation.

Most upset was a contributor named Thomas Lord, who parodied the academic language of Critical Code Studies, writing:

> But, basically—the . . . wait let me drop into jargon . . . "the center of this for-
> mation of CCS discourse is defined by the conjunctive nexus of formerly sep-
> arated discursive forms, joined here by an ironic and nihilistic comparison of
> discordant measures of value and meaning."

Lord's parody of academic philosophy mocks both what he views as its pompous style and its pseudo-intellectualism, a result of layering interpretations upon interpretations. While Lord and others involved in this discussion do concede that there is a meaning in code and that philosophical and political readings are also important, the sarcasm in early reactions against CCS express a sense of the interpretive incursion of CCS as an assault on a protected domain. Rather than a distrust of literary interpretation, this defensiveness seems to be a response to the premises of the philosophy and the leanings of the politics, in the broader sense, being applied to code.

Here and in his other comments on the thread, Lord, perhaps inadvertently, emphasizes the specialized language of two divergent discourse communities. On the one hand, he is enraged by the use of an obfuscated philosophy-speak that is being used to express fairly simple and obvious truths. On the other hand, he resists humanist forays into the explication of "the complexities of technical vocabulary formation." As he explains, "Here in programming land, we also use other ordinary language words in strange ways. We talk about correctness, expressiveness, abstraction, composition," although he admits that "in and *around* programming languages, we manage to not confine our use of those terms to their strict technical sense." So while he calls for the use of "plain English," or a critical discourse without specialized terms (aka jargon), he builds a bulwark around the specialized language of computer programming against the barbarians of critical theory.

Certainly, CCS needs to attend to the specialized vocabulary of computer science as well as appropriate usage, both formal and informal, of this vocabulary within a variety of communities. However, what is at stake here has little to do with plain speech; rather, the threat comes from the left-leaning political points of view encoded in the particular "jargon." Plainly, what irks some programmers about CCS is not its highfalutin language, but the politics that the ideological language of critical theory brings to the putatively pure, functional language (computer source code). Such programmers are invested in a vision—a fantasy, CCS would suggest—of their work as apolitical, completely outside the context of social and political culture. Indeed, that is a political fantasy that the methods of Critical Code Studies can dispel, but not without creating some discomfort.

A WORM NAMED ANNAKOURNIKOVA

The discussion on Lamda the Ultimate appears at first glance to be a general reaction to the incursion of humanities-style interpretation of code into the culture of programming, but the specific source of the hostile response was an essay I wrote that analyzed a computer worm named annakournikova, along with several works of code poetry, through the theoretical lens of heteronormativity. Circulating at the turn of the millennium, the annakournikova worm arrived as an e-mail seeming to offer photographs of Anna Kournikova, the tennis player known just as much for her modeling career as for her domination on the WTA Tour. Opening the file, which was actually Virtual Basic Script, executed code that reproduced the file and sent the e-mail to the victim's entire address book. In my essay, I positioned the code poetry as being disruptive to existing social norms while, by contrast, I claimed, the worm operated in a manner analogous to heteronormativity. To accept any part of this argument, the reader would have to at least entertain the premise of heteronormativity—a prospect that would mark me, the essay's author, as what conservative online communities refer to as a SJW or Social Justice Warrior, their label for actors with progressive agendas and, implicitly, baseless arguments.

However, it was not only the ideological critique implicit in the term "heteronormativity" that was provocative; so, too, was my actual analysis. For rather than arguing that heteronormativity is merely present in code, I argued that the annakournikova worm operated with the *logic* of heteronormativity.[3] The parallel works something like this: like a malware worm, norms of society are registered and accepted by members and are then repeated and circulated by them without their conscious awareness. The worm that circulates through the unwitting participation of those promised pictures of the tennis ingénue (with a wink) is not just similar to heteronormativity, it epitomizes that reproductive logic. Consider a similar line of argumentation that Tara McPherson presents when she examines the way the logic of Unix conflicted with the socially progressive changes of the Civil Rights movement. Such interpretations are based on abstractions of underlying logic both in their discussions of technology and society, rather than the denotations of specific software processes. In other words, the annakournikova worm was not built on heteronormative code (whatever that might mean) but was instead an agent of a heteronormativity that reproduces itself across a computational system in a way analogous to how heteronormativity reproduces itself across human culture.

The offensiveness of these structural readings—as evinced by Lord's response to my heteronormativity argument—is rooted in their theoretical framing. But there is a deeper level of suspicion here, a sense that criticism performs a kind of sleight of hand with technological objects, imposing and inscribing on them political dynamics by means of an obfuscated set of rhetorical moves. Theory acts, as it were, like another worm replicating itself throughout the academy. Surely, this caricatured narrative battle between left-leaning humanists and conservative scientists has been depicted for decades, reemerging periodically in the discussion of absurd-sounding titles of Modern Language Association (MLA) papers or reports of radical art projects that have garnered paltry federal grants. But critiques of Critical Code Studies often reference a particular moment in literary history—the debate between scientific theorists and postmodernist critics known as the "Science Wars." Lane Wilkinson writes on his blog, Sense and Reference, "I'm baffled by the silliness of some of the Postmodernism 2.0 stuff like 'Critical Code Studies,' 'The Ethno-Hermeneutics of jQuery,' or "Postcolonial Client-Server Architecture.'" Wilkinson's attack is not on the general aspects of this poststructuralist reading, but particularly on the application of countercultural critiques to the field of science. By joining the jargon of literary criticism with arbitrary aspects of programming, he presents the methods of CCS as equally arbitrary.

It is not my intention to reignite the Science Wars by renewing the attack on scientific knowledge—if there ever was one. Bruno Latour and C. P. Snow have presented many ways to bridge that divide, as have other writers, including those appearing in this volume. Instead, I would argue, in the plainest possible language, that scholars working in the realms of science should not fear that critical theory is out to get them or to trivialize scientific discovery through the hocus pocus of hermeneutics. We cannot build a velvet rope around code (and other artifacts of science) to protect it from the interpreting hooligans and marginalized peoples of the digital humanities (or who wish to transform it), perhaps most definitely because, in increasing numbers, those hooligans and marginalized peoples are writing code of their own.

Code Reading in Action

Over the past decade, Critical Code Studies has proved itself to be more than mere free associations on the constructs of programming or a progressive political assault on the realm of computer science. Strong code readings are grounded in a thorough understanding of the functioning of the code, the software and hardware constraints that shape it, and the history of its development and circulation. The word "critical" underscores the role of theoretical humanistic lenses even as it emphasizes the importance of interpretation to this work. The critical stance supports the questioning of existing power structures that influence and are enacted through production of code. However, its interpretations of the sign systems of code are not limited to a particular political perspective. Instead, its methods and interpretation offer a bridge between the disciplines of computer science and the humanities. By treating code as something that is not an inevitable, natural, or purely objective structure, it moves beyond the progress narrative of pragmatics, asking what forces, social and material, shaped the development of the code. It explores the rhetoric and semiotics, the connotations and contexts, uncovering histories and assumptions as well as consequences and implications of the choices made in developing code, programming languages, and programming environments. The following examples demonstrate how Critical Code Studies does not serve merely to document the social history of code, but also to illuminate new ways of presenting and exploring the origins and structures of code and the way its form complements and complicates its functioning.

TRANSBORDER IMMIGRANT TOOL

Critical Code Studies has continued to examine provocative—and politicized—works of media art, such as the codebase of the Transborder Immigrant Tool.[4] This mobile phone application, written by the Electronic Disturbance Theater (EDT), is an example of software whose authors considered the code part of the poetic work and expected it to be read and interpreted, another sign of the impact of the growing community of CCS scholars. The tool aims to sustain undocumented border crossers by directing them to caches of water in the desert and by playing them poetry that discusses a range of content, including practical techniques for surviving in the desert. The code was written in Java Platform, Micro Edition (J2ME) for a Motorola phone and was made available online during the 2010 CCS conference at the University of Southern California (USC) by co-developer Brett Stalbaum.

Before a scholar can build a CCS interpretation, he or she must first know how the code functions. My interpretive process thus began by tracing through the functioning of the code, consulting with Stalbaum when I had questions about how it operated. In Stalbaum's code, I explored unusual structures and naming conventions, and I was struck by the use of what seemed to be a metaphor of water witching that appeared in one of the method declarations:

Function: public void witchingEvent(TBCoordinates mc)

This call to "witchingEvent" is triggered when a water cache has been located near the current position of the phone. Water witching or dowsing names the practice of searching for water by walking around with a stick and waiting for it to be drawn toward the water. Surprisingly, this high-tech, GPS-driven location device drew its conceptual metaphor from a folk practice that relies not on the latest mobile-phone widgetry but instead on wood sticks that seem to know where water is hiding. Divining through the history of TBT's source code, so to speak, I found that this section was written by then-undergraduate Jason Najarro, for whom the witching metaphor was so resonant he created presentations about it.[5]

In using the metaphor of dowsing, the programmers were doing something both political and provocative—they aligned the tool with the Mayan technologies that the EDT group learned from the Zapatistas.[6] These are the technologies of cultures that cannot be contained within Western epistemes, technologies of disruption and provocation that Rita Raley calls "tactical media." The function call and its calculations, re-envisioned as an act of divination, shape the meaning of the tool.

Is such a reading of a metaphor an affront to programmers? It shouldn't be, but because the reading hinges on what computer scientists would call an "arbitrary" portion of the code—that is, a human-specified value that has no significance in the programming language—it may be prone to criticism. After all, the function could just as easily have been named "XYZZY." Function names are unlike primitives such as "public" or "void," which have fixed syntactical values in Java. In fact, in a discussion on the HASTAC Scholars forums, Evan Buswell warns against CCS grounding its interpretations in these arbitrary aspects. In his comment, he imagines a future in which CCS is "wildly successful," one in which "CCS practitioners are maybe brought into courtrooms to establish the evil intentions of some maniacal programmer bent on threatening democracy." Buswell argues that should this scenario come to fruition:

> there will be an invisible line between CCS and CS, protecting the core from
> the periphery, insulating and separating from critique the power structure of
> code itself, and constructing a discourse of "good code" and "bad code" to go
> along with the discourse of "good business" and "bad business" that tends to
> dominate naive anti-capitalist critique. ("The Essence of Code")

In such a world, Critical Code Studies would be relegated to superficial critiques of arbitrary elements of code, leaving it incapable of speaking to the forces at work in technoculture. That is to say, it could speak to the ornamentation but not the architecture of the world of computation. To contribute fully to the analyses already under way in computer science, Critical Code Studies cannot merely dwell on the arbitrary elements or the comments included in code. It must pursue the aspects of the code that are fundamental to the chosen language and the structure of the specific program. It cannot rely merely on high-level abstractions of the logic of the program. At the same time, it should not neglect the arbitrary, for those elements are most explicitly written for human readers.

10 PRINT CHR$(205.5+RND(1)); : GOTO 10

The methods of Critical Code Studies are not dependent on large bodies of code or the names of methods and variables contained within it. A code reading can emerge out of even one line of code, using that line not as an end but as an entry point to an exploration of technoculture. Such a reading emerged from a discussion in the first Critical Code Studies Working Group, held online in 2010. In a "code critique" thread, Nick Montfort posted the code for a one-line program written in BASIC for the Commodore 64, one that produces what most people see as a random maze pattern scrolling on the screen. At first, I thought Nick must either be joking or performing a sneaky kind of trolling. "Interpret this!" he seemed to be saying, throwing down the gauntlet.

In this context, the methods of CCS as demonstrated here would not work so well. There were no variables with echoes of natural language, no controversial social context, and no comments. Yet if CCS could not handle this program, I believed, the approach would be proved intellectually bankrupt. The result: a book coauthored by ten people and published by MIT Press (and free to download[7]) and at least one other journal article. These works tackle many aspects of the code, including the pseudo-randomness of RND, the culture of one-liners, the PETSCII set of characters that makes this concise program possible, along with various cultural contexts such as the place of BASIC, the C64, mazes, and home computing in the early 1980s—all factors that add resonance to this tiny code snippet. Taken together, these projects provide an example of collaborative code reading by scholars with backgrounds in both computer science and the humanities.

One small example might illustrate the kinds of critiques we performed. While writing the book, we authors would often refer to the program as 10 PRINT. But at some point, we began to wonder why the 10 was there at all. Most contemporary programming languages do not use line numbers as BASIC did, yet unless a person was executing BASIC on the command line, she would need to number the lines. Starting with 10 and increasing by 10s was a convention, since it offered the opportunity to add lines before or after any given line. I can remember writing lines 15, 16, 17 of a program and worrying that I had used up all the intervening space.

In other words, while the 10 allows for the program to loop, the 10 itself was an arbitrary designation; it could have been 1 or 15 or 105, or the one-line program could have been written without the line number altogether. The 10, then, becomes a sign of the program's partiality and potential. 10 PRINT is the first (or 10th) line of a potentially much longer program. This might seem to be a small insight, except that it indicates how all programs are partial and potential components of other programs. Code is not merely a discrete set of instructions and comments but a sign of possibility, akin to Barthes's distinction between work and text, in which the Text is the infinite field of discourse, but the Work is a particular instantiation, always partial ("From Work to Text").

Such theorization helps us understand the nature of code as a sign system. It is at once a practical system for programming and a semiotic system for communicating other messages, including possibility and even wit. The one-line BASIC program acted as a hub from which we could explore many spokes of analysis. Our readings did not challenge existing norms with fancy neologisms, nor did we dwell on provocative politics. Instead, we showed how a single line of code could provide access to its history and its hardware, and how a meditation on one line of code could serve as a heuristic for understanding computational culture.

While reading this one-line program might seem to be a conservative act, it in fact liberates code for additional readings. Within the world of computers, we were able to examine the historical moment that made this code so exciting, which included discussions of the platform, the advent of home computing, and the development and spread of BASIC as a relatively accessible programming language. Scholars wrote new code, including ports to other programming languages and a maze-walking program that tested the solvability of the on-screen puzzle. Beyond the realm of computer culture, moreover, we were able to reveal the connections between this influential program and other artistic and artisanal communities, from dance to stitchcraft, where this pattern-making knowledge was also required. To tie the computational artistry of a line of code to the material (but equally procedural) artistry of handicraft is a radical act, one that dissolves a conventionally held separation between digital and analog forms of art and between the modern technology of computers and the ancient technology of needlework. Interpreting this one line of code was not, then, an act of description or documentation, but of creating new and at times unexpected paths to understanding.

PROJECT FOR TACHISTOSCOPE

Critical Code Studies can also reveal aspects of the functioning of a piece of software that are not apparent by observing its output, and consequently, change the way we understand the software itself. For example, in another collaborative book project, written with Jessica Pressman and Jeremy Douglass, I employ the methods of Critical Code Studies to interpret a work of electronic literature, "Project for Tachistoscope [Bottomless Pit]"[8] by William Poundstone. "Project" is a work of Flash animation that presents the story of a massive crater that has opened up near a highway construction project. The story describes this inexplicable fathomless pit, the people who try to interpret it, and the community that must grapple with it. The interface of Poundstone's project presents a noisy, pulsating swirl of color and images that make it difficult to understand the story, which is displayed to the reader one word at a time.[9]

The piece itself remediates the notion of a tachistoscope—a category of devices that typically display a single image for a short amount of time—by flashing additional words at the reader between the words of the story. Although these words appear too quickly to be fully comprehended, the reader can detect their presence, since the words of the story are displayed in black while these others are displayed in white.

We caught our first snapshots of these words when Jeremy created a sequence of screenshots of the piece. To discover what these words might be, we then used a Flash decompiler to access the Flash source file (.fla). Flash files must be compiled—or converted from source code to a machine-readable format—before they can be embedded in web pages or otherwise viewed. A Flash decompiler allows that viewer to examine the underlying source code by creating a functionally equivalent version of the original code. In other words, the resultant code is actually a re-creation generated by the decompiler, although images and sound files pass through unchanged. Thus the decompiled code is a kind of translation of the source file, lacking the specific programming choices of the original source file. The resulting code cannot be read as closely, since it does not contain the exact signs used by the programmer. Because of this limitation, we ultimately asked Poundstone to share with us the .fla file used to create the piece.[10]

While we had some sense of the subliminal words flashing on the screen before looking at the code, they remained unreadable. We assumed that they were being randomly selected to appear in the work at a random interval, based on the fact that the same words did not appear in the same place or order every time the work was executed. On inspecting the code, however, we discovered something unexpected: the words were not displaying on the screen at random intervals; instead, they were flashing continuously. What was random was when those words would appear in white and hence be more detectable to the human eye. Moreover, the words were not being presented in a random order but in the exact same order each time. The work, as it turned out, displayed a perpetual alternation between words: first a subliminal word (in black or white), then a story word.

This discovery completely changed the way we had been interpreting the work. Rather than seeing this work as the product of random combinatorics, we realized that the list of subliminal words was hand-curated—that is, the list was created knowing when each word would appear in relation to the story words, at least on the first pass through the piece.[11] With access to the Flash source file (.fla), we discovered that the subliminal words always appeared in white, their most noticeable form, during an animation sequence entitled "fixation crosses," in which four white crosses flutter by in four ordinal directions (NW, NE, SW, SE). These fixation crosses, we hypothesized, prepped the eye to notice the white text. That suggestive name "fixation crosses," with echoes in optometry and cognitive science, would not have been available for interpretation without access to the code.

While the name "fixation crosses" is arbitrary, the ways in which the subliminal words are displayed is not. The name is "arbitrary" in the sense that its choice is not significant to the way the code is processed. But the arbitrary and the procedural both become significant when placed against this tale of, among other things, an indeterminate sign. The "Pit" of the story is a signifier whose signified cannot be determined, one that destabilizes every effort to measure it. Although neither the code nor the Flash file represent the "bottom" of the Pit, they do give us access to layers of signification of this work that the author/programmer fashioned while creating this piece.

At the level of the code, the work of the digital humanist is to interpret the significance of these particular choices against the paradigm of possible choices and within the context of their social and material traces. The danger is to pretend that the code "just works"—that the code's construction lacks intention and, therefore, that we can avoid interpretation. Choices are made throughout the process of programming—choices made by people in complex social situations—and those choices are informed by a perspective on the world and will impact the world. This impact is registered not only explicitly, as in the case of code that models terrorist movements or climate change, but also subtly, as it communicates ideas and worldviews to those who read it. Humanists reading code are doing more than merely changing their own oil; they are learning the hieroglyphic systems that are the lingua franca of the digital age. Their ability to trace and explicate meaning will enhance the understanding of code and identify the messages encoded in each program.

The future of Critical Code Studies is married to the future of the digital humanities, even if both decide to change their names (again) down the road. That future will depend on the ability of those developing computational technology and those interpreting it to communicate with one another in a way that is, if not amicable, at least symbiotic. The two-worlds model may be encoded into many parts of our cultural self-portraits, yet we cannot let the suspicions and sarcasm completely derail efforts toward shared inquiry.

NOTES

1. Both of these topics were the focus of weekly discussions in the 2014 online Critical Code Studies Working Group. The discussion on "Feminist Code" was led by Arielle Schlesinger with Jacqueline Wernimont and Ben Wiedermann, and the discussion on "Postcolonial Critical Code Studies" was led by Roopika Risam, Adeline Koh, and Amit Ray.

Schlesinger herself had been the subject of a spiraling flame war on the discussion board Reddit and parody on the code repository site GitHub, incited by her proposal for a feminist programming language.

2. http://lambda-the-ultimate.org/user/4902.

3. McPherson offers a similar "operates with the logic of" argument in "Why Are the Digital Humanities So White?"

4. My readings of this code appear in a 2013 article in *Digital Humanities Quarterly* and in an in-progress online book called *Border Codes,* written on the ANVC Scalar platform (http://scalar.usc.edu/nehvectors/border-codes/index).

5. See a poster from one of Najarro's presentations here: http://www.tacticalmedia files.net/mmbase/attachments/4950/xborder.pdf.

6. Ricardo Dominguez tells an exemplary story of "Mayan technologies" in which a boy uses a stick to send a military helicopter back in the direction from which it came (Bond and Frank).

7. http://10print.org.

8. http://collection.eliterature.org/1/works/poundstone__project_for_tachisto-scope_bottomless_pit.html.

9. Paratexts accessed through the work's start pages situate the project within the world of concrete poetry and also subliminal advertising, as certain tachistoscopes have been built to measure the effect of priming, testing the effects of quickly flashed visual information (see discussion in chapter 4 of Pressman, Marino, and Douglass, 101–4).

10. The full ActionScript source code, visualizations, backgrounds on the tachisto-scope, and other resources are available in our online companion to our book, featured on the collaborative research platform we designed, called ACLS Workbench. See http://scalar.usc.edu/aclsworkbench/reading-project/.

11. Since the story words and subliminal words loop at different rates (there are far fewer subliminal words), it would be unlikely that the author would try to plan the order the words display in the 2nd, 3rd, nth cycles of the story.

BIBLIOGRAPHY

Barthes, Roland. "From Work to Text." In *Textual Strategies: Perspectives in Poststructuralist Criticism,* ed. Josue V. Harari, 73–81. Ithaca, N.Y.: Cornell University Press, 1979. http://courses.wcupa.edu/fletcher/special/barthes.htm.

Berlant, Lauren, and Michael Warner. "Sex in Public." *Critical Inquiry* 24, no. 2 (January 1, 1998): 547–66. doi:10.2307/1344178.

Blas, Zach. *transCoder | Queer Technologies,* code, October 31, 2007. http://users.design.ucla.edu/~zblas/artwork/transcoder_archive/. http://users.design.ucla.edu/~zblas/thesis_website/transcoder/transcoder.html.

Bond, Mindi, and Raphie Frank. "Ricardo Dominguez, Artist and Electronic Civil Disobedience Pioneer." *The Gothamist,* November 29, 2004. http://gothamist.com/2004/11/29/ricardo_dominguez_artist_and_electronic_civil_disobedience_pioneer.php.

Brown, Travis. "Critical Code Studies." *Lambda the Ultimate* (blog), November 5, 2010. http://lambda-the-ultimate.org/node/3944.

Buswell, Evan. "The Essence of Code: Code Is Not the Essence." *HASTAC Scholars Forum: Critical Code Studies.* http://hastac.org/forums/hastac-scholars-discussions /critical-code-studies#comment-17497.

Electronic Disturbance Theater. *Transborder Immigrant Tool: A Mexico/U.S. Border Disturbance Art Project,* 2008. http://bang.transreal.org/transborder-immigrant-tool/.

Hayles, N. Katherine, and Anne Burdick. *Writing Machines.* Cambridge, Mass.: MIT Press, 2002.

Marino, Mark C. "Code as Ritualized Poetry: The Tactics of the Transborder Immigrant Tool." *Digital Humanities Quarterly* 7, no. 1 (2013). http://www.digitalhumanities .org/dhq/vol/7/1/000157/000157.html.

———. "Critical Code Studies." *Electronic Book Review.* Electropoetics (blog), December 4, 2006. http://www.electronicbookreview.com/thread/electropoetics/codology.

———. "Disrupting Heteronormative Codes: When Cylons in Slash Goggles Ogle Anna-Kournikova." In *Proceedings of the Digital Arts and Culture Conference, 2009.* eScholarship, University of California, Irvine, December 12, 2009. http://escholarship.org/uc /item/09q9m0kn#.

———. "Field Report for Critical Code Studies." *Computational Culture,* November 9, 2014. http://computationalculture.net/article/field-report-for-critical-code-studies-2014.

———. "Of Sex, Cylons, and Worms: A Critical Code Study of Heteronormativity." *Leonardo Electronic Almanac* 17, no. 2 (April 30, 2012): 184–201. http://www.leoalmanac.org /vol17-no2-of-sex-cylons-and-worms/?utm_source=rss&utm_medium=rss&utm_ campaign=vol17-no2-of-sex-cylons-and-worms.

McPherson, Tara. "Why Are the Digital Humanities So White? or Thinking the Histories of Race and Computation." In *Debates in the Digital Humanities,* ed. Matthew K. Gold, 139–160. Minneapolis: University of Minnesota Press, 2012.

Middleton, James. "Anna Virus Writer Offered IT Job." *IT News from V3.co.uk,* February 20, 2001. http://www.v3.co.uk/v3-uk/news/1998007/anna-virus-writer-offered-it-job.

Montfort, Nick, Patsy Baudoin, John Bell, Ian Bogost, Jeremy Douglass, Mark C. Marino, Michael Mateas, Casey Reas, Mark Sample, and Noah Vawter. *10 PRINT CHR$ (205.5+RND(1)); : GOTO 10.* Cambridge, Mass.: MIT Press, 2012.

Poundstone, William. *Project for Tachistoscope [Bottomless Pit],* 2005. http://collection.elit erature.org/1/works/poundstone__project_for_tachistoscope_bottomless_pit.html.

Pressman, Jessica, Mark C. Marino, and Jeremy Douglass. *Reading Project: A Collaborative Analysis of William Poundstone's Project for Tachistoscope [Bottomless Pit].* Iowa City: University of Iowa Press, 2015.

Raley, Rita. *Tactical Media.* Minneapolis: University of Minnesota Press, 2009.

Russo, Julie Levin. "The Slash Goggles Algorithm." *LiveJournal, Thearchive2,* April 10, 2008. http://community.livejournal.com/thearchive2/1465.html.

Sokal, Alan D. "Transgressing the Boundaries: An Afterword." *Dissent* 43, no. 4 (1996): 93–99.

———. "Transgressing the Boundaries: Toward a Transformative Hermeneutics of Quantum Gravity." *Social Text* 46/47 (1996): 217–52.

Warner, Michael. "Introduction: Fear of a Queer Planet." *Social Text* 29 (January 1, 1991): 3–17. doi:10.2307/466295.

Warner, Michael, and Social Text Collective. *Fear of a Queer Planet: Queer Politics and Social Theory.* Minneapolis: University of Minnesota Press, 1993.

Wilkinson, Lane. "Join the Digital Humanities . . . or Else." *Sense & Reference* (blog), January 31, 2012. http://senseandreference.wordpress.com/2012/01/31/join-the-digital-humanities-or-else/.

Where Is Methodology in Digital Humanities?

TANYA E. CLEMENT

For the very idea of "practices" has a satisfyingly concrete ring to it, if no longer through that classical (and singular) opposition to "theory," as something that (in the plural) installs us immediately in the interstices of effective social power, in its minutest details.

—Evan Watkins, *Work Time: English Departments and the Circulation of Cultural Value*

In a 2009 *Digital Humanities Quarterly* piece, Christine Borgman asks, "Where are the social studies of digital humanities?" Suggesting that ethnographic and other social studies of scientific information work have significantly shaped how scholars have come to understand scholarly cyberinfrastructure in the sciences, she argues that the practices of digital humanists should be similarly studied. And while most digital humanists do not employ the qualitative methods of data gathering to which Borgman refers, such as survey research, observations, and interviews, perhaps the absence of these methods indicates that DH it is still not clear where such methods might fit within the epistemological landscape of the humanities. After all, social scientists have long studied—and often directly impacted—scholarly information system development in the sciences using these familiar methods. By contrast, digital humanists are using methods that are largely new to the humanities, and perhaps for this reason, we are less adept at expressing how these forms of study map to our theoretical concerns.

How we validate and share knowledge within and between epistemological frameworks, whether it is the humanities or the social sciences, has much to do with how we articulate the link between our methods and our theories. Situating seemingly positivist social science methods within a humanist framework is about more than the interpretive methods we might employ. Likewise, collaborating with social scientists or impacting social science studies, which are also often shaped by cultural studies, critical race theory, feminist inquiry, or postcolonialism, requires more than staking a claim to constructivist theories. In ethnographic studies such as those Borgman cites, an articulation of methodology helps the researcher describe a systematic approach to fieldwork and data analysis methods, one that ultimately facilitates a deeper engagement with theory. This chapter therefore aims to distill a range of methodological perspectives employed in the study of information systems in the social sciences and digital humanities, with the goal of suggesting bridges not only between the social sciences and digital humanities but between digital and traditional humanities.

I begin with a brief review of studies on information work in the social sciences and the digital humanities in order to situate these at once disparate and interconnected discourse communities. Then, by focusing on the methodological perspectives that underpin crucial projects in each field, I show how each understands the links between their methods and their theories. This attention allows us to understand the theoretical implications of adopting methods that are more familiar to the social sciences in DH as well as to identify the theoretical implications of digital humanities methods for the humanities writ large.

Establishing Social Science Methodology in Information Work

Information systems and the people who work with them have long been studied by social scientists. Michael Buckland, among the most well-known theorists of information, identifies three meanings of the term: information as knowledge, information as thing, and information as process. For Buckland, information-as-knowledge is intangible since it is based on personal, subjective, and conceptual understandings. Information-as-thing has materiality, however, since to communicate these understandings they have "to be expressed, described, or represented in some physical way, as a signal, text, or communication" within a system (2). The systems that these information workers typically work with include computers and networking technologies, whether they are stand-alone or embedded in a larger system,[1] but information-as-thing allows the social scientist to isolate information objects associated with specific forms of information work from the systems that engage those objects (whether that object is digital or not) as culturally informed processes—for example, the sculptures and exhibits of a museum or gallery; the books, documents, and taxonomies of a library; the DNA or microscope of a scientific lab; the code, bits, and bytes of computer programmers; the numbers and graphs of data analysts, and so on. An investigation of how workers interact with and through these information objects and systems through social-scientific means often yields insights about how information is understood in those fields.

At the same time, much social science information work scholarship is undergirded by a desire for a better understanding of information-as-process—what Foucault would call "an archaeology of knowledge"—or the systems of power and influence that shape information systems and therefore knowledge production, identity construction, and intersubjectivity. Social science researchers work with disempowered communities to better understand systems of power and resistance in the modern metropolis (Burawoy); study the relations of employment and the role of the worker in the constitution of a worker's identity (Orr); and study interpretive flexibility and human agency in information technology development and use in large, multinational software consulting firms (Orlikowski). Embedding themselves, sometimes as workers in these communities, these researchers attempt to foreground their own research practices in their studies of others.[2] Of particular interest to digital humanists, Christopher Kelty's *Two Bits: The Cultural Significance of Free Software* and Matthew Hull's *Government of Paper: The Materiality of Bureaucracy in Urban Pakistan* are ethnographic studies in information work of which the objects of study are text and technology; their subjects concern the creation, dissemination, and authorization of knowledge; their goals are to explore "recursive publics" and the political economies of paper, respectively. Other social scientists, such as those to whom Borgman refers, also consider how the universal claims of science are localized as a result of unspoken, ontological, epistemological, and practical diversities in the day-to-day worlds of scientific labs (Knorr-Cetina; Sommerlund; Voskuhl).[3] These studies share a theoretical kinship with humanistic studies concerning information and knowledge production, even as they employ divergent methods.

Qualitative social scientific methods in information and knowledge work typically focus on the direct observation of practices rather than on reviews of theories or findings (Geertz "Thick Description"). Social scientists employ such methods through standardized procedures, which are considered essential for conducting a qualitative study that yields valid and rigorous scholarship. Howard Becker's seminal 1996 essay, "The Epistemology of Qualitative Research," maintains that scholars who employ quantitative methods justify their results by proving that their data is reliable (i.e., repeatable), but those who rely on qualitative methods are more concerned with showing that their data is accurate and precise (or based on close observation) and broad (based on a wide range of variables). In other words, researchers who engage in qualitative methods are especially conscientious about their methods producing accurate data—as close to objective as one can get—so that their results can be considered valid by their peers, who typically find quantitative methods more exact (Becker).

In such studies, an articulation of methodology helps researchers reinforce the systematic nature of their chosen approach. As I will argue, this is an act that ultimately facilitates a deeper engagement with theory. Consider that social scientists view *technique* as a particular and situated way of applying a *method* or systematic approach, and *methodology* as the reciprocal relationship between *method* and *theory* (Katz; Burawoy, 271). Data produced outside of a theoretical framework is considered merely "sociological aestheticism" (Geertz, "Thick Description"), simply description (Katz), or at worst, "haphazard" and "fortuitous" (Snow, Morill, and

Anderson, 184). In the dominant model of social science scholarship, therefore, the researcher includes an explicit statement about which theories he or she is engaging within any initial account of his or her methodological conditions (Snow, Morill, and Anderson, 194). This theory is described in the context of the study, including how the theory was formed and how the particular setting of the study compares to that formation, as well as any co-related historical factors such as how the theory has been used in the past or how it is discussed in current scholarship (195). This form of explicit engagement with theory is crucial in social science epistemologies that warrant a degree of scientific objectivity.

Establishing Digital Humanities Methodology in Information Work

Digital humanists also operate on information-as-thing (the word, the line of poetry, the page, the piece of code) as well as understand information as information-as-process—the continual state of becoming informed through understandings that are constantly shifting. The study of information work in digital humanities and of digital humanists as information workers has been primarily concerned with the cultural contexts that influence these shifting understandings—what we might also describe as knowledge production—especially as these contexts relate to the academy. Johanna Drucker, Kathleen Fitzpatrick, Julia Flanders, John Unsworth, and many others have written about the processes of scholarly knowledge production in changing publication and employment practices, for example. Anne Balsamo, N. Katherine Hayles, Alan Liu, and Patrik Svensson have each published extended studies on the future of researchers and educators in the humanities and arts—a future in which, as a result of a postindustrial value system, literature and the arts are increasingly undervalued.[4] These examples demonstrate the overarching concern of digital humanists with the cultural contexts of academe and how the changing nature of information work will alter the future of the humanities.

What is needed to connect this body of work to the discourse of information work in the social sciences is a more precise articulation of how digital humanists themselves function as information workers. In fact, Liu provides a taxonomy of the knowledge worker that is particularly helpful in understanding digital humanists as information workers:

> Knowledge workers =
> Academic intellectuals +
> (technical + professional + managerial) intelligentsia +
> trailing edge clerical workers (Liu, *Laws of Cool*, 392)

Broadly speaking, digital humanists are typically academic intellectuals and "intelligentsia," and their information work might include research, writing, and publication, project conceptualization, teaching, and service to the institution and the field at large. Doing this work within the context of information technologies can include (among a variety of activities), algorithm development and implementation; coding and encoding; e-mailing; data curation, management, and analysis; generating and analyzing statistics; social networking; meeting virtually; note-taking and publication; user experience and user testing; as well as database, software, web, and visualization development and interpretation. Noting that his definition of the knowledge worker is a class-based concept, Liu reminds us that information work is a process of knowledge production that is embedded in culture. As such, this list is not exhaustive; it does not include the social infrastructure development work that supports these activities with technology such as curriculum development, fund-raising, networking, staffing, and general project management, but it makes the point well: the digital humanist can be defined as a knowledge worker *and* an information worker.

And yet there is a prevailing notion in the social sciences that humanists are not trained to study themselves as information workers. For instance, the Information Work Research Group in the School of Information at the University of Texas at Austin, of which I am a part, trains graduate students in social scientific methods—that is, direct, in situ observations and semistructured interviews—out of the sense that such methods provide an "essential means for understanding what information professionals actually do at work, why they do, and how they do it," digital humanists included.[5] Borgman attributes the differences between humanists' "fluid" methods and more exacting social scientific methods to the fact that humanities scholars tend to learn methods that are specific to content areas and through independent research rather than as a "common substrate of research methods courses and practices that span the social sciences" (Borgman, *Big Data, Little Data, No Data,* 164). The implication is that a level of scientific objectivity is lacking in the humanist's more subjective approach to studying knowledge production and information work.

Indeed, some digital humanists openly discount the need for the objective stance that is central to social science research. For example, Liu calls his study a "census, a propaedeutic, an introduction" in lieu of "a more scientific study," and likens his reading of "cool" websites to the act of "thrusting one's hand into the water to see if it is cold, hot, or lukewarm" (*Laws of Cool,* 183; 233). Similarly, in her survey of social science studies on issues of attention in the digital age, Hayles notes that "few scholars in the humanities have the time—or the expertise—to backtrack through cited studies and evaluate them for correctness and replicability" (*How We Think,* 68). Arguing that "perhaps our most valuable yardstick for evaluating these results . . . is our own experience," Hayles simultaneously promotes a de-siloing of knowledge work, maintaining that "the scientific research is valuable and should not be ignored" (68). To be sure, these examples leverage experiential knowledge with other interpretive data-gathering methods, such as archival work and close reading. But in their nods to the value of social science research, Liu, Hayles, and other digital humanists implicitly deny their own need for a systematic repeatable method and at times openly disavow a desire to be "scientific" at all.[6]

Certainly, digital humanists are deeply concerned with employing accurate and variable as well as systematic methods in their studies. John Unsworth, for instance, calls methods "primitives" and lists activities such as discovering, annotating, comparing, illustrating, referring, representing, and sampling as among the methods employed in humanities knowledge work. The European Union's Digital Research Infrastructure for the Arts and Humanities initiative has gone so far as to create a Taxonomy of Digital Research Activities in the Humanities (TaDiRAH), which includes three broad categories: *research activities, research objects,* and *research techniques. Research techniques* include a long list of topic areas about which we are used to seeing debates in DH, including concordance-building, crowdsourcing, encoding, gamification, topic modeling, and versioning. In this case*, research activities,* which includes capture, creation, enrichment, analysis, interpretation, storage, dissemination, and meta-activities (such as assessing, community building, project management, and teaching and learning), in effect extend Unsworth's list of primitives to add methods typically employed in a digital context.[7] There is indeed a broad range of topics and methods in which digital humanists engage as we pursue our inquiries into information-as-process.

It is telling, then, that most critiques of DH—both from the social sciences and the humanities—do not point to a lack of accuracy, variability, or other limitation of method. Rather, most critiques of DH point to a decoupling of method from the theoretical perspectives that would ordinarily help situate the kind of intellectual effort being engaged (Drucker; Hall; Liu, "Where Is Cultural Criticism in the Digital Humanities"; McPherson, "Why Are the Digital Humanities So White"?). To frame the issue another way, consider how reductive it would seem to describe the mere presence of the techniques and methods as *doing digital humanities.* It would be like saying that *doing ethnography* simply entails establishing relationships, watching people, transcribing interviews, and keeping a diary (Geertz, "Thick Description"). Digital humanities research must include enough detail or "evidence" to form accurate and convincing accounts, and accounts are much more accurate when they reflect as broad a spectrum of perspectives as possible. These imperatives can be achieved—to a varying degree—through many types of methods, but situating digital humanities within a humanist epistemological framework must also entail an explicit articulation of our methodological perspectives, or how our techniques are tied to theory. Digital humanities scholarship that does not engage with theory risks being perceived as unconcerned with interpretive, situated, and subjective knowledge production, and therefore displaced from the epistemic culture of the humanities. Articulating our methodology, moreover, gives us an opportunity to explain *why* we do what we do, which in turn allows us to argue for the specific contributions of our findings to ourselves, to other humanists, to those possible collaborators in other disciplines who rely on methodology as a signpost, and to the world.

Methodological Perspectives in DH Information Work

In contrast to social science scholarship on information work, digital humanities studies of information work often lack methodological discussions—even while *methodological perspectives,* as I term them, are always at play. *Methodological perspectives* are akin to what Sandra Harding has called "methodological features" in feminist social science inquiry—the empirical and theoretical resources, intellectual rationales, and relations between subject and object of study—that, once identified, help a researcher to pinpoint how they are applying "the general structure of scientific theory to research on women and gender" (Harding, *Feminism and Methodology,* 9). In the context of DH, using the term *methodological perspectives* rather than *methodological features* underscores the fact that even so-called features are subjective and influenced by one's situated epistemic culture.[8]

In digital humanities, we reflect our methodological perspectives when we choose to study certain texts (or certain things *as* texts) or when we discuss why methods are best employed through certain techniques—why deformance in Adobe Photoshop can advance our thinking about the hermeneutics of visual art (Samuels and McGann), for example; or how algorithmic thinking with word frequencies might advance our thinking about how gender roles play out in *King Lear* (Ramsay, "Reconceiving Text Analysis"); or how surface reading with social network analysis allows us to articulate the archival silences in Thomas Jefferson's archive (Klein). These and other examples show us methodological perspectives (a "thinking through" of the link between techniques, methods, and theories) already present in literary scholarship in digital humanities. More often than not, however, these ties are implicit—the means to the end is either foregrounded in exclusion of a productive critique, or the research strategy is subsumed by a finding that the researcher argues has been "discovered" rather than constructed.

But methodological perspectives in the humanities and social sciences can overlap, which means that digital humanists must be even more diligent about articulating how our perspectives are situated within a humanist epistemological framework. That is, new methods in digital humanities such as statistical analysis, visualization, or ethnography do not exist in a vacuum. If digital humanists choose to employ methods that are more common to the social sciences, we must understand the relevant articulation work that surrounds similar kinds of methods in the social sciences. Or consider the reverse: theories in feminist inquiry, postcolonial studies, and activism have never been solely humanistic research perspectives; scholars from outside the humanities also school themselves in those histories before applying their methods. In other words, theories that engage self-reflexivity as a methodological perspective are essential to scholarship in the humanities.[9] But reflexive awareness is also at the foundation of methodological perspectives in qualitative social science research—research that has been deeply influenced by constructivist paradigms.[10] There is a general understanding in the social sciences—the same that should be reflected in digital humanities work—that methodological perspectives, as driven by the historical, present, and perceived future context of a project, shape and are shaped by practical and theoretical concerns.

A reflexive understanding of knowledge production and information-as-process is a significant research perspective that translates across information studies in the social sciences and digital humanities. Examining similar methodological perspectives in information work research in the social sciences—namely, authority creation, hermeneutics, and becoming answerable—informs how we might apply humanist theories to research on information-as-process in the digital humanities. Comparing these perspectives from the viewpoint of social science and digital humanities studies not only allows us to develop a better understanding of methodological perspectives in general, but also offers specific examples of how these similar perspectives play out in different epistemic cultures. Though shared across disciplines, these perspectives ultimately reflect unique epistemes through their employment of technique and method in individual studies. Learning to express these differences is vital not only for digital humanists who seek to situate their work in conversation with social science research, but also for those who seek to situate themselves in common as humanists.

AUTHORITY CREATION

Concerns about the validity and relevance of research are prevalent in the social sciences and digital humanities alike, especially as research paradigms evolve in accordance with rapidly changing information and knowledge economies (Becker, Harpham).[11] Concurrent with these concerns are additional anxieties about how to establish authority and validate scholarly work in such evolving topologies. Considered together, humanistic and social scientific studies of information work demonstrate how authority creation constitutes a methodological perspective, one that can help us understand the value of the new forms of inquiry that arise within the context of evolving technologies and techniques. Such a perspective is epistemologically performative, shaping expectations about what practices comprise good scholarship even as those practices evolve.

In ethnographic studies of information work, for example, an ethnographer's presence at a field site (or multiple sites) for extended periods of time has long been essential for establishing the authority and validity of her ethnographic study. At present, however, ethnographers have new opportunities for observing and participating in communities through online forums, networks, and virtual worlds, and as a result, the means by which authority is established through field "presence" has shifted (Horst and Miller; Collins and Durington; and Boellstorff et.al). These shifts have facilitated new opportunities for rendering information work outside of scientific labs "observable" for social science research.[12] They have also opened up new data "traces"—conversation transcripts, institutional records, source code, transaction logs, or version histories—for scholarly analysis. These traces of data, in turn, have placed renewed focus on authority creation, as ethnographers have focused on new forms of inscription such as elaborate experimentations in self-ethnographies and data visualizations in order to establish authority in this context (Beaulieu, "From Co-Location to Co-Presence," 459). Mindful that scholarship cannot be constructed through quantitative trace data analysis alone, other scholars such as Geiger and Ribes (2011) argue that observing such traces must be achieved alongside more traditional interviews and observations, which allow for a qualitative understanding of the cultures—the activities, people, systems, and technologies—that contribute to their production. Their methodological perspective therefore includes adapting new to old epistemic traditions.

In digital humanities, studies in new kinds of information work have also exposed new ways to create authority while simultaneously unearthing deep-rooted assumptions tied to publishing and promotion traditions. Online peer-reviewed publications, scholarly electronic editions, specifications, research tools, research blogs, and hypermedia and new media works each provide an opportunity to consider how authority in the humanities has traditionally been established. Susan Schreibman, Laura Mandell, and Stephen Olsen identify two essential aspects of digital scholarship that break with epistemic tradition, thereby making such scholarship difficult to assess in terms of its intellectual contributions: first, humanities scholars are, for the most part, "ill equipped" to evaluate the nature of intellectual work in digital humanities scholarship; second, much digital humanities scholarship is about digitization and increased access to or the development of digital infrastructure. This scholarship draws on the methods and practices associated with scholarly editing, bibliography, and philology, activities that have been long regarded as less scholarly or rigorous (124–25). As a response, Geoffrey Rockwell has developed a taxonomy for new types of digital publications, demonstrating how a consideration of authority creation as a methodological perspective can engage theoretical issues related to historical context, community impact, and the projected sustainability of research (Rockwell, 160).

In any study in which one employs techniques or methods that are well documented and theorized in another epistemic culture, or in which one hopes to impact how knowledge is produced across epistemic borders, the scholar's own authority is brought into question. A single example from digital humanities literature shows the potential risks for digital humanists who seek to establish their authority in DH information work studies with*out* an understanding of social science methodological concerns. In Julia Flanders's essay "Time, Labor, and 'Alternate Careers' in Digital Humanities Knowledge Work," she tells her personal origin story as an "alternative academic" (alt-ac) or nontenure-track academic in a research university. In the essay, Flanders focuses on the work practices and roles of digital humanists, but her method is personal reflection—an approach that she at once likens to and distances from social scientific work by denying its objectivity; she calls it "quasi-anthropological" and "self-study." On the one hand, Flanders rightly distances her essay from a more traditional social scientific study since "self-study" has not been a traditional method in that field. On the other hand, social science researchers have done much work articulating self-reflective ethnographic approaches to studying information work. Working as an apprentice in a bookmaking workshop, for example, Daniela Rosner uses an autobiographical account ("The Material Practices of Collaboration") to position herself as her own research subject. From this position, Rosner argues, she can better focus on the social and functional role of book artifacts. By denying self-study as a valid approach to information work in digital humanities, we potentially raise concerns about the methods of authority creation in DH that are implicitly tied to theories of power, influence, and privilege—questions of *whose* information work may be discoverable—especially when the authority to speak is in large part based on experience.

DH scholars such as those involved in #transformDH[13] and postcolonial digital humanities have indeed engaged in important work that attempts to broaden and dismantle systems of authority, power, and influence.[14] But overt discussions about the ties between authority creation in digital humanities methods and the methods, such as ethnography as well as visualization or data analysis, that are also employed in sister fields are still lacking.[15] New methods of research, such as those employed in DH work, can and should be viewed as opportunities for interrogating traditional assumptions. But without sufficient reflection, such methods can establish limited forms of skill or experience as authority—a turn that would limit the reach and impact of DH in the humanities.

HERMENEUTICS

Authority creation is at the foreground of recent conversations in large part because our hermeneutical methods, and therefore our principles of interpretation, have begun to shift within the context of information technologies. For example, digital humanists have become quite proficient at arguing for new objects of study in these contexts including code (Chun), databases (Presner), hard drives (Kirschenbaum, *Mechanisms*), lab spaces (Svensson, "From Optical Fiber to Conceptual Cyberinfrastructure"), magnetic tape (Sayers), the MP3 (Sterne), and platforms (Manovich). Even in light of these and other studies, however, the epistemic culture of digital humanities, which scholars such as Svensson argue have evolved expressly from humanities computing, still treats the text as the primary object of study, with linguistic analysis remaining as a central, unexamined method in the field (Svensson, "Humanities Computing as Digital Humanities").

Indeed, while the studies mentioned demonstrate the expanding scope of objects to read, the hermeneutical methods associated with reading remain largely unarticulated. As Hayles describes close reading ("that sacred icon of literary study"), for example, it is "the one thing virtually all literary scholars know how to do well and agree is important" (58). There is also common agreement that close reading a text can help to uncover (in the context of New Critical theories) affective fallacy, allusions, ambiguity, irony, intentional fallacy paradox, patterns, tension, and unity (Parker); likewise, a researcher can conduct *surface* (Klein), *suspicious* (Felski), and *symptomatic* readings that interpret words as evidence of a text's ideology. That reading is universally understood as a reliable hermeneutical method in the humanities means that humanists are not typically required to argue for it as a method.

To be sure, new hermeneutical methods in digital humanities represent unique opportunities for researchers to articulate methodological perspectives—that is, ties between theory and technique—that concern the very nature of interpretation. Hayles, for example, uses her study of reading methods to compare existing techniques and to explore new ones, such as *hyperreading* through associative links or *distant reading*—using computational methods to reveal patterns (61, 73). These methods of reading in digital humanities have been provocative in meta-conversations about what interpreting through such methods means, as well as how such methods shape the production of meaning (Drucker; Liu, "The Meaning of the Digital Humanities"), but more often than not, studies in the digital humanities do not discuss alternative methods as they relate to theories concerning the different modes of making meaning.[16]

Ethnographic studies that situate the hermeneutics of reading as an alternative practice can therefore provide useful examples of methodological perspectives that acknowledge the theories they engage. In his study "Deep Play: Notes on the Balinese Cockfights," for instance, Clifford Geertz explains that ethnographic methods require "examining culture as an assemblage of texts," since cultural forms are akin to "imaginative works built out of social materials" (27). For Geertz, what makes the cockfight "readable" is his rendering of the cockfight as a text through "thick description." Through his analysis, description is simultaneously revealed as a method through which the ethnographer arrives at conclusions about how a culture produces, perceives, and interprets meaning, and as a method that is nevertheless heavily shaped by the ethnographer (Geertz, "Thick Description"). Treating cultures as an assemblage of texts emphasizes how the interpretive act of reading is only one among many hermeneutical methods for thinking through the formation of culture.

Geertz's methodological inquiry into his "search of meaning" illuminates the central issue at stake in the call for increased attention to alternative hermeneutical practices in digital humanities as well. For instance, digital humanists have focused on data visualization, new forms of publication, and critical making as interpretive modes of knowledge representation, but often without explicit statements about how the use of these technologies might impact larger theoretical concerns. Scalar, for example, was designed as a publishing platform for making multimedia scholarship more accessible, allowing for textual and audiovisual materials to be read in nonlinear sequence (McPherson, "Designing for Difference"). The necessity of having to treat the audiovisual materials as static objects in a database, however,

precludes an understanding of these materials as emergent events for which meaning changes and evolves, as well as any means for computational engagement with
the media objects themselves—such as audio or video analysis. Similarly, critical
making projects that seek to interrogate the "resistance" of materiality through
technology (Nowviskie, chapter 15 in this volume) or the "disobedience" of technology itself (Oroza, interviewed by Alex Gil in chapter 16 in this volume) are
required to do so within the established pathways of proprietary technological formats such as those needed by a 3D printer or, in Oroza's case, a communist dictator-
ship—both of which are regimes of influence that must be theorized. In such cases,
digital humanists must be able to articulate the hermeneutical methodologies that
might help foreground the multiplicity of cultural influences at play in the sociotechnical systems we use in our interpretive work.[17] Foregrounding methodological
perspectives that show a concern for hermeneutics—especially the hermeneutics of
reading—can serve as a primary means by which we might better situate our new
methods in the context of humanistic interpretive work.

BECOMING ANSWERABLE

The idea in the social sciences and the popular press that in this, the age of big data,
the humanities might be simply "blurring with the sciences" (Borgman, "The Digital Future Is Now"; Leroi), is compounded by the fear in the humanities—not altogether unrelated—that digital humanities is blurring with the corporate culture of
the information work space (Kirschenbaum, "What Is 'Digital Humanities'"). Consequently, we have seen a renewed call to activism in digital humanities information
work—what Donna Haraway might call "becoming answerable" to the fact that the
humanities are diametrically opposed in object, subject, and purpose from both
the sciences (social and otherwise) and corporate cultures.[18]

Some digital humanists have taken up this call through social actions that are
both policy-based[19] as well as project-based. By and large, however, these actions
have reflected traditional humanist methodologies. The projects featured through
the #transformDH hashtag and Tumblr, for example, apply traditions of radical
inquiry to digital and new media work in the humanities. Lothian and Phillips
identify these projects as agents of social and cultural transformation, ones that
can help to diversify DH scholarship and break down institutional silos, but the
methods they employ fall squarely within a familiar range—increasing access to
alternative perspectives by making previously unacknowledged documents discoverable (exemplified by Adeline Koh's "Chinese Englishmen" project); creating provocative art pieces (Zach Blas's Queer Technologies project); giving voice
to underrepresented communities (Women Who Rock project); and collaborating
in community-based, politically engaged knowledge production (From the Center
project). Though important and indeed potentially radical, the methods of these
projects typify common humanistic tactics for dismantling information regimes

by "transforming digital technologies so that they become more socially responsive to social and cultural inequities" and "more resistant to predatory capitalistic practices," as Hayles describes (18). These projects present necessary critiques of social systems through acts of inclusion, provocation, and disruption. In terms of information work, however, many of the techniques they employ are methodologically problematic since they rely on unexamined information technologies.

A complementary trend has emerged in the social sciences in which studies seek to become answerable on behalf of their findings about the social and cultural biases of information infrastructures by actively dismantling those same problematic systems. When applied to studies of information work, such a methodology is often characterized by using redesigns—or modifications on the level of coding and encoding—to expose and then examine the invisible social orders that influence and are influenced by information technologies.[20] These radical digital projects, such as those that seek to interrogate spatial and temporal mappings (Drucker and Nowviskie; Meeks and Gossner) or taxonomic systems (Kim; Feinberg, Carter, and Bullard) do so by dis- and reorienting the traditional logics behind databases and interfaces. In each of these cases, the authors—some of whom have published as digital humanities scholars and all of whom are influenced by both information studies and the humanities[21]—reorient seemingly objective representations of life and culture—space, time, and image—through changes in encodings, both computational and taxonomic, in order to show how these "invisible infrastructures" (Star) are instantiating situated, interpretive, and subjective perspectives in digital cultural heritage resources.

In digital humanities, such techniques must be employed with explicit ties to humanistic goals, but any additional links to theory that we can make when we describe how we achieve these goals will deepen and broaden their impact. For example, Evans Watkins and Janice Radway, literary theorists who have employed interviews and observations in their studies of, respectively, the daily practices of the English professoriate and the situated practices of women reading novels, have done so in the context of Marxist and reader response theories deeply familiar to literary study. While their methods are not traditional for the humanities, the subject matter and the theories they engage—in other words, their methodological approach to becoming answerable—situates this work squarely in the humanities.[22] Significantly, these theorists have also been heavily cited by social science researchers who value similar methods and seek to learn from the observed activities of readers and scholars in the humanities. It follows, then, that when digital humanists employ methods from outside of the humanities, they must explicate the links between their methods and their theories so that their work can be situated in the field, and in relation to other disciplines, as a contribution to humanist knowledge production.

Methodological perspectives in the social sciences and the humanities might jointly engage reflexive processes and constructivist paradigms, issues of authority creation and power relations, questions of hermeneutics and interpretive stances, and the desire to become answerable to the publics with whom we do our most important knowledge work, but the goals and values of these two epistemic cultures are still diverse. Typically, humanists have been interested in methods that employ idiographic investigations, while social scientists have engaged in nomothetic explanations. In other words, humanists have generally analyzed individual texts, objects, communities, and cultures in order to understand situated, subjective phenomena, while social scientists—even those who apply ethnographic methods—"try to see how society works, to describe social reality, to answer specific questions about specific instances of social reality" (Becker). In contrast, humanists produce "uncertain knowledge," or "knowledge that solicits its own revision in an endless process of refutation, contestation, and modification" (Harpham, 30). Perhaps it is our penchant for uncertain knowledge that elicits the view that digital humanities is uniquely poised, among all humanistic fields, to produce scholarship that will impact how we think about and develop new scholarly information infrastructures (Borgman, "The Digital Future is Now").

As Borgman suggests, we can learn from the social scientists who have impacted and continue to impact how information-as-process is conducted. But if we learn to describe what has thus far remained implicit in our own ways and modes of research, we must also begin to teach. Digital humanists must articulate these methods to ourselves and to others, because to do so is to understand where we can build bridges across diverse discourse communities, where we can learn from each other. In the humanities, for example, the connections between methods of close reading and the politics of reading suspiciously or symptomatically are easily intuited, but the connections between the objectivist methods that are regularly employed in other epistemic cultures and the theories that encourage uncertain knowledge production are not easily ascertained. As humanists, we must be explicit about our desire to distinguish ourselves from the objective stances that are still praised in social science epistemologies when what we do is deliberately open-ended, circular, situated, subjective, or personal; but we must also know when theories about situated knowledge production have deeply impacted scholarship in sister fields. Indeed, such theories should also impact ours. To articulate methodology—that crucial link between method and theory—is to explain our work to potential collaborators, in both the humanities and social sciences, and to those to whom we are accountable, as activists and as educators: our administrators, our students, and the world.

NOTES

1. Scholars in science and technology studies (STS) also rely on organization and management scholarship in workplace studies in which researchers study workers including consultants, doctors, or engineers in the context of particular organizations (Garcia

et al.) as well as the information work practices of traditional information institutions including libraries, archives, and museums that collect, preserve, interpret, and disseminate various kinds of information (Marty; LeMaistre et al.).

2. This kind of fieldwork is exemplified in the work of scholars such as Daniela Rosner, who considers "object bias" in Computer-Supported Cooperative Work (CSCW) studies. From a reflexive position, Rosner focuses on the social and functional role of artifacts as objects that are spatial and temporal flows with emergent compositional elements and constituent surfaces.

3. Other examples might include Latour and Woolgar's ethnography of the scientific laboratory life (1986); Bowker and Star's ethnography of infrastructure and metadata (2000); Suchman's ethnography of technology design and production and consumption and use (2006); and Geiger and Ribes's trace ethnography of log data (2011).

4. These studies include Liu's *The Laws of Cool* (2004), Balsamo's *Designing Culture* (2011), Svensson's four-part series on the emergence of Digital Humanities in the *Digital Humanities Quarterly* (2009, 2010, 2011, 2012), and Hayles's *How We Think* (2012).

5. This definition is from a grant proposal narrative that is not publicly available.

6. This stance is unlike social scientists such as Donna Haraway and Sandra Harding, who use a feminist epistemology to critique objectivist stances and to claim that valid scientific methods require that we claim our situatedness on what we are able to see (Harding, *Whose Science? Whose Knowledge?*, 106; Haraway, 583).

7. Other good examples include Hayles's coverage of different modes of reading (57–68) and her work close reading telegraph manuals alongside electronic and paper-based postmodern literature, Liu's survey across business and management literature (*Laws of Cool*, 76–175) and his close reading of "cool" websites from the 1990s (*Laws of Cool*, 176–285), and the Stanford Literary Lab Pamphlets, which focus on texts that range hundreds of years and techniques that include topic modeling, sentiment analysis, and visualization techniques.

8. That epistemology has bearing on the methodological discussion is not lost on Harding. In *Feminism and Methodology,* she notes that her recommendation for employing these three methodological features is meant to counteract "traditional" theories of knowledge. "Traditional" methodological features in her treatment of the topic, however, are those that are common to social science investigations. I am consciously situating this conversation squarely in the humanities episteme by choosing the alternative term "methodological perspective."

9. Harpham defines the objective of humanities scholarship as "self-understanding" (23) and Gilman calls this reflexivity "the self-conscious awareness of the methodological approaches that one uses" (384). Menand also identifies reflexive processes as the defining feature of humanistic knowledge by arguing that in "developing tools for understanding ourselves" and "everything in the world of values"—what Latour calls "states of affairs" (232)—humanists are instantiating "the fact of situatedness" that ultimately leads to a necessary skepticism to objectivity and positivism (Menand, 15). For Stanley Fish likewise, this skepticism means that humanists understand the constructed nature of "the cultural

systems within which we live and move and have our beings" as "the given" or "normative" (377). This investment in the constructed nature of knowledge production in all fields means methodological perspectives in the humanities must reflect an understanding that knowledge is "knowing, observer dependent, emergent, and process-driven rather than entity-defined" (Drucker, 87).

10. In "the Chicago School," originating at the University of Chicago in the 1940s and 1950s, ethnography was considered an empirical, scientific study and ethnographic writings typically began to include methodology sections (and books on methodology and epistemology) that shied away from more subjective (historical research) or objective (statistical techniques) methods. Valid data was achieved through in situ observation that provided insight into the participant's interpretations of events. Such insights were often the result of gaining the confidence of and having and showing empathy for subjects. As in literary study, ethnographers made a postmodern, postcolonialist turn in the 1980s and 1990s that is reflected in books that challenged the efficacy (and ethics) of ethnography as an objective or impartial look at the world and insisted, instead, on the potential of fieldwork that produced subjective, contingent, and situated knowledges (Adler).

11. Becker's response is to assure his audience that qualitative methods, while not objective in the same way as quantitative methods, are still valid in the context of older and new methodological traditions. Harpham's remarks in "Beneath and beyond the 'Crisis in the Humanities'" are a response to what McGann calls a general "malaise" that has had humanities scholarship and education in a "holy mess for some time" (McGann, 72) and are also meant to assure his audience that humanist inquiries are still valid—in that they are still relevant—within the context of global economies and advanced information technologies.

12. For a social science researcher like Anne Beaulieu, that has meant new means for studying the information work of women's studies scholars through online forums and listservs ("Mediating Ethnography"). Through a methodological perspective concerned with authority creation and gendered information work, Beaulieu engages feminist theories that are concerned with making previously unseen work observable and therefore discoverable as new subjects for study.

13. #transformDH, http://transformdh.org/.

14. Postcolonial Digital Humanities, http://dhpoco.org/.

15. One concern, as Drucker points out, is that the "cultural authority" of visualization, publishing, and design technologies are still claimed by fields in the sciences and technology (85).

16. In direct response to topic modeling and visualization techniques, Liu has called this "the meaning problem in the Digital Humanities" based on projects that perform "tabula rasa interpretation" or "the initiation of interpretation through the hypothesis-free discovery of phenomena" ("The Meaning of the Digital Humanities," 414).

17. Chun and Balsamo are excellent examples of this kind of methodological perspective at work in digital humanities. Blanchette gives an excellent overview of critical making in particular from the social science perspective.

18. Posner has made this call in her keynote at the Keystone Digital Humanities Conference, which she has published on her blog. In *The Laws of Cool*, Liu warns that in the age of "millennial knowledge" or "knowledge that is antihistorical (anti-obsolescent). . . . The centrality of the challenge to academic knowledge thus stands starkly revealed: [corporate] knowledge work is not just indifferent to humanistic knowledge, it opposes it on principle" (6), while in her book, Hayles writes, "If the Traditional Humanities are at risk of becoming marginal to the main business of the contemporary academy and society, the Digital Humanities are at risk of becoming a trade practice held captive by the interest of corporate capitalism" (53–54). Finally, Drucker is concerned with the ramifications of DH's wholesale adoption of visualization techniques that "come entirely from realms outside the humanities—management, social sciences, natural sciences, business, economics, military surveillance, entertainment, gaming, and other fields," arguing that humanistic principles are at best peripheral to the methodological premises of these other disciplines, but more often than not that these other methodologies are "at odds with—even hostile to—humanistic values and thought" (86). In the context of these concerns, Liu situates the work of literature and art as committing necessary "disruptions" in the flow of informationalism (*Laws of Cool*, 427). "The creative arts," Liu writes, "as cultural criticism must be the history not of things created . . . but of things destroyed in the name of creation" (8).

19. The ACH (Association for Computers and the Humanities) has gone to great lengths to help support open access and fair use in DH by joining the DH community in filing two amicus briefs in lawsuits related to digitization of in-copyright and orphaned works in the Google Books and HathiTrust corpora. Spearheaded by Matthew Jockers, Matthew Sag, and Jason Schultz on behalf of the DH community, the briefs describe "how DH scholars employ innovative data-mining techniques in ways consistent with fair use, and how scholarship could be held back if this kind of research is not well supported by the courts." As of October 11, 2012, based in part on the evidence from these briefs, the United States district court ruled favorably for continued fair use in digital research ("Brief of Digital Humanities and Law Scholars").

20. Haraway has warned that the science community considers a history of knowledge production as "histories of the technologies" (587) rather than a history of the communities that use these technologies. As a reflection of Haraway's work as well as the work of others such as Harding and Suchman, ethnographic studies have considered technologies, instead, as ways of life and ways of social orders.

21. While some of these examples come from DH scholarship, these authors, as professors and graduate students in iSchools or professionals in libraries are scholars whose work has been heavily influenced by both the humanities and information studies. The work done by Feinberg, Carter, and Bullard describes a process in which they purposefully use selection, description, organization, and arrangement to explicate resource collections as forms of rhetorical expression.

22. Guided by feminist inquiry, Radway seeks to understand how romance novels impact gender relations. Accordingly, Radway's methods include using in situ observations

and interviews to study these dynamics since these methods allow her to shift her focus away from the reified literary text and the implied reader and toward actual, situated women reading the text. Watkins identifies the practices that must (and do) promote disruptions in the formation of human capital in which graduates from English departments inevitably engage.

BIBLIOGRAPHY

Adler, Peter N. *Membership Roles in Field Research.* Newbury Park, Calif.: SAGE Publications, Inc., 1987.

Balsamo, Anne. *Designing Culture: The Technological Imagination at Work.* Durham, N.C.: Duke University Press, 2011.

Beaulieu, Anne. "From Co-Location to Co-Presence: Shifts in the Use of Ethnography for the Study of Knowledge." *Social Studies of Science* 40, no. 3 (2010): 453–70.

———. "Mediating Ethnography: Objectivity and the Making of Ethnographies of the Internet." *Social Epistemology* 18, no. 2–3 (2004): 139–63.

Becker, Howard S. "The Epistemology of Qualitative Research." In *Contemporary Field Research: Perspectives and Formulations* (2nd ed.), ed. Robert M. Emerson, 317–30. Prospect Heights, Ill.: Waveland Press, 2010.

Blanchette, Jean-François. "A Material History of Bits." *Journal of the American Society for Information Science and Technology* 62, no. 6 (2011): 1042–57.

Boellstorff, Tom, Bonnie Nardi, Celia Pearce, T. L. Taylor, and George E. Marcus. *Ethnography and Virtual Worlds: A Handbook of Method.* Princeton, N.J.: Princeton University Press, 2012.

Borgman, Christine L. *Big Data, Little Data, No Data: Scholarship in the Networked World.* Cambridge, Mass.: MIT Press, 2015.

———. "The Digital Future Is Now: A Call to Action for the Humanities." *Digital Humanities Quarterly* 3, no. 4 (2009).

Bowker, Geoffrey C., and Susan Leigh Star. *Sorting Things Out: Classification and Its Consequences.* Cambridge, Mass.: MIT Press, 2000.

Breglia, Lisa. "The 'Work' of Ethnographic Fieldwork." In *Fieldwork Is Not What It Used to Be: Learning Anthropology's Method in a Time of Transition,* ed. James D. Faubion and George E. Marcus, 129–42. Ithaca, N.Y.: Cornell University Press, 2009.

Buckland, Michael K. "Information as Thing." *Journal of the American Society for Information Science* 42, no. 5 (1991): 351–60.

Burawoy, Michael. *Ethnography Unbound: Power and Resistance in the Modern Metropolis.* Berkeley: University of California Press, 1991.

Chun, Wendy Hui Kyong. *Programmed Visions: Software and Memory.* Cambridge, Mass.: MIT Press, 2013.

Collins, Samuel Gerald, and Matthew Slover Durington. *Networked Anthropology: A Primer for Ethnographers.* Milton Park, Abingdon, Oxon; New York: Routledge, 2014.

Drucker, Johanna. "Humanistic Theory and Digital Scholarship." In *Debates in the Digital Humanities,* ed. Matthew K. Gold, 85–95. Minneapolis: University of Minnesota Press, 2012.

Drucker, J., and B. Nowviskie. "Speculative Computing: Aesthetic Provocations in Humanities Computing." In *A Companion to Digital Humanities,* ed. S. Schreibman, R. Siemens, and J. Unsworth. Malden, Mass.: Blackwell Publishing, 2004. doi: 10.1002 /9780470999875.ch29.

Feinberg, Melanie, Daniel Carter, and Julia Bullard. "Always Somewhere, Never There: Using Critical Design to Understand Database Interactions." *Proceedings of the 32nd Annual ACM Conference on Human Factors in Computing Systems.* New York: ACM, 2014. 1941–1950. ACM Digital Library. Web. November 5, 2015. CHI '14.

Felski, Rita. "The Hermeneutics of Suspicion." *ACLA 2014–2015 Report on the State of the Discipline of Comparative Literature,* February 21, 2014. http://stateofthediscipline .acla.org/entry/hermeneutics-suspicion.

Fish, Stanley. "Theory's Hope." *Critical Inquiry* 30, no. 2 (2004): 374–78.

Fitzpatrick, Kathleen. *Planned Obsolescence.* Media Commons Press, 2009. http://mcpress .media-commons.org/plannedobsolescence/.

Flanders, Julia. "Time, Labor, and 'Alternate Careers' in Digital Humanities Knowledge Work." In *Debates in the Digital Humanities,* ed. Matthew K. Gold, 292–308. Minneapolis: University of Minnesota Press, 2012.

Forsythe, Diana E. " 'It's Just a Matter of Common Sense': Ethnography as Invisible Work." *Computer Supported Cooperative Work (CSCW)* 8, no. 1–2 (1999): 127–45.

Garcia, A. C., M. E. Dawes, M. L. Kohne, F. M. Miller, and S. F. Groschwitz. "Workplace Studies and Technological Change." *Annual Review of Library and Information Science* 40 (2006): 393–487.

Geertz, Clifford. "Deep Play: Notes on the Balinese Cockfight." In *Myth Symbol and Culture,* special issue, *Daedalus* 101, no. 1 (1972): 1–37.

———. "Thick Description: Toward an Interpretative Theory of Culture." In *The Interpretation of Cultures, 3–30.* New York: Basic Books, 1973.

Geiger, R.S., and D. Ribes. "Trace Ethnography: Following Coordination through Documentary Practices." *2011 44th Hawaii International Conference on System Sciences (HICSS) IEEE Xplore* (2011): 1–10.

Gilman, Sander L. "Collaboration, the Economy, and the Future of the Humanities." *Critical Inquiry* 30, no. 2 (2004): 384–90.

Habell-Pallán, M., S. Retman, and A. Macklin. "Notes on Women Who Rock: Making Scenes, Building Communities: Participatory Research, Community Engagement, and Archival Practice." *NANO* 1.5 (July 2014). http://nanocrit.com/issues/5/notes-women -who-rock-making-scenes-building-communities-participatory-research-commu nity-engagement-and-archival-practice.

Hall, Gary. "Toward a Postdigital Humanities: Cultural Analytics and the Computational Turn to Data-Driven Scholarship." *American Literature* 85, no. 4 (2013): 781–809.

Haraway, Donna. "Situated Knowledges: The Science Question in Feminism and the Privilege of Partial Perspective." *Feminist Studies* 14, no. 3 (1988): 575–99.

Harding, Sandra G. *Feminism and Methodology: Social Science Issues.* Bloomington: Indiana University Press, 1987.

———. *Whose Science? Whose Knowledge?: Thinking from Women's Lives.* Ithaca, N.Y: Cornell University Press, 1991.

Harpham, Geoffrey Galt. "Beneath and Beyond the 'Crisis in the Humanities.'" *New Literary History: A Journal of Theory and Interpretation* 36, no. 1 (2005): 21–36.

Hayles, N. Katherine. *How We Think: Digital Media and Contemporary Technogenesis.* Chicago; London: University of Chicago Press, 2012.

Horst, Heather A., Daniel Miller, and Heather Horst, eds. *Digital Anthropology.* London; New York: Bloomsbury Academic, 2012.

Hsu, Wendy F. "Digital Ethnography toward Augmented Empiricism: A New Methodological Framework." *Journal of Digital Humanities* 3, no. 1 (2014).

Hull, Matthew S. *Government of Paper: The Materiality of Bureaucracy in Urban Pakistan.* Berkeley: University of California Press, 2012.

Jockers, Matthew L., Matthew Sag, and Jason Schultz. "Brief of Digital Humanities and Law Scholars as Amici Curiae in Authors Guild v. Google." SSRN Scholarly Paper ID 2102542. Rochester, N.Y.: Social Science Research Network, 2012.

Katz, J. "From How to Why: On Luminous Description and Causal Inference in Ethnography (Part 1)." *Ethnography* 3, no. 1 (2001): 63–90.

Kelty, Christopher M. *Two Bits: The Cultural Significance of Free Software.* Durham, N.C.: Duke University Press, 2008.

Kim, David. "'Data-izing' the Images: Process and Prototype." In *Performing Archive: Curtis + the Vanishing Race,* by Jacqueline Wernimont, Beatrice Schuster, Amy Borsuk, David J. Kim, Heather Blackmore, and Ulia Gusart (Popova). Scalar, 2013. http://scalar.usc.edu /works/performingarchive/data-izing-the-photos?path=network-view-of-curtis-images.

Kirschenbaum, Matthew G. *Mechanisms: New Media and the Forensic Imagination.* Cambridge, Mass.: MIT Press, 2008.

———. "What Is 'Digital Humanities,' and Why Are They Saying Such Terrible Things about It?" *Differences* 25, no. 1 (2014): 46–63.

Klein, Lauren F. "The Image of Absence: Archival Silence, Data Visualization, and James Hemings." *American Literature* 85, no. 4 (2013): 661–88.

Knorr, Karin. *The Manufacture of Knowledge: An Essay on the Constructivist and Contextual Nature of Science.* Oxford: Pergamon, 1981.

Knorr-Cetina, K. *Epistemic Cultures: How the Sciences Make Knowledge.* Cambridge, Mass.: Harvard University Press, 1999.

Koh, Adeline. "Addressing Archival Silence on 19th Century Colonialism—Part 1: The Power of the Archive," *Adeline Koh* (blog), March 4, 2012. http://www.adelinekoh .org/blog/2012/03/04/addressing-archival-silence-on-19th-century-colonialism-part -1-the-power-of-the-archive/.

Latour, Bruno. "Why Has Critique Run out of Steam? From Matters of Fact to Matters of Concern." *Critical Inquiry* 30, no. 2 (2004): 225–48.

Latour, Bruno, and Steve Woolgar. *Laboratory Life: The Construction of Scientific Facts,* reprint ed. with introduction by Jonas Salk. Princeton, N.J: Princeton University Press, 1986.

Lave, J. *Apprenticeship in Critical Ethnographic Practice.* Chicago: University of Chicago Press, 2011.

LeMaistre, Tiffany, Rebecka L. Embry, Lindsey L. Van Zandt, and D. Bailey. "Role Reinvention, Structural Defense, or Resigned Surrender: Institutional Approaches to Technological Change and Reference Librarianship." *The Library Quarterly* 82, no. 3 (2012): 241–75.

Leroi, Armand Marie. "One Republic of Learning: Digitizing the Humanities." *New York Times,* February 13, 2015. http://www.nytimes.com/2015/02/14/opinion/digitizing -the-humanities.html?_r=1.

Liu, Alan. *The Laws of Cool: Knowledge Work and the Culture of Information.* Chicago: University of Chicago Press, 2004.

———. "The Meaning of the Digital Humanities." *PMLA* 128 no. 2 (2013): 409–23.

———. "Where Is Cultural Criticism in the Digital Humanities?" Paper presented at the panel on "The History and Future of the Digital Humanities," Modern Language Association convention, Los Angeles, January 7, 2011.

Lothian, Alexis, and Amanda Phillips. "Can Digital Humanities Mean Transformative Critique?" *Journal of E-Media Studies* 3, no. 1 (2013).

Lynch, Michael. *Art and Artifact in Laboratory Science: A Study of Shop Work and Shop Talk in a Research Laboratory.* London: Routledge and Kegan Paul, 1985.

Manovich, Lev. *Software Takes Command.* New York: Continuum Publishing Corporation, 2013.

Marcus, George E., and Dick Cushman. "Ethnographies as Texts." *Annual Review of Anthropology* 11 (1982): 25–69.

Marty, P. F. "Unintended Consequences: Unlimited Access, Invisible Work, and the Future of the Information Profession in Cultural Heritage Organizations." *Bulletin of the American Society for Information Science and Technology* 38, no. 3 (2012), 27–31.

McCarty, Willard. *Humanities Computing.* New York: Palgrave Macmillan, 2005.

McGann, Jerome. "Culture and Technology: The Way We Live Now, What Is to Be Done?" *New Literary History* 36 no. 1 (2005): 71–82.

McPherson, Tara. "Designing for Difference." *Differences* 25, no. 1 (2014): 177–88.

———. "Why Are the Digital Humanities So White?" In *Debates in the Digital Humanities,* ed. Matthew K. Gold, 85–95. Minneapolis: University of Minnesota Press, 2012.

Meeks, E., and K. Grossner. "Topotime: Representing Historical Temporality." In *Proceedings of the Digital Humanities 2014 Conference.* Lausanne.

Menand, Louis. "Dangers Within and Without." *Profession* (2005): 10–17.

Orlikowski, Wanda J. "The Duality of Technology: Rethinking the Concept of Technology in Organizations." *Organization Science* 3, no. 3 (1992): 398–427.

Orr, Julian E. *Talking about Machines: An Ethnography of a Modern Job.* Ithaca, N.Y.: ILR Press, 1996.

Parker, Robert Dale. *How to Interpret Literature: Critical Theory for Literary and Cultural Studies,* 3rd ed. New York: Oxford University Press, 2014.

Posner, Miriam. "What's Next: The Radical, Unrealized Potential of Digital Humanities." *Miriam Posner* (blog), July 27, 2015. http://miriamposner.com/blog/whats-next-the -radical-unrealized-potential-of-digital-humanities/.

Presner, Todd. "The Ethics of the Algorithm: Close and Distant Listening to the Shoah Foundation Visual History Archive." Forthcoming in *History Unlimited: Probing the Ethics of Holocaust Culture.* Cambridge: Harvard University Press, 2015. http://www .toddpresner.com/wp-content/uploads/2014/12/Presner_Ethics_Dec2014.pdf.

Radway, Janice A. *Reading the Romance: Women, Patriarchy, and Popular Literature,* rev. ed. Chapel Hill: University of North Carolina Press, 1991.

Ramsay, Stephen. "In Praise of Pattern." *TEXT Technology* 14, no. 2 (2005): 177–90.

———. "Reconceiving Text Analysis: Toward an Algorithmic Criticism." *Literary and Linguistic Computing: Journal of the Association for Literary and Linguistic Computing* 18 no. 2 (2003): 167–74.

Rockwell, Geoffrey. "On the Evaluation of Digital Media as Scholarship." *Profession* 1 (2011): 152–168.

Rosner, Daniela K. "The Material Practices of Collaboration." In *Proceedings of the ACM 2012 Conference on Computer Supported Cooperative Work,* 1155–64. New York: ACM, 2012.

Samuels, Lisa, and Jerome J. McGann. "Deformance and Interpretation." *New Literary History* 30, no. 1 (1999): 25–56.

Sayers, Jentery. *"How Text Lost Its Source: Magnetic Recording Cultures."* PhD diss., University of Washington, 2011.

Schreibman, Susan, Laura Mandell, and Stephen Olsen. "Introduction: Evaluating Digital Scholarship." *Profession* 1 (2011): 123–201. http://www.mlajournals.org/doi/abs/10.1632 /prof.2011.2011.1.123.

Snow, David A., Calvin Morill, and Leon Anderson. "Elaborating Analytic Ethnography: Linking Fieldwork and Theory." *Ethnography* 4, no. 2 (2003): 181–200.

Sommerlund, Julie. "Classifying Microorganisms: The Multiplicity of Classifications and Research Practices in Molecular Microbial Ecology." *Social Studies of Science* 36, no. 6 (2006): 909–28.

Star, Susan Leigh. "The Ethnography of Infrastructure." *American Behavioral Scientist* 43, no. 3 (1999): 377–91.

Sterne, Jonathan. *MP3: The Meaning of a Format.* Durham, N.C.: Duke University Press Books, 2012.

Suchman, Lucy. *Human-Machine Reconfigurations: Plans and Situated Actions,* 2nd ed. Cambridge; New York: Cambridge University Press, 2006.

Svensson, Patrik. "Envisioning the Digital Humanities." *Digital Humanities Quarterly* 6, no. 1 (2012).

———. "From Optical Fiber to Conceptual Cyberinfrastructure." *Digital Humanities Quarterly* 5, no. 1 (2011).

———. "Humanities Computing as Digital Humanities." *Digital Humanities Quarterly* 3, no. 3 (2009). http://digitalhumanities.org/dhq/vol/4/1/000080/000080.html.

———. "The Landscape of Digital Humanities." *Digital Humanities Quarterly* 4, no. 1 (2010).

TaDiRAH. "Taxonomy of Digital Research Activities in the Humanities." *Dariah,* July 18, 2014. http://tadirah.dariah.eu/vocab/index.php.

"technique, n." *OED Online.* Oxford University Press, December 2014.

Turkle, Sherry. *Life on the Screen.* New York: Simon and Schuster, 2011.

Unsworth, John. "Scholarly Primitives: What Methods Do Humanities Researchers Have in Common, and How Might Our Tools Reflect This?" Humanities Computing: Formal Methods, Experimental Practice, King's College symposium, London, May 13, 2000.

Voskuhl, Adelheid. "Humans, Machines, and Conversations: An Ethnographic Study of the Making of Automatic Speech Recognition Technologies." *Social Studies of Science* 34, no. 3 (2004): 393–421.

Watkins, Evans. *Work Time: English Departments and the Circulation of Cultural Value.* Stanford, Calif.: Stanford University Press, 1989.

Resistance in the Materials

BETHANY NOWVISKIE

Most mornings, these days—especially when I am the *first* to arrive at the Scholars' Lab—I'll start a little something printing on our Replicator. I do this before I dive into my e-mail, head off for consultations and meetings, or (more rarely) settle in to write. There's a grinding whirr as the machine revs up. A harsh, lilac-colored light clicks on above the golden Kapton tape on the platform. Things become hot to the touch, and I walk away. I don't even bother to stay, now, to see the mechanized arms begin a musical slide along paths I have programmed for them, or to watch how the fine filament gets pushed out, melted and microns-thin—additive, architectural—building up, from the bottom, the objects of my command.

I'm a lapsed Victorianist and book historian who also trained in archaeology, before gravitating toward the most concrete aspects of digital humanities production—the design of tools and online environments that emphasize the materiality of texts and the physicality of our every interaction with them. I suppose I print to feel productive, on days when I know I will otherwise generate more *words* than *things* at the Scholars' Lab, the digital humanities center I direct at the University of Virginia Library. Art objects, little mechanisms and technical experiments, cultural artifacts reproduced for teaching or research—cheap 3D printing is one affirmation that words (those lines of computer code that speak each shape) always readily become things. That they kind of . . . *want to*. It's like when I learned to set filthy lead type and push the heavy, rolling arm of a Vandercook printing press,[1] when I should have been writing my dissertation.

I peek in, as I can, over the course of a morning. And when the extruders stop extruding, and the whole beast cools down, I'll crack something solid and new off the platform—if a colleague in the lab hasn't done that for me already. (It is a satisfying moment in the process.)

Sometimes, though, I come back to a mess—a failed print, looking like a ball of string or a blob of wax. Maybe something was crooked, by a millimeter. Maybe the structure contracted and cracked, no match for a cooling breeze from the open door. Or maybe my code was poor, and the image in my mind and on my screen failed to make contact with the Replicator's sizzling build-plate—so the plastic filament that should have stuck like coral instead spiraled out into the air and cooled and curled around nothing. Those are the mornings I think about William Morris.

Not too long ago we could never have imagined humanities computing becoming so mainstreamed as to have a cutesy acronym in "DH," or cluster hires everywhere, or a dedicated office at the National Endowment for the Humanities and common campus centers, full-time strategists, and digital humanities librarians—much less frustrated outsiders and active (rather than passive) detractors. In those days, as a grad student in the late 1990s, I apprenticed under Jerome McGann, building an online collection of Pre-Raphaelite art and literature called the *Rossetti Hypermedia Archive*.[2] Jerry had recently been interviewed[3] for *Lingua Franca* by a then-unknown, twenty-six-year-old tech writer (Steven Johnson[4]) and had thrown a little Morris at him, by way of explaining the embodied frictions that become beautifully and revealingly evident when you move scholarly editorial practice, born in book culture, from print to digital media: "You can't have art," said William Morris, the designer, poet, and master craftsman of the Victorians, "without resistance in the material."

It's a compelling line, reproduced (somewhat mechanically and often slightly mangled) all over, but only rarely contextualized or traced back to its source. Morris's erstwhile son-in-law, Henry Halliday Sparling, reports it in his 1924 study of the Kelmscott Press—not as the general, vatic pronouncement it often appears to be, but as part of the designer's extended complaint about a newfangled device: the typewriter. For many years, I thought this an odd quarrel for Morris to pick.

"Morris condemned the typewriter for creative work," Sparling tells us, saying that "anything that gets between a man's hand and his work, you see, is more or less bad for him. There's a pleasant feel in the paper under one's hand and the pen between one's fingers that has its own part in the work done." Morris goes on to extol a nicely proportioned quill over the steel pen, and to condemn the pneumatic brush, "that thing for blowing ink on to the paper—because they come between the hand and its work, as I've said, and again because they make things too easy. The minute you make the executive part of the work too easy, the less thought there is in the result. *And you can't have art without resistance in the material.* No! The very slowness with which the pen or the brush moves over the paper, or the graver goes through the wood, has its value." So far, so good, but then Morris—whom I believe had never used a typewriter—concludes the passage a little awkwardly: "And it seems to me, too, that with a machine, one's mind would be apt to be taken off the work at whiles by the machine sticking or what not" (Sparling).

I'm generally with Morris until the final turn. Isn't "the machine sticking or what not" just another kind of maker's resistance? A complication we might identify, make accessible—which is sometimes to say tractable—and overcome? After all, the "executive part of the work," its carrying-out, should never be made "too easy." Isn't a sticky typewriter—as something to be worked against or through—a defamiliarizing and salutary reminder of the material nature of every generative or transformative textual process?

But as I reflected on "Avenues of Access" (the theme at the presidential panel of the 2013 MLA convention, for which this talk was prepared), I came to understand. Morris's final, throwaway complaint is not about that positive, inherent resistance—the friction that makes art—which we happily seek *within the humanities material we practice upon*. It's about resistance unhealthily and inaccessibly located in a *tool set*. Twentieth-century pop psychology would see this as a disturbance in "flow" (Csíkszentmihályi). Twenty-first-century interaction design seeks to avoid or repair such user experience flaws. And, closer to home, *precisely this kind* of disenfranchising resistance is the one most felt by scholars and students new to the digital humanities. Evidence of friction in the means, rather than the materials, of digital humanities inquiry was everywhere evident in the program of the MLA convention. It was likewise written in frustration all over the body of proposals and peer reviews for a conference of much greater disciplinary, linguistic, generational, and professional convergence that I chaired later that same year, the annual meeting of the Alliance of Digital Humanities Organizations, DH 2013.[5]

When established digital humanities practitioners and tool builders are feeling overly generous toward ourselves (as we occasionally do), we diminish our responsibility to address this frustration by naming it the inevitable "learning curve" of humanities computing. Instead, we might confess that among our chief barriers to entry are poorly engineered and ineptly designed research tools and social systems, the creation of which is a sin we perpetrate on our own growing community. It's the kind of sin easily and unwittingly committed by jacks-of-all-trades. (And I will return to them, to us, in a minute.) But it is worth reflecting that tensions and fractures and glitches of *all* sorts reveal opportunity.

When Morris frets about "the machine sticking or what not," it is with an uncharacteristic voice. He offers the plaint of a passive tool user—not of the capable artisan we are accustomed to, who might be expected to fashion and refine and forge an intimate relationship with the instruments of his work. The resistance in the typewriter Morris imagines, and the resistance digital humanities novices feel when they pick up fresh tool sets or enter new environments, is different from the productive "resistance in the material" encountered by earlier generations of computing humanists. It's different from that happy resistance *still felt* by hands-on creators of humanities software and encoding systems.

Until quite recently every self-professed digital humanist I knew was deeply engaged in tool building and in digitization: the most fundamental and direct kinds of humanities remediation. The tools we crafted might be algorithmic or procedural—software devices for performing operations on the already-digitized material of our attention—or patently ontological: conceptual tools like database designs and markup schema, for modeling humanities content in the first place. These were frameworks simultaneously lossy and enhancing, all of them (importantly) making and testing hypotheses about human texts and artifacts and about the phase changes these objects go through as we move them into new media. No matter the type, our tools had one thing in common: overwhelmingly, *their own users* had made 'em, and understood the continual and collective *remaking* of them, in response to various kinds of resistance encountered and discovered, as a natural part of the process of their use. In fact, this constructivist and responsive maker's circle was so easily and unavoidably experienced as *the new, collaborative hermeneutic* of humanities computing, as *the work itself,* that—within or beyond our small community—we too rarely bothered to say so.

So much for the prelude. Three crucially important factors, all touching on modes of access, are converging for humanities computing today. I believe we are at the most critical juncture for the welfare of digital research of any in my eighteen years of involvement in the field. The first factor I will share with you sets unheard-of conditions for real, sustained, and fundamentally new advancements in humanities interpretation. The second defamiliarizes our own practice so thoroughly that we just might all (established and new actors alike) feel levels of "resistance" adequate to allow us to take advantage of the first. But I lose heart when I think about the third. I will walk through them one by one.

The first of my three factors starts with the massive, rapid, and inexorable conversion of our material cultural inheritance to digital forms. Handcrafted, boutique digitization by humanities scholars and archivists (in the intrepid, research-oriented, hypothesis-testing mode of the 1990s) was jarred and overwhelmed by the mid-2000s advent of mass digitization, in the form of Google Books. Least-common-denominator commercial digitization has had grave implications not only for our ability to insert humanities voices and perspectives in the process, but also for our collective capacity *and will* to think clearly about, to steward, and to engage with physical archives in its wake. A decade on, as a community of scholars and cultural heritage workers, we have only just begun to grapple with the primary phase change of digitization-at-scale, when we have become (for the most part) bystanders at the scene of a second major technological shift.

I gestured at it in the images with which I began my talk.[6] Momentous cultural and scholarly changes will be brought about not by digitization alone but by the development of ubiquitous digital-to-physical conversion tools and interfaces. What will humanities research and pedagogy do with consumer-accessible 3D fabrication? With embedded or wearable, responsive and tactile physical computing devices? What will we do with locative and augmented reality technologies that can bring our content off the screen and into our embodied, place-based, mobile lives? Our friends in archaeology and public history, recognizing the potential for students and new humanities audiences, are all over these developments and trends. Writers and artists have begun to engage. And I believe that scholarly editors, paleographers, archivists, and book historians will be the next avid explorers of new digital materialities. But what might other literary scholars do? What new, interpretive research avenues will open up for you, in places of interesting friction and resistance, when you gain access to the fresh, *full circuit* of humanities computing—that is, the loop from the physical to the digital *to the material text and artifact* again?

The second factor I want to address has a twinned potential. It could be dangerously inhibiting or productively defamiliarizing for our field. Currently it's a little of both, resting on the uncomfortable methodological and social axis of embodied inquiry. A clear call from people who feel barred from participation in the tool-building side of the digital humanities has led our software developers' community to talk about things long internalized—about *what goes unspoken* or is illegibly expressed in day-to-day DH practice. And, frankly, if it were not for some measure of annoyance at that much-quoted false binary of "hack vs. yack," we might, as a group, have remained disinclined to speak—disinclined to voice the ways in which we see *tacit knowledge exchange* in code-craft and digital humanities collaboration contributing to a new hermeneutic, a new way of performing thoughtful humanities interpretation.[7] You might call this interpretive practice *exegesis through stage-setting*. It comes into focus as interface and architecture, through our own deliberate acts of communal, mostly nondiscursive humanities systems design. The work we do is graphical and structural and interactive. It is increasingly material and mobile, and it is almost never made alone. Whatever it is, like any humanities theorizing, it opens some doors and shuts others, but it's a style of scholarly communication that differs sharply from the dominant, extravagantly vocal and individualist verbal expressions of academic humanities of the last fifty to sixty years. And, like any craft, it will always be under-articulated.

The call prompting new introspection about the nature of DH work comes most strongly from women, minority scholars, and other groups underrepresented in software development, responding in their turn to an aggressively male global tech culture that is (on a good day) oblivious to its own exclusionary practices and tone. Now, all this is much more the case *outside of the digital humanities* than within it, and in truth, I find the humanities a piss-poor battleground for a war that should be fought in primary and secondary STEM education. But the prompt *to make accessible the unspoken in digital humanities* also comes not only from people who feel they have lacked the basic preparation to engage, but from those who lack the time and tools: largely from contingent faculty and scholars in under-resourced or largely teaching-focused schools—people newly interested in digital humanities but feeling unable to play along with their counterparts from research institutions.

These scholars would find the murmurings of the digital humanities developers' community sympatico and sincere. But our conversations are pretty much sub rosa now and (part of the problem) are happening in places either technologically inaccessible to most humanities faculty or so coded as "unscholarly" as to be ignored by them. We're doing what we can,[8] from our end, to fix that, including by hosting events such as the Scholars' Lab's NEH-funded summit, "Speaking in Code."[9] But will it *matter*? Maybe not to this discipline, to the scholars in attendance at MLA conventions. Literary critics and cultural theorists may not (after the current digital humanities bubble bursts) ultimately wish to engage in a brand of scholarly communication that places less premium on argument and narrow, expert discourse, and more on the implicit embodiment of humanities interpretation in *public production* and open-source, inter-professional *practice*. For the most part, though, I suspect many of our colleagues *just can't tell*: to them, everyone with direct access to the means of digital humanities production speaks, sometimes literally, in code.

When I'm feeling sad about this stuff, I turn, again, to William Morris. As a self-help strategy, that yields mixed results: "In the Middle Ages," he tells us in *Art and Labour*, "everything that man made was beautiful [eh.], just as everything that nature makes is always beautiful; [yeah?] and I must again impress upon you the fact that this was because they were made mainly for use, instead of mainly to be bought and sold. . . . [hmm.]" He continues: "the beauty of the handicrafts of the Middle Ages came from this, that the workman had control over his material, tools, and time."[10]

I began by suggesting that there are *three* new conditions at play in this, our late age of the digital humanities. The first dwells in phase changes: the ability of scholars to engage not only with the physical-to-digital conversions that characterized the first sixty years of humanities computing, but with new, digital-to-physical technologies like fabrication and augmented reality. The second builds on the notion of embodied inquiry and tacit understanding to suggest the emergence of a new hermeneutic from the digital humanities—a mode of humanities interpretation that rests more in the design of systems, interfaces, and user experiences than in verbal or written expression. But it is the final condition that speaks most closely to Morris's notion of "control over . . . material, tools, and time." This is the rise of casual and alternative academic labor. To get at it, though, I must briefly address a market that has come to be called "alt-ac:" the increasing recruitment of humanities PhDs to full-time, hybrid, scholarly professional positions in places like libraries, IT divisions, and digital humanities labs and centers. Real advantages and new opportunities for the humanities are attendant on this development. Properly trained and supported, long-term, "alternative academic" faculty and staff are potential leaders in your institution. They are uniquely positioned to represent and enact the core values of our disciplines; to serve as much-needed translators among scholars, technologists, and administrators; and to build technical and social systems suited to the work we know we must do. Absent their energetic involvement in shaping new structures in higher education, I am convinced that digital humanities will only scale *as commodity tool-use for the classroom*—not as a generative research activity in its own right.

But they, like far too many of our teaching faculty, are subject to the increasing casualization of academic labor. Positions in digital humanities centers are especially apt to be filled with soft-money (or short-term, grant-funded) employees. In a field whose native interdisciplinarity verges on inter-professionalism, full-time, long-term digital humanities staff already struggle against the pressure to become jacks of all trades and masters of none. How can grant-funded digital humanities journeymen find the time and feel the stability that leads to institutional commitment, to deep engagement and expertise, and to iterative refinement of their products and research findings? And the situation is worse for more conventionally employed, adjunct academics. If the vast majority of our teaching faculty become contingent, what vanishing *minority* of those will ever transition from being passive digital tool users to active humanities makers? Who among them will find time to feel a productive resistance in her materials?

Casualized labor, at a systemic level, begets commodity tool sets, frictionless and uncritical engagement with content, and shallow practices of use. I am not an uncritical booster of the tenure system, nor am I unaware of the economic realities of running a university, but I find it evident that, if we fail to invest institutionally and nationally in full-time, new-model, humanities-trained scholarly communications practitioners, devoted to shepherding and intervening in the conversion of our cultural heritage to digital forms and the new manifestations of digital culture—and if we permit our institutions to convert a generation of scholars to at-will teaching and digital humanities labor—humanities knowledge workers of all stripes will lose, perhaps forever, control over Morris's crucial triad: our material, our tools, and our time.

We cannot allow this to happen at any stage of the game, but most especially today, it seems to me—as I listen to a community struggle to articulate the relationship between interpretation and craft, and as I crack some warm artifact off the printer of a morning. We've come to a moment of unprecedented potential for the material, embodied, and experiential digital humanities.

How do we, all together, intend to experience it?

NOTES

1. http://vandercookpress.info.
2. http://rossettiarchive.org/.
3. http://linguafranca.mirror.theinfo.org/9505/repossession.html.
4. http://en.wikipedia.org/wiki/Steven_Johnson_%28author%29.
5. http://dh2013.unl.edu.
6. Slides from the talk are available at http://nowviskie.org/handouts/slides/resistance-slides.pdf.
7. For more on straw man uses of "hack vs. yack," see my 2014 blog post, "On the Origin of 'Hack' and 'Yack,' reproduced as chapter 7 in this volume.
8. http://www.adelinekoh.org/blog/2012/05/21/more-hack-less-yack-modularity-theory-and-habitus-in-the-digital-humanities/#comment-807.

9. "Speaking in Code" was a 2013 summit for humanities software developers, the self-described goal of which was "to give voice to things that are almost always tacitly expressed in our work: expert knowledge about the intellectual and interpretive dimensions of DH code-craft and unspoken understandings about the relation of that work to ethics and inclusion, scholarly method, and humanities theory and critique." A kit for hosting your own #codespeak event is available at http://codespeak.scholarslab.org.

10. William Morris delivered the lecture "Art and Labour" at least ten times between 1884 and 1886. It is reproduced in LeMire's *The Unpublished Lectures of William Morris* and at https://www.marxists.org/archive/morris/works/1884/art-lab.htm.

BIBLIOGRAPHY

Csíkszentmihályi, Mihály. *Flow: The Psychology of Optimal Experience*. New York: Harper & Row, 1990.

Jones, Steven E. *The Emergence of the Digital Humanities*. New York: Routledge, 2013.

LeMire, Eugene D. *The Unpublished Lectures of William Morris*. Detroit: Wayne State University Press, 1969.

Sparling, H. Halliday. *The Kelmscott Press and William Morris, Master-Craftsman*. London: Macmillan, 1924.

Interview with Ernesto Oroza

ALEX GIL

The possibility of full and equal participation in the digital humanities has become the focus of much recent discussion around the diversity, defini-tion, and scope of the field. Many of those who feel left out argue that a lack of funding or infrastructural support can pose an insurmountable barrier to digital humanities work. Some wait for a grant to hire developers to carry out their visions, others for a fully funded DH center at their universities to "support" them. In my estimate, the sense of exclusion based on access to infrastructure or funding comes from a failure to recognize that many individuals and groups in the United States and abroad do not have recourse to such infrastructure or funding and are already doing valuable work. We need not wait for the affordances of infrastructure. In fact, I would argue that scholars adopting an infrastructure prematurely, or receiving a large grant for a project, might keep themselves from acquiring an intimate knowl-edge of the digital technologies they seek to employ and, by extension, from the means of producing their own digital humanities knowledge.

Through my work with Global Outlook::Digital Humanities—a special-interest group of the Alliance for Digital Humanities Organization charged with breaking down the barriers that hinder communication and collaboration between scholars around the world—and more recently, the Group for Experimental Methods in the Humanities—dedicated to the rapid prototyping of speculative ideas in the humani-ties—I've come to view the barrier-to-participation question through a global lens. How can one work with computers in the humanities when one is situated in a place where the hardware is more than a decade old, or where the Internet connection is unreliable, if it exists at all? How can one "do digital humanities" when one earns a living outside of a cultural or academic institution, or when one must do one's work hiding from the authorities? How can one begin to understand digital humanities knowledge produced under such conditions, whether practiced in the Global South or in that global south that de facto inhabits the North in its underserved and there-fore marginalized populations?

My own answers to these questions have recently found an unlikely echo in the work of Cuban designer, architect, and theorist Ernesto Oroza. Oroza's web project, Architecture of Necessity,[1] presents a compelling example of digital curation, but his most important contribution to our conversations about diversity, definition, and scope—and by extension barrier-to-entry—comes from his work as an impromptu ethnographer of Cuba's DIY culture. In this work, he not only describes the practices of a people who have embraced a hacker ethos, but also develops several concepts that are immediately applicable to the domain of digital humanities. One of these, "the architecture of necessity," emerges from the example of Havana, a city that has grown according to an unpredictable logic, despite repeated attempts at planning, centralizing, and legislating. The digital humanities has also grown in the space between ambitious, well-funded, and meticulously planned projects and a bevy of prototypes and one-offs. The difference can be caricatured by comparing a robust digital collection built by libraries using Fedora and a quick-and-dirty digital archive built on Omeka by a professor and a graduate student. But in the end, the aggregate—the true shape of the field—begins to resemble the Havana that Oroza describes.

Another concept, the "Moral Modulor," refers to an individual who finds a way to make his or her environment livable—literally—with very few resources at hand. These intrepid urbanites transform the world around them by ignoring certain codes and expectations and by appropriating what is readily available. The Moral Modulor cannot afford to wait for a government grant and yet must learn how to "make a window," to borrow a phrase, in order to ensure survival. As opposed to Le Corbusier's *modulor*, a physical scale based on human proportions to bridge discrepancies in measurement, the Moral Modulor provides us with a moral scale to bridge divergent measures. The proportion is need, and its basic units are survival and love. Imagine now if we were to build our new republic of letters, our digital humanities, using this ruler.

My favorite of Oroza's concepts, "the technology of disobedience," describes objects employed with complete disregard for their intended use: a tray used as an antenna, a clothes dryer used as a house fan. A truly disobedient technologist is never happy with a black box. The black box exists to be opened and tinkered with, or used for a purpose not found in the manual. As a graduate student, I once used the diff algorithm to help me detect transpositions in texts, by simply dumping every longest common subsequence[2] into a table and rerunning the algorithm. I called it "the poor man's fuzzy matching," for lack of a better term. At the time, I didn't have the conceptual framework to realize that I was engaged in an act of technological disobedience!

In the following interview with Oroza, I try to tease out some of his ideas so as to introduce his thinking for a digital humanities audience, while at the same time *not losing sight of the particular geopolitical situation that gave rise to his work.* I hope that readers can extrapolate from our conversation and begin to answer

questions of need, affordance, and purpose for their own projects, whether begin-
ner or advanced. It is also my hope that, in this glimpse of the Cuban DIY scene,
readers will be prompted to consider how their DH work may connect to projects
at the intersection of computing and the humanities that are rooted in other communities and environments.

ALEX GIL (AG): Since I saw the video "Cuba's DIY Inventions from 30 Years of Isolation"[3] on YouTube, I've been trying to get my hands on all your works online and on
paper. Your concepts—architecture of necessity, technological disobedience, Moral
Modulor, to name a few of the most important—have become very important for
my own thinking on what a few of us are calling minimal computing.[4] As you know,
this interview will appear in *Debates in Digital Humanities*[5] *2016*. Although no definition holds for long, we could say for now that digital humanities refers to a wide
range of practices at the intersection of computing (GIS, data wrangling, web design,
etc.) and the humanities (history, literature, art, music, etc.). Your concepts and work
have much to say to our field, and my hope for this interview is that we could tease
out those contributions. Thank you again for agreeing to do it.

Growing up in Santo Domingo, I saw much of what you call the architecture
of necessity—not as much as Cuba, to be fair, but enough for me to recognize right
away what you were pointing to. Santo Domingo was also a "ciudad sin terminar"
[an unfinished city], as Alejo Carpentier would call it.[6] If I understand you correctly, what is wrong in this picture, regardless of the economic causes—capitalism
or socialism—is the concept of finishing itself attached to the desire for "development." My first question to you, then, is one that you ask us: "What is a finished
stairway?"[7]

ERNESTO OROZA (EO): First of all, let me thank you for the opportunity to discuss
these ideas.

The question does not seek an answer, just points toward a possibility: in asking, I propose.

In the text, the question points to several readings. The first—and it is a question
that many pose within the field of architecture—assumes urban and architectural
regulations as conceptual and textual architectures that can be challenged, and that
allow for interventions. In other words, some Cubans understand the legal code
as a physical space rife with potentialities and limitations, with fulcrums, inconsistencies, enclosures, gaps. A second reading points in another direction, as you
point out, to us as citizens, and to the weight of our preconceptions and social
commitments in our daily actions. I'm speaking of our notions of progress, quality, beauty, and social status. The charge applies to the urban regulators, architects,
and governments, as well as to the populations that live in conditions of urgency.

To make matters worse, in our poor countries we only know the models—the
material world we aspire to—through the media, print ads, and audiovisuals like

movies or soap operas, or from photos our family members send us from "developed" countries. Our attempt to imitate these concepts and material cultures wears away our economies. And we often fail because we simply don't have the productive means.

In this sense, it's a shame that the cost of a stair doesn't simply respond to the size and the type of materials employed, the cost of the legal process—permits, licenses—the design cost, or the labor involved. To these essential costs to make a stair you have to add the cost of making a stair that meets social and class exigencies and commitments. What to make? A balustrade that references colonial architecture or a simple, functional, and austere railing? I've been able to verify that some of these houses, oozing with concrete and urgent family needs—in response to a context full of restrictions—end up generating enormous costs due to formal and class exigencies.

Besides the idea of the complete, the finished, the idea of progress contains other qualifiers we can use to reformulate the question. We have been convinced that we need whole objects, polished surfaces, coherent forms. Sometimes these demands come from the past. For example, all new buildings in Cuba, even if they are built using contemporary means and to respond to current needs, are required by urban law to correspond and integrate with—in formal terms—the old buildings around it. Then we have the demand that comes from the future—Progress—and the one that lurks from the past: the demand to guard tradition, to correspond to the symbolic power of the colonial presence, which we now believe forms part of our cultural capital.

In relation to the question of what is expected of us, in recent years I've found some confluences with the thought of Julio García Espinosa, the author of *Por un cine imperfecto*[8] [Toward an Imperfect Cinema]. Specifically with the ideas he develops in his film *Son o no son*.[9] In this movie, García Espinosa, who wrote and directed it, has a choreographer ask the following question: "What are they expecting from us?" For the choreographer, immersed in an ontological debate, to make a musical show for an international tourist audience in Cuba means minimizing the complexity of the cultural product of the island and to assume the codes of understanding and tastes of the middle class—which, as Julio says, is neither a class, nor has taste. The question of the choreographer continues: "Where can our [underdeveloped] countries find women of the same size, who look the same, all capable of raising their legs at the same time?! Too much is expected from us indeed!!" While the choreographer speaks, the camera pans over a motley crew of very different human biotypes and ethnicities.

AG: In our first conversation, you warned me, just in case, not to fetishize work done out of necessity. I agree that the danger is real. Hopefully our audience will be self-aware enough to see the real contribution of those who must operate out of necessity as the contribution of peers, and perhaps to agree with you, that we would benefit enormously to adopt some of these practices without the financial necessity to do so. This brings us to the idea of necessity itself, and its correlate, the Moral Modulor:[10]

> The Moral Modulor, unlike the "Corbusierean" Modulor, is a human being at the same time as a measuring tool. He embodies the human potential to understand urgency and inscribe it in space. He adds, to the order established by human dimensions, the moral dimension that necessity recovers.

I hear two possible interpretations of the word "necessity" here. We can think of necessity as constraint, but we can also hear it as moral demand: "What do we need to do?" How do you see these two possibilities play out in the Moral Modulor?

EO: The Moral Modulor is a very specific social being for me. The concept came from concrete, lived experiences. I would see the Moral Modulor every morning in Lawton, the neighborhood where I used to live in Havana; on many occasions, I was the Moral Modulor. The Moral Modulor is an individual who has the impulse to rebuild human life, and this is something he does for his children or for his family. With no means, his days are busied with searching for food, water, resources, or finding a roof. This character is similar to the individual who lives "below zero" as described by Glauber Rocha, or the sub-proletariat of Pasolini. This new Modulor perceives the world on a very precise moral frequency: he only sees what is useful. As he travels around the city he only sees potential stairs, windows, doors, or walls. His condition allows him to discriminate against the superfluous or the useless. When he builds a space, the Modulor rejects from its construction social or urban contracts. From his buildings we see evacuated all the stupid pressures that we accept from context and society.

This Modulor not only inscribes his physical and spiritual dimensions on space, he also traverses the city, observes, asks, appropriates, copies, gathers, and negotiates. An example that shows how this individual operates are the windows that appear spontaneously in blind side façades—these blind façades exist because another building that stood on the side no longer exists. These buildings have not been repaired or painted for decades. The Moral Modulor takes a hand out of the window, which he himself created with a hammer and a chisel, and paints the border of the window as far as his arm can reach. Moral and anthropometric inscription, this gesture has the value of re-signifying that this house belongs to him and that a family lives here.

AG: In *Rikimbili* you notice "des modèles de comportement face aux technologies et surtout face à cette autorité et cette vérité supposée des produits capitalistes" [models of behavior in the face of technologies, and above all, in the face of the authority and the supposed claim to truth of capitalist products]. You call these

Figure 16.1. The work of The Moral Modulor. Havana, 2010. Photo by Beatriz Dooley.

models "désobeissance technologique" [technological disobedience]. You go on to describe the contours of the phenomenon:

> Les pratiques productives du début des années quatre-vingt-dix s'inscrivent sommairement dans le registre de la réparation et de la récupération d'objets issus d'une réalité matérielle vieillie, insuffisante et pauvre. L'individu préten- dait simplement élaborer un succédané instantané, un objet ou une solution transitoire qui résoudrait son problème jusqu'à la disparition de la crise. . . . À force d'ouvrir les objets, de les réparer, de les fragmenter et de s'en servir à sa convenance, le Cubain finit par mépriser les signes qui font des produits occi- dentaux une unité ou une identité fermée. (20–21)

> [The productive practices of the 1990s inscribe themselves summarily in the register of reparation and recuperation of objects borne out of an aging, insuf- ficient, and poor material reality. The individual pretended simply to elaborate an instant substitute, a transitory object or solution to solve a specific problem until the crisis subsided. . . . Forced to open the objects, to fix them, to frag- ment them and use them at their convenience, Cubans ended up rejecting the signs that make an occidental product whole or possessing a closed identity.]

In this passage I hear a transformation of consciousness, almost a class consciousness, that leads to the culture of technological disobedience that you so shrewdly
document and extol. Debating your work recently with a friend, he argued that what
you describe here is just "hacker culture." Although I argued for the cultural specificities of the Cuban phenomenon, I would like you to weigh in. What, if anything,
is of universal or at least extra-Cuban in the phenomenon you describe? What is
specific to the Cuban context? At the end of the day, are we talking about a global
"hacking" phenomenon?

EO: I think we have all been pushed to this situation globally, no matter where we
live. The artifacts that Cubans took apart and altered in Cuba are industrial objects
that belong to the same logic that is being "hacked" and questioned everywhere
on the planet. I'm referring to industrial objects informed by logics of limited use,
exclusive technical principles, commodified lifestyles, and abusive production
relationships. The difference I would draw from "hacker culture" and the Cuban
phenomenon is that in Cuba everyone participates. Everyone takes apart the fan, the
telephone, the washer machine, the car. Nelida, my mother-in-law, was doing these
things in my house long before I was. I was too absorbed studying radical Italian
architecture from the 1960s to notice my mother-in-law was doing radical design
in our own home, whenever the fan broke or we needed a new water line. I think
when the hacker movement includes stay-at-home parents, doctors, sportsmen,
musicians, workers, then both phenomena will be homologous and your friend will
be completely right. What we share in this global saga is the unexpected turn of the
Arvatovian object: beings are the ones who can now see through opaque objects!

AG: You mention your mother-in-law. I have seen my mother do these sorts of things
since I was a little boy: practical solutions for a million things using empty plastic
bottles, cans, sticks, whatever. This sort of culture seems to be passed on in Santo
Domingo through an oral and matrilineal tradition. Could we say that technological
disobedience has a feminist component, or at the very least matriarchal?

EO: Yes, women assume enormous responsibility for the survival of the family. They
organize activities, lead by example, inspire, push. They understand the biological
rhythms of the house, the interrelation of all activities, the subplots of need, and not
only as a reaction to the masculine tendency to delegate responsibility.

I wrote a brief text in the 1990s about this. It began like this: "We will win, *mami*,
I swear." I dedicated it to the mother, but also to the girlfriend, to the spouse. We
Latinos use the word *mami* in a wider range than maternity. I continued: ". . . let the
voices of power say what they please, I know that she is the one who throws us into
the weightless abysm of utopia, with her breath on the nape, beyond emptiness and
money in flight." Cuban women assumed the compromise with survival. Many were
very ready. The older ones because of the so-called "escuelas hogaristas" [home-ed

schools], prior to the revolution. The young ones because of the large presence of women in technical careers, many of them staying alone as the men quickly emigrated to the United States looking for opportunities to send remittances.

AG: The Coca-Cola Company has launched "the 2nd Lives" campaign[11] ostensibly to help consumers recycle their bottles. This campaign shows us that capitalist giants can appropriate "technologies of disobedience" for their own purposes, in this case to whitewash the fact that they produce those plastic bottles in the first place. Technology produced under the conditions you describe in your book *Objets réinventés* seems almost impossible to trademark by their creators, and yet companies like Coca-Cola seem perfectly capable of turning them into commodities. In your estimate, should technological disobedience continue to take place outside of trademark or copyright law? Perhaps in their fissures?

EO: I hope their executives pay more attention. Thousands of users on YouTube are telling Coca-Cola to get out of the food market and move to other sectors away from drinks. The videos show all the great ways Coca-Cola can be used for removing grease or rust, specifically in order to clear electrical batteries, pots, and toilets. They soon will understand, thanks to the vernacular imagination, that they should be addressing other needs and not competing with other drinks.

But I prefer not to make such a clear cut between the economically established industrial imaginary and the popular imaginary without means. Coca-Cola was a popular idea. The car as well as electricity were astute ideas that consolidated themselves economically because, among other things, they found the necessary economic means to expand and consolidate. Popular culture also uses standards to disseminate its artisanal ideas, even if standardization is an industrial idea. It's important to rethink the positive impact that popular culture has on generic and standardized objects, usually stigmatized in contemporary cultural discourses because of the alleged damage they bring to regional cultures. The truth is that the standardized object behaves like a vector for the spread of astute ideas, a flammable material in intellectual terms. In the 1990s, for example, Cuba had no TV antennas; suddenly the roofs were covered by peculiar antennas made out of aluminum trays. These standardized trays were designed to ration food in school and worker cafeterias in socialist countries. Because everyone knew the tray in Cuba—and it was the only piece of available metal—the dissemination of the antenna was immediate after some Cuban made the first one.

To come back to your question, this action by Coca-Cola, which has less pathetic precedents in ColaLife [a system to distribute medicine in Africa], is showing us that when an infrastructure auto-hacks itself, it subverts the political component behind reuse and refunctionalization. But Coca-Cola is not changing the state of affairs for the better. On the contrary, they make it worse. Ultimately, though, it doesn't matter what they do. Renewed answers will always come from the resistance.

AG: In a certain sense, the relationship between the tech industry and the precarious academic is that of the industrialized countries and Cuba. Major technologies happen to us. From my desk I observe four phenomena. First, there is the *resigned use,* where researchers adapt to the tools that fell from the clouds, that they could understand—obedience. Second, the *use that changes the technology,* equivalent to your "refonctionnalisation." In this second one we can place a large portion of digital humanists. The third, of course, is those who truly *reinvent.* And, finally, a small but growing minority that are interested in *reparation.* How do you see connections between the work you do and the digital world?

EO: I understand your parallels, but I'm not sure if the relations you propose are equivalent. The Cuban problem is exacerbated by the absence of relations between Cuba and industrial countries. In any case, Cuba has relations with markets, mostly secondhand, free-duty zones in Panama and Taiwan, for example. So we have contact with the worst industrial and technological problems today: low-quality objects, decontextualized utensils, products that become obsolete on the production line. This relation also has enormously adverse impacts on the island's economy because of the excessive accumulation of the endearingly named *Objetos ociosos y de lento movimiento* ["lazy and slow moving objects"]. The numbers offered by the government of products sitting in warehouses, enormous lots obtained dearly in the duty-free zones of Panama, now rotting because of the reluctance of the Cuban consumer to acquire them at retail prices, are alarming. The government should liberate them in bulk and people would find a way to reuse the materials in other ways, to serve other functions.

Now that I've added this caveat to your question, let me try to answer. First of all, I think digital humanists won't be able to escape their precarious condition. And this fate is both stimulating and fruitful. The behavior of Cubans today in relation to the crisis can indeed be extrapolated to many other sectors of modern life experiencing exclusion and difficult access to resources. Misery is not an alternative, but an individual with consciousness of her needs and finding solutions for herself is. In my experience, answers ooze from circumstances. Sometimes reparation is the only way. Sometimes reinvention, reuse, or refunctionalization are inevitable or irreplaceable. Sometimes, many times, these gestures can be combined, answers contaminate one another, they turn hybrid.

It seems obvious to me that these activities will be ever more present in the digital realm because of the growing range of services provided online and the monopolies of some software providers. At the same pace that our lives become digital, inequalities are transferred and spread in the new medium, and there they will encounter astute answers, detours, and appropriations. From the breakdown in your question, I see the digital humanist as the change agent, who not only will seek astute solutions, but who will fight against the status quo. Perhaps this will distinguish them from the Cuban who deployed her inventiveness to survive, but did not try to change the general conditions around her.

Last night, while answering your questions, my MacBook Pro laptop cable broke. I noticed because of the burnt smell. My first reaction was to find the cost of a new one on the Internet. You can't find it for less than $30, and a minimum of five to fifteen days delivery. It was that, or work for half an hour following instructions on YouTube to make the repairs. This thing had no screws! I had to use a saw!

April 29, 2015

NOTES

This interview was conducted in Spanish and translated into English by Alex Gil.

    1. http://architectureofnecessity.com/.

    2. That is, the longest exact string in sequential order shared by to the two texts compared by Juxta.

    3. https://www.youtube.com/watch?v=v-XS4aueDUg.

    4. http://blros.github.io/mincomp/.

    5. http://dhdebates.gc.cuny.edu/.

    6. http://architectureofnecessity.com/la-habana-ciudad-sin-terminar/.

    7. http://www.ernestooroza.com/architecture-of-necessity/.

    8. http://www.cinefagos.net/index.php?option=com_content&view=article&id=434:por-un-cine-imperfecto&catid=30&Itemid=60.

    9. http://www.imdb.com/title/tt0078296/.

    10. http://www.ernestooroza.com/tag/moral-modulor/.

    11. https://www.youtube.com/watch?v=DN72umTfAsg.

Digital Humanities Knowledge: Reflections on the Introductory Graduate Syllabus

SCOTT SELISKER

Syllabi themselves not only map out a (necessarily limited) picture of the field, but they also make an argument for what kind of knowledge is being produced in the course. In considering this argument, I found myself, like my colleagues at other institutions, balancing a broad-as-possible introduction to DH tools with some instruction on how DH fits into disciplinary research questions and, relatedly, having to decide how much coding to teach. Because my students and I considered these course design questions together, we began as a class to consider the knowledge that DH produces as a productive encounter between humanistic and computational styles and forms of thought.

Tools and Research Questions

I found in my syllabus and others that a natural way to organize the introductory DH syllabus is through the variety of tools that digital humanists use, such as markup languages and content management systems, data mining, network visualization, and so forth. But starting with the tool can have its own kinds of limitations, and there is often some distance between describing a tool's capabilities (and limitations) and formulating a solid disciplinary research question with it. Over the course of the semester, my students and I developed a provisional criterion for what marks a "mature" stage of digital humanities as a field: its ability to connect digitally obtained evidence with other forms of evidence and to integrate digital work into the research questions other, non-DH scholars are asking. This criterion offered less a marker for what is (and is not) "mature" scholarship than it gave us, as a class, a strategy for reading and using this scholarship: how can we, as students, understand the ties between computationally obtained evidence and the research questions that are driving our fields now? I believe one of my students was the source of a phrase that came up several times in our classroom as we moved from week to week, from one digital humanities method or tool to another: "Is this a tool in search of a research question?" We would mine our readings to construct ways in which the tools could be used in the *service* of one or more disciplinary research questions.

As we progressed, I came up with a list of research foci where the integration of digital tools seemed particularly promising beyond the archival, bibliographic, and textual studies with which humanities computing began. Weeks after I compiled my personal list—new sociologies of literature and culture, media theory and history, and science and technology studies—I saw that it had already been compiled (or strongly implied) in Alan Liu's expanded version of "Where Is Cultural Criticism in the Digital Humanities?"[1] (about which I'll have more to say soon). The experience led me to conceive of advanced DH courses as those that could leave aside the "bus tour" of tools and methods and start with research questions that could make use of digital and nondigital evidence. The first of these courses that I have planned out will be a course on "Social Networks and Information Culture." (I should note, however, that Lauren F. Klein's[2] and Andrew Goldstone's[3] recent courses, built in different ways around the theme of "data," seem to balance admirably between a sustained thematic focus *and* the breadth of an introductory survey.)

How Much Programming?

The DH syllabi that I have seen seem to vary most widely in their approach to the amount of technical skills they intend to teach. My own initial model was like that of the THATCamp workshop: in the second half of each week's seminar, we would go to the computer lab and get started using a new tool. I initially envisioned more guided instruction on programming basics, but the wide range of students' abilities made this approach less practical than simply giving individual guidance, as needed, to each of the thirteen students. I think an excellent course could be built around Python or R (and they have, in the cases of Matt Wilkens's[4] and Andrew Goldstone's[5] syllabi), but I decided to err on the side of shallowness and breadth, making each lab a sort of hands-on session for a technique we had seen used in a reading. In the first couple of lab sessions, for instance, we set up basic WordPress or Drupal installations in order to see how database-driven websites work, an activity that set us up to talk about online archives and questions about databases. In another lab, we walked through the process of downloading and visualizing our social networks from Facebook or Twitter. In others, we tried out topic modeling, other distant reading techniques, and so on. On the negative side here, we were never able to go into much depth in the lab, but on the positive side, we got to work hands-on, at least a little, with most of the techniques we read about. While most of the guided work tended toward very modest goals, the independent project work time in the last five or six weeks seemed much more successful. There, students went into more depth with the methods that they thought they could connect with data for their own research questions.

I was particularly surprised by the ways that students built on their own strengths in devising their projects. One pair of students made a rich database of nineteenth-century publication data using some prior advanced knowledge of Excel, and that was all they really needed to reach some compelling conclusions. One student created a simple virtual world as a way to get more familiar with Unity3D, based on a bit of prior programming experience. Another devised a Python script to distant-read a particular theme throughout the corpuses of several nineteenth-century authors. Several students worked intensively with me during labs and office hours to figure out or troubleshoot tasks that had them stumped (e.g., getting data into the right format to work with a D3.js visualization). And much of this work plugged into papers that provided strong disciplinary contexts for the questions they asked of their data, and they did so very well. (So, by our own criterion, I suppose, the student projects were rich in "mature" DH scholarship.)

The Knowledges of DH

That question about the amount of programming to include led me and my students, collectively, to ask what it is that we ought to be teaching and learning in a digital humanities course. Surely, even programming-intensive DH courses teach forms of expertise that cannot be reduced to basic skills. A noteworthy moment of insight on this question came from our reading the Liu essay mentioned previously: "Where Is Cultural Criticism in the Digital Humanities?" We read the essay as part of a discussion of the most heated DH debates on the questions of diversity and theory in the digital humanities. Liu's essay is widely cited in discussions of diversity, in particular, so I imagined we would discuss it in that light.

Instead, we found ourselves talking (and I found myself thinking more afterward) about the turns at the end of his essay, where, in considering the roles of "instrumentality" in scholarship, Liu also seems to be rethinking the kind of knowledge that DH scholarship produces. He writes:

> The appropriate, unique contribution that the digital humanities can make to cultural criticism at the present time is to use the tools, paradigms, and concepts of digital technologies to help rethink the idea of instrumentality. The goal, as I put it earlier, is to think "critically about metadata" (and everything else related to digital technologies) in a way that "scales into thinking critically about the power, finance, and other governance protocols of the world." Phrased even more expansively, the goal is to rethink instrumentality so that it includes both humanistic and STEM fields in a culturally broad, and not just narrowly purposive, ideal of service. (In *Debates in the Digital Humanities* 2012 edition, 490–509, 501)

I think Liu is suggesting that getting our hands dirty with digital tools (both by using computational techniques and by studying computational culture) puts us in a position where our metacommentary could produce fresh insights about the forms and technologies of knowledge in the contemporary moment. I like this notion because it suggests that the main benefit of humanists using "big data," for example, is *not* simply some well-mapped and well-ordered fingertip command of all the data of culture. Rather, what we get is a more robust understanding of "big data" as an *idea* and as a cultural phenomenon, an understanding that comes from trying to square this new form of knowledge with humanistic strategies of thinking. (Indeed, Liu's chapter in the present volume asks how we can approach big data through a modified understanding of the text's formal unity.)

For me, this insight happily supersedes the old "hack vs. yack" debate from the early days of DH. On the one hand, "hacking" makes scholars and students more active and insightful consumers of technology, which is one way of saying that it provides the kinds of digital literacy—the ability to create and manipulate content—that I believe ought to be an essential part of a twenty-first-century liberal arts education. Nevertheless, the know-how of "hacking" ought not to be confused with special expertise, since much DH work, including tool building, can be and often is done with sub-bachelor's-level computer science knowledge. Following this thinking, digital humanities courses give humanities practitioners literacy, not expertise; our expertise as humanists has always been in our strategies for rethinking and reframing difficult but important questions. To put the point I draw from Liu another way: the "theory" (or "yack") DH needs is broader than a particular canon of interdisciplinary thinkers and broader than calls for diversity, both of which are important and also deserve continual rethinking and renewal. Theory, as a historicist, self-reflexive, and interdisciplinary account of culture, stands to be enlarged and also renewed through *our* encounters with the forms, media, and techniques of contemporary information culture. The chance to think more about such opportunities has me excited to teach my next DH seminar.

NOTES

After I finished teaching my first digital humanities graduate seminar, I wrote this lightly revised blog post to reflect on a few of the questions I had seen colleagues grappling with on the level of course design. What is it that we teach, exactly, when we teach digital humanities at the graduate level, and how can we balance disciplinary training in a home discipline (like literature) with the kinds of technical training that are necessary to doing much of the work we call digital humanities? My mandate at the University of Arizona was to create an introduction to digital humanities in literary studies that could also benefit students coming from other disciplines, and in the class seven English literature students joined with four students in library science, one in creative writing, and one in gender and women's studies. We split the weekly session each week into a discussion and a lab component. In planning the syllabus, I had useful conversations with Matthew Wilkens, Andrew Goldstone, and Chris Forster, and I perused syllabi generously posted online by Alan Liu, Rita Raley, Miriam Posner, and Lauren F. Klein. My own syllabus is online now, too.[6]

1. http://dhdebates.gc.cuny.edu/debates/text/20.

2. http://lkleincourses.lmc.gatech.edu/data13/schedule.

3. http://www.rci.rutgers.edu/~ag978/litdata/syllabus.

4. http://mattwilkens.com/teaching/digital-humanities-graduate-seminar-spring-2014.

5. http://www.rci.rutgers.edu/~ag978/litdata/syllabus.

6. http://u.arizona.edu/~selisker/images/SeliskerENGL596K.pdf.

PART III

DIGITAL HUMANITIES AND ITS PRACTICES

Alien Reading: Text Mining, Language Standardization, and the Humanities

JEFFREY M. BINDER

For all the talk about how computers allow for new levels of scale in humanities research, new debates over institutional structures, and new claims to scientific rigor, it is easy to lose sight of the radical difference between the way human beings and computer programs "read" texts. Topic modeling, one of the most touted methods of finding patterns in large corpora, relies on a procedure that has little resemblance to anything a human being could do. Each text is converted into a matrix of word frequencies, transforming it into an entirely numerical dataset. The computer is directed to create a set of probability tables populated with random numbers, and then it gradually refines them by computing the same pair of mathematical functions hundreds or thousands of times in a row. After a few billion or perhaps even a few trillion multiplications, additions, and other algebraic operations, it sutures words back onto this numerical structure and presents them in a conveniently sorted form. This output, like the paper spit out by a fortune-telling machine, is supposed to tell us the "themes" of the texts being analyzed. While some of the earliest computational text-analysis projects, like Father Roberto Busa's famous collaboration with IBM on the *Index Thomisticus,* began by attempting to automate procedures that scholars had already been doing for centuries, topic modeling takes us well beyond the mechanical imitation of human action (Hockey). When we incorporate text-mining software into our scholarly work, machines are altering our interpretive acts in altogether unprecedented ways.

Yet, as Alan Liu has argued, there has been relatively little interchange between the scholars who are applying these computational methods to literary history and those in fields like media studies who critically examine the history and culture from which this computational technology emerged ("Where Is Cultural Criticism in the Digital Humanities?"). Many scholars of technology, including Lisa Gitelman, Wendy Hui Kyong Chun, Tara McPherson, and David Golumbia, have argued that the seemingly abstract structures of computation can serve ideological ends; but scholars who apply text mining to literary and cultural history have largely skirted the question of how the technologies they use might be influenced by the military and commercial contexts from which they emerged (Gitelman, *Paper Knowledge*; Chun, *Control and Freedom*; McPherson, "Why Are the Digital Humanities So White?"; Golumbia, *Cultural Logic of Computation*). As a way of gesturing toward a fuller understanding of the cultural context surrounding text-mining methods, I will give a brief account of the origins of a popular technique for topic modeling, Latent Dirichlet Allocation (LDA), and attempt to situate text mining in a broader history of thinking about language. I identify a congruity between text mining and the language standardization efforts that began in the seventeenth and eighteenth centuries, when authors such as John Locke called for the stabilization of vocabularies and devalued "literary" dimensions of language such as metaphor, wordplay, and innuendo as impediments to communication. I argue that, when applied to the study of literary and cultural texts, statistical text-mining methods tend to reinforce conceptions of language and meaning that are, at best, overly dependent on the "literal" definitions of words and, at worst, complicit in the marginalization of nonstandard linguistic conventions and modes of expression.

While text-mining methods could potentially give us an ideologically skewed picture of literary and cultural history, a shift toward a media studies perspective could enable scholars to engage with these linguistic technologies in a way that keeps their alienness in sight, foregrounding their biases and blind spots and emphasizing the historical contingency of the ways in which computers "read" texts. What makes text mining interesting, in this view, is not its potential to "revolutionize" the methodology of the humanities, as Matthew Jockers claims, but the basic fact of its growing influence in the twenty-first century, given the widespread adoption of statistical methods in applications like search engines, spellcheckers, autocomplete features, and computer vision systems. Thinking of text-mining programs as objects of cultural criticism could open up an interchange between digital scholarship and the critical study of computers that is productive in both directions. The work of media theorists who study the ideological structures of technology could help us better understand the effects that computerization could have on our scholarly practice, both in explicitly digital work and in more traditional forms of scholarship that employ technologies like databases and search engines. On the other side, experimenting with techniques such as topic modeling in a critical frame could support a more robust analysis of the cultural authority that makes these technologies seem natural at the present moment, baring the ideological assumptions that underlie the quantification of language, and creating, perhaps, a renewed sense of the strangeness of the idea that words can be understood through the manipulation of numbers.

Models of Language

"Topic modeling" does not refer to any single method, but rather to a number of distinct technologies that attempt to determine the "topics" of texts automatically. The

implementation most commonly used in the humanities is a program called MAL-
LET, developed by Andrew McCallum and others and based on an algorithm developed by David Blei (Blei, Ng, and Jordan, "Latent dirichlet allocation"; McCallum,
MALLET). Provided with a collection of text files, MALLET can produce "topics"
that look, in the output of the program, like this:

> passions passion pleasure person love pride object hatred humility
> men interest natural society property actions justice human moral
> reason nature give principles general observe relations common subject
> idea ideas objects existence mind perceptions impressions form time
> object imagination relation effect present mind idea experience force

This model was trained using the text of David Hume's *Treatise of Human Nature*,
divided into Hume's relatively short sections. Each line represents a "topic"—a cluster of words that tend to appear together in the same section. MALLET presents
these topics as lists of words (e.g., "passions passion pleasure . . ."), starting with the
word most strongly affiliated with the topic and proceeding downward. The program associates each text with one or more of these topics, which constitute a guess
as to what that text is "about." There is no certainty to this process; the topics are
produced by an approximate method and so the results are slightly different every
time the program is run. The meaning of the results is further complicated by the
fact that the "topics" in the output do not necessarily correspond to anything for
which a simple description might exist. In many cases, they seem to be based more
on sets of discursive conventions than on what we normally think of as "topics," and
the results often include one or more topics that are totally inscrutable. Interpretation emerges as a key issue, especially given that the method depends on a complex
set of assumptions that are colored by the institutional situation from which topic
modeling emerged.

   The idea of using a computer to automatically identify "topics" is in large part a
product of the desire to exploit the increasingly large amount of text that was being
distributed electronically in the late twentieth century. While the earliest attempts at
automated "topic detection" go back to the 1960s, the field expanded greatly starting around 1990. (For an example of a very early attempt, see Borko and Bernick.)
Many of the efforts from the 1990s dealt primarily with text from newswires and
were designed for applications in finance and national security. The major accomplishments of this period include a software package known as SCISOR (System for
Conceptual Information Summarization, Organization, and Retrieval), developed
in the early 1990s, and the DARPA-funded Topic Detection and Tracking initiative,
which ran from 1996 to 1997 (Jacobs and Rau; Allan et al.). The primary goal of the
DARPA initiative, which drew participants from Carnegie Mellon University and
the University of Massachusetts, was to come up with a way of automatically detecting the occurrence of major world events, such as volcanic eruptions and political

elections, through the text analysis of news feeds. The methods developed for this project mostly worked in a different way from the topic-modeling software that is now most familiar in the humanities. Instead of dealing with static collections of texts, they were designed to process continuous text feeds that changed from one topic to another at irregular intervals. One of the primary functions of the software was to determine when these transitions took place.

The topic-modeling techniques most commonly used in DH emerged around the same time as these projects, but they came from an area of research that was more oriented toward static collections than continuous news feeds. One of the most influential methods to emerge from this area is Latent Semantic Indexing (LSI), which was introduced in 1990 by Deerwester et al. ("Indexing by Latent Semantic Analysis"). Unlike the methods designed for the "segmentation" of newswire text, LSI and the other methods it inspired are meant to work with collections of discrete documents. The most common LSI-derived methods of topic modeling also depend on the "bag of words" assumption. Under this assumption, the computer takes no account of sentence divisions, syntax, or even the relative positions of words, considering only how frequently each word type appears in each document. Using these frequencies, LSI identifies clusters of associated words ("topics") and links them to particular documents, something that can serve two major purposes. First, as the name Latent Semantic Indexing suggests, it can be used as a subject index, helping users find documents that are relevant to particular topics; and second, it produces a "reduced description" of the corpus that can be used to visualize patterns in a large amount of text.

In the original version of LSI, the topics are computed through a more-or-less arbitrary procedure that was empirically found to produce reasonable results for the test dataset, a collection of information science abstracts (Deerwester et al., 19; Blei, Ng, and Jordan, 994.). In 1999, Thomas Hofmann developed a new variant of LSI based on a probabilistic model, a mathematical construct that offers a sort of rationale for the method (Hofmann, "Probabilistic Latent Semantic Indexing"). Texts, the model asserts, are composed of mixtures of certain "topics," each of which has an associated vocabulary; a text about, for instance, fishing and economics is most likely to contain words that are strongly associated with these topics. Hofmann's procedure can be used to determine the "topic" definitions that best fit a given collection of text based on this model. In 2003, David Blei, Andrew Y. Ng, and Michael I. Jordan introduced a further modification of the method called Latent Dirichlet Allocation (LDA), which is the variant used by MALLET and remains the most popular form of topic modeling among humanists (Blei, Ng, and Jordan; McCallum). LDA uses a similar model to Hofmann's, but it adds a mathematical function called a *Dirichlet distribution* to determine the probabilities of certain topics occurring together. Adding this function makes the model fully *generative,* which means, in a computer-science context, that it offers a complete mathematical description of the process by which the input texts were (hypothetically) generated, including a way of determining the probabilities of specific outcomes. (For a general introduction to generative modeling in relation to other forms of machine learning, see Jebara.) The generative model underlying LDA is something like this: first, the writer picks a "mixture" of topics to write about; then the writer constructs the text word-by-word by first randomly choosing a topic from the mixture and then picking a word based on the probability table for that topic. This generative model allows a computer to perform two complementary operations: a topic-modeling program can "learn" what words are associated with what topics based on a corpus of text; then, it can use this model to infer the likely topics of other texts.

It should be apparent from my admittedly rough description that this form of statistical modeling carries a heavy weight of epistemological baggage. Prominent among the disciplinary norms that govern the legitimacy of evidence and methodology in machine learning is the idea that the performance of the tools should be judged against a "gold standard" that defines the correct output—a practice that assumes the desired result to be both fixed ahead of time and accessible through some means outside of the method itself (Juckett). The institutional formation from which text-mining software emerged has also influenced the sorts of language for which it is designed. As I noted previously, the original version of LSI was initially tested with information science abstracts. The paper that introduces LDA draws its examples from AP and Reuters news articles, while Blei's later work has included models based on articles from the journal *Science,* the *Yale Law Journal,* and the *New York Times* (Blei, Ng, and Jordan; Blei, "Probabilistic Topic Models"; Blei, "Topic Modeling and Digital Humanities"). The sorts of text on which these methods are generally tested have a number of commonalities. They are primarily written in a standard dialect and orthography; they tend to privilege the informational over the aesthetic dimensions of language; and they primarily consist of prose. Many of the examples used in testing these methods are also, it is worth noting, the sorts of text that the military-industrial apparatus would have a clear interest in mining. The language commonly used in articles about topic modeling—articles by Hofmann and Blei describe users going on "quests" for information in collections of texts that bear "hidden" or "latent" meanings—is suggestive of the ultimate purpose of the technology (Hofmann; Blei, "Probabilistic Topic Models"). By automatically determining what large numbers of documents are "about," the software can help operators find and "extract" what they need from texts that are assumed to be repositories of information.

While LDA has proved to work reasonably well when applied to texts that are outside of its original purview, including nineteenth-century novels, literary criticism, and early eighteenth-century essays, it is reasonable to ask whether the results it produces are affected by the assumptions that went into the development of the software.[1] One scholar who has considered the biases of topic modeling while employing it in humanistic research, Lisa Marie Rhody, argues that topic models of poetry must be read in a different way from those based on scientific journals

("Topic Modeling and Figurative Language"). A reason, she suggests, is that poetry characteristically uses a relatively large amount of figurative language and produces meaning in a much wider variety of ways than do "non-figurative" texts. An attempt to topic model poetry thus encounters particular interpretive difficulties, but it also "illustrates how figurative language resists thematic topic assignments and by doing so, effectively increases the attractiveness of topic modeling as a methodological tool for literary analysis of poetic texts." In the topic model that she produced based on the Revising Ekphrasis[2] collection of poetry, Rhody finds that some of the most interesting "topics" correspond less to what poems are "about" than to particular poetic traditions. She argues, in particular, that a topic with the top words "death life heart dead long world blood earth man soul men face day pain die" corresponds to the language of elegiac poetry, and she uses it to highlight elegiac qualities in poems by African American poets that are not explicitly about death.

While Rhody frames her argument in terms of a "caricatured" view that hyper-emphasizes the figurative nature of poetry, the distinction between figurative and non-figurative language is slightly misleading as an explanation of why topic modeling works particularly well with scientific texts. Many phrases occur repeatedly in scientific abstracts that are arguably figurative: ideas being "underlined" and "highlighted," "first steps" toward solutions, "root causes" of problems. From the perspective of topic modeling, what is important is not that words be used literally, but that the vocabularies of texts correlate with their topics in a uniform fashion. Scientific language fits this requirement particularly well in part because it is produced within a system of overlapping subdisciplines that have distinctive lexicons. The slippery question of whether well-worn phrases like "root cause" are figurative is beside the point; what is important to a topic-modeling program is that this formula is repeated commonly in engineering abstracts but is relatively rare in physics, which makes it a potential distinguishing factor between the two disciplines.[3] In addition to having to work with highly specialized technical vocabularies, scientific writers are encouraged to stick with established usages rather than inventing novel expressions for things that have already been described, which creates highly repetitive patterns in word usage that facilitate the detection of topics.[4] Because of the tight control of the vocabulary to be used within each specialization, the process of scientific writing hews very close to the generative model by which LDA assumes texts were written—much closer, I venture, than the process of writing poetry, although Rhody's example shows that some poetic traditions do have distinctive vocabularies that topic modeling can detect.

The assumption that word choice follows uniformly from the "topic" of a text—whatever we take the "topics" to represent—presumes a sort of linguistic standardization that is historically bound up with structures of authority. As John Guillory has noted, while we now tend to see a plain and direct style as the default for most forms of writing, rhetoricians in the early-modern period placed a greater value on *copia,* a style that involves a profusion of different ways of saying the same thing ("The Memo and Modernity"). The idea that words should have fixed meanings was largely a product of the latter half of the seventeenth century, when authors like John Locke, Thomas Sprat, and John Wilkins began to see the fluidity of language as an obstruction to clear thought.[5] The compilation of dictionaries for European languages, which began in earnest around that time, created a newly sharp division between standard and nonstandard uses of words, largely based on which usages were "authorized" by their inclusion in the works of eminent writers. It also sharpened the divisions between languages; as Benedict Anderson argues, the "lexicographic revolution" led Europeans to see languages as the property of particular groups, creating imagined communities of German, French, and English speakers where previously there had been a profusion of local dialects (84). This shift in the way Europeans thought about language enabled the creation of highly uniform styles like the ones now used in scientific writing and gave a greater stability to the word usage of many other forms of writing, reducing both variation for variation's sake and many regionalisms. The reason topic modeling does particularly well at identifying themes in technical and informational genres like news articles, abstracts, and encyclopedia entries is that they actively strive to follow this sort of standard, sticking for the most part to usages that have the force of authority behind them.

While topic modeling's affinity for uniform language can be accounted for if the collection of texts is fairly homogeneous, as in Blei's collection of newspaper articles and Rhody's collection of poetry, it becomes a more difficult problem when the method is applied to a corpus that includes texts of various types with varying relations to linguistic standards. When trained on collections that include mostly standardized text but some text that follows other conventions—as is the case with many collections of nineteenth-century fiction—topic models tend to relegate the nonstandard words to a small number of topics while excluding them from the rest of the model. For example, Matthew Wilkins's topic model of the Wright American Fiction corpus[6] includes these two topics: "uv wuz ez hev wich hed sed sez ther ef" and "dat master slave negro massa slaves white black dis dey" (Wilkins, *100-topic model of the Wright American Fiction corpus*). The language of the mock-rustic characters of humorists like David Ross Locke, Charles Farrar Browne, and George William Bagby gets its own topic, while the spellings that some novelists used to represent African American speech are mixed together with words having to do with slavery. Topic modeling is fairly good at distinguishing languages, something that could potentially be useful, but this tendency to separate linguistic conventions could easily become problematic if we are not extremely careful in how we interpret the results. To the extent that it is relegated to its own topic, orthographically distinctive text is prevented from influencing the other topics in the model. If we are to use the other topics as a way of tracking themes or "discourses" in the collection, we are effectively excluding the words of characters who are presented in caricature from affecting our results, repeating the structure of authority that enables their speech to be coded as nonstandard.

LDA is not just tuned to work best with standardized (and, one might say, hegemonic) forms of language; it also structures its results in a way that encourages interpretation in terms of the standardized meanings of words. In chapter 45 in this volume, Tanya Clement discusses a property common to many text-mining techniques, a dependence on the assumption that "the Word" is a stable and inherently meaningful unit of language ("The Ground Truth of DH Text Mining"). The tendency of text-mining programs to accentuate the stability of words results, in part, from the way in which statistical methods tend to smooth out individual discrepancies so as to emphasize the overall patterns in a dataset. This smoothing is not an accident, but a necessary result of the need to avoid what statisticians call *overfitting* (Dietterich). A model that exactly accounts for every nuance of a dataset tends to be too complex to be useful—to take an image from Jorge Luis Borges, it is like a map that is as large as the territory it represents—and thus, some cases that deviate from general trends have to be ignored (Borges, "On Exactitude in Science"). Though the practicalities of modeling require the smoothing-out of differences, this process is an ideologically loaded way of dealing with language, and the much-vaunted comprehensibility of topic models depends on it. Each "word" in the output of a topic-modeling program stands for many instances of that word in the input, each one with a unique syntactic context that the model largely ignores. An interpretation of these aggregate-words can easily slide into the assumption that all of these instances can be encompassed by a single meaning.

An example of this smoothing-out of instabilities in word meaning occurs in Matthew Jockers's book *Macroanalysis*. After introducing the idea of topic modeling, Jockers presents two topics from a model of the Stanford Literary Lab's corpus of novels. Jockers proceeds to interpret the appearance of the word *stream* in the list of top words for one of these topics, alongside *indian, indians, chief, savages, warriors, men, party*, etc.:

> In conjunction with the much larger company of other words that the model returns, it is easy to see that this particular use of *stream* is not related to the "jet stream" or to the "stream of immigrants" entering the United States in the 1850s. Nor is it a word with any affiliations to contemporary "media streaming." This *stream* refers to a body of flowing water. (127)

Here Jockers seems to be doing something familiar to literary critics: determining the meaning of a word based on context. But the "particular use" of *stream* to which Jockers is referring is neither a word type (the word *stream* considered in the abstract) nor a word token (a particular instance of the word in a text)—it is an entry in a probability table that was generated through an approximate optimization method. This unit does not correspond to a single "use" of a word in any usual sense, but rather derives from patterns among many different instances of the word in the corpus. Although some of these instances might refer to a body of flowing water, there is no guarantee that they all use the word in the same sense—there are, for instance, at least a few dozen references to a "stream of settlers" in nineteenth-century texts that discuss conflicts between Europeans and Native Americans, and if these are present in Jockers's corpus they would likely be included in the topic he discusses.[7] In attempting to determine what the *stream* in the topic model "refers to," Jockers interprets this abstract composite as if it were the same type of thing as a word token in a literary text, a move that presupposes the stability of the word's signification in the parts of the corpus covered by the topic. This sort of interpretation-in-aggregate is not necessarily illegitimate if we recognize it for what it is, but Jockers's application of simple and familiar terms of interpretation to a topic model belies the very complex and potentially problematic set of assumptions that underlie what he is doing in this passage.

The bias toward standardized forms of language is present not only in topic modeling, but in many other text-mining methods that depend on statistical analysis of words. The affinity of these methods for particular forms of language becomes readily apparent in an exchange between Jockers and Annie Swafford about Jockers's *Syuzhet* program (Jockers, "Revealing Sentiment and Plot Arcs with the Syuzhet Package"). This package uses sentiment analysis software to guess the emotional valence of each sentence of a novel and plots an "arc" that is derived from these results. In a blog post, Swafford points out a number of problems with this method, among them the inability of sentiment analysis to account for the nuances of literary language ("Problems with the Syuzhet Package"). Responding to the latter problem, Jockers admits his frustration: "Things like irony, metaphor, and dark humor are the monsters under the bed that keep me up at night" ("Some thoughts . . ."). The difficulty of accounting for these aspects of language in projects like *Syuzhet* seems to stem from the fact that all of the sentiment analysis methods presently available are designed to suit the language of, in Swafford's words, "a tweet or product review" ("Continuing the Syuzhet Discussion"). In other words, Jockers's analysis depends on a tool designed to suit the contemporary descendants of the Enlightenment project of rationalizing language and standardizing the meanings of words. Although some of the problems that Swafford points out are specific to the software that *Syuzhet* uses, many other text-mining techniques share the tendency to work best with texts that straightforwardly follow standard usages while treating the existence of "non-literal" language, when they deal with it at all, as a problem to be solved. If we are to adopt text-mining tools in humanistic research, we will need to take account of the assumptions they make about language and how those assumptions could serve ideological interests.

Alien Reading

Although these observations suggest that there are good reasons for scholars to be wary of the adoption of text-mining software in the humanities, it would be a mistake simply to dismiss it as irrelevant to our concerns. In his 2014 article, "Theorizing Research Practices We Forgot to Theorize Twenty Years Ago," Ted Underwood forcefully points out that literary scholars outside of the digital humanities have already been using text-mining software on a regular basis for decades in the form of databases and search engines, but we have done little to theorize the role that these technologies play in scholarly practice (64). Many of the databases scholars commonly use already depend on generative models and other text-mining techniques for correcting scanning errors and accounting for spelling variants. In the present day, it is virtually impossible for scholars to avoid text-mining software altogether, even if many of us only encounter it indirectly through platforms like Google or JSTOR. If, as scholars, we are to engage with these technologies on our own terms, then we will have to find a way of making their roles in humanistic research a matter of active concern. Experimenting with text-mining programs in English departments could serve as a safeguard against the possibility that we unknowingly absorb these tools into our practice without reflecting on the assumptions about language and knowledge that underlie them and considering the effects they could have on our work.

The unreflective computerization that Underwood points out presents a particular problem in the present moment because of a current trend toward user interfaces that cover up the complexity of what goes on inside the machine. As Lori Emerson argues in *Reading Writing Interfaces,* the naturalistic interfaces of modern computers make their operations seem much simpler and more familiar than they really are, encouraging a passive, consumer-like orientation towards the computer rather than a deep understanding of it (1–19). The interfaces of tablet computers especially make heavy use of elements that mimic the behavior of physical objects, appealing to very familiar intuitions about how objects behave. This makes the devices easy to use up to a point, but it gives the typical user little insight into how they work. Search engines can similarly be much more complex than their user interfaces suggest, employing sophisticated algorithms for cleaning up and indexing texts, identifying synonyms, and determining the "relevance" of results that depend on strong assumptions about language and that could potentially introduce biases into research. While many text-mining programs present their results using familiar terms like *word, topic,* and *similarity,* the mathematical structures underneath are often fundamentally different from the ways in which human beings ordinarily understand these concepts. The apparent simplicity of interfaces like the search box allows us to use these technologies in our scholarship without confronting the complexity of what they do and the ways in which their designs might conflict with our precepts as scholars.

While Underwood responds to this problem with an embrace of statistical modeling, it is also possible to employ text-mining programs without accepting the thinking behind them, pushing back against naturalistic user interface design by drawing attention to aspects of the software that conflict with a humanistic view of interpretation. This approach would involve encountering text mining as an alien form of reading—alien both in the fact that it emerged from a discipline with very different concerns from our own and the fact that it is performed by a machine, the sort of nonhuman agent that Ian Bogost has sought to understand with his idea of *alien phenomenology* (Bogost). Rhody's work with topic modeling is one example of a project that employs text-mining technologies while keeping in mind the ways in which their assumptions might clash with the concerns of humanists. I would like to suggest an approach that goes further into a critique of the technology itself, engaging with text-mining tools as embodied, historically situated cultural productions that are potentially problematic. Understanding the extent to which our use of digital tools can reinforce hegemonic views of language requires a sort of scholarship that takes up a critical, perhaps even antagonistic attitude toward computerized modes of processing language. One thing that we, as humanists, can do to further this goal is to experiment with text-mining programs in a context that enables us to brush them against the grain, analyzing their assumptions and showing how they are positioned in the wider intellectual and cultural scene of the twenty-first century—writing, as it were, the *Tristram Shandy* to information science's *Essay concerning Human Understanding*.

This statement could perhaps be accused of encouraging the sort of navelgazing focus on methodology that, as Cameron Blevins argues in chapter 26 of this volume, has characterized recent work in digital history; but we need not consider text-mining practices in isolation from the rest of the world ("Digital History's Perpetual Future Tense"). Sterne's *Tristram Shandy* is much more than just a satire of Locke's call for the stabilization of words; it situates this impulse among many other aspects of the life of the eighteenth-century English middle class and its relationship to the intellectual culture of its past. In a long view, text-mining software is a part of the same history that literary critics study, a twenty-first-century expression of a standardizing impulse that has had a productive (if sometimes hostile) interchange with imaginative literature for centuries and that bears complex relationships to older practices of industrial management, library organization, and philology.[8] These histories are relevant to many of the questions that more traditional forms of literary scholarship ask, bound up as they are with age-old practices of reading and writing like excerpting, cataloging, and the creation of grammars. A critical engagement with text-mining software can also help us understand those aspects of computational methods that are genuinely new, especially the use of statistical methods. Experimenting with text-mining software can highlight the strangeness of computational technology in comparison to what has come before—a strangeness that, to use a commonplace from the field of media studies, those of us who live on the cusp of its emergence may be much better poised to see than future generations.

Engaging with text mining as an alien form of reading requires that we resist attempts to present computational results in forms that readily appeal to our assumptions and intuitions about language. The ease with which we can identify the "words" in the output of MALLET with our usual notion of the word makes it too easy to overlook the radical difference between how these units function in the program and the ways in which words can work in a human mind. While we cannot expect everyone who uses text-mining software to attempt a complete understanding of what is going on inside the computer, we should at least make an effort to appreciate the extent to which the tools we use are unknown to us, especially given the possibility that what happens inside could serve ideological ends. One can get a vivid sense of the gap between machine reading and our intuitive conceptions of language by examining the entries to Darius Kazemi's National Novel Generating Month,[9] an annual contest that challenges people to write a computer program that generates a 50,000 word novel (*NaNoGenMo 2014*). Most of the results are essentially unreadable, serving more as comments on process and algorithm than as ways of producing something that really resembles a novel, and they often ultimately direct our attention back on the role of computation itself in the generative process. For instance, Sean Connor's entry produces a randomized novel[10] by piecing together sequences of words and punctuation marks from L. Frank Baum's fourteen Oz novels. This is one paragraph of the output:

> " Same with me , please , " interrupted the girl Ruler for judgment. Again the passage turned abruptly , this time the huge scaly jaw of Choggenmugger was severed in twain and the beast advanced along the road . ("The Quantum Supposition of Oz")

The program that generated this text is based on a Markov chain model, the same sort of generative model that is commonly used in regularizing texts for the purposes of search engines, among many other applications. Although we cannot draw any major conclusions about how the technology works by reading specific examples of output, the practice of generating text using statistical models that were primarily designed for the processing of existing texts can be useful simply as a reminder of the fact that these models only loosely correspond to the way human languages work. The statistical methods that exist at present diverge in many ways from our ordinary expectations about what a text should look like, something that becomes much easier to see when one employs them for writing rather than for reading.

Text-generation programs have been employed for a number of purposes in the humanities, not all of which are specifically critical of the technology underlying them. Stephen Ramsay's *Reading Machines* proposes an Oulipan approach to literary criticism in which computerized transformations serve to enable richer and more complex interpretations of texts (15–17). Others, such as Mark Sample, have connected text generation to Lisa Samuels and Jerome J. McGann's idea of "deformance," a practice that creates modified versions of texts as a way of exploring their autopoietic capabilities (Sample, "Notes towards a Deformed Humanities;" Samuels and McGann, "Deformance and Interpretation"). For instance, Sample's Twitter account "This is Just to Say" (@JustToSayBot[11]) produces randomly generated parodies of William Carlos Williams's poem of the same name, replacing the sweet and cold plums with something different every time. But it is also possible to think of text generation more as an interrogation of the technology itself than as a way of encountering literary texts. One way of understanding how a text generator could serve as a critique of technology is through Sean Sturm and Stephen Turner's idea of *digital caricature*. Drawing on the work of the philosopher Vilém Flusser, Sturm and Turner suggest that we think of computation as "a caricature of thinking," a diminished imitation of mental operations that can potentially be viewed as a joke (para. 30–31). Finding humor in the "drop-down menu-isation" that computers impose on design, they argue, involves understanding it not just in terms of symbolic logic, but also from the perspective of "a region of primitively evolved drives" that computers lack (para. 33). The failures of methods like the Markov chain model to produce convincing imitations of novels can serve as caricatures in just the sense that Sturm and Turner discuss, eliciting laughter because they reveal the machine's incongruity with the social world in which we expect writing to take place. While computer scientists will undoubtedly develop better software that can create more convincing imitations of human writing, employing these programs as jokes allows us to revel in their present limitations, taking the opportunity they provide to show how the mechanisms underneath the software differ from human intelligence. Given the increasing inescapability of digitally inflected modes of thought, Sturm and Turner suggest, the best way to understand what it means to be human today is to laugh at computers.

But while digital caricature can serve a useful purpose by provoking an awareness of the difference between human and machine reading, it cannot substitute for a historical perspective on these technologies. The absurd text created by novel generators can give us a visceral sense of how computational models differ from our intuitive understandings of language, but it can only get us so far in understanding how those models relate to ideology. For this we need to supplement our experimentation with text-mining methods with research that situates them historically—both in the short term, looking at the institutional contexts from which they emerged, and in the long term, looking at how they relate to the histories of linguistic thought, philosophy, communication, and labor organization. This is an area where scholars of literature and intellectual history could have a particularly productive interchange with media theorists who critically study contemporary technology. Text-mining systems are playing increasingly large roles in our lives, our teaching, and our scholarship, and digital humanists, especially those who are versed in both statistical modeling and literary theory, are uniquely positioned to examine the linguistic ideologies that underlie them. Placing text mining in dialogue with the past could be useful not just for theorizing the implications of new scholarly tools like search engines, but also for interpreting historical texts in ways that are of particular relevance to the present shift from print to digital reading. To do this, we need a different form of scholarship from the one that applies a computer science methodology to the study of literary history. A media-studies approach would engage with programs like MALLET as cultural artifacts from the twenty-first century, products of a mechanization of language that is in some ways similar to views that have been put forth in the past, and that is in some ways new.

NOTES

1. Jockers models nineteenth-century novels in *Macroanalysis,* 118–153; Goldstone and Underwood apply topic modeling to literary criticism in "The Quiet Transformations of Literary Studies." Collin Jennings and I created a topic model for Joseph Addison and Richard Steele's *The Spectator,* available to view online at http://networkedcorpus.com /spectator/topic-index.html.

2. http://www.lisarhody.com/revising-ekphrasis.

3. I draw this conclusion from a search of the Thomson Reuters *Web of Science* database.

4. For an anecdote about a PhD student in biology being excoriated for writing "like a poet," see Ruben.

5. See Locke, *An Essay concerning Human Understanding,* especially 437–65; Sprat, *History of the Royal Society of London*; and John Wilkins, *An Essay towards a Real Character.*

6. http://wilkens.github.io/wright-topics.

7. The HathiTrust database returns 329 results for "stream of settlers" together with "Indians," constituting at least thirty distinct books.

8. On one connection between computers and industrialism, see McPherson. On accounting as a precedent for hypertext, see Duguid. On the relationship between computational linguistic techniques and philology, see Lennon.

9. https://github.com/dariusk/NaNoGenMo-2014.

10. https://github.com/spc476/NaNoGenMo-2014/blob/master/TheQuantum SuppositionOfOz.txt.

11. https://twitter.com/JustToSayBot.

BIBLIOGRAPHY

Allan, James, Jaime Carbonell, George Doddington, Jonathan Yamron, and Yiming Yang. "Topic Detection and Tracking Pilot Study Final Report." *Proceedings of the DARPA Broadcast News Transcription and Understanding Workshop.* Lansdowne, Va.: February 1998.

Anderson, Benedict. *Imagined Communities: Reflections on the Origin and Spread of Nationalism.* London: Verso, 2006.

Blei, David M. "Probabilistic Topic Models." *Communications of the ACM* 55, no. 4 (2012): 77–84.

———. "Topic Modeling and Digital Humanities." *Journal of Digital Humanities* 2, no. 1 (Winter 2012). http://journalofdigitalhumanities.org/2–1/topic-modeling-and-digital-humanities-by-david-m-blei.

Blei, David, Andrew Y. Ng, and Michael I. Jordan. "Latent Dirichlet Allocation." *Journal of Machine Learning Research* 3 (2003): 993–1022.

Bogost, Ian. *Alien Phenomenology, or What It's Like to Be a Thing.* Minneapolis: University of Minnesota Press, 2012.

Borges, Jorge Luis. "On Exactitude in Science." In *Collected Fictions,* trans. Andrew Burley, 325. New York: Penguin, 1999.

Borko, H., and M. D. Bernick. "Automatic Document Classification." *Journal of the ACM* 10, no. 3 (April 1963): 151–62.

Chun, Wendy Hui Kyong. *Control and Freedom: Power and Paranoia in the Age of Fiber Optics.* Cambridge, Mass.: MIT Press, 2008.

Connor, Sean. "The Quantum Supposition of Oz." *NaNoGenMo 2014.* https://github.com/spc476/NaNoGenMo-2014/blob/master/TheQuantumSuppositionOfOz.txt.

Deerwester, Scott, Susan T. Dumais, George W. Furnas, Thomas K. Landauer, and Richard Harshman. "Indexing by Latent Semantic Analysis." *Journal of the American Society for Information Science* 41, no. 6 (1990): 391–407.

Dietterich, Tom. "Overfitting and Undercomputing in Machine Learning." *ACM Computing Surveys* 27, no. 3 (September 1995): 326–27.

Duguid, Paul. "Material Matters: Aspects of the Past and the Futurology of the Book." In *The Future of the Book,* ed. Geoffrey Nunberg, 63–102. Berkeley: University of California Press, 1996.

Emerson, Lori. *Reading Writing Interfaces: From the Digital to the Bookbound.* Minneapolis: University of Minnesota Press, 2014.

Gitelman, Lisa. *Paper Knowledge: Toward a Media History of Documents.* Durham, N.C.: Duke University Press, 2014.

Goldstone, Andrew, and Ted Underwood. "The Quiet Transformations of Literary Studies: What Thirteen Thousand Scholars Could Tell Us." *New Literary History* 45, no. 3 (Summer 2014): 359–84.

Golumbia, David. *The Cultural Logic of Computation.* Cambridge, Mass.: Harvard University Press, 2009.

Guillory, John. "The Memo and Modernity." *Critical Inquiry* 31, no. 1 (Autumn 2004): 123–29.

Hockey, Susan. "The History of Humanities Computing." In *A Companion to Digital Humanities,* ed. Susan Schreibman, Ray Siemens, and John Unsworth. Malden, Mass.: Blackwell, 2004. http://www.digitalhumanities.org/companion.

Hofmann, Thomas. "Probabilistic Latent Semantic Indexing." *Proceedings of the Twenty-Second Annual International SIGIR Conference.* New York: ACM, 1999.

Jacobs, P. S., and Lisa F. Rau. "SCISOR: Extracting Information from Online News." *Communications of the ACM* 33, no. 11 (November 1990): 88–97.

Jebara, Tony. *Machine Learning: Discriminative and Generative.* New York: Springer: 2004.

Jockers, Matthew L. *Macroanalysis: Digital Methods and Literary History.* Urbana: University of Illinois Press, 2013.

———. "Revealing Sentiment and Plot Arcs with the Syuzhet Package." *Matthew L. Jockers* (blog), February 2, 2015. http://www.matthewjockers.net/2015/02/02/syuzhet.

———. "Some thoughts on Annie's thoughts . . . about Syuzhet." *Matthew L. Jockers* (blog), March 4, 2015. http://www.matthewjockers.net/2015/03/04/some-thoughts-on-annies-thoughts-about-syuzhet.

Juckett, David. "A Method for Determining the Number of Documents Needed for a Gold Standard Corpus." *Journal of Biomedical Informatics* 45, no. 3 (June 2012): 460–70.

Kazemi, Darius. *NaNoGenMo 2014.* https://github.com/dariusk/NaNoGenMo-2014.

Lennon, Brian. "Machine Translation: A Tale of Two Cultures." In *A Companion to Translation Studies,* ed. by Sandra Bermann and Catherine Porter, 135–46. New York: John Wiley & Sons, 2014.

Liu, Alan. "Where Is Cultural Criticism in the Digital Humanities?" In *Debates in the Digital Humanities,* ed. Matthew K. Gold, 490–509. Minneapolis: University of Minnesota Press, 2012.

Locke, John. *An Essay concerning Human Understanding* (1690). London: Penguin Classics, 1998.

McCallum, Andrew Kachites. *MALLET: A Machine Learning for Language Toolkit.* 2002. http://mallet.cs.umass.edu.

McPherson, Tara. "Why Are the Digital Humanities So White? or Thinking the Histories of Race and Computation." In *Debates in the Digital Humanities,* ed. Matthew K. Gold, 139–160. Minneapolis: University of Minnesota Press, 2012.

Ramsay, Stephen. *Reading Machines: Toward an Algorithmic Criticism.* Urbana: University of Illinois Press, 2011.

Rhody, Lisa M. "Topic Modeling and Figurative Language." *Journal of Digital Humanities* 2, no. 1 (Winter 2012). http://journalofdigitalhumanities.org/2–1/topic-modeling-and-figurative-language-by-lisa-m-rhody.

Ruben, Adam. "How to Write Like a Scientist." *Science Careers,* March 23, 2012. http://sciencecareers.sciencemag.org/career_magazine/previous_issues/articles/2012_03_23/caredit.a1200033.

Sample, Mark. "Notes towards a Deformed Humanities." *Sample Reality,* May 2, 2012. http://www.samplereality.com/2012/05/02/notes-towards-a-deformed-humanities.

Samuels, Lisa, and Jerome McGann. "Deformance and Interpretation." *New Literary History* 30, no. 1 (1999): 25–56.

Sprat, Thomas. *History of the Royal Society of London, for the Improving of Natural Knowledge.* Royal Society, 1667.

Sturm, Sean, and Stephen Francis Turner. "Digital Caricature." *Digital Humanities Quarterly* 8, no. 3 (2014). http://www.digitalhumanities.org/dhq/vol/8/3/000182/000182.html.

Swafford, Annie. "Continuing the Syuzhet Discussion." *Anglophile in Academia: Annie Swafford's Blog,* March 7, 2015. https://annieswafford.wordpress.com/2015/03/07/continuingsyuzhet.

———. "Problems with the Syuzhet Package." *Anglophile in Academia: Annie Swafford's Blog,* March 2, 2015. https://annieswafford.wordpress.com/2015/03/02/syuzhet.

Underwood, Ted. "Theorizing Research Practices We Forgot to Theorize Twenty Years Ago." *Representations* 127, no. 1 (Summer 2014): 64–72.

Wilkins, John. *An Essay towards a Real Character, and a Philosophical Language.* London, 1668.

Wilkins, Matthew. *100-topic model of the Wright American Fiction corpus.* http://wilkens.github.io/wright-topics/#.

My *Old Sweethearts*: On Digitization and the Future of the Print Record

ANDREW STAUFFER

Energetic digitization efforts of the past two decades have created a world of surrogates for printed books. The Google Book project made huge inroads into the born-analog content of libraries, with a particular emphasis on open-stack collections. Other agents such as HathiTrust, and commercial entities such as Gale/Cengage, have also been assiduous in providing digital access to print materials of earlier eras via scanned copies.[1] Particularly for non- or medium-rare materials printed between 1830 and 1923 (the beginning of industrial printing up to the copyright limit), this has meant wide access to full-text content and page images.[2] One downstream effect of these massive collections of photo-facsimiles has been a renewed attention to bibliographic detail: we see pages, everywhere. And we notice things about them as interfaces, as designs, and as material that eluded us in modern editions. In some ways, the print record is available to us like never before. However—and this is my polemic—it is also occluded in crucial ways that have troubling implications not only for scholarship but also for the institutions that stand at the center of humanistic activity generally: libraries.

The problem is this: academic libraries are now questioning the value of maintaining extensive print collections of non-rare materials that have been scanned and are freely available online.[3] After all, most patrons prefer to consult older books via Google or HathiTrust (or more modern editions of their textual content) when they can (Anderson). Use of the non-rare legacy print collections is dropping, and at the same time libraries are facing urgent demands for digital databases, collaborative spaces, and the newer, in-copyright books that claim more shelf space each year. That is, various pressures (money, space, convenience) are driving the nineteenth- and early twentieth-century books off the shelves. An obvious solution is to downsize the print holdings in the stacks, either moving them to offsite storage or de-accessioning them in reliance on interlibrary loan if the print version is really needed. In pursuit of this effort, library policy leaders are pursuing ideas of "collective collections"—managing (and managing down) our national holdings of little-used printed books and journals in regional, and eventually national, collaborative arrangements (Dempsey et al.; Lavoie, Malpas, and Shipengrover). Librarians are now developing preservation and access models wherein the use of non-rare, out-of-copyright, already-digitized physical materials is increasingly an eccentric requirement.[4] With all of their content online, who still needs these books?

Scholars do, as it turns out. I am going to pass lightly over some large issues such as the value of serendipitous discoveries in the stacks (Alves; Carr),[5] the importance of the library as a built space for historical encounters, and the somatic and affective appeal of the codex as such. (For a perspective on the particular value of humanities materials in libraries, see Woolwine.) I want to focus our attention instead on the library as a more complex ecosystem of information than our digital catalogs and electronic text corpora comprehend. Insofar as we resolve whole ranges of "copies" to a single catalog entry and/or a scanned version of a single copy, we strip the print record of its meaningful variety. As we all know, when we abstract and formalize printed books in order to make them operational in a digital environment, we lose detail. We don't ever really "put a book online" or even "digitize" a book: rather, we create a model that allows certain affordances and eliminates others. As Jerome McGann has written, "After we digitize the books, the books themselves remain. . . . Perhaps the greatest of the false promises of digitization is that its simulations will save our books. . . . If our book heritage is to be saved, we will have to chose to save it intact, not simulate it electronically" (132). Scanned books still exist in the world, somewhere, as part of a much larger family of copies whose significance can only be grasped in the aggregate. Bibliography and textual scholarship attempt that grasp.

None of this would be a huge worry if books were mostly staying on the shelves, or if our access to collections was not increasingly mediated by layers of digital cataloging—that is, by metadata. Metadata is not the enemy, of course: it has potential to reveal books and their relations in ways far beyond analog classificatory systems. But it can also lead to oversimplifications—the too-few-buckets problem—especially under conditions of straitened resources and efficiency mandates. Insofar as scholars and students get to books primarily via online searches that lead to offsite retrieval—or interlibrary loan requests or (most commonly) the click of a Google Books link—they will be misled by the apparent singularity and self-identity of the copy they encounter. Moreover, librarians pursuing significant downsizing of their collections based on the number of copies in OCLC World-Cat (a common metric for de-accessioning, along with usage numbers) will be winnowing a multiform collection whose significant variations lie hidden behind blandly aggregated metadata, given current library cataloging standards. ("If an item can easily be obtained from other libraries, it can be safely weeded" [Tyckoson, 69].) In addition, the further we as an academic culture move away from ready access to the actual print record (the real books), the more unlikely it is that scholars will cultivate the baseline bibliographic familiarity out of which comparative discovery can only grow.

As specialists in medieval and early-modern eras know well, books reflect the multiple hands of their makers and users: the contingencies and processes, the tactical moves, the errors and accidents, the exfoliation of possibilities—the texture of the communicative circuit. They are temporally layered objects, variable from other copies at the point of production in myriad ways, and accruing meaningful evidence of use chronically throughout their individual existences in the world (they are sort of like people, in those ways). All of this is true of books printed after the handpress period as well (that is, via increasingly mechanical, industrial processes), although people tend to forget the fact. Insofar as we allow single-copy scans to stand in for entire editions and conflate multiple copies into a single WorldCat entry, we are encouraging the growth of bibliographic monocultures, editing away the details in the interests of efficiency.[6] With such protocols, we are enabling a flattening of the human record in all of its variability, and the humanities suffer thereby.

As I have said, material printed between 1830 and 1923 is the most vulnerable: mostly out of copyright, frequently available in full text online, usually not valuable to collectors, sometimes in deteriorating condition due to the wood pulp paper and cheaper production values of the era, and often assumed even by scholars to be standard, identical copies created by machines in the age of the stereotype and the steam press. Also, there is a lot of it, and it is little-used by patrons. No wonder libraries are trying to move much of this material offsite or abandoning commitments to their copies altogether. When someone really needs to see a physical copy of, say, the 1902 edition of James Whitcomb Riley's *An Old Sweetheart of Mine,* that person can get it via interlibrary loan.

So I decided to test the implications of that logic by requesting as many copies of the 1902 *Old Sweetheart* as my interlibrary loan office would supply at once. This book was chosen somewhat haphazardly as a subject, based on research into editions likely to reside in a large number of circulating collections in the United States. Riley was a popular American poet of the later nineteenth century and was often published in kitschy formats that circulated widely as gift-books during his era. This particular edition features numerous illustrations by Howard Chandler Christy and decorative embellishments by Virginia Keep.[7] Working from a single World-Cat entry that indicated over 100 copies held in member libraries, I made requests for ten of these copies, including the University of Virginia copy in the set. I would have asked for more, but the interlibrary loan (ILL) office expressed its displeasure; and in any case, ten copies were enough to make my point, for now.

Placed side-by-side, these ten *Old Sweetheart*s began to tell a story.

The first thing one notices are the varying bindings, visible even in a black and white photograph: the burgundy cloth, blue-green cloth, gray cloth, and library buckram reveal an obvious layer of variation among these supposed duplicates. Individual weathering to each binding has produced different gradations of color

Figure 19.1. Copies of the 1902 edition of *An Old Sweetheart of Mine* obtained via ILL from Richard Bland College, U Tennessee, UNC-Charlotte, Louisiana State U, Olivet Nazarene, Kenyon, West Virginia U, Duke, Vanderbilt, and U Virginia.

within the groupings as well, both of the publisher's cloth and the stamped designs on it. Various library stamps, stickers, and barcodes are also visible on the exteriors. So even from this distance, having not even opened the books, we can see evidence of two species of variability: different bindings at the point of production, and different post-publication patterns of change.

It is beyond my scope in this brief chapter to present an exhaustive catalog of the ways in which each of these copies differs from its peers. It is enough to say that no two copies are exactly alike, and to express my belief that, were I to examine all of the copies of this edition from the various libraries in WorldCat, that same truth would hold to some degree. It remains for me to register a few examples to help convey a sense of the bibliodiversity preserved in multiple copies of a single edition. According to WorldCat and the interlibrary loan system that undergirds the "collective collections" movement, these are all interchangeable duplicates.

Publishers' Information

All ten copies have the same copyright statement on the reverse of the title-leaf: "Copyright, 1902/ The Bowen-Merrill Company." But on the title page itself, four copies have "Bowen-Merrill" listed as the publisher, five copies have "Bobbs-Merrill," and one has "Grosset and Dunlap." The company changed the "Bowen" to "Bobbs" in January 1903, in the midst of the print run, in part accounting for the mixed state of attribution here (Russo and Russo, 92). On the spines of these books, three copies are stamped "Bowen Merrill," five have "Bobbs Merrill," one has been rebound, and one has "Grosset and Dunlap." These are distributed across the burgundy and blue-green bindings, with Grosset and Dunlap the odd man out in gray, printed in a smaller format. A bibliographer could use these variants as an aid to determining the chronological order of the different states of the first edition.

Text of the Poem

Seven of the copies have the word "song" in stanza 18, where the other three have the word "shout." Eight of the copies have an exclamation point after the word "come" in stanza 34, and two have a period instead. Seven copies have a lower-case letter "t" at the opening of the third line of stanza 36, and three have a capital "T." These variations do not cluster together in immediately recognizable sets, nor do they map directly to the varying publisher information or to the binding colors. Textual scholarship requires such details to establish the genealogy of a work: does "song" or "shout" represent Riley's final intention for stanza 18? Which word should we reproduce in a modern version? What about our punctuation and capitalization choices? Rather than just choosing randomly, scholars use evidence of the kind contained in these multiple copies to produce new editions.

Preliminary and End-Leaves

In addition to decorative endpapers, this edition has eleven preliminary leaves and three end-leaves, including various vignettes of the narrator and his sweetheart as children and adults, printed in pale pink (as well as a half-title, title page, dedication page, list of illustrations, and an epigraph). The pink vignettes are variously faded across all copies, coming through bright and clear in some and barely visible in others. One copy has shuffled the order of the front matter so that the half-title comes two pages earlier than in other copies. Another copy omits one page of the opening vignette illustrations. The copy rebound in buckram lacks the rear endpapers entirely. In choosing which copies to retain in our "collective collection," we need to have a better sense of condition, or else we risk choosing faded, damaged, or incomplete copies to represent the edition. Without the kind of cross-copy comparison that diversity in library collections enables, bibliographical description is hamstrung by a lack of evidence and can only proceed by guesswork.

Figure 19.2. Alternate engravings from the 1902 *An Old Sweetheart of Mine.*

Illustrations

Two copies show subtle differences in at least one of the illustrations, suggesting something complex about the ways they were engraved and reproduced. A much fuller study would be necessary to survey and explicate the variants across all of the illustrations and designs as printed, but for now, we can simply say that not all "old sweethearts" are the same.

Here she is: see any differences between these two (Figure 19.2)?

Look closely, for example, at the roses she is plucking.

In Figure 19.3 you can see the flowers on the left seem to be pulled toward her, whereas those on the right are shooting up more vertically, with extra stems. Further, in the latter image, the rose in the sweetheart's hand is accompanied by three lines

Figure 19.3. Alternate engravings from the 1902 *An Old Sweetheart of Mine* (detail).

of background texture, leading to a ghostly (uncolored) rose above right, all absent in the other version. These small variations provide evidence of a forked printing history and multiple states of the engravings, something that would require the examination of many copies to trace. We might discover something about the way Christy worked as an illustrator, or the nature of the reproductive process used by the publisher. But in any case, these variable roses serve as a nice representation—part metaphor, part synecdoche—for the presence of rich, unnoticed bibliodiversity in the stacks, an ecosystem under threat in the new information economy.

User Marks

In four copies, previous owners have written their names. The University of Virginia copy has a gift inscription that reads, "This is my message/ for you—/

December 1903 / D / Can you decipher it?" The bookplate indicates it was a gift from R. N. Watts, who seems to have been serving as secretary to Austin, Texas chapter of the YMCA around the time of the inscription (thanks, Google Books). Using large libraries of digital surrogates like those found at Google and Hathi, we can begin to trace the lives recorded in the print volumes. In this way, scholars may illuminate patterns of book use and reading in previous eras when print dominated the media landscape. We can help "decipher" their individual messages via digital search, opening up a hybrid research environment in which digital models and physical records illuminate one another. My *Book Traces* project (http://booktraces. org) is one attempt in this direction, a crowdsourced site encouraging the discovery of historical user-modified volumes (primarily marginalia and inscriptions) in the circulating collections of libraries. Thanks to a grant from the Council for Library Information Resources (CLIR), librarians at the University of Virginia are working to catalog such volumes in our main humanities library in the Book Traces @ UVA initiative. As these copies of *Old Sweetheart* demonstrate, user modifications are only one way that copies differ, but marginalia and inscriptions are easily spotted locally without the need for cross-copy comparison, and thus they provide a pragmatic vector for conserving variety in the stacks.

In the event, *An Old Sweetheart of Mine* was a happy choice for this experiment, not only because of the multifaceted variation among copies of the 1902 edition, but because the poem itself resonates with the bookish forms that contain it. The narrator presents a series of nostalgic memories of a childhood girlfriend, indulged in an upstairs study among "old bookshelves" while his wife and children are out of the way. In its first published version (1889), the poem begins,

> As one who cons at evening o'er an album, all alone,
> And muses on the faces of the friends that he has known,
>
> So I turn the leaves of Fancy, till, in shadowy design,
> I find the smiling features of an old sweetheart of mine.

In Riley's poem, remembering the beloved is like browsing through a picture album, a book of souvenirs made up of "the leaves of Fancy." The poem suggests the close ties between consciousness and codices, between books and identity, in the great age of industrial printing. These were the platforms, these the interfaces, upon which readers in the nineteenth and twentieth centuries elaborated their social relationships and emotional lives. Their apparent sameness from a distance (are not all old sweethearts the same?) is belied by their utter individuality once examined and known (no, each one is different). Yet as a cultural object, this Riley book moves in the other direction as well, predicated as it is on the similarity of middle-class romantic feelings across an incalculable range of readers. Put harshly, the book trades in sentimental cliché: a Hallmark card on steroids, this edition of *An Old Sweetheart*

Figure 19.4. Another version of the publisher's binding for the 1902 *An Old Sweetheart of Mine.*

of Mine needs to be relatable to be salable: the reader needs to be able to imagine that *Mine* as his own. In this way, it becomes a fascinating thing to contemplate, a little microcosm of the uncertain relation of the one to the many, the individual to the mass public, that characterizes modern questions of identity, and animated the entire scene of literary production in an era of general literacy. Its bibliographic variety-within-sameness puts a particularly fine point on the issue.

It is no surprise that Riley's poem and its accompanying paratexts vary across editions and reprintings: but the range of variation *within a single edition*—pointing to numerous states of that edition invisibilized by aggregating common metadata—should give us pause before we declare them all duplicates.

After the exercise with interlibrary loan copies of the 1902 *Old Sweetheart,* I started looking for other copies of this edition at used bookstores and found one—printed with "Bowen-Merrill" on the copyright page, but "Bobbs-Merrill" on the title page and spine, like some of the others—with an alternate binding, as shown in Figure 19.4.

And so possibilities proliferate. My limited interlibrary loan experiment did not net this one, but it well might have if I had pushed through to obtain other libraries' copies. Here, an alternate "Christy girl" graces the cover, another representation of the "old sweetheart," caught in the act of reading: her finger poised within the volume, a look of reverie on her musing face. Like our narrator, she turns "the leaves of Fancy," perhaps of her own eponymous volume, the one she inspired and the reader holds.

The poem itself, "An Old Sweetheart of Mine," ends with an uxorial twist: it turns out that the apparently neglected wife downstairs *is* the "old sweetheart," who shows up at the end in her own "living presence," as domestic bliss subsumes the "truant fancies" of erotic memory. It seems an apt allegory for the reappearance of the book in our hands, as we move from the "leaves of Fancy" of virtual reading back to the "living presence" of the physical volumes. Riley's point is that love requires both the memories and the embodied form, the virtual sweethearts of the past and her living self before him. Humanities scholarship also needs both worlds to thrive: digital and analog, virtual and historical, abstract and particular. Matthew Kirschenbaum[8] and Bethany Nowviskie[9] have often said that "love will find a way" to preserve our cultural inheritance. If that is true, then let me add a corollary proposition: we are going to need as many *Old Sweethearts* as we can get.

NOTES

1. For a relatively recent survey of nineteenth-century materials online, see Stauffer.

2. This access has been notoriously troubled not only by copyright issues but by the poor metadata and image quality of the Google scans. See Nunberg and also Darnton.

3. See Grafton for more on changing library priorities in the digital age.

4. See, for example, Schoenfeld and Housewright for the 2009 Ithaka Strategy and Research Report, "What to Withdraw: Print Collections Management in the Wake of Digitization," which notes that "due to a decline in faculty interest in print preservation both locally and remotely in recent years, the political necessity of maintaining even remote access to print collections will probably remain a requirement only in the medium term" (12–13).

5. Carr gives a recent counter-perspective on serendipity as a problem (predicated on the accidental).

6. One thinks of the agricultural monocultures that Michael Pollan has condemned in *The Botany of Desire* and elsewhere, the biodiversity movement aimed at mitigating the Holocene (or Sixth) extinction, and even the neurodiversity movement in the autism

community, all of which speak to the fundamental importance of preserving variety as a human and natural good. Books are not naturally occurring phenomena of course, but their historical variability and evidentiary complexity evoke a similar logic of long-view plenitude versus short-term efficiency.

7. *Bibliography of American Literature* 16657. See entry for "An Old Sweetheart of Mine," in Russo and Russo, 90–92. They identify only two states of this edition; there are plainly many more.

8. An Interview with Matthew Kirschenbaum, August 12, 2013, http://blogs.loc.gov /digitalpreservation/2013/08/whats-a-nice-english-professor-like-you-doing-in-a-place -like-this-an-interview-matthew-kirschenbaum/.

9. *Bethany Nowviskie* (blog), September 19, 2011, http://nowviskie.org/2011/dh -wonks-step-this-way/.

BIBLIOGRAPHY

Alves, Julio. "Unintentional Knowledge: What We Find When We're Not Looking." *Chronicle of Higher Education* 59, no. 41 (2013). http://chronicle.com/article /Unintentional-Knowledge/139891.

Anderson, Richard. "Print on the Margins." *Library Journal*, 136, no. 11 (2011): 38–39. http://lj.libraryjournal.com/2011/06/academic-libraries/print-on-the-margins -circulation-trends-in-major-research-libraries/.

Carr, Patricia. "Serendipity in the Stacks: Libraries, Information Architectures, and the Problems of Accidental Discovery." *College and Research Libraries* (2015). http://crl .acrl.org/content/early/2015/01/01/crl14-655.full.pdf.

Darnton, Robert. "Google and the Future of Books." *New York Review of Books*, February 12, 2009. http://www.nybooks.com/articles/archives/2009/feb/12/google-the-future -of-books/.

Dempsey, Lorcan, Brian Lavoie, Constance Malpas, Lynn Silipigni Connaway, Roger C. Schonfeld, J. D. Shipengrover, and Günter Waibel. *Understanding the Collective Collection: Towards a System-wide Perspective on Library Print Collections.* Dublin, Ohio: OCLC Research, 2013. http://www.oclc.org/research/publications/library/2013/2013 -09r.html.

Grafton, Anthony. "Apocalypse in the Stacks: The Research Library in the Age of Google." *Daedelus* 138, no. 1 (Winter 2009): 87–98.

Lavoie, Brian, Constance Malpas, and J. D. Shipengrover. *Print Management at "Mega-scale": A Regional Perspective on Print Book Collections in North America.* Dublin, Ohio: OCLC Research, 2012. http://oclc.org/content/dam/research/publications/library /2012/2012-05.pdf.

McGann, Jerome. *A New Republic of Letters: Memory and Scholarship in the Age of Digital Reproduction.* Cambridge, Mass.: Harvard University Press, 2014.

Nunberg, Geoffrey. "Google's Book Search: A Disaster for Scholars." *Chronicle of Higher Education*, August 31, 2009. http://chronicle.com/article/Googles-Book-Search-A/48245/.

Russo, A. J., and D. R. Russo, eds. *A Bibliography of James Whitcomb Riley*. Indianapolis: Indiana Historical Society, 1944.

Schoenfeld, Roger, and Ross Housewright. "What to Withdraw: Print Collections Management in the Wake of Digitization." *Ithaka S+R Research Report,* September 1, 2009. http://www.sr.ithaka.org/research-publications/what-withdraw-print-collections -management-wake-digitization.

Stauffer, Andrew. "Digital Scholarly Resources for the Study of Victorian Literature and Culture." *Victorian Literature and Culture* (2011): 39, 293–303.

Tyckoson, David A. "Perspectives on Weeding in Academic Library Collections." In *Rethinking Collection Development and Management,* ed. Becky Albitz, Christine Avery, and Diane Zabel, 59–76. Santa Barbara, Calif.: ABC-CLIO, 2014.

Woolwine, David E., "Collection Development in the Humanities and Social Sciences in a Transitional Age: Deaccession of Print Items." (2014). *Library Philosophy and Practice (e-journal).* Paper 1173. http://digitalcommons.unl.edu/libphilprac/1173.

Argument, Evidence, and the Limits of Digital Literary Studies

DAVID L. HOOVER

There are many kinds of literary arguments, and two ways they vary are in the extent to which they deploy evidence and in the nature of that evidence. Here I want to discuss a small sampling of these varieties of argument and evidence and how they intersect with and affect or limit the usefulness of digital approaches to literary studies. I will argue that at least some approaches (intentionally) devalue evidence and use arguments that barely deserve the name. The specious attractiveness of such approaches is dangerous to the unwary and has the potential to damage further how the humanities are viewed both by the public at large and by disciplines with approaches that are more closely based on evidence. Finally, I will look more closely at two problematic discussions of the nature of evidence and argument in the digital humanities and suggest ways that digital methods might improve them.

Argument and Evidence in (Digital) Literary Studies

I begin with a brief look back at a famous hoax. Alan Sokal, a New York University physicist, submitted "Transgressing the Boundaries: Toward a Transformative Hermeneutics of Quantum Gravity" to *Social Text*. When the journal published it (Sokal, "Transgressing the Boundaries") without having anyone who knew anything about science read it, Sokal revealed to the editors of *Lingua Franca* that it was a hoax (Sokal, "A Physicist Experiments with Cultural Studies"). This fiasco resonates in many ways with the all-too-common lack of respect for argument and evidence in literary studies before and since the hoax (see Guillory for a thorough discussion of the hoax in a broader context). Sokal put it this way:

> *Social Text*'s acceptance of my article exemplifies the intellectual arrogance of Theory—postmodernist *literary* theory, that is—carried to its logical extreme. No wonder they didn't bother to consult a physicist. If all is discourse and "text,"

then knowledge of the real world is superfluous; even physics becomes just
another branch of cultural studies. If, moreover, all is rhetoric and language
games, then internal logical consistency is superfluous too: a patina of theoretical sophistication serves equally well.

Incomprehensibility becomes a virtue; allusions, metaphors, and puns
substitute for evidence and logic. My own article is, if anything, an extremely
modest example of this well-established genre. (Sokal, "A Physicist Experiments with Cultural Studies," 52)

I do not think Sokal's wonderful proposal that gravity is a social construct is "an
extremely modest example," but egregious examples of the misuse of argument and
evidence in literary studies help to explain why his spoof was not so far beyond the
pale as to alert the editors of *Social Text* to its nature. To take just two examples I
have discussed elsewhere, consider Stanley Fish's argument in his influential *Is
There a Text in This Class* that there is nothing about Faulkner's "A Rose for Emily"
that prevents it from being read as a story about Eskimos (347), or Jerome McGann's
argument in his prize-winning *Radiant Textuality* that Joyce Kilmer's "Trees" is
actually a good modernist poem about God having sex with trees since "only God
can *make* a tree" (29–52). (See Hoover, "Hot-Air Textuality" and "The End of the
Irrelevant Text," for discussion of these and other examples.) Both of these arguments were intended as provocations and as invitations to rethink interpretation,
but such arguments, and the tolerance for them that made Sokal's hoax possible,
have, I think, damaged the public perception of literary studies. Worse yet, some
scholars may, because of the prestige of those making the arguments and the venues
in which they appear, come to think of such arguments as legitimate and acceptable outside the provocative discussions in which they first appeared. I turn now
to two discussions of digital humanities that explicitly take up the question of evidence and argument.

Ramsay's Reading Machines *and Virginia Woolf's* The Waves

In *Reading Machines: Toward an Algorithmic Criticism,* Stephen Ramsay suggests that computational studies of literature remain marginalized because they lack
"bold statements, strong readings, and broad generalizations" (2). They are too cau-
tious, too scientific, to interest literary critics, who value opening texts to new interpretations more than they value solving problems (10–11). (My discussion here is
based, in part, on Hoover, "Making Waves," and Plasek and Hoover.) Ramsay quotes
from a feminist discussion of *The Waves* (Woolf) that he says challenges the digital humanities:

> In this essay I want to resituate *The Waves* as complexly formulating and refor-
> mulating subjectivity through its playful formal style and elision of corporeal

materiality. The Waves models an alternative subjectivity that exceeds the dominant (white, male, heterosexual) individual western subject through its stylistic usage of metaphor and metonymy. . . . Focusing on the narrative construction of subjectivity reveals the pertinence of *The Waves* for current feminist
reconfigurations of the feminine subject. This focus links the novel's visionary
limitations to the historic moment of Modernism. (Wallace, 295–96)

Ramsay argues that

Wallace frames her discourse as a "resituation" of Woolf's novel within several
larger fields of critical discourse. This will presumably involve the marshaling
of evidence and the annunciation of claims. It may even involve offering various "facts" in support of her conclusions. But hermeneutically, literary critical
arguments of this sort do not stand in the same relationship to facts, claims,
and evidence as the more empirical forms of inquiry. There is no experiment
that can verify the idea that Woolf's "playful formal style" reformulates subjectivity or that her "elision of corporeal materiality" exceeds the dominant Western subject. (Ramsay, *Reading Machines,* 7)

Literary criticism's problematic relationship to facts, claims, and evidence seems
more like a bug than a feature, but I think John Guillory is right in arguing that "if
positivism is a holistic or totalizing ideology that reserves the name of knowledge
only for the results of the scientific method (narrowly defined), it does not follow
that the critical disciplines must be based on a counter-holism in which everything
is interpretation, in which the very possibility of a positive knowledge is called into
question" (Guillory, 504). A reexamination and interrogation of Ramsay's algorithmic provocation will clarify these issues.

The Waves consists of alternating monologues by three male and three female
characters, an experimental technique that has invited critical comment about what
axes of difference or unity characterize the novel:

Are Woolf's individuated characters to be understood as six sides of an individual consciousness (six modalities of an idealized Modernist self?), or are
we meant to read against the fiction of unity that Woolf has created by having
each of these modalities assume the same stylistic voice?

It is tempting for the text analysis practitioner to view this as a problem
to be solved—as if the question were rhetorically equivalent to "Who wrote
Federalist 10?" The category error arises because we mistake questions about
the properties of objects with questions about the phenomenal experience of
observers. . . . We may ask "What does it mean?" but in the context of critical
discourse this is often an elliptical way of saying "Can I interpret (or read) it
this way?" (Ramsay, *Reading Machines,* 10)

It is not clear to me that Woolf creates a "fiction of unity" in *The Waves*. One could argue instead that separating the voices of six "different" characters creates a "fiction of diversity." (For a thorough recent discussion of the various views about the similarities and differences among the voices in *The Waves,* see Balossi, *A Corpus Linguistic Approach to Literary Language and Characterization,* chaps. 1–2.)

COMPUTATIONALLY TRACTABLE AND COMPUTATIONALLY INTRACTABLE QUESTIONS

There is, I suggest, a hierarchy in the tractability of various literary claims to a computational investigation, though I am not suggesting an equation of tractability with value or importance. Clearly many tractable problems will be of limited interest to literary scholars (are Faulkner's sentences longer than those of Henry James?). "We should expect six different voices (or one unified voice) in *The Waves*" seems a computationally intractable claim, a matter of interpretation. Evidence might be adduced in its favor, but such evidence would necessarily be oblique and the argument for it largely a matter of persuasion. "*The Waves* has a 'playful formal style' also seems intractable. The style does not seem playful to me, but it is difficult to imagine how convincing evidence could be brought to bear on the question." (Evidence to support or contest the argument that the style is "experimental" would be easier to produce.) "*The Waves* displays an 'elision of corporeal materiality,' in contrast, seems more amenable to an argument based on evidence." The claim that Woolf elides "corporeal materiality" surely has implications for the vocabulary of the text that could be tested computationally and statistically. I reject Ramsay's claim that it is a category error to treat the question of whether the voices of the six monologues in *The Waves* are the same or different as a problem to be solved. It seems instead an important question that is quite amenable to digital humanities methods—methods that have been extensively tested in the area of authorship attribution (where Ramsay accepts the idea of solvable problems). I will make the bold claim that the six voices are demonstrably different. I should emphasize here that the fact that a problem is computationally tractable does not mean that a definitive or certain solution is necessarily possible; nor does the fact that a problem is computationally intractable mean that a legitimate and effective argument cannot be made about it.[1]

In an attempt to provoke discussion rather than solve a problem, Ramsay treats the six monologues as a corpus of documents and investigates them with tf-idf, a measure from the field of information retrieval that is used (in multiple variations) in many search engines.[2] Simply put, a tf-idf score is the frequency of a word multiplied by the total number of documents and divided by the number of documents containing the word. These scores, he suggests, should identify each monologue's characteristic words more effectively than a traditional word-frequency list that is dominated by very frequent words shared by most texts. (The overwhelming evidence of the last thirty years that the most frequent words are very effective for authorship attribution problems makes this argument less than compelling.) Tf-idf scores are lower for function words and higher for speakers' characteristic words because the frequencies of words used by only one speaker are multiplied by six (six total documents divided by the one in which the word occurs), while the frequencies of words used by all six speakers are multiplied by one (six total documents divided by the six in which the word occurs) (Ramsay, *Reading Machines,* 11). After identifying each speaker's most characteristic words, Ramsay reveals that he has actually used a slightly different formula that includes a log function (to reduce the effect of a word's appearance in only one speaker) and prevents the scores from becoming negative.[3] The purpose of the alterations in the formula "is not to bring the results into closer conformity with 'reality,' but merely to render the weighting numbers more sensible to the analyst" (*Reading Machines,* 15). Yet the variants are not "merely" at the whim of the analyst; they have testable consequences.

TF-IDF AND THE QUESTION OF CHARACTER-INDIVIDUALIZATION IN *THE WAVES*

But let us travel a bit further with Ramsay by looking at his list of the words with the highest tf-idf scores in Louis's monologue (I have added the raw frequency of each word). He suggests that "few readers of *The Waves* would fail to see some emergence of pattern in this list" (Ramsay, *Reading Machines,* 12). For example, *western* seems to echo Louis's concern about his *Australian accent* and *England* (all four of these words are in Louis's top twenty-five). But actually *western, wilt,* and *thou* appear in Louis's monologue only in quotations from a sixteenth-century poem. Ramsay's intervention raises interesting questions: Why choose this algorithm? How do the results affect our emerging reading of *The Waves*? (*Reading Machines,* 15). But how to answer these questions? Ramsay also ignores some interesting questions: Would other algorithms give similar results? Should Louis's quotations be considered *his* speech (and retained?) or the anonymous author's (and omitted?). My own answer is that the anonymous author's words are not Louis's words for the purposes of characterizing his speech. Louis's repeated quotation of this poem and the nature of the author and the quotation are certainly significant in characterizing him, but I would distinguish between his mention of words and his use of them.[4] (The styles of the six monologues are obviously not characterized only by their vocabularies, but discussing the vocabulary separately seems reasonable.) Some of the questions I have just raised are not computationally tractable, and other analysts would give answers different from mine. Ramsay has argued that computational analyses are often too reductive, but here his own argument suffers because it rejects any attempt to answer the questions in a reasonable way.

The tf-idf algorithm was designed to retrieve relevant documents rather than to characterize or analyze them, but my point is not that any particular choice of algorithm is definitively correct or incorrect. Rather, the choice of algorithm is important

Table 20.1. Louis's Most Characteristic Words

WORD	TF-IDF	FREQ.
mr	5.917	10
western	5.729	9
nile	5.518	8
australian	5.002	6
beast	5.002	6
grained	5.002	6
thou	5.002	6
wilt	5.002	6
pitchers	4.675	5
steel	4.675	5
attempt	4.276	4
average	4.276	4
clerks	4.276	4
disorder	4.276	4
accent	3.916	14
beaten	3.76	3
bobbing	3.76	3
custard	3.76	3
discord	3.76	3
eating-shop	3.76	3
england	3.76	3
eyres	3.76	3
four-thirty	3.76	3
ham	3.76	3
lesson	3.76	3

and its consequences need more discussion if we are to achieve more than mere provocation. In any case, Ramsay's lists of the words with the highest tf-idf scores for each of the six characters suggest a possible answer to whether we should read the novel as six voices or one. The differences are surely real, though Ramsay is right in suggesting that they still need to be interpreted. As I will soon clarify, the legitimacy of treating Louis as if he were a real person also needs further discussion.

Trying to recreate Ramsay's analysis reveals further interesting points. First, and probably least controversial, is his omission of the long final chapter of *The Waves* from his analysis. This chapter is all in Bernard's voice, and it begins "Now to sum up," showing that it is likely to be quite different from the rest of the novel. I have also removed it from my analysis, and Burrows does the same (206), as does Balossi (84). Ramsay (personal communication) agrees that he should have noted this. Even after removing the final chapter, however, calculating the tf-idf scores for Louis's words shows that Ramsay's analysis and mine yield different word frequencies. His score for *beast* requires six occurrences, for example, not the five my analysis finds. Although there is a sixth occurrence in the omniscient narration at the beginning of the fifth chapter, the difference in frequencies seems to be a result of different tokenizations: *beast's* also occurs only in Louis's monologue, and this implies that Ramsay's tokenization must break words at apostrophes. Another indication of this is that *Bernard's* does not occur among the men-only words later in Ramsay's discussion, even though it occurs in all the men and none of the women. His score for *accent* indicates thirteen occurrences, not the fourteen I found, but Rhoda's most characteristic words include *them*— and *accent* occurs once as *accent*—. This presumably reduces his count by one. What constitutes a word is a surprisingly complex question, but counting *them*— and *accent*— as different words from *them* and *accent* while counting *beast* and *beast's* as the same word seems at best debatable (see Hoover, "The Trials of Tokenization," for a discussion). The rarity of the characteristic words identified by tf-idf makes questions of tokenization much more important than they would be if more frequent words were involved. Tf-idf also strongly privileges words limited to one character: only *accent* is used by more than one speaker.

The identification of characteristic words is problematic in another way. *Low,* one of Bernard's characteristic words, also occurs once in the sections of omniscient narration that begin the chapters of the novel. Analyzing only the six monologues seems reasonable, but should words that also occur in the narration be counted as Bernard's characteristic words? (Some consider Bernard to be modeled on Woolf herself [Ramsay, *Reading Machines,* 13].) The possibility of including the omniscient third-person narration seems intriguing but problematic, not least because it has fairly well-known differences from the "speech" of the six monologues (see Biber). Including the narration would remove *low, canopy, bowled,* and *brushed* from Bernard's most characteristic words and *beast, steel,* and *discord* from Louis's. What questions does this raise? Is there a reasoned and rational way to answer them? Asking them should deepen and inform our discussion of the novel.

TF-IDF AND THE QUESTION OF A GENDER DIVISION IN *THE WAVES*

Most algorithms for computational approaches come from authorship attribution, where ostensibly correct answers exist. But Ramsay is certainly right that the existence of "correct" answers to questions like "Do the men and women speak differently?" or "Do the six characters have distinct and consistent voices?" is precisely at issue. Although these characters are literary constructs created by a single author rather than authors themselves, many studies have shown that some authors' characters can profitably be treated as if they were individuals (see Burrows, for example). Furthermore, if we attempt to distinguish individual voices where none really exist, the attempt will simply fail. Ramsay shows us provocatively that all three women share only fourteen words that are used by none of the men, but that all three men share ninety words that are used by none of the women (*Reading Machines,* 13–14):

Women-words:

shoes, Lambert, million, pirouetting, antlers, bowl, breath, coarse, cotton, diamonds, rushes, soften, stockings, wash

Men-words:

boys, possible, ends, church, sentences, everybody, Larpent, tortures, feeling, office, united, felt, rhythm, weep, heights, wheel, able, however, banker, accepted, hundred, Brisbane, act, included, ourselves, alas, inflict, poetry, approach, irrelevant, power, background, knew, arms, baker, language, destiny, banks, Latin, letters, became, meeting, lord, block, neat, poet, board, novel, reason, brake, observe, respect, burnt, oppose, telephone, central, pointing, waistcoat, certainly, sensations, beak, chose, sheer, chaos, cinders, story, difficult, clamour, suffering, endure, course, torture, forgotten, crucifix, troubling, friend, distinctions, use, god, distracted, waste, king, doctor, watched, notice, ease, willows, ordinary, edges, works

These lists are indeed provocative, as Ramsay suggests: many of the words even seem disturbingly stereotypical. He goes on to say that "critics who have argued for a deep structure of difference among the characters—one perhaps aligned along the gender axis—might also feel as if the program vindicates their impressions. Is there a gender divide? Yes; the characters are divided along the gender axis by a factor of 6.4285 to 1" (Ramsay, *Reading Machines*, 14). But he then remarks that the algorithm that produces this difference "has no more claim to truth value than any ordinary reading procedure" (14–15), and that his analysis does not settle the question of whether there is a gender divide in *The Waves*. I think this last claim is right, though not because the question cannot be settled.

Attempting to recreate Ramsay's analysis of the genders reveals a few discrepancies like those in his list of Louis's distinctive words. For example, the men-only words *banker* and *Brisbane* appear in Neville's and Bernard's monologues only as imagined quotations from Louis. My list of men-only words, unlike Ramsay's, also includes *Bernard's* because my tokenization does not break words at apostrophes. Bernard's only use of *Bernard's*, however, is in a quotation from his girlfriend, which one might consider deleting as not really Bernard's language. But the girlfriend is actually imaginary. Given that the novelist Virginia Woolf has invented the monologue of her imaginary novelist Bernard, does Bernard's invented dialogue for his imaginary girlfriend count as his "own" language? Why? Why not? I think her language should count as Bernard's here, but discussing these kinds of computationally intractable decisions, I suggest, could deepen and enrich a conversation about *The Waves*.

More significantly, Ramsay's provocative ratio of ninety men-only to fourteen women-only words rests problematically on the amounts of text by the two genders. Even without Bernard's final chapter, there are about 35,000 words by the men and only 20,000 by the women, a discrepancy that explains the preponderance of men-only words. To "prove" this one could simply cut each male monologue to the length of its corresponding female monologue. Corresponding how? Matching longest to longest, shortest to shortest? Why? I have chosen a different "deformation," randomizing the lines of each monologue and cutting each one to 6,067 words, the length of the shortest (Susan's), equalizing each character's contribution. Why? Why not just take the first 6,067 words of each? (Answer: so as not to test all of Susan's language against only the first part of the language of the other characters.) This deformed text produces thirty-one women-only and twenty-nine men-only words.

Ramsay is right that the algorithm merely begins the argument, but the provocative revelation that the men share more words than the women is deceptively and inappropriately provocative: it rests merely on the lengths of the monologues. Why the male monologues are longer is also a provocative question, especially as the monologues of all three men are longer than the longest monologue by any of the women. Nevertheless, the nature of the male and female words remains provocative and suggestive for a conversation about gender in *The Waves*:

All Men, No Women:

boys, feeling, poet, dropped, letters, waste, weep, swing-doors, office, oppose, wheel, hundred, waistcoat, however, telephone, ease, suffering, board, arms, Bernard's, sheer, beak, possible, bag, lord, approach, god, friend, able

All Women, No Men:

pavement, bedroom, stockings, wash, shoes, wander, hide, tennis, step, soften, front, shelter, settle, million, music, matter, Lambert, diamonds, fills, rushes, breath, pulls, shot, fling, real, cotton, pirouetting, coarse, branch, bowl, antlers

My deformation's doubling of women-only words raises questions of its own and warns against over-interpreting the lists. Obviously, the men use some of these women-only words in the parts I left out, a problem exacerbated by the rarity of these words: the highest frequency of any of the words I have listed is four. All this suggests a reconsideration of the initial decision to use tf-idf and a search for a method that can cope in a reasonable way with the variation in how much the characters of each gender speak.

CHARACTER-INDIVIDUALIZATION IN *THE WAVES* REVISITED

Examining *The Waves* in the light of Ramsay's provocation raises so many intriguing questions that they cannot all be addressed here, but the question of character-individualization can be revisited by using the same deformation I used for examining the men-only and women-only words. I identified the fifty most characteristic

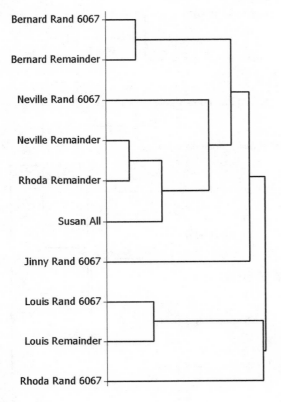

Figure 20.1. Tf-idf and Character-Individualization (words with the 20 highest tf-idf scores).

words of these six sections of 6,067 randomly chosen words from each character using Ramsay's tf-idf formula. I then tested how well they group with the remainders of the longer monologues using cluster analysis, starting with all 300 words (in descending tf-idf order), then reducing the number gradually. The best result, for the twenty most distinctive words, is shown in Figure 20.1.[5]

Bernard's and Louis's sections group together, while Neville's and Rhoda's fail (Jinny and Susan have too little text for two sections). A simple word frequency list, however, correctly groups all four in many analyses, providing a tentative answer to the question of whether the voices are distinct. (The only adjustment I made here was to base the word list on the six random 6,067-word sections only, to equalize the amount of text by each character.)

Selecting the most characteristic words for each monologue using Zeta (Craig and Kinney) also produces many perfect results (see Figure 20.2, based on the twenty most characteristic words). This very different method, which measures consistency of use rather than frequency, confirms the distinctness of the voices and, like tf-idf, also eliminates the most frequent words. It also suggests, as does the analysis of the most frequent words, that Susan's narrative is unusual compared to the others, not just shorter. Agreement between kinds of evidence gathered in two distinct ways strengthens an argument.

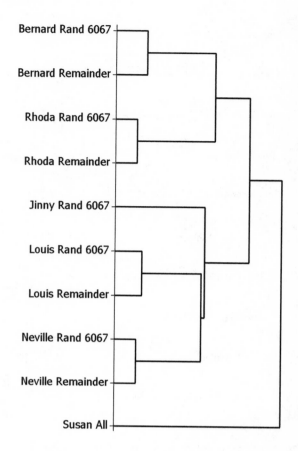

Figure 20.2. Zeta and Character-Individualization (20 most characteristic words).

Finally, testing the six characters in 2,000-word sections with two-word sequences (based on the six full monologues, minus Bernard's final chapter) also yields some completely correct clusters (see Figure 20.3 for an analysis based on the 900 most frequent two-word sequences) and reconfirms the distinctiveness of Susan's monologue.

As I have noted, Ramsay suggests that treating the question of whether the six characters in *The Waves* share "the same stylistic voice" as a problem to solve is a "category error," and that the proper question—one computers cannot answer—is "Can I interpret (or read) it this way?" (*Reading Machines*, 9–10). Critics still *can* read the novel as a single stylistic voice, and the six monologues undoubtedly share many characteristics. There is, after all, a Woolf style that should distinguish her from other authors and a *Waves* style that should distinguish it from her other novels. In spite of a host of very interesting remaining questions about the status of algorithms, arguments, and evidence, however, the bold claim that there *are* six distinct character voices in *The Waves* seems strongly confirmed. Reading them as the "same stylistic voice" should require at the very least some recognition that they are quite easy to distinguish, especially because, as more than twenty-five years of research has shown, even different authors are sometimes much more difficult

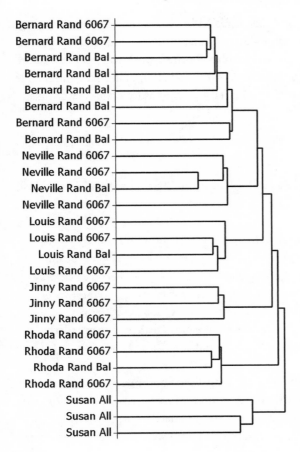

Figure 20.3. Two-Word Sequences and Character-Individualization (900 most frequent two-word sequences).

to distinguish than this.[6] An analysis of the monologues divided into 3,000-word sections and based on the 800 most frequent words suggests that the early chapters, when the characters are children, are also significantly different from the adult chapters (see also Balossi, *A Corpus Linguistic Approach,* chap. 6 and app. E). The fact that the characters do not group completely by gender in most of the analyses I have described also suggests a tentative negative answer to the question "Do the men and women speak differently?" that is different from Ramsay's answer. More analysis would be needed to see how this answer should be qualified, but the results I have described suggest that the characters are more distinct than the genders, a conclusion that agrees with much previous work (for a discussion of the strengths of various signals in texts, see Jockers, *Macroanalysis,* ch. 6). The grouping of the early sections of the text (when the characters are children) by gender suggests an intriguing direction for further research into the gender question that might be folded into Wallace's feminist discussion of the novel.

Ramsay's provocative intervention is valuable for forcing us to reexamine our methods and focus on questions of interest to traditional literary scholars. But further analysis of his provocation and his algorithms suggests that more attention to the text, to the nature and function of the algorithms, and to method can prompt bold claims that rest on a sounder foundation—claims that can improve and deepen the discussion, not just make sure it continues. Further work will help us explore the boundary between computationally tractable and computationally intractable questions and the significance of that boundary for the future of literary criticism.

Stanley Fish on Argument, Evidence, and Method in the Digital Humanities

In "Mind Your P's and B's: The Digital Humanities and Interpretation," Stanley Fish remarks, by way of introduction, that

> Halfway through "Areopagitica" (1644), his celebration of freedom of publication, John Milton observes that the Presbyterian ministers who once complained of being censored by Episcopalian bishops have now become censors themselves. Indeed, he declares, when it comes to exercising a "tyranny over learning," there is no difference between the two: "Bishops and Presbyters are the same to us both name and thing." That is, not only are they acting similarly; their names are suspiciously alike. (Fish, "Mind Your P's and B's")

He goes on to argue the phonetic similarity of *bishop* and *presbyter* and to claim that in the sentences following Milton's equation of these words "'b's' and 'p's' proliferate in a veritable orgy of alliteration and consonance."

I will return to these specific claims, but I want to start at the end of his comments and work backward. Fish says that the "interpretive proposition" that Milton believes that the censors have turned into their oppressors led him to notice the prevalence of [p] and [b] in the passage. He argues as follows:

> The direction of my inferences is critical: first the interpretive hypothesis and then the formal pattern, which attains the status of noticeability only because an interpretation already in place is picking it out.
>
> The direction is the reverse in the digital humanities: first you run the numbers, and then you see if they prompt an interpretive hypothesis. The method, if it can be called that, is dictated by the capability of the tool. (Fish, "Mind Your P's and B's")

I do not think that Fish is right that inference usually works this way in literary studies. Surely it is also quite common to notice a phrase, a plot twist, a quirk of characterization, or some other detail that acts as a discovery tool and leads to an interpretation, once further details are integrated into a coherent whole. He is certainly right that evidence only becomes fully meaningful and valuable when it is integrated into an interpretation, but just as certainly wrong that a pattern only attains "noticeability" because an already-existing interpretation is "picking it out." Surely a reader needs no interpretation to notice the alliteration at the beginning of Hopkins's "The Windhover":

I caught this morning morning's minion, king-
dom of daylight's dauphin, dapple-dawn-drawn Falcon, in his riding
Of the rolling level underneath him steady air

As in any field of inquiry, there are multiple methods and multiple approaches in digital humanities, and Ramsay's critique, as I have just discussed, has been that digital humanities is too *much* hypothesis-driven, too positivistic, too definite. Yet the example Fish critiques really is problematic. He notes that computational tools can identify patterns we cannot see for ourselves, so that we cannot know in advance what a computational analysis will show, and he suggests that digital humanities practitioners therefore proceed randomly or on whim. In the example he mentions, a computational analysis shows that nineteenth-century American fiction mentions many international locations, a fact that leads the analyst to suggest that it was more "outward looking" than previously thought. Here Fish rightly points out that we cannot know whether this claim is true without a great deal more investigation: there are many possible reasons for the presence of a large number of international locations, though probably not the "infinite" number Fish claims. I have argued, in my discussion of McGann's claim that "The Snow Man" is a noun-heavy poem, that the claim is not meaningful until we know how many nouns is normal (Hoover, "Hot-Air Textuality" and "The End of the Irrelevant Text"); similarly, the mere presence of many international locations may surprise the analyst, but that surprise is not very meaningful until we know how it compares to something other than the analyst's expectation (British novels of the same period, for example) and how the international locations function in the texts.

Fish goes on to discuss Ramsay's project of deforming texts and multiplying interpretations, and his praise of "screwing around" as a method (Ramsay, "The Hermeneutics of Screwing Around"). He concludes as follows:

But whatever vision of the digital humanities is proclaimed, it will have little place for the likes of me and for the kind of criticism I practice: a criticism that narrows meaning to the significances designed by an author, a criticism that generalizes from a text as small as half a line, a criticism that insists on the distinction between the true and the false, between what is relevant and what is noise, between what is serious and what is mere play. Nothing ludic in what I do or try to do. I have a lot to answer for. (Fish, "Mind Your P's and B's")

Those who have followed the many phases of Fish's career, especially those of us who remember "the Eskimo 'A Rose for Emily,'" may find this statement somewhat surprising. More important, many of us who have been doing digital humanities for a very long time have more in common with this orientation than Fish understands. I doubt that criticism *can* (even if it should) narrow interpretation to the author's meanings—an idea that has been very unpopular in literary criticism for a long time (including in Fish's own work), but narrowing interpretations, focusing on even the smallest details, and insisting on a distinction between what is relevant and what is noise, between "what is serious and what is mere play," are all very much mainstream in many approaches to digital humanities. Yet, even "screwing around" can be valuable as a method, and I have often argued that one benefit of digital tools and methods is that they help us to uncover details and facts that we would not have noticed otherwise.

I have argued that "mere play" is not sufficient, and although it seems unwise to "generalize" from "a text as small as half a line," as Fish says he does, it is certainly important at times to focus even on a single word. As a simple example, I have argued that the single instance of the word *arrow* in William Golding's *The Inheritors,* in which he imagines a Neanderthal society that does not use or even understand such weapons and refers to arrows many times as *twigs,* is an error (Hoover, *Language and Style,* 147–48). Although distant readings, like those of Moretti, can be valuable, I find more valuable the close readings of most work done in the previous twenty-five years of what is now called digital humanities—work that very often features detailed, minute, and hypothesis-driven analysis of texts.

ARGUMENT, EVIDENCE, AND *AREOPAGITICA*

Now I want to take up Fish's specific example and try to mind his "p's" and "b's" a little more carefully. As a consequence, he will have still more to answer for, though not in the way he suggests. As I have noted, Fish says that Milton declares that "Bishops and Presbyters are the same to us both name and thing." But consider this phrase from *Areopagitica* in context:

> if some who but of late were little better then silenc't from preaching, shall come now to silence us from reading, except what they please, it cannot be guest what is intended by som but a second tyranny over learning: and will soon put it out of controversie that Bishops and Presbyters are the same to us both name and thing. (Milton, *Areopagitica*)

Milton does not quite assert that Bishops and Presbyters are the same and that their names are suspiciously similar. It seems inappropriate to ignore the conditional future meaning of the statement. *If* these things come to pass, it will remove all question that Bishops and Presbyters are the same: a weaker foundation on which to base Fish's observation of the importance of [p] and [b]. It even seems uncertain that *name* here means the words *bishops* and *presbyters* rather than "reputation," as it does elsewhere in Milton's essay; for example, in "Dionysius Alexandrinus was . . . a person of great name in the Church for piety and learning" and "fain he would have the name to be religious, fain he would bear up with his neighbours in that."

What comes next is worse:

> In both names the prominent consonants are "b" and "p" and they form a chiasmic pattern: the initial consonant in "bishops" is "b"; "p" is the prominent consonant in the second syllable; the initial consonant in "presbyters" is "p" and "b" is strongly voiced at the beginning of the second syllable. The pattern of the consonants is the formal vehicle of the substantive argument, the argument that what is asserted to be different is really, if you look closely, the same. That argument is reinforced by the phonological fact that "b" and "p" are almost identical. Both are "bilabial plosives" (a class of only two members), sounds produced when the flow of air from the vocal tract is stopped by closing the lips. (Fish, "Mind Your P's and B's")

Are [b] and [p] really the prominent consonants in both words? The initial [b] of *bishops* and the initial [p] of *presbyter* clearly qualify, but the [p] of *bishops* is surely less prominent than the medial [sh] in the stressed first syllable (especially when the following [s] robs the [p] it of its aspiration). The [z] and [t] of *presbyters* both seem more prominent than the "b" at the beginning of the unstressed second syllable, and the first [z] is reinforced by the final [z]. The claim that the [b] of *presbyters* is "strongly voiced" is both unclear (is it spoken strongly or with strong voicing?) and doubtful. Compare the much more salient [b] of *prebendary, proboscis,* or *preboreal,* where it begins the second, stressed syllable. Furthermore, Fish never explains why chiasmus should be considered a sign of similarity rather than of difference. Still further, how significant is the chiasmus in the full consonant sequence?

[b] — [sh] — [p] [s] vs [p][r] — [z] — [b] — [t] — [r] [z]

Fish also claims that "the phonological fact that 'b' and 'p' are almost identical" reinforces his argument, ignoring the fact that the voicing difference between [p] and [b] is crucial in English and many other languages, that it also distinguishes [t] from [d], [k] from [g], [f] from [v], [s] from [z], [ch] from [j], and [sh] from [zh], making it arguably the most important difference/differance in the English consonant system. We might say that if Milton really means that the words *bishops* and *presbyters* sound suspiciously alike, he is on shaky ground.

After claiming that the sentences that follow his quotation from Milton demonstrate a "veritable orgy of alliteration and consonance," Fish gives a partial list of words containing "p" or "b" and continues as follows:

Even without the pointing provided by syntax, the dance of the "b's" and "p's" carries a message, and that message is made explicit when Milton reminds the presbyters that their own "late arguments . . . against the Prelats" should tell them that the effort to block free expression "meets for the most part with an event utterly opposite to the end which it drives at." The stressed word in this climactic sentence is "opposite." Can it be an accident that a word signifying difference has two "p's" facing and mirroring each other across the weak divide of a syllable break? Opposite superficially, but internally, where it counts, the same.

There is a wealth of confusion here, but first consider the final confused notion that *opposite* has two "p's" separated by a syllable break. This is true for print, but there is only one [p] sound in *opposite*, belonging unequivocally to the first syllable. Indeed, Fish's entire argument might seem more defensible if he concentrated on spelling rather than sound, but he repeatedly emphasizes sound, and the spelling similarity between *bishops* and *presbyters* is hardly compelling. Bishops and Prelates may be alike, but Milton's point is that the effect of censorship will truly *be* opposite from its intent. Could Milton really be using two written "p's," only one pronounced, in a word signifying difference to support the identity of *bishop* and *presbyter* based on the reversed positions of the [p] and [b] sounds in the two words? I suppose it is possible, but it is not unreasonable to hope for better kinds of argument and evidence than this. Although Fish describes his quotation from Milton as a "climactic" sentence, it is worth noting that the sentence does not end with "meets for the most part with an event utterly opposite to the end which it drives at," but rather continues, after a colon, with "instead of suppressing sects and schisms, it raises them and invests them with a reputation," and goes on to emphasize censorship's likely encouragement of the growth of sects. Can it be an accident that "suppressing" also contains two "p's" facing each other across a syllable break? Surely "yes" is a possible answer for both "suppressing" and "opposite."

Further, is it really true that the dance of [p] and [b] "carries a message"? Does Fish's list of words with these consonants constitute "a veritable orgy of alliteration and consonance"? There is no way to answer these questions without knowing if the dance and density are unusual (as Fish later suggests). And it would help if Fish gave us some rationale for his choice of what words with [p] and [b] to include in his list. If Milton is playing with contrast/similarity, should the listed words be related thematically? Should only content words count? Only stressed words? (Fish only lists nouns, verbs, and adjectives.)

Fish suggests that a full argument for his hypothesis would have to demonstrate that Milton intentionally put the pattern of [p] and [b] in the text, building an argument from the counts of the sounds to his intention and back, partly by citing other places Milton plays with sound in a similar way. Fish claims that, given only twenty-one consonants in the alphabet of twenty-six letters, he would have to "separate the patterns produced by the scarcity of alphabetic resources (patterns to which meaning can be imputed only arbitrarily) from the patterns designed by an author." Undeniably, accidental patterns must be distinguished from meaningful ones, but Fish unfortunately again equates spelling with sound here, even though he explicitly argues that Milton is playing with sound. Twenty-one of the letters of the alphabet may typically be called consonants (<y> is bit problematic), but there are not twenty-one consonants in English. Many letters represent more than one sound (<c f g s x z>, for example), and some consonants must be indicated with combinations of letters (<th>, <ch>, <sh>, <ng>), some of which also represent more than one sound (ba*th* vs ba*the*).

The mere fact that Fish noticed the prevalence of [p] and [b] in *Areopagitica* because of Milton's equation of *bishop* and *presbyter* is completely irrelevant to whether or not the question can or should be studied computationally. Fish's method of collecting evidence only after adopting a preliminary hypothesis is even somewhat problematic because of the danger of self-fulfilling prophecy, but a computational (and consistent) method of counting [p] and [b] sounds in texts is entirely compatible with Fish's method and could help him persuade us that the pattern might be intentional. I have not performed a computational analysis, but a check of many passages of the same size by Milton's contemporaries reveals passages from Joseph Hall's *An Humble Remonstrance* (a tract that Milton probably had a hand in answering) that show higher proportions of words with [p] and [b] than the passage Fish analyzes. Further, the parts of *Areopagitica* that precede the alleged equation of *bishop* and *presbyter* show proportions of [p] and [b] that are almost identical to those of the passages following it. Is this what we should expect if Milton is intentionally using a high frequency of the two sounds to imply that bishops and presbyters are the same?

I have only suggested some directions for a more comprehensive and reliable analysis of *Areopagitica*, but such an analysis would surely enhance and deepen the discussion of Fish's hypothesis that Milton is using the prevalence of [p] and [b] to argue that bishops and presbyters are the same. Digital humanities is far from being antithetical to his argument, which seems to cry out for the very precision and accuracy that computational approaches can provide.[7]

Conclusion

Digital literary studies offers no panacea, and its tools and methods can never eliminate the importance of literary intuition and close reading. There is plenty of room for a productive and vigorous discussion of what kinds of literary questions can profit from computational approaches, what kinds cannot, and what the differences between them mean for the practice of literary criticism. The results of studies using digital tools and methods must, like any results arrived at by any method, still be interpreted and must still be integrated into coherent rhetorical arguments. New methods, tools, and results must also be rigorously interrogated, questioned, tested, and replicated. Digital methods can provide new evidence and even new kinds of evidence in support of literary claims, and can make new kinds of claims possible. They can also make some claims untenable. In addition to allowing for "distant" kinds of readings of enormous collections of texts that are simply too large to be studied otherwise, the extraordinary powers of the computer to count, compare, collect, and analyze can be used to make our close readings even closer and more persuasive. Perhaps the availability of new and more persuasive kinds of evidence can also inspire a greater insistence on evidence for literary claims and push traditional literary scholars in some productive new directions. I would not argue that digital methods should supplant traditional approaches (well, maybe some of them). Instead, they should be integrated into the set of accepted approaches to literary texts.

NOTES

1. I have argued that the question of whether dictation caused the change from Henry James's early to late style is also computationally tractable (Hoover, "Modes of Composition in Henry James"). Even interpretation seems amenable to new kinds of evidence from giant natural language corpora (Louw; Hoover, *Language and Style in The Inheritors*; Hoover, "The End of the Irrelevant Text"; Hoover, "Some Approaches to Corpus Stylistics"), though some corpus approaches have more in common with postmodern theory (Hoover, Culpeper, and O'Halloran, *Digital Literary Studies*, chaps. 6–7).

2. Ramsay's initial formula is tf-idf = tf *(N/df), where "tf" is the term frequency (the frequency of the term in the corpus), "N" = the number of documents (here, the six monologues), and "df" = the document frequency (the number of documents containing the term); see Ramsay, *Reading Machines*, 11.

3. My attempt to duplicate Ramsay's results revealed that he actually uses a somewhat different formula. Many formulas exist, but for the four I tested, twenty of the twenty-five most characteristic words are the same. For similar problems reproducing Ramsay's tf-idf scores, see Forster.

4. In his brief but suggestive and valuable discussion of the monologues of *The Waves*, John Burrows goes a bit further than I have in removing pseudo dialogue from the monologues, a practice that reduces Susan's part from the 6,067 words I analyze to 5,690 (Burrows, 191, 205–7).

5. Cluster analysis is an exploratory method often used in authorship studies. There is no space here for a full discussion, but the method compares similarities and differences among the frequencies of all the words being analyzed in all of the texts and groups most closely those texts that use the words in the most similar way. The closer to the left of the graph that they form a cluster, the more similar two texts are. In Figure 20.1, Neville Remainder and Rhoda Remainder are the two most similar (the up-down proximity of Bernard Remainder to Neville Rand 6067 is not meaningful). The words are not truly

randomly chosen because I have only sorted the lines of the text using a randomizing function, but this is random enough for my purposes.

6. Lexical and semantic differences among the six monologues are strongly confirmed using quite different methodology and in much greater detail in Balossi's impressive corpus linguistics study of characterization in this novel (Balossi, *A Corpus Linguistic Approach*, see especially chaps. 6–8).

7. In a more informal context and blog post, Mark Liberman performed a quick test of Fish's claim that this section of the Milton contains a preponderance of "p" and "b" and found it (somewhat) lacking; see Liberman, "The 'Dance of the p's and b's': Truth or Noise?" This post and a succession of comments on it show that other readers were also bothered by many of the problems I cite in Fish's argument.

BIBLIOGRAPHY

Balossi, Giuseppina. *A Corpus Linguistic Approach to Literary Language and Characterization: Virginia Woolf's The Waves*. Amsterdam: John Benjamins, 2014.

Biber, Douglas. *Variation across Speech and Writing*. Cambridge: Cambridge University Press, 1988.

Burrows, John F. *Computation into Criticism*. Oxford: Clarendon Press, 1987.

Craig, Hugh, and Arthur Kinney. *Shakespeare, Computers, and the Mystery of Authorship*. Cambridge: Cambridge University Press, 2009.

Fish, Stanley. *Is There a Text in This Class?* Cambridge, Mass.: Harvard University Press, 1980.

———. "Mind Your P's and B's: The Digital Humanities and Interpretation." *New York Times*, January 23, 2013. http://opinionator.blogs.nytimes.com/2012/01/23/mind-your-ps-and-bs-the-digital-humanities-and-interpretation/?_r=0.

Forster, Chris. "With Thanks to Woolf and emacs, Reading 'The Waves' with Stephen Ramsay," February 13, 2013. http://cforster.com/2013/02/reading-the-waves-with-stephen-ramsay/.

Guillory, John. The Sokal Affair and the History of Criticism. *Critical Inquiry* 28, no. 2 (2002): 470–508.

Hoover, David L. "Hot-Air Textuality: Literature after Jerome McGann." *Text Technology* 14, no. 2 (2005): 71–103.

———. *Language and Style in The Inheritors*. Lanham, Md.: University Press of America, 1999.

———. "Making Waves: Algorithmic Criticism Revisited." DH2014, University of Lausanne and Ecole Polytechnique Fédérale de Lausanne, July 8–12, 2014.

———. "Modes of Composition in Henry James: Dictation, Style, and *What Maisie Knew*." *Henry James Review* 35, no. 3 (Fall 2014): 257–77.

———. "Some Approaches to Corpus Stylistics." In *Stylistics: Past, Present and Future*, ed. Yu Dongmin, 40–63. Shanghai: Foreign Language Education Press, 2010.

———. "The End of the Irrelevant Text: Electronic Texts, Linguistics, and Literary Theory." *Digital Humanities Quarterly* 1, no. 2 (2007). http://www.digitalhumanities.org/dhq /vol/1/2/000012/000012.html.

———. "The Trials of Tokenization." DH2015, University of Western Sydney, Australia, June 29–July 3, 2015.

Hoover, David L., Jonathan Culpeper, and Kieran O'Halloran. *Digital Literary Studies: Corpus Approaches to Poetry, Prose, and Drama.* London: Routledge, 2014.

Jockers, Matthew L. *Macroanalysis: Digital Methods and Literary History.* Urbana: University of Illinois Press, 2013.

Liberman, Mark. "The 'Dance of the p's and b's': Truth or Noise?" *Language Log*, January 26, 2012. http://languagelog.ldc.upenn.edu/nll/?p=3730.

Louw, Bill. "Irony in the Text or Insincerity in the Writer? The Diagnostic Potential of Semantic Prosodies." In *Text and Technology,* ed. M. Baker, G. Francis, and E. Tognini-Bonelli, 157–76. Philadelphia: Benjamins, 1993.

McGann, Jerome J. *Radiant Textuality: Literature after the World Wide Web.* New York: Palgrave, 2004.

Milton, John. *Areopagitica.* Available at http://www.dartmouth.edu/~milton/reading _room/areopagitica/text.shtml.

Plasek, Aaron, and David L. Hoover. "Starting the Conversation: Literary Studies, Algorithmic Opacity, and Computer-Assisted Literary Insight." DH2014, University of Lausanne and Ecole Polytechnique Fédérale de Lausanne, July 8–12, 2014.

Ramsay, Stephen. *Reading Machines: Toward an Algorithmic Criticism.* Urbana: University of Illinois Press, 2011.

———. "The Hermeneutics of Screwing Around; or What You Do with a Million Books." In *Pastplay: Teaching and Learning History with Technology,* ed. Kevin Kee, 111–20. Ann Arbor: University of Michigan Press, 2014.

Sokal, Alan D. "A Physicist Experiments with Cultural Studies." In *The Sokal Hoax: The Sham That Shook the Academy,* ed. *Lingua Franca,* 49–53. Lincoln: University of Nebraska Press, 1996.

———. "Transgressing the Boundaries: Toward a Transformative Hermeneutics of Quantum Gravity." *Social Text* 46/47 (1996): 217–52.

Wallace, Miriam L. "Theorizing Relational Subjects: Metonymic Narrative in *The Waves*." *Narrative* 8 (2000): 294–323.

Woolf, Virginia. *The Waves.* London: Hogarth Press, 1931.

Pedagogies of Race: Digital Humanities
in the Age of Ferguson

AMY E. EARHART AND TONIESHA L. TAYLOR

In their 2013 essay, "Can Digital Humanities Mean Transformative Critique?" Alexis Lothian and Amanda Phillips ask, "What would digital scholarship and the humanities disciplines be like if they centered around processes and possibilities of social and cultural transformation as well as institutional preservation? If they centered around questions of labor, race, gender, and justice at personal, local, and global scales?" (Lothian and Phillips). As digital humanities scholars invested in critical race studies, we share their concerns, and we applaud the recent work in the field that draws attention to these questions. But we are also invested in the development of a practice-based digital humanities that attends to the crucial issues of race, class, gender, and sexuality in the undergraduate classroom and beyond. Our *White Violence, Black Resistance*[1] project merges foundational digital humanities approaches with issues of social justice by engaging students and the community in digitizing and interpreting historical moments of racial conflict.[2] The project exemplifies an activist model of grassroots recovery that brings to light timely historical documents at the same time that it exposes power differentials in our own institutional settings and reveals the continued racial violence spanning 1868 Millican, Texas, to 2014 Ferguson, Missouri.

An Activist Model of Grassroots Recovery

As our cultural heritage is being transferred from print to digital form, we must ensure that we do not perpetuate known biases. In the previous volume of *Debates in the Digital Humanities,* one of this chapter's authors, Amy Earhart, critiques the digital "canon that skews toward traditional texts and excludes crucial work by women, people of color, and the GLBTQ community," advocating for an activist model of grassroots recovery projects to expand current digital offerings (316). This model could also help to allow broader participation in canon expansion. Rather than the current digital project model, one that relies on a high degree of expertise and knowledge, as well as substantial funding, grassroots recovery approaches emphasize the use of entry-level technology and broad partnerships, with particular attention to community and student participation. We select technologies with low entry points so as to encourage this range of participation. Here we disagree with those who see digital humanities projects as too complex or too difficult for introductory courses, such as Peter J. Wosh, Cathy Moran Hajo, and Esther Katz. We reject an approach that "relies more on describing and critiquing projects than examining the challenges inherent in creating digital projects," instead maintaining that embedded skills development is possible within such courses, and that undergraduates may make meaningful contributions to digital projects (Wosh, Hajo, and Katz). We are also concerned that an overreliance on high-end technologies in digital humanities projects necessarily excludes those outside of well-funded, elite academic institutions. As we watched news from Ferguson and later Baltimore, it became apparent that citizens on the ground were closest to the news and were using social media to share their experiences. We view this as a compelling reason to keep skills at an accessible level so that they can translate from the classroom to the community. In our classrooms, we teach "small" digital humanities skills such as data collection, metadata application, and analysis. We are invested in working with community activists and students, both of whom have much to add to scholarly work. Accordingly, we structure our projects to provide entry points for a range of collaborators. Ours are projects that can grow over time. The careful structuring of a classroom exercise allows for the development of an increasingly complex and sophisticated project as budgets and skills grow.

A collaborative project between this chapter's authors and the students in their respective classes at Prairie View A&M University (PVAMU) and Texas A&M University (TAMU), *White Violence, Black Resistance,* provides an important example of how grassroots projects can teach research, recovery, and digitization skills while expanding the digital canon—in this case, as it relates to race, violence, and Texas politics.[3] *White Violence, Black Resistance* privileges the recovery of historic primary sources and literary products languishing in our university special collection and archives. Accordingly, Earhart has focused on the recovery and curation of primary materials related to the Millican riot, an 1868 race riot in Texas, while Taylor has collected materials related to Prairie View A&M women. As we were collecting and digitizing these materials, the United States was hit with waves of violence against black bodies. As the murders of Mike Brown and Eric Garner made the news, our historic project gained additional contemporary significance. Activists' use of social media to document and draw attention to recent events reaffirmed our desire to include local communities in our projects. Taylor, who began to collect tweets associated with the hashtags #ICantBreathe, #BlackLivesMatter, #BLM247, #Ferguson, and #JusticeforMikeBrown, was shocked by the eerie echoes of the language used during the coverage of the Millican riot and how it was replicated in contemporary coverage of violence against African American men. It redoubled our desire to broaden the digital canon with respect to white violence and black resistance, since those issues remain crucial to our understanding of contemporary events.

By viewing our project as activist in nature, we are able to tap into alternative understandings of project development. Most digital humanities work is premised on an acquisition model, wherein a project or center must accrue money, staff, space, and hardware so as to complete meaningful digital projects. We wondered how we might, instead, think about a dispersal model, one designed to decenter traditional power structures by shifting power centers, eliminating funding needs, and reducing the necessity for advanced technical knowledge. What does it mean to create a truly student-centered project? What does it mean to rethink archival ownership? How do we redefine the relationship between scholarship and community? Might we allow subject specialists who lack high-end technical skills to participate in digital projects? *White Violence, Black Resistance* was designed to answer such questions as we leveraged expertise and resources across historical areas of divide. We also followed the lead of GO::DH co-founder Alex Gil, who argues that diversity of approach is the key to access (see also chapter 16 in this volume for Ernesto Oroza's interview with Alex Gil). Indeed, resources and support vary by borders and by institution and are fundamentally local. In our project, citizen scholarship and community interest in the recovery and analysis of historical and cultural materials provide invaluable resources. In designing our project, we have prioritized the development of a space for community activists and citizens to participate.[4]

TAMU and PVAMU: System Institutions with a Twin Past

We are acutely concerned with inequitable distributions of digital humanities resources and labor, given the divergent histories of our home institutions, Texas A&M University (Earhart) and Prairie View A&M University (Taylor). Prairie View A&M University first opened in 1876 as Alta Vista Agriculture & Mechanical College for Colored Youth, the same year that Texas A&M University was opened as the land grant Agricultural and Mechanical College.[5] During segregation, the two universities were divided by race, and they continue to be divided by resources. Though the state constitution in Texas clearly indicates that both are "universities of the first class," they have not seen the funding allocations that would realize this (Woolfolk, 27–28). Rather, the campuses continue to be marked by a separation of race and resources that constructs Texas A&M as a predominantly white (PWI) research university and Prairie View as a historically black (HBCU) teaching university.

Over the course of our collaborative project, certain practical implications of this racially charged history became apparent. For instance, Taylor discovered that the two universities have had different attitudes toward the development of special collections materials (Gabriel; Owens). Certain types of preservation were viewed as a drain on limited resources that exacerbated existing power differentials. According to an informant, the racial tensions and pressures of creating a space:

for the education of Negroes meant that keeping paper and stuff was seen as *the white man's job* [emphasis spoken]. You know something that white folks did. And could do better. You had folks that really believed that. So they thought that if they, you know, A&M, wanted to keep stuff then folks would let them. Never mind this meant they could care less about us or what really happens up here, but you know, we kept what we could when folks would know better. (Anonymous Informant No. 2)[6]

The inequitable treatment of HBCU libraries within larger university systems is a pervasive problem. Irene Owens documents the difficulties that such libraries have faced in terms of space, personnel, and collections, and the library at Prairie View A&M is no exception ("Stories Told yet Unfinished").[7] Funding issues for a variety of campus-related preservation projects at PVAMU have only recently begun to be addressed. We view our project as another way to help equalize the imbalance between institutions. For example, Taylor discovered, during her time working on the PV women's materials, that many PVAMU-related documents had been moved to the TAMU special collections. Yet the materials were often stored haphazardly in back rooms at the main campus, effectively hidden from the cataloging system and therefore from use. Through our collaboration, we have been able to find partners at both institutions to help review the collections. The Dean of TAMU has promised to return the materials pending the findings of the investigation; the process of repatriation has begun.

White Violence, Black Resistance reminds us of the range of means by which power differentials are replicated within the academy. When we selected Omeka as our platform, we each asked our institution to host the software on a campus server. Omeka is available either as a free software program that an individual or organization can install and run on a server, or as a for-fee service through which the software is hosted by the Roy Rosenzweig Center for History and Media (RRCHNM) at George Mason University. We initially hoped to install the software on our own servers, as there is greater ability to customize the site with local control. Unfortunately, hosting the Omeka software proved difficult. Texas A&M University has strict rules that prohibit faculty from running small-scale servers, making a self-run Omeka installation out of the question. Earhart's interest in using Omeka began a formal inquiry into content management systems run by the TAMU library, but at this date neither the library nor the Initiative for Digital Humanities, Media, and Culture (the IDHMC, TAMU's digital humanities center) have installed Omeka. So, institutional support of this sort of collaborative pedagogical work proves challenging at Texas A&M University. To complete the project, Earhart used her research funding to purchase access to an RRCHNM-hosted Omeka installation. Taylor, on the other hand, found Prairie View A&M University supportive of Omeka hosting due to its pedagogical applications. Taylor was able to secure the annual purchase of Omeka access through university funds for student research and faculty development, yet she was unable to persuade the university to support Omeka on its own servers due to concerns over student access to Omeka as a data curation space. The launch of the project through Omeka, then, was impacted by our universities' understandings of their respective missions—teaching versus research—and institutional rules about server access.

The divergent missions of these universities also impact the ability of their faculties to access research funding, whether through conference travel or release time. When our paper on *White Violence, Black Resistance* was accepted at Digital Humanities 2014 in Lausanne, Switzerland, for example, Taylor was unable to secure travel funding, so Earhart attended and presented the paper with Taylor skyping in to the session. But other institutional structures present greater impediments to the project's success. Taylor was able to locate a GIS specialist, Noel Estwick, who taught her students basic mapping approaches to historical data, a partnership nearly impossible at TAMU, where tenure and promotion requirements encourage faculty to privilege research productivity over pedagogical training. Through the project, we have learned that successful partnerships must circumvent the limitations of specific institutions and find strength in partnerships that remove barriers. Rather than assuming that the research institution has greater resources, our partnership reminds us that every institution can make valuable contributions to carefully constructed projects.

Such partnerships require careful management of the ownership of materials and digital content, however. Given the past history of removal of resources from PVAMU to TAMU, we carefully considered symbolic markers of ownership in the project. We decided that individual pieces of the project might be housed on the respective scholars' institutional server, but that the project website needed to be neutral, a space deliberately unaffiliated with either university in its domain registration and visual branding. We chose a Google Sites page as a federating space in which to gather our materials and eschewed institutional labels or logos.[8] Given a history of institutional exploitation, we wanted to emphasize in simple ways that Texas A&M and its affiliated faculty and students were not going to co-opt materials or work from Prairie View A&M. At the same time, we wanted to individuate the projects and give students control over their engagement with them. The discrete representation of individual digital objects within Omeka allowed students to delineate their own items while at the same time contributing to a larger project. Omeka became a bridge through which we could model student research across the two universities, emphasizing individual archival collection and collaborative moments of interaction between the classes.

DIY Digital Projects: Choosing Tech and Teaching Choices

Central to the recovery project has been a sense that historical and cultural narratives have often erased Prairie View and other primary black towns and spaces in Texas and within our university system. Will G. Thomas III and Elizabeth Lorang argue for "an alternative modality of engagement with the digital on our campuses—one built around reciprocity, openness, local community, and particularity." We view projects like our current work as a way of disrupting such erasures, using carefully constructed technological projects to spread digital cultural empowerment through both universities and student bodies. Much as we saw activists using Twitter to promote change during #BlackLivesMatter campaigns, we too see technologies as opening spaces of intervention. Here we also agree with the FemTech-Net whitepaper that Internet technology "strains the capacity for respect and the appreciation of the nuances of diverse backgrounds which increases the intensity of the work that must be done by teachers and organizers of the learning process."

To locate the voices, spaces and places where African American contributions have been most actively present, yet also actively erased or silenced, we have been careful to create digital structures that reveal rather than conceal. Such erasure, we found, occurs both symbolically and literally. Our project intervenes in current structures of production through the digitization and dissemination of materials about white violence and black resistance found buried in difficult-to-access archives, crumbling newspapers, analog and/or transcribed oral histories, and unknown journals. We focus on the recovery of cultural objects that have been underrepresented in digital archive collections, artifacts that discuss the racial violence, tensions, and other aggressions (micro and macro) in our localized Texas environment. This project brings to light the very different university and social structures in which our students reside. For Taylor's predominantly black students, the recognition of historical racism and violence against African Americans is far less surprising than it is to Earhart's predominantly white students. In Earhart's class, students often struggle to come to terms with the horrific mutilation and lynching of a black Methodist minister, Reverend George Brooks, that occurred a mere twenty minutes' drive from campus.[9] The difference in student perceptions of the Millican race riot mirrors national understandings about violence and race. After Ferguson, numerous polls showed that black and white Americans perceived race issues very differently. For example, a December 2014 Gallup poll, cited in *U.S. News and World Report,* revealed a statistically significant difference in the view of racism (Cook). The same patterns are replicated in our classrooms, reminding us of how significant it is to engage students in such complex and troubling history.

When Taylor discusses the idea of erasure with her students, she is careful to focus on how individual stories have often been silenced. As V. P. Franklin reminds in his text, *Living Our Stories,* the voices of African Americans are crucial to the American project. While the slave narrative is the first, and, Franklin argues, the only real American literary tradition, it gives birth to a power inherent in the names and naming of black lives. Franklin impresses on his reader that in the telling of the stories there is a resistance to silence and erasure. The power of the narrative is held within the black body telling the story. For students engaged in the digitization of documents, it becomes important to name as many aspects of the document, such as the author, the place of publication, and the race of the participants, as possible. This naming happens in the creation of a plain but common language system used for metadata. It also gives both Earhart and Taylor an opportunity to discuss how racial descriptors that may have once been in vogue can change over time. In conversations with students, there have been deep discussions about the use of racial descriptors that appear in historic newspapers and photo captions. So where Franklin would argue that there is power in the telling of the stories, we would assert that there is particular power in the story of metadata as a searchable discourse that expands or contradicts the data. For this reason, we encourage students to think about how the use of descriptive terms of race such as "colored," "negro," "white," and "mulatto" function historically and contemporarily, in both historical documents and our current digital project.

In Taylor's class, students worked on projects related to the Prairie View Women's Oral History Project, which redresses the fact that very few of the published histories of the university mention the women who were on the staff or faculty of the institution. Among the oral histories collected from women who have had a thirty-year or longer relationship to the university, students interviewed Dr. E. Joahanne Thomas-Smith, the longest serving upper-level woman administrator in PVAMU history.[10] Students uncovered a number of women who came to Prairie View and returned as staff or faculty members, including Lucille Bishop Smith. After finding that there was little mention of the first women who attended Prairie View A&M, students discovered evidence of a washerwoman on staff in 1878 (unnamed in the annual report) as well as female students in attendance. The project collects narratives, personal papers, photographs, and audio and video recordings related to the growth, development, and maintenance of the university, its students, faculty, staff, and surrounding community through a "deep dig" into the university archives, expanding the digitized canon of works collected and archived by the university. The items that students located were often well known to senior community members but missing from the official digital archive.

In Earhart's class, students researched a local history event, the Millican race riot of 1868, a conflict that occurred in Millican, Texas, a town located fifteen miles from Texas A&M University campus.[11] Details remain unclear, but we believe that Reverend George Brooks, a local Methodist preacher, former Union soldier, and Union League organizer, led his congregants to drive a Klan parade out of Millican, which sparked several days of conflict and the deaths of numerous black Millicans, including Brooks. The event was covered by newspapers across the globe, yet when the event is discussed by scholarship a watered-down version with glaring inconsistencies is presented. For example, in *Still the Arena of the Civil War: Violence and Turmoil in Reconstruction Texas, 1865–1874,* Mary Jo O'Rear notes that in response to the supposed lynching of Miles Brown, the black militia "took Brown's boss, plantation owner Anthony Holiday, hostage" (275). Students' research of newspaper archives, marriage documents, and Census materials reveal that the relationship between the Holiday or Halliday family and the black community is complex. Andrew and William Holiday, sons of the former Brazos County plantation owner Samuel Holiday, were involved in the riot as well as black freedmen who share the surname Holiday, suggesting that they were either owned by the Holiday family or were relatives of the white Holidays. Clearly the complexities of the local situation demand recovery to bring the riots and the participants into focus.

The *White Violence, Black Resistance* site functions as a common space for the two courses as well as a classroom space. While we are interested in producing a high-quality research project, we continue to position student learning and shared inquiry before the production of the archive. This is a crucial distinction, as we do not want to lose student agency and participatory learning in our desire for a finished site. Paul Fyfe calls the interaction between classroom and research "a terrific opportunity to join students in shared projects of inquiry and explore new aspects of the discipline" (85). To this end, we evaluate student learning based on tasks completed within a project during the course through carefully constructed markers of assessment. For example, students are asked to apply metadata to the individual items that they include in the Omeka site. To facilitate this task, we workshop the project with a metadata specialist in the library and incorporate a discussion of the limitations of metadata, which is particularly important when dealing with the complexities of race. We also ask students to write reflections on the experience of applying metadata so as to have them apply humanities interpretations to technological functions. As Lindsay Thomas and Dana Solomon note, "Asking students to use, break, and comment on a project currently in development—and then, ideally, repeating this cycle—transforms how they think about the project itself and about their roles as researchers, students, and developers." Finally, we see students as part of a process of creation and fully expect that materials that they create will undergo review and revision similar to the peer review process of scholarship. We remind students that they will be given credit for the work they produce. At the same time, we make clear that process-oriented projects mean that various partners might revise items submitted to projects, much as an editor would suggest revision to scholarly articles and books.

Here we understand digital pedagogies as closely akin to the way writing and communication has been taught. Process remains the central goal, not just product. Accordingly, students take an active role in the project, some driving to local sites related to the project to collect graveyard records and others seeking relatives whom they might interview about ties to Prairie View A&M University. Students select particular areas of interest with which to engage, giving students ownership and responsibility for constructing their own attributed sections of a larger federated site. We are focused on what E. Leigh Bonds calls a "methodology of experimentation—of teacher and student producing knowledge rather than delivering/receiving it" ("Listening in on the Conversations"). Crucial to our belief in a student-centered, activist project we follow the principles of the Collaborators' Bill of Rights for attribution.[12] Accordingly, each student was given a form to fill out that requests students opt in or out of the public display of the project. While we might require that students complete work on the project for the class for credit and grades, we must give students the right to opt out of the public display due to safety concerns or privacy issues.

A focus on points of resistance is central to student learning. Just as we as faculty collaborators interrogate moments of resistance in our partnership, we encourage students to understand how points of resistance in their own work, in the historical narrative, or the technical interface reveal crucial moments of engagement and insight. Instead of following a lockstep approach to a text, we ask the students to creatively interrogate the text within a broader context. As Ann Hawkins argues, "the textual condition I find most commonly in my students: [is] a textual boredom." By asking students to engage with the consideration of how such resistances shape knowledge, the project spurs student engagement and skills development. Omeka's use of Dublin core metadata provides one such moment of interrogation. Dublin core metadata is a fifteen element form of description that is purposefully "broad and generic" (Metadata Innovation). While the broadness of the metadata makes it broadly applicable, the danger of such a metadata form is a loss of the specific contours of certain cultural experiences. Application of metadata forces students to consider their materials as nuanced and complex. Instead of merely conducting close readings of materials, as would happen in a traditional literature or communication studies course, the application of metadata helped to push students to confront crucial concepts that we teach in our courses. For example, the software defines the creator category as "an entity primarily responsible for making the resource" (Omeka). Students questioned how to apply the creator category to newspaper article reprinted or extensively quoted in other newspaper publications. They also wondered how to attribute the creator of oral histories passed down from parent to child and preserved by the black community. Such questions help us to reframe the way that ownership becomes culturally constrained.

Most powerful is the ability of such projects to shift the relationship between student, teacher, and community. "In such networked humanities projects, . . ." notes Alan Liu, "the paradigm changes to one in which the teacher and student stop looking through the text just at each other, turn shoulder to shoulder, and both look at a different kind of project they are building together—one that, as in the case of a Web site, allows them to look *through* it to a public able to look in reverse at *them*" (314). The ability to have students work with faculty and to allow the public to view the type of work that we accomplish is powerful, particularly within the current environment of distrust of the academy. Students are interested in classroom activities that have an impact, and "there is clear evidence that students are not dominated by new media (as the NEA reports)," according to Tanya Clement, "but instead feel an increased sense of creative control and therefore a desire to participate in society and actively engage in 'generative practices' that herald social change" ("Multiliteracies").

Students who participate in our digital projects uniformly note that the work is a highlight of their college career, a project that meant something important to them and to their learning experience. The community benefits from our work as well through expanded access to the topics we are investigating. Many of the resources related to our project, such as contemporary newspaper accounts, are paywalled. As university faculty we have access to a substantial number of resources that remain unavailable to the general public, whether digital, such as digital newspaper databases, or physical, the permission to examine archives. As we have received feedback from the interested public regarding our project, it is clear that the inequities of access have impacted what the interested novice might be able to learn about these events. Hence, we have focused on collecting and making open access to primary resources related to the events we are exploring.

Our work has revealed that the print record tells only one piece of the story of such racial conflicts, so we have turned to the local community to flesh out the record through oral histories. Contemporary newspaper reports give the numbers of dead in the Millican riot from zero to sixty persons. Oral histories from the local black community suggest that the number was far greater than reported. By including oral histories we present other stories and perspectives, learning from local communities with long memories of such events. Such projects encourage our students to interact with the community, to move off of the campus grounds, while also expanding their understanding of cultural and historical events. The opportunity to work with the community also provides student agency. Saklofske, Clements, and Cunningham note that "students need not only collaborate with academic colleagues, but also with their wider community. The mutable nature of the digital environment demands flexibility, so that students can be allowed to bring their own ideas, knowledge, questions and topics into the learning environment, as opposed to the strict set of guidelines that might be imposed by an instructor of administration." While acknowledging that such freedom could seem "daunting" to students, "we must recognize various means of knowledge contribution through unique and differing methods of communications" (Saklofske, Clements, and Cunningham). For students this has meant a greater connection to the events and people of the past. Moreover, students are empowered to think critically about the ways that *not* digitizing the stories of the local community further silences them. Students working with the Prairie View Women's Oral History Project recognize that Prairie View's rural location and agricultural focus allows for a localized knowledge of history that is often invisible to those outside the university community. Curating digital exhibits with the aid of community members provides needed institutional and social memory context. To ensure that local knowledge is not exploited or misrepresented, projects are created in collaboration with community members and the faculty member.[13] Of course, a connection to the local community needs to be carefully navigated. Given the historical past of our universities, community members rightly fear exploitation. Any connections to the community need to be carefully built, paying attention to power dynamics.

At a moment where black bodies are under threat, attention to the historical roots of such violence is crucial. Through the engagement of students and the community *White Violence, Black Resistance* creates a digital record of past violations that have a direct impact on how we understand Ferguson, Mike Brown, Trayvon Martin, and other such contemporary events. Student exploration of the historical events through primary documents provides an important space for students to come to terms with such events and to position these historical events in relationship to current events. The creation of digital canons where such events are erased allows us to believe that such acts are random occurrences of a few individuals rather than systemic actions that have origins within American culture. Through careful attention to historical inequities within our institutions, with the attention to power dynamics between students, faculty, the university, and our communities, our project provides a model of digital humanities engagement with complex issues of race and social justice while also providing needed expansion of the digital record.

NOTES

1. http://sites.google.com/site/bkresist.

2. *White Violence, Black Resistance,* https://sites.google.com/site/bkresist/.

3. Currently, the digital canon is skewed by the types of projects that seem most likely to receive funding. Funding is often reliant on granting agencies that must make decisions based on impact. Impact is often measured by interest in a subject or author, which means that better-known authors, more canonical authors, are necessarily more likely to be funded than those seemingly noncanonical or lesser-known authors. Jessica DeSpain and Elizabeth Lorang have tracked NEH funding awards and argue that "from 2006–2016, the combined totals of Digital Humanities Start-up Grants, Implementation Grants, Digging into Data Grants, and Fellowships, as well as Collaborative and Scholarly Editions and Translations Grants indicate that out of 691 grants, only 34 have women's work as a subject—5 percent of funded projects. The statistics for grants considering underrepresented cultures is slightly higher, at 14 percent."

4. Other digital projects are built on community interaction. See *History Harvest,* http://historyharvest.unl.edu, and *eBlack Champaign Urbana,* http://eblackcu.net. Thank you to Paul Fyfe for suggesting these resources. We are also exploring partnerships within our community. One local group, the Camptown Texas Ten Counties Historical Explorers, has a history of exemplary work in documenting African American experiences in Texas. They have successfully documented the Camptown Cemetery in Brenham, Texas, and have been working to obtain historical markers to commemorate the Millican riot and other black history events. The knowledge possessed by individuals who participate in the group is rich and often underestimated by scholars.

5. Prairie View A&M University became a land grant university in 1890 when the Morrill Act was expanded to include "Negro-Land Grant Institutions."

6. Participants in the Prairie View Women's Oral History Project are allowed to choose to have their interviews remain confidential; in some cases the names of participants are withheld by mutual agreement.

7. Owens also has a helpful discussion of the inequitable treatment of HBCU libraries.

8. We recognize that the choice of Google as a neutral space runs counter to many in digital humanities who are concerned with Google's control and ownership of materials. Our project, however, uses Google as the federating space, with project and partnership descriptions linking to individual project materials housed on other servers.

9. Contemporary newspaper reports indicate that Brooks was mutilated before lynching. Reverend George Brooks's body was only identifiable by his previously missing finger on his right hand (Nevels, 21).

10. Dr. Flossie M. Byrd is the second longest serving woman administrator with twenty-seven years of service (she was a Dean of the College of Home Economics for twenty-three years). Mrs. R. B. Evans is likely the third longest serving woman administrator as Dean of Women, and Dr. Thomas-Smith is the longest, as her appointment in administration is ongoing. Dr. Thomas-Smith was Provost and Senior Vice President of Academic Affairs for eighteen years. She served in administrative roles for nearly thirty-nine years and has been at PVAMU for forty-seven years.

11. The town is located 36.5 miles from Prairie View, Texas.

12. Collaborators' Bill of Rights, NEH whitepaper, http://mith.umd.edu/offthetracks/recommendations/.

13. Just under half of the students that have participated in the curation and collection work on the Prairie View Women's Oral History Project have had one or more family member(s) previous attend PVAMU. The majority of these students were not from the Prairie View or Waller County communities. So while they had an intimate family connection to the university, they tended to not have the same familiarity with the surrounding community. This required both students and professor to think more critically about the connections to community and the location of narratives.

BIBLIOGRAPHY

Anonymous Informant no. 2. Interview by T. L. Taylor. *Prairie View Women's Oral History Project,* March 2014.

Bonds, E. Leigh. "Listening in on the Conversations: An Overview of Digital Humanities Pedagogy." *CEA Critic* 76, no. 2 (July 2014). https://muse.jhu.edu/login?auth=0&type=summary&url=/journals/cea_critic/v076/76.2.bonds.pdf.

Clement, Tanya. "Multiliteracies in the Undergraduate Digital Humanities Curriculum: Skills, Principles, and Habits of Mind." In *Digital Humanities Pedagogy: Practices, Principles, and Politics,* ed. Brett D. Hirsch. Cambridge, Mass.: Open Book Publishers, 2012. http://www.openbookpublishers.com/htmlreader/DHP/chap15.html.

Cook, Lindsey. "Blacks and Whites See Race Issues Differently." *U.S. News and World Report, Data Mine* (blog), December 15, 2014. http://www.usnews.com/news/blogs /data-mine/2014/12/15/blacks-and-whites-see-race-issues-differently.

DeSpain, Jessica, and Elizabeth Lorang. Unpublished NEH Grant Application, 2015.

Earhart, Amy E. "Can Information Be Unfettered? Race and the New Digital Humanities Canon." In *Debates in Digital Humanities*, ed. Matthew K. Gold, 309–18. Minneapolis: University of Minnesota Press, 2012.

Earhart, Amy E., and Toniesha L. Taylor. *White Violence, Black Resistance*. http://sites .google.com/site/bkresist.

"FemTechNet Whitepaper." *FemTechNet Commons*. http://femtechnet.newschool.edu.

Franklin, V. P. *Living Our Stories, Telling Our Truths: Autobiography and the Making of African-American Intellectual Tradition*. New York: Oxford University Press, 1996.

Fyfe, Paul. "How to Not Read a Victorian Novel." *Journal of Victorian Culture* 16, no. 1 (2011): 84–88.

Gabriel, Jamillah R. "Academic Libraries at Historically Black Colleges and Universities." Unpublished paper, 2009. http://academia.edu.

Gil, Alex. "Global Perspectives: Interview with Alex Gil." *4humanities: Advocating for the Humanities*. http://4humanities.org/2013/01/interview-with-alex-gil/.

Hawkins, Ann R. "Making the Leap: Incorporating Digital Humanities into the English Classroom." *CEA Critic* 76, no. 2 (July 2014). https://muse.jhu.edu/login?auth=0&type= summary&url=/journals/cea_critic/v076/76.2.hawkins.pdf.

Liu, Alan. *The Laws of Cool: Knowledge Work and the Culture of Information*. Chicago: University of Chicago Press, 2004.

Lothian, Alexis, and Amanda Phillips. "Can Digital Humanities Mean Transformative Critique?" *Journal of e-Media Studies* 3, no.1 (2013). http://journals.dartmouth.edu /cgi-bin/WebObjects/Journals.woa/1/xmlpage/4/article/425.

"Metadata innovation." *Dublin Core Metadata Innovation*. http://dublincore.org.

Nevels, Cynthia S. *Lynching to Belong*. College Station: Texas A&M Press, 2007.

Omeka. http://omeka.net.

O'Rear, Mary Jo. "A Free and Outspoken Press: Coverage of Reconstruction Violence and Turmoil in Texas Newspapers, 1866–1868." In *Still the Arena of Civil War: Violence and Turmoil in Reconstruction Texas, 1865–1874*, ed. Kenneth W. Howell, 267–84. Denton: University of North Texas Press, 2012.

Owens, Irene. "Stories Told yet Unfinished." *Journal of Library Administration* 33, no. 3–4 (2001): 165–81.

Saklofske, Jon, Estelle Clements, and Richard Cunningham. "They Have Come, Why Won't We Build It? On the Digital Future of the Humanities." In *Digital Humanities Pedagogy: Practices, Principles, and Politics*, ed. by Brett D. Hirsch. Cambridge, Mass.: Open Book Publishers, 2012. http://www.openbookpublishers.com/htmlreader/DHP/chap13.html.

Thomas, Lindsay, and Dana Solomon. "Active Users: Project Development and Digital Humanities Pedagogy." *CEA Critic* 76, no. 2 (July 2014). http://muse.jhu.edu /login?auth=0&type=summary&url=/journals/cea_critic/v076/76.2.thomas.html.

Thomas, Will G., III, and Elizabeth Lorang. "The Other End of the Scale: Rethinking the Digital Experience in Higher Education." *Educause Review,* September 15, 2014. http://er.educause.edu/articles/2014/9/the-other-end-of-the-scale-rethinking-the-digital-experience-in-higher-education.

Woolfolk, George. *Prairie View: A Study in Public Conscience 1878–1946.* New York: Prager 1962.

Wosh, Peter J., Cathy Moran Hajo, and Esther Katz. "Teaching Digital Skills in an Archives and Public History Curriculum." In *Digital Humanities Pedagogy: Practices, Principles, and Politics,* ed. Brett D. Hirsch. Cambridge, Mass.: Open Book Publishers, 2012. http://www.openbookpublishers.com/htmlreader/DHP/chap03.html.

Here and There: Creating DH Community

MIRIAM POSNER

round springtime, when universities are making offers for jobs that start in the fall, I tend to get a few similar e-mails. I am junior enough that I know a lot of people just leaving grad school (whether from library school, a PhD program, or a master's program) and as universities continue to build DH centers, these people are getting snapped up to help spark DH activity elsewhere. So around May, they are e-mailing me (and probably a lot of other people, too) to ask: Where do I start? What do I need to know?

I have been frank about what I think of taking someone fresh out of grad school, giving her a temporary gig, and expecting her to be the sole torchbearer for some amorphous DH initiative.[1] In brief, it is a bad idea, for a lot of different reasons. It is not fair to the person the institution is hiring, because she will spend her entire tenure trying desperately to impress you at this impossible task so that she can keep her job. And it is not fair to that person's university community, which deserves continuity, focus, and the attention of someone who cares about the big picture.

But a number of people have good gigs that involve an element of community-building. And there are also a lot of people who have been working in libraries or other units for some time and are newly tasked with the responsibility of building interest in and capacity for digital humanities on their campuses.

So for a while now, I have had a mental list of things that I tell my friends who are getting started on the job of building a DH initiative on their campus. If at all possible, I try to do it over a drink. This work is not easy, and it is very sensitive, and I have only learned what I know by making terrible mistakes. So in a minute, I will give you that list of suggestions for building and sustaining a digital humanities community at a university.

But first, I wanted to talk briefly about what I think it means to create a community. We often use the term to describe a group of people who are fairly like-minded or interested in the same goal. I am not sure, though, that this is the definition that is important to me. At UCLA, for example, that would not necessarily work, because we are all so different. In fact, my favorite thing about UCLA is that our students come from everywhere. LA is the home of the Korean taco and the bacon-wrapped matzo ball. I have been inspired and energized by this diversity, and it has helped inform my ideas about what it means to be a community.

For me, community happens when people are genuinely invested in seeing each other succeed. This does not happen by being nice to each other—although there is nothing wrong with that, per se. It happens by recognizing and rewarding other people's work. We depend too much in the academy on the currency of prestige and what some have called "*hope labor*"[2]—the idea that it is okay for your labor not to be rewarded now, because it may pay dividends down the road (Kuehn and Corrigan). The unpaid internship is the classic example. A durable community forms when people are valued and rewarded for their labor, and it worries me that in the excitement of doing digital humanities, people's labor sometimes gets erased. This is why I will not circulate unpaid internship announcements to our students and why I won't accept volunteer help, even though we have no program budget to speak of. If labor is valuable, the university should reward it, and we all should recognize it, too.

There are times when the notion of community seems meaningless or even oppressive to me, especially as it becomes dispersed across time and space and used as a way to determine whether someone is recognizably one of us. But on the ground, with people I work with, then, yes, it does matter. In fact, many days, it is the *only* thing that matters to me, including digital humanities or the university as an enterprise or whatever. It is a way of measuring whether I am fulfilling my obligations to other people, and they to me. And if I am not, then I do not really see the point of continuing. "Creating community" is really a method of asking myself, Are the people I interact with recognized, valued, and attended to? Of course, I fail at this all the time—we all do, we are human—but a durable community, the kind I care about, recognizes that people are fallible but connected to each other, bound by ties of mutual respect and obligation that are stronger than niceness or civility.

That said, beyond rewarding people for their work and recognizing their essential humanity, there are some basic rules I have learned over the years for helping people to create connections with each other while building a digital humanities program. A lot of these rules, I think, could apply to building any new program.

You Are a Disruption in the Force

When people anticipate challenges to getting DH activity off the ground, they often anticipate technophobia (which, as I will explain, is a fairly misguided fear) or a dearth of technical expertise. But let's be real. If anyone sees you as a threat, it is because you represent a shift in the institution's power balance. Your time is an investment the university is making and, through no fault of your own, that investment may come from withdrawing an investment somewhere else. Or—again, through no fault of your own—you may be seen as the entering wedge for a new program conceived by a controversial administrator. You cannot control this, but it is important to understand the larger social and political context of the institution so that you can try to address the real source of people's concerns.

Go to Coffee with One New Person Every Week

The best way to get to know more people is to be a human being who is interested in other human beings. A lot of us academic types are introverts—myself included—and there is always something kind of terrifying about going to coffee with no particular agenda to talk to someone who may or may not like you. But I find that it is helpful to give yourself a little quota. E-mail one person per week and then cross that task off your list. This can seem trivial, but you will be surprised at what a difference it makes. People really appreciate the gesture, even if the coffee itself is kind of awkward. Months later, they remember that you made the effort and that you expressed interest in what they are doing.

Promise Nothing

So now that you are going out to coffee with new people every week, the temptation is to agree to whatever they want you to do, so that they will like you. Resist! You are on a listening tour. You are sympathetic, you are interested, but you are not making any promises. This is not just so that you will avoid being burdened with tasks too soon. It is also because the single most damaging thing a new campus unit can do is to break its promises. Goodwill and reputation are irreplaceable. If you agree to something you cannot actually do, you have broken people's trust.

Obtaining Server Space Is the Hardest Computing Problem in the World

You are ready to dig in and want to test something out, so you just need to throw up a quick WordPress instance to test a plugin. All the server administrators have to do is give you some server space. And the next thing you know, it is five years later and you are still hammering out details of the MOU and wondering what happened to the person you used to be.

It is the most hilariously awful problem in doing DH at a university, and almost nobody has got this figured out. I know people who are secretly running servers under their desks, buying their own server space, or running projects off Google Drive. On the one hand, it is completely absurd, because how in God's name are you supposed to do anything if you cannot put stuff on the Web? On the other hand, it is a problem that goes to the heart of one of the most difficult questions DH is dealing with right now—specifically, who is going to deal with the damn thing down the road? If your site gets hacked, are you expecting the sysadmins to leap out of bed at three in the morning to fix it? My advice—which I believe originally comes from Bethany Nowviskie—is to request a virtual private server and offer to sign a memorandum of understanding stating that you are expecting no support or maintenance of anything on the server. To this, I would add that, realistically, you should expect the process of getting server space to take at least a year. Yes, I am serious. This is why I encourage people who are negotiating their new DH jobs to try to negotiate for server space in their hiring package.

Work with the Existing Culture

When you are getting something off the ground, it is a really smart idea to work with models that are already familiar to people at your university. For example, if the humanities center offers working groups, you might propose one on the digital humanities. If there is a standing faculty meeting, present there rather than holding your own meeting. If there is an existing program for pedagogy grants, perhaps you can team up with that organization to offer a grant for DH courses. You want your initiative to be legible and to fit in with the existing system of incentives at your university.

Nobody Comes to Workshops

This is hyperbolic, and there are a lot of exceptions, but if you raise the issue of DH training among veterans, chances are, you will hear this refrain from a good number of people. It really seems like people *should* come to workshops, because they *say* they want to learn new skills. If you survey people, they will say that skill building is their number-one priority. And yet. You offer the damn workshop and no one shows up. It is the worst. So if faculty, staff, and students say they want workshops, why don't they come? I think that even if people are unwilling to articulate it, there are a few reasons workshops do not work:

1. It is a one-shot. Things seem so clear in the moment, with an instructor there, and then you get home and the data has not been prepared or cleaned for you, or you come up with a question and there is no one to ask. I am afraid I think workshops are just of fairly limited utility, in terms of building skills. They can be quite effective in sparking people's interest and broadcasting what your unit can offer, but for giving people a solid foundation in a new skill, workshops are too brief.
2. They are not tied to work people actually care about, when they care about it. People tend not to *know* they will need OpenRefine a few weeks down

the road—until it becomes incredibly urgent to clean up a spreadsheet. It is really hard for people who are starting out to anticipate the obstacles they will encounter until they are faced with them.

3. Their efficiency works against them. If you have put together a workshop, you know how much work it is. You have to get the dataset, clean the dataset, put it somewhere people can find it, troubleshoot the software, plan out the steps, etcetera, etcetera. You *have* to do this if you want to get through all the material in an hour. But guess what? THAT PREP WORK IS WHAT DOING DH IS. All that garbage prep work is what we spend most of our time doing. This seamless processing of data is a fantasy world!

4. You do not have a relationship with the instructor or participants. Most people are basically interested in other people. Most people at a university are kind of desperate for a low-stakes way to get to know and hang out with people. Workshops just aren't it—you meet with a bunch of strangers and never see them again.

At UCLA, we have had better success with immersive training—dedicated days or even weeks that people have set aside to train themselves. After a year of unattended workshops, I was shocked when we announced registration for a two-day grad-student bootcamp[3] and had to close registration in an hour because we were full. The demand is there—we just were not offering the training in the right format. This kind of training is effective because it is intensive and people clear the decks for it—but it is also effective because it is fun. People want to hang out with and get to know other people who are interested in similar things, and that is just not going to happen in an hour-long library workshop. A two-day long bootcamp, and even a week-long training opportunity, is not the ideal. The ideal is long-term collaboration with people you come to know and trust over the years. So I would recommend following up an immersive training event with a working group or some other regular meeting place where people can see each other and continue to build relationships.

Think about Your Follow-Through

In my experience, people see places like the University of Virginia Scholars' Lab and the Roy Rosenzweig Center for History and New Media at George Mason University and get really excited about stickers and cool websites and T-shirts. Those places have fantastic outreach, and when people are starting up a center, they want to mimic them. But what is less obvious is that all those places spend a ton of energy building the infrastructure that allows them to actually deliver on the promise of their publicity. You need to know what you can and cannot offer to people before you hang out your shingle. This is another case where I say: Take it slow, take it steady, and really listen to people. What kind of help can you really offer people? If it is consultations, great—but what are the limits of that help? Can people expect you to be on call for years down the road? If it is visiting people's classrooms, that is great, too—but does that mean you will be answering students' e-mails and helping design assignments? Be clear about what you can and cannot offer people, and be frank about your limitations. Keep track of the unmet needs of people in your community so that you can make a case to get the support you need to meet them later. Again, take it slow, start small, and stay human.

Go Where the Deals Get Made

If you care about outreach, you need to go where faculty and students are. While it is a nice gesture to hold a mixer at the library, this is not where the wheeling-and-dealing happens. It happens at department talks and lectures and screenings. You have to go to these events if you want people to notice you and take you seriously, particularly faculty and grad students. Showing up to a seminar or lecture demonstrates to people that you are interested in being part of their community, too, and when you show that you are engaged and asking good questions, it demonstrates that you do, in fact, get what the humanities is—you are not just a Twitter account and a smartboard operator.

Survey Sparingly and with Skepticism

Libraries in particular love to do surveys, and in some ways it seems like the most natural thing in the world to find out what people want from your DH center. But I will tell you right now what people want: they want you to scan their stuff and enter data for them. Maybe someone should be doing that for people, but it is not what a DH center needs to be doing. If we just did what people told us they wanted, we would be answering people's e-mail and picking up their library books. You need to have a strong sense of the community you want to build, and you need to be forceful in articulating it. Don't wait for people to tell you what to do—do what you know is right. Here, I find Bethany Nowviskie's notion of *"lazy consensus"* really helpful.[4] If no one else cares enough to weigh in on a decision, you make it. You do not need the entire university to vote on it.

Erase the Words "Luddite" and "Technophobia" from Your Vocabulary (Unless You Study the Nineteenth-Century British Working Class)

There are a lot of reasons people may not be super-stoked about a new DH center, and it is frankly lazy to attribute these concerns to a fear of technology. In my experience, people who truly just fear technology are pretty few and far between. I am not even sure I have ever met someone like that. The *much* more likely scenario is that people, especially faculty, consider digital humanities flash-in-the-pan Dean candy. This is probably the most pressing criticism you will face, and you need to take it very seriously. DH has been complicit with some of the over-the-top rhetoric about what it can do—if not by outright making exaggerated claims, then by not objecting when reporters and administrators call us the next big thing. Understandably, there is now a lot of fallout from that inflated rhetoric. So how do you respond? By being a human being. By demonstrating that you care about the humanities more than you care about the digital. By going to people's talks and asking good questions and continuing to read and think and demonstrate that you care about being a good citizen of your university. Most important, by not assuming that people who do not like DH are being irrational. You won't win everyone over, but that's okay. Your job is not to win a popularity contest, and you can respond much more substantively to people's concerns if you learn not to take them personally. I often have to repeat to myself, "People's beef is with digital humanities; it is not with me, Miriam Posner, the human being."

Find Your Librarian Allies

Some but not all DH jobs are based in the library. Either way, librarians can be your best friends. They know how the university works, they are the world's experts on the art of gentle persuasion, and they know how stuff actually gets done. In addition to all that, they know things that you need to know. If you are going to do a digital project well, you need to adhere to basic principles of information science, like metadata standards and the organization of data. Librarians know this, and you need them to help you with it. Librarians are your natural allies, even though, as I have said elsewhere,[5] the library as an institution is not always the most congenial place to do DH.

Beware the Flash

There is an anxiety in the air right now about coming up with the best, brightest, shiniest DH project that gets featured in the *New York Times*. This worry is particularly acute if your DH unit is trying to prove itself, and even more pressing if your own job is contingent. You need people to notice what you are doing so that they will keep paying you to do it. There are some great projects out there that are really eye-catching and big and cool. But for the most part, I do not think these projects are the right choices for places that are just starting out.

In a way, this is a question about what you want. Do you want a small set of superstar faculty with awesome projects? Or do you want a community of people who learn together, support each other, and trust each other? My preference is for the latter, even though it is not as shiny. You don't get NEH start-up grants for showing people how to build Omeka exhibits and make maps, but why on earth are we building these tools if we don't want people to use them? So when, in your first year, someone comes to you with a sprawling monster of a project that will eat up all of your resources, I say *run*. Or, more precisely, don't run—but work with that person to come up with a plan for starting very small and scaling up as capacity grows. This means, incidentally, that your institution needs to have some tolerance for a ramp-up period, which is part of why I think hiring a contingent person to start a DH program is a bad idea.

Remember Why You Are Doing DH

I know as well as anyone that in the jostling for prestige and budget that comes with working in a university, it is easy to forget why you got into this field in the first place. But teaching reminds me why I am doing it at all. For me, my job is about the students. Everything else is noise. Loud noise, sometimes, but noise. There are other reasons universities exist, like to support research and preserve knowledge and serve the larger community. And maybe those are your reasons for getting into the digital humanities. The important thing is to remind yourself that you are not doing it to build one project or your center's brand. You are doing this work to serve the larger functions that universities are supposed to perform. This helps me prioritize my work and when I am tired and frustrated, it keeps me going. In the end, my loyalty is not to the digital humanities—it is to knowledge, and sharing knowledge.

They say if you love something, you need to be prepared to let it go. I love the digital humanities—it has been incredibly generous to me professionally, and I have mentors who care about my success with a warmth I did not anticipate or deserve. But I have responsibilities on the ground, too, to the people in my immediate community. And if digital humanities as it is articulated elsewhere is not right for what my community needs, then there are times I need to let it go.

And of course, the nice part is that a commitment to one's local environment can only make DH as a whole stronger, and weirder, and more durable. Slow, small, and human are strange watchwords for a field that is distinctive for its speed, size, and technology. But they are not bad guidelines for connecting people together.

NOTES

This essay was first delivered on September 18, 2014, at the Digital Frontiers conference (University of North Texas) and published on Miriam Posner's blog the same day.

1. "The Digital Humanities Postdoc," *Miriam Posner's Blog*, May 7, 2012, http://miriamposner.com/blog/the-digital-humanities-postdoc/.

2. http://www.polecom.org/index.php/polecom/article/view/9.

3. http://dhbasecamp.humanities.ucla.edu/bootcamp/.

4. "Lazy Consensus," *Bethany Nowviskie* (blog), March 10, 2012, http://nowviskie .org/2012/lazy-consensus/.

5. http://www.escholarship.org/uc/item/6q2625np.

BIBLIOGRAPHY

Kuehn, Kathleen, and Corrigan, Thomas F. "Hope Labor: The Role of Employment Prospects in Online Social Production." *The Political Economy of Communication* 1, no. 1 (May 2013). http://www.polecom.org/index.php/polecom/article/view/9/64.

The Sympathetic Research Imagination: Digital Humanities and the Liberal Arts

RACHEL SAGNER BUURMA AND ANNA TIONE LEVINE

The field of digital humanities has seen an increasing interest in the theory and practice of the preparatory, intermediate steps of the research process. The slow, interpretive, and unglamorous aspects of DH work—data cleaning and corpus preparation and even metadata management—are increasingly acknowledged and even celebrated as valuable and central. Despite the field's well-known and much-debated emphasis on "making tools," with its corresponding privileging of deliverable products, DH has come to strongly value not just open access to tools or datasets, but openness of process.[1] This emphasis on the visibility and significance of process coheres around the particularities and idiosyncratic features of the workflows of both personal and collective research. And digital humanities practices like the use of open research notebooks, the publication of Zotero libraries, and the sharing of research artifacts on new platforms also have strong affinities with the recent renewal of interest in the longer history of related practices in the humanities—histories of note-taking, intersections between humanities work and information science, and media archaeologies.[2] These fields of study share a common project: making the labor and practices that constitute the history and present of humanities research visible and communicable on a human scale.

This emphasis on the value of the research process has another, if less widely recognized, home, one we want to claim as an alternative intellectual origin for digital humanities work: liberal arts classrooms of all kinds in all sorts of institutions.[3] Undergraduate research has long emphasized process over product, methodology over skills, and multiple interpretations over single readings.[4] Our current understanding of the role of research as a part of liberal arts education has been shaped by an accident of institutional history, one in which the departmentalized structure of the research university came to be awkwardly yoked to a generalist undergraduate liberal arts education designed to form citizens, not train professional scholars. Cohering around discipline-specific majors and organized primarily around departments, the liberal arts curriculum resolves its apparent contradictions by asking students to engage in imagining what it means to "think like" a literary critic, an anthropologist, or a computer scientist. This "thinking like" involves a crucial suspension of disbelief—what might be described as a sympathetic imagining—since most English, anthropology, and computer science majors will neither become professional scholars nor take jobs significantly shaped by the particular practices of their undergraduate academic fields of study.

Liberal arts learning therefore requires a simultaneous commitment to and distance from a student's chosen field(s) of study.[5] But the practice of liberal arts can transform this odd positioning into an advantage; seeing some aspects of a field or discipline as it is, students also see it and even experience it as it could otherwise be. Practicing basic lab methods, learning to cite in a specific disciplinary style, tracking an article's sources back to an archive, or conducting an ethnographic interview all require a student to envision a range of possible practices and outcomes—to learn, but also to partly reimagine, the iterative, recursive, and enduring aspects of the research process and its shaping conventions.

Seeing the research process both as it is for oneself and as it might be for someone else—what we might think of as a sympathetic research imagination—also lies at the core of archive-centric digital humanities projects.[6] Such projects, which offer new curations and organizations of digital texts, objects, metadata, and other artifacts, also have a double mission. By defining a domain or parameters for what they include, what access they allow, and how they organize and present their data, they create new knowledge formations or bring to light materials that have been undernoticed, hidden, or excluded from existing scholarly or public narratives. At the same time, they offer users the ability to reorganize materials in order to build their own narratives and interpretations—to imagine how the archive might be read differently. Some have even suggested that the chief value of such projects is the degree of "interactivity offered to users who wish to frame their own research questions" (Unsworth). Framing new constellations of texts and artifacts as contributions to knowledge, digital archives allow researchers of all kinds to parse and reorganize the archive's contents in order to create new interpretations.

The same sympathetic research imagination we find in the liberal arts classroom—that double imagining of a discipline's research practices and protocols from within and without, for oneself and for imagined others—also governs both the high-level decisions about and the day-to-day work of such archival projects. Building an archive for the use of other researchers with different goals, assumptions, and expectations requires sustained attention to constant tiny yet consequential choices: "Should I choose to ignore this unusual marking in my transcription, or should I include it?" "Does this item require a new tag, or should it be categorized using an existing one?" "Is the name of the creator of this document data or metadata?" "Does this occurrence 'count' as the type of event I'm attempting to record?"

"Which of these fields will be available as facets for search?" "Is it ethical to open this particular version of this document to public view? And is it legal?" The ability to envision multiple research processes and imagine potential research questions becomes central as contributors evaluate how their decisions open up or close down possibilities for the project's audience. The liberal arts research imagination guides and informs the often-tedious yet only seemingly rote process of data entry, transcription, and debugging, the sometimes disenchanting but crucially important backbone of digital archive projects.

Black Liberation 1969[7]—a project chronicling Swarthmore College's black protest movement during that year—offers an example of a digital archive of primary sources and historical interpretations, one created by collaboration between faculty, students, librarians, and information technologists within the context of a liberal arts college.[8] It is led by Swarthmore Professor Allison Dorsey, in collaboration with Swarthmore Digital Scholarship and Initiatives Librarian Nabil Kashyap, the students of the Black Liberation 1969 class, and student and alumni research assistants.[9] Built with the kind of research imagination we have described, the site's design as well as its interpretive materials work to make the creators' choices as transparent as possible while also remaining usable to researchers engaging with the primary sources. *Black Liberation 1969* has a specific mission—to "finally [bring] forward the experiences of the black students who organized and executed a series of nonviolent direct actions and negotiations at Swarthmore College" in 1969—but its guiding directive is pointedly open-ended. The project documentation explains that it "challenges visitors to reconsider the stories that have previously constituted the official narrative and to engage with the black experience of Swarthmore in this critical period." Rather than offer a single counter-narrative to users, the project creates room for multiple readings by offering new material for researchers to explore and use. *Black Liberation 1969* formalizes this mission in its organizational distinction between "collections,"[10] which maintain "the organization of the documents as they were originally found," and "exhibits,"[11] which are student-curated topical presentations of collections that provide visitors with interpretations and visualizations of the different events and struggles of this period.

The history of the *Black Liberation 1969* project illustrates how the materials of a research project might be gathered by students, professors, and librarians into a liberal arts classroom and then be transformed for an expanded audience that might use them to build new narratives of their own or make narratives previously submerged by a dominant institutional narrative newly visible. The first iteration of the *Black Liberation 1969* digital archive was an inward-facing Omeka database created to house primary documents for a course taught by Professor Dorsey in the History department at Swarthmore in the fall of 2014. Only later did work begin to transform the documents discovered during this collective research toward a new history of the black student protest movement at Swarthmore College—interviews,[12] mimeographed syllabi,[13] photos,[14] student organization records,[15] newspaper[16] articles—into an outward-facing site. Built for the research needs of the students and the course first, the project's second phase was designed to reimagine the archive for other audiences and publics. *Black Liberation 1969* thus shows how collaborations among faculty, librarians, and students can reframe the kind of rigorous research that takes place in the context of the liberal arts classroom—through the significant labor of database-building, metadata creation, and interface design—both to make the work of research more visible and to let specific audiences beyond the walls of the classroom learn about students' interpretations of their research materials and create their own.

Despite sharing a name with the fall 2014 Swarthmore College class that collaborated to create it, the *Black Liberation 1969* site represents only one part of the collective research project. In addition to collaborating with Professor Dorsey to create the site, collections, and exhibits, students in the class wrote and presented interpretive essays at a symposium and also created interpretive art projects[17] that were displayed around campus. This constellation of projects implicitly insists that the digital archive is only one aspect of a larger research effort involving many people and several stages. And the digital archive reveals and preserves work, extends audiences, and allows a new kind of access, but refuses to suggest that what is digitally visible is the most important aspect of the larger social life of rigorous humanistic research.

Black Liberation 1969 is an especially intensive example of a joined practice of pedagogy and scholarship that is much more widespread than dominant narratives about the relations among liberal arts, humanities research, pedagogy, and the digital humanities currently acknowledge. We offer our interpretation of this project as the beginning of how we might rewrite the history of digital humanities work in order to put a capaciously defined liberal arts and its research imagination at the center. We see a secret history of digital humanities in the generative compromises produced by the practice of liberal arts education in a higher education landscape dominated by research universities, generative compromises that are encoded in one of the common forms—the digital archive—that digital humanities projects take. This view does not therefore imagine a pedagogy of or for the digital humanities, nor does it make an argument about the role of digital humanities in a liberal arts education. Instead, we call for a digital humanities that more intentionally acknowledges the centrality of the research imagination, and a digital humanities that imagines the liberal arts classroom—real and imaginary, existing and prospective—as its origin and at its center.

NOTES

1. Dennis Tenen, in chapter 9 in this volume, notes some of the problems of this emphasis on tools, advising that digital humanists should place the emphasis instead on nurturing "meaningful change in our communities" and on "standards and best practices" for existing tools' use.

2. See, for example, work represented at the 2012 "Take Note" conference at Harvard University, the work of Lisa Gitelman on the media history of documents, of Simon Reader on the notebooks of Victorian writers, and of Deidre Lynch on the nineteenth-century album.

3. Research rarely features in our accustomed stories about undergraduate humanities education or liberal arts education, but research in the humanities classroom has a long history of its own. For just one example of the how the teaching of early twentieth-century professor of literature Caroline Spurgeon emphasized the process of note-taking and the undertaking of serious research at the undergraduate level, see www.acls.org /news/10-8-2014.

4. We have tended to think that digital tools and platforms for exhibit-building, text visualization, and mapping are opening up new forms of undergraduate research—and in some ways they certainly do. But in fact we might as easily or as often claim that they make existing forms of research long familiar to the liberal arts classroom newly visible, as digital platforms and tools permit sharing work at multiple stages—citation-gathering, preparatory blogging, drafts, collaborative work—as well as a proliferation of publication platforms. Claims that "collaborative undergraduate research in the humanities . . . represents a departure for the norm for small liberal arts colleges" could in one view be expanded to describe a relative absence of collaborative undergraduate research in the humanities on any campus (Alexander and Davis). On the other hand, one could argue, as we do, that collaborative research is in fact a common but under-described part of undergraduate humanities classrooms.

5. We wish to note here that we deliberately speak of liberal arts pedagogy and classrooms rather than institutions, since the sort of pedagogy we discuss is associated with small residential liberal arts colleges and may be intentionally cultivated by them at an institutional level, but perhaps is as often found in classrooms of the research university, the extension school, or the community college.

6. Rhetorically, most accounts of the value of liberal arts education tend to swing back and forth between variously phrased celebrations of its ability to produce vocation-ready transferable skills in students and a range of defenses of learning for learning's sake. Rhetorics of digital humanities pedagogy tend to intensify this bifurcation, doubling down by either celebrating technical skills or by advocating for the freedoms of deformance and play in the classroom. Without claiming that either of these types of arguments are invalid, we suggest that the experience of most undergraduate students while studying an academic discipline in a liberal arts style or context falls into this murkier and perhaps more interesting territory.

7. http://blacklib1969.swarthmore.edu.

8. In her well-known essay taxonomizing seven types of DH projects, Miriam Posner calls these kinds of projects "archives of primary sources"; most of what we are arguing here applies as well to work on digital scholarly editions and some other kinds of text analysis projects in which decisions about selecting, cleaning, and formatting the texts to be mined and transformed require the same kind of sympathetic research imagination.

See Posner's blog post, "How Did They Make That?" http://miriamposner.com/blog/how
-did-they-make-that/.

    9. See *Black Liberation 1969*'s complete credits page here: http://blacklib1969.
swarthmore.edu/credits.

    10. http://blacklib1969.swarthmore.edu/collections-gallery.

    11. http://blacklib1969.swarthmore.edu/exhibits-list.

    12. http://blacklib1969.swarthmore.edu/interviews.

    13. http://blacklib1969.swarthmore.edu/items/browse?collection=12.

    14. http://blacklib1969.swarthmore.edu/items/browse?collection=14.

    15. http://blacklib1969.swarthmore.edu/items/browse?collection=8.

    16. http://blacklib1969.swarthmore.edu/items/browse?collection=1.

    17. http://www.swarthmore.edu/news-events/black-liberation-1969-student
-projects).

BIBLIOGRAPHY

Alexander, Bryan, and Rebecca Frost Davis. "Should Liberal Arts Campuses Do Digital Humanities? Process and Products in the Small College World." In *Debates in the Digital Humanities,* ed. Matthew K. Gold. Minneapolis: University of Minnesota Press, 2012. http://dhdebates.gc.cuny.edu/debates/text/25.

Unsworth, John. "What Is Humanities Computing and What Is Not?" In *Defining Digital Humanities: A Reader,* ed. Melissa Terras, Julianne Nyhan, and Edward Vanhoutte, 35–48. Farnham: Ashgate, 2013.

Lessons on Public Humanities from the Civic Sphere

WENDY F. HSU

Traditionally, public humanities has meant either widening the readership of humanities scholarship or working in cultural heritage institutions like museums, archives, galleries, and libraries. My own adventure in the public sector, working with the City of Los Angeles Department of Cultural Affairs (DCA) as an ACLS Public Fellow, has broadened my understanding of the evolving value of humanities participation in the public sphere. I view my role within the department as fluctuating between technologist—someone who designs and prototypes emergent forms of technology with a public purpose in mind—and interpreter—someone who explains the meanings of technology adoption in the context of democratic participation, civic awareness, government transparency, and public-sector labor. Professional experience with civic technology offers opportunities to rethink the digital public work in the humanities. By evoking lessons on public inclusion, community-driven inquiry, and public-benefit design, I hope that we as humanists can be inspired to contribute to the public while participating as partners with the public.

Early and In-process Inclusion

The first lesson from my work in public-sector technology is the importance of early and in-process inclusion. Allowing for the public to participate in the design and development of a project from its very beginning demonstrates the principle of building *with* and not *for*. "Community-driven technologies," as civic technology advocate Laurenellen McCann explains, should be "built at the speed of inclusion—the pace necessary not just to create a tool but to do so with in-depth communal input and stewardship—and directly respond to the needs, ideas, and wants of those they're intended to benefit."[1] At DCA, I have learned that developing digital projects at the speed of inclusion entails an in-process involvement of the public.

Getting community input throughout the project lifecycle can help inform decision making related to content organization, interaction paths, and information design.

Soon after I came on board at DCA, I was charged with developing an agency-wide social media plan. City officials had lifted the ban on social media at the department level only a few months before my arrival. Navigating public expectations for government responsiveness and informational transparency, the department saw opportunities to reorient itself to the new domain of communications afforded by social media. Within this new terrain, I forged ahead with a social media pilot program, experimenting with interactions with the public over social media while learning from the public how social media could augment access to and understanding of DCA's programming, services, and process. With this purpose, I live-tweeted a grant workshop and received public feedback on obscure content areas related to our grants program. Based on this feedback, I organized an internal meeting with the grants division to discuss our definitions of geographical equity. This interaction inspired the idea of a webinar as a means to deliver workshop content and, more broadly, challenged the program to rethink its analog, paper-based operation. Here, the inclusion of the public early in the development process allowed my colleagues to gain insights into how we could restructure our content and delivery platforms.

Humanities scholars do not do very well in bringing the public into our design and development processes. The assumption that scholarship is inherently a form of "public good" is not a productive place to start a conversation with those outside of the academy (Stommel). In a Twitter post from the #uwdh conference on April 17, 2015, Jesse Stommel noted that Kathleen Fitzpatrick's emphatic remark over "the importance of thinking about scholarship and academic work as a public good." My experience at the DCA has shown that we should think of public work in the humanities as a process, not a product, and that we should do more to include the public at earlier phases of our work. Content and design considerations should be informed by conversations with the public, whether over social media or in civic contexts like town hall meetings. Using the digital to learn from the public is a listening practice, one that yields more efficacious and engaged public humanities work.

Problem Scoping and Inquiries with the Community

Another key lesson from the civic tech world is that problem solving begins and ends with community building. Problem solving, in the civic and public sector, takes place on teams with various stakeholders, including citizens, residents, community organizers, and policy and advocacy specialists. In this context, civic technologists organize events such as hackathons and datathons not only to solve problems, but also to determine problems based on the participants' concerns, needs, and interests. Defining community problems that can feasibly be solved is an important goal of such events.[2]

At a datathon about neighborhood change and gentrification in northeast Los Angeles that I helped organize with Occidental College's Center for Digital Liberal Arts, I learned how to build consensus around problem identification and scoping requirements from a group consisting of citizens, residents, organizers, activists, parents, local government workers, and city officials. Driven by pragmatic needs, these problems—related to shelter, transportation, finance, healthcare, and education—can be challenging in terms of feasibility. At the first workshop, we asked participants to brainstorm questions and write them down on Post-it notes. Participants recorded inquiries about the correlation between displacement and redlining practices by local banks; business ventures recently established in the area; the aesthetic and cultural signs of gentrification; and the relationship between bicycle infrastructure and the vibrancy of local business. The academic historians, sociologists, art historians, and urban planners in the room then collaborated with members of the community to explore these problems, each stakeholder providing respective expertise so that together the group could transform their collective insights into feasible solutions.

Humanities scholars do not often venture into the public as we do our work. As stewards of culture, we seem to feel more comfortable when analyzing culture from a distance than when rolling up our sleeves and participating in civic and community actions. Our vision for problem solving often requires a much longer time scale, one characterized by what Rita Felski has described as "painstaking inquiry" ("Critique and the Hermeneutics of Suspicion"). Humanities scholars often shy away from a fixed solution either because they are more interested in problematizing solutions than solving problems, or because they prefer to defer solutions for others to figure out. Occasionally, they make gestures toward solutions as a form of speculation, as in a short remark in a concluding paragraph. Because they rarely offer specific recommendations for immediate progress, the contributions of humanities scholars seem less relevant to conversations about pressing community problems. Instead of analyzing social and cultural patterns from a distance or in solitude, however, we humanities scholars could stand to set aside our roles as subject specialists and learn to scope problems and explore possible solutions contributed by community workers, working with those who have frontline experiences with solution proposition and implementation. Collective ideation, or the co-interpretation of a shared problem, is among the first steps to realizing the public purpose of humanities work.

Design and Making as Civic Actions

At a lecture at the Columbia Global Center in Amman, Jordan, Gayatri Spivak argues that "the task of the humanities is to teach literature and philosophy in such a way that people will be able to imagine what a socially just world should be."[3] Spivak's evocation places humanistic thinking in the realm of social justice and imagination. Imagination is in essence an interpretive act, and interpretation provides the foundation for the humanistic practices of visioning, speculating, and reflecting. But interpretation can also lead to creative modes of humanist expression, such as making and design. By transforming critical thought into action, design can provide an exercise for imagining a different reality (Dunn and Raby). This form of speculative design can animate thoughts and evoke questions about *what* and *how* related to mobilizing imagined ideas for social justice.

At the core of my work at DCA is an attempt to reimagine how the department as a public agency can participate in the current information- and technology-driven economy. While researching best practices, I must interpret the affordances of certain technologies and their impact on society in order to design interactions that embody public values and the humanist ideals of equity and justice. My goal is to contribute to an instance of digital governance that demonstrates democracy through public participation, education, and information transparency. While leading the department's website redesign, I challenged myself to think about how to create an accessible and meaningful platform, one that offers services and facilitated interactions for our constituency across cultural, ethnic, linguistic, generational, and socioeconomic boundaries. Public-benefit design means lowering the barrier of entry and maintaining the integrity of public participation, while not making assumptions about the public(s) you are serving.

Making and prototyping constitute another method for staging critical intentions. At the DCA, I created prototypes that can serve as rhetorical vehicles for setting new standards of practice in the field of civic technology. While developing the DCA social media plan, for example, I learned that private interests such as product awareness and customer service tend to drive the design and practice of social media in government.[4] As a critical response, I produced the *DCA Social Report*[5] (Hsu and Moreau), an information kit that promotes public-benefit social media practices and tools including metrics and other methods of evaluation. Furthermore, this document also demonstrates digital and short-form information curation as a platform of public information service. I experimented with the form of a report, publishing the document as a microsite and licensing it with Creative Commons standards. This openness is intended to further the public mission of engagement and transparency through design.

Process can also be an object of design, especially for institutional or organizational change. My most prominent design project so far is Lab at DCA, a digital literacy and innovation incubator for city staff. At its core, Lab at DCA is a design intervention of staff training at the City of Los Angeles. Taking cues from digital humanities training initiatives such as the Praxis Program at the University of Virginia and the Digital Summer Institute at Occidental College, I designed a lab curriculum based on a digital literacy model.[6] The creation of Lab is a response to the lack of resources for digital workforce development and the city's outdated technological tools and infrastructures. The Lab's co-learning structure also mitigates institutional hierarchy, as expressed by its top-down management and siloed reporting system, and empowers lower-level staffers who are otherwise at the mercy of the efficiency-driven managerial practices.

Digital humanists are good at expressing our cultural critiques by making things: a database, a website, or a hypertext edition of an analog book. We have also figured out ways to stage interventions within the institutions in which we work, reconfiguring legacy research paradigms as librarians and Alt-Ac-ers and establishing new learning standards by redesigning curricula. As Lab at DCA demonstrates, these skills can translate to the public sphere. I urge digital humanists, especially those with digital making or design skills, to apply their experience to projects with a public purpose.

Designing with (and not for) the public could mean the participation in the following domains of action: (1) organizing public projects with a civic cause through the design of a web interface, a database, or hashtag campaign, and setting a common agenda at community tech events such as hackathons and datathons; (2) prototyping a community-driven digital object such as an oral history archive, a multimedia document, a digital library, or public information products such as web maps or data visualizations; (3) intervening in a civic or public process in a way that furthers a humanist agenda—for example, civic pedagogy, public cultural stewardship, or critical race/gender/sexuality/class/labor/immigrant politics. I offer these suggestions with the hope that humanities scholars will participate in design work and interventions that benefit the community and activate social justice.

Coworking across Lines of Power

Communities can emerge across lines of power, but communications that lead to opinion formation can further divide strong and weak publics. According to Nancy Fraser, a strong public encompasses decision-making power that a weak public doesn't have.[7] Even within a weak public without the power of governance, the differentiation of power can be reinforced by intellectual politics upheld by institutions of knowledge production. Whether justified or not, those with positions within or in proximity to academic institutions are closer to this power center.[8] Public participation begins from a place of humility. Civic actions stem from dialogues across lines of power. Community events like datathons and hackathons are valuable not because they advance technology for the sole purpose of solving problems, but because they use data and technology as a context of organizing and coworking toward community solutions. Humanists, I urge you to leverage your knowledge of the digital as a tool of community building. Working, listening, and making in proximity with communities will bring us closer to the co-imagination of a socially just world.

NOTES

1. The "Build With, Not For" conversation is currently prominent among civic designers and technologists. For more, read McCann. At the 2015 Personal Democracy Forum meeting in New York in June 2015, two consecutive breakout sessions explored this topic in the format of interactive workshops with documentation.

2. There have been critiques about how the eagerness for technology solutions could end up driving civic technologists' search for a problem to be solved. This impulse toward solution has ramifications when tech solutions are often framed as products available on the market, thus reinforcing the market logic of technology in the private sector. For more on this subject, see Shaw.

3. For more on this conception of humanities education, read Spivak, "Can There Be a Feminist World?"

4. DCA Social Report is meant to be an interrogation of the utility of the existing social media primers for government. I describe how governments can critically adapt private-sector tools, approaches, and values for a public interest in an essay-length introduction to the report. See Hsu, "Introductions: Why This Report?"

5. http://dcaredesign.org/socialreport.

6. Similar to its literary counterpart, digital literacy as a civic framework calls for a baseline understanding of the building blocks, like grammar and vocabulary, of what make up the current media landscape. In this new landscape, formal and content qualities of information are radically recontextualized by the Internet. For the civic workforce, it is no longer sufficient to be able to generate and critique work materials in print-based or other analog formats. For more on digital literacy for government work, see Hsu, "Digital Literacy for Civic Staff." On digital literacy and political affordances of the Web, see Maier, "Digital Literacy, Part 1: Cadence."

7. Nancy Fraser's formulation of strong and weak public is a critical response to Habermas's bourgeois public sphere. Fraser notes that Habermas's theoretical formation does not consider the empirical reality of social inequality and overlooks existing power stratifications. Fraser's work serves as a good reminder for how humanities scholars may position their work and its political implications vis-à-vis the public ("Rethinking the Public Sphere").

8. Similarly, Emily Shaw advocates for civic technologists to consider the power relations within the public in their work. Locating government as a center of power, Shaw evokes that those who are the most distant from government are the least empowered in the world of civic technology. She advises civic technologists to consider the voice and the needs of the power-distant individuals in their work (Shaw, "Civic Wants, Civic Needs, Civic Tech").

BIBLIOGRAPHY

Birchall, Clare. "'Data.gov-in-a-box': Delimiting Transparency." *European Journal of Social Theory,* March 1, 2015. doi: 10.1177/1368431014555259.

Drazin, Adam. "Design Anthropology: Working On, With, and For Technologies." In *Digital Anthropology*, ed. Heather A. Horst and Daniel Miller, 245–65. New York: Berg, 2012.

Dunn, Anthony, and Fiona Raby. *Speculative Everything: Design, Fiction, and Social Dreaming*. Cambridge, Mass.: MIT Press, 2013.

Fraser, Nancy. "Rethinking the Public Sphere: A Contribution to the Critique of Actually Existing Democracy." *Social Text,* no. 25/26 (1990): 56–80.

Felski, Rita. "Critique and the Hermeneutics of Suspicion." *M/C Journal* 15, no. 1 (2012). http://journal.media-culture.org.au/index.php/mcjournal/article/viewArticle/431.

Hsu, Wendy. "Digital Literacy for Civic Staff, Why Lab at DCA, Part 1." *Lab at DCA* (blog), August 1, 2015. http://dcaredesign.org/lab/digital-literacy-for-civic-staff-why-lab-at-dca-part-1/.

———."Introductions: Why This Report?" *DCA Social Report,* August 2, 2015. http://dcaredesign.org/socialreport/about-dca-report/.

Hsu, Wendy, and Jack Moreau. *DCA Social Report,* July 5, 2015. http://dcaredesign.org/socialreport.

Lab at DCA. http://dcaredesign.org/lab.

Latour, Bruno. *Pandora's Hope: Essays on the Reality of Science Studies*. Cambridge, Mass.: Harvard University Press, 1999.

Luff, Paul, Jon Hindmarsh, and Christian Heath. *Workplace Studies: Recovering Work Practice and Informing System Design*. Cambridge: Cambridge University Press, 2000.

Maier, Andrew. "Digital Literacy, Part 1: Cadence." *UX Booth*, October 3, 2013. http://www.uxbooth.com/articles/digital-literacy-part-1-cadence/.

McCann, Laurenellen. "Building Technology With, Not For Communities: An Engagement Guide for Civic Tech." Medium.com, March 30, 2015. https://medium.com/@elle_mccann/building-technology-with-not-for-communities-an-engagement-guide-for-civic-tech-b8880982e65a.

Neff, Gina. *Venture Labor: Work and the Burden of Risk in Innovative Industries*. Cambridge, Mass.: MIT Press, 2013.

Schrock, Andrew. Forthcoming. "Civic Hacking as Data Activism and Advocacy: A History from Publicity to Open Government Data." In *New Media and Society*.

Shaw, Emily. "Civic Wants, Civic Needs, Civic Tech." *Sunlight Foundation* (blog), September 29, 2014. http://sunlightfoundation.com/blog/2014/09/29/civic-wants-civic-needs-civic-tech/.

Spivak, Gayatri. "Can There Be a Feminist World?" *Public Books,* May 15, 2015. http://www.publicbooks.org/nonfiction/can-there-be-a-feminist-world.

Stommel, Jesse (@Jessifer). "#uwdh @kfitz has emphasized several times today the importance of thinking about scholarship and academic work as a public good,'" Twitter post, April 17, 2015. https://twitter.com/jessifer/status/589078243074039809.

PART IV

DIGITAL HUMANITIES AND THE DISCIPLINES

The Differences between Digital Humanities and Digital History

STEPHEN ROBERTSON

The digital humanities is what digital humanists do. What digital humanists do depends largely on academic discipline but also on level of technical expertise. Each discipline, with varying degrees of intensity, has over the years developed a set of favored methods, tools, and interests that, although shared with other disciplines remains connected to the discipline. The task of the digital humanities, as a trans-curricular practice, is to bring these practitioners into communication with each other, and to cultivate a discourse that captures the shared praxis of bringing technologies of representation, computation, and communication to bear on the work of interpretation that defines the humanities.

—Rafael Alvarado, University of Virginia, USA, Day of DH 2011

Digital humanities as it is currently constituted has not erased the differences between academic disciplines. Digital humanists share a commitment to collaboration, openness, and experimentation; a set of software tools, such as Voyant, Palladio, or Omeka; and a group of venues such as THATCamp. But disciplinary sources, questions, and approaches shape their projects, as well as their choice and use of digital tools.[1] The *Companion to Digital Humanities*, the edited collection that has become a convenient touchstone for the emergence of the field that has succeeded humanities computing, reflects these diverse practices. It contains chapters on work in different disciplines, followed by chapters on "Principles," "Applications," and "Production, Dissemination, Archiving" (Schreibman, Siemens, and Unsworth). However, at the time of the *Companion*'s publication in 2004, work with digital technology and media still received little recognition in academic disciplines, and many practitioners held junior positions or were located in the interstices of institutions (Rockwell). In those circumstances, the attraction of an interdisciplinary digital humanities as a professional home overshadowed the disciplinary differences within it. Digital humanities became a big tent (Terras; Svensson).

Much has changed since 2004. The use of digital technology and media are now recognized, if not always embraced, by most of the major humanities professional organizations. Strands of digital sessions now appear in conference programs for major and more specialized conferences: digital history, for example, can be found in the American context not only at the annual meetings of the American Historical Association (AHA) and Organization of American Historians, but also smaller organizations such as the Southern Historical Association, the Urban History Association, and the International Congress on Medieval Studies.[2] The AHA will soon adopt standards for assessing digital scholarship for promotion and tenure, joining the Modern Language Association and the College Art Association.[3] Job advertisements in history, English, art history, archaeology, and media studies now include a regular sprinkling of positions requiring expertise in digital technology, some even as the primary field. Undergraduate and graduate courses, certificates, and masters programs in digital humanities are appearing in a diverse range of institutions. At the same time, in a predictable corollary to this growing acceptance, digital humanities has been the target of attacks in scholarly and more popular publications. In almost all cases, what is labeled digital humanities in those critiques is in fact digital literary studies, effectively casting the big tent as housing only a single discipline.[4]

In this moment, our focus needs to shift back to disciplinary difference within digital humanities.[5] The audiences to which we are now seeking to explain our work are increasingly not only administrators and funding agencies whose broad remits echo the breadth of digital humanities, leaving us to elaborate only the digital. Instead, we are engaged more at the local level, with individual scholars, teachers, students, and groups beyond the academy who rarely see their interests and projects in such broad terms. As a result, to them digital humanities is doubly unintelligible, requiring us to persuade them of the credibility and relevance of both the digital and the interdisciplinary. Their willingness to engage with digital humanities is often further reduced by their association of the term with attacks on digital literary studies. A conversation instead about digital history, for example, allows explorations of the specific technologies and approaches that offer the most possibilities for the sources, questions, and teaching of historians. As Ryan Cordell perceptively notes in regards to teaching digital humanities, a "rapid introduction to as many methods and tools as possible" provides only a "glancing understanding of any aspect," whereas "a more focused introduction to a few tools, methods, and theoretical conversations" within a disciplinary focus provides "fewer but more well-developed skills from which they can build" (see chapter 36 in this book on "How Not to Teach Digital Humanities").

Moving forward, we would be better served by reimagining digital humanities not as single all-encompassing tent but as a house with many rooms, different spaces for disciplines that are not silos but entry points and conduits to central spaces where those from different disciplines working with particular tools and media can gather.

Each of the many disciplinary rooms would have a distinctive character, reflecting a particular contribution and orientation to the field.

In this chapter, I explore digital history's use of the Web and computational tools as two areas that distinguish the discipline within digital humanities, and from digital literary studies in particular. In singling out digital literary studies as a counterpoint, I seek to disrupt the recent tendency in both scholarly and popular discussion to equate that field with digital humanities. Beyond that historically contingent assertion of difference, I aim to redirect attention to academic disciplines as central to what different digital humanists do in order to make clear what the field offers scholars in those disciplines. A common reaction to the argument I make here has been to point to a handful of projects that do not fit the patterns which I identify, and on that basis, dismiss the importance, if not the existence, of disciplines within digital humanities. To be clear, disciplinary difference in digital humanities is not a binary, in which approaches are the preserve of particular disciplines and entirely absent from others. Rather, difference is a spectrum of emphasis, with varying degrees of interest in methods, tools, and values. Looking for projects that do not fit the differences I identify is not the test of the argument; rather, the key is establishing which projects are exceptions and which are exemplars.[6]

The most common use to which digital humanists, including some historians, have put the Web has been the distribution and presentation of material to other scholarly researchers. Such a use of the Web in digital literary studies, for example, is clear in the *Companion to Digital Humanities*; audiences other than scholars barely receive a mention. Matthew Kirschenbaum, in exploring the user interface of the *William Blake Archive*, did respond to complaints that it was "not particularly easy to use" and "chock-full" of "scholarly trappings" by noting that "while we are happy to have users from many different constituencies, the site's primary mission has always been expressly conceived as scholarly research" ("So the Colors Cover the Wires"). Perry Willett's discussion of the audience for electronic texts noted similar tensions and likewise put "general readers" to one side (Electronic Texts). An orientation to a scholarly audience continues to characterize the newer generations of projects, such as the *Shelly-Godwin Archive*.[7] Such uses of the Web to present both primary sources and scholarship were also the focus of the account of digital history offered by William Thomas in the *Companion to Digital Humanities* ("Computing and the Historical Imagination"). Like electronic editions and other TEI projects, digitized archives such as *Valley of the Shadow*, the project that Thomas helped lead, or my own *Digital Harlem*, for that matter, were designed to meet the needs and interests of the scholars who created them.[8] As David Parry notes, placing them online made them publicly available, but did not expand the scope of their audience ("Be Online or Be Irrelevant"). They remained accessible, relevant, and useful primarily to those scholars and their colleagues—and to the incidental audiences of genealogists, who search historical databases for individuals, and readers seeking copies of literary texts.[9] As Sheila Brennan reminds us in her contribution to this collection, your audience is those for who you design a project, not those who can find it (see chapter 32, "Public, First").

Notwithstanding Thomas's focus on historians using the Web to reach other scholars, since the earliest days of the Web, historians created online projects for audiences rarely addressed by other digital humanists. Many of the early practitioners of digital history were social historians and radical historians committed to democratizing the creation of the past and to collaborating with teachers to enhance and diversify the history taught in high schools and universities. Their pursuit of those goals gave digital history a distinctive emphasis on using the Web to reach classrooms and the wider public. In the American context, the availability of funding through the U.S. Department of Education's Teaching American History program and the NEH Education Programs and Public Programs facilitated these projects.[10] Professional recognition was also forthcoming: beginning in 2004, the American Historical Association's James Harvey Robinson Award for the most outstanding contribution to the teaching of history was given to online projects on four consecutive occasions.[11] In addition, the field of public history has given work with audiences beyond the classroom a place within the historical profession for which there is no equivalent in other disciplines in digital humanities—although it should be noted that that place is not in the mainstream of the profession. Public history grew from a movement in the 1970s to apply history to real-world issues, but in the United States it has only relatively recently gained support and recognition within research-oriented institutions and professional organizations.[12] That digital history is recognized within public history is clear from the NCPH's Outstanding Public History Project, which has been awarded to three online projects since 2008.[13]

The work of the Roy Rosenzweig Center for History and New Media[14] (RRCHNM), founded in 1994, provides examples of how digital historians used the Web to reach both audiences in classrooms and among the wider public. Roy Rosenzweig established the center with the mission of using digital technology and media "to democratize the past—to incorporate multiple voices, reach diverse audiences, and encourage popular participation in presenting and preserving the past."[15] RRCHNM's earliest online projects were collaborations with the American Social History Project created with and for teachers. *History Matters: The U.S. Survey Course on the Web*, launched in 1998, included historical sources like those found in digital archives, but annotated by historians and packaged with online forums with leading historians and teachers, syllabi annotated by teachers, projects created by history students, and interviews with distinguished teachers who shared their strategies and techniques for using the historical sources in the classroom.[16] Other projects explored the French Revolution and highlighted the new fields of world history and the history of childhood and youth, and recent history, such as the events of 1989.[17] *Teachinghistory.org* pursued this work on a particularly large scale, building on and disseminating the results of more than 1,000 *Teaching American History* projects, providing both history content and teaching materials and bringing together different communities concerned with history education.[18] The audience for these sites continues to grow: well into its second decade, and lacking design features now expected on the Web, *History Matters* nonetheless attracts increasing numbers of visitors each year: 2.1 million unique visitors and just over 3 million visits in 2014. That same year, *Teachinghistory.org* saw its audience grow to 1.6 million unique visitors and just over 3 million visits.

RRCHNM also used the Web to develop public history projects involving audiences beyond the classroom. Early projects focused on collecting and preserving the past, in collaboration with a variety of communities. *ECHO* fostered communication and dialogue among historians, scientists, engineers, doctors, and technologists in order to develop and disseminate methods to collect and preserve the recent history of science, technology, and industry.[19] The *September 11 Digital Archive*,[20] a collaboration with the American Social History Project at the CUNY Graduate Center, collected digital material related to the attacks both through a web interface and direct collecting. The *Hurricane Digital Memory Bank* further developed that approach, adding the geolocation of contributions and using extensive outreach activities and strategic partnerships with more than twenty universities, museums, state humanities councils, media outlets, nonprofit relief groups, and grassroots empowerment groups.[21] In the *Bracero History Archive,* a web-accessible repository facilitated many parties working together to build a collection of oral histories with Bracero guest workers and other types of historical evidence of their experiences, and then present it with supporting materials and teaching resources.[22] *Gulag: Many Days, Many Lives* and *Objects of History* involved collaborations with Russian museums and the National Park Service, and with the National Museum of American History, respectively, to build and present exhibits.[23] While historians also use the Web to distribute and present material to other scholars, the practice of placing material online to reach and collaborate with the wider public, and to reach teachers and students in classroom settings, has become established and professionally recognized within history to an extent that distinguishes digital history within digital humanities.

Digital history is distinctive within digital humanities in a second area—its use of computational tools. This distinction is less intense than that in the use of the Web. Historians can be found using mapping, text analysis, and network software, the three types of computational tools favored in the digital humanities, as well as 3D modeling, image analysis, and social media. However, digital historians have turned to digital mapping to a greater extent than other disciplines in the digital humanities, adopting it as their favored computational tool. For example, of the list of digital humanities projects maintained by John Levin and adopted by the Geo-Humanities Special Interest Group of ADHO, almost two-thirds are historical projects.[24] It is certainly the case that digital mapping is not as central to history as it is to archaeology, but mapping has long been a part of record keeping the practices of archaeology. The turn to digital mapping in history is not continuous with older practices to the same extent. If maps have appeared in historical scholarship, historians have until recently written about the past with little attention to space, notwithstanding the discipline's definition around nations and cities.

The distinctive prominence of mapping in digital history is a product of both the spur to mapping that the spatial turn provided to historians and of the more limited availability, until recently, of historical material to which text analysis tools could be applied. In the last decade, historians have given renewed attention to space and place as part of spatial turn in the humanities—which began in the 1970s with a focus on perceptions and representations, that, as Karen Haltunen put it, "tended to the metaphorical" and employed the "idiom of borders and boundaries, frontiers and crossroads, centers and margins," and extended in the early 2000s to a concern with "spatial issues more materially" (2).[25] It was this more recent development that provided a spur to mapping; visualization was not as necessary a part of exploring spatial perceptions and language.

At the same time, mapping tools became more accessible and useful to historians seeking to extend the spatial turn to the material. The first computational mapping tools, GIS software, which appeared in the early 1960s and became more widely available in the early 1980s, were, and still are, expensive, complex, and cumbersome and operate only on computers running Windows. Moreover, this software was designed for precise, quantitative data that could be parsed in highly structured tabular databases and cartographic maps that emphasized generalization. It fit uneasily with the sources that most historians use, which are characterized by ambiguity, uncertainty, uniqueness, and with the discipline's move away from statistical analysis after the 1970s. A small group of historians did adopt GIS software and continue to work within its limitations, under the umbrella of the Social Science History Association and its journal, *Social Science History*, and largely disconnected from digital history. In the last decade, the development of the geospatial web has made mapping available and accessible to digital historians, with web mash-ups allowing maps to be created and iterated with unprecedented ease. Web mapping platforms such as Google Maps, MapQuest, CartoDB, Palladio, and Neatline do not have the same quantitative orientation as GIS software, allowing a diversity of spatial data to be visualized.[26] More advanced and customized web mapping is also now possible using open-source tools such as Leaflet, GeoServer, d3.js, and OpenLayers. With these tools, historians explored a range of questions and topics: urban development, housing, ghettos, moviegoing, language use, sound, industries ranging from iron to cutlery, events such as bombing, military recruitment, the slave trade, slave revolts, and gaining freedom from slavery, the spread of disease, witchcraft accusations, feminist activism, and the circulation of correspondence.[27] These tools are obviously available to all digital humanists, and other disciplines have also experienced the spatial turn. So, while those factors help explain the prominence of mapping in digital history, they do not explain its relatively lesser place in the practice of other disciplines within digital humanities.

Digital historians have often used the geospatial web as a platform for presenting historical sources. Maps allow the visual display of information, and for the organization and integration of different sources on the basis of their shared geographic location. The first two winners of the AHA's Roy Rosenzweig Prize for Innovation in Digital History[28] were mapping projects built on Google Maps: *Digital Harlem: Everyday Life, 1915–1930* (which I created with collaborators at the University of Sydney) and Bobby Allen's *Going to the Show*. *Digital Harlem* offered a visualization of everyday life through maps of locations, events and individuals' lives, using information extracted from legal records, newspapers, and other published and archival texts.[29] *Going to the Show* mapped the locations of movie venues in North Carolina between 1896 and 1922, combined with an archive of related material.[30] More recent examples include: *Mapping the Republic of Letters*,[31] which traces the circulation of correspondence among enlightenment intellectuals using prototype browser-based tools now being developed as an open-source platform, Palladio; *The Roaring Twenties*, which displays the location of sounds and noise complaints in 1920s New York City, initially using Google Maps, before shifting to MapQuest; and *Photogrammar*, which located 170,000 photographs taken by staff of the Farm Security Administration in the 1930s and 1940s, using Leaflet and CartoDB.[32]

Historians have also used web maps that display historical data as part of their analysis of those sources. The interactive, iterative features of digital maps make them research tools, a means of discovering as well as displaying knowledge. Not only are mapped sources placed in their geographic contexts, but selections of those sources can be mapped, different layers of sources can be juxtaposed, and the scale can be zoomed from the level of individual buildings out to neighborhoods, cities, and regions. Viewing these maps can reveal spatial patterns not evident from reading the texts, relationships that facilitate comparisons and prompt questions. The answers to those questions are not on the maps, but in the sources from which they are derived. So mapping a range of sources using *Digital Harlem*,[33] for example, highlighted a more extensive and expansive white presence in the neighborhood, leading to questions about the nature of a range of interracial encounters, when they occurred, and the extent to which life in this black neighborhood could be lived apart from whites (Robertson, White, and Garton). Similarly, *Visualizing Emancipation* mapped the position of Union troops and a range of emancipation events drawn from *Official Records of the War of the Rebellion* and other sources to trace the spread of emancipation during the Civil War and explore the relationship between the presence of troops and enslaved men and women's escape from bondage (Ayers and Nesbit).[34]

Less often, historians have created maps to illustrate arguments or present the answer to questions, forgoing some interactivity and ability to query the data in order to highlight a particular analysis. *Slave Revolt in Jamaica, 1760–1761*, for example, offers an animated narrative map of a slave revolt built using Leaflet. That map allows the user to move within the timeline, but in no other way to affect the map. *Mapping Occupation*[35] presented a spatial narrative that coupled a text with a series of maps to explore the Union Army's occupation of the Reconstruction South. Icons on some of maps can be clicked to reveal the underlying data and the scale can be adjusted, but otherwise the maps are limited to illustrating a particular argument.[36]

The relative prominence of mapping in digital history is also a product of historians' limited use of the textual analysis tools. It is not the case that historians have been unable to see ways to use text mining and topic modeling in their research. To the contrary, historians were among the first digital humanists to experiment with such tools. Dan Cohen[37] made early use of data from Google books, and he went on to be part of the *With Criminal Intent*[38] project that data-mined the Old Bailey trials (*Searching for the Victorians*; *Data Mining with Criminal Intent*). Sharon Block[39] and Rob Nelson employed topic modeling. Block explored the eighteenth-century *Pennsylvania Gazette* ("Doing More with Digitization"). Nelson explored the Confederacy's paper of record during the Civil War (*Mining the Dispatch*[40]). But until recently, little work has built on those experiments.

One explanation for the relatively limited use of text analysis tools by historians is a lack of digitized sources. As Dan Cohen noted in 2008, "Unless we can have machines scan, sort, and apply digital techniques to the full texts of documents, we can't do sophisticated digital scholarship" (Cohen et al., "Interchange"). Sources that are central to historical scholarship have been digitized and made machine-readable on a far lesser scale than those on which literary studies relies. In part, this reflects the fact that historians rely more on documents that are not published or printed. Making what is digitized accessible to computational tools is a more expensive and time-consuming task in the case of those sources than with published sources. The optical character recognition (OCR) software that extracts text from images currently only works with printed texts, meaning that handwriting must be transcribed. Although the *Proceedings of the Old Bailey*, one of the best-known and most widely used digitized collections, used manual keying as part of its digitization process, transcription is beyond the resources of most institutions and employed largely only through crowdsourcing.[41] Much of the early digitization of historical sources was highly selective, chosen from larger collections to answer specific research questions or to make available well-known or popular documents.[42] Both forms of collection have limited attraction to a wider audience of researchers, especially given the premium the profession places on original research.[43] Contrast the use of the *Valley of the Shadow*[44] and the *Proceedings of the Old Bailey*:[45] the former is a pioneering virtual archive of sources selected by Edward Ayers for a comparative investigation of two communities in American Civil War; the latter is a collection of all the surviving editions of the published accounts of trials that took place at the Old Bailey. Although the *Valley* project produced a path-breaking digital article in the *American Historical Review* and a prize-winning book, and has been widely used in teaching, I could identify only one other scholar who used it for research.[46] As of July 2015, by contrast, 401 publications cite the *Proceedings*.[47]

In addition, many of the historical sources that are digitized are only accessible by search, in databases that do not have an API or other means of accessing the complete data. This is particularly true of the commercial databases that contain digitized newspapers, a published source widely relevant to historical research and less so to other fields in digital humanities. Sixteen of the most important American newspapers and nine of the leading African American newspapers, for example, can only be found in *Proquest Historical Newspapers*. While those databases allow researchers to search text generated by OCR, the results that are returned are only images of the page, containing no machine-readable text. Not only is there no means of bulk export, but the licensing agreements expressly prohibit data mining. Both Proquest and Gale Cengage have announced plans to open up their databases to computational analysis, but it remains unclear at what cost and by what means.[48] Peter Leonard and Lindsay King did obtain access to Proquest's Vogue Archive and their project, *Robots Reading Vogue*, shows what would be possible with access to these collections, combining an Ngram viewer, topic modeling, a frequency analysis for advertising, and a visual analysis of magazine covers. Those visualizations link to articles in *Vogue*, providing an alternative to search as a gateway into the archive—assuming that you are affiliated with an institution that subscribes to the Proquest database.[49]

In the absence of such interfaces, however, the closed and sometimes shrouded character of commercial products has encouraged historians and other humanities scholars to be simply consumers of digital content, to accept the search interfaces provided by vendors as the means by which to conduct research in digitized sources rather than looking to tools like topic modeling software. Studies of research practices have shown that many humanities scholars rely on search, beginning with Google search to identify sources, and proceeding to full text keyword searching to research within digitized collections (Rutner and Schonfeld; Kemman, Kleppe, and Scagliola; Chassanoff). So naturalized has search become that few recognize that it is not, as Ted Underwood points out, "a finding aid analogous to a card catalog . . . [but] a name for a large family of algorithms that humanists have been using for several decades to test hypotheses and sort documents by relevance to their hypothesis" (65). It can be a powerful method, disrupting the hierarchies and categories of information established in the past. Full-text search examines every publication in a database, not simply those that have become canonical, and every word in a publication, working from the bottom up rather than from the top down—for example, from the journal to the issue to the article, as a researcher in a library would. In the case of newspapers, full-text search checks many words that researchers likely would not have read when browsing, where their focus is on particular sections and headlines, not the advertisements, schedules, and notices that make up the bulk of most papers. In the case of archival collections, search can remove information from the context of the institution that structured the collection; it can, in Tim Hitchcock's words, de-center institutions in favor of individuals ("Digital Searching"). But search is also a limited method. Search struggles to deal with what lies outside a set of results. In returning only the terms one enters, a search filters out any alternative hypotheses. For historians, this poses particular challenges, as the language and ways of organizing knowledge in the past often differ significantly from contemporary terms and patterns of thought. If we use the wrong search terms, we literally misread our sources. And working with interfaces that tell us how many results we found without reference to how many results were possible, it is not always clear just how significant those results might be. In the case of most newspaper databases, search also returns individual stories, removed from their place on the page and in newspaper as a whole. In other words, search radically decontextualizes the results it produces.[50] Text mining and topic modeling can offer a different perspective that addresses those limits and complements search and other approaches to historical research.

Recognition of the value of topic modeling as a complement to search is one of several factors that have led to more use of text analysis by historians. Digitized historical sources open to text mining and topic modeling are also beginning to become more available. In the U.S. context, a key development is the Library of Congress' ongoing *Chronicling America* project.[51] Now approaching 9.5 million pages, this collection of newspapers from across the nation is not just freely available, but is also equipped with an API, allowing researchers to extract large datasets. However, although *Chronicling America* contains a rich selection of newspapers, it does not include the major papers in Proquest's databases. Nor does the collection cover the same date range as *Proquest Historical Newspapers,* being limited to the years before 1923 that are out of copyright. And the more limited resources of this project means that the OCR-generated text is uncorrected and consequently marred by numerous errors.[52] OCR accuracy is greater in commercial products, but just how much more accurate is impossible to know, as the companies do not release that information, notwithstanding how important it is to assessing the significance of search results.

A small number of historians have already text mined *Chronicling America*. As part of their *Mapping Texts* project, Andrew Torget and Jon Christensen used word counts, named entity extraction, and topic modeling to examine language patterns in Texas newspapers.[53] In a more focused study, Cameron Blevins used named-entity extraction with two of those Texas newspapers to explore what they revealed about the imagined geography of the United States in a period understood as one of integration and incorporation. What he found and reported in the first digital history article to appear in the *Journal of American History* ("Space, Nation, and the Triumph of Region[54]) was that, at odds with the prevailing view, the newspaper was focused on region, not nation.[55] In *An Epidemiology of Information: Datamining the 1918 Flu Pandemic,*[56] E. Thomas Ewing and others from Virginia Tech employed topic modeling and segmentation and tone classification on a set of twenty newspapers to explore the transmission of disease-related information (Ewing et al.). *Chronicling America* is also serving as a basis for research projects in literary studies. Ryan Cordell's *Viral Texts* project traces networks reprinting texts in nineteenth-century newspapers.[57] Elizabeth Lorang and others are developing an image classifier to identify poetry in newspapers, in order to explore the magnitude of poetic content in the press (Lorange et al.). And Lauren Klein and her collaborators at Georgia Tech are using abolitionist newspapers as the case study in their project to build *TOME,* a tool to visualize topic-modeling results (Klein).

Beyond work with newspapers, other noteworthy historical text analysis projects include two explorations of the *Digital National Security Archive* that are grappling with an even more fragmentary source and bringing digital methods to the field of diplomatic history, one of the discipline's most methodologically conservative fields. Micki Kaufman's multi-award-winning "'Everything on Paper Will Be Used Against Me': Quantifying Kissinger," employs a variety of text analysis methods to explore Henry Kissinger's memoranda and teleconference transcripts.[58] The *Declassification Engine* project, led by Matthew Connelly and David Madigan, looks at the full range of documents in the archive to explore official secrecy through analysis of redacted text and declassified documents.[59] Michelle Moravec's work using text analysis tools in women's history is important not only for bringing digital history to another field where it has been slow to find a place, women's history, but also as an example of the kind of work an individual scholar can do without a formal technical background or extensive institutional or grant support. Among other projects, Moravec has used corpus linguistics to explore gender in the *History of Women's Suffrage* —Elizabeth Cady Stanton, Susan B. Anthony, Matilda Joslyn Gage, and Ida Husted Harper's multivolume record of the suffrage movement ("'Under this name she is fitly described'"). Moravec's current project, *The Politics of Women's Culture,* also features text analyses of Women's Liberation Movement periodicals to explore networks within the movement.[60]

Building on this work, responding to the emerging opportunities, and working to obtain more access and additional digitized sources will require historians to confront their reliance on search as a research method and its limits as an approach to understanding digitized sources. Scholars that are simply searching collections with an API like the *Proceedings of the Old Bailey* or *Chronicling America* as part of their research—and many are, judging by the character of publications citing the *Proceedings of the Old Bailey* and *Chronicling America*—are missing an opportunity to put those search results into context.[61] The need to contextualize searches applies even to the use of digitized collections to recover the history of ordinary individuals, an important dimension of what the era of "big data" offers historians (Hitchcock,

"Big Data, Small Data"). Recent text analysis projects, together with these imperatives, make it likely that the limited use of text analysis tools that currently distinguishes digital historians will become less marked in the future.

Signs of a trend toward text analysis are a reminder that disciplinary differences in digital humanities are not fixed or immutable. They grow from the interests and questions that characterize a discipline at a given time, and which attract awards and recognition, and from the sources used to explore those topics, and which have been digitized and made machine-readable and available to researchers. All those elements are subject to change. Notwithstanding that fluidity, at any given time disciplinary differences are present. Discussions of digital humanities that do not recognize the different sources, approaches, and questions of humanities disciplines limit the audience they will engage and can even alienate humanities scholars who do not see their field represented. In so doing, they create a barrier to interest and to entry to the field. It does not matter how big the tent is if the entrance is narrow. To engage more scholars in digital humanities requires approaching them in disciplinary terms and showing how the values and practices of digital humanities can help them pursue their disciplinary projects. Discussions with historians, for example, need to begin with digital mapping and to present text analysis in relation to the historical sources accessible to computational tools, and to the other methods, such as search, that scholars have been using to explore those sources. Once scholars can see the value of digital humanities to their discipline, once they have entered not a big tent, but a room devoted to their field within a house shared with other disciplines, then they are in a position to engage with digital humanities as an interdisciplinary field. As Tom Scheinfeldt argues, "Understanding what makes us distinctive will help us better see what in our practices may be of use to our colleagues in other disciplines and to see more clearly what they have to offer us" ("The Dividends of Difference"). This chapter represents an effort to understand the distinctive features of digital history, arguing that historians are different in the way they use the Web and in the computational tools they currently favor. To test and sharpen that analysis requires other scholars to take up the task of understanding what makes their disciplines distinctive within the digital humanities.

NOTES

1. For an introduction to the values of the digital humanities, see Spiro, "This Is Why We Fight." For an exploration of debates over the extent to which those values are present in digital humanities, see Kirschenbaum, "What Is "Digital Humanities."

2. Southern History Association, http://sha.uga.edu/2013 Program for web.pdf; Urban History Association, http://uha.udayton.edu/2012Conf/UHA_Conference_2012_Complete_Oct_12_2012.pdf; International Congress on Medieval Studies, http://scholarworks .wmich.edu/cgi/viewcontent.cgi?article=1051&context=medieval_cong_archive.

3. Ad Hoc Committee on Professional Evaluation of Digital Scholarship by Historians, "Guidelines for the Professional Evaluation of Digital Scholarship in History," April 2015, http://historians.org/teaching-and-learning/current-projects/committee-on-professional-evaluation-of-digital-scholarship-in-history; MLA, "Guidelines for Evaluating Work in Digital Humanities and Digital Media," 2012, https://www.mla.org/guidelines_evaluation_digital; College Art Association, http://www.collegeart.org/news/2014/10/29/mellon-foundation-awards-grant-to-caa-to-partner-with-sah-on-digital-scholarship-guidelines/.

4. The blog post on which this chapter is based was written in response to "In the Shadow of the Digital Humanities," a special issue of *Differences* 25, no. 1 (2014), and Adam Kirsch's article in the May 2014 issue of *The New Republic*, "Technology Is Taking over English Departments: The False Promise of Digital Humanities." What was striking to me at the time was the almost complete absence of any mention of digital history in discussions purportedly about the field of digital humanities. See Robertson, "The Differences between Digital History and Digital Humanities."

5. For two other recent calls to make this switch, see Scheinfeldt, "The Dividends of Difference," as well as Ryan Cordell's "How Not to Teach Digital Humanities," chapter 36 in this volume.

6. That is not a straightforward task. We lack comprehensive compilations of digital humanities projects. There are numerous lists that highlight small numbers of projects as examples of particular approaches or fields within digital humanities, encouraging the tendency to focus on such projects without a sense of how they reflect what is being done in digital humanities as a whole.

7. Shelly-Godwin Archive, http://shelleygodwinarchive.org/about.

8. *Valley of the Shadow: Two Communities in the American Civil War*, http://valley.lib.virginia.edu; *Digital Harlem: Everyday Life, 1915–1930*, http://digitalharlem.org.

9. On readers as audiences for electronic editions, see Willet. On searching for names as an incidental use of *The Proceedings of the Old Bailey, 1674–1913*, see "Getting Started," http://www.oldbaileyonline.org/static/GettingStarted.jsp.

10. For digital historians work with teachers and students, see Brier, "Where's the Pedagogy?"; Robertson, "CHNM's Histories: Collaboration in Digital History"; Robertson, "CHNM's Histories: Digital History & Teaching History"; and Dorn, "Is (Digital) History More than an Argument about the Past?"

11. James Harvey Robinson Prize Recipients, http://www.historians.org/awards-and-grants/past-recipients/james-harvey-robinson-prize-recipients.

12. For a brief definition of public history, see National Council on Public History (NCPH), "What Is Public History?" http://ncph.org/cms/what-is-public-history/. The two major American historical organizations only adopted guidelines on evaluating public historians for tenure and promotion in 2010. See Working Group on Evaluating Public History Scholarship, "Tenure, Promotion, and the Publicly Engaged Academic Historian: A Report."

13. NCPH Outstanding Public History Project Award, http://ncph.org/cms/awards/public-history-project-award/.

14. http://chnm.org.

15. About RRCHNM, http://chnm.gmu.edu/about/. Grant proposals and reports for RRCHNM projects can be found at *RRCHNM20,* http://20.rrchnm.org.

16. More About History Matters, http://historymatters.gmu.edu/expansion.html.

17. *Liberty, Equality, Fraternity: Exploring the French Revolution,* http://chnm.gmu.edu/revolution/; World History Matters, http://worldhistorymatters.org/; *Children and Youth in History,* http://chnm.gmu.edu/cyh/; *Making the History of 1989,* http://chnm.gmu.edu/1989/.

18. About the Project, http://teachinghistory.org/about.

19. *ECHO: Exploring and Collecting History Online,* http://echo.gmu.edu; grant proposals and reports at *RRCHNM20.*

20. http://911digitalarchive.org.

21. *The September 11 Digital Archive,* 911digitalarchive.org; *Hurricane Digital Memory Bank,* http://hurricanearchive.org.

22. *Bracero History Archive,* http://braceroarchive.org.

23. *Gulag: Many Days, Many Lives,* http://gulaghistory.org; *Object of History,* http://objectofhistory.org.

24. "DH GIS Projects," *Anterotesis,* http://anterotesis.com/wordpress/mapping-resources/dh-gis-projects/; "Humanities GIS Projects," *GeoHumanities,* http://geohumanities.org/gis. Of the 143 projects in the list that involve more than the digitization of maps, 92 are historical projects. I did not include in the count of historical projects five projects related to book publishing that straddle the boundary between literary and historical studies. The list includes all the digital mapping projects that I have been able to identify.

25. For the spatial turn, see also Guldi, "What Is the Spatial Turn?"; Robertson, "Putting Harlem on the Map"; White, "What Is Spatial History."

26. For a more detailed, insightful guide to spatial humanities and its relation to GIS, see Bodenhamer, Corrigan, and Harris, *The Spatial Humanities.*

27. "DH GIS Projects," http://anterotesis.com/wordpress/mapping-resources/dh-gis-projects/.

28. http://www.historians.org/awards-and-grants/past-recipients/roy-rosenzweig-prize-recipients.

29. *Digital Harlem: Everyday Life, 1915–1930,* http://digitalharlem.org.

30. *Going to the Show,* http://docsouth.unc.edu/gtts/.

31. http://republicofletters.stanford.edu/index.html.

32. *Mapping the Republic of Letters,* http://republicofletters.stanford.edu; *The Roaring Twenties,* http://vectorsdev.usc.edu/NYCsound/777b.html; *Photogrammar,* http://photogrammar.yale.edu.

33. http://digitalharlem.org.

34. See also *Visualizing Emancipation,* http://dsl.richmond.edu/emancipation/.

35. http://mappingoccupation.org/index.html.

36. *Slave Revolt in Jamaica,* http://revolt.axismaps.com; *Mapping Occupation,* http://mappingoccupation.org.

37. http://www.dancohen.org/2010/10/04/searching-for-the-victorians/.

38. http://criminalintent.org.

39. http://www.common-place.org/vol-06/no-02/tales.

40. http://dsl.richmond.edu/dispatch/pages/home.

41. See "Technical Methods," Old Bailey Online, http://www.oldbaileyonline.org /static/Project.jsp#methods. The largest and longest-running crowdsourced transcription project is Transcribe Bentham, http://blogs.ucl.ac.uk/transcribe-bentham/. In the United States, the Smithsonian has a large transcription project; https://transcription.si.edu. On a smaller scale, *Papers of the War Department,* a project of RRCHNM, uses Scripto, a plugin for Omeka; see http://wardepartmentpapers.org/transcribe.php. That open-source platform allows smaller institutions to undertake crowdsourced transcription.

42. See also the other problems in the British case discussed by Tim Hitchcock in "Digitising British History since 1980."

43. For an example of historians' concern about the completeness of digital collections, see Chassanoff, "Historians and the Use of Primary Sources in the Digital Age."

44. http://valley.lib.virginia.edu.

45. http://www.oldbaileyonline.org/.

46. A search of Google Scholar identified only one article reporting research using the project. Ayers and his colleague Scott Nesbit have made use of the *Valley* in another project: *Visualizing Emancipation.*

47. "Old Bailey Proceedings Online: Citations Bibliography," https://www.zotero.org /groups/old_bailey_proceedings_online_citations_bibliography.

48. "Gale Leads to Advance Academic Research by Offering Content for Data Mining and Textual Analysis," news release, November 17, 2014, http://news.cengage. com/library-research/gale-leads-to-advance-academic-research-by-offering-content -for-data-mining-and-textual-analysis/. See also the much more ambivalent response of representatives of Cengage and D. H. Thomson at the seminar on "Mining digital repositories" at the Dutch Koninklijke Bibliotheek in 2014: http://blog.kbresearch.nl/2014/04/13 /how-to-maximise-usage-of-digital-collections/.

49. *Robots Reading Vogue,* http://dh.library.yale.edu/projects/vogue/.

50. I have found two other accounts of the impact of search as a historical research method particularly useful: see Mussell, "Doing and Making: History as Digital Practice," and Nicholson, "The Digital Turn."

51. *Chronicling America,* http://chroniclingamerica.loc.gov.

52. The exemplar in this area is *Trove,* which currently makes freely available almost 900 Australian newspapers and over 17 million pages, and benefits from less restrictive copyright law in being able to include content published up to 1954. It provides an API, allows users to tag and comment, and has been extremely successful in recruiting its users to correct OCR generated text. See http://trove.nla.gov.au.

53. "Assessing Language Patterns: A Look at Texas Newspapers, 1829–2008," http:// language.mappingtexts.org.

54. http://jah.oxfordjournals.org/cgi/content/full/jau184?ijkey=unucsImiwNrelaF& keytype=ref.

55. See also Blevins, "Mining and Mapping the Production of Space," an accompanying essay to the *Journal of American History* article.

56. http://vtechworks.lib.vt.edu/bitstream/handle/10919/46991/An Epidemiology of Information Project Research Report_Final.pdf?sequence=1.

57. About the Viral Texts Project, http://viraltexts.org.

58. *"Everything on Paper Will Be Used Against Me:"* Quantifying Kissinger, http://blog.quantifyingkissinger.com.

59. *The History Lab*, http://www.history-lab.org.

60. Digital History, http://michellemoravec.com/122-2/.

61. For publications citing *Chronicling America*, see NEH, "National Digital Newspaper Program Impact Study 2004–2014."

BIBLIOGRAPHY

Ayers, Edward L., and Scott Nesbit. "Seeing Emancipation: Scale and Freedom in the American South." *Journal of the Civil War Era* 1, 1 (March 2011): 3–24.

Blevins, Cameron. "Mining and Mapping the Production of Space: A View of the World from Houston," 2014. http://web.stanford.edu/group/spatialhistory/cgi-bin/site/pub .php?id=93.

———. "Space, Nation, and the Triumph of Region: A View of the World from Houston." *Journal of American History* 101, no. 1 (June 2014): 122–147.

Block, Sharon. "Doing More with Digitization: An Introduction to Topic Modeling of Early American Sources." *Common-Place* 6, no. 2 (January 2006). http://www.common -place.org/vol-06/no-02/tales/.

Bodenhamer, David, John Corrigan, and Trevor Harris, eds. *The Spatial Humanities: GIS and the Future of Humanities Scholarship.* Bloomington: Indiana University Press, 2010.

Brier, Stephen. "Where's the Pedagogy? The Role of Teaching and Learning in the Digital Humanities." In *Debates in Digital Humanities,* ed. Matthew K. Gold. Minneapolis: University of Minnesota Press, 2012. http://dhdebates.gc.cuny.edu/debates/text/8.

Chassanoff, Alexandra. "Historians and the Use of Primary Sources in the Digital Age." *The American Archivist* 76, no. 2 (2013): 470–471.

Cohen, Dan. "Searching for the Victorians." October 4, 2010. http://www.dancohen .org/2010/10/04/searching-for-the-victorians/.

Cohen, Dan, Michael Frisch, Patrick Gallagher, Steven Mintz, Kirsten Sword, Amy Murrell Taylor, William G. Thomas III, and William J. Turkel. "Interchange: The Promise of Digital History." *Journal of American History* 95, no. 2 (2008): 442–451.

Cohen, Dan, Tim Hitchcock, and Geoffrey Rockwell, et al. "Data Mining with Criminal Intent: Final White Paper," August 31, 2011. http://criminalintent.org/wp-content /uploads/2011/09/Data-Mining-with-Criminal-Intent-Final1.pdf.

Dorn, Sherman. "Is (Digital) History More than an Argument about the Past?" In *Writing History in the Digital Age,* ed. Kristen Nawrotzki and Jack Dougherty. Ann Arbor: University of Michigan Press, 2013. http://quod.lib.umich.edu/d/dh/12230987.0001.001/.

Ewing, E. Thomas, Samah Gad, Bernice L. Hausman, Kathleen Kerr, Bruce Pencek, and Naren Ramakrishnan. *An Epidemiology of Information: Datamining the 1918 Flu Pandemic.* Project Research Report, April 2, 2014. http://vtechworks.lib.vt.edu/bit stream/handle/10919/46991/An%20Epidemiology%20of%20Information%20 Project%20Research%20Report_Final.pdf?sequence=1.

Guldi, Jo. "What Is the Spatial Turn?" *Spatial Humanities,* 2011. http://spatial.scholarslab. org/spatial-turn/.

Haltunen, Karen. "Groundwork: American Studies in Place—Presidential Address to the American Studies Association, November 4, 2005." *American Quarterly* 58, no. 1 (March 2006): 1–15.

Hitchcock, Tim. "Big Data, Small Data and Meaning," *Historyonics* (blog), November 9, 2014. http://historyonics.blogspot.com/2014/11/big-data-small-data-and-mean ing_9.html.

———. "Digital Searching and the Re-formulation of Knowledge." In *The Virtual Representation of the Past,* ed. Mark Greengrass and Lorna Hughes, 81–90. London, Ashgate, 2008.

———. "Digitising British History since 1980." *Making History: The Changing Face of the Profession in Britain.* Institute for Historical Research, 2008. http://www.history.ac.uk /makinghistory/resources/articles/digitisation_of_history.html.

Kemman, Max, Martijn Kleppe, and Stef Scagliola. "Just Google It." In *Proceedings of the Digital Humanities Congress 2012,* ed. Clare Mills, Michael Pidd, and Esther Ward. Sheffield: HRI Online Publications, 2014. http://www.hrionline.ac.uk/openbook /chapter/dhc2012-kemman.

Kirschenbaum, Matthew G. " 'So the Colors Cover the Wires': Interface, Aesthetics, and Usability." In *A Companion to Digital Humanities,* ed. Susan Schreibman, Ray Siemens, John Unsworth. Oxford: Blackwell, 2004. http://www.digitalhumanities.org/companion/.

———. What Is "Digital Humanities" and Why Are They Saying Such Terrible Things about It?" *Differences* 25, 1 (2014): 46–63.

Klein, Lauren. "Talk at Digital Humanities 2014," DH Lab, July 24, 2014. http://dhlab.lmc .gatech.edu/news/talk-at-digital-humanities-2014/.

Lorang, Elizabeth, Leen-Kiat Soh, Maanas Varma Datla, Spencer Kulwicki. "Developing an Image-Based Classifier for Detecting Poetic Content in Historic Newspaper Collections." *D-Lib Magazine* 21, 7/8 (July/August 2015). http://www.dlib.org/dlib /july15/lorang/07lorang.html#n18.

Moravec, Michelle. " 'Under this name she is fitly described': A Digital History of Gender in the *History of Woman Suffrage,*" March 2015. http://womhist.alexanderstreet .com/moravec-full.html#en7.

Mussell, James. "Doing and Making: History as Digital Practice." In *History in the Digital Age,* ed. Toni Weller, 79–94. London: Routledge, 2013.

National Council on Public History. "What Is Public History?" http://ncph.org/cms/what-is-public-history/.

National Endowment for the Humanities. "National Digital Newspaper Program Impact Study 2004–2014," September 2014. http://www.neh.gov/files/divisions/preservation/ndnp_report_2014_0.pdf.

Nelson, Robert. *Mining the Dispatch.* Digital Scholarship Lab, University of Richmond. http://dsl.richmond.edu/dispatch/pages/home.

Nicholson, Bob. "The Digital Turn." *Media History* 19, no. 1 (2013): 59–73.

Parry, David. "Be Online or Be Irrelevant." *AcademHack,* January 11, 2010. http://academhack.outsidethetext.com/home/2010/be-online-or-be-irrelevant/.

Robertson, Stephen. "CHNM's Histories: Collaboration in Digital History." Author's blog, October 14, 2014. http://drstephenrobertson.com/blog-post/chnms-histories-collaboration-in-digital-history/.

———. "CHNM's Histories: Digital History & Teaching History." Author's blog, October 27, 2014. http://drstephenrobertson.com/blog-post/digital-history-teaching-history/.

———. "The Differences between Digital History and Digital Humanities," Author's blog, May 23, 2014. http://drstephenrobertson.com/blog-post/the-differences-between-digital-history-and-digital-humanities/.

———. "Putting Harlem on the Map." In *Writing History in the Digital Age,* ed. Kristen Nawrotzki and Jack Dougherty. Ann Arbor: University of Michigan Press, 2013. http://quod.lib.umich.edu/d/dh/12230987.0001.001/.

Robertson, Stephen, Shane White, and Stephen Garton. "Harlem in Black and White: Mapping Race and Place in the 1920s." *Journal of Urban History* 39, no. 5 (2013): 864–880.

Rockwell, Geoffrey. "Inclusion in the Digital Humanities." *Philosophi.ca,* September 7, 2011. http://www.philosophi.ca/pmwiki.php/Main/InclusionInTheDigitalHumanities.

RRCHNM20. Roy Rosenzweig Center for History and Media (RRCHNM) 20th Anniversary Conference, George Mason University, November 14–15, 2014. http://20.rrchnm.org.

Rutner, Jennifer, and Roger Schonfeld. "Supporting the Changing Research Practices of Historians (ITHAKA S+R, 2012)," December 10, 2012. http://www.sr.ithaka.org/sites/default/files/reports/supporting-the-changing-research-practices-of-historians.pdf.

Scheinfeldt, Tom. "The Dividends of Difference: Recognizing Digital Humanities' Diverse Family Tree/s." *Found History,* April 7, 2014. http://foundhistory.org/2014/04/the-dividends-of-difference-recognizing-digital-humanities-diverse-family-trees/.

Schreibman, Susan, Ray Siemens, John Unsworth, eds. *A Companion to Digital Humanities.* Oxford: Blackwell, 2004. http://www.digitalhumanities.org/companion/.

Spiro, Lisa. " 'This Is Why We Fight': Defining the Values of the Digital Humanities." In *Debates in Digital Humanities,* ed. Matthew K. Gold. Minneapolis: University of Minnesota Press, 2012. http://dhdebates.gc.cuny.edu/debates/text/13.

Svensson, Patrik. "Beyond the Big Tent." In *Debates in Digital Humanities,* ed. Matthew K. Gold. Minneapolis: University of Minnesota Press, 2012. http://dhdebates.gc.cuny.edu/debates/text/22.

Terras, Melissa. "Peering inside the Big Tent: Digital Humanities and the Crisis of Inclusion." Author's blog, July 26, 2011. http://melissaterras.blogspot.com/2011/07/peering-inside -big-tent-digital.html.

Thomas, William. "Computing and the Historical Imagination." In *A Companion to Digital Humanities,* ed. Susan Schreibman, Ray Siemens, and John Unsworth. Oxford: Black-well, 2004. http://www.digitalhumanities.org/companion/.

Underwood, Ted. "Theorizing Research Practices We Forgot to Theorize Twenty Years Ago." *Representations* 127, 1 (Summer 2014): 64–72.

White, Richard. "What Is Spatial History?" *Spatial History Project,* February 1, 2010. https://web.stanford.edu/group/spatialhistory/cgi-bin/site/pub.php?id=29.

Willett, Perry. "Electronic Texts: Audiences and Purposes." In *A Companion to Digital Humanities,* ed. Susan Schreibman, Ray Siemens, and John Unsworth. Oxford: Black-well, 2004. http://www.digitalhumanities.org/companion/.

Working Group on Evaluating Public History Scholarship. "Tenure, Promotion, and the Publicly Engaged Academic Historian: A Report." AHA Perspectives, September 2010. http://www.historians.org/perspectives/issues/2010/1009/1009new3.cfm.

Digital History's Perpetual Future Tense

CAMERON BLEVINS

In 2008, historian Tom Scheinfeldt made a prediction. He believed that the practice of history was moving away from big ideas about ideology or theory and toward an emphasis on "forging new tools, methods, materials, techniques, and modes or work." The blog post titled "Sunset for Ideology, Sunrise for Methodology?" outlined the rise of digital history as a field. That same year, the *Journal of American History* published an interchange between leading digital historians titled "The Promise of Digital History." Together, Scheinfeldt's blog post and the *Journal of American History* interchange embodied a feeling of newness, excitement, and tantalizing potential surrounding the future of a field that was about to take off. In fact, the word "new" appeared more than one hundred times in the *Journal of American History* interchange—eclipsed only by the words "digital" and "history" ("Interchange: The Promise of Digital History").[1] A brilliant sunrise was hiding just over the horizon.

Seven years later, the rhetoric surrounding digital history feels much the same as 2008. The 2015 American Historical Association (AHA) Conference included some twenty panels on digital history. A remarkable number of their abstracts and titles (including the title of my own panel) featured words like "promise," "possibilities," "opportunities," and, perhaps most ubiquitously, "potential"—"the potential of digital humanities approaches" (Hulden), "the potential of digital tools" (Vincent Brown), "the potential of hypertext for history" (Appelbaum), "the potential of the archive in the digital era" (Desai). In short, the digital turn "has the potential to profoundly change the way we think and work as historians" (Nancy Brown et. al.) Reading these abstracts in 2015, one would think the sunrise of methodology was still hovering just over the horizon.

The ongoing rhetoric of "potential" and "possibility" is especially curious given the field's very real advancements. The annual AHA conference now showcases dozens of digital history projects each year (Shrout). History departments are increasingly offering courses on digital methods at both the graduate and undergraduate level (Bush; Hajo; Heppler; Kramer; McDaniel). Historians have built a suite of widely used digital tools, from reference-management software to web-publishing platforms for archival collections, maps, and timelines.[2] Online exhibits and interactive websites have allowed historians to reach an audience that stretches far beyond the walls of the academy.[3] Digital history's methodological sun is no longer lurking over the horizon; it has already come up. So what explains the disconnect between rhetoric and results? Why does the field seem to be stuck in a perpetual future tense?

There are many reasons for historians to frame digital methodology in terms of its future potential. The most obvious is that digital history is a relatively young field with much of its growth having taken place only in the past decade. A focus on technology means keeping an eye on the future, as new tools arise or certain platforms become obsolete. There is an element of strategic salesmanship as well. It is easier to pitch projects to university administrators, funding agencies, and skeptical colleagues if the enterprise is framed as innovative and forward-looking. But there is a subtler reason why digital history operates in a perpetual future tense. Although the sunrise of methodology has cast its light across much of the historical profession, one area still remains in the shadows: argument-driven scholarship. In terms of using technology specifically to advance academic claims about the past, digital history has largely overpromised and underdelivered.

For academic historians, the enterprise of historical research is synonymous with making arguments. Doctoral dissertations and monographs present arguments about the past, while job committees and tenure review boards evaluate the originality and impact of these arguments. There is, of course, much more to doing history than just making arguments, but this kind of scholarship has been the primary measuring stick in the academy for the past half-century. Argumentation is still the fulcrum of academic history. So long as this remains the case, it poses a problem for digital historians. Because as a field, digital history has largely pivoted away from making academic arguments. We have instead poured our energies into other historical practices: digitizing and archiving sources, designing online collections and exhibits, building tools and platforms, and incorporating digital media into the classroom. These projects may incorporate scholarly claims and interpretations about the past, but argumentation is rarely their central purpose. These are the areas where the sunlight of methodology has shone brightest and where digital history has achieved its most impressive accomplishments. By comparison, academic argument-driven scholarship remains in the shadows. Few of us want to acknowledge this gap, but it is a major reason why historians continue to use the future tense of "potential" and "possibility" despite two decades of successfully applying digital methods within archival, pedagogical, and public history initiatives.[4]

It is time for academic historians to close the gap. This essay explains how and why this gap developed by tracing digital history's genealogy over the past several decades. It focuses on two historical traditions that are most frequently linked to digital history: quantitative history and public history. Both have left their imprint on the field, but in opposite ways. Quantitative history serves primarily as a cautionary tale, while public history acts a template for the current practice of digital history. This particular genealogy has steered digital historians away from advancing explicit, scholarly claims about the past. For digital historians interested in these kinds of arguments, it is time to devote far more of our time and energy to making them. A renewed commitment to generating argument-driven scholarship will help push the field out of its perpetual future tense.

Argument and Genealogy

In the 1960s, quantitatively inclined historians turned to computers, social-science methods, and statistical analysis to make arguments about the past. A "cliometric" cohort of economic historians rose to particular prominence within this quantitative turn, perhaps none more than Robert Fogel and Stanley Engerman. In *Time on the Cross: The Economics of American Negro Slavery* (1974), Fogel and Engerman used statistical analysis to argue that slavery in the nineteenth-century United States was both more profitable and more benign than previously thought. For many historians, *Time on the Cross* embodied everything that was wrong with quantitative history, from its reliance on limited datasets to its dismissal of less quantifiable aspects of history such as ideology or power. Cliometricians may have been able to calculate exactly the average number of whippings a slave received each year, but they had far less to say about what that violence meant and the ways in which these enslaved men and women created meaning in their lives (Gutman; Weiss; Thomas III). By the 1980s and 1990s, the cultural and linguistic turn had eclipsed quantitative approaches. In the words of historian Ed Ayers, "Rather than SPSS guides and codebooks, innovative historians carried books of French philosophy and German literary interpretation. . . . The first computer revolution largely failed" (Ayers, "The Past and Futures of Digital History").

Quantitative history's controversies and limitations cast a long shadow across the historical profession. Many historians who studied quantitative methods in graduate school still shudder at the memory of laboriously coding punch cards or wading through unreadable statistical charts and tables. Others vaguely conflate the entire quantitative history movement with the lack of empathy and argumentative overreach embodied by Fogel and Engerman's *Time on the Cross*. As one joke went at the time, "If a cliometrician were to write the history of the crucifixion . . . he would begin by counting the nails" (Haskell). It wasn't the numbers themselves that provoked this kind of backlash; it was the use of those numbers to make positivistic arguments. The caricatured view of quantitative history was that it reduced the past into a laboratory in which the historian-as-scientist could run experiments, test hypotheses, and reach empirically verifiable conclusions. Historians are wary of being tarred this way by the brush of scientific positivism, and this fear holds particular resonance for digital historians. Using computers and quantitative data to make historical arguments runs the risk of echoing the work of cliometricians, with all the baggage that comes with that association. Digital historians are much more eager to distance themselves from the mistakes of their quantitative predecessors than they are to proudly carry forward their methodological mantle. This is an unfortunate part of quantitative history's legacy: a fear of argumentative overreach based on numerical evidence (Sewell Jr.).[5]

The cautionary shadow cast by the quantitative history movement is a real one, but it does not fully explain digital historians' lack of academic argumentation. The looming specter of scientific positivism might frame *how* we make historical arguments, but they do not necessarily dissuade us from making them. It is simply that argument-based scholarship does not rank especially high on the field's priority list. For example, one of the most successful digital history projects released in 2014, *Histories of the National Mall*, uses a mobile interface to explore the place-based history of Washington, D.C.'s National Mall.[6] The project certainly offers an historical interpretation of the National Mall: rather than the neatly curated and organized landscape with which we are familiar, the National Mall was, for much of its history, an unregulated space defined by messiness and multiplicity. But this interpretation—the kind of traditional argument with which academic historians are familiar—is implicit rather than explicit, not least because the project is aimed at tourists and visitors rather than a handful of specialized history professors. Academic argumentation takes a backseat to the project's larger goals and interventions: building a user-friendly mobile platform, narrating compelling stories about the Mall's history, and facilitating exploration and discovery. As a paragon of modern digital history, *Histories of the National Mall* seems utterly divorced from the kind of quantitative history conducted by cliometricians during the 1970s. Instead, it exemplifies a different historical practice that has shaped the current field of digital history: public history (Leon).

As Tom Scheinfeldt, Stephen Robertson, and other digital historians point out, public history can make a strong claim as digital history's true progenitor. When digital history began to take root in the 1990s, it found its most fertile ground in archival collection, digitization, and presentation. From an early stage, the historians and institutions that did the most to adopt new media and technology digital innovations were also deeply involved in the world of libraries, education, archives, and museums (Scheinfeldt, "Dividends of Difference"; see also chapter 25 by Robertson in this volume). Early projects like *The Valley of the Shadow* at the University of Virginia, an online repository related to the Civil War, or the City University of New York's multimedia textbook *Who Built America?* became the primary models for digital history products (Thomas III, "Computing and the Historical Imagination").[7] The priorities and interests of early pioneers like Roy Rosenzweig laid down the path for future digital historians to follow. Rosenzweig's own Center for History and New Media, which he founded at George Mason University in 1994, became one of the institutional epicenters for the emerging field of digital history. Over the next two decades, the majority of the Center's projects were public history initiatives, and in 2005 Rosenzweig and his colleague Daniel Cohen authored one of the field's foundational texts: *Digital History: A Guide to Gathering, Preserving, and Presenting the Past* (Robertson, "CHNM's Histories"; Cohen and Rosenzweig).[8] The volume was, in effect, a guide to the practice of *public* history in a digital age.

Early digital historians interested in public history often launched initiatives that targeted a particular audience: history teachers and students (Robertson, "CHNM's Histories"). *History Matters*, for instance, was an early digital history collaboration produced by two of the field's most influential institutional leaders: the American Social History Project at the City University of New York and the Center for History and New Media at George Mason University.[9] It offered high school and college teachers and their students in U.S. history survey courses a gateway for accessing primary documents, resources, and guides. Much like public history projects, these teaching initiatives were primarily concerned with using new media and the Web to reach a more general audience outside of the academy. The goal of expanding access to the past (in this case, expanding access for specifically teachers and students) took precedence over using digital tools to craft new academic arguments about the past.

During the late 1990s, the rise of hypertext also helped shape the young field of digital history. Hyperlinks presented digital historians with the opportunity to recast traditional historical narratives into radically new electronic formats. In the early 2000s, the *American Historical Review* (one of the historical profession's premier academic journals) published several articles that, to varying degrees, engaged with hypertext, new media, and nonlinear historical narrative (Darnton; Ethington; Thomas III and Ayers). The revolutionary possibilities of hypertext found fertile ground in the wake of the field's wider "linguistic turn," which critiqued the underlying assumption that historical narratives were an objective reflection of past realities. In this context, hypertext was a way to detonate the tidy beginnings, middles, and ends that historians artificially impose on the past. The historical profession's broader interest in hypertext and nonlinear narratives ultimately proved fleeting, but for many early digital historians it was an important step in challenging traditional approaches to studying the past. These early works of hypertext history focused primarily on using digital methods to explore the new *forms* that historical scholarship might take in a digital medium. Although some of them incorporated tools like GIS to reach new findings and build new arguments about the past, their larger interventions centered primarily around how these findings and arguments were communicated and consumed. Once again, argumentation about the past itself often took a backseat to other interests and priorities.[10]

Of all the different genealogical strands that helped foster digital history's emergence during the early 1990s and 2000s—public history, pedagogy, and hypertext—public history proved to be the most influential and enduring. More so than teaching and far more so than hypertext, public history came to define how people, especially other historians, understood the practice of digital history. Projects completed during these early years became the template for what constituted and defined the field. Today, digital history is all but synonymous with digital *public* history.[11] The syllabi of digital history courses typically cover topics like digitization, copyright, and website design. Assignments in these courses frequently take the form of an online website, collection, or exhibit (Bush; Hajo). One of the largest grant-makers for digital history initiatives, the National Endowment for the Humanities' Office of Digital Humanities, has dispensed millions of dollars over the past several years to historical projects. Most of its grant recipients focus on cultural heritage initiatives, online archives, museum collections, digital preservation, databases, tool building, and software design.[12]

To borrow from historian Sherman Dorn, the "first-mover" advantage of early digital historians in the 1990s and early 2000s helped set the agenda for the field as it coalesced (Dorn). At the top of this agenda was an overriding ideology: to democratize access to the past. The rise of the World Wide Web offered a powerful vehicle to achieve this goal. In fact, there was a strong parallel between the democratizing impulse of public history and the democratizing potential of the early Web. Rosenzweig and Cohen, for instance, ended their 2005 book *Digital History* with a "larger message—that all historians can use the web to make the past more richly documented, more accessible, more diverse, more responsive to future researchers, and above all more democratic" (Cohen and Rosenzweig, 248). Digital history was imbued with an early and overriding commitment to empower all kinds of people, not just professional historians, to interact with the past more easily, more flexibly, and more directly.

Public history's ideology has had an overwhelmingly positive influence on digital history. A commitment to public engagement and accessibility has democratized both the consumption and production of history. Expanding the audience has simultaneously allowed digital history's practitioners to expand the *kind* of work that they do: building new textual search interfaces like Bookworm, developing open-source software like Omeka, or redefining the scope of national archives like the Digital Public Library of America or the National Library of Australia (Cohen; Sherratt).[13] It is a field that has become predicated on ambitious collaborative projects conducted with a broad audience in mind. This is the enduring legacy of public history within the practice of digital history today.

Yet in borrowing from the priorities and values of public history, digital historians have simultaneously turned away from argument-driven academic scholarship. It is not that public historians do not make arguments. Every online exhibit or archive offers an interpretation about the past, explicitly or implicitly. But argumentation is not the organizing objective of public historians in the same way that it is for modern academic historians. To give one example, the National Council on Public History states that public history prioritizes "an interest and commitment to making history relevant and useful in the public sphere" ("What Is Public

History?"). Debates over arguments, claims, and interpretations might have their place in public history, but they are not as central as the goal of making the past accessible, relevant, and useful for a wide audience.[14] And despite calls for change, the opposite is too often true in the academy, where accessibility, relevance, and public engagement frequently take a backseat to scholarly arguments, claims, and interpretations.

At first glance, public history's emphasis on accessibility embeds history within the digital humanities landscape. Digital history's commitment to democratizing access to the past, for instance, dovetails with the "openness" of the broader digital humanities, which Lisa Spiro describes as one of the field's "core values" (Spiro). But in other ways, digital history's genealogy and its move away from academic argumentation sets it apart from other disciplines. The difference is especially telling when compared to digital literary studies, which has embraced argument-driven scholarship in recent years with far more enthusiasm. Public-facing initiatives certainly played an important role in the field's growth, most prominently with the Text Encoding Initiative (TEI), a long-standing project to define a schema for digitizing and encoding texts. But argument-driven analysis exerts a much stronger influence on digital literary studies compared to digital history. Statistical studies in authorship attribution and stylistics stretched back for decades, and these kinds of literary analysis were featured prominently in 2004's *A Companion to Digital Humanities* (Burrows; Craig). Franco Moretti's analytical concept of "distant reading," meanwhile, has come to define how many people view and define the field of digital literary studies, so much so that Moretti won the National Book Critics Circle Award for criticism in 2014 (Moretti, "Conjectures on World Literature"; Moretti, *Distant Reading*). The enormous attention paid to analytical approaches like "distant reading" has grown so large that other digital literary projects such as preservation, curation, annotation, and encoding—public history's closest literary cousins—are being marginalized (Cordell).

In digital literary studies, the scales have tipped toward argument-driven scholarship such as "distant reading" rather than archival and digital publication practices. In digital history, that balance is entirely reversed. There is no Franco Moretti or "distant reading" in history. Instead, public history projects garner far more popular attention than argument-driven academic analyses (Onion, "Five of 2014's Most Compelling Digital History Exhibits and Archives"; Onion, "Five More Digital Archives and Historical Exhibits We Loved"). Compared to our literary colleagues, digital historians have pushed academic arguments into the background in favor of public-facing projects. The difference between the two fields is partly an issue of sources. Historians rely on an archive that does not readily lend itself to digitization, much less digital analysis. After all, a printed novel like *Middlemarch* is much more digestible for a computer than the handwritten scrawl of a probate will or a mortgage deed (see chapter 25 of this volume). Although digital literary scholars had something of a head start in terms of their source base, the archival lag between machine-readable texts and unpublished documents does not fully explain the argument gap between literature and history. Source availability matters less than what the two fields want to do with them and how those goals have been prioritized. To offer a caricature of recent years: in digital literary studies the predominant goal has been to use digital sources to generate arguments. In digital history, the predominant goal has been to make those sources available and accessible.

The Case for Argument

Digital historians should be proud of their field's genealogy and public history's path-defining role within it. With all due respect to our colleagues in English or classics, no other discipline in the humanities has committed itself so wholeheartedly to public engagement and access. One could argue that online historical exhibits, collections, and archives reach larger and more diverse audiences than any other kind of humanities work. These digital history projects are some of the strongest rebuttals we have for critics who bemoan the humanities' eroding position in society or growing irrelevancy in the digital age. In this context, a call for more argument-based academic scholarship might seem odd. After all, shouldn't academic historians spend less time debating with one another and more time making the past accessible to nonacademics? This dichotomy between accessibility and argument is, of course, a false one; we can and indeed should do both. But as it currently stands, argument lags far behind accessibility in the way that digital historians practice their craft.

We rarely acknowledge the widespread absence of academic argumentation in digital history. To take an example from my own work: in 2010, I wrote a blog post about the diary of an eighteenth-century Maine midwife named Martha Ballard, first made famous in the early 1990s by historian Laurel Ulrich's prize-winning *A Midwife's Tale* (Blevins, "Topic Modeling Martha Ballard's Diary"; Ulrich). The post described how I used topic modeling[15] to analyze about 10,000 diary entries written by Ballard between 1785 and 1812. Topic modeling is a technique that generates groups of words more likely to appear with each other in the same documents (in this case, diary entries). For example, one of the topics the tool identified in Ballard's diary contained the following words: *gardin, sett, worked, clear, beens, corn, warm, planted, matters, cucumbers, gatherd, potatoes, plants, ou, sowd, door, squash, wed, seeds*. As a human reader, it is clear that these are words about gardening. Once the program identified this topic, it measured the topic's relative presence within all 10,000 diary entries—essentially tracking when Martha Ballard wrote about gardening in her diary. Aggregating the topic's presence across all of the entries into a single representative "year" produced a thumbprint of a typical New England growing season, one that spiked dramatically in the late spring and early summer before slowly tailing off during the autumn months.

The blog post about topic modeling is probably the most widely read piece of historical writing I have produced in my career. Five years after I wrote it, the post has been viewed more than 10,000 times and appeared on the syllabi of at least twenty different courses (Bush; Gibbs; Wilkens). It has been cited in books, journal articles, conference presentations, grant applications, government reports, white-papers, and, of course, other blogs (Jockers 22, 124; Tangherlini and Leonard, 728; Meeks and Weingart; Kushkuley; Guiliano; Fox; Yang, Torget, and Mihalcea; Posner). Lost amidst all of this attention, however, was the fact that there was little new or revelatory in my writing *about the past itself.* It made no new interpretations about women's history or colonial New England or the history of medicine. It largely showed us results that we already knew—like the fact that people in Maine did not plant beans in January—or visualized patterns that had already been analyzed in far richer detail by historian Laurel Ulrich in *A Midwife's Tale.* Outside of a few scattered and underdeveloped sentences, interpretive historical arguments were almost entirely absent from the blog post.

My post's contributions were illustrative and methodological rather than interpretive and historical. I showed how a topic-modeling tool could ingest 10,000 diary entries and, in a matter of seconds, spit out the major themes of those entries and track them over time. And, like a magic trick, it could do this without understanding the semantic meaning of a single word, connecting Martha Ballard's "gardin" and "beens" regardless of how she spelled them. Near the end of the post I wrote, "Topic modeling offers a new and valuable way of interpreting the source material." Maybe so, but left unsaid is the fact that I did not actually use the method to build an original interpretation about Martha Ballard and her world. I was content to outline the method and its results while stopping just short of argument. Instead, I stuck to the familiar script we so often deploy when talking about digital methods and historical research, writing about "the potential for topic modeling in historical source material" (Blevins, "Topic Modeling Martha Ballard's Diary). In short, digital history's perpetual future tense.

Trying to locate explicit, historical arguments in digital history projects can often feel like a game of "Where's Waldo?" This is partly because academic historians have been content to follow the templates laid down by public history or pedagogical projects. There are vastly more examples to follow of historical collections built using Omeka than there are of argument-driven historical scholarship using digital methods. Digital projects may begin with a focus on producing purely academic research, but many of them ultimately end up taking the form of online exhibits or collections of primary sources. Meanwhile, even when historians use digital methods specifically for the purposes of research and analysis, they often focus far more on the data and the methodology (and the methodology's potential) than on interpreting the results—just as I did with my blog post on Martha Ballard. Explicit arguments about the past tend to fade into the background or melt away entirely.

There are exceptions, of course. To take one example, historian Benjamin Schmidt posted a series of blog posts[16] detailing his research that used a nineteenth-century ship's logs to map historical maritime patterns (Schmidt, "Reading Digital

Sources"). In these posts, Schmidt first spends considerable time discussing the digital source base itself:[17] how the archive was originally collected, the reasons and process behind its digitization, and its gaps and limitations (Schmidt, "Logbooks and the Long History of Digitization"). He goes on to outline[18] the methodology[19] he used, including an innovative application of machine-learning algorithms to extract a particular subsample from the archive (Schmidt, "Machine Learning at Sea"; Schmidt, "When You Have a MALLET"). All of these posts give crucial context for Schmidt's captivating visualizations[20] of that data, including ghostly animations of thousands of individual voyages traversing the globe (Schmidt, "Visualizing Ocean Shipping").

Schmidt does not stop at advancing new analytical methods or designing beautiful visualizations: he uses the data, the methods, and the visualizations to make new arguments about the past. In particular, Schmidt reinterprets nineteenth-century American maritime history, reorienting it away from an interconnected commercial network and toward a conceptualization of the ocean as a site of industrial extraction and pillaging[21] (Schmidt, "Data Narratives and Structural Histories"). It is exactly the sort of explicit and substantive historical claim that is so frequently absent from digital history works, including my own blog post on Martha Ballard's diary. What is so compelling about Schmidt's work is the way that he blends discussions of methodology, data, and visualization (the familiar terrain of digital historians) together with scholarly interpretations about maritime history and the American state (the familiar terrain of academic historians). It is an admittedly difficult juggling act to pull off, but one that more of us should attempt.

To be clear: it is not the responsibility of digital historians to suddenly reorient their priorities toward academic argumentation. A historian working in cultural heritage preservation cannot be expected to drop everything to intervene in obscure historiographical debates. And making scholarly arguments does not mean that we have to abandon the core values that have made digital history such a thriving field. Public engagement and accessibility can and should shape our arguments about the past. Even more important, I hope that digital historians continue to push the boundaries of what "counts" as historical scholarship beyond the traditional definition privileged by what Edward Ayers terms the academy's "monographic culture" (Ayers, "Does Digital Scholarship Have a Future?"; Dorn; Scheinfeldt, "Where's the Beef?"). But those of us who *are* interested in academic arguments need to get on with making them.

There are two major reasons for digital historians to engage more forcefully with argument-driven scholarship. The first reason is pragmatic. A turn away from argumentation erects a wall between digital history and the academy. There is currently widespread curiosity from traditional academics in digital methodology, but the barriers to entry are steep. Some of these barriers center on technological learning curves or funding issues, but a less acknowledged barrier is that the field's most prominent projects do not necessarily line up with the interests and practices of academic historians. The American Historical Association, for instance, has awarded its Roy Rosenzweig Prize for Innovation in Digital History almost entirely to libraries and archives for online collections of documents ("Roy Rosenzweig Prize Recipients"). While scholars might admire and benefit from these projects, many will not want to invest their time and energy in building them. For academic historians who have trained, worked, and built their careers on the basis of making arguments, digital history's current landscape can seem like an unfamiliar place. And while it is unfair to expect the field of digital history to bend its priorities wholesale to reflect the needs of academics, we should also consider the extent to which our projects would benefit from the thematic knowledge, expertise, and experience of academic historians. A more explicit emphasis on generating argument-driven scholarship would give these scholars a more inviting avenue through which to participate in the field.

The second, and more important, reason that digital history should reengage with argumentation is that making arguments is a fundamentally valuable and necessary way to further our collective understanding of the past. History is an interpretive process, and argumentation is a means of making that interpretive process explicit. After all, not every interpretation is equally good. Arguments backed by evidence allow others to evaluate the quality of those interpretations—to confirm them, to critique them, and to build upon them. It is easy to forget that Robert Fogel and Stanley Engerman's *Time on the Cross* received enthusiastic initial accolades from the popular press when it was first published in 1974. Academic historians were the ones who led the counterattack against their interpretations. The book suffered from many weaknesses, but a lack of argumentation was not one of them. By positing explicit arguments about, say, the profitability of antebellum slavery, Fogel and Engerman allowed other scholars to evaluate and ultimately reject their conclusions. Four decades later, academic historians waded into a related debate about the nature of the Confederate flag in the wake of the June 2015 shooting at a black church in Charleston, South Carolina. When they argued that the flag is a symbol of white supremacy rather than benign regional heritage, they were drawing on a rich historiographical tradition of academic research, argument, and debate stretching back more than a century (Richardson). The controversies surrounding *Time on the Cross* and the Confederate flag were far more than just ivory tower academics quibbling over arcane historical details. Both examples involved very real stakes: how the United States understands the legacy of its enslavement of millions of black men and women.

Whether in 1974 or 2015, academic argumentation is still a crucial means of advancing a conversation about the past. It is not the only way to have that conversation, but it is a necessary one. So far, digital history has largely shied away from this kind of conversation. Instead, digital history has thrown itself into other conversations with other participants. Our field's genealogy means that many of those conversations are centered on libraries and archives, museums and classrooms. Digital historians have contributed far more to public history than we have to argument-driven scholarship. When we do engage in academic conversations, we often elide the priorities of the other participants while lapsing into a vague future tense of promise and possibilities. It is time to spend less time talking about digital history's potential to generate new arguments about the past and more time actually making them.

NOTES

This chapter is a revised version of Cameron Blevins, "The Perpetual Sunrise of Methodology," *Cameron Blevins* (blog), January 5, 2015. http://www.cameronblevins.org/posts /perpetual-sunrise-methodology/. Many thanks to Matthew Gold, Stephen Robertson, and Dennis Tenen for their feedback.

1. Word-count figures ignore common English stop-words such as "the," "and," "of," etc.

2. http://zotero.org/; http://omeka.org/; http://neatline.org.

3. http://www.becomingrichardpryor.com/pryors-peoria/; http://mallhistory.org/.

4. Two critiques to the necessity of traditional academic arguments can be found in Dorn and in Scheinfeldt ("Where's the Beef?").

5. Scott Weingart writes on the scientific model in the humanities in Weingart, "Appreciability & Experimental Digital Humanities"; Weingart, "Do Historians Need Scientists?"; Weingart, "Digital History."

6. http://mallhistory.org.

7. http://valley.lib.virginia.edu/; http://ashp.cuny.edu/who-america/.

8. The twenty-year anniversary of the *Roy Rosenzweig Center for History and New Media* in 2014 featured a round-up of all the projects conducted at the center: http://20 .rrchnm.org/items/browse/type/project.

9. http://historymatters.gmu.edu/.

10. Many thanks to Stephen Robertson for pointing out the role of hypertext in digital history's genealogy.

11. Both Lara Kelland and Mary Rizzo warn of the dangers of public history being marginalized under the umbrella of digital humanities and losing its drive and ability to challenge traditional power structures. Those fears might apply to the broader field of digital humanities, but this is not the case within digital history, where public history holds a tremendous degree of influence (Kelland; Rizzo).

12. NEH Office of Digital Humanities Press Room (March 2013) http://www .neh.gov/divisions/odh/grant-news/announcing-23-digital-humanities-start-grant-awards -march-2013; NEH Office of Digital Humanities Press Room (July 2013) http://www.neh .gov/divisions/odh/grant-news/announcing-6-digital-humanities-implementation -grant-awards-july-2013; NEH Office of Digital Humanities Press Room (March 2014) http://www.neh.gov/divisions/odh/grant-news/announcing-20-digital-humanities-start -grant-awards-march-2014; NEH Office of Digital Humanities Press Room (July 2014) http://www.neh.gov/divisions/odh/grant-news/announcing-seven-digital-humanities -implementation-grants-july-2014.

13. http://benschmidt.org/projects/bookworm-info/; http://omeka.org; http://dp.la /info/2013/04/18/message-from-the-executive-director/; http://www.nla.gov.au/our -publications/staff-papers/from-portal-to-platform.

14. Public history is an incredibly diverse field that in many ways defies tidy categorizations. For an introduction to the field and its diversity, see Weible.

15. http://en.wikipedia.org/wiki/Topic_model.

16. http://sappingattention.blogspot.com/2012/11/reading-digital-sources-case -study-in.html.

17. http://sappingattention.blogspot.com/2012/10/logbooks-and-long-history-of .html.

18. http://sappingattention.blogspot.com/2012/11/machine-learning-on-high-seas .html.

19. http://sappingattention.blogspot.com/2012/11/when-you-have-mallet-every thing-looks.html.

20. http://sappingattention.blogspot.com/2012/04/visualizing-ocean-shipping.html.

21. http://sappingattention.blogspot.com/2012/10/data-narratives-and-structural. html.

BIBLIOGRAPHY

Appelbaum, Yoni. "Open Sources: Realizing the Potential of Hypertext for History." American Historical Association, New York City, January 2–5, 2015. https://aha.confex .com/aha/2015/webprogram/Paper17502.html.

Ayers, Edward L. "Does Digital Scholarship Have a Future?" *Educause Review* 48, no. 4 (2013): 24. http://www.educause.edu/ero/article/does-digital-scholarship-have-future.

———. "The Past and Futures of Digital History." Virginia Center for Digital History, 1999. http://www.vcdh.virginia.edu/PastsFutures.html.

Blevins, Cameron. "Topic Modeling Martha Ballard's Diary." *Cameron Blevins* (blog), April 1, 2010. http://www.cameronblevins.org/posts/topic-modeling-martha-ballards -diary/.

Brown, Nancy, Rachel Kantrowitz, Ashley Sanders, and Nora Slonimsky. "Digital Tools: From the Archive to Publication." American Historical Association, New York City, January 2–5, 2015. https://aha.confex.com/aha/2015/webprogram/Session12161 .html.

Brown, Vincent. "Mapping a Slave Revolt: Digital Tools and the Historian's Craft." American Historical Association, New York City, January 2–5, 2015. https://aha.confex .com/aha/2015/webprogram/Paper17474.html.

Burrows, John. "Textual Analysis." In *A Companion to Digital Humanities (Blackwell Companions to Literature and Culture),* ed. Ray Siemens, John Unsworth, and Susan Schreibman. Oxford: Blackwell Publishing Professional, 2004. http://www.digital humanities.org/companion/view?docId=blackwell/9781405103213/9781405103213. xml&doc.view=print&chunk.id=ss1-4-4&toc.depth=1&toc.id=0.

Bush, Erin. *H390: The Digital Past* (syllabus), 2014. George Mason University. http://h390 .erinbush.org/.

Cohen, Dan. "Welcome to the Digital Public Library of America." *Digital Public Library of America,* April 18, 2013. http://dp.la/info/2013/04/18/message-from -the-executive-director/.

Cohen, Daniel, and Roy Rosenzweig. *Digital History: A Guide to Gathering, Preserving, and Presenting the Past on the Web.* Philadelphia: University of Pennsylvania Press, 2005.

Cordell, Ryan. "On Ignoring Encoding." *Ryan Cordell* (blog), May 8, 2014. http://ryan cordell.org/research/dh/on-ignoring-encoding/.

Craig, Hugh. "Stylistic Analysis and Authorship Studies." In *A Companion to Digital Humanities (Blackwell Companions to Literature and Culture),* ed. Ray Siemens, John Unsworth, and Susan Schreibman. Oxford: Blackwell Publishing Professional, 2004. http://www.digi talhumanities.org/companion/view?docId=blackwell/9781405103213/9781405103213 .xml&doc.view=print&chunk.id=ss1-4-1&toc.depth=1&toc.id=0.

Darnton, Robert. "An Early Information Society: News and the Media in Eighteenth-Century Paris." *American Historical Review* 105, no. 1 (February 2000). http://isites .harvard.edu/fs/docs/icb.topic1389220.files/darnton%20early%20info%20society .pdf.

Desai, Menan. "The South Asian American Digital Archive: History and Community-Based Archives." American Historical Association, New York City, January 2–5, 2015. https://aha.confex.com/aha/2015/webprogram/Paper16147.html.

Dorn, Sherman. "Is (Digital) History More than an Argument about the Past?" In *Writing History in the Digital Age,* ed. Kristen Nawrotzki and Jack Dougherty. Ann Arbor: University of Michigan Press, 2013. http://writinghistory.trincoll.edu/.

Ethington, Philip J. "Los Angeles and the Problem of Urban Historical Knowledge." *American Historical Review* 105, no. 5 (2000). http://www.usc.edu/dept/LAS/history/histo rylab/LAPUHK/Text/LAPUHK.pdf.

Fogel, Robert William, and Stanley L. Engerman. *Time on the Cross: The Economics of American Negro Slavery.* New York: Norton, 1974.

Fox, Andrea. "Bit by Bit: Tapping into Big Data." Library of Congress, Digital Preservation, March 12, 2014. http://digitalpreservation.gov/documents/big-data-report-andrea -fox0414.pdf.

Gibbs, Fred. *Digital Methods for the Humanities.* University of New Mexico, 2014. http:// fredgibbs.net/courses/digital-methods/.

Guiliano, Jennifer. "Topic Modeling for Humanities Research." Grant Application, Digital Humanities Start-Up Grants, Level 1. National Endowment for the Humanities, Office of Digital Humanities, 2011. http://www.neh.gov/files/grants/university_of_maryland _topic_modeling_for_humanities_research_level_i_grant.pdf.

Gutman, Herbert G. *Slavery and the Numbers Game: A Critique of Time on the Cross.* Urbana: University of Illinois Press, 1975.

Hajo, Cathy Moran. *HIST GA.2033: Creating Digital History.* New York University, 2014. http://creatingdigitalhistory.wikidot.com/syllabus.

Haskell, Thomas L. "The True & Tragical History of 'Time on the Cross.'" *New York Review of Books,* October 2, 1975. http://www.nybooks.com/articles/archives/1975/oct/02/the-true-tragical-history-of-time-on-the-cross/.

Heppler, Jason. *History 205F: Digital History: Sources, Methods, Problems* (syllabus), 2014. Stanford University. http://jasonheppler.org/teaching/hist205f.2014/.

Hulden, Vilja. "American Debates over the Meaning of Labor Unionism Examined with Digital Humanities Tools." American Historical Association, New York City, January 2–5, 2015. https://aha.confex.com/aha/2015/webprogram/Paper17330.html.

"Interchange: The Promise of Digital History." *Journal of American History* 95, no. 2 (2008): 452–91. http://www.journalofamericanhistory.org/issues/952/interchange/.

Jockers, Matthew. *Macroanalysis: Digital Methods and Literary History.* Urbana: University of Illinois Press, 2013.

Kelland, Lara. "The Master's Tools, 2.0." *Public History Commons,* May 5, 2014. http://publichistorycommons.org/the-masters-tools-2-0/.

Kramer, Michael. *History 393–31: Approaching Digital History* (syllabus), 2014. Northwestern University . https://curricula.mmlc.northwestern.edu/digitalhistoryseminar/syllabus/.

Kushkuley, Sophie. "Trend Analysis in Harper's Bazaar," In *Workshop on Computational Linguistics for Literature,* 84–87. Montreal: Association for Computational Linguistics, 2012. http://aclweb.org/anthology/W/W12/W12-2512.pdf.

Leon, Sharon M. "Histories of the National Mall: Place-Based Public History." *AHA Today,* March 30, 2015. http://blog.historians.org/2015/03/histories-national-mall-place-based-public-history/.

McDaniel, W. Caleb. *HIST 318: Digital History Methods* (syllabus), 2014. Rice University. http://digitalhistory.blogs.rice.edu/syllabus/.

Meeks, Elijah, and Scott B. Weingart. "The Digital Humanities Contribution to Topic Modeling." *Journal of Digital Humanities* 2, no. 1 (April 9, 2013). http://journalofdigitalhumanities.org/2–1/dh-contribution-to-topic-modeling/.

Moretti, Franco. "Conjectures on World Literature." *New Left Review,* January–February 2000, 54–68.

———. *Distant Reading.* London: Verso Books, 2013.

Onion, Rebecca. "Five More Digital Archives and Historical Exhibits We Loved in 2014." *Slate,* December 30, 2014. http://www.slate.com/blogs/the_vault/2014/12/30/historical_documents_online_five_digital_archives_we_loved_in_2014.html.

———. "Five of 2014's Most Compelling Digital History Exhibits and Archives." *Slate,* December 29, 2014. http://www.slate.com/blogs/the_vault/2014/12/29/historical_documents_online_five_best_digital_archives_from_2014.html.

Posner, Miriam. "How Did They Make That?" *Miriam Posner's Blog,* August 29, 2013. http://miriamposner.com/blog/how-did-they-make-that/.

Richardson, Heather Cox. "White Southern Hate, Stripped Bare for All to See." *Salon,* July 5, 2015. http://www.salon.com/2015/07/05/white_southern_hate_stripped_bare_for_all_to_see/.

Rizzo, Mary. "Every Tool Is a Weapon: Why the Digital Humanities Movement Needs Public History." *Public History Commons,* November 12, 2012. http://publichistorycommons.org/every-tool-is-a-weapon/.

Robertson, Stephen. "CHNM's Histories: Collaboration in Digital History." *Dr. Stephen Robertson* (blog), October 14, 2014. http://drstephenrobertson.com/blog-post/chnms-histories-collaboration-in-digital-history/.

——. "CHNM's Histories: Digital History & Teaching History." *Dr. Stephen Robertson* (blog), October 27, 2014. http://drstephenrobertson.com/blog-post/digital-history-teaching-history/.

"Roy Rosenzweig Prize Recipients." *American Historical Association.* http://www.historians.org/awards-and-grants/past-recipients/roy-rosenzweig-prize-recipients.

Scheinfeldt, Tom. "The Dividends of Difference: Recognizing Digital Humanities' Diverse Family Tree/s." *Found History,* April 7, 2014. http://foundhistory.org/2014/04/the-dividends-of-difference-recognizing-digital-humanities-diverse-family-trees/.

——. "Sunset for Ideology, Sunrise for Methodology?" *Found History,* March 13, 2008. http://foundhistory.org/2008/03/sunset-for-ideology-sunrise-for-methodology/.

——. "Where's the Beef? Does Digital Humanities Have to Answer Questions?" In *Debates in Digital Humanities,* ed. Matthew K. Gold. Minneapolis: University of Minnesota Press, 2012. http://dhdebates.gc.cuny.edu/debates/text/18.

Schmidt, Ben. "Data Narratives and Structural Histories: Melville, Maury, and American Whaling." *Sapping Attention* (blog), October 30, 2012. http://sappingattention.blogspot.com/2012/10/data-narratives-and-structural.html.

——. "Logbooks and the Long History of Digitization." *Sapping Attention* (blog), October 12, 2012. http://sappingattention.blogspot.com/2012/10/logbooks-and-long-history-of.html.

——. "Machine Learning at Sea." *Sapping Attention* (blog), November 1, 2012. http://sappingattention.blogspot.com/2012/11/machine-learning-on-high-seas.html.

——. "Reading Digital Sources: A Case Study in Ship's Logs." *Sapping Attention* (blog), November 15, 2012. http://sappingattention.blogspot.com/2012/11/reading-digital-sources-case-study-in.html.

——. "Visualizing Ocean Shipping." *Sapping Attention* (blog), April 9, 2012. http://sappingattention.blogspot.com/2012/04/visualizing-ocean-shipping.html.

——. "When You Have a MALLET, Everything Looks like a Nail." *Sapping Attention* (blog), November 2, 2012. http://sappingattention.blogspot.com/2012/11/when-you-have-mallet-everything-looks.html.

Sewell Jr., William H. "Confessions of a Former Quantitative Historian." In *Logics of History: Social Theory and Social Transformation,* 22–80. Chicago: University of Chicago Press, 2005.

Sherratt, Tim. "From Portals to Platforms: Building New Frameworks for User Engagement." Staff Papers. Hamilton, New Zealand: National Library of Australia, November 5, 2013. http://www.nla.gov.au/our-publications/staff-papers/from-portal-to-platform.

Shrout, Anelise Hanson. "Digital Projects at the AHA (now with Projects from THAT-Camp)." *Anelise H. Shrout* (blog), January 6, 2015. http://www.anelisehshrout.com /digital-projects-at-the-aha/.

Spiro, Lisa. " 'This Is Why We Fight': Defining the Values of the Digital Humanities." In *Debates in Digital Humanities*, ed. Matthew K. Gold. Minneapolis: University of Minnesota Press, 2012. http://dhdebates.gc.cuny.edu/debates/text/13.

Tangherlini, Timothy R., and Peter Leonard. "Trawling in the Sea of the Great Unread: Sub-Corpus Topic Modeling and Humanities Research." In "Topic Models and the Cultural Sciences," special issue, *Poetics* 41, no. 6 (December 2013): 725–49.

Thomas III, William G. "Computing and the Historical Imagination." In *Companion to Digital Humanities*, ed. Ray Siemens, John Unsworth, and Susan Schreibman. Oxford: Blackwell Publishing Professional, 2004.

Thomas III, William G., and Edward L. Ayers. "An Overview: The Differences Slavery Made: A Close Analysis of Two American Communities." *American Historical Review* 108, no. 5 (December 2003): 1299–1307.

Ulrich, Laurel Thatcher. *A Midwife's Tale: The Life of Martha Ballard, Based on Her Diary, 1785–1812*. New York: Vintage, 1991.

Weible, Robert. "Defining Public History: Is It Possible? Is It Necessary?" *Perspectives on History*, March 2008. http://www.historians.org/publications-and-direc tories/perspectives-on-history/march-2008/defining-public-history-is-it-possible-is -it-necessary.

Weingart, Scott. "Appreciability & Experimental Digital Humanities." *The Scottbot Irregular* (blog), February 4, 2014. http://www.scottbot.net/HIAL/?p=40224.

———. "Digital History, Saturn's Rings, and the Battle of Trafalgar." *The Scottbot Irregular* (blog), December 15, 2014. http://www.scottbot.net/HIAL/?p=41109.

———. "Do Historians Need Scientists?" *The Scottbot Irregular* (blog), February 11, 2014. http://www.scottbot.net/HIAL/?p=40349.

Weiss, Thomas. "Review Essay of *Time on the Cross: The Economics of American Negro Slavery* by Robert Fogel and Stanley Engerman." *Economic History Association: EH.Net*, Project 2001: Significant Works in Economic History, 2001. http://eh.net /book_reviews/time-on-the-cross-the-economics-of-american-negro-slavery/.

"What Is Public History?" *National Council on Public History*. http://ncph.org/cms /what-is-public-history/.

Wilkens, Matthew. *English 90127: Digital Humanities Graduate Seminar* (syllabus), 2014. Notre Dame. http://mattwilkens.com/teaching/digital-humanities-graduate -seminar-spring-2014/.

Yang, Tze-I., Andrew J. Torget, and Rada Mihalcea. "Topic Modeling on Historical Newspapers." Paper for the 2011 ACL Workshop on Language Technology for Cultural Heritage, Social Sciences, and Humanities, Portland, Oregon, June 2011. http://digi tal.library.unt.edu/ark:/67531/metadc83799/.

Collections and/of Data: Art History and the Art Museum in the DH Mode

MATTHEW BATTLES AND MICHAEL MAIZELS

Where the world becomes picture, the system . . . comes to dominance.

—Martin Heidegger, "The Age of the World Picture" (1938)

The Photographic Turn

Compared to other humanities disciplines, art history has a relatively recent origin story for the birth of an "empirical" version of the field. While nineteenth-century historians enshrined the Thucydidean rejection of supernatural causes and moral lessons as the mythical foundation for fact-based history, efforts to objectively map and understand the development of art (read: Western art) were still very much inchoate at the time (Suessmann, 85). This is not to say that there had been no attempts to systemically narrate the history of art-making. Such eighteenth-century thinkers as Johann Winkelmann and Gotthold Lessing sought to replace a prior emphasis on hagiography with a new approach that privileged stylistic analysis and historical argumentation. Although Winkelmann and Lessing might have been able to directly observe some of their objects of investigation, they could not necessarily compare one object with another, nor could they share those comparisons visually with their readers (Potts, 136; for more on the intellectual roots of the discipline of art history, see Mansfield, *Art History and Its Institutions*). One might argue that the beginnings of modern art history, as a field, are inseparable from the technology—photography—that made such interobject comparisons possible. To understand how the possibilities of "digital art history" and "the digital museum" have been uniquely construed within the larger constellation of DH, it is therefore necessary to probe the long-standing, discipline-specific ambitions (as well as suspicions) for mobilizing representations not only to stand in for, but also to order, associate, and authorize works of art.

Art history's origin myth centers on a particularly ritualized performance of that photographically mediated comparability: the lantern-slide lecture. (For more on the centrality of the slide lecture to the historiography and self-identity of art history, see Nelson.) In darkened auditoriums, founding figures such as Aby Warburg, Heinrich Wölfflin, and Jacob Burkhardt enacted a new kind of learning, one in which pairs of great masterworks could be conjured up, thereby placing them in direct dialogue with one another. Viewers saw the development of stylistic attributes—the pointed tip of the Gothic arch, the theatrical lighting of Caravaggesque painting—unfold across space and time. Indeed, the work of these scholars seeded a range of art historical movements, each with ambitions to explain the evolution of the plastic arts.

The slide lecture maintains a powerful grip on the collective art-historical imagination; it is the format through which art historical most often training begins, and it is by far the most popular means by which the discipline spreads its views and virtues to the mass of uninitiated undergraduates. Considered more broadly, however, the slide is part of an assemblage of critical, curatorial, and historical visual documentation that affects preservation practice and print production. In point of fact, the slide is only one of a much larger set of examples of how the notion of the photographic has been integral to art history since its beginnings. While projected lantern-slides may be useful for communicating with a broad audience, for example, they have significant drawbacks as research aids. They were expensive to make, easy to destroy, and unwieldy in groups of more than two or three. For this reason, another photographic form, one with an uncannily contemporary valence—the comprehensive image collection, consisting of surrogates printed variously on paper and glass or kept as negative stock—emerged at scholarly centers such as the Frick Collection, the Warburg Library, and Bernard Berenson's Villa I Tatti, giving shape to a wholly new discipline. The scope of such collections still outstrips all but the most recent repositories of digital images. Collecting surrogates intensively in the first two decades of the twentieth century, the eminent collector and scholar Bernard Berenson was able to supplement his own massive holdings with an encyclopedic collection of 300,000 photographs of art objects, most of which dated to the Italian Renaissance (Cohen).

Much reflection on the effect of photographic reproduction on art has followed Walter Benjamin, who saw the photograph as a force that "emancipates the work of art from its parasitical dependence on ritual" (224). Beyond the impact on the "aura" of individual objects adumbrated by Benjamin, however, it is important to see how photographic reproductions of artworks have worked as more than mere surrogates. For they also made art available to forms of ordering based fundamentally in writing, and especially print: tables, files, catalogs, and lists. As Geoffrey Bowker (*Memory Practices in the Sciences*) has shown in the case of nineteenth-century geology, such practices were useful in assembling disparate materials into a unified time series, shaping aesthetic experience into a manageable historicity. Gathered

Figure 27.1. The Biblioteca of Bernard Berenson's Villa I Tatti in Florence, where
Berenson, assembled the apparatus for art-historical research, including vast collections of
photographic reproductions for comparative purposes.

and sorted into boxes, trays, and carousels, deposited into image archives and collections of many kinds, the slide was a crucial element in a kit of parts for reifying and performing explanations of aesthetic experience, an archipelago of visualized, commodified, and institutionalized reinscription of images and objects. Seen in this light, the institution of the slide was also a key element in early twentieth-century art history's preliminary gestures toward quantitative and combinatorial practices presently familiar in the digital humanities.

Despite their scale, these archives mimicked in basic conceit the organizing principle of the art museum, an institution that had emerged more than a century before. Early art museums, many of which began as royal collections, provided an important manifestation of coalescing nationhood (their art, our collection) as well as an expression of the Victorian-era drive for unified, orderly knowledge, characteristic of a time when "international classifications were developed . . . facts could be split apart, sorted into pigeonholes, and reassembled in new ways" (Bowker, *Memory Practices in the Sciences*, 29). Such developments were powerfully at work in the constitution of art history as well. By presenting a representative selection of Italian masterworks, for example, gentlemen-scholars steeped in the historical literature could glean insights into the development of naturalistic lighting in the Quattrocento. These insights represented a transfer of intellectual and cultural capital parallel to that involved in the colonial transport of cultural goods. Scholars in Germany, France, and later, the United States would become the world leaders in the analysis of artworks from the long history of the Mediterranean (Mansfield, "Art history in Greece and Cyprus," 291), and this analysis was performed and represented in the galleries of encyclopedic museums. Photographic archives fulfilled a similar, albeit much less public-facing function. By drawing together an array of representations of world art objects, the photographic archive formed a stable center, a privileged position of viewing, from which the nascent art historian could survey the production of geographically and chronologically dispersed artifacts (see Latour).

For Andre Malraux, the French theorist and cultural diplomat, this photographic archive could fulfill the potential of the museum by turning its original mission inside out. (For further discussion of the centrality of Malraux's ideas to the rise of "global art history," see Allan.) The museum had not simply served to collect and preserve artworks of important artistic heritage that might otherwise be scattered and lost to the vicissitudes of history—it had essentially created the concept of artistic heritage, and arguably art itself, through its collections. "The Middle Ages were as unaware of what we mean by the word 'art' as were Greece and Egypt, who had no word for it," Malraux wrote in his treatise *Voices of Silence*. Because the linkages between the Mediterranean and the European, or the medieval and the classical, were not to be found within the originating cultural contexts of the material, they had to be drawn out through the retrospective gaze of the art historian. As he explains, while the "common link . . . between a 'Venus' which was Venus, a crucifix which was Christ crucified, and a bust," may be hard to define, the objects could nevertheless be put into dialog if considered not as culturally-specific artifacts but simply as 'three 'statues'" (Malraux, 53; this discussion is informed by Foster, 100). In Malraux's distinctly Kantian thought, all traces of staked interest—in any aspect of the object that might have informed an original context, meaning, or usage—could be stripped away in order to situate an art object within the ostensibly neutral epistemological framework of the museum.

As with the slide, these vast collocations of surrogate images do more than simply represent widely distributed objects; they also make them sortable, comparable, classifiable, and reducible to orders. Indeed, such classificatory assemblages serve as epistemological and practical precedents for the database, which, as Lev Manovich (*The Language of New Media*) has argued, discloses meaning not discursively or syntagmatically but paradigmatically, as a structure of possible relations. In this move toward flatness and fungibility, ordering effaces or supersedes narrative accounts— grounded in particularities of material, technique, and place—of art and its makers. Predictably, this conception generated considerable backlash from a number of different directions. On one hand, a global art history—one capable of being put into practice through the transnational circulation of images—seemed inherently, problematically Eurocentric. It served to flatten the production all of cultural artifacts into an undifferentiated "art" to be sorted and classified by a Western scholar constantly reinforcing his own position at the center. Moreover, an image-based art history appeared untenable from an epistemological as well as ethical vantage.

Photographic images introduce many kinds of distortions—of original installation contexts, material construction and history, weight, scale, and color—and thus the validity of formal comparisons (especially of cross-cultural examples) seemed radically in doubt (see Preziosi, 403–503).

These tensions—between a world-historical system and the specificities of the local; between a thing and its representation; between a new technology and an old subject of inquiry—still frame the art-historical reception of the digital turn. Indeed, it was frequently as a fulfillment of the photographic legacy that the earliest experiments in digital art collections were typically seen (Foster, 109; Nelson, 414). More recent, ambitious projects such as the Google Art Project or Art.sy's "artistic genome" are particularly redolent of Malraux's ambition to build an edifice of images from which nothing would remain missing. These projects do not originate in any digital-humanities-inflected version of academic art history; instead, they represent commercial attempts to generate and mine value from accumulations of visual abundance. And yet it is worth noting that analogous textual corpora—Google Books most obviously and emphatically, but also Project Gutenberg and the larger ecosystem of digitized textual material, many of them commercial products—were likewise not the product of DH-identified centers or practices. DH practitioners not only make use of such resources, but provide critical reflection on their hybrid origins and dubious commercial and technological entanglements. In comparison to textual studies, however, art history's analytic, computational, and critical encounter with vast repositories of digital images is in its infancy.

Project Outlines: *The Lightbox and* S.M.S. *NOs 1–6*

To work with large collections, databases of surrogate images, and the metadata that coordinate them, art historians and curators face both theoretical and practical challenges. The dichotomy may be ready-to-hand, but it is unavoidable: arguments developed in exhibitions express and contend with norms and assumptions that both undergird and undermine theory; scholarly arguments in art history, meanwhile, normatively are expected to survive the tests of spatialization and performativity associated with gallery installation. Two projects associated with metaLAB (at) Harvard have sought to tangle with these challenges. One proceeds as a provocative encounter with theoretical adumbrations of metadata and descriptive practice in collections; the second takes up a practical and curatorial struggle with the folk-theoretical contentions of a body of mid-twentieth-century art practice. Neither is offered as a comprehensive solution to the tensions that characterize art history's disciplinary encounter with "big data" in its successive manifestations. Rather, they are presented here as case studies and anecdotes from the field.

The first project, *Lightbox,* is a participatory installation of data and media for the Lightbox Gallery, an exhibition space and media platform in the Harvard Art

Figure 27.2. The Lightbox Gallery in the Harvard Art Museums, showing the screen with the object map, above which are mounted the projectors that display data visualizations on the window shades opposite. Photographed February 2015.

Museums. The project offers an interface through which museum visitors can use the screen array to navigate and interactively manipulate, on-screen, metadata associated with the collection on display in the galleries. *Lightbox* seeks to enact a critical turning-around, an interrogation not so much of artworks themselves but the digital means by which we so frequently know them.

The design of the installation constantly reinforces the dialogue (and difference) between the digital objects and their material referents, exploring the differing meanings of words like "object," "image," and "data" at work in information science and curatorial practice. While a spectrum of museums and museologies have been since legible long before the rise of digital media, the perspective offers special salience in the present context, one in which information networks act as cybernetic systems of aesthetic immanence, mediators of the modes and forms defined as art by the disciplines that claim and structure the museum.

A second project, *S.M.S. NOs 1–6s,* presents a digital survey of William Copley's *S.M.S.* (1968), an editioned set of multimedia artworks produced over the course of a single year. Although the artworks were entirely analog, *S.M.S.* was in many ways a predecessor of contemporary experiments in multimedia publishing: every two months subscribers would receive a small folder filled with assembly-art projects, music, poetry books, games, and other assorted objects produced by artists including Marcel Duchamp, John Cage, Bruce Nauman, La Monte Young, Dick Higgins, and Hollis Frampton. The project alluded to and utilized technologies of information transmission both old and new—ranging from semaphore and telegraphy

Figure 27.3. In 1967, the artist and dealer William Copley, drawing inspiration from Duchamp's *Boite en Valise,* began to assemble a set of editioned portfolios that were designed to make art accessible to those beyond the wealthy collector class.

to magnetic tape and fair-use copyright statutes—as a means of breaking free of the notion of the artwork as a singular, stable, bounded object.

Complementing a 2014–15 exhibition at the Davis Museum at Wellesley College, our web-based *S.M.S. NOs 1–6s* illustrates the ways in which digital tools can be mobilized toward a kind of digital *translation* of a set of objects. Expressed on an iPad, the interface presents images of the small *S.M.S.* objects with a degree of the kineticism that was integral to their original presentation. These objects were initially made to be handled: books opened and read, DIY kits assembled, puzzles solved, and music unwound and listened to. Although any digital mediation irrevocably alters the experience with the artwork, our interface offers a translation of these objects, in keeping with their original spirit, into a new digital space. Users are now able to interact with digital avatars of each *S.M.S.* object: flipping it over, turning its pages, listening to its audio, or activating its intended motion. The project can be accessed at http://sms.sensatejournal.com/.

As curatorial and scholarly practices incorporate computational and data-intensive tools and methods, art historians struggle afresh with the collision of orders and epistemes prefigured in the discipline's encounter with photographic reproduction and large-scale image sets: conflicts of narrative and database, of particularized connoisseurship and comprehensive analysis, of micro-scale accounts of objects with the elucidation of systems at the macro scale. Specifically, we aim not only to provide interested computational thinkers with culturally or epistemologically significant datasets, but also to foster dialogue in which the rich interpretative traditions of the humanities can work to historicize our own sociotechnical moment. By emphasizing the ways in which our culture has long attempted to picture a perfectly complete representation of the world's knowledge—from the medieval *compendia* up through Malraux's encyclopedic museum of photographs—we can gain greater theoretical and practical purchase on the aspirations and limitations of our contemporary fascination with the possibilities of big data. As interventions in this history, *Lightbox* and *S.M.S. NOs 1–6s* are meant to suggest a specific aspirational epistemology: that in both theoretical argument and curatorial practice, art history in the digital context should attend to not only the powers and benefits of technology, but its norms and assumptions as well.

Lightbox: Theorizing Data in the Art Historical Mode

Compared to textual studies, art history and visual analysis still lack a robust toolkit for "distant looking," albeit with notable (and rapidly maturing) exceptions.[1] The *Lightbox* installation is informed by two overlapping metaLAB research interests related to this desire for wider perspectives: first, to explore the practical manipulation of metadata to answer new kinds of questions in the study of visual culture; and second, to seek in such metadata traces of past practices of collection and description, tracing changes in the constitution and ordering of collections and the objects they contain over time. (For a thorough and searching example of this second interest, see Loukissas.) The first interest signals a recognition of the power of practices termed "distant reading" in text-focused digital humanities domains through technical systems such as text mining, network visualization, and geospatial analysis.

The *Lightbox,* it should be admitted, is no solution to this problem. It is not a research tool, but an expressive demonstration of certain aspects of the museum's disciplinary identity and the polyvalent nature of the art collection, tracing a line from academic canons of taste to art markets, public discourse, and constructions of cultural heritage. The *Lightbox* installation reflects these contradictory and overdetermining strands not by means of linear argument, but through a database-driven structuration and animation of collections and the media and metadata that index them. Design and development of the *Lightbox* installation drew on metaLAB's hybrid strengths, combining elements of architectural design, software development, and scholarly practice.[2] Crucially, however, the project is motivated by a desire to grapple with the theoretical framing of objects, their description and classification, and the transformations wrought in this theoretical space by the advent of the digital. Before offering a description of the installation, then, an account of this theoretical framing would be useful.

The project relies on two concepts—first, the "boundary object," and second, the "epistemic virtue"—as heuristic tools for thinking about the function of the twenty-first-century art museum. The concept of the "boundary object," which originates with S. L. Star and J. R. Griesemer, is crucial to our understanding of the museum as a site of methodological *agon* and discipline formation. Star and Griesemer examine the way in which objects in museums both "inhabit several intersecting social worlds . . . and satisfy the informational requirements of each of them" (393). While Star and Griesemer were writing about objects in a natural-history museum, works of art in galleries may be seen in the same light, as they serve as nodes in flows of epistemes and sites for the coordination of practice among scholars, curators, conservators, and the viewing public. Such negotiations, as Lorraine Daston and Peter Galison have shown, tend to cohere around "epistemic virtues": norms and assumptions, rarely articulated but often performed, that stabilize understandings of the order, meaning, and value of ideas (18). Taken together, the "boundary object" and the "epistemic virtue" provide a useful armature for understanding collaborations among database managers, interface designers, and curators in the art museum.

In *Lightbox,* metaLAB fixed on one boundary object above all: the idea of the "object" itself, in its multiple and overlapping negotiations in computer science, art history, and the craft practices of exhibition and conservation. The back-and-forth of practice in the art museum churns through definitions of the "object" as an object of desire, an artifact rendering knowledge of lost time, a fungible commodity in a marketplace, or a cloud of data to be virtually embodied. Evaluating and enacting these definitions takes the negotiation of such epistemic virtues as comparison, historicization, access, and appreciation. In their collaborative address of the "object," different constituencies have differing stakes in the museum's enterprise of preservation, exhibition, and knowledge production.

In the museum database, these negotiations take a notable turn, as the historical panoply of the descriptive apparatus deployed by these constituencies (including card-based accessions records, tabular inventories, and textual bibliographies, exhibition records, and provenance files) is collapsed, systematized, and made digitally fungible and interoperable. Since the mid-twentieth century, this transformation has taken place across a spectrum of systems from mainframe and terminals, through the desktop personal computer, to distributed, web-native interfaces. As discussed in the first section of this chapter, throughout much of that transformation, a regnant epistemic hierarchy (which emerged in the era of Berenson and Warburg and came to maturity in the Malrauxian twentieth century) was largely conserved: objects are things of transcendent value, of aura, with connections to deep time and the wellsprings of invention; salient comparisons among them balance aesthetic appreciation with a global historicity of visual culture. The digital records that index these objects were designed to be wholly subservient to the work of historicizing, interpreting, and evaluating them.

With the coming of the World Wide Web, however, this political and epistemic balance begins to shift. Diverse, disaggregate genres and formats (sculptures and coins, textiles and texts, oil paintings and electronic images) have coalesced into a new class of "digital objects" of ascendant practical and political value. Sets of loosely connected media and metadata are being assembled into objects of a new kind, with powerful online presences, commanding programmatic agencies and transmedial powers. The agents of these digital objects put new epistemic virtues into play: access, openness, and interoperability take up residence alongside comparability, historicity, and aesthetic appreciation. These virtues and boundaries are expressed in classifications and orderings of objects that often are rendered invisible by the normative modes of description and presentation that operate in galleries, exhibitions, and catalogs raisonnés. (For a rich analysis of the role of invisibility in classification schemes, see Bowker and Star, *Sorting Things Out.*) The aggregative, universalizing purposes Malraux lent to words like "art" or "sculpture" for purposes of a museum without walls, the online art museum in the twenty-first century deploys around the word "object" in the context of the wall-less web.

In the museum, digital objects at present are encoded in JavaScript Object Notation (JSON), a data format that disciplines assemblages of discrete and disparate information into closely articulated textual "arrays." The JSON data format is offered as an "open" standard, in contrast to proprietary data formats developed by the vendors of commercial systems for managing collections in libraries and museums. More than this, though, it is also a vernacular: JSON's instrumental syntax also expresses the norms and practices of a community of technologists committed to concepts of collaboration, community, and "openness" in the development of software. It also encodes practical definitions of such concepts as "object," "array," and normative valuations of qualities like "flatness" and "hierarchy" that are entangled with moral and ideological commitments of the open-source and free software movements. As a mode of structuring data, it is expressive of emergent epistemic virtues associated in the digital realm with these movements and allied communities: accessibility, openness, semantic computability, and interoperability.[3] The "objects" in question (referred to by the "O" in the acronym "JSON") live between the curly bracket braces of JavaScript syntax; they render qualities of the material objects of art-historical interest as discrete, linked, computable information. The museum objects to which they refer—coded elsewhere as unique bodyings-forth of genius, material specificity, and aesthetic impulse, comparable but ultimately irreducible—are thus computationally domesticated to the database, the rigors of the TCP/IP protocol, and the virtues of the open web. And yet unlike Daston and Galison's draftsmen, who rendered neurons or crystals in ways that subordinated artisanal effects of visual invention to the theoretical dispositions of scientists, today's designers and web programmers act on museum objects in ways that reflect the cultural capital amassed by digital projects in a networked age.

In the *Lightbox,* metaLAB sought to explore this tangle by way of the agency and rhetoric of design. In its final form, the installation offers an "object map" on its display screens, consisting of an array of thumbnail images of all of the objects on display in the museum galleries (ca. 1,400 objects, about sixth-tenths of one percent of the museum's collection in toto). Visitors use a wireless controller to explore this object map; when an object is selected, a display of its record image and associated metadata fills the screens. Upon selection of a given object, the first state of the object display screen offers an array of object-intensive media and information; the location of the object in the museum is given, surrogate images are displayed, and a histogram showing the proportions of colors in the digital record image of the object is rendered.

This histogram presents the color values not of an object in a museum gallery, but of a web-native digital object, an immutable mobile readily transportable across browsers and platforms. It is rendered from data derived by an algorithm that analyzes the record object as a digital file and identifies the various percentages of color data conveyed in the form of web-native hexadecimal values in the RGB color model. It makes no distinction between background colors, frames, or other parts of the image that are peripheral to the object itself. Thus in histograms of ancient coins, the black of the background typically predominates, while histograms of sculptural

Figure 27.4. *Lightbox* installation, "Object Map," with record image (center), information on location of the object in the gallery (left), and a color histogram displaying proportions of RGB color values in the record image (right). The histogram displays black (derived from the background) as the major color, clearly demonstrating the algorithm's treatment of the digital image, and not the material object, as the "object" of analysis. (The record image, it is worth pointing out, already offers a phenomenological fiction, displaying obverse and reverse of the coin at once.)

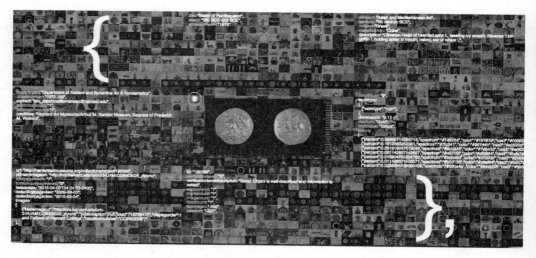

Figure 27.5. *Lightbox* installation, "Object Map," with thumbnails of objects on display serving as background to two instantiations of the digital object: the record image (center), framed with metadata in JSON. To the viewer, the image represents the object; to the computer, the object is the encoded metadata enclosed in curly brackets.

objects tend to reflect the cool grays of the galleries' normative white walls. The design and presentation of these color data provoke viewers to consider the differences between the experience of color in the museum gallery or when viewing an image on a screen as compared to the phenomenon of color-as-data "experienced" by digital systems. In this uncanny phenomenology, reflective surfaces reduce to dappled, mappable mosaics; the computer makes no distinction between figure and ground, object and support, picture and frame. *Lightbox* uses design and technology to explore the spectrum of perception and affect across technical and human encounters with the collection, to expose the grain of technical and interpretive negotiations implied by the computational access of museum collections.

The reordering and *re*presentation not only of color data, but of a comprehensive selection of metadata fields, allows the visitor to explore how art objects are described and indexed for computational manipulation and scholarly investigation. By resorting the collections successively according to these fields, the visitor is able to play with strategies for organizing objects in galleries, museum databases, and interactive, web-based search tools. These sortings also are expressed in a series of graph-based data visualizations in the projection opposite the screens, with bar-graph visualizations placing the selected object and the search term in the context of the collection as a whole, rendering visible ebbs and flows in museum acquisition, cultural and historical areas of strength and interest, and the clustering of practices of description among genres, media, and cultural areas.

The *Lightbox* installation makes visible not only changes in museum practices of collection development, description, and interpretation (which it does only

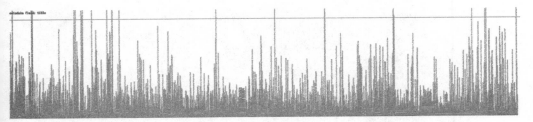

Figure 27.6. An instance of the projected data visualization, this one ordering the collection according to the field "title," displaying the text contexts of that field as vertical "bars" of text. Although scale and interposition render these lines of text all but illegible, we elected to include them in the visualization, as patterns of resonance and repetition make visible practices of naming and describing artworks across the collections.

gesturally, performatively, and not in any comprehensively scholarly sense, to be sure). It also offers a glimpse of how data systems past and present coexist palimpsestically in databases, on websites, and in museum galleries; it plays visually with the forms data have taken in systems of inventory, registration, and access; and it explores the extent to which the computational address of objects in museum collections—like the digital instantiation of all kinds of objects—involves acts of translation and negotiation. Finally, the installation explores museum objects as boundary objects caught in the digital-material divide. We discover that these objects are never stable entities, but sites of negotiation, cascades of epistemic virtues balanced variably across galleries, exhibition catalogs, and online databases. This scholarly conjecture is realized in the first instance through the acts of design and making that constitute the installation—acts that not only indicate the imbrication of boundaries and virtues, but perform and enact them as well. Fundamental aspects of the design—decisions whether to include color data, whether to make digital images modifiable or analyzable on-screen, and degrees of balance between curatorial exposition and digital "transparency"—enacted the cascade of virtues and the confusion of boundaries at every point. As a project, then, the *Lightbox* is a demonstration of the conjecture it seeks to index and frame: that knowledge in the museum is a constructed thing, always in the making.

S.M.S. NOs 1–6:[4] A Narrative of Art-Historical Data in Practice

A desire to unsettle the object-ness of the art object, thereby disrupting the circuitry of the institutions dedicated to their cultural valuation, also formed the bedrock of a much different historical project. In 1967, the artist and dealer William Copley felt that he was at the end of his rope. Reeling from the closure of his Los Angeles gallery—one of the first institutions to introduce Marcel Duchamp and Man Ray to West Coast audiences—and the fallout from his second divorce, Copley returned to New York to seek a new direction. Feeling, in his words, that "Shit Must Stop," he

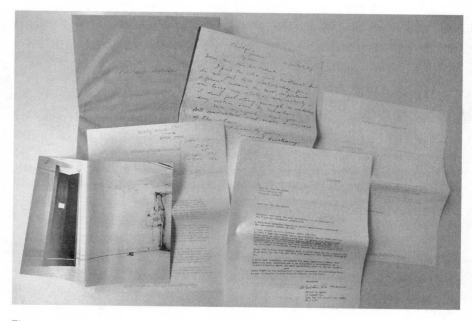

Figure 27.7. Drawing on the connections he had built as a dealer, Copley brought together an impressive range of artists for the *S.M.S.* project, including Marcel Duchamp, Man Ray, Roy Lichtenstein, La Monte Young, and Walter de Maria.

began to envision ways of circumventing the gallery and collector system and assembled a set of editioned portfolios that were designed to make art accessible to those beyond the wealthy collector class. Although Copley paid all participants the same modest $100 honorarium, he spent nearly the remainder of his savings producing luxurious, exacting replicas of each artist's work in an edition of 2,000. This enormous edition size—and the affordable price of $125 for the entire project—enabled a much broader swath of the public to collect the internationally recognized artists contained in the *S.M.S.* portfolios. Within the next months, the first bimonthly issue of *S.M.S.* was on its way to subscribers.[5]

But what differentiates *S.M.S.* from better-known meditations on the theme of art as a kind of reproduction—for example, in the work of Andy Warhol or, later, Sherrie Levine—was the emphasis on technologies of information transmission as both the vector and model for artistic creation as copy-making. The productions of *S.M.S.* are unmistakably a product of the moment that gave rise to the modern data-driven society, and they willfully, imaginatively, and playfully engage with topics like cryptography, random number generation, and the panoply of technologies for moving information over long distances. While Walter de Maria explored the notion of art by telephone, Hannah Weiner used historical flag-signaling languages in her poetry, and Dick Higgins contributed a word-puzzle based on the principle of code switching. Even the generic cardboard mailer box was adorned with Morse code that repeatedly spells out "S-M-S."[6] In this way, Copley's *S.M.S.*

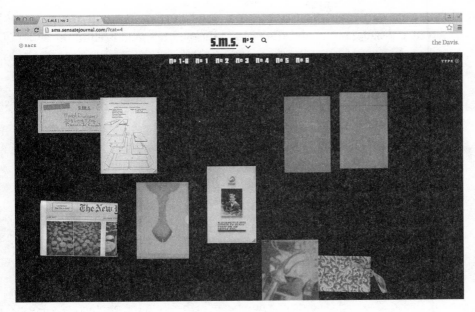

Figure 27.8. The *S.M.S.* interface reproduces the effect of receiving a portfolio in the mail and pouring the contents onto a coffee table in order to thumb through the books, play the audio, and assemble the kits. By enabling viewers to pinch, expand, and shuffle each object, the system reprises the tactility and kineticism that was integral to the original presentation of this material.

functions as an early example of information technology imagined as giving rise to something very much unlike Malraux's totalized museum without walls, a world in which artistic proliferation produces endless difference rather than encyclopedic completeness.

For this reason, *S.M.S.* provides an ideal subject through which to think about the possibilities for digital art history in new ways. The specific venture we discuss came about through an opportune collaboration between the Davis Museum at Wellesley College and *Sensate,* an experimental scholarly and media practice journal. While the Davis Museum was interested in showcasing its holdings of the complete set of the *S.M.S.* portfolios, *Sensate* sought an innovative way to present material from *S.M.S.,* in large part because the multiplatform, media-rich nature of *S.M.S.* positions it as a kind intellectual ancestor of contemporary, experimental journals. Thus while the physical exhibition strove to make these objects singular and accessible—for example, by producing a select number of replica objects that museum patrons could handle and explore—the digital project was designed to capitalize on this parity between form and content. In other words, if *S.M.S.*—with its thematic interests in information technology, avant-garde experimentalism, and transcending a received set of rarified confines—might be considered a predecessor of *Sensate,* the publication ought to allow the latter to shed a new and specific light on the former.

Given the attention that Copley devoted to how the *S.M.S.* objects were to be received and handled by subscribers, the solution presented itself in the area of interface design. To devise the user's pathway through the information, we used small printouts of each work to mark a place for that object in the portfolio. As we moved these small copies (of small copies) around on a large table, we realized that this arrangement could function as a very generative interface. Users could be presented with digital versions of each object seemingly spilled onto a horizontal surface, an experience that would reproduce the effect of receiving a portfolio in the mail and then, as was intended, pouring the contents onto a coffee table in order to thumb through the books, play the audio, and assemble the kits. By enabling viewers to "touch" each object to magnify or reorder it, we would be able to reprise the tactility and kineticism that was integral to the original presentation of the material.

Because most objects in the original *S.M.S.* were comprised of an outside cover and inside contents, we elected to treat these virtual, resizable representations as "covers" for unique digital objects. When users click on each object, they are taken to an "interiors" page that contains a number of high-resolution photographs—of all sides of all parts of the object, as well as several "action shots" of the parts being put into use.[7] For example, in Arman's *Torture Device for Color,* viewers could see not just details of the screws and Plexiglas plates, but how these bits of hardware were to be assembled into a miniature vise that could squeeze a tube of paint to the point of explosion. These simulations made it newly possible for members of the public to read prose and poetry works by figures including John Cage, George Reavey, and Nicolas Calas, as well as to listen to Marcel Duchamp's *contrepètries* and Diane Wakoski's *The Magellanic Clouds,* a unique piece of spoken-word poetry recorded directly onto cardboard.

Like all such projects, *S.M.S. NOs 1–6* was threaded through with instances in which our ambitions ran up against the singularity of our objects under consideration. Beyond the basic questions of media preservation—which has impacted both the long-term survival of the *S.M.S.* objects themselves as well as framed decisions about the life of our project going forward—these issues shed light on the epistemological stakes of doing digital art history. Namely, we aimed to produce a kind of digital catalog raisonné, an authoritative volume that would comprehensively document the contents of the *S.M.S.* portfolios. But the question of what constituted comprehensiveness quickly became more complicated than we realized. When attempting to create standards for the photographic presentation of these objects, we ran again and again into the irreducible heterogeneity of the portfolios. We decided on a policy to photograph everything front and back—but should we present viewers with thirty-six identical-looking photographs of the flat black backs of John Giorno's playing cards? What about an object like Alain Jacquet's *Three Color Separations,* a set of three color transparencies that have no clearly specified arrangement and thus no single "back"?

Figure 27.9. The digital version of Arman's *Torture Device for Color* not only gives viewers details of the screws and Plexiglas plates, but shows how these bits of hardware were to be assembled into a miniature vise that could squeeze a tube of paint to the point of explosion.

It was in this attempt to square a documentary circle that we most clearly saw the collision between *S.M.S.* and the museum/gallery world of which the portfolios were originally couched as a refusal. In their sheer internal difference, media-based ephemerality, and irreducible strangeness, the *S.M.S.* objects are particularly ill-suited for traditional museum practices grounded in the analysis of freestanding, stable artworks produced by recognized, well-understood makers. Yet, both *S.M.S.* and the Davis Museum were transformed, however slightly, by the encounter. One the one hand, Copley could never have envisioned that the museum would become an important vector through which his beloved *S.M.S.* would be disseminated and preserved. Similarly, our *S.M.S.* exhibition became the first time that the Davis Museum partnered with an external scholarly journal to distribute high-resolution images that not only depict works in its collection, but also digitally simulate the original conditions of their reception. This is a museum without walls in the most un-Malrauxian sense, one that uses the dissemination of photographic images not to produce an encyclopedic compendium of artifacts stripped from their context, but a transcription of a set of works that attempts to preserve, and even potentially further, an original set of intentions, meanings, and uses.

Art History and Curatorial Practice in the DH Mode

The advent of "data" as a category of popular discourse and interdisciplinary negotiation has inaugurated an era of both anxiety and excitement in the humanities.

The excitement originates from those who see in the approach taken to "data" by technologists and scientists models for the practical and epistemological address of topics of abiding interest in the humanities: texts, objects, and images, but also lives, values, and affective experience. These things, too, are data, we are wont to say; they disclose aspects of their uncanny depths to quantitative perspectives made possible by the rise of computation. "Our" data, moreover, tied as they are to art, literature, architecture, music, and the full panoply of human expressive ambition, offer a glamour and an interest missing from data generated in other social contexts. And what of the anxiety? It emerges from the very same place: from the recognition that humanities topics, terms, and objects of study rarely look like the kinds of data found salient and manipulable—rendered meaningful—in computational contexts.

And yet it is precisely in connection with this last point—with the meaning-making nature of computational approaches to "data" writ large—that the humanities finds its bearings as a set of interpretive and critical practices. For all the real power and instrumental impact of computational efforts, and for all the cool implacability with which machines and algorithms seem to pick data apart, to fix their natures and discern their associations, these acts and analyses still take place as ineluctably human constructs, in inescapably human contexts. As we apply our assemblages of machines to the making or discovery of meaning in data, we face long-standing challenges to historicize, to interpret, and to tell stories. Our machines enter into these evaluative moves neither in originary nor terminal positions—neither as the dawn of a new age nor as the teleological culmination of what has come before—but in the midst of the churning cycle of human encounters with the world.

These humanistic gestures and predispositions, expressed through the *S.M.S.* publication and the *Lightbox* installation, gather force and importance as they emerge in our specific institutional milieus: art museums and an interdisciplinary research group situated in institutions of higher education. Both installation and exhibition, with their associated programs of design, knowledge production, and scholarly reflection, must be judged ultimately on their entanglement with and impact on an emerging generation of thinkers and makers. Asking students, as well as colleagues and the visiting public, to reflect on and explore the theoretical underpinnings that inform the description of the object in digital terms (as in the case of *Lightbox*), or to reflect on norms of ephemerality, materiality, and networked communication that both precede and overspill the advent of the digital (as in the case of *S.M.S.*), is to ask them to ponder the powers and agencies of computation in terms not only of efficacy and instrumentality, but in terms of technical, academic, and aesthetic translation and negotiation. It is our purpose to ground a generation fully (and indeed normatively) convinced by the powers and possibilities of digital technology in the vital and salutary work of interpretation, evaluation, and appreciation that remains at the heart of the humanistic disciplines, however they are formulated in formal, professional, and institutional terms. Computation is powerful, but not all-powerful; the work of framing its epistemological limits is essentially a humanistic endeavor.

NOTES

1. Representative initiatives include Getty Research Portal (portal.getty.edu) and Provenance Index (http://www.getty.edu/research/tools/provenance/) and metaLAB's own Curarium (curarium.com). Notable as well are various participatory research projects developed under the aegis of Zooniverse, which facilitate lay contributions to large-scale projects in image analysis; an example in a humanities field is the Ancient Lives Project (https://www.zooniverse.org/project/ancientlives). Lev Manovich's ImagePlot software (http://lab.softwarestudies.com/p/imageplot.html) approaches problems in large-scale visual analysis with distinctive flair and ambition.

2. Practical expression of these ideas in the form of rendered digital images, displays of metadata, and visual analysis of collections data were developed by metaLAB creative technologists Jessica Yurkofsky and Krystelle Denis, with architectural renderings from metaLAB designer James Yamada supporting the design process by demonstrating how conjugations of data and media would play out in the physical space of the gallery.

3. JSON, like other digital media and data formats, wants a fuller interpretation, sensitive to humanistic and sociotechnical dimensions, which space precludes here. For exemplary projects, see Sterne and also Montfort et al.

4. http://sms.sensatejournal.com/.

5. The bulk of the information presented in this section derives from an interview conducted by the author with Billy Copley, William Copley's son, and director of the Copley Estate, on October 30, 2014. The best published treatment of the *S.M.S.* appears in Mizota.

6. The Morse code forms a black border around the outside of the mailing envelope, a reference to Copley's Letter Edged in Black Press, which produced and distributed the portfolios. According to convention, an envelope with a black border contained a death notice, and as such, Copley's press was designed to serve warning to the conservative, gallery-based art world.

7. The web-based presentation of these photographs was made possible by the generosity of the William Copley Estate, which retained copyright over all of the works included in *S.M.S.* in order to ensure that their dissemination would be unimpeded by the creators of the works themselves, who might later seek to reclaim rights over the distribution of likenesses of their work. Our interface was produced in collaboration with our incomparable designer, Ayham Ghraowi.

BIBLIOGRAPHY

Allan, Derek. "André Malraux and the Modern, Transcultural Concept of Art." *Literature and Aesthetics* 15, no. 1 (2005): 79–98.

Benjamin, Walter. "The Work of Art in the Age of Mechanical Reproduction." In *Illuminations: Essays and Reflections,* ed. Hannah Arendt, trans. Harry Zohn, 217–52. New York: Schocken, 1969.

Bowker, Geoffrey. *Memory Practices in the Sciences.* Cambridge, Mass.: MIT Press, 2008.

Bowker, Geoffrey, and Susan Leigh Star. *Sorting Things Out: Classification and Its Consequences.* Cambridge, Mass.: MIT Press, 1999.

Cohen, Rachel. *Bernard Berenson: A Life in the Picture Trade.* Jewish Lives Series. New Haven and London: Yale University Press, 2013.

Daston, Lorraine, and Peter Galison. *Objectivity.* Cambridge, Mass.: MIT Press, 2007.

Foster, Hal. "The Archive without Museums." *October* 77 (Summer 1996): 97–119.

Latour, Bruno. "Visualisation and Cognition: Drawing Things Together." *Knowledge and Society Studies in the Sociology of Culture Past and Present* 6 (1986): 1–40.

Loukissas, Yanni. *The Life and Death of Data,* 2014. http://lifeanddeathofdata.org/.

Malraux, Andre. *The Voices of Silence.* Translated by Stuart Gilbert. London: Paladin, 1974.

Manovich, Lev. *The Language of New Media.* Cambridge, Mass.: MIT Press, 2001.

Mansfield, Elizabeth, ed. *Art History and Its Institutions: Foundations of a Discipline.* New York: Psychology Press, 2002.

———. "Art History in Greece and Cyprus." In *Art History and Visual Studies in Europe: Transnational Discourses and National Frameworks,* ed. Matthew Rampley, 379–92. Leiden: Brill Publishing, 2012.

Mizota, Sharon. "Shit Must Stop." Special issue, *Art on Paper* 13, no. 4 (May/June 2009).

Montfort, Nick, Patsy Baudoin, John Bell, Ian Bogost, Jeremy Douglass, Mark C. Marino, Michael Mateas, Casey Reas, Mark Sample, and Noah Vawter. *10 PRINT CHR$(205.5+RND(1)); : GOTO 10.* Cambridge, Mass.: MIT Press, 2014.

Nelson, Robert. "The Slide Lecture, or the Work of Art 'History' in the Age of Mechanical Reproduction." *Critical Inquiry* 26, no. 3 (Spring, 2000): 414–34.

Potts, Alex. *Flesh and the Ideal: Winckelmann and the Origins of Art History.* New Haven, Conn.: Yale University Press, 2000.

Preziosi, Donald. "Globalization and Its Discontents." In *The Art of Art History: A Critical Anthology,* ed. Donald Preziosi, 403–8. Oxford: Oxford University Press, 1998.

Star, S. L., and J. R. Griesemer. "Institutional Ecology, 'Translations,' and Boundary Objects: Amateurs and Professionals in Berkeley's Museum of Vertebrate Zoology, 1907–1939." *Social Studies of Science* 19, no. 3 (August 1989): 387–420.

Sterne, Jonathan. *MP3: The Meaning of a Format.* Durham, N.C.: Duke University Press, 2012.

Suessmann, Johannes. "Historicising the Classics." In *Thucydides and the Modern World: Reception, Reinterpretation, and Influence,* ed. Katherine Harloe and Neville Morley, 77–92. Cambridge: Cambridge University Press, 2012.

Archaeology, the Digital Humanities, and the "Big Tent"

ETHAN WATRALL

There has been much discussion about "the big tent" as the metaphor that defines and delineates the boundaries of the digital humanities. In some cases, such as at the University College London Centre for Digital Humanities (Warwick et al.), the "big tent" is framed quite broadly, defined not by traditional disciplinary boundaries but by practice. Kathleen Fitzpatrick,[1] on the other hand, defines the "big tent" as "a nexus of fields within which scholars use computing technologies to investigate the kinds of questions that are traditional to the humanities, or, as is more true of [her] own work, who ask traditional kinds of humanities-oriented questions about computing technologies." Whatever the perspective on the "big tent," the metaphor has inevitably led to debate as to who is in this "tent" and who is not.

Curiously, archaeology and archaeologists (especially anthropological archaeologists) are largely absent from this discussion. Archeologists rarely publish in the same places as scholars who identify themselves as digital humanists. For the most part, archaeologists do not seek funding from the agencies and programs to which digital humanists commonly turn. It is also quite rare to see archaeologists at digital humanities conferences, meetings, or workshops. Prominent digital humanities conferences (or un-conferences, as the case may be) such as THATCamp or Digital Humanities are almost never attended by archaeologists. In fact, many scholars in the archaeological community are not even aware that the digital humanities exist. To extend the "big tent" metaphor, most archaeologists (especially anthropological archaeologists) are so far away from the tent that they cannot even see it.

This state of affairs is puzzling, as archaeology articulates quite nicely with many of the fields of study that have self-identified as being part of the digital humanities, such as history or classics. Furthermore, archaeologists have long been invested in a wide variety of innovative digital technologies and practices. Computational archaeology (which eventually evolved into digital archaeology) dates to the late 1950s—not long after the rise of humanities computing, the precursor to DH. Regardless of the obvious connections between the two domains, there exists a significant missed opportunity, since issues of discipline and disciplinary-based epistemologies have resulted in a curious disconnect. Indeed, archaeology has a great deal to offer digital humanities, in terms of data-driven scholarship, public engagement, and experiential learning. By exploring several critical points of interchange between archaeology and the digital humanities, this discussion reveals new pathways to fruitful engagement, interaction, and collaboration.

An Abbreviated History of the "Digital" in Archaeology

In archaeology, which has a strong tradition of focusing on practical methodologies, computers and computation have largely fallen under the domain of method rather than theory; they have most often been thought of and used as tools to better understand, interpret, and communicate the archaeological past. One might even go so far as to argue that, of all the domains in the humanities and humanistic social sciences that explore cultural heritage, archaeology is the one with the greatest emphasis on and acceptance of methodology as a vital part of the discipline's scholarly inquiry. However, archaeological method is inextricably intertwined with archaeological theory; in many cases, the two are inseparable. Low-level archaeological theory, as described by scholars such as Michael Schiffer, involves observations and interpretations that result in data about the archaeological record. These observations and interpretations are inherently theory-driven and only emerge from methodologically driven lab and fieldwork.

The roots of digital archaeology (which was originally referred to as computational archaeology) date back further than many people might think. While George Cowgill cites several tantalizing examples in the late 1950s, the best-known and most influential computational archaeology project comes courtesy of James Deetz's seminal work on Arikara ceramics, carried out in the early 1960s. In that project, Deetz employed an IBM704 mainframe at the MIT Computation Laboratory to analyze stylistic variation across an assemblage of 2,500 rim sherds[2] from the central South Dakota Medicine Crow site, hoping to expose "stylistic coherence" (*Dynamics of Stylistic Change in Arikara Ceramics*).

Deetz's work was extremely important, as it suggested that computers were excellent tools for statistical, typological, chronological, or stylistic analysis of large, exceedingly complex, and messy sets of data—a hallmark of archaeology. In this regard, Deetz's work, as well as those who followed him (e.g., M. Ascher and R. Ascher; G .L. Cowgill) engaged with the notion of "big data" before the term ever existed.

In those early years, computational archaeology also capitalized on something that computers do well: information storage. Archaeological work generates a massive amount of data—data that needs to be stored, curated, and accessed. This is not just a matter of volume, but also of variety. Any given archaeological project can collect ceramic material, lithic material (stone tools and their manufacturing by-products), faunal material (animal bone, horn, soft tissue, etc.), floral material (plant seeds, stems, pollen, residue, etc.), architectural and structural remains, human skeletal remains, spatial and map data, epigraphic material, remote sensing data (LIDAR, electrical resistivity, magnetometry, etc.), and geological materials (soil, etc.). It is not out of the ordinary for an average archaeological site to have thousands, if not tens of thousands, of artifacts, each of which might have multiple characteristics that must be measured and recorded. Early on, computers provided a critical platform for storing, preserving, and accessing this vast and complex array of archaeological data.

The earliest experiments with digital data storage took place in the early 1960s. Unfortunately, as Chenhall ("The Archaeological Data Bank") reported, there were more problems than successes. The three major problems were that: (1) despite the claims of major computer manufacturers, hardware and software had only just reached the point where they were barely adequate for dealing with archaeological data; (2) facilities to support the storage and preservation of archaeological data in electronic form were exceedingly uncommon; and (3) there was no consensus among archaeologists as to what types of data should be stored and how that data should be collected. In today's terms, one might say, simply, that the cyberinfrastructure for these projects did not exist.

As computer hardware and software evolved and became more accessible, so did archaeological digital data storage projects. The more successful efforts were closely tied to museum-based efforts, such as the British Museum Association IRGMA, the Smithsonian Institution Information Retrieval System, and the General Retrieval and Information Processor for Humanities Oriented Studies (GRIPHOS)—many of which were part of the Museum Computer Network (MCN) (see Chenhall; Scholtz and Chenhall). One non-museum project worth highlighting took place at the Arkansas Archaeological Survey (AAS) which in 1972 was awarded a National Science Foundation grant to determine the problems and possibilities, including time factors and costs, of recording and storing large quantities of archaeological data electronically (Scholtz and Chenhall). This project employed the GRIPHOS system to provide an information storage, search, and retrieval infrastructure for Arkansas Archaeological Survey (AAS) site files,[3] the Harrington Caddoan collection (housed in the Museum of the American Indian), the AAS faunal collection, and the AAS human skeletal collection (Scholtz and Chenhall; Urban and Misunas). While it may seem ironic, the greatest accomplishments of the AAS GRIPHON project were not its successes, but its problems. Scholtz and Chenhall clearly recognized that there were enormous theoretical and methodological concerns, such as data standards, usage best practices, and lack of training infrastructure, that needed to be overcome before archaeological digital data repositories (in modern parlance) could be effectively leveraged in everyday archaeological practice.

In 1971, the University of Arkansas Museum hosted the Archaeological Data Bank Conference. Funded by the Wenner-Gren Foundation for Anthropological

Research, the conference brought together archaeologists from the private and the public sectors and academia in order to explore the utility of databases in archeological research. The conference represents the first time that a community of archaeologists had convened to address the collection, storage, and preservation of archaeological data in electronic form. The conference was particularly noteworthy because it signaled a recognition of the need for professional infrastructure that supported scholarly communication on issues of computational archaeology. The recognition of this need eventually led to the foundation of the Computer Applications and Quantitative Methods in Archaeology (CAA) organization in 1973, and the *Archaeological Computing Newsletter* in 1984—both of which continue to this day.

By the mid-1980s, desktop computers had become effective tools for data visualization and archaeological imagery. Desktop computers facilitated the spread and adoption of geographic information systems (GIS)—probably one of the most important applications in computational archaeology (and in archaeology in general). GIS not only allowed for the visualization of spatial and map-based data in the context of survey and documentation of archaeological resources, but it also allowed for both the analysis and modeling of archaeological sociospatial data (Kvamme; Bevan and Conolly; Byerly et al.). GIS is also noteworthy because it provided a standards-based framework for sharing spatial archaeological data, maps, and tables.

In addition to using GIS, many archaeologists turned to desktop computers for drafting purposes. Computer-assisted design (CAD) software allowed archaeologists to produce a wide variety of maps and illustrations. The strength of CAD in this regard rested in the ability of the archaeologist to create and generate highly detailed and geometrically accurate plans, profiles, and feature maps at various scales and with differing emphases, without time-consuming redrafting (Duncan and Main). The larger promise of CAD, however, rested in the ability to visualize sites or structures with full 3D geometry. Until that point, all 3D imagery had been created manually by archaeological illustrators. CAD allowed archaeologists to easily manipulate (scale, rotate, transform) 3D imagery of archaeological features, landscapes, artifacts, and structures without having to manually redraw. More recently, advances in surveying equipment, particularly the total station,[4] has made capturing and recording 3D data much easier. This, in combination with the 3D capabilities of CAD, has led to some extremely detailed, complex, and accurate examples of 3D models of archaeological material (Eiteljorg II). In addition to serving as part of the archaeological record-keeping process, these 3D models were also used as the foundation for reconstructing, illustrating, visualizing, or envisioning the past—either for scholarly purposes or public consumption. The height of this trend was reached (and is currently still very much ongoing) in robust 3D visualization and virtual reality projects, many of which, at least partially, used 3D CAD data as the starting point for 3D models.

The emergence of the desktop computer as a powerful tool for archaeological inquiry was accompanied by the beginnings of an important shift in terminology.

Up until this point, "computational archaeology" was the commonly used term for the domain. However, at least partially in recognition that the term "computational" spoke to algorithmic processes instead of to a medium, the term "digital archaeology" began entering the disciplinary vernacular at this time (Lock; Zubrow).

Digital archaeology was bolstered by the introduction of the CD-ROM, which had the capacity to deliver rich media experiences that would have a powerful impact on teaching and learning in both formal and informal settings. The most notable archaeological example was *Adventures in Fugawiland*.[5] Originally published in 1990, *Adventures in Fugawiland* was designed to introduce students to the fundamentals of archaeological research by allowing them to simulate fieldwork experiences. The simulation—calling it a "game" would be a misrepresentation—was developed by T. Douglas Price and Anne Birgitte Gebauer of the University of Wisconsin. Students worked with a realistic topographical map containing numerous fictional prehistoric sites located in "Fugawiland," chose sites to excavate on-screen, examined what they found, and answered questions about their findings. Students could refer to abundant help modules, including a regional plot providing a graph of the abundance of different site characteristics in Fugawiland. *Adventures in Fugawiland* enjoyed several editions and was used as course material in many anthropology classes throughout North America.

By contrast, the emergence of the World Wide Web in the mid-1990s did not have as much of an impact on digital archaeological practice as some might think; rather, it fueled already existing practices and helped them evolve. Databases and digital repositories benefited from living in a networked information ecosystem. GIS data, such as maps and tables, were more easily shared and distributed over the Web. If we were to identify the one area that benefited the most from the birth of the Web, however, it would be public archaeology. At its core, public archaeology protects and advocates for archaeological heritage sites and resources through public education, outreach, and engagement. The Web extended the reach of traditional efforts, helping archaeologists engage larger audiences through the use of rich media.

Unfortunately, the Web as a scholarly publishing platform in archeology has yet to meet its true potential. There are several examples of online journals, the most noteworthy being the venerable *Internet Archaeology*.[6] However, these journals remain peripheral to traditional models of scholarly publication and have not made a significant impact to date.

Reasons for the Disconnect?

The disconnect between archaeology and the digital humanities persists, in spite of their similar and at times intertwined historical trajectories. This is a result of both discipline and epistemology. The digital humanities, as both a domain and a label, has its roots in the humanities—in disciplines such as literature, rhetoric, history, and media studies. Anthropological archaeology is a social science, not a humanities discipline.

It would of course be unfair not to acknowledge that this statement is compressing and oversimplifying complex disciplinary issues. There has long been push and pull between anthropological archaeology as a social science and anthropological archaeology as a humanities discipline. For anthropological archaeology, the shift from humanistic inquiry to social science began in the late 1950s with the seminal work of Willey and Phillips (1958) and the emergence of New Archaeology (a term that was later replaced by Processual Archaeology in recognition that the focus of the discipline should be on the study and reconstruction of "cultural processes"). The new methodological approaches of this processual-based research paradigm favored logical positivism, the use of quantitative data, and the scientific method (specifically a hypothetico-deductive model).

There exists a divide within anthropology itself that is pertinent to this discussion. Forming along subdisciplinary lines, the divide generally has sociocultural anthropology and linguistic anthropology aligning intellectually with the humanities, while physical anthropology and archaeology are aligning themselves firmly with the social sciences—and in some cases the natural sciences. This divide, and the intellectual foundation thereof, has resulted in a great deal of friction within the field. In 2010, for example, the executive board of the American Anthropological Association (AAA) adopted a long-range planning document that removed the word "science" from the description of the association's mission. This change, which the executive board had assumed would be uncontroversial, instead resulted in a firestorm of criticism (Lende). Many archaeologists and physical anthropologists were furious, arguing that the change minimized their contributions to the discipline. The AAA insisted that it was not seeking to marginalize any of its members or the subfields that they represent and reintroduced the notion of scientific inquiry into the association's mission statement (Wood). Despite this, many archaeologists and physical anthropologists remain very frustrated that the AAA would even consider making a change that would so clearly privilege one mode of scholarly inquiry over another.

A distinction should to be made between anthropological archaeologists and those humanist scholars who self-identify as archaeologists—or more precisely, between anthropological archaeology and humanist archaeology. Generally speaking, "humanist archaeology" refers to disciplines such as classical archaeology or Egyptology, whose framework is one of humanistic inquiry and that largely think of archaeology as method, a toolkit to be used to address questions framed by their own disciplinary epistemologies. Anthropological archaeology, on the other hand, is a subdiscipline of anthropology. It is guided and informed by a theory and practice intended to systematically and rigorously understand the organization, operation, and evolution of human societies based on the study material culture.

The oftentimes mistaken assumption about anthropological archaeology is that it is concerned exclusively with the study of the distant past. In fact, anthropological archaeology is just as interested in the recent past as it is the distant past. Historical archaeology is concerned with applying archaeological methods and theory to better understanding historical contexts for which written records exist. Historical archaeology is particularly adept as exploring those groups who were not privileged by being the focus of written records, such as the enslaved, indentured laborers, the working class, women, and children. In some cases, archaeologists are even quite interested in the present. Ethnoarchaeology is engaged in the study of modern human groups through the combined lens of ethnography and archaeological method and theory. One of the best-known examples of ethnoarchaeology is the work of Lewis Binford. During the late 1960s, Binford undertook ethnographic fieldwork among the Nunamiut people in Alaska in order to better understand the periglacial environment of the Middle Paleolithic (300,000 to 30,000 years ago). He saw the hunter-gatherer subsistence strategies of the Nunamiut as a way to understand the archaeology of the Mousterian, a Middle Paleolithic European tool tradition (Binford).

Points of Commonality, Collaboration, and Cross-Fertilization

Despite the fact that the disconnect between the digital humanities and anthropological archaeology is rooted in issues of discipline and disciplinary-based epistemologies, there are exciting points of commonality between the two domains and the possibility for method and practice from archaeology to fertilize DH. As previously mentioned, archaeology articulates quite nicely with many of the fields of study that have self-identified as being part of the digital humanities, such as history and the classics. Furthermore, archaeologists have been and continue to be heavily invested in a wide variety of innovative digital technologies and practices. Going forward, what is needed is an articulation of points of commonality so as to suggest specific opportunities for fruitful future interaction. What follows is not intended to be exhaustive. Indeed, there are several domains, such as agent-based modeling and GIS, which are not addressed. Instead, several logical places where a dialogue between digital humanities and archaeology might begin are proposed.

DATA

Archaeologists are at home with massive amounts of data that is often incredibly complex, varied, and messy (both in practical and statistical terms). Large-scale excavations, especially those that span multiple years, regularly cope with tens of thousands of artifacts—and in many cases, hundreds of thousands of artifacts. This is to say nothing of data that comes from geomorphic, geologic, limnological, palynological, and chemical sources, among others. The sheer volume and complexity of archaeological data is often difficult to communicate to nonarchaeologists.

While archaeologists generally agree on what might be called methodological meta-standards, the discipline as a whole exhibits variety in the kinds of data recorded and exactly how data are recorded. This is not the result of gross theoretical differences, nor should it be perceived as a failure of archaeology as a social science. Instead, it is the result of the complex and varied nature of archaeological materials and research. The geographic region where archaeologists work, as well as the temporal and cultural areas within which they work, have a significant impact on the kinds of data they collect and the way in which they collect it. The kinds of artifacts recovered from a Paleolithic site in France, for example, differ from the kinds of artifacts recovered from the excavation of a historical nineteenth-century farmstead in Nova Scotia.

Some of the earliest attempts to apply computers to archaeological problems were focused on electronic data. As such, archaeologists have become quite experienced at addressing issues of capturing, collecting, preserving, analyzing, accessing, and sharing large amounts of digital data. Given the complex nature of archaeological data, archaeologists have also been actively engaged in exploring issues of data standards, including the dichotomy between taxonomy and folksonomy. In this regard, archaeologists have an enormous amount to share with digital humanists on the subject of collecting, recording, preserving, accessing, and analyzing large corpora of data. There are a number of noteworthy archaeological data repositories and projects that speak to this experience including Open Context, tDAR, and ADS.

Developed by the Alexandria Archive Institute,[7] Open Context[8] is a free, open-access platform for the online publication of primary data from archaeological research. Open Context originally emerged as a way for scholars and students to easily find and reuse content created by others. Open Context's technologies focus on ease of use, open licensing frameworks, informal data integration and, most important, data portability. The Digital Archaeological Record (tDAR) differs from Open Context in that it is a traditional preservation repository. tDAR[9] is a digital archive that houses archaeological data, reports, dissertations, books, images, coding sheets, and typologies. The Archaeological Data Service (ADS) is similar to tDAR in that its goal is the preservation and access of archaeological data. ADS[10] differs from tDAR in that it is a constellation of digital archives that contain site reports, site descriptions, project descriptions, datasets, theses and dissertations, and papers that are accessible through ArchSearch, a federated search tool. All of the content is accessible through ArchSearch. Beyond the sheer volume and variety of content in ADS, which is housed at the University of York, the project is particularly important because it serves as a national-level archaeological infrastructure for heritage bodies, universities, and private archaeological firms.

PUBLIC EDUCATION, OUTREACH, AND ENGAGEMENT

Archaeology has long been deeply invested in public engagement and outreach. In fact, there is a distinct domain within archaeology that focuses exclusively on the topic—Public Archaeology. Much like public history, public archaeology is interested in transforming scholarly archaeological work (in many creative ways) to be consumed by those outside the academy. Public archaeology differs from public history in that the primary driving goal is to protect and advocate for archaeological heritage sites and resources through public education, outreach, and engagement. Community archaeology, a specific area of practice within public archaeology, is focused very acutely on local engagement. Community archaeology is set apart from the more general practices of public archaeology in that it seeks to equitably and equally engage local communities in the planning and implementation of research projects that are of direct interest to them (Trigger; Pyburn). Community archaeology oftentimes also has a very strong focus on social and community justice. Both public and community archaeology signal an important recognition of how archaeology is perceived and interpreted in the public eye. Community archaeology, in particular, recognizes and balances the ethics and identities that are bound to research of the past (Merriman).

In public archaeology, community engagement is facilitated using a variety of tools including public lectures, pamphlets, nonscholarly books, fixed or traveling museum exhibits, public workshops, bus tours, and school visits. Many of these activities are aggregated and publicized broadly as "Archaeology Days" (Michigan Archaeology Day, Spiro Mounds Archeology Day), "Archaeology Months" (Florida Archaeology Month, Saskatchewan Archaeology Month, Scottish Archaeology Month), and archaeology festivals (Festival of British Archaeology).

Public archaeology commonly strives for the inclusion of members of the public in original archaeological research, excavation, and preservation. It is not uncommon for archaeological projects to have a framework for including local community members in their excavations. In such cases, members of the public are treated very much like other project personnel and are recognized—even celebrated—for their contributions in all publications and site reports. In this regard, public archaeology has long embraced the idea of citizen scholarship and has naturally developed sets of logistical, ethical, and procedural frameworks to manage public involvement. An excellent example of such a project is the USDA Forest Service Passports in Time program,[11] which provides structured opportunities for the public to work on archaeology and historic preservation projects alongside Forest Service archaeologists in national forests throughout the United States. These practices and programs have much to offer, given the recent interest in public crowdsourcing and citizen scholarship in the digital humanities.

Public archaeology has become increasingly invested in digital media as a platform for public engagement, outreach, and education. Archaeologists have embraced digital media as a method to extend and expand public engagement. Two excellent examples in this regard are the Thames Discovery Programme[12] and the Michigan State University Campus Archaeology Program.[13] Both projects effectively leverage blogs, social discussion platforms, and social media sharing platforms to engage and educate the public as to their activities. Another excellent example is the Portable Antiquities Scheme.[14] Based at the British Museum and administered by a network of Finds Liaison Officers (FLOs) located in museums and archaeology services throughout the country, the Portable Antiquities Scheme is a platform that facilitates and supports the submission and recording of archaeological objects found by members of the public in England and Wales. The Portable Antiquities Scheme is particularly important as it is an example of crowdsourcing the archaeological record within the context of larger social and political concerns. A final example of note is Micropasts,[15] a collaboration between the University College London Institute of Archaeology and the British Museum and a web platform that facilitates research-based collaboration between full-time academic researchers, volunteer archaeological and historical societies, and other interested members of the public. The project supports the creation of both crowdfunding campaigns and crowdsourcing projects. Crowdsourcing projects on Micropasts include the transcription of archive cards from 1947–48 excavations at the ancient Egyptian site of Amara West,[16] photomasking of 3D objects from the collections of the Palestine Exploration Fund,[17] and the creation of Roman amphorae profiles that can be converted into 3D solids.[18] Micropasts not only facilitates the performance of public archaeology, but also exists as a research project that explores and improves how academics, professionals, and the volunteering public cooperate with one another (Bonacchi et al).

MODELS OF EXPERIENTIAL LEARNING

In recent years, the philosophy of "building as a way of knowing" has taken firm root in the digital humanities. Well-respected DH scholars such Stephen Ramsay have argued passionately that one can acquire a far deeper understanding of tools, technologies, platforms, and systems through development rather than passive analysis and commentary. This approach has spawned an exciting philosophy of teaching as well as curricula and programs that stress building, hacking, doing, and critical play.

While relatively new in the digital humanities, a similar model has existed in archaeology for many years. Given that archaeology is so keenly focused on methodology and practice, students are required to develop a variety of applied skills during their education. These skills, which are taught in class-based, volunteer, and practicum settings, are always hands-on and almost always carried out on actual archaeological data and collections. There is very little sense of separating students from professional practice by a veil of intellectual stimulation.

One of the most important components of this model is the archaeological fieldschool. A requirement of all undergraduates who wish to pursue archaeology in a professional capacity, either to enter graduate school or Cultural Resource Management, the fieldschool is a period of time, typically ranging from four to eight weeks, in which students work on an archaeological site in order to learn the process of field archaeology and explore the many tangible and intangible skills required to be an archaeologist. During the fieldschool, students engage in all aspects of an archaeological project: survey, excavation, record keeping, artifact analysis and lab work, public outreach, and sometimes even publication. As such, the archaeological fieldschool is an excellent model to which DH can look for highly successful, applied learning experiences.

However, the fieldschool is not just an instructional experience, but also an opportunity for undergraduates to get acquainted with the culture of archaeological practice. Given that the digital humanities has long thought of itself as an interdisciplinary community of practice, the archaeological fieldschool also has much to teach about the process of professional acculturation.

Concluding Thoughts

We need not dwell on the reasons for the disconnect between the digital humanities and archaeology. Instead, we should look for tangible and actionable solutions that will bring the two domains together in fruitful engagement, interaction, and collaboration. As discussed, several areas, such as data management, public engagement, and experiential learning, provide useful starting points.

To move beyond these discrete areas of intersection will require additional spaces of dialogue—an epistemological and disciplinary neutral ground, so to speak. One might argue that seemingly interdisciplinary digital humanities meetings and events are the perfect meeting ground for archaeologists and digital humanists. But to those archaeologists who are aware of such events—and there are not many, quite frankly—such conferences do not seem like neutral spaces. From the perspective of the archaeologist, these conferences are attended by humanists who spend time discussing humanist topics. Even the Digital Humanities Conference, the flagship conference of the DH community, which ostensibly embodies the interdisciplinarity of the domain, is dominated by papers primarily influenced by trends in digital literary studies. To most archaeologists, papers discussing stylometrics, TEI, or algorithmic criticism are impenetrable and of no professional use. Digital humanists must therefore work to communicate their domain to anthropological archaeologists. I am not suggesting that all of the responsibility for engagement should fall on the digital humanities; there are of course some archaeologists who are already actively engaged with the digital humanities community and are very much of aware of the challenges of such a collaboration. However, an initial handshake, an intellectual "hello, nice to meet you," is still needed between the two domains. Until then, archaeologists will forever be outside of the "big tent," looking in.

NOTES

1. http://chronicle.com/blogs/profhacker/author/kfitzpatrick/.

2. "Sherd" in an archaeological term for a broken piece of a ceramic (pottery) artifact—usually a vessel. A "rim sherd" is a sherd that comes from the rim of the vessel. See https://www.le.ac.uk/ulas/services/ceramic_analysis.html.

3. In the United States, each state maintains a record of all documented archaeological sites in that state. These are commonly referred to as a state's "site files."

4. A total station is an electronic/optical instrument used in modern surveying and mapping. A total station combines features of a theodolite to measure angles in the horizontal and vertical planes and the features of an electronic distance meter to measure distances from the instrument to a particular point. See https://en.wikipedia.org/wiki/Total_station.

5. The first version of *Adventures in Fugawiland* were actually delivered on a 3.5 inch floppy disk. However, subsequent editions were distributed on CD-ROM.

6. http://intarch.ac.uk/.

7. http://alexandriaarchive.org.

8. http://www.opencontext.org.

9. http://www.tdar.org.

10. http://ads.ahds.ac.uk.

11. http://www.passportintime.com.

12. http://www.thamesdiscovery.org.

13. http://campusarch.msu.edu.

14. http://www.finds.org.uk.

15. http://micropasts.org/.

16. http://crowdsourced.micropasts.org/app/amaraWest1947.

17. http://crowdsourced.micropasts.org/app/photomaskingPEF/.

18. http://crowdsourced.micropasts.org/app/amphs1/.

BIBLIOGRAPHY

Ascher, Marcia, and Robert Ascher. "Chronological Ordering by Computer." *American Anthropologist* 65, no. 5 (1963): 1045–52.

Bevan, Andrew, and James Conolly. "GIS, Archaeological Survey, and Landscape Archaeology on the Island of Kythera, Greece." *Journal of Field Archaeology* 29, no. 1/2 (2002): 123–38.

Binford, Lewis. *Nunamiut Ethnoarchaeology.* Waltham, Mass.: Academic Press, 1978.

Bonacchi, C., A. Bevan, D. Pett, and A. Keinan-Schoonbaert. "Crowd- and Community-Fuelled Archaeological Research. Early Results from the MicroPasts Project." In *Proceedings of the Conference Computer Applications and Quantitative Methods in Archaeology (CCAQM Paris),* April 22–25, 2014.

Byerly, Ryan M., Judith R. Cooper, David J. Meltzer, Matthew E. Hill, and Jason M. LaBelle. "On Bonfire Shelter (Texas) as a Paleoindian Bison Jump: An Assessment Using GIS and Zooarchaeology." *American Antiquity* 70 (2005): 595–629.

Chenhall, R. G. "The Archaeological Data Bank: A Progress Report." *Computers and the Humanities* 5, no. 3 (1971): 159–69.

———. "The Description of Archaeological Data in Computer Language." *American Antiquity* 32, no. 2 (1967): 161–67.

———. "The Impact of Computers on Archaeological Theory: An Appraisal and Projection." *Computers and the Humanities* 3, no. 1 (1968): 15–24.

Cowgill, George L. "Archaeological Applications of Factor, Cluster, and Proximity Analysis." *American Antiquity* 33, no. 3 (1968): 367–75.

———. "Computer Applications in Archaeology." *Computers and the Humanities* 2, no. 1 (1967): 17–23.

Deetz, James. *The Dynamics of Stylistic Change in Arikara Ceramics.* Urbana: University of Illinois Press, 1965.

Duncan, J., and P. L. Main. "The Drawing of Archaeological Sections and Plans by Computer." *Science & Archaeology* 20 (1977): 17–26.

Eiteljorg II, Harrison. "Computing for Archaeologists." In *A Companion to Digital Humanities,* ed. Susan Schreibman, Ray Siemens, and John Unsworth, 20–30. Malden, Mass.: Wiley-Blackwell, 2005.

Fitzpatrick, Kathleen. "Reporting from the 2010 Digital Humanities Conference." *Chronicle of Higher Education ProfHacker* (blog), July 13, 2010. http://chronicle.com/blogs/profhacker/reporting-from-the-digital-humanities-2010-conference/25473.

Kvamme, K. L. "Geographic Information Systems in Regional Archaeological Research and Data Management." *Archaeological Method and Theory* 1 (1989): 139–203.

Lende, Daniel. "Anthropology, Science, and Public Understanding." *Neuroanthropology* (blog), December 1, 2010. http://blogs.plos.org/neuroanthropology/2010/12/01/anthropology-science-and-public-understanding.

Lock, Gary. *Using Computers in Archaeology: Towards Virtual Pasts.* London: Routledge, 2003.

Merriman, N. *Public Archaeology.* London: Routledge, 2004.

Pyburn, A. K. "Public Archaeology, Indiana Jones, and Honesty." *Archaeologies: Journal of the World Archaeological Congress* 4, no. 2 (2008): 201–4.

Ramsay, Stephen. "On Building." *Stephen Ramsay Blog,* January 11, 2011. http://stephenramsay.us/text/2011/01/11/on-building/.

Ramsay, Stephen, and Geoffrey Rockwell. "Developing Things: Notes toward an Epistemology of Building in the Digital Humanities." In *Debates in the Digital Humanities,* ed. Matthew K. Gold, 75–84. Minneapolis: University of Minnesota Press, 2012. http://dhdebates.gc.cuny.edu/debates/part/3.

Schiffer, Michael B. "The Structure of Archaeological Theory." *American Antiquity* 53, no. 3 (1988): 461–85.

Scholtz, Sandra, and Robert Chenhall. "Archaeological Data Banks in Theory and Practice." *American Antiquity* 41, no. 1 (1976): 89–96.

Terras, Melissa. "Present, Not Voting: Digital Humanities in the Panopticon." Plenary address presented at DH2010, London, England, July 10, 2010.

Trigger, Bruce. *A History of Archaeological Thought.* New York: Cambridge University Press, 1993.

Urban, Richard, and Marla Misunas. "A Brief History of the Museum Computer Network." *Encyclopedia of Library and Information Sciences.* Boca Raton: CRC Press, 2007.

Warwick, C., S. Mahony, J. Nyhan, C. Ross, M. Terras, U. Tiedau, and A. Welsh. "UCLDH: Big Tent Digital Humanities in Practice." Paper presented at DH2011, Stanford, California, June 19–22, 2011.

Whallon, Robert, Jr. "The Computer in Archaeology: A Critical Survey." *Computers and the Humanities* 7, no. 1 (1972): 29–45.

Willey, Gordon R., and Philip Phillips. *Method and Theory in American Archaeology.* Chicago: University of Chicago Press, 1958.

Wood, Peter. "Anthropology Association Rejecting Science?" *Chronicle of Higher Education Innovations* (blog), November 29, 2010. http://chronicle.com/blogs/innovations/anthropology-association-rejecting-science/27936.

Zubrow, Ezra. "Digital Archaeology: A Historical Context." In *Digital Archaeology: Bridging Method and Theory,* ed. Patrick Daly and Thomas L. Evans, 8–27. London: Routledge, 2005.

Navigating the Global Digital Humanities: Insights from Black Feminism

ROOPIKA RISAM

As the field of digital humanities has grown in size and scope, the question of how to navigate a scholarly community that is diverse in geography, language, and participant demographics has become pressing. An increasing number of initiatives have sought to address these concerns, both in scholarship—as in work on postcolonial digital humanities or #transformDH—and through new organizational structures like the Alliance of Digital Humanities Organization's (ADHO) Multi-Lingualism and Multi-Culturalism Committee and Global Outlook::Digital Humanities (GO::DH), a special interest group of ADHO. From the work of GO::DH in particular, an important perspective has emerged: digital humanities, as a field, can only be inclusive and its diversity can only thrive in an environment in which local specificity—the unique concerns that influence and define digital humanities at regional and national levels—is positioned at its center and its global dimensions are outlined through an assemblage of the local. This idea was at the core of my Digital Humanities 2014 talk, in which I suggested that accent is a fitting metaphor for negotiating the relationships among local contexts. Similarly, at Digital Diversity 2015, Padmini Ray Murray insisted, "Your DH is not my DH—and that is a good thing." Claire Warwick reiterated this idea in her DHSI 2015 keynote speech, suggesting that local institutions and cultures are critical to digital humanities practice. Additionally, in her talk at the Canadian Society of Digital Humanities and Association for Computers and the Humanities joint conference in 2015, Élika Ortega posited, "All DH is local DH." The insistent resurfacing of this theme at digital humanities conferences signals a critical need for sustained theorization of the relationship between local and global in scholarship and practice.

Taking the need for further examination of local–global connections within the digital humanities as its basis, this chapter clarifies the stakes of theorizing this dimension of digital humanities. I look to black feminist epistemology and its emphasis on intersectionality as a model for mediating between the universal and the particular and for attending to the tensions between local and global in the digital humanities.

Examining the lessons for digital humanities to be learned from black feminism, I discuss the challenges of maintaining the threads that cohere the field on a global scale as well as the local specificities that enrich its practices.

As a multidisciplinary field of study changing the nature of scholarly communication, digital humanities faces not only the challenges of interdisciplinarity but also the difficulty of navigating the global scope of its practitioners. This scope brings with it thorny questions about how digital humanities practices are defined; how to decenter the dominance of the United States, United Kingdom, and Canada within the field; and how to make space for multilingual contributions to scholarship. Given the availability of digital scholarship online, the tendency of digital humanists to maintain a robust web presence, and a preference for making scholarship accessible, digital humanities seems like a radically open field. Yet it is not immune to the challenges that plague any interdisciplinary and global field: negotiating competing methodologies, proliferating institutional expectations, multiple audiences, and manifold practices. These are similar concerns that provoked anxieties among black feminist scholars within the U.S. academy when critical theory began gaining currency in the humanities, and Barbara Christian's essay "The Race for Theory" includes a number of insights about the difficulties of negotiating difference that are relevant to the local–global conundrum within digital humanities.

In the late 1980s, black feminist scholars recognized that the sea change underway in literary studies within the U.S. academy raised concern that the hard-won gains of Black studies were in peril. Although black feminists had successfully created spaces for their scholarship in the academy in the 1960s and 1970s, they worried that the popularity of critical theory would eclipse their contributions. Understandable anxieties about the rise of "theory" generated rancor within the academy as neoconservative tomes like Allan Bloom's *The Closing of the American Mind* (1987) and Roger Kimball's *Tenured Radicals* (1990) accused literary scholars of brainwashing young minds, muddying distinctions between high and low culture, devaluing great books of Western civilization, and failing to promote democracy.

For black feminist scholars, theory presented challenges to their recognition within literary studies. Where would the specificities of African diasporic women's experiences—the unique confluence of race, gender, class, nation, and other identity categories—have a place in the decidedly Eurocentric theory that was gaining currency within the humanities? From outside of black feminism, this concern might seem unwarranted. For example, Marxist approaches to literature and culture are grounded in questions of capital and power, and postcolonial studies takes up the dynamics through which European colonizers racialized and othered most of the world's population—issues germane to black feminist work. Yet these approaches are not only situated in continental philosophy but also are nonspecific, taking as their basis not the historical specificity of women of the African diaspora but the broader issue of how power operates discursively.

Christian speaks to these concerns in her groundbreaking essay "The Race for Theory," arguing that the uncritical embrace of theory in the academy can be dangerous. Based on continental philosophy and rooted in European epistemology, she argued, theory emerged from the experiences of a dominant culture built on the subjugation of black people. As a result, the rise of theory required black feminists to communicate in a language fundamentally alien to their own; it risked prescriptive readings, restrictions on creativity, and less diversity of thought within the field. Christian did not view theory as dynamic enough to accommodate modes of thought that foreground intersectional analyses, particularly of race and gender. The term "intersectionality" was coined in 1989 by black feminist legal scholar Kimberlé Crenshaw, who perceived that neither antiracist nor feminist movements adequately accounted for the unique needs of black women whose experiences are shaped by both race and gender. Intersectionality, she argued, could provide an interpretive lens to account for both. Subsequently, Crenshaw's term has been used more expansively to speak to the need for analysis that accounts for multiple axes of privilege and oppression, not only race and gender but also sexuality, ability, nation, and so on. But for Christian, this valuable lens was endangered by the rise of theory.

Nearly thirty years after the advent of theory, literary studies seem to be amidst another transformation—a digital one. There exist a number of parallels between the anointing of theory in the humanities and the increasing interest in the digital humanities: both gained popularity in times of crisis within higher education; both engender concerns that method may profane the purported sacredness of literary texts; and both have raised questions about the place for complex questions of difference in the argot of the day. Christian's call for the importance of foregrounding difference and resisting flattening of specificities that emerge from practice offers useful guidance for attending to the tension between local and global articulations of digital humanities.

Among the challenges of negotiating difference in the global digital humanities is how digital humanities is defined at both local and global levels. Debates over the role of tools within its practices demonstrate competing local needs subtending the global. In the U.S. context, the way Christian represents theory, with its "preoccupations with mechanical analyses of language, graphs, algebraic equations" (53), evokes debates over whether digital humanities is overly focused on tool and method, to the detriment of critical analysis (Nowviskie; Posner; Cecire), or whether theories emerge from the process of building (Ramsay; Rockwell; Scheinfeldt). As Bethany Nowviskie has noted, the binary implied between "hack" and "yack" is a false one (see chapter 7 of this volume). Despite the significance of this debate in the U.S. context, the concern is a local one of varying relevance to digital humanities on the global stage. This is a case in which situating the issue of tool building in its local contexts heeds Christian's warning that theory not rooted in practice becomes elitist and exclusive. For example, the possibility of critiquing an emphasis on building within digital humanities is taken for granted in the United States. The choice to build—or not—is an unaffordable luxury in other digital humanities communities around the world. In India, for example, many local languages are underrepresented in digital scholarship because optical character recognition does not recognize them. Building new tools to account for these languages is crucial to cultural preservation—it is not a choice. In this case, critiquing the practice of tool building may be the privilege of digital humanists working with the Roman alphabet because they can use existing tools, even if they are aware of their limitations. Taking the local U.S. debate as a global one—as so often happens—elides the contexts that shape digital humanities practices in other communities.

Therefore, defining the digital humanities in a global context requires reflection on the plurality of circumstances that inflect local practices. This is not only a matter of tools but also one of method. As Isabel Galina has noted, "Methods that have worked effectively in one cultural setting may fail spectacularly in another (and vice versa) and certain reasoning of how things should work does not apply similarly in other frameworks" ("Is There Anybody out There?"). Another matter is funding for digital humanities scholarship—both a lack of funding for scholars from low-income economies and fiscal disparities between scholars working in research and teaching intensive institutions. Moreover, local cultural contexts influence practices; despite a general predisposition in the United States to the idea that information wants to be free, not all communities want their cultural heritage digitized, whether because of cultural expectations for how knowledge should be transmitted, as in many indigenous communities, or for matters of safety, as among trans* communities. The practices shaped by these cultural traditions or codes constitute local forms of digital humanities and must be accounted for in the move to the global.

The challenge is not to let hegemonic local forms—such as practices or debates taken for granted in the United States—overdetermine the definition of digital humanities globally. Here is another case in which Christian's insistence on the centrality of black feminist thought to theory provides an important model for negotiating difference in the digital humanities. Christian argued that critical theory was effecting a willful erasure of black feminist theory. She noted that black feminist scholars had been "doing" theory for a long time, but that those contributions were written out by poststructuralist theory. In the drive to articulate a global digital humanities, attention to the intersecting forces that shape local practices is integral to ensuring that definitions are not excluding existing practices that go unrecognized because they emerge outside of the tools and practices that have dominated international conferences and journals.

Another difficulty in conceptualizing the global contours of digital humanities is the centrality of U.S., U.K., and Canadian practices that define the field globally. Melissa Terras's infographic, "Quantifying Digital Humanities," maps locations of digital humanities centers around the world and suggests the dominance of these three countries (see Figure 29.1).

Quantifying Digital Humanities

—————————— COURTESY OF UCL CENTRE FOR DIGITAL HUMANITIES ——————————

Digital Humanities research and teaching takes place at the intersection of digital technologies and humanities. DH aims to produce and use applications and models that make possible new kinds of teaching and research, both in the humanities and in computer science (and its allied technologies). DH also studies the impact of these techniques on cultural heritage, memory institutions, libraries, archives and digital culture.

Digital Humanities is difficult to quantify. Here we present all available statistics reguarding individuals and resources, to explore the scope of the field.

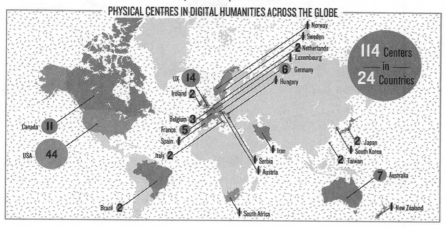

Figure 29.1. Terras's *Quantifying Digital Humanities.* Via UCL Centre for Digital Humanities Flickr page. Reproduced under a Creative Commons 2.0 License.

Just as Christian raised concerns over the ways that theory centered the heirs of European philosophy, relegating the rest of the world to the peripheries, so too, it seems, the centers of digital humanities produce their own margins. The dominance of these three countries in this map reflects a tendency of digital humanities scholarship around the world to take them as their centers. If global digital humanities can only be understood through its local practices, then the act of mapping these practices reveals its contours with greater accuracy. Such work is evident in Alex Gil's project *Around DH in 80 Days,* which offers a map that challenges perceptions of the global landscape and definitions of digital humanities (see Figure 29.2).

The project emerged from Gil's habit of sending colleagues e-mails with annotations of digital humanities projects from around the world. To launch the map-based version of the project, he crowdsourced digital scholarship from all regions, recruited regional editors, and facilitated eighty days of entries to plot a global vision of digital humanities. The map that resulted highlights contributions to the digital humanities that decenter the United States, United Kingdom, and Canada.

In spite of ongoing work to rewrite the maps of global digital humanities, a troubling trend appears in digital humanities citations: erasure of local difference. Staci

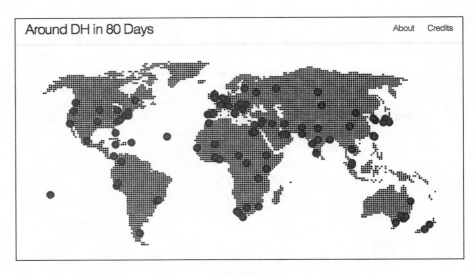

Figure 29.2. Alex Gil's *Around DH in 80 Days*. Image from http://arounddh.org. Reproduced under a Creative Commons 3.0 License.

Stutsman's analysis of digital humanities syllabi has demonstrated that the same handful of theorists from these countries (Susan Hockey, Lev Manovich, Matthew Kirschenbaum, Dan Cohen, Franco Moretti, and Stephen Ramsay) is being taught repeatedly, with little variation. These are, indeed, the same names that recur in digital humanities scholarship in South Africa, Nigeria, India, and South Korea, regardless of their relevance to local context. There is an imperative here to move from a logic that centers the Global North—advanced industrial and high-income economies—in digital humanities toward embracing the diversity of practices around the world and the intersecting forces that shape them. This instance recalls Christian's parallel between the race for theory within the academy with the colonial race for Africa, the systematic colonization of the continent by European powers in the late eighteenth and early nineteenth centuries. She imagines the world of literary studies being similarly overrun with continental philosophy, prescribing ways of reading for Africana literature that originate in methodologies derived from theory, not from within the African diaspora itself. In the global scope of the digital humanities, the dangers of such colonial dynamics are pressing. As Gil has argued, "The United States is very provincial in these matters" ("A Non-Peer-Reviewed Review"). Yet such provincialism is troubling because the influences that define the digital humanities in the United States—or indeed the United Kingdom or Canada—are local but are often easily taken for global. The dominance of scholarship from these countries in the digital humanities demonstrates the ongoing need for locally situated scholarship and indigenous frameworks that theorize questions of the digital through the specificities of its on-the-ground practices worldwide.

Another challenge to articulating a global digital humanities is the question of language. English has occupied the position of *lingua franca* in the field, despite the variety of languages spoken by its practitioners and welcomed at its international conference. Christian similarly notes that the rise of theory allowed for those well versed in its language to exert undue influence on the production of scholarship, marginalizing people of color in general and black women in particular. Although Christian's use of language in this case refers to the technical language, or jargon, of critical theory, a comparison is apt because she observes that such language effaces the possibilities for African American vernacular English within scholarship. Marginalization of languages other than academic forms of English is a critical issue in the digital humanities. Analysis of digital humanities journals, as Domenico Fiormonte has suggested, shows that "DH is monolingual regardless of the country and/or working institution/affiliation of authors" ("Towards a Monocultural [Digital] Humanities"). An implication, he suggests, is not just that digital humanities scholarship is being written in English but that English language sources are primarily the ones being cited. This compounds the hegemony of Anglophone digital humanities within the field. At the Digital Humanities 2014 conference, Élika Ortega and GO::DH organized a whisper campaign to facilitate translation of conference presentations. As Ortega notes, through the project GO::DH learned that there are significantly more languages represented at the conference than the languages in which presentations could be given (at that time English, French, German, Italian, or Spanish, now those five plus one language of the organizing country). Along with GO::DH, which is developing a Translation Toolkit, ADHO's Multi-Lingualism and Multi-Culturalism Committee is in the process of identifying and implementing practices at the Digital Humanities conference to negotiate the fraught question of language. This is certainly an area in which the tensions between local and global practices of digital humanities meet a practical challenge. However, as Galina has suggested, digital humanists are well positioned to build tools and databases or design protocols to assist in translation. Indeed, this is an issue in which cooperation across ideological and economic differences will make the field richer.

The digital divides that shape the digital humanities do so unevenly. Local contexts matter and reflect linguistic, cultural, and social difference. Each location, as well as local communities within national contexts, is uniquely constituted in a matrix of intersecting factors that shape practices. The barriers to speaking of a truly global digital humanities are great, from significant differences in practices to the overdetermining influence of the United States, United Kingdom, and Canada to the dominance of English. As black feminist responses to the rise of theory suggest, the growing popularity of scholarly conversations risk flattening difference unless they carefully privilege diversity, multiplicity, and plurality. Only by defining, situating, and building on local contexts can we understand what digital humanities looks like at the global scale.

BIBLIOGRAPHY

Cecire, Natalia. "Introduction: Theory and the Virtues of Digital Humanities." *Journal of Digital Humanities* 1, no. 1 (2011). http://journalofdigitalhumanities.org/1-1 /introduction-theory-and-the-virtues-of-digital-humanities-by-natalia-cecire/.

Christian, Barbara. "The Race for Theory." *Cultural Critique*, no. 6 (Spring 1987): 51–63.

Crenshaw, Kimberlé. "Mapping the Margins: Intersectionality, Identity Politics, and Violence Against Women of Color." *Stanford Law Review* 43, no. 6 (July 1991): 1241–99.

Fiormonte, Domenico. "Towards a Monocultural (Digital) Humanities." *Infolet*, July 12, 2015. http://infolet.it/2015/07/12/monocultural-humanities/.

Galina, Isabel. "Is There Anybody out There? Building a Global Digital Humanities Community." Keynote speech at the Digital Humanities 2013 Conference, University of Nebraska–Lincoln. Lincoln, Nebraska, July 19, 2013. http://humanidades-digitales.net/blog/2013/07/19/is-there-anybody-out-there-building-a-global-digital -humanities-community/.

Gil, Alex. "A Non-Peer-Reviewed Review of a Peer-Reviewed Essay by Adeline Koh." @ *elotroalex* (blog), April 20, 2015. http://elotroalex.webfactional.com/a-non-peer -reviewed-review-of-a-peer-reviewed-essay-by-adeline-koh/.

Nowviskie, Bethany. "On the Origin of 'Hack' and 'Yack.'" *Bethany Nowviskie Blog*, January 8, 2014. http://nowviskie.org/2014/on-the-origin-of-hack-and-yack/.

Ortega, Élika. "RedHD: Open, Collective, and Multilingual Work Dynamics." Presentation at the Canadian Society of Digital Humanities and Association for Computers and the Humanities Joint Conference, University of Ottawa, Canada, June 3, 2015. http:// slides.com/elikaortega/deck-2#/.

———. "Whispering/Translating during DH2014: Five Things We Learned." *Readers of Fiction*, July 21, 2014. http://linkis.com/tLMeK.

Posner, Miriam. "Some Things to Think about before You Exhort Everyone to Code." *Miriam Posner Blog*, February 29, 2012. http://miriamposner.com/blog/some-things-to -think-about-before-you-exhort-everyone-to-code/.

Ramsay, Stephen. "On Building." *Stephen Ramsay Blog*, January 11, 2011. http://stephen ramsay.us/text/2011/01/11/on-building/.

Ray Murray, Padmini. "Locating the Digital Humanities in India: Internationalisation, Globalisation, and Localisation." Plenary presentation at Digital Diversity 2015, University of Alberta, Edmonton, Canada, May 9, 2015.

Risam, Roopika. "Other Worlds, Other DHs." Presentation at Digital Humanities 2014 Conference, Lausanne, Switzerland, July 9, 2014. http://www.slideshare.net/roopsi1 /other-worlds-other-dhs-roopika-risam.

Rockwell, Geoffrey. "Inclusion in the Digital Humanities." *philosophi.ca* (wiki), September 7, 2011. http://www.philosophi.ca/pmwiki.php/Main/InclusionInTheDigitalHumanities.

Scheinfeldt, Tom. "Where's the Beef? Does Digital Humanities Have to Answer Questions?" In *Debates in Digital Humanities,* ed. Matthew K. Gold. Minneapolis: University of Minnesota Press, 2012. http://dhdebates.gc.cuny.edu/debates/text/18.

Stutsman, Staci. "Digital Humanities vs. New Media: A Matter of Pedagogy." HASTAC Blog, November 17, 2013. https://www.hastac.org/blogs/stacistutsman/2013/11/17/digital-humanities-vs-new-media-matter-pedagogy.

Warwick, Claire. "The End of the Beginning: Supporting and Sustaining DH Institutions." Keynote speech at the Digital Humanities Summer Institute 2015, University of Victoria, Canada, June 2015. http://victoria.events/event/8607/the-end-of-the-beginning-building-supporting-and-sustaining-digital-humanities-institutions.

Between Knowledge and Metaknowledge: Shifting Disciplinary Borders in Digital Humanities and Library and Information Studies

JONATHAN SENCHYNE

Early in the summer of 1918, Maude Dickinson, a student in the Library School of the University of Wisconsin, filed her final library science degree project, "History of Paper-Making in the United States: A Contribution to a Bibliography." Dickinson was learning the principles and practices of enumerative bibliography: compiling, categorizing, and relating information about information. Today, we might also characterize work of this general sort as metadata and linked data creation. But from the early modern period to Dickinson's early twentieth century and beyond, the form of library science known as bibliography was essential for the creation, dissemination, and organization of knowledge.[1] Today, when I consult Dickinson's bibliography in my research on the history of the book in America, I am, in a way, entering into trans-temporal collaboration with her.

Dickinson's role in this collaboration is very clear when I look at a curious feature on the last page of the typescript, her time tally. It reminds me of the hours of information labor I am spared from doing myself.[2] On the final page of her bibliography, Dickinson reports the following:

	TIME
Getting acquainted with the subject	6 hours
Gathering and arranging material	115 [hours]
Typing	32 [hours]
Total	153 hours (Dickinson, 32).

Figure 30.1. Maude Dickinson's logged hours of information work.

Dickinson's 153 hours of information work in 1918 may seem like an odd starting point for a consideration of the relationship of library and information studies (LIS) education to the digital humanities. These hours highlight, however, the long history of complex interrelations between knowledge workers in American colleges and universities. As Julia Flanders wrote in the inaugural volume of *Debates in the Digital Humanities*,[3] "Every hour of faculty work is brought into being by hundreds of hours of time spent maintaining the physical and administrative space within which that work is conducted: libraries, network, payroll, buildings, and all the rest of it" (Flanders, 293). Dickinson's training in LIS is representative of a tradition in which librarians are concerned largely with "all the rest of it" over "the subject" with which they become "acquainted" but do not specialize. Distinct from specialized faculty work, Flanders argues that information work in the academy tends to operate at the level of "metaknowledge," or "the organization and management of knowledge *across* and *apart from* specific subject areas" (Flanders, 302).

The emergence of the digital humanities in specialized disciplines and librarianship alike necessitates a recalibration of this allocation of knowledge and practice. DH in the disciplines has brought discussion of metaknowledge—data structures, archival and editorial standards, digital curation and representation—into the graduate education of disciplinary specialists. But what about in LIS graduate education, where metaknowledge training has long been the standard model? To train digital *humanities* librarians, unique from digital librarians or generalist academic librarians, LIS programs and students need to spend more than a figurative six hours on a humanities subject compared to 147 hours organizing and representing information about it.

I take Dickinson's temporal division of knowledge labor as symbolic of divisions that have been fairly consistent in LIS education and practice from Dickinson's time until ours. Undergraduate and then graduate degrees in LIS programs prepared a largely female workforce for employment in public libraries, K–12 schools, colleges, and universities (and sometimes private firms) as metaknowledge workers whose professional focus was management and organization of diverse forms of information about nearly any subject. Of course, LIS education has never been fully subject-area agnostic. There has long been specialized training in youth and literacy, for example. But when it comes to disciplinary academic knowledge, an academic librarian traditionally might train to understand the norms and trends in scholarly communication in the humanities, rather than the deeply specialized debates in fields such as nineteenth-century American literary history.

In the last five years, the accelerated proliferation of digital humanities research, the centers that support it, and the scholar-practitioners it employs has changed both the division of labor and the division of knowledge between "content" training in academic subspecialties and metaknowledge training in LIS. Because participation in DH research (as researcher or literate reader) requires varying levels of familiarity with academic subspecialties, computer science, information organization, data management, and design practice, undergraduate and graduate programs in content disciplines (e.g., history and English) as well as metaknowledge disciplines (e.g., LIS) find themselves trying to figure out new calibrations of training in content and form, disciplinary knowledge, and technical systems. What do these shifting boundaries between humanities content and information science mean for LIS education and practice in the coming years? As graduate education in specialist humanities fields increasingly turns attention to topics like metadata and organizational schema, LIS graduate education should turn some of its focus to discipline-specific humanities education in order to produce capable and relevant DH librarians. The model wherein librarian Maude Dickinson spent 147 hours gathering, arranging, and representing (e.g., typing) information about topics as varied as the wind while academic specialists spend 147 hours creating small pieces of new knowledge will not suit DH librarians going forward because disciplinary-specific knowledge and information management metaknowledge are mutually constitutive in DH work. In short, digital humanities librarianship implies something distinct from librarianship or digital librarianship in general. That "something" is a relation to the content disciplines from which it flows: the humanities.

Why would LIS students need to study cultural theory or literary history? What sort of LIS education, typically at the master's level, will these new DH-oriented jobs require? "Digital humanities librarian," as a discrete position, is a relatively new title, yet as I write this chapter there happen to be two open searches for positions with that title at U.S. universities. Other currently open searches are not explicitly calling for "digital humanities librarians" but are within this purview: data analytics and visualization librarian, digital initiatives librarian, and digital research services librarian for arts and sciences.[4] What these jobs look like on the ground will vary by institution and local context, as with any job, but they might share some by-now familiar characteristics. For example, in formalized DH labs and "drop-in" DH consultation models alike, librarians frequently act as the threshold between humanities faculty and student specialists and computer scientists. DH librarians use their training in metaknowledge, broad humanities practices, and information science practices to translate concepts and values across diverse audiences and project participants. In DH projects, librarians are often something like the necessary and useful friction where the rubber hits the road. This approach is largely consistent with ways of thinking about librarianship that Maude Dickinson would have recognized in 1906. A little familiarity with the discipline (getting acquainted with the subject), a lot of work in organization and management (gathering and arranging material), and some time executing technical applications (typing, or today, coding). This rather traditional division of intellectual labor is even reflected in one of the best online resources for digital humanities librarianship, the web community "dh+lib."[5] I invoke this vibrant and important community not to criticize it or its representation of DH and librarianship, but instead, to reflect on its name, which figures the field imaginary as the sum of two distinct disciplines. The librarian is the transactional "plus" or "and" between two entities. Take DH, add in libraries and librarians.

But this formulation of the encounter between DH and librarianship poses a number of problems. For one, a content-agnostic model of LIS training does not accurately reflect the reality of twenty-first-century DH librarianship, or even of twenty-first-century archival practice. Students currently pursuing archives special-izations, for example, often wonder[6] whether they will need MA or PhD degrees in history or another humanities discipline to be competitive for coveted positions in highly specialized archives (Cobb). The Society of American Archivists points out[7] in its advice for interested students that archivists "receive graduate degrees in his-tory of library science . . . some have degrees in both fields . . . a PhD is often preferred for higher ranking positions in academic institutions" ("So You Want to Be an Archi-vist"). The reason for this is often that good archival practice frequently requires adapting and innovating systems and methods of intake, preservation, storage, and retrieval according to the unique qualities of the materials, the habits and ques-tions of scholars and users, and the relationship of the materials to their history and interpretation.[8] Put simply, archivist work has always been about more than putting interchangeable "content" in the appropriate Hollinger box, and sometimes being able to do that work effectively requires advanced study in the content discipline.

In practical terms, this is a challenge for graduate students wondering whether they need to double up degrees, studying archival science as well as, say, early Ameri-can history if they intend to seek a job at institutions like the American Antiquarian Society, the Library Company, or other highly specialized collections. It does not mitigate the harmful effects of unnecessary "credential creep"[9] in DH hiring, where a confluence of a buyer's job market and uncertainty over what the relatively new field is and requires has resulted in inappropriately overstating requirements for DH jobs. Amanda Gailey and Dot Porter have argued that search committees may require a PhD when an MA or MLS will do, simply because there are enough PhDs looking for work or because faculty on hiring committees are more familiar with the PhD as a credential (Gailey and Porter). But the possibility remains that content-agnostic LIS master's training legitimately may not prepare candidates enough for the job, just as traditional humanities PhD programs do not necessarily train candidates to become curators, archivists, or librarians.

Many LIS students who want to pursue DH work are faced with a steep tech-nological learning curve with information systems and coding. And students today focus a great deal of their LIS education developing these skills and literacies. This is akin to studying archival science: what are the digital systems of preservation, access, and manipulation at our disposal? I would argue that, as with some archi-vist students, students pursuing DH librarianship will also face a learning curve in the humanities specialties. Just as archival work requires more than "content plus acid free storage," DH work requires more than "content plus content man-agement system," or "content plus topic modeling application." Editing and repre-senting texts digitally often requires developing or altering content management and web display systems that are responsive to the unique qualities of the mate-rial or to the scholarly methodologies of particular academic communities. To be done well, this requires disciplinary knowledge and familiarity with disciplinary cul-tures. How does the history of interpreting Emily Dickinson's construction of the fascicles—small gatherings of manuscript poems that Dickinson sewed together in codex form—matter for their representation and manipulation online, for example? The answer to that question varies depending on whether one's interpretation of the fascicles is closer to Sharon Cameron's suggestion that they be read as books, or Alexandra Socarides's counterargument that Dickinson was more intentional about the relation of one poem to another on individual sheets.[10] How would this difference in possible interpretations be registered in a digital representation of these material texts? Omeka, the digital archive and exhibition tool, cannot help you make a decision about Socarides's claims over Cameron's. And it cannot help you know to ask the question in the first place, which is possibly the most important step. But the difference for scholarship is crucial: when represented online, do the digital surrogates of the fascicles encourage readers to understand them as book-like objects, or do they offer a way to investigate and manipulate them as individual sheets? Platforms like Omeka cannot expand to support these new possibilities without scholar-practitioners who can envision them.

These challenges are, of course, currently met by many individual DH researchers, teams, and labs. For certain people, their interests and skills have led them to both special disciplinary knowledge and technical (or meta) knowledge—here I think of people exactly like Flanders or Bethany Nowviskie, who model the scholar-practitioner ideal.[11] More frequently, DH brings diverse individuals, with different skillsets, into lab environments where librarians, computer scientists, and historians or literary critics come together to theorize problems and meet technological challenges together: the NULab for Texts, Maps, and Networks; the Maryland Institute for Technology in the Humanities; and the Scholars' Lab at UVA, to name only a few. Practitioners such as Flanders and Nowviskie will still come to this work organically through the idiosyncrasies of their skills and interests. But, as "DH librarian" becomes codified as a job title, LIS students will increasingly come into programs wondering what is necessary to become one. "Do all the things" is not the most useful advice, even if it contains a kernel of truth. Short of "do it all," I fear that technological training will be offered as an answer to the question of DH librarian education, at the expense of disciplinary content knowledge.

In the next five years, we will need to see more active collaboration between iSchools/LIS departments and humanities graduate programs in order to create courses and programs that prepare DH librarians and DH disciplinary specialists side by side. Practically speaking, if we hope our students develop DH labs and other scenes of vibrant collaborative research, why expect those spaces and relationships to emerge *ex nihilo* at some future date? In broader terms, we must recognize, as Elizabeth Maddock Dillon and Nicole Aljoe have urged, that digital practice in the humanities needs "traditional" forms of humanist inquiry for its continued innovation and relevancy. In their work creating a TEI-encoded archive of early Caribbean texts, for example, the problem of how to "mark up" the unnamed enslaved people and "embedded" slave narratives in these texts required innovations in the

TEI markup itself. This insight, and the innovation of TEI that it led to, depended on a deep knowledge of theory and criticism in the history of slavery, of Afro-Caribbean literature, and of Atlantic and black Atlantic studies.[12] Of course, Dillon and Aljoe are part of the NULab team, which includes librarians and computer scientists whose roles include working with, and expanding the boundaries of, digital tools in the humanities lab.

So, why would I like LIS grad students to know more about cultural theory, the black Atlantic, or book history? Why won't an additive "plus lib" be sufficient? The risk for librarians of thinking of librarianship as an add-on to DH work, instead of as an integral and organic part of teams and processes, is that the roles once held by librarians risk being filled by people with other training. This may be a good thing in some cases, but it also risks the loss or devaluing of important LIS-specific training, knowledge, and structures.

We are now witnessing humanities PhD programs trying to incorporate more training in metaknowledge, organization of information, and digital tools—areas that have long been the purview of LIS education. The #alt-ac model, for example, is one way that disciplinary specialists have been widening their preparation for and approach to employment, frequently with courses in LIS departments/iSchools. Other programs like the Council on Library and Information Resources (CLIR) postdoctoral fellowship program, and, depending on the placement site, the American Council of Learned Societies (ACLS) Public Humanities postdoctoral fellowship, are explicitly oriented toward "offer[ing] recent PhD graduates the chance to help develop research tools, resources, and services while exploring new career opportunities" ("CLIR Postdoctoral Fellowship Program"[13]). The CLIR program places holders of humanities PhDs into short-term positions in academic libraries and research centers, often as a first step toward a career in libraries. It is a source of frustration to some in the library profession that no LIS degree is required for positions like these, and the pattern will likely become increasingly prevalent as more people take the #alt-ac path from a specialized PhD to various forms of knowledge work in and around colleges and universities. Graduate training in the academic disciplines increasingly incorporates LIS training and looks positively on employment in both traditional and new types of knowledge work. Or, as in the case of the CLIR fellowships, sometimes the specialized knowledge and training of "library curious" scholars with advanced research degrees is valued highly enough that it replaces an LIS degree as a qualification for employment in academic settings where DH and related work is done.

LIS training should come closer to a middle ground with humanities disciplinary graduate training, and LIS students and faculty would do well to become similarly interested and engaged with specialized humanities disciplinary work. Students entering LIS grad programs with the goal of being a DH librarian should seek to leave grad school knowing as much about habits of thought and questioning in the humanities as they know about digital tools. They should be able to call upon their training to participate seriously in seminar-style conversations about historiography, theory, and traditions of criticism. They should be able to use appropriate technologies for the kind of DH work to which they are drawn, whether it be digital resource and data management or text mining. And they should develop a facility with technology such that they will be able to learn new technologies as they emerge in the field in the future. This is a tall order, and it begins to sound again like "do all the things." But those of us who have some control over curriculum can make these educational outcomes easier to pursue. Offer joint programs where students pursuing either an LIS or a humanities degree can work side by side, taking courses in both theory and technology, I say. Faculty and students across disciplines must pursue and train for DH as a thing in and of itself, a demanding thing that requires both/and knowledge. DH must not be an add-on, either to an academic discipline (Civil War poetry but with DH) or to a profession (DH but with librarians).

In other words, DH is exciting precisely because it holds out a promise to think in new ways about the synthesis of content and form, and about the production of knowledge. In both humanities and LIS programs, DH is a reminder that disciplinary knowledge depends on the ways that fields produce, organize, and represent information. As we prepare students in both of these fields to encounter DH from different perspectives, we must accord disciplinary knowledge and metaknowledge equal weight no matter which "side" our approach is from: the content disciplines or the information science "side." To close with Maude Dickinson's student project: for too long, academics and librarians have treated content (like academic scholarship on papermaking) and form (like bibliographies created and access curated by librarians) as separate kinds of work done by separate kinds of workers. We are at a moment when that separation of intellectual and physical labor serves neither scholars nor librarians well. Soon "DH plus lib" will be thought of simply as DH. For the sake of the field and the employability of library and information school graduates, LIS education must attend more closely to discipline-specific work.

NOTES

Thank you to Lauren Gottlieb-Miller and Bronwen Masemann, my colleagues in the School of Library and Information Studies at the University of Wisconsin–Madison, for discussing these issues with me. Thanks also to the editors of this volume for their extremely helpful comments on drafts of this work.

1. On the history of bibliography as information management, see Blair.

2. For a study of the importance of information labor and the consequences of its frequent invisibility, see Downey.

3. http://dhdebates.gc.cuny.edu/debates/text/26.

4. These searches were found by taking an unscientific survey of job listings at *dh+lib,* http://acrl.ala.org/dh/category/jobs/, and the Digital Library Federation, http://www.diglib.org/topics/jobs/, in early June 2015.

5. See *dh+lib,* http://acrl.ala.org/dh.

6. https://www.linkedin.com/grp/post/52874-235380641.

7. http://www2.archivists.org/profession.

8. Take, for example, the work of information professionals in tribal libraries, archives, and museums—institutional contexts where sovereign power, colonial power, and indigenous knowledge traditions frequently make Euro-American ideas about culture and information (like the unqualified good open access) inappropriate.

9. http://mediacommons.futureofthebook.org/alt-ac/pieces/credential-creep -digital-humanities.

10. See Cameron, *Choosing Not Choosing,* and Socarides, *Dickinson Unbound,* for context on whether the poems in Dickinson's fascicles should be read and interpreted as intentionally related to one another, as if in book form, or not. What interests me in this context is that the space afforded users to encounter with the digital surrogates of the fascicles will bear on the way they are interpreted.

11. Here I point to the multifaceted approach to education and employment that Flanders outlines in "Time, Labor, and 'Alternate Careers.'"

12. See Dillon and Aljoe, "The Early Caribbean Digital Archive," and Aljoe et al., "Obeah and the Early Caribbean Digital Archive."

13. http://www.clir.org/fellowships/postdoc.

BIBLIOGRAPHY

Aljoe, Nicole N., Elizabeth Maddock Dillon, Benjamin J. Doyle, and Elizabeth Hopwood. "Obeah and the Early Caribbean Digital Archive." *Atlantic Studies: Global Currents* 12, no. 5 (2015): 258–66.

Blair, Ann. *Too Much to Know: Managing Scholarly Information before the Modern Age.* New Haven, Conn.: Yale University Press, 2010.

Cameron, Sharon. *Choosing Not Choosing.* Chicago: University of Chicago Press, 1993.

"CLIR Postdoctoral Fellowship Program," Council on Library and Information Resources. http://www.clir.org/fellowships/postdoc.

Cobb, Tanya. "Do Archives Job Applicants Need a Second Master's Degree?" Society of American Archivists, *LinkedIn* Group. https://www.linkedin.com/grp/post/52874-235380641.

dh+lib. http://acrl.ala.org/dh/.

Dickinson, Maude V. *History of Paper-Making in the United States: A Contribution to a Bibliography.* Madison: University of Wisconsin Library School, 1918.

Dillon, Elizabeth Maddock, and Nicole Aljoe. "The Early Caribbean Digital Archive: Recovery and Remix." Conference paper prepared for African American Expression in Print and Digital Culture, University of Wisconsin–Madison, September 20, 2014.

Downey, Greg. "Virtual Webs, Physical Technologies, and Hidden Workers: The Spaces of Labor in Information Internetworks." *Technology and Culture* 42, no. 2 (2001): 209–35.

Flanders, Julia. "Time, Labor, and 'Alternate Careers' in Digital Humanities Knowledge Work." In *Debates in the Digital Humanities,* ed. Matthew K. Gold, 292–308. Minneapolis: University of Minnesota Press, 2012. http://dhdebates.gc.cuny.edu/debates/text/26.

Gailey, Amanda, and Dot Porter. "Credential Creep in the Digital Humanities." *#alt-academy, Media Commons,* May 6, 2011. http://mediacommons.futureofthebook.org/alt-ac/pieces/credential-creep-digital-humanities.

"So You Want to Be an Archivist: An Overview of the Archives Profession." Society of American Archivists. http://www2.archivists.org/profession.

Socarides, Alexandra. *Dickinson Unbound: Paper, Process, Poetics.* New York: Oxford University Press, 2013.

"Black Printers" on White Cards: Information Architecture in the Data Structures of the Early American Book Trades

MOLLY O'HAGAN HARDY

Since Isaiah Thomas incorporated his research for his ambitious *The History of Printing in America*[1] (1810) into the collections of the American Antiquarian Society (AAS), which he founded in 1812, the Society has held the most data on the early American book trades in North America and the Caribbean. The bulk of this information exists on twenty-five drawers of cards in our reading room and is known as the Printers' File.[2] Culled from biographies, reference books, and newspapers, the data detail the work of some 6,000 printers, publishers, editors, binders, and others involved in the book trades up to 1820.

We are now transforming all of this data, both from the cards and from our General Catalog,[3] into a digital resource. In an effort to augment the types of queries our data can answer, to link our data to related datasets, and to allow greater access to a resource that is currently only available in our reading room, we are reorganizing, reordering, and in effect "digitizing" this data. In the transformation, the information architecture governing the data will change, and this change illustrates how data structure can both make and obscure meaning. The loss in this case is not data about the printers themselves, but instead it is information about the zeitgeist in which the data were assembled. As Alan Liu reminds us, digital humanists need to show that critical thinking about our resources "scales into thinking critically about the power, finance, and other governance protocols of the world" ("Where Is Cultural Criticism"). Insofar as such protocols are inscribed on and in the very structures of data—be they index cards, library catalogs, or databases—attention to them is especially crucial at times of change and at moments of reordering and reorienting our data. The opportunity to make the important critical move that Liu argues for therefore requires attention to the critical making of libraries and archivists in the decades that came before the digital turn.

Book historians (and the more steeped in bibliography and cataloging one is, the more I think this is true) have long been keenly aware of the importance of how

Figure 31.1. This is one of the 25 drawers of the Printers' File. Each card in the Printers' File has a person's name at the top. Courtesy of the American Antiquarian Society.

information is structured. In her contribution to the 2012 edition of *Debates in the Digital Humanities,*[4] Joanna Drucker identifies such an awareness with the critical editing and online repositories built in the early 1990s, but we might trace such an awareness much further back if we are to look at the history of cataloging and bibliography in this country, and of course even further back, if we turn our gaze across the Atlantic. But the point that I want to make here is less about origins than it is about Drucker's concern that what she terms "capta" and defines as "interpretation rather than data" is lost in the creation of humanist "data." And she is right: if we fail to reflect on a given system's "capta," systems of interpretation and an analysis of the work they do might well be lost. Attention to the processes and procedures of the past generations' data creators—librarians and archivists—allow us to see how information structures governing data are a form of "capta" themselves. As Lisa Gitelman and Virginia Jackson argue in the introduction to *"Raw Data" Is an Oxymoron*[5] (16): "starting with data often leads to an unnoticed assumption that data are transparent, that information is self-evident, the fundamental stuff of truth itself. If we're not careful, in other words, our zeal for more and more data can become a faith in their neutrality and autonomy, their objectivity." Drucker warns us that something is lost—and I will provide an example of that—and then Gitelman and Jackson remind us that there is no stripping down of data to some neutral place, that ordering is interpretation. The transformation of the Printers' File verifies that observation as well.

Composed almost singularly by Avis Clarke, librarian at AAS from 1927 until 1970 when she retired, the Printers' File is an example of a largely bygone era of massive bibliographic data collection by individuals. In the early twentieth century, increasingly institutionalized special collection libraries had come to rely on the female clerical worker. Barbara Mitchell concludes her essay on this transformation of the male librarian's authority to the female cleric's bureaucratic function in the period:

> Seen within its technological, cultural and social context, the rise of the card catalogue, and the concomitant entrance of female clerical workers into increasingly bureaucratized libraries, was a pivotal point not only in the history of libraries. The great library catalogues, early technology systems that would endure for decades, were catalysts for an extraordinary moment of institutional growth and change. (Mitchell, 147)

Clarke was an indefatigable and, if rumors are true, somewhat eccentric workhorse whose output lasted a staggering forty-three years in the middle of the twentieth century. Here she is pictured, typing up one of thousands of cards she created.

These cards, and the name authority work they have contributed to, have been of inestimable value to AAS catalogers and researchers alike as they write and rewrite the history of early American, Caribbean, Scottish, Irish, and English printing and all of the labors associated with it.

Figure 31.2. Avis Clarke at her typewriter, where she worked from 1927–70. Courtesy of the American Antiquarian Society.

The transformation of the Printers' File into a digital resource has rendered visible some of these hitherto "unnoticed assumptions" that Gitelman and Jackson describe. The Printers' File is in effect a prosopography, tracing the business and at times personal lives of thousands of people involved in and around the early American book trade and the people who dictate this structure. Each of the salmon-color cards in the twenty-five drawers details the life of an individual.

One person might have more than one card, but always—or almost always—there is a name at the top of the card to remind the user that it is the category of "person" that is organizing this inquiry (Figure 31.1). In this sea of salmon cards, there is however an exception: four white cards that have the title "Black Printers" at their top, instead of a person's name. The cards then list a number of African American printers active in the trade from the eighteenth to the early twentieth centuries. Why are these cards included? How did they come to disrupt the information structure that governs this data? And what do we make of such a disruption?

The answer can be found in our institutional records,[6] which trace the building of our collections and in so many ways reflect and inform the history of information science and librarianship in this country. In the AAS archives there is correspondence between California Historical Society[7] librarian James Abajian and AAS associate librarian Fred Bauer, Jr. In June 1975, Abajian sent a general query to a number of university libraries and a few independent libraries about his latest project: "I am preparing for publication a monograph concerning U.S. 19th and early 20th century black printers, type founders, and ink and paper makers. If you have any references to blacks engaged in either this field or peripheral areas, I should very much appreciate receiving Xerox copies of them." Bauer promptly responded with

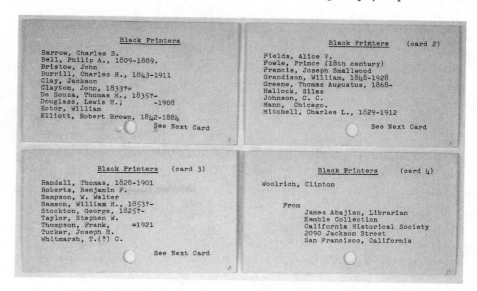

Figure 31.3. White cards that are now part of the Printers' File. These resulted from the Abajian's letter to Bauer. Courtesy of the American Antiquarian Society.

a list of reference books Abajian might consult and told him of the Printers' File. Bauer lamented that the Printers' File could not really be of help because of the way it was organized. He wrote, "Unfortunately, we do not have any entry to our Printer's [*sic*] Catalog by sex or race (color). This great resource can only be tapped through the Surname of the printer." In response, Abajian adjusted his query, forwarding "a selected list of such printers is attached for whatever can be done with it" (Correspondence in "AAS Records").

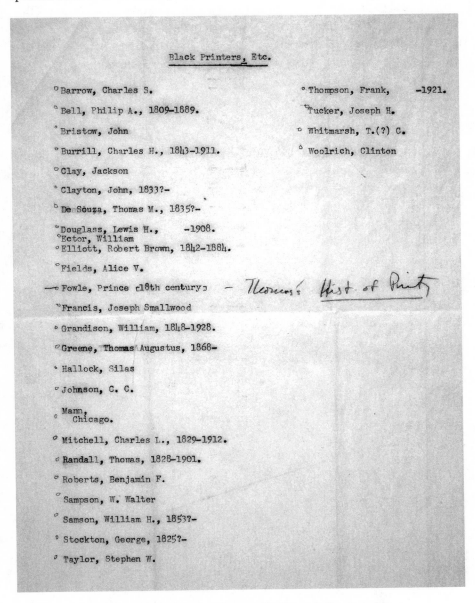

Figure 31.4. Appendage in letter from James Abajian to Fred Bauer Jr. Courtesy of the American Antiquarian Society.

Bauer was pleased to have the list, responding that he hoped "to turn up some information as we proceed with our cataloging" and asking Abajian for permission to include it in the File. Bauer again bemoaned the Printers' File's insufficiency: "Since we are still working in the period 1640–1830," he wrote, "we have only a slight chance to discover any of the people you have found, but we shall try. Please keep us advised of your results for we would welcome any additional information for our Printers' file."[8] It is Abajian's list that became the four 3×5 white index cards.

Placed at the start of the "B"s, these cards, now understood in the context of this exchange, speak to an absence in the history of the American trades: the names of these "black printers" are there because Abajian sought data that Bauer regrettably could not supply. In other words, their inclusion signifies exclusion.

There is much more to be said about these cards as outliers, about the political and social conditions in which these men and women of the book trades worked and the reasons their work is obscure, and about the zeitgeist in which Abajian sought information about them. For my purposes here, I want to say simply that, through rupture, these cards call attention to the forces at play as this huge amount of information was structured. In digitizing the data, we will note the race, insofar as we know it, of all members of the trade so that the uniqueness of these cards will be lost.

The gray scale in which we have scanned the cards allows one to distinguish between a salmon card and a white card, but there will be no place to field the card

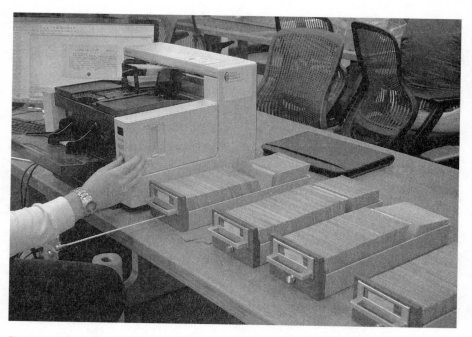

Figure 31.5. Scanning of the Printers' File cards. Courtesy of the American Antiquarian Society.

color: 4 entries out of some 6,000 hardly warrant their own column in a spreadsheet. We will however be including information about what Bauer lamented the lack of in his letter to Abajian: the "sex or race (color)" of these historical figures insofar as we know it. In the digital resource, the "black printers" can be found by simple querying of the data, as if these names had always been there. These names will not stand out because they are on white cards, but instead will exist in the same ontology as all the others in the dataset. The cards themselves, however, remind us that our organization of data, no matter how neutral we imagine it to be, is built out of and therefore reflects on a particular moment—that it is performing a kind of "capta" through its very organization within a system that can never itself be neutral because its creation, like the data it captures, is a humanist endeavor.

NOTES

1. http://catalog.mwa.org/vwebv/holdingsInfo?bibId=286959.
2. http://www.americanantiquarian.org/printers-file.
3. http://www.americanantiquarian.org/catalog.htm.
4. http://dhdebates.gc.cuny.edu/debates/text/34.
5. http://mitpress.mit.edu/books/raw-data-oxymoron.
6. http://catalog.mwa.org/vwebv/holdingsInfo?bibId=357400.
7. http://www.californiahistoricalsociety.org.
8. Jonathan Senchyne of the University of Wisconsin first drew my attention to these letters.

BIBLIOGRAPHY

Correspondence in "AAS Records, 1912-," 1979 1970. Box 394. American Antiquarian Society, Worcester, Massachusetts.

Drucker, Johanna. "Humanistic Theory and Digital Scholarship." In *Debates in the Digital Humanities,* ed. Matthew K. Gold. Minneapolis: University of Minnesota Press, 2012. http://dhdebates.gc.cuny.edu/debates/text/34.

Gitelman, Lisa, and Virginia Jackson. *"Raw Data" Is an Oxymoron.* Cambridge, Mass.: MIT Press, 2013.

Liu, Alan. "Where Is Cultural Criticism in the Digital Humanities?" In *Debates in the Digital Humanities,* ed. Matthew K. Gold. Minneapolis: University of Minnesota Press, 2012. http://dhdebates.gc.cuny.edu/debates/text/20.

Mitchell, Barbara. "Boston Library Catalogues, 1850–1875: Female Labor and Technological Change." In *Institutions of Reading: The Social Life of Libraries in the United States,* ed. Thomas Augst and Kenneth Carpenter, 119–47. Amherst and Boston: University of Massachusetts Press, 2007.

Public, First

SHEILA A. BRENNAN

A s a public historian who has practiced in both analog and digital modes, I am attuned to the articles in the *Chronicle* and conversations—on Twitter, at meetings, and at conferences—from traditional and alt-academics who see digital and online projects as a means for sharing academic research with "the general public." Skeptics ask why academics have lost their publics, while proponents point to popular digital humanities projects (Bender). It is important to recognize that projects and research may be available online, but that status does not inherently make the work digital public humanities or public digital humanities. Public history and humanities practices—in either digital or analog forms—place communities, or other public audiences, at their core.

Digital humanities scholars and practitioners are defined by the digital, which makes the difference in their humanities scholarship. Public historians and public humanities scholars are defined by the "public," even when definitions of these practices are contested (National Council on Public History; Lubar). Suzanne Fischer offers a useful way of describing public history as "cracking open history as a democratic project, and doing it transparently, in public." She also suggests that while public historians work with specific audiences on projects, they also have "a duty to serve particular communities" ("On the Vocation of Public History"). Public digital humanities, then, should be identified by the ways that it engages with communities outside of the academy as a means for doing digital humanities scholarship.

Research projects, online textbooks, tools, course websites, online journals, or social networks are not inherently "public" digital humanities projects merely because they have a presence on the Web. Working in public—an intentional approach to working and sharing research and practices—does not equate to doing public digital humanities. Similarly, launching a project website or engaging in social media networks does not necessarily make a project discoverable, accessible, or relevant to anyone other than its creators. Doing any type of public digital humanities work requires an intentional decision from the beginning of the project that identifies, invites in, and addresses audience needs in the design, as well as the approach and content, long before the outreach for a finished project begins. Public historians and other professionals working at cultural heritage institutions have learned that by not seeing "the public" as real people they have sometimes viewed "the public" as an unidentified "other." By examining the roots of public history, scholars interested in creating public digital humanities projects can avoid these pitfalls and see their work as part of a long tradition of publicly engaged scholarly work.

Public History Roots

Public digital humanities, digital public history, and digital public humanities all have strong roots in public history. In the United States, the practice of public history can be traced back to the early nineteenth century, when white women and men of means volunteered their time to save and preserve community stories, objects, and places (Kammen; West). The federal government got involved in the history business in the late nineteenth and early twentieth centuries. Federal history and museum programs, such as the National Park Service and Smithsonian Institution, were grounded in practices borrowed and adopted by scientists and naturalists and used in publicly funded spaces (Meringolo). Government civil servants assumed responsibilities to care for, interpret, and collect materials on behalf of citizens. Many of these practitioners also belonged to professional organizations in equal numbers with academic historians, such as the American Historical Association. Technological advances in preservation and research materials during the mid-twentieth century (e.g., microfilm) led to standardizing and specializing practices of archivists, for example, and to a growing divide among academic historians and practicing public historians (Townsend). These practitioners often did not identify their work as "public history"; rather, some referred to this work as "applied history" (National Council on Public History). Their work was, and still is, service-driven, carrying with it a significant amount of intellectual labor and institution building. Individuals practicing within or collaborating with cultural heritage institutions and university libraries, as may be the case for digital humanities scholars, continue this tradition of service-driven work that shapes and contributes to new forms of scholarship.

The public history movement that we know today emerged in universities in the 1970s, responding both to the employment crisis in the United States (and the marketability of history majors) and to the social and labor history movements that engaged communities in questioning existing social, political, and cultural structures and inequalities (Stanton, xiv)—including those embedded in cultural heritage institutions. In the late twentieth century, many self-identified public historians continued to view the "public" as generalized and passive. Public history may have offered scholars new ways of communicating (e.g., through museum exhibits), but as Denise Meringolo observed, many scholars did not rethink the structures and relationships involved in that communication flow (*Museums, Monuments*, xxi). Oral historians, like Michael Frisch, filled that gap by encouraging all historians to think of their role as facilitators. By recording conversations with the unfamous, they could save and make available for the public record the lives and histories of ordinary citizens. Frisch popularized the term and philosophy of "shared authority," as integral to public history practices before the birth of the modern web browser (Frisch). Tom Scheinfeldt has argued that because these public history practices from the mid- to the late twentieth century were "highly technological, archival, public, collaborative, political, and networked," they represent another branch in the broad genealogy of digital humanities ("Dividends of Difference").

A key figure in this genealogy is labor historian Roy Rosenzweig, who saw potential to broaden and diversify the historical enterprise using digital means. Roy's passion motivated him to found the Center for History and New Media[1] in 1994 to use digital media to democratize history by incorporating multiple perspectives and inviting everyday citizens to contribute their own stories for new digital collections built to document major events and the histories of their own communities.[2] To some, this mission may have sounded utopian, but Roy was practical. He believed that all scholars, but historians in particular, shared responsibility for documenting, saving, and preserving historical evidence in analog and digital formats (Rosenzweig). This meant historians could, and should, build digital projects and platforms that would be used, and useful, and never isolated from the larger networks of libraries, archives, and museums. This foundation in public history makes the Roy Rosenzweig Center for History and New Media (RRCHNM) different from most digital humanities centers; as a result, most of its projects are created for and with audiences outside of academia and serve as models for public digital humanities work.

Doing Public Digital Humanities

Each public digital humanities project must begin by identifying audiences outside of the academy. To help see audiences as people with interests, lives, agendas, and challenges, some digital project teams borrow techniques from user-centered design and create user personas. The Smithsonian Learning Lab[3] offers a good example for the process of creating named personas that represent real teachers, the primary audience for the Learning Lab's new digital initiative (Milligan). Understanding audiences is not a skill most humanities scholars are taught in graduate school, but it is a key element for successful digital projects.

Identifying and collaborating with specific audiences helps public digital humanities projects be relevant, useful, and usable. This means working with those groups to identify the needs of a potential platform, assess its functionality, and then measure its effectiveness for communicating ideas. The *Histories of the National Mall* project team from the Rosenzweig Center for History and New Media identified tourists and individuals new to the D.C. area (e.g., summer interns) as the primary audiences for its mobile public history project.[4] Before customizing an Omeka site, the team tested the site architecture, content, functionality, and terminology with different users using paper mock-ups. Once the site was prototyped in Omeka, the team spent time on the National Mall with friends and family members to test different iterations of the site before the beta launch. This type of audience identification and evaluation is even more important for software projects. During its original grant, the Omeka team surveyed museum professionals before, during, and after the beta release and conducted focus group testing to gauge needs, assess the effectiveness of the software to meet those needs, and explore the usability of the Omeka software.[5] While time-consuming, these steps are necessary to include in the work plan of any digital project to ensure its success.

Projects must be accessible to those identified as potential audiences in a number of important ways. First, any public digital humanities project should be designed such that people of all abilities can use and access it on the Web. Second, projects should be built in ways that reach primary audiences on the platforms they regularly use. This may mean designing a light mobile framework to reach people who only access the Web from handheld devices. If users communicate on one specific social media space, the project should be there. If users speak multiple languages, the platform choice must allow for that content to be accessible in those languages. Third, the language, symbols, and navigational paths embedded in the digital project must be understandable by its users and participants. A public digital humanities project should never make the audience feel dumb or unwelcome in that space. Fourth, names are important. Projects should be named after something meaningful to the targeted audiences, or something that is intentionally not associated with a familiar term. Omeka, for example, fits into the latter category. The Swahili term embodies what the web publishing platform is designed to do: display or lay out wares; to speak out; to spread out; to unpack. Because the word itself was unfamiliar for most users, it could take on the meaning of a new piece of software. The name of *Histories of the National Mall,* on the other hand, directly tells tourists visiting the National Mall that the site is about the history of that public space. Acronyms and clever naming can work for some digital humanities projects, but it is best not to alienate or mislead users.

Developing a public digital humanities project is a challenging process that requires building a team with many different skills sets. When a team lacks expertise in public humanities, it should find public humanities scholars with whom to collaborate. There is often a public historian or a community activist who is eager to share knowledge and experience with audience engagement. Digital humanities project teams that incorporate and invite voices from user communities in the early stages will build fabulous new digital things that are relevant, useful, and productive for those targeted users. To do public digital humanities, the "public" needs to come first. Always.

NOTES

1. Formally known as the Roy Rosenzweig Center for History and New Media (RRCHNM) at George Mason University, http://chnm.gmu.edu/.

2. The *September 11 Digital Archive* is an example, http://911digitalarchive.org/.

3. http://learninglab.si.edu/news/2015/03/our-personas-introducing-naomi-javier -samantha-and-nicole.

4. *Histories of the National Mall,* http://mallhistory.org/.

5. Omeka, http://omeka.org/.

BIBLIOGRAPHY

Bender, Thomas. "How Historians Lost Their Public." *Chronicle of Higher Education,* March 30, 2015. http://chronicle.com/article/How-Historians-Lost-Their/228773/.

Fischer, Suzanne. "On the Vocation of Public History." *#alt-Academy: Alternative Academic Careers,* May 7, 2011. http://mediacommons.futureofthebook.org/alt-ac/pieces /vocation-public-history.

Frisch, Michael H. *A Shared Authority: Essays on the Craft and Meaning of Oral and Public History.* Albany: State University of New York Press, 1990.

Kammen, Michael. *Mystic Chords of Memory: The Transformation of Tradition in American Culture.* New York: Knopf, 1991.

Lubar, Steven. "Seven Rules for Public Humanists." *On Public Humanities* (blog), June 5, 2014. https://stevenlubar.wordpress.com/2014/06/05/seven-rules-for-public-humanists/.

Meringolo, Denise D. *Museums, Monuments, and National Parks: Toward a New Genealogy of Public History.* Amherst: University of Massachusetts Press, 2012.

Milligan, Darren. "Our Personas: Introducing Naomi, Javier, Samantha, and Nicole." *Smithsonian Learning Lab.* Accessed March 25, 2015. http://learninglab.si.edu/news/2015/03 /our-personas-introducing-naomi-javier-samantha-and-nicole/.

National Council on Public History (NCPH). "What Is Public History?" http://ncph.org /cms/what-is-public-history/.

Rosenzweig, Roy. "Scarcity or Abundance? Preserving the Past in a Digital Era." *American Historical Review* 108, no. 3 (2003): 735–62. http://chnm.gmu.edu/essays-on -history-new-media/essays/?essayid=6.

Scheinfeldt, Tom. "The Dividends of Difference: Recognizing Digital Humanities; Diverse Family Trees." *Found History,* April 7, 2014. http://foundhistory.org/2014/04/the -dividends-of-difference-recognizing-digital-humanities-diverse-family-trees/.

Stanton, Cathy. *The Lowell Experiment: Public History in a Postindustrial City.* Amherst: University of Massachusetts Press, 2006.

Townsend, Robert B. "The AHA on the Path to Public History." *Public History Commons,* March 9, 2015. http://publichistorycommons.org/the-aha-on-the-path-to-public -history/.

———. *History's Babel: Scholarship, Professionalization, and the Historical Enterprise in the United States, 1880–1940.* Chicago: University of Chicago Press, 2013.

West, Patricia. *Domesticating History: The Political Origins of America's House Museums.* Washington, D.C.: Smithsonian Institution, 1999.

PART V

DIGITAL HUMANITIES AND ITS CRITICS

Are Digital Humanists Utopian?

BRIAN GREENSPAN

*As [King Utopus] set a vast number of men to work, he, beyond all men's
expectations, brought it to a speedy conclusion. And his neighbours, who at first
laughed at the folly of the undertaking, no sooner saw it brought to perfection
than they were struck with admiration and terror.*

—Thomas More, *Utopia*

*We live in capitalism. Its power seems inescapable. So did the divine right of
kings. Any human power can be resisted and changed by human beings.*

—Ursula K. Le Guin

What We Mean When We Say "Utopia"

Articles, blogs, and tweets about the digital humanities turn repeatedly, anxiously,
and sometimes hopefully to the topic of utopia. But just what do digital humanists mean when they talk about utopia? The problem in describing any project
as "utopian" is that there are always *other* utopias, an alterity within utopia itself
that blurs its contours, making it less an island than an archipelago. Utopias can
be systemic or iconoclastic, absolute or relative, abstract or concrete; they can be
failed, fictional, ambiguous, or actually existing in the form of communes, phalanster-
ies, or kibbutzim, and embodying a range of politics from anarchism to liberalism
to libertarianism. There are femtopias, queer utopias, and Afro-futurist utopias, as
well as technological, critical, degenerate, and satiric utopias. They can be heuristic
or systemic, eternal or persistent, revolutionary or catastrophic. There are pocket
and blueprint utopias, utopias of spatial form, and process utopias, which can be
archaeological, ontological, or architectural in mode. So it is not surprising that digital humanists should hold widely variant notions about utopia. More than simply
a matter of fuzzy nomenclature, these conflicting understandings of utopia convey
differing ideological orientations toward scholarship, technology, and the future.

Digital humanists who invoke *utopia* often do so to signify a hopeful horizon of expanded possibility and openness; yet, in the same breath, many (mis)label as *utopian* any projects considered naïve, impractical, or impossible, if not downright dangerous. Ruth Levitas characterizes the fallacies of this pervasive anti-utopian outlook:

> The political case against utopia is not new. It argues that where there is vision, the people perish. It imputes to utopia both a claim to perfection, which is then dismissed as impossible, and the imposition of uniformity on utopia's inhabitants, rejected as immoral. It argues that utopia can be realised only by violence and maintained only by political repression. ("For Utopia," 31–32)

Some digital humanists rely upon anti-utopian sentiment as a check against the overtly utopian elements of their research, suggesting a fundamental ambivalence or anxiety toward the utopian. For instance, Patrik Svensson accurately describes DH in decidedly utopian terms as a scholarly enterprise characterized by "grand, sweeping statements" and "far-reaching visionary discourse" expressing a "visionary and hopeful" attitude toward technology's "transformative" potential ("Envisioning," ¶¶30, 11, 19). Yet, he insists that "what the digital humanities needs is an inclusive and forward-looking (not necessarily utopian) vision" (¶116), and is careful to avoid statements that he considers "all-pervasive, overly utopian or ungrounded" (¶163). Svensson's apprehension toward grand, "overly utopian" statements reproduces a familiar anti-utopian bias that dates to post–World War II liberals like Karl Popper and Isaiah Berlin, who saw any attempt to depict the social and cultural totality as overly totalizing and potentially totalitarian, a slippery slope of false cognates typically justified with reference to Stalin, Mao, and the evils of state socialism (Jacoby, 42–45; Moylan, *Scraps,* 121–31). This liberalism is clear in Svensson's own design parameters for DH, which propose not a "singular vision" but a "visionary space" governed by parameters like "mutual respect" and "disciplinary grounding" ("Envisioning," ¶¶117, 10). Svensson wants DH to transform not only the humanities and university, but also, "if appropriate and mutually beneficial, . . . industry, cultural institutions and the art world" (¶139), but his suspicion of totality prevents him from proposing a DH that sets out to transform the world at large.

Svensson is not alone in embracing patently utopian ideals while identifying utopianism with the least salutary aspects of digital culture. Elsewhere in this volume (see chapter 38), Richard Grusin notes the future-oriented nature of DH and its affect of "hope," "growth," "optimism," and "new beginnings." Yet, he also derides the "'utopian' vision of a higher education whose future is dominated by MOOCs" (81). For Grusin, "the convergence of neoliberal calculus and digital utopianism" (87) is responsible for exacerbating the divide within the humanities between critical skills and production skills, between yack and hack, creating a new class of precariously employed educational workers. He raises crucial concerns about how the division between critique and production within DH, along with its tendency to value collaborative work more highly than individual scholarly labor, risks exacerbating neoliberal imperatives within higher education (89). In the process, however, he collapses utopianism in general with that determinist strain of mainstream techno-utopianism that grew out of the American hippie counterculture and agrarian communal movement of the 1960s, a history documented by Fred Turner. By so doing, Grusin cuts DH off from the long utopian tradition of pedagogical reform and the utopian mission described by Miguel Abensour as "the education of desire"—that is, teaching "'desire to desire, to desire better, to desire more, and above all to desire in a different way'" (Thompson, 97).

The positions of both Grusin and Svensson are characteristic of the "double bind of Utopian discourse" that Neil Fraistat observes within the digital humanities, which promises broad transformations to scholarship, but "at a level of abstraction that forces us ultimately either to credit it as meaningful, or dismiss its entire enterprise" (2). Fraistat makes a useful distinction between the recognition of DH's "Utopian promise" of "inclusivity, openness to critique, self-reflexivity, and the ability to be transformed as well as being transformational," and the alternate "Dystopian figuration" of DH as the tacit ally of neoliberal capitalism: "For DH is a field whose master discourse includes such keywords as 'innovation,' 'disruption,' 'transformation,' and, yes, 'entrepreneurship.' All of these terms contain trap doors to the dark side, ..." (8–9). I am sympathetic with Fraistat's critique of creeping neoliberalism, as well as his emphasis on the digital humanities' "active pursuit of the speculative, the possible, the counter-factual, the conjectural, the alternate reality, and the Utopian" (23). But Fraistat ultimately truncates the critical potential of utopianism by linking it primarily to the Romantic self-reflection of William Godwin and Percy Shelley. He thereby short-circuits the link between digital humanities and the utopianism of post-enlightenment thinkers like Fourier, Saint-Simon, Marx, Engels, and Kropotkin, along with the entire tradition of technological utopias and dystopias that evolved in response to industrial and postindustrial capitalism, from Samuel Butler, Ignatius Donnelly, and H. G. Wells to Octavia Butler, William Gibson, and Ursula K. Le Guin. While it is true that the range of utopian concerns and discursive genres was greatly expanded by Godwin and other eighteenth-century authors (Pohl), it was only in later decades that utopian speculation took up the anti-propertarian elements of More's *Utopia* programmatically, and took aim at overcoming the contradictions and alienation of modern life under capitalism.

Far from exacerbating the problems associated with neoliberal capitalism, the speculative disruptions of utopian discourse offer digital humanists a way to think through them. More than just a double-bind between transformative and skeptical thought, utopianism represents a mode of critical thinking that actively engages the "dystopian figuration" of the dark side. Especially in its most abstract and improbable forms, utopian speculation enables precisely the sort of institutional self-critique that Grusin and Fraistat recommend, one that opens outward beyond scholarly disciplines and onto a broader social critique. Whether literary, visual, or cinematic in form, and whether optimistic or apocalyptic in tone, utopian and dystopian texts alike engage in a mode of imaginative construction or "architecture" that is at the same time a form of estrangement and critical thinking (Levitas, *Utopia as Method,* 197). Utopias offer hopeful models for overcoming capitalism's contradictions by negotiating the apparent divide between critique and production, as well as the antinomy of individual and collective desires, "that no-man's-land between the individual *actant* and the social totality" (Jameson, *Archaeologies,* 206).

Digital humanists often display an anxious attraction to utopian discourse, but they also tend to distrust the idea of utopia, leading them to misrecognize the utopian impulse driving their own engagement in grand, technologically innovative projects that reshape paradigms of scholarly collaboration and property. The digital humanities would benefit from a more informed and rigorous engagement with the understandings of utopia as advanced within utopian studies—maybe the only field that is more interdisciplinary, community-oriented, and hopeful. Utopian scholars, for their part, have not only been slow to adopt digital humanities perspectives and methodologies, but have barely begun to address the mediality of utopian expression. While utopianists avidly consume SF stories about futuristic technologies, they retain a decided media bias toward fictional narratives in print, which they implicitly position as a universal medium appropriate to the study of universal social progress. This situation has started to change, with a number of mostly younger utopianists (including Jill Belli, Stephanie Boluk, Frank Crocco, Krzysztof Maj, Peter Sands, and Adam Stock) exploring everything from digital pedagogies, dystopian digital games, and "happiness" apps to virtual- and augmented-reality media. Bart Simon and Darren Wershler are studying the utopian dimension of *Minecraft,* while Michelle Tiedje is using R to map the transnational networks of nineteenth-century utopian reformers and their literature, an entirely new approach to the study of intentional communities. The 2014 Imaginaries of the Future Leverhulme International Network workshop in Montreal featured talks on the utopian dimension of digital architecture, networks, locative media, and wearable devices by Christina Constandriopoulos, Delfina Fantini van Ditmar, Jill Didur, and Isabel Pedersen.[1] A number of undertakings by "utopian entrepreneurs" (Laurel) are also helping to build bridges, including the Alternate Reality Games (ARGs) designed by Jane McGonigal to promote social progress, and Kari Krauss's ARG *Dust,* which uses a post-apocalyptic scenario to encourage teenagers to think about humanity's prospects for a distant future. Ed Finn's Project Hieroglyph offers a digital platform for near-future SF narratives, while Stephen Duncombe's Kickstarter project *(open) Utopia* provides "a complete edition of Thomas More's *Utopia* that honors the primary precept of Utopia itself: that all property is common property," published under a Creative Commons license and linked to Social Book and Wikitopia. And both the North American Society for Utopian Studies and the European Utopian

Studies Society have begun to implement open online portals to digital collections and other resources for utopian scholars.

The news from the other side of the fence is less promising. That digital humanists have not shown more interest in utopian studies is curious, given that many of the tools they use every day were anticipated over a century ago by the likes of Edward Bellamy, H. G. Wells, and E. M. Forster, whose utopian worlds are replete with anticipations of teleconferencing suites, on-demand libraries, and the Internet of Things, which together constitute a rich archive of imaginary media. Such inventions are what the utopian philosopher Ernst Bloch calls *novums,* "the unexpectedly new, which pushes humanity out of its present towards the not yet realized" (Moylan, "Locus," 159). The use of technological novums to connect the past to our collective future also inspires and organizes the lion's share of DH projects. No one expresses the utopian longings we invest in innovative media better than Jeffrey T. Schnapp and Matthew Battles, whose beautifully designed volume, *The Library Beyond the Book,* hints through historical snapshots and speculative future scenarios at how real or imaginary archival technologies might fulfill their civic mission by remaining "ever attentive to the voice of a collectivity" (124).

Although often characterized as static blueprints for perfection, utopias in fact tend to be open-ended and provisional: even More's original *Utopia* has been described as a narrative experiment in dynamic textualities involving a unique form of "spatial play" that allows many different social and textual configurations to coexist within a single representation (Marin). Ever since, utopias have critiqued the status quo through speculative forms of invention not unlike what Jentery Sayers calls "tinkering," and which Fredric Jameson describes as a kind of "puttering," "a hobby-like activity, which anyone can do in their own spare time, at home, in your garage or workshop, that organizes the readership of the Utopian text, a better mousetrap which you also can emulate" (*Archaeologies,* 34–35). The concept of tinkering is one way that both utopians and digital humanists address the radical unfinalizability of their projects, which are often of a scale or degree of experimentalism that defy closure and completion.

Utopian scholars devote endless energy to recovering, curating, and preserving the partial and fragmented record of this experimental archive, an undertaking that could only benefit from closer engagement with text-encoding standards and protocols for open-access archives. After all, More's *Utopia* is less a city than an archive without walls. As Travis DeCook explains, because More's Utopians live the good life, they do not need to record it: "while Utopia lacks both rhetorical storehouses and archives of specialized knowledge such as legal and religious texts, the Utopian commonwealth itself is a kind of storehouse, an institutional archive in which good action is preserved through time" (DeCook, 11). But if the figure of the universal archive provides the very model of utopian narrative and social organization, it does so only in an allegorical register, as an intimation of a revolutionary social totality that cannot yet be mapped (Wegner, "Here or Nowhere"). That is why the closer we get to actually achieving the archive without walls, the harder it becomes to recognize as classically utopian, and the more we risk misrecognizing its transformational significance. So Matthew Kirschenbaum has argued that Google Books is realizing "what were once utopian dreams of digitizing all of the world's book-based knowledge" ("Remaking of Reading," §3), implying that technology is moving us beyond mere dreaming and into the reality of a universal library. Kirschenbaum suggests that we need practical measures like XML standards to save scholarship from what he sees as an impractical utopianism, while downplaying the figurative and socially transformative qualities of a global, universal library. Perhaps we should not be surprised that those who actually invent and adopt new scholarly technologies are often reluctant utopians. Even Marx and Engels felt the "scientific" socialism they advocated in *The Manifesto of the Communist Party* to be at odds with earlier utopian socialists like Fourier and Saint-Simon, whom they characterized as "a subjective imaginative abstraction from the divisions of class society" (Geoghegan, 29). Still, while studying a million books is no longer impossible, the very scale of such an undertaking estranges conventional scholarly practices and continues to resonate with older utopian dreams of a perfect social order arising from the total archive,[2] even if many digital humanists resist that notion.

Digital humanists dream and talk big: big tents, big data, global networks, and "massive addressability" (Witmore) are the stuff of DH,[3] intimating new forms of collective belonging brought about by revolutionary technologies—and sometimes by their catastrophic failure. In her keynote for the ADHO 2014 Digital Humanities conference, Bethany Nowviskie invoked the sublime trope of "deep time" and the problem of "communicating across millennia," popularized by science-fiction author Gregory Benford, to situate the sundry conservation and preservation efforts of digital humanists in relation to the mass extinction that inevitably awaits our planet:

> What is a digital humanities practice that grapples constantly with little extinctions and can look clear-eyed on a Big One? Is it socially conscious and activist in tone? Does it reflect the managerial and problem-solving character of our 21st-century institutions? Is it about preservation, conservation, and recovery— or about understanding ephemerality and embracing change? Does our work help us to appreciate, memorialize, and mourn the things we've lost? Does it alter, for us and for our audiences, our global frameworks and our sense of scale? Is it about teaching ourselves to live differently? ("Digital Humanities in the Anthropocene," §8)

Amid countless scientific and science-fictional scenarios for our planetary demise, Nowviskie's moving proleptic elegy carves out spaces of hope rooted in the decay of notions of work, progress, resilience, and individual freedom closely associated with neoliberal capitalism.

Philip E. Wegner has examined the opposition between apocalyptic and science-fictional thinking that structures Nowviskie's talk. Citing Jameson's maxim that "it is easier to imagine the end of the world than to imagine the end of capitalism" (Jameson, "Future City," 76), Wegner argues that post-apocalyptic narratives tend toward a conservative return to history that leaves the status quo intact. However, there has evolved a parallel narrative genre, which he dubs the "critical post-apocalypse," that "both interrogate[s] the pseudo-event of a supposed apocalypse . . . and then educat[es] the reader's desire for an authentic event: not the end of *the* world, but the end of *a* world, that of the current socio-political or symbolic order we call global or neo-liberal capitalism" (Wegner, *Shockwaves,* 94). Nowviskie's narrative can be considered a critical post-apocalypse that emphasizes the close connections between utopian and dystopian thought: not only does she interrogate various representations of global ecological collapse, but the toolkit she proposes comprises temporalities on multiple scales, including both digital recovery projects and more ephemeral experiments, while activating both collective memory and speculative, future-oriented projects that disrupt dominant notions of progress and sustainability. Her address ultimately hesitates between the conservative desire to curate "bits against our ruins" and the more radical desire to anticipate a rupture in the very temporality of the digital humanities. And yet, by connecting time on a geological scale to both an enhanced awareness of the uneven development of global computing resources and the Occupy movement, she underlines the urgency of linking DH to radical dreaming, oppositional politics, and materialist critiques of the status quo.

Admittedly, such apocalyptic utopian scenarios are less common in DH than the practice of speculative world-building in a realist mode. Digital humanists have built impressive historical models and simulations to show how the world was or might have been, such as the *Virtual Paul's Cross Project*,[4] Dempsey et al.'s stunning *Pudding Lane*[5] recreation, or Kevin Kee's *Niagara 1812*.[6] Utopians, by contrast, exercise more freedom to speculate about how the world might be otherwise, imagining alternate realities that diverge from the factual record and that typically contain too many self-contradictions to be modeled or implemented with precision: the utopia's "unabashed and flagrant otherness gives it a power which is lacking in other analytical devices. By playing fast and loose with time and space, logic and morality, and by thinking the unthinkable, a utopia asks the most awkward, the most embarrassing questions" (Geoghegan, 2). Joanna Drucker, for one, has insisted on the importance of reimagining computation through humanistic principles for the purpose of "showing interpretation, modeling it, making a composition space in which ambiguity and contradiction can coexist" ("Humanistic Theory")—in other words, a space very much like More's *Utopia*. With Bethany Nowviskie, she has advocated "speculative computing" practices grounded in "aesthetic provocations" that resist "logical, systematic knowledge representation" and instead "engage subjective and intuitive tools . . . as primary means of interpretation in computational environments" (Drucker, "Speculative Computing," 431–32). Still, some digital humanists privilege production over speculation. In a 2014 issue of *Journal of Digital Humanities* devoted to world-building, Noah Wardrip-Fruin falls squarely on the side of achievable design: "Speculating about what the world 'might' look like in the future is easy. More challenging, though, is realizing that speculative vision through the design process" (¶3). To claim that speculation is easy runs counter not only to Drucker's case for humanistically informed computing, but also to Jameson's well-known argument that we are no longer constitutionally able to imagine a world other than the one we inhabit—that is, to imagine a world beyond capitalism—which is why utopias are always doomed to fail (Jameson, "Progress versus Utopia"). And yet, these failures are productive, since they indicate the barriers and blinds spots that prevent us from imagining another reality entirely.[7] For Jameson, utopia is the impulse that leads us to imagine the transition to another world even as it whispers, "not yet" (*Archaeologies*, 232–33).

The insistence on the value of failure is a mantra that digital humanists share with utopian scholars. Dustin Grue, Teresa M. Dobson, and Monica Brown made this connection in a study of how secondary students break their own interpretive rules while tagging literary fiction in XML. The authors explain this continuous interpretive failure and renewal of rule systems with reference to arguments by Bloch and Theodor Adorno that the inevitable failure of utopian visions does not destroy hope, but rather sustains it through a critique of the status quo ("Reading Practices and Digital Experiences," 246–47). As important as their findings are for our understanding of reading habits, I am not convinced that interpretive heuristics—the assumptions people make and discard while reading a text—are necessarily utopian in the Blochian sense, which entails anticipation in the present of a future, messianic rupture in history itself that heralds the transition to another society entirely. It is the difference between a radical system failure leading to full-scale revolution, and the kind of iterative failure of hypotheses allowing gradual progress through small tweaks and piecemeal reform that describes the everyday method of most digital humanists. Julia Flanders has even lamented the retreat from the revolutionary discourse of early hypertext studies, which associated digital textuality with

> potentially dramatic political consequences. . . . But in more recent years, the language of revolution has not retained its critical bite or its pervasiveness. In its place we can see a softer kind of incremental progressive vision in, for instance, the grant-proposal rhetoric that promises to "broaden access," improve educational outcomes, and create "new ways of thinking" without upsetting fundamental institutional structures. (Flanders, ¶3)

This incremental approach is the way of the "realistic utopia" that Levitas associates with a specifically American form of pragmatism, "a civic religion," in Richard Rorty's phrase, "that substitute[s] utopian striving for claims to theological knowledge," not worrying "about eternity" or any messianic truth, and focusing instead on achieving a "global egalitarian utopia" modeled ultimately on the American Constitution (Levitas, *Utopia as Method,* 133–34). Digital humanists retrace the pragmatist's path from theology to democracy whenever they draw a line of influence from Father Busa's *Index Thomisticus* to current text-encoding initiatives.

The secular mission of realistic utopianism proceeds through a far more modest rhetoric than the hopeful, critical, progressive, and broadly transformative sense of utopia that appears in the *Manifesto,* which proclaims,

> Digital Humanities have a utopian core shaped by its genealogical descent
> from the counterculture-cyberculture intertwinglings of the 60s and 70s.
> This is why it affirms the value of the open, the infinite, the expansive, the
> university/museum/archive/library *without walls,* the democratization of culture and scholarship, ... (*The Digital Humanities Manifesto 2.0,* ¶13)

Within the *Manifesto,* "Utopian" signals an open-access approach to scholarship so liberating that it bears comparison with May/June 1968, one of those rare points in history that could be called a *concrete utopia* in Bloch's sense, a moment in which hopes for a radically different future are acted out in the objective reality of the present (Moylan, "Locus of Hope," 159). Of course, DH is hardly about to trigger general strikes or civil unrest, but the rhetoric of the manifesto genre invites such hyperbole. For the *Manifesto's* authors, the utopian core of the digital humanities can be summed up as an ethos of "participation without condition," a less obviously inflated claim.

Todd Presner, one of the *Manifesto's* authors, has elaborated on this notion of a participatory culture that is "open-ended, nonhierarchical, and transmigratory, aimed at reestablishing contact with the nonphilosophical. 'Participation without condition' is not a principle that can be willed into place, but rather an ideal to build toward through imaginative speculation and ethically informed engagement, . . ." (60–61). Presner suggests that "speculative making" practices, such as the many compelling geospatial installations built on his *HyperCities* platform, can provide transformative, material models of possible futures that are more open and participatory. By connecting DH "to the vaguely utopian dimensions" of critical theorists like Bloch, Adorno, Walter Benjamin, and Herbert Marcuse, Presner opens the door for a broader consideration of the utopian critical tradition within DH, although doing so risks calling into question his ideal of "participation without condition." After all, utopias are never truly open access; they always come with conditions for belonging. Even More's *Utopia* placed conditions on its citizens: they all had to spend two years working the farms, men could not have premarital sex or marry till the age of twenty-two, and those who grew too old and sick were expected to volunteer to be euthanized. Likewise, as Svensson points out, some feel that digital humanists place conditions on admission to their big tent, whether in the form of text-based research, coding skills, demonstration of some degree of self-reflection on the tools we use, or even attendance at THATCamps or ADHO conferences (Svensson, "Beyond the Big Tent"). Presner himself delineates several conditions of participation in the form of critical principles that underwrite certain DH projects, including "a respect for multiplicity and difference through the creation of trusted social bonds, an approach to historical documentation that builds from the fragments of participatory discourse, and a concept of archivization made possible by the contingent material technologies of communication" (64). Far from throwing open the doors to all comers, a genuinely utopian DH would posit the conditions, codes, and protocols of participation necessary for creating and sustaining the ideal community, even as it acknowledges this community always to be not yet realized.

From Dark Side to Dialectics

If DH is to be truly game-changing in the epochal terms that Nowviskie and the *Manifesto* frame it, then the difference that DH makes cannot be left at a vaguely open respect for difference that merely reflects the broader liberal-democratic-capitalist context. The ideal of a frictionless "participation without condition" represses another model of organization and inclusion, one in which antagonism is not only accepted but constitutive. I want to suggest that attempts to explain the constitution of the digital humanities repeatedly raise the spectre of utopian communism, only to sublimate it into less overtly antagonistic forms of collaboration and critique.

In the epigraphic disclaimer to his provocative essay on the dark side of DH, "*I am not now, nor have I ever been, a digital humanist*" (79), Grusin playfully associates DH with crypto-communism in a denial of sympathies that, albeit facetious, is symptomatic of the insistent liberalism masking the digital humanities' uneasy relation to committed communal thinking. As Jodie Dean contends, this squeamishness to even mention communism reflects the dominant attitude not only of conservatives and liberal anti-utopians, but of the radical Left as well. In *Blog Theory*, Dean argues from a Lacanian perspective that today's subjects neither desire nor enjoy digital media, but are merely caught in a repetitive loop of psychic drive. On her view, failure is neither the "useful result" of high-risk experimentation (Spiro, 29) nor allegoric of our inability to imagine a world beyond capitalism (Jameson, "Progress versus Utopia"), but a symptom of the forms of "communicative capitalism" that increasingly dominate our social interactions: "we enjoy failure. Insofar as the aim of the drive is not to reach its goal but to enjoy, we enjoy our endless circulation, our repetitive loop. We cannot know certainly; we cannot know adequately. But we can mobilize this loss, googling, checking Wikipedia, mistrusting it immediately. . . . Failure . . . is functional for communicative capitalism; it's our ensnarement in the loop of drive" (Dean, *Blog Theory*, 121–22). Dean has since extended this argument to the macropolitical scale, arguing that the contemporary Left is likewise caught in the loop of drive by the loss of its desired object, the "communist horizon": "For the Left, democracy is the form the loss of communism takes. Rather than fighting for a collective ideal, engaging in a struggle on behalf of the rest of us, the Left repetitively invokes democracy, calling for what is already there" (Dean, *Communist Horizon*, 65). Dean contends that, with its insistence on democracy and participation, the Left turns its back on a common commitment to the political project of opposing capitalism—that is, to communism, which names "the sovereignty of the people, and not the people as a whole or a unity but the people as the *rest of us*" (69). Her argument builds on attempts by Alain Badiou, Slavoj Žižek, Susan Buck-Morss, Bruno Bosteels, and others, in the wake of neoliberalism's ascendancy and the 2008–2009 global market collapse, to reclaim the idea of communism from its perversion in the state socialist programs of Lenin, Stalin, or Mao, figures that anti-utopians still trot out as evidence of the dangers of visionary thinking.

Following Dean, I suggest that digital humanists' repeated emphasis on failure, community, collaboration, and images of totality are really partial drives expressing a desire for something else: namely, a social order entirely beyond capitalism and its underpinnings in the academic, scholarly publishing, and high-tech industries. What the digital humanities really want is communism, which Dean defines as "our collective steering of our common future for our common good" (*Communist Horizon*, 87). Nor will a greater commitment to crowdsourcing and open access alone fix the problem: as Dean notes, "capitalism is a system that constitutively exploits people, not one that constitutively excludes them" (*Communist Horizon*, 105), and expanding participation in itself only extends the reach of the existing scholarly, educational, publishing, and intellectual property regimes. Digital humanists' embrace of a participatory ethic intimates our utopian desire for a more inclusive totality, even as it plays into the exploitation of surplus labor that governs the system of proletarianization. Not unlike the contemporary Left, we are willing to engage the idea of the crowd only when it is divested of its unruly character and historical associations with the revolutionary proletariat. The ideology of participation without condition, regulated through crowdsourcing platforms and protocols for accessibility and interoperability, allows digital humanists to indulge in "a fantasy of multiplicity without antagonism, of difference without division" (*Communist Horizon*, 228).

Admittedly, Dean risks characterizing the Left in monolithic terms, and her critique of communicational capitalism likewise generalizes to the point that all networked communication and social media amount to nothing but participation for its own sake, a form of "whatever being" that grants users a sense of belonging without demanding true commitment (*Blog Theory*, 67). Nor am I suggesting that digital humanities ought to function in the manner of the party, which Dean takes as essential for organizing our "collective desire for collectivity" (*Communist Horizon*, 20). DH is not a party (or, for that matter, a discipline, crowd, public sphere, or intentional community) so much as it is an *organized network*, in Ned Rossiter's

sense of a nonhierarchical institutional form that emerges alongside digital communications media, filling the gap left by the collapse of both civil society and political
society into neoliberal markets. "Orgnets" make utopian speculation concrete by
helping to organize the unevenly developed topography of the digital networks and
immaterial labor that together produce what Rossiter calls, after autonomist Marxism, "the common"—that is, "life as it resides within relations immanent to media
of communication" (Rossiter, 195).[8]

Contemporary theorists of the Left talk incessantly about information and communication networks, but rarely exhibit anything beyond a loosely metaphorical
understanding of them. That is where DH comes in: we are uniquely positioned to
critique the ways that new media exacerbate the enclosure of immaterial labor both
inside and outside of the academy, and to develop, test, and implement the platforms
and protocols through which networked communities are identified, engaged, and
empowered to contribute to the common. Participatory and crowdsourced projects have the potential to challenge the flexible notions of work that Grusin rightly
blames for precarity in the academic workforce, but only if we take participation
to mean a great deal more than performing the free labor of deciphering captchas,
metatagging HTML, Mechanical Turk piecework, or other forms of "crowdmilking"
(Scholz). If DH projects are to be collective in a committed and redemptive sense,
rather than merely fetishes of democratic liberalism, then they need to focus on
the struggle, antagonism, and violence that attends capitalism everywhere (Dean,
Communist Horizon, 61), including our classrooms, scholarly associations, publishing consortia, and other sites of knowledge creation and mobilization. We need
to recognize the mechanisms through which intellectual property law constrains
digital productivity, how digital collections remediate conventional archival powers
and privileges, and the ways in which our projects both produce the common and
enable its enclosure. We must ensure that the open-access archives and tools that
we build and give away are autonomous from the system of rent—not by merely
exploiting information networks or taking our exodus from them, but by adapting
these tactics into robust strategies and protocols that foreground, discourage, and
resist the expropriation and valorization of the common.

The new models of participation and dissemination that we develop for literary
or historical scholarship not only can shed light on movements like Occupy, but in
a kind of social tinkering, they can be integrated with older models of organization,
whether cooperatives, communes, soviets, or syndicates, as well as those speculative
modes of sociality and "visions of alternatives" that comprise the "positive aspects"
of utopian expression (Fitting, 14). Above all, we can stop mistrusting the utopianism of our own solutions—a mistrust shared by many detractors of DH—and
instead use our expertise working with large datasets to build speculative models
that dream large and fail spectacularly, auguring forth transformative images of collectivity, and holding open a place for entirely new paradigms beyond technological

progress and the upgrade path that we cannot yet imagine. We can design our tools to be at once user-friendly and estranging, opening up marvelous new worlds that educate our collective desire for something else entirely. Otherwise, even the most progressive DH practices will remain at best a form of speculative leftism, a "purification of the notion of communism" through the "philosophical appropriation of radical emancipatory politics" (Bosteels, *Actuality,* 24; 33).

We need not accept Dean's definitions as the last word; after all, her very emphasis on antagonism and division "suggests that we have not yet decided on what the 'common' in communism refers to (Martel, 701). We could turn to Bruno Bosteels, who suggests that, "[l]ike democracy when properly understood, communism would name this invariant process whereby the people constitute themselves as people" ("Speculative," 752). Or we could return to Marx, who called communism "the *real* movement which abolishes the present state of things"—a statement that Dean (following Peter Hallward) glosses "[n]ot as immediate insurrection or as prefiguration but rather as *the expansion of voluntary cooperation*" (Dean, "Response," 828). What we cannot do is continue to ignore what the idea of communism might mean for the digital humanities in particular, and vice versa. Digital humanists have crucial perspectives to bring to the redefinition and redeployment of communist ideals by theorists like Sylvain Firer-Blaess and Christian Fuchs, who observe strong resemblances between Wikipedia's voluntary self-management and the form of participatory democracy that Marx and Engels envisioned, postulating an "info-communist" mode of production. We can learn from Joss Hands's "platform communism," which analyzes "the relationship between the digital as an actually existing realm and the horizon of communist possibility" (14), while bringing to his analysis a closer engagement with platform studies and a more rigorous conception of digital networks. And we can build on the work of Nick Dyer-Witheford in *Cyber-Marx* and elsewhere, turning his critiques of the exploitation of digital labor to bear on our own practices.

Above all, we can embrace the insights of utopian studies, without which we risk misrecognizing the visionary significance of our own impossibly large projects. If some remain apprehensive about or resistant to DH, let it be not because of our alleged instrumentality or neoliberalism, but because we loudly call for hopeful alternatives to the current state of affairs, even if they are not yet clearly defined. The truly dark side of DH is its fear of radical social change, which prevents us from recognizing emergent scholarly and pedagogical protocols as what they might yet become: raw materials for building another world entirely.

NOTES

1. I am grateful to many of these scholars for their feedback on earlier versions of this chapter, in particular Jill Belli, Sarah Brouillette, Claire Curtis, and Peter Sands, and

to those who provided feedback at Western University's 2012 Digital Humanities' Speaker Series, where I originally presented these ideas. I also wish to thank the Social Sciences and Humanities Research Council of Canada and the Leverhulme Trust Foundation for their generous support.

2. In our panel on "Utopia and the Digital Humanities" at the 2014 annual meeting of the Society for Utopian Studies, Carolyn Lesjak presented a compelling analysis of the extent to which the scale of Franco Moretti's method of distant reading world literature functions as a utopian allegory of the historical and social totality.

3. As Paul Fyfe pointed out to me, some digital humanists also think small. Global Outlook::Digital Humanities has established a minimal computing working group, and even distant reading has alerted us to the necessity of matching patterns in large textual or visual corpora to local sites of meaning in a "blended approach" that unifies "the macro and micro scales" (Jockers, 26).

4. http://vpcp.chass.ncsu.edu.

5. http://journalofdigitalhumanities.org/3-1/pudding-lane-recreating-seventeenth-century-london.

6. http://kevinkee.ca/articles/project/niagara-1812.

7. Ruth Levitas has warned that this concept of utopia as blind spot and failure, as that which has always not yet come into being, runs the risk of "sidestepping the substance of imagined alternatives" (*Utopia as Method,* 124). She proposes a parallel mode of utopian design, the "Imaginary Reconstitution of Society" (IROS), that I suspect would provide digital humanists with valuable insights into their speculative world-building practices. Jameson himself has appeared to recant his earlier position that imagining utopia is constitutionally impossible, although he might well have simply confirmed it. In his plenary address for the 2013 meeting of the Society for Utopian Studies, he argued that the possibility of a communist utopia today depends on the delineation of a clear utopian program, and posited as his "American Utopia" a version of Lenin's "dual power," which describes the coexistence of an official government with unofficial organizations or networks that provide practical services. Jameson puckishly suggested that such an arrangement would require the universal conscription of all Americans into a "citizen army," in the wake of the Post Office and the Mafia's failure to fit the bill. The talk triggered much debate among the assembled delegates as to the extent of utopian irony its author was deploying.

8. For an explanation of the common and its relation to autonomist Marxism, see Hardt.

BIBLIOGRAPHY

Bosteels, Bruno. *The Actuality of Communism.* Brooklyn, N.Y.: Verso, 2014.
———. "The Speculative Left." *South Atlantic Quarterly* 104, no. 4 (Fall 2005): 751–67.
Dean, Jodi. *Blog Theory: Feedback and Capture in the Circuits of Drive.* Cambridge: Polity, 2010.
———. *The Communist Horizon.* Brooklyn, N.Y.: Verso Books, 2012.

————. "Response: The Question of Organization." *South Atlantic Quarterly* 113, no. 4 (Fall 2014): 821–35.

DeCook, Travis. "Utopian Communication." *SEL Studies in English Literature 1500–1900* 48, no. 1 (Winter 2008): 1–22.

Dempsey, Joe, Daniel Hargreaves, Daniel Peacock, Chelsea Lindsey, Dominic Bell, Luc Fontenoy, and Heather Williams. "Pudding Lane: Recreating Seventeenth-Century London." *Journal of Digital Humanities* 3, no.1 (Spring 2014). http://journalofdigital humanities.org/3–1/pudding-lane-recreating-seventeenth-century-london.

"The Digital Humanities Manifesto 2.0." June 2009. http://www.humanitiesblast.com /manifesto/Manifesto_V2.pdf.

Drucker, Joanna. "Humanistic Theory and Digital Scholarship." In *Debates in the Digital Humanities,* ed. Matthew K. Gold. Minneapolis: University of Minnesota Press, 2012. http://dhdebates.gc.cuny.edu/debates/text/34.

Drucker, Joanna (and Bethany Nowviskie). "Speculative Computing: Aesthetic Provocations in Humanities Computing." In *A Companion to Digital Humanities,* ed. Susan Schreibman, Ray Siemens, and John Unsworth, 431–47. Oxford: Blackwell Publishing, 2004.

Duncombe, Stephen, ed. *(Open) Utopia, by Thomas More.* Wivenhoe/New York/Port Watson: Minor Compositions/Autonomedia, 2012. http://theopenutopia.org.

Dyer-Witheford, Nick. *Cyber-Marx: Cycles and Circuits of Struggle in High-Technology Capitalism.* Urbana: University of Illinois Press, 1999.

Finn, Ed. Project Hieroglyph. http://hieroglyph.asu.edu.

Firer-Blaess, Sylvain, and Christian Fuchs. "Wikipedia: An Info-Communist Manifesto." *Television & New Media* 15, no.2 (2014): 87–103. http://fuchs.uti.at/wp-content/Wiki pedia.pdf.

Fitting, Peter. "The Concept of Utopia in the Work of Fredric Jameson." *Utopian Studies* 9, no. 2 (1998): 8–17.

Flanders, Julia. "The Literary, the Humanistic, the Digital: Toward a Research Agenda for Digital Literary Studies." In *Literary Studies in the Digital Age: An Evolving Anthology,* ed. Kenneth M. Price and Ray Siemens. New York: Modern Language Association, 2012. https://dlsanthology.commons.mla.org/the-literary-the-humanistic-the-digital/.

Fraistat, Neil. "The Promise(s) of Digital Humanities." Lecture delivered at Tufts University, April 10, 2014. http://mith.umd.edu/wp-content/uploads/2014/05/The-Promises-of -Digital-HumanitiesaaDH.pdf.

Geoghegan, Vincent. *Utopianism and Marxism.* London: Methuen & Co. Ltd., 1987.

Gold, Matthew, ed. *Debates in the Digital Humanities.* Minneapolis: University of Minnesota Press, 2012. http://dhdebates.gc.cuny.edu.

Grue, Dustin, Teresa M. Dobson, and Monica Brown. "Reading Practices and Digital Experiences: An Investigation into Secondary Students' Reading Practices and XML-Markup Experiences of Fiction." *Literary and Linguistic Computing* 28, no. 2 (2013): 237–48.

Hands, Joss. "Platform Communism." *Culture Machine* 14 (2013). http://www.culture machine.net.

Hardt, Michael. "The Common in Communism." In *The Idea of Communism,* ed. Costas Douzinas and Slavoj Žižek, 131–44. London: Verso, 2010.

Jacoby, Russell. *The End of Utopia: Politics and Culture in an Age of Apathy.* New York: Basic Books, 1999.

Jameson, Fredric. "An American Utopia." Presentation at the Society for Utopian Studies Annual Meeting, Charleston, S.C., November 14–17, 2013. https://www.youtube.com /watch?v=MNVKoX40ZAo.

———. *Archaeologies of the Future: The Desire Called Utopia and Other Science Fictions.* New York: Verso, 2005.

———. "Future City." *New Left Review* 21 (2003): 65–79.

———. "Progress versus Utopia; Or, Can We Imagine the Future?" *Science Fiction Studies* 9, no. 2 (1982): 147–58.

Jockers, Matthew L. *Macroanalysis: Digital Methods and Literary History.* Chicago: University of Illinois Press, 2013.

Kee, Kevin. *Niagara 1812.* http://kevinkee.ca/articles/project/niagara-1812.

Kirschenbaum, Matthew G. "The Remaking of Reading: Data Mining and the Digital Humanities." National Science Foundation Symposium on Next Generation of Data Mining and Cyber-Enabled Discovery for Innovation, Baltimore, 2007. http://www .csee.umbc.edu/~hillol/NGDM07/abstracts/talks/MKirschenbaum.pdf.

Krauss, Kari M. "DUST: Long-Term Thinking Activities." Author's blog, February 25, 2015. http://www.karikraus.com.

Laurel, Brenda. *Utopian Entrepreneur.* Cambridge, Mass.: MIT Press, 2001.

Levitas, Ruth. "For Utopia: The (Limits of the) Utopian Function in Late Capitalist Society." *Critical Review of International Social and Political Philosophy* 3, nos. 2–3 (2000): 25–43.

———. *Utopia as Method: The Imaginary Reconstitution of Society.* London: Palgrave Macmillan, 2013.

McGonigal, Jane. *Reality Is Broken: Why Games Make Us Better and How They Can Change the World.* New York: Penguin, 2011.

Marin, Louis. *Utopics: The Semiological Play of Textual Spaces.* Amherst, N.Y.: Humanities Press International, 1984.

Martel, James. "Division Is Common." *South Atlantic Quarterly* 113, no. 4 (2014): 701–11.

Marx, Karl. *The German Ideology.* 1845. Marxists Internet Archive. https://www.marxists .org/archive/marx/works/1845/german-ideology.

Moylan, Tom. "The Locus of Hope: Utopia versus Ideology." *Science Fiction Studies* 9, no. 2 (1982): 159–66.

———. *Scraps of the Untainted Sky: Science Fiction, Utopia, Dystopia.* Boulder: Westview Press, 2000.

Nowviskie, Bethany. "Digital Humanities in the Anthropocene." Presentation at the ADHO Digital Humanities Annual Conference, Lausanne, July 7–12, 2014. http://nowviskie .org/2014/anthropocene.

Pohl, Nicole. "Utopianism after More: The Renaissance and Enlightenment." In *The Cambridge Companion to Utopian Literature,* ed. Gregory Claeys, 51–78. Cambridge: Cambridge University Press, 2010.

Presner, Todd. "Critical Theory and the Mangle of Digital Humanities." In *Between Humanities and the Digital,* ed. Patrik Svensson and David Theo Goldberg, 55–68. Cambridge, Mass.: MIT Press, 2015.

Presner, Todd, David Shepard, and Yoh Kawano. *HyperCities: Thick Mapping in the Digital Humanities.* Cambridge, Mass.: Harvard University Press, 2014.

Rossiter, Ned. *Organized Networks: Media Theory, Creative Labour, New Institutions.* Rotterdam: NAi, 2006.

Sayers, Jentery. "Tinker-Centric Pedagogy in Literature and Language Classrooms." In *Collaborative Approaches to the Digital in English Studies,* ed. Laura McGrath. Logan: Computers and Composition Digital Press/Utah State University Press, 2011. http:// ccdigitalpress.org/cad/Ch10_Sayers.pdf.

Schnapp, Jeffrey T., and Matthew Battles. *The Library Beyond the Book.* Cambridge, Mass.: Harvard University Press, 2014.

Scholz, Trebor. "Crowdmilking" (blog), March 9, 2014. http://collectivate.net/journal isms/2014/3/9/crowdmilking.html.

Spiro, Lisa. "'This Is Why We Fight': Defining the Values of the Digital Humanities." In *Debates in the Digital Humanities,* ed. Matthew K. Gold. Minneapolis: University of Minnesota Press, 2012. http://dhdebates.gc.cuny.edu/debates/text/13.

Svensson, Patrik. "Beyond the Big Tent." In *Debates in the Digital Humanities,* ed. Matthew K. Gold. Minneapolis: University of Minnesota Press, 2012. http://dhdebates.gc.cuny .edu/debates/text/22.

———. "Envisioning the Digital Humanities." *Digital Humanities Quarterly* 6, no. 1 (2012). http://digitalhumanities.org/dhq/vol/6/1/000112/000112.html.

Thompson, Edward Palmer. "Romanticism, Moralism, and Utopianism: The Case of William Morris." *New Left Review* 1, no. 99 (1976): 83–111.

Turner, Fred. *From Counterculture to Cyberculture: Stewart Brand, the Whole Earth Network, and the Rise of Digital Utopianism.* Chicago: University of Chicago Press, 2010.

"Virtual Paul's Cross Project: A Digital Recreation of John Donne's Gunpowder Day Sermon," 2014. http://vpcp.chass.ncsu.edu.

Wardrip-Fruin, Noah. "An Introduction to Alex McDowell's 'World Building.'" *Journal of Digital Humanities* 3, no. 1 (Spring 2014). http://journalofdigitalhumanities.org/3-1 /an-introduction-to-alex-mcdowells-world-building-by-noah-wardrip-fruin.

Wegner, Phillip E. "Here or Nowhere: Utopia, Modernity, and Totality." In *Utopia Method Vision: The Use Value of Social Dreaming,* ed. Tom Moylan and Raffaella Baccolini, 113–30. Ralahine Utopian Studies Vol. 1. Oxford: Peter Lang, 2007.

———. *Shockwaves of Possibility: Essays on Science Fiction, Globalization, and Utopia.* Ralahine Utopian Studies Vol. 15. Frankfurt: Peter Lang, 2014.

Witmore, Michael. "Text: A Massively Addressable Object." In *Debates in the Digital Humanities,* ed. Matthew K. Gold. http://dhdebates.gc.cuny.edu/debates/text/28.

Ecological Entanglements of DH

MARGARET LINLEY

Ecological metaphors run rampant throughout the digital humanities, shaping the way the discipline thinks about electronic space and time and how it maps interactions between humans and technologies as well as between different media. While ecological metaphors model the discipline's paradigmatic self-understanding and underlying assumptions, there has been little discussion of the implications and consequences of this development for the field as currently constituted. Tracing modern ecological thought from its genesis in the Enlightenment and nineteenth-century evolutionary biology through the late twentieth-century emergence of media ecology theory within media studies, this chapter takes up the challenge of understanding what is at stake in the systemic presence of ecological metaphors circulating the field of digital humanities today, from the "trees" Franco Moretti cuts from evolutionary theory to the proliferation of "genetic texts," "media species," and "born digital objects." Following the work of major promoters of ecological thought, I ask what it means to think about digital ontologies in terms of species—with life cycles spanning birth, evolution, and extinction and with complex interactions involving enmeshments, mutations, migrations, and adaptations across platforms and through time—as well as of environments, networks, and systems entailing massive and dynamic interactions of "processes and objects, beings and things, patterns and matter" (Fuller, 2).

A new cultural logic is emerging in the ecological metaphors for imagining digital experience as well as in practices of ordering, modeling, networking, and mapping a world characterized by ubiquitous data and responsive programming. Rather than representing a radical break with the past, this new rationality builds on and extends the connectivity and continuities analyzed in frameworks developed through modern environmental thought and the media ecology tradition. Ecology composes the forms of material culture that unfold in processes of continuity and ordering of disparate, discontinuous scales of existence from the local to the global, thereby linking the very nexus of the digital and the humanities to planetary consciousness. An interrogation of the momentous and material impacts of the traffic in ecology at the same time that the earth appears increasingly vulnerable to the effects of human-technological intervention emerges as a pressing task of digital humanities today.

Political Ecology

I begin with two distinct ways of narrating the connection between the digital and the humanities. The first is exemplified by Alan Liu's introduction[1] to *A Companion to Digital Literary Studies* ("Imagining"), which characterizes the relation between the digital and the literary as a story of a "new media encounter," one which is actually not new at all but rather a familiar retelling of "first contact" scenes between traditional and emergent media that have recurred through history. As Liu explains, "New media, it turns out, is a very old tale." Liu's quarrel with the veneration of the present is one that often underpins understandings of new media, a position that echoes Lisa Gitelman and Geoffrey Pingree's influential argument that "all media were once 'new media'" (Gitelman and Pingree, xi). But Liu adds two important insights to the debate. First, he observes that the "first contact" scene of media transition is analogous to that of colonial encounter, one weighted with modernization processes that bear uneven power dynamics that cut across racial, gender, class, age and other social divides. Second, he argues, this scene unfolds formulaically, in a dialectical encounter of ideological oppression or "enchantment" followed by a reversal involving opposition, critique, and resistance, and finally, a mixing of the old and new in "whole imaginative environments" (Liu, "Imagining"). In short, the resolution to the allegory of "first contact" is a translation to the multidimensional and dynamic space of media ecology.

Liu provides a useful starting point for thinking about the ecological turn in the digital humanities because his analysis of its transformative force, as well as his exploration of its often surprising and unpredictable effects on what it means to be human, leans heavily on the trope of media ecology. Worried about literature's potential extinction in a society where the "digital is the great new medium," Liu sees media ecology as a space of hope for both literature and the humanities. In this formulation, media ecology denotes a mixed environment in which human identity can be asserted and sustained through imagination reconceived as *poiesis,* a term that blends technological and creative forms of making.[2]

"Macroanalysis," the name that Matthew Jockers uses to describe his approach to large-scale literary computing and its revolutionary potential, could not be more different. Jockers's application of large-scale computational techniques to the study of literary history is, of course, part of the quantitative trend associated with popular buzzwords like "distant reading" (Moretti), "culturomics" (Michel et al.),[3] and "big humanities"[4] (Marciano). Here the "star" of the digital humanities has shifted from the "new" to the "big," from the accelerated temporality of media change to the scaled-up spatiality of mass data analysis. Yet Jockers, like Liu, also draws on the ecology metaphor to frame his methodology. According to Jockers, "the study of literature should be approached not simply as an examination of seminal works but as an examination of an aggregated ecosystem or 'economy' of texts" (32). While Jockers understands ecosystems as economic structures, he shares with Liu an awareness of the politically loaded stakes of his position, throwing down the gauntlet with a bravado that emphasizes the contentious entanglements of text mining within the ecological framework: Jockers writes, "At the risk of giving offense to the environmentalists, what is needed now is the literary equivalent of open-pit mining or hydraulicking" (9). Digging quite literally into data, Jockers eschews traditional literary hermeneutics in favor of analytical methods more common to the sciences, social sciences, and business. In describing his work, however, he employs terms that underscore the impossibility of employing such methods in a condition of complete objectivity, as some might hope. As Matthew Gold[5] responds to this same passage, "one doesn't need to be an environmentalist to be a bit uneasy about such a scenario" ("Facts, Patterns").

Despite employing language that equates computational literary analysis with surface mining, Jockers exhibits no hesitation in subscribing to the traditional concept of imagination, or to the distinctively romantic sense of discovery also espoused by Liu.[6] Indeed, Jockers imagines his macroanalytic method as a complement to familiar literary methods of analysis. When describing his own scene of encounter between the literary imagination and the digital, however, Jockers offers a rather different take. Remarking on the sudden and rapid migration of scholars to the bourgeoning field of digital humanities, Jockers notes that the motivation is the "promise of opportunity," likely a "direct by-product of having such a wealth of digital material with which to engage" (11). Thus, "with apologies" to the "natives of the [digital] tribe" (of which Jockers includes himself), he explicitly acknowledges that "the streets of this 'new' world are paved with gold and the colonizers have arrived" (12).

As though responding directly to Liu's invocation of Keats's "On First Looking into Chapman's Homer," a poem of colonial mastery and technological domination, Jockers seizes the digital literary ecology unquestionably as a realm of opportunity, speculation, and ultimately, exploitation. His language invokes the ecological archetype of digital space as empty, virginal, uncharted territory mixed with a memory of the mythical American frontier and the rugged individualism that it supports.[7] Here, data is figured as a natural resource, one that can be exchanged in a cultural capital market. In a reading that conflates form with the economic forces and political power of resource capitalism, Jockers appears to collapse data interpretation into abstraction, reduction, extraction, and conversion. Alternatively, perhaps Jockers's targeting of environmentalists is intended as a challenge to the affective labor that binds some humanists to an organic ecological worldview.

The contrast—between Liu's assertion of the human at the center of digital ecology and Jockers's reinstatement of the instrumental attitude toward the environment that has dominated Western culture since the Industrial Revolution—might give us pause, especially since the Industrial Revolution is also one of the proposed dates for the beginning of the much vaunted anthropocene[8] era.[9] What are the purposes served by this framework within the bourgeoning field of digital humanities, we might then ask? Why are we building and analyzing digital systems as ecosystems at the moment when entire natural ecosystems are being eradicated, "living as we do in a continually worsening state of environmental crisis verging on catastrophe" (McKusick, 34).[10] Is there a relation between these developments?

Media Ecology

In referencing Keats and the romantic concept of the imagination, Alan Liu implicitly gestures toward the significance of the English Romantic poets in the formation of contemporary conceptions of nature, even as he disregards it as a nineteenth-century source of media ecology. On the alliance between technology and Romanticism, we must instead turn to Walter Ong, an influential figure in the media ecology intellectual tradition who, in a 2002 speech to the Media Ecology Association[11] (http://www.media-ecology.org/), declared that we live in an interconnected "ecological age." According to Ong, Romanticism's mirroring of technology is the product of domination over nature through the noetic abundance, both the buildup and bringing forth of knowledge, enabled by the rise of print culture and the spatialization of information, including the development of knowledge storage and retrieval systems (*Rhetoric*, 279). It is well worth our attention to consider how this nexus of communications and information technologies and the speculative disposition of romantic knowledge toward other worlds (e.g., Keats's "wild surmise") continues to manifest in various social and institutional settings today, including in emergent academic fields of inquiry such as the digital humanities.

"Media ecology" is an ambiguous term that circulates in multiple ways to describe the dynamic complexity of media difference, media change, and media systems, and that helps foreground key features of information and communications technologies. Among the most crucial is how media forms constitute vital and dynamic cultural environments. Thus, a central tenet of media ecology is that media are not mere tools but function rather both *within and as* environments, and thereby shape human perception and cognition, forms of discourse, and patterns of social behavior. A medium's physical properties therefore define the nature of communication; any changes in modes of communication have an effect on individual perceptions, expressions, values, and beliefs, as well as those of the society as a whole.

While it is not the aim of this chapter to compare media ecology with digital humanities, clearly there are meaningful links to be made. Just as the "big tent" of digital humanities is loosely organized around "a common methodological outlook" (Kirschenbaum, "What Is Digital Humanities,"[12] 4) with a high degree of heterogeneity and inclusion of other epistemic traditions (Svensson,[13] 37), media ecological perspectives and practices emerged out of a range of disciplines from communications, literature, and media studies to education, history of science and technology, behavioral sciences and psychology, urban studies, sociology, anthropology, cybernetics, and information studies. At the same time, it should be acknowledged that media ecology—perhaps more than digital humanities—has been shaped by certain key individuals: Marshall McLuhan, whose proverbs would come to define the digital age, and Neil Postman, who is strongly influenced by McLuhan.[14] In a statement reminiscent of John Muir, the American naturalist and founder of the Sierra Club,[15,16] Postman defines media ecology as the study of "media as environments"[17] and their effects on "people's cognitive habits, their social relations, their political biases, and their personal values" ("The Day Our Children Disappear," 382). In common with the founding spirit of the modern environmentalist movement, Postman's definition suggests a holistic understanding of ecological connectedness through media, whereby technology operates as part of the material landscape in which individuals and social groups interact.

The substantial stakes in any figuration of what counts as technical or medial knowledge and the conditions of its production, whether in the form of new media or data, are apparent in the digital humanities from the start as well and feature prominently in the discipline's self-proclaimed inaugural 2004 volume, *A Companion to Digital Humanities*,[18] which marked a "turning point" by bringing together a wide range of theorists and scholars to examine and reflect for the first time on "digital humanities as a discipline in its own right" (Schreibman, Siemens, and Unsworth, xiii). Exploring possibilities and problems arising from attempts at designing "built environments" for humanistic inquiry, the *Companion* especially foregrounds epistemological and infrastructural questions of standards for creating taxonomical systems and metadata structures crucial to electronic reliability, sustainability, and interoperability. Computers could thus seem reassuringly familiar, enabling "a very old impulse" (Crane,[19] 46) toward enlightenment forms of systematic knowledge management and classification, only at a more intensive and expansive scale. The counterpoint to the quest for technological control is, as Ong points out, the romantic domination over nature, which is not far removed from aims of progress, expansion, and gain inherent to the scene of new media encounter critiqued by Liu and the spectacle of data extraction described by Jockers. Not surprisingly, voices emerge in the *Companion* calling for reflection on how computational tools and techniques participate in the making of the world and thus become problematic when they are insufficiently critiqued or allowed to remain invisible (Smith,[20] 315).[21]

Extending this awareness that computers are more than tools but instead function, in the tradition of media ecology, both within and as environments, Matthew Kirschenbaum conceives of digital space as its own milieu, observing that "the desktop environment governs the behavior of the browser software, whose features and functions in turn directly affect many aspects of the user's interaction with the site's internal design and content" ("So the Colors Cover the Wires,"[22] 524) or, by extension, is housed within other social or institutional ecosystems. Importantly, such gestures toward ecological thinking in the early phase of the developing digital humanities render the object of knowledge stable and identifiable, a thing to be queried and managed within the realm of comprehension. While these perspectives are consonant with the tropism of environments and effects instituted three decades earlier by Postman in the founding moment of media ecology, they do not necessarily see it as their responsibility to understand the implications of digital work in the context of systems and infrastructure with broader social, political, or cultural implications.

If, as Gitelman and Jackson suggest, data have always been in some sense "precisely *not* the domain of humanist inquiry" (3), the ubiquity of data today only serves to heighten the relevance of the media ecologists' attempt to comprehend the planetary magnitude of networked information and communications structures. Media systems understood at such scale and complexity point toward enormous social, political, and cultural fragility, instability, and risk, which Postman articulates in cataclysmic terms of "assault," "threat," and "crisis":

> Technological change is neither additive nor subtractive. It is ecological. I mean "ecological" in the same sense as the word is used by environmental scientists. One significant change generates total change. . . . A new technology does not add or subtract something. It changes everything . . . when an old technology is assaulted by a new one, institutions are threatened. When institutions are threatened, a culture finds itself in crisis. (*Technopoly*, 18)

While Postman's dramatic rendering of the consequences of technology gone awry may seem a world apart from the concerns of digital humanists, that is far from the case. Rather, Postman's technological angst is very much oriented toward digital humanities debates over the status of digital tools and whether they are commensurate with humanities research. Whereas in the previous volume of *Debates in the Digital Humanities*,[23] Johanna Drucker[24] describes the assumptions embedded in platforms and protocols built by nonhumanists as "at odds," "hostile," "an anathema," or "antipathetic" to humanistic thought and values ("Humanistic Theory," 86), Stephen Ramsay and Geoffrey Rockwell[25] counter that the various roles involved in making, conceiving, and transforming are hardly clear-cut, and a "fear of automated scholarship—an automatic writing" may underlie such objections to humanities tools and tool building ("Developing Things," 83; Ramsey, "On Building"). As different as these perspectives may be, they share a desire for humanists to make tools in their own image alongside a simultaneous awareness that those tools also make us. Ramsay and Rockwell's spectre of automated scholarship and Drucker's story of how research instruments and technical environments convert "relativist" humanists to "positivists" ("Humanistic Theory," 88) represent scenarios that differ in degree rather than kind from Postman's dark ecological vision.

Postman's technological pessimism is thus a version writ large of central unresolved concerns around *techne* within digital humanities today, an unease that
brushes up against the limits of the conceptual contradiction inherent in the concept of romantic nature that Ong first identified. The computer as a tool or medium
can only enable mastery if humans (and humanists) retain control over its operations. Within this familiar Gothic allegory, the computer will take on more lifelike
capacities that will put it beyond restraint, becoming potentially threatening and
dehumanizing. As such, the romantic sublime, the space of "wild surmise" and
Frankensteinian experiments, cannot help but breed monstrous offspring with the
capacity to mutate, adapt, and evolve beyond human intention, thereby wreaking
havoc on their makers and the world. Directly challenging this perennial cautionary tale against controversial technologies, Bruno Latour reminds us in his post-
environmental rereading of *Frankenstein* that this modern narrative of increasing
"human mastery *over* and freedom *from* Nature"—with "Nature" understood in
Ong's terms as an outcome of modern technology—can be redescribed as the
increasing "*attachments* between things and people" ("Love Your Monsters").[26]
It is not the invention that is flawed but rather the failure to cultivate and care for
the technological creation. Drawing hope from Latour's prospect of ever-increasing
intimacy with the new natures we are constantly generating, Bethany Nowviskie
persuasively argues that now is precisely the time of the digital humanities—that
we are living in the moment when the work we undertake, the systems we create,
and the tools we build have deep and enduring connections to the incomprehensi-
ble scale of geological time precisely because our practice potentially grapples daily
with the technological, environmental, and ethical conditions of the present ("Digital Humanities at the Anthropocene").[27] As such, what is needed now more than
ever is a searching and actively engaged digital humanities.

Nature's Economy

The entanglements of nature and technology thoroughly overdetermine ecological
metaphors, but that should not blind us to the epistemological and practical work
they perform. Returning to the polarization within digital humanities around the
concepts of "new media" and "data driven," it is not hard to see how it becomes
impossible to separate the rhetoric of resource extraction that Matthew Jockers
deploys from environmental politics. Ironically, Alan Liu's views on the mediated
status of nature have also long functioned as something of a lightning rod for
ecocritics. More than twenty-five years have passed since Liu declared that "there
is no nature" except as "the name under which we use the nonhuman to validate
the human" (*Wordsworth*, 38). His much-contested new historicist position that
nature is politically constituted through particular forms of government (*Wordsworth*, 104) continues to provoke those unwilling to give up the faith in an authentic, autonomous nature.[28] In our present moment, when historians and theorists of

deep geologic time are calling for a radically different kind of historicism, one that would take account of massive temporalities and tangled human and nonhuman influences in the shaping of the planet, we might do well to turn to the past in order to situate the ecological metaphors that run rampant through the digital humanities. In so doing, we might also begin to realize the rich potential—as well as the challenges—suggested by the intersection of communications, globalization, and the quest for a sustainable future.

As with the term "media ecology," the history of "ecology" is itself also deeply rooted in the past. German zoologist Ernest Haeckel coined "oecology" in 1866, belatedly naming the modern history of ecology that began more than a century earlier as a more comprehensive view of the "earth's fabric of life" (Worster, x). Two broad perspectives arose alongside ecological thought: balance and coexistence on the one hand, and dominion over nature through reason and industriousness on the other. Religious beliefs and scientific tenets combined during the Enlightenment to support emerging social values that associated nature with productivity and efficiency in keeping with economic aims of progress, expansion, and profit—goals conducive not only to the spread of industrial capitalism but to imperialism and globalization as well. The historical and ideological undercurrents of Haeckel's scientific coinage thus extend well beyond Darwinian evolution and Linnaean taxonomy, or "economy of nature," to mix with values of industrial capitalism. The contrasting branch of modern ecological thought, arising during the Industrial Revolution and often referred to as "romantic ecology" after Jonathan Bate's influential 1991 study, follows eighteenth-century naturalist Gilbert White's understanding of the physical world in terms of interdependence, connectedness, and holism. Proponents of harmonious balance run headlong against the modern faith in technology, while the hierarchical perspective sees nature as an instrument at the service of maximum human production and progress. Significantly, however, romantic nature is a divided concept, torn by an understanding of the world as "a place of vital sustenance and peaceful coexistence," on the one hand, and on the other "a nightmare vision of a world threatened by imminent environmental catastrophe" (McKusick, 29). This dialectical critical tension within romantic ecology challenged scientific rationalism, the values and institutions of liberal capitalism, and superiority over nature in Western religion and continues today to provide inspiration to environmental activism.

This 200-year tradition, one that opposes the tendencies of enlightenment ideals of conquest, industrial capitalism, and technological progress to ideas of a nature associated with physical and psychic health, wholeness, and refuge, is the major impetus behind both the modern environmental movement and the reflections of media ecologists. It is therefore no coincidence that media ecology emerged at the same time as environmental ecology was rapidly popularized as a source of ethical guidance in the wake of widespread recognition of environmental crisis of the 1960s. The political, economic, and social connotations of ecology running through the twentieth-century media theory intellectual tradition and spilling over into the digital humanities today were thus imbued in its very origins—including its complicity with Western ideologies of development (Huggan and Tiffin)—and intensified under the threat of nuclear annihilation in the 1960s and 1970s.[29]

Reflecting one of the major tendencies of romantic ecology, a central premise of media ecology is that the way in which a society organizes and transmits perceptions and knowledge about the world strongly affects the nature of those perceptions and the way we come to know the world. As a result, any environmental change will ultimately impact the survival of everything within the ecology as well as the system itself. The holism usually attributed to romantic ecology gets incorporated in the reflexivity of media ecological thought, which Ronald Deibert summarizes as premised on:

> the basic materialist position that human beings, like all other organisms, are vitally dependent on, and thus influenced by, the environment around them . . . [and] approach their environment . . . through a complex web-of-beliefs, symbolic forms, and social constructs into which they are acculturated and through which they perceive the world around them. (*Parchment, Print, and Hypermedia*, 43)

Deibert additionally emphasizes that such transformations must be approached historically, contrasting media environments across time and tracing changes in the technology of communication for their effects on the evolution of the social and political order. This humanist strain is especially strong in Bonnie Nardi and Vicki O'Day's examination of the ecological metaphor for the way it attempts to make greater space for human intervention in a technologically oriented world, turning a spotlight on human activities served by technology rather than technology as tool (*Information Ecologies*, 49). Nardi and O'Day's emphasis on human agency at the local level of information ecologies parallels the privileged attachment to place in much environmental thought and summons the ecology metaphor to counteract the opposing tendency within the medium theory tradition, which expresses a pessimistic view of media based on a deterministic logic of technology that is systematic, all-encompassing, and autonomous.

These fundamentally different ways of implementing ecological thought both within the environmental tradition and media studies have significant implications for the use of similar metaphors in the digital humanities, offering potent vehicles for the kind of searching, engaged, active stance Nowviskie advocates for digital humanists toward the materialist, political, and ethical conditions of our practices. When the emphasis is on the systemic interpretation, the resulting view is that of technological determinism. If, on the other hand, the emphasis is on the local particularity of the ecosystems and the situatedness of human actors within it, the focus shifts toward a more agential, activist view. The point here is not whether an anthropological perspective is better than a technocentric one, but rather that both are anthropocentric, suggesting an impossible separation of ourselves from the non-human world. Given that we, our technologies, and nature cannot be disentangled, as Latour suggests, we might examine the ecological metaphors we similarly live by in digital humanities contexts in order to understand how they both limit and open our understanding of, and active engagement with, the new intimacies and attachments that are emerging in an era understood not only on a digital scale but an environmental one as well.

Whereas for Postman there is a hierarchical separation between humans and the environment to which they are subject, even as that environment is understood as a complex message system, for McLuhan the personal and social consequences of any medium result from the new spatial awareness introduced in the electronic age, which he thought could be best described as a technological extension of the human sensorium "to involve us in the whole of mankind and to incorporate the whole of mankind in us" (*Understanding Media,* 4). This new sense of scale drives McLuhan's belief that the world had turned into a "global village" and cannot be dissociated from the impact of space exploration and the images of the planet it engendered.[30] Reflecting on the significance of this moment when new media technologies enabled humans to see the earth as a whole from space for the first time, providing environmentalist and imperialist alike with a powerful icon supported by the slogan "think globally, act locally," McLuhan writes:

> Perhaps the largest conceivable revolution in information occurred on October
> 17, 1957, when Sputnik created a new environment for the planet. For the first
> time the natural world was completely enclosed in a man-made container. At
> the moment that the earth went inside this new artifact, Nature ended and
> Ecology was born. "Ecological" thinking became inevitable as soon as the
> planet moved up into the status of a work of art. ("At the moment of Sputnik the
> planet became a global theater in which there are no spectators only actors," 49)

Published in 1974, the McLuhan article anticipates Liu's sense of nature constituted in politicized acts of mediation, here seen not through landscape politics but rather through the impact of the Soviet launch of the first artificial earth satellite, which in turn set off the space race, the creation of NASA, the Apollo project, and the first moon landing. Encapsulating the Western inheritance of global meanings, the enduring achievement of the space project was not so much knowledge gained about the moon, which was its ostensible purpose, but rather an altered image of the earth (Cosgrove, 257), the most iconic of which is the famous photograph variously referred to as the "blue marble" or "blue planet" taken during the final Apollo flight in 1972.

Despite its Cold War origins, the affectively charged and deeply political image of a precious, isolated globe suspended alone against a stark, black background

was quickly appropriated and turned into a commodity. The environmental movement (Friends of the Earth[31] founded in 1969, Earth Day[32] inaugurated 1970, and
the whole-earth movement associated with James Lovelock's *Gaia,* 1978) and institutions wanting to advertise their own technological advancement (airlines, tele-
communications and computer companies, government offices, and global financial corporations) together embraced the visual allegory of the planet's harmony
and fragility, a permanently destabilized, networked globe at once bearing the hope
of human aspiration and the potential for human destruction. Crucially, this static
image of ecological unity and vulnerability, imperial inclusiveness and domination, conjures a dynamic system of informational exchange, rendering networks and
nature alike both figurative and rich sources of figuration or metaphor (as McLuhan
suggests) and thus endlessly available for a range of cultural, political, and commercial purposes.

A celebrated image of space enterprise, one simultaneously intimate and mac-
rocosmic, sorrowful and hopeful, the "blue marble" thus leaves a legacy that captures
the complexity that media ecology has to offer digital humanities. As a summary of
the abstract density of global systems in a relatively simple and concrete image that
emphasizes synthesis, holism, and self-regeneration (Heise, 63), the photograph
points toward its counterpoint in the history of technical evolution: not Bethany
Nowviskie's cosmic elegy of "common ground and shared fate" ("Digital Humanities in the Anthropocene"),[33] itself a beautiful and haunting expression of romantic
ecology, but media archeologist Siegfried Zielinski's visualization of the collapse of
space and time that occurs with the change in perspective from a humanized earth
to an insidious human-made instrument of destruction (*Deep Time of the Media*).
Shifting from an anthropocentric view of earth to the deep time of the anthropocene, Zielinski imagines that the 35mm camera used to take the "stunning pictures
of the blue planet" from the Mir space station "was simply thrown out the escape
hatch" while the space station continues its orbit (2).[34]

Ecosystems

Where media theorists such as Zielinski, as well as Ursula Heise, see allegory and
narrative in the iconic images of technical excess, information specialist Paul N.
Edwards perceives global data. For the latter, the "blue marble" prompts the question:
"How did the earth become a system?" The epistemology of digital space suggested
by the ecological understandings evinced in the exemplary work of Liu and Jockers
(outlined at the outset of this chapter) implies that electronic environments have a
cosmology of their own, opening a space to deterritorializing moves that make it
hard to situate and historicize the work that goes on there. While it would seem that
the pathway linking media ecology and environmentalism with digital humanities
could go no further than the deep time of outer space, the rise of big data and systems
theory ensures there is another way to read the mediated informational abundance

that constitutes the "blue marble" moment. Which is to say, the connections linking media ecology to digital humanities arise as much out of the pattern seeking
and analyses of big data, specifically in communication sciences of cybernetics, as
it does from the new media encounter.

Jerome McGann takes up precisely this task of locating the meaning of digital knowledge work in the dimensional space of electronic environments in his
contribution to *A Companion to Digital Humanities*. Also embracing ecological
metaphors, McGann invokes systems theory to describe the differences between
electronic coding practices and bibliographic environments:

> Like biological forms and all living systems, not least of all language itself,
> print and manuscript encoding systems are organized under a horizon of co-
> dependent relations. That is to say, print technology . . . is a system that codes
> (or simulates) what are known as autopoietic systems. ("Marking Texts of Many
> Dimensions," 200)

In framing his critique of digital textual editing with the cognitive biological theory of Humberto Maturana and Francisco Varela, McGann evokes the earlier convergence between media ecology and cybernetics, starting in the mid-twentieth
century when biological metaphors were deployed frequently to describe parallels between complex organic systems and emergent computer architecture and,
more importantly, to attempt to mimic the former.[35] The term "cybernetics," coined
by Norbert Weiner and developed in the 1940s and 1950s to denote the study of
homeostatic mechanisms governing systematic behavior, focused on information,
irrespective of content, and the efficiency of its transmission. The media ecology
movement reinserted communication back into its social, political, and historical
contexts, and especially through the work of Gregory Bateson, ecological systems
came to be understood not only as natural but also as social and technological
(Kaizen, 87).

For Maturana and Varela, who apply systems theory to living organisms, biological systems are circular and self-referring by nature, continually self-reproducing
according to their own internal logic using their own material, as when a cell self-
divides and thereby reproduces from its own elements. McGann glosses this process
of autopoiesis as "self-maintenance through self-transformation" (McGann, "Marking Texts," 201). As such, all living organisms are "autopoietic" unities or closed systems while remaining open in material exchange with their environment. Through
interactions with the environment (openness) while nevertheless maintaining circular integrity of organization (closure), autopoietic systems, and thus all living
things, are "cognitive systems, and living [is] a process of cognition" (Maturana and
Varela, 13).

In urging the liveliness of traditional textual systems, McGann maintains
that manuscript and print technologies provide "arresting models for information

technology tools"; in so doing, he also echoes Bateson on artistic production as a special means of communication precisely in its self-reflexivity. Art self-consciously reflects on the conditions of its own transmission in the very act of transmission.[36] Sifting a similar perspective through the life sciences work of Maturana and Varela, McGann argues that traditional textualities, "like gene codes," make of themselves "as part of their simulation and generative processes . . . a record of those processes." A poem may be "like biological forms and all living systems," but it is a special case, as "a machine of creation and reflection" (McGann, "Marking Texts," 202).

Electronic models have yet to be developed for displaying and replicating the self-reflexive operations of bibliographic tools, however. Markup models like TEI impose on dynamic textuality an abstract taxonomy of hierarchically organized elements defined in advance and cannot take account of the multiplicity of the work as it is produced through the interpretive process. Consequently, McGann calls on digital humanists to build dynamic, topological models for mapping the space of digital operations (203), but the question remains today whether the particular limitations of digital processing that he identifies can be addressed adequately by such important infrastructural projects as TAPoR (Text Analysis Portal for Research). Tools for text analysis, though indispensible to tasks of archiving, record keeping, searching, and linking, remain bound, according to McGann, by the hierarchical, two-dimensional limits of their basic markup structure.[37] Returning to this topic a decade later, McGann's position has not changed: text processing has not yet exploited the possibilities of digital space to develop equivalent textualities that would be analogous to the codex form in complexity and expressiveness (McGann, *New Republic,* chaps. 5 and 6).[38]

Whereas McGann insists that the ideal topological approach needs to be imagined as "applied textual autopoiesis," of which the codex provides the most effective model, Andrew Piper argues that only by letting go of the bibliographical will we be able to move toward a topological hermeneutics. Rather than seek digital tools that can imitate the dynamic space of the book, we need to alter "our visual and cognitive relationship to the text" ("Reading's Refrain," 377). Piper elaborates a specifically literary topology comprised of familiar conventional literary features; topology is concerned "above all else" with textual relationality and, "like a book, it is a technology of reading" (378). However, the similarities end there. Topology does not refer directly to real space, is not accompanied by a stable textual referent, and lacks a basic ontology (378). Literary topologies are spatial, numerical, historical, graphical, and explicitly ecological. In fact, Piper explains that because topologies attempt to observe relations between books beyond their discrete material boundaries, they are "far more ecological [than books] in nature" (378).

Beginning, like McGann, with the question of the basic unit of textual analysis, Piper similarly loads his argument with biological metaphors, for example, "lexical molecules" (the basic units of the literary topology can extend from a word, such as phoneme or letter, to larger analytical categories, including publication or genre) and "lexical chromosomes" (a set of the most frequent significant words of a work). However, he quickly emphasizes that a literary topology is not interested in fixing the meaning of words or in creating controlled vocabularies and taxonomies; rather the focus is "fields" rather than corpora or archives of language and texts. The redundancy and ambiguity inherent to traditional literary hermeneutics of representation but expelled from TEI, to McGann's regret, is released in Piper's literary topology into "a field of contingent multiplicities" and a "more nuanced sense of discursive being" (Piper, "Reading's Refrain," 383). Here then would seem to be the answer to McGann's call to imagine a digital processing program that would, autopoietically as it were, "short-circuit a number of critical predilections that inhibit our received, commonsense wisdom about our textual condition" (McGann, "Marking Texts," 203).

Given that Piper's collaborator, Mark Algee-Hewitt, and Matthew Jockers both hail from Moretti's Stanford Literary Lab[39] and are associated additionally with Piper's .txtLab[40] at McGill University, it is not surprising that some of their reflections on quantitative analysis and text mining are imbued with Moretti's evolutionary methodology (see Piper and Algee-Hewitt). Addressing recent debates around the relative values of close and distant reading, Piper contends that topology offers a method for the systematic analysis of large amounts of data but also, unlike close or distance reading, makes scale itself an object of knowledge. He offers "scalar reading" and "dispersive reading" as alternatives (Piper, "Reading's Refrain," 382, 394), with the latter bringing into view the vast majority of words, typically articles and prepositions, often filtered out of computational analysis as stop words.

Piper's topological approach is ecological in its understanding of the complexity of literary systems and linguistic environments as well as in its balance between systemic modes of analysis and attention to the local and particular: the dynamic, the emergent, the multidimensional. Through his nuanced theorization of literary topology, Piper attempts to sidestep the controversies associated with text mining. Despite careful attention to language, as well as to the critical tension surrounding the application of computational techniques to humanities questions, Piper does not, however, reflect explicitly on the implications of his invocation of ecology metaphors to frame and express his argument. The failure to do so occludes the significance of ecology as a mode of analyzing quantitative reading in terms of processes of mediation and also formally segregates topology from the political and ethical imperatives implied in its dynamic continuities with material practices and environmental impacts of the kind writ large in the "blue marble" moment.

Mutations

In spite—or perhaps because—of the semantic richness and ideological thickness of the term "ecology," it may be the best word we have for the "massive and dynamic interrelation of processes and objects, beings and things, patterns and matter," as

Matthew Fuller suggests (2). Fuller, who has explored contemporary media ecologies more thoroughly than anyone, understands media environments as each having and creating its own dimensions of relationality, a multitude of forces that might be political, material, aesthetic, historical, affective, and so on. The space of digital media may appear infinite but, according to Fuller, it is fully contingent upon the supposedly "inevitable" interpretative perspectivalism of the human subject (or critic) that grasps the dimensions of relationality which constitute and intersect that space. Fuller's insights into the nature of digital media ecologies exemplifies McLuhan's statement that the "'message' of any medium or technology is the change of scale or pace or pattern that it introduces into human affairs" (*Understanding Media,* 8). Fuller's version of media ecology also resonates with McGann's grasp of the potentiality of digital space as n-dimensional, and is echoed as well in Piper's scalar literary topology—that is, in the multidimensional "textual relationality" that would allow the compositional dynamics of the topology to travel in more than one direction.

If Fuller's perspectivalism would seem to move toward anthropocentric fantasies of disembodiment, his work insists that the materiality of media hinges on their existence as both informational and physical objects. Media in their particular specificity can be grasped then by paying attention to the way they connect, mix, interrelate, create patterns and variations, and open new conditions of interactions on various spatial and temporal scales. This technological dynamism arising from concrete matters and circumstances, which in some cases may look like the liveliness of life itself, is best described as ecological. Fuller's work is thus pivotal to thinking about the ubiquity of computation and mediation in everyday life and points toward three important material thresholds for digital humanities today: the new materialisms of bioinformatics and the "trans-corporeality" of human/nonhuman relations;[41] the new topologies of architectural and infrastructural spaces; and the new temporalities of the archive or evidence of the human record. Some of the most important work in and around the digital humanities is moving in these directions.

New materialisms call attention to how the intermingling of biology and technology has launched a wealth of metaphors that circulate widely through popular and academic culture. Fuller himself draws on this metaphoricity when he declares that "a media ecology is a cascade of parasites" (174). Katherine Hayles makes a similar point, that owing to their deep interpenetration, print and "born digital" media are "best considered as two components of a complex and dynamic media ecology," which operate like "biological ecotomes" in a wide variety of relationships, including competition, cooperation, mimicry, symbiosis, and parasitism (*Electronic Literature,* 160). Pushing the evolutionary metaphor further, Lev Manovich considers how biological adaptation models the way algorithmic software collapses distinctions between form and matter to combine available techniques and thereby produce unique media "species" (*Software Takes Command,* 167 ff.). Alan Liu's "first contact" allegory with its generic attraction, repulsion, and synthesis flourishes in this

ubiquitous computing context, switching easily from imperial to organic and informational materialities. Translated into software environments, media techniques
become unbundled from their physical bases and translated into data elements
through algorithmic generation or other technical means to produce new unfore-
seen combinations attracting a host of ecological metaphors variously highlighting
biological, reproductive, and evolutionary functionality. Liu's allegory reminds us,
however, that such new digital processes and products are hardly free from political, economic, and other socially motivated stakes.

For Jussi Parikka, self-generating worms, viruses, bugs, and parasites reveal
essential traits of the logic of digital culture. Taking his cue from Bruno Latour's
attention to the nonhuman actors that inhabit digital society, Parikka argues that
the virality that abounds online today holds "essential keys to unraveling the logics
of software that produce the ontological basis for much of economical, societal, and
cultural transactions of modern global networks" ("Universal Virtual Machine").[42,43]
Viruses, like McGann's poems, engage in autopoiesis, whereby they self-reproduce
and, in interacting with the digital communications environment, regenerate the
whole media ecology, networking, copying, or self-replicating. While the cultural fascination with such uncannily lifelike processes has popularized monstrous autonomous mutations of mythic (and memetic) proportions, the biological basis of digital
culture participates in distributed life processes on dimensions that are technical,
social, political, and commercial, "changing the landscape of the living" (Coole and
Frost, 16). In calling into question the nature of the human subject of the digital
humanities as well as the tools and techniques we have used to generate that concept,
new materialisms help us grasp the blurring of bodies, objects, and contexts as well
as the interactions of different orders of matter in the biotechnological and digital
technological developments that define our networked existence. In addition, new
materialisms encourage digital humanities to reflect on McLuhanesque anthropocentric incorporations of the world in us (e.g., the global village) and actively foster
an understanding of how human and nonhuman assemblages and systems that are
fundamentally open-ended and generative, with a constant propensity for change,
are enmeshed in dense webs of historically situated social, economic, and technological relations.

New topologies bring into focus the changes in the conceptualization of space
in the era of distributed and ubiquitous software. These changes extend well beyond
the textual dimensions explored by McGann and Piper, and even the cosmic exploration of big data encapsulated in the images of the whole earth from space. The
intermingling of species begins at home, layering the experience of even the most
mundane and familiar physical environments.[44] Given the increasing integration
of the digital, what we now call the "Internet of Things" and "cloud computing" into
the built and experienced environment, as well as whatever might be called a natural one, we are no longer able to ignore the effects of "the systems ecology of interface and our mutating adaptations," Johanna Drucker explains ("Reading Interface,"

218–19). For Drucker, interfaces will increasingly saturate our experience of the world—no longer representational but performative and constitutive—and thus a fundamental problem for human identity.

Proliferating interfaces link the sensorial capacity for feedback with the users of intelligently networked space (Halpern). Out of emergent biotechnological ecologies spring a range of new forms of administration, management, and productivity. In this way, data becomes the site of abundance once attributed to nature, with an almost palpable sensual appeal that has no relation to its content, a reminder of Jockers's zeal for "open-pit mining" of literary texts. Alan Liu focuses on large-scale online social networking to ask about the nature of the new knowledge produced by the collective intelligence of the "the hive mind," given that the crowd has been a "core problem of modernity" since at least the French Revolution ("The Meaning of the Digital Humanities," 412). Tobias Blanke's research on digital infrastructure is also interested in the unpredictable and unknowable nature of crowd knowledge, not as a problem but as a source of energy that might be harnessed through networked cloud infrastructures to power the new digital economy (*Digital Asset Ecosystems*). And Steven Jones explores the disciplinary effects within institutional ecologies of "platform thinking"; as it turns conventional forms and formats of scholarly communication inside out, scholarly production today frequently takes place in collaborative, networked workshops, now called makerspaces, of creation (*Emergence of Digital Humanities*, 174).

New temporalities of media archeology point us toward insights from past new media, searching for "the forgotten, the quirky, the non-obvious, practices and inventions" (Parikka, *What Is Media Archaeology*, 2). Media archeology is thus also about history making, cultural memory, and the storage systems of the archive as well as the creative practices about and shaped by mixing with technical media. It takes its methods from geology as much as evolutionary biology, thinking in terms of the sedimentation and layering of time and matter. Through excavations of the past, the old suddenly becomes new and innovation speeds headlong into obsolescence. In this context, Bolter and Grusin's concept of remediation helps illuminate how old media never die and new media are never fully distinguishable from the resurgence of past forms they embody, and Alan Liu's new media encounter is an event that is enfolded within, rather than an exchange between, artifacts. Media archeology especially involves refocusing attention radically on the technical thing and its nonhuman temporality, ascertaining its potentiality for material agency in history (Ernst). Media are thus nonscribal record keepers of culture, storing traces of the political and social conditions of their physical origins and epistemological orientations.

Media archeology enriches the digital humanities by including software, data structures, and interfaces in addition to hardware in cultural heritage archives while complicating its anthropocentric emphasis with a nonhuman privileging of (digital) object time and space. Even more than we might find in the posthumanism of the new materialities, the trajectory of media archeology points directly to media ecology. Parikka's work offers an exemplary meditation on the ways that media have helped us grasp earth as an object (as in the "blue marble" photograph) at the same time that the earth provides the materials that enable media (*Geology of Media*). No less important, it explains how calculation-based and data-centric forms of recording history will ultimately conflict with the humanist tradition of recounting the past through stories—not only those that envision hope for humanity through technological progress, but also those that narrate the post-apocalyptic tragedy of a future that begins with the end.

Ecological awareness challenges the digital humanities to think big—bigger than big data to a perspective that, as Timothy Morton suggests, is simultaneously vast and profound yet intrinsically uncanny (*The Ecological Thought*, 50–58). Such a perspective asks that we consider how orienting ourselves toward a sense of scale might provide a method of thinking about the particularity and limitations of the intellectual work we do and technical things we make. In so doing, it might also encourage advocacy, engagement, action, and participation as well as an ethics of responsibility, sustainability, and conservation. But added to this process are also questions about human and nonhuman interactions, distributed networks, and complex systems, to which humans—however the term may now be defined—adapt along with other species and orders of matter with the capacity for evolution, mutation, self-replication, and migration. On the one hand, this points to a world of interdependence, coevolution, holism, even balance and harmony; on the other, it suggests risk, vulnerability, impending crisis, and catastrophe itself. In an age when mass extinction and environmental destruction is a fact of daily life, and when the devastating record of human presence is written into the earth's crust for what would seem to be time immemorial, ecological thinking offers a point of entry to the planetary relations of our most quotidian affairs.

As the possible implications of the ecology metaphor suggest, the tradition of ecology has a rich cultural and political history, with deep roots both in science and the humanities. The challenge for digital humanities is to sharpen its use of metaphor so that its arguments can be made more carefully and more exacting. Digital humanists are well aware that metaphors embody dispositions toward the world and that our concepts of technology are often interlaced with highly charged figurations. So why has this issue not yet been taken up more explicitly? If one of the implications of the ecological metaphor is activism, action, and responsibility, perhaps Alan Liu got it right after all when he chided digital humanities for not being ready to take up full responsibility because:

> the field does not yet possess an adequate critical awareness of the larger social, economic, and cultural issues at stake. The side of the digital humanities that descends from humanities computing lacks almost all cultural–critical

awareness, and the side that descends from new media studies is indiscriminately critical of society and global informational "empire." ("The State of Digital Humanities," 11)

Ecological thinking demands more than this, calling out for ethical awareness as well. It pushes against our humanist reluctance about new ways of creating meaning through human-machine collaborations of simulation, modeling, and probabilistic topologies.

Perhaps Johanna Drucker is correct when she qualifies the theoretical apparatus deriving from systems ecology and new materialisms as "not strictly speaking, the domain of humanists"—an odd position given that her work has become increasingly invested in ecological metaphors ("Performative Materiality").[45] Perhaps ecological perspectives can too easily serve what to some seems a clichéd "holistic" or naïve cultural politics, a battle that, according to Tanner Higgin, many digital humanists take as having "already been won,"[46] or, as Gary Hall would have it, merely become an "accepted convention of political critique" ("Has Critical Theory Run Out of Time,"[47] 130). Certainly one of the most frequent uses of the ecological metaphors occurs in defining the field of digital humanities itself, positing the field as a system (Charlie Edwards, "The Digital Humanities and Its Users")[48] or as a media ecology specifically, as we have just seen (Jones), although it is just as likely that digital humanities is more than one ecology. Whether the ecology metaphor serves to express action and intervention or substitute for action or critical reflection; whether it serves systematization and classification, cross-disciplinary knowledge or capitalist and entrepreneurial values; or whether media simply serves to beget media (Hayles and Pressman, xi) or software (Manovich) or some other digital mutation, the ecology metaphor does all these things and then some. More than any one answer, we need to pursue the uses that the ecological metaphor has and continues to serve in framing the field of digital humanities, what sorts of arguments and positions are implied in its deployment, what conditions of possibility it enables, and what affordances it offers for users.

NOTES

1. http://www.digitalhumanities.org/companion/view?docId=blackwell /978140 5148641/9781405148641.xml&chunk.id=ss1-3-1&toc.depth=1&toc.id=ss1-3-1&brand =9781405148641_brand.

2. This line of thinking clearly has affinities with utopian thought. On the utopianism of the digital humanities, see chapter 33 in this volume by Brian Greenspan, "Are Digital Humanists Utopian?"

3. http://www.sciencemag.org/content/331/6014/176.

4. http://bighumanities.net.

5. http://blog.mkgold.net/2015/04/20/facts-patterns-methods-meaning-public -knowledge-building-in-the-digital-humanities.

6. In fact, one of the most popular appeals of literary text analysis of large corpora is precisely this amenability to "the rhetoric of discovery" (Gold).

7. The same charges leveled against Franco Moretti's model of "distant reading" apply here too, of course: charges of covert imperialism and globalizing imperatives along with promotion of the inequalities of neoliberalism and statistically based so-called rational ideology. See Bode and also Serlen, "The Distant Future?" Importantly, however, Matthew Gold ("Facts, Patterns, Methods, Meaning") notes a marked difference between Moretti's "sense of wonder, showmanship, and play" and Jockers's more precisely scientific approach almost a decade later, which he attributes to the "increasing pressure on DH researchers to find, present, and demonstrate results." Scott Weingart similarly notes a shift between Moretti and Jockers, but for him the difference rests on the switch from "reading" to "analysis" ("Liveblogged Review of *Macroanalysis* by Matthew L. Jockers").

8. http://www.igbp.net/download/18.316f18321323470177580001401/13763 83088452/NL41.pdf.

9. The term anthropocene is attempting to define the human species as a geological force; see Crutzen and Stoermer. It is a source of much debate as to whether such a geological period exists and, if so, how it should be defined, and a great deal has been written on the topic; of particular relevance to digital humanists are Chakrabarty; Boes and Marshall; and especially Nowviskie.

10. See Dyer-Witheford and de Peuter for a Marxist take on similar questions in the context of the digital gaming industry.

11. http://www.media-ecology.org.

12. http://dhdebates.gc.cuny.edu/debates/text/38.

13. http://dhdebates.gc.cuny.edu/debates/text/22.

14. Indeed, this may have contributed to media ecology's survival during the decades of McLuhan's decline (roughly mid-1970s to mid-1990s) as well as his recuperation as media prophet of the cyber age, represented in his resuscitation by *Wired* magazine in the early 1990s as the patron saint of digital culture.

15. http://www.sierraclub.org.

16. Muir, who founded the Sierra Club in 1892, is known for observing that "when we try to pick out any thing by itself, we find it hitched to everything else in the universe. See Muir, as well as the Sierra Club website for a discussion of this quote and its source: http://vault.sierraclub.org/john_muir_exhibit/writings/favorite_quotations.aspx; http://vault .sierraclub.org/john_muir_exhibit/writings/my_first_summer_in_the_sierra/chapter_6.

17. Media Ecology Association, "What Is Media Ecology?" http://www.media-ecology .org/media_ecology/#What%20is%20Media%20Ecology?%20%28Neil%20Postman%29.

18. http://www.digitalhumanities.org/companion/view?docId=blackwell/978 1405103213/9781405103213.xml&chunk.id=ss1-1-3&toc.depth=1&toc.id=ss1-1-3&brand =default.

19. http://digitalhumanities.org:3030/companion/view?docId=blackwell/978 1405103213/9781405103213.xml&chunk.id=ss1-2-4&toc.depth=1&toc.id=ss1-2-4&brand =9781405103213_brand.

20. http://digitalhumanities.org:3030/companion/view?docId=blackwell/978 1405103213/9781405103213.xml&chunk.id=ss1-4-3&toc.depth=1&toc.id=ss1-4-3&brand =9781405103213_brand.

21. In chapter 31 of this volume, " 'Black Printers' on White Cards," Molly O'Hagan Hardy argues that book historians (without whom the bibliographic metadata infrastructure of the humanities would not exist) have always been keenly aware of how data is structured; data not only emerges from a partial and historically specific place but cannot be separated from what Johanna Drucker terms "capta" or interpretation ("Humanistic Theory," 89).

22. http://www.digitalhumanities.org/companion/view?docId=blackwell/ 9781405103213/9781405103213.xml&chunk.id=ss1-5-4&toc.depth=1&toc.id=ss1-5-4 &brand=default.

23. http://dhdebates.gc.cuny.edu/book.

24. http://dhdebates.gc.cuny.edu/debates/text/34.

25. http://dhdebates.gc.cuny.edu/debates/text/11.

26. http://thebreakthrough.org/index.php/journal/past-issues/issue-2/love -your-monsters.

27. http://nowviskie.org/2014/anthropocene.

28. On the longevity of this debate see, for example, Gifford, 15; Bate, 19; McKusick, 15 and 17; Dewey Hall, 121.

29. On the ecological tradition see, for example, Worster; McIntosh; Clark; Egerton; and Westling.

30. Heise, 22–28. See also Jasanoff, 310–22; Cosgrove, 254–67; Paul Edwards, 1–3; and Sloterdijk, 19–26.

31. http://www.foe.org/about-us.

32. http://www.earthday.org/earth-day-history-movement.

33. http://nowviskie.org/2014/anthropocene.

34. For more about the anthropocene, see the International Geosphere-Biosphere Programme, http://www.igbp.net/globalchange/anthropocene.4.1b8ae20512db692f2a 680009238.html.

35. See Laue's brief but excellent discussion of the centrality of biological metaphors that inform cybernetics and systems theory and in turn frame computer architecture ("How a Computer Works"). The history of twentieth-century cybernetics presented in N. Katherine Hayles's now classic study, *How We Became Posthuman,* is reworked in provocative new directions in Johnston (*The Allure of Machinic Life*); Lydia Liu (*The Freudian Robot*); and Halpern (*Beautiful Data*).

36. Gregory Bateson, "Creative Imagination," cited in Kaizen. In his analysis of play among animals, Bateson concluded that "metacommunication" was necessary and thus not unique to humans; see "Theory of Play and Fantasy," also cited in Kaizen.

37. TAPoR, Discover Research Tools for Textual Study, http://www.tapor.ca/.

38. Johanna Drucker similarly argues in *A Companion to Digital Humanities* in favor of exploring and incorporating speculative methods of inquiry into digital humanities scholarship and especially to experiment with procedures that might produce "aesthetic provocation" (Drucker with Nowviskie "Speculative Computing," 443). Almost a decade later, she finds not much has changed. Interface design is "stuck in print imitation" limiting explorations of new hybrid, fluid, and n-dimensional screen spaces ("Diagrammatic Writing," 100).

39. https://litlab.stanford.edu.

40. http://txtlab.org.

41. Eugene Thacker defines "bioinformatics" as the science and business that arises at the nexus of molecular biology, math, statistics, and computing methods applied to solve biological problems (*Biomedia*, 32–62). Stacy Alaimo defines "trans-corporeality" as the contact zone between human bodies and more-than-human nature, underlining the enmeshment between humans and ecologies (11–22).

42. http://vxheaven.org/lib/mjp02.html.

43. See also Thacker's essays on the conceptual underpinnings of network thinking in relationships between technology, biology, and politics ("Networks, Swarms, Multitudes: Part One" and "Part Two").

44. Johanna Drucker examines the notion of interface as a boundary space, suggesting that the "ambient triggers" and "smart" environments offering commercial and cultural opportunities for the integration of stored and programmed information into daily life will "increasingly make the world we navigate into an interface" ("Reading Interface," 218).

45. http://digitalhumanities.org/dhq/vol/7/1/000143/000143.html.

46. http://mediacommons.futureofthebook.org/content/cultural-politics-critique-and-digital-humanities.

47. http://dhdebates.gc.cuny.edu/debates/text/14.

48. http://dhdebates.gc.cuny.edu/debates/text/31.

BIBLIOGRAPHY

Alaimo, Stacy. *Bodily Natures: Science, Environment, and the Material Self.* Bloomington: Indiana University Press, 2010.

Bate, Jonathan. *Romantic Ecology: Wordsworth and the Environmental Tradition.* London: Routledge, 1991.

Bateson, Gregory. *Steps to an Ecology of Mind.* Chicago and London: University of Chicago Press, 2000.

Blanke, Tobias. *Digital Asset Ecosystems: Rethinking Clouds and Crowds.* Oxford: Chandos Publishing, 2014.

Bode, Katherine. *Reading by Numbers: Recalibrating the Literary Field.* London: Anthem, 2012.

Boes, Tobias, and Kate Marshall. "Writing the Anthropocene: An Introduction." *Minnesota Review* 83 (2014): 60–72.

Bolter, Jay David, and Richard Grusin. *Remediation: Understanding New Media.* Cambridge, Mass.: MIT Press, 1999.

Cali, Dennis D. "On Disciplining Media Ecology." *Explorations in Media Ecology* 10, no. 3–4 (2012): 335–46.

Chakrabarty, Dipesh. "The Climate of History: Four Theses." *Critical Inquiry* 35, no. 2 (Winter 2009): 197–222.

Clark, Timothy. *The Cambridge Introduction to Literature and the Environment.* Cambridge: Cambridge University Press, 2011.

Coole, Diana, and Samantha Frost. "Introducing the New Materialisms." In *New Materialisms: Ontology, Agency, and Politics,* ed. Diana Coole and Samantha Frost, 1–43. Durham, N.C.: Duke University Press, 2010.

Cosgrove, Denis. *Apollo's Eye: A Cartographic Genealogy of the Earth in the Western Imagination.* Baltimore: Johns Hopkins University Press, 2001.

Crane, Greg. "Classics and the Computer: An End of the History." In *A Companion to Digital Humanities,* ed. Susan Schreibman, Ray Siemens, and John Unsworth, 46–55. Oxford: Blackwell, 2004. http://digitalhumanities.org:3030/companion/view?docId=blackwell/9781405103213/9781405103213.xml&chunk.id=ss1-2-4&toc.depth=1&toc.id=ss1-2-4&brand=9781405103213_brand.

Crutzen, Paul J., and Eugene F. Stoermer. "The Anthropocene." *IGBP Newsletter* 41 (May 2000): 17–18. http://www.igbp.net/download/18.316f18321323470177580001401/NL41.pdf.

Darwin, Charles. *The Origin of Species: A Variorum Text,* ed. Morse Peckham. Philadelphia: University of Pennsylvania Press, 1959.

Deibert, Ronald J. *Parchment, Print, and Hypermedia: Communication in World Order Transformation.* New York: Columbia University Press, 1997.

Drucker, Johanna. "Diagrammatic Writing." *New Formations* 78 (2013): 83–101.

———. "Humanistic Theory and Digital Scholarship." In *Debates in the Digital Humanities,* ed. Matthew K. Gold, 85–95. Minneapolis: University of Minnesota Press, 2012. http://dhdebates.gc.cuny.edu/debates/text/34.

———. "Performative Materiality and Theoretical Approaches to Interface." *DHQ* 7, no. 1 (2013). http://digitalhumanities.org/dhq/vol/7/1/000143/000143.html.

———. "Reading Interface." *PMLA* 128, no. 1 (January 2013): 213–20.

Drucker, Johanna with Bethany Nowviskie. "Speculative Computing: Aesthetic Provocations in Humanities Computing." In *A Companion to Digital Humanities,* ed. Susan Schreibman, Ray Siemens, and John Unsworth, 431–47. Oxford: Blackwell, 2004. http://digitalhumanities.org:3030/companion/view?docId=blackwell/9781405103213/9781405103213.xml&chunk.id=ss1-4-10&toc.depth=1&toc.id=ss1-4-10&brand=9781405103213_brand.

Dyer-Witheford, Nick, and Greig de Peuter. *Games of Empire: Global Capitalism and Video Games.* Minneapolis: University of Minnesota Press, 2009.

Edwards, Charlie. "The Digital Humanities and Its Users." In *Debates in the Digital Humanities*, ed. Matthew K. Gold, 213–32. Minneapolis: University of Minnesota Press, 2012. http://dhdebates.gc.cuny.edu/debates/text/31.

Edwards, Paul N. *A Vast Machine: Computer Models, Climate Data, and the Politics of Global Warming*. Cambridge, Mass: MIT Press, 2010.

Egerton, Frank N. *Roots of Ecology: Antiquity to Haeckel*. Berkeley: University of California Press, 2012.

Ernst, Wolfgang. *Digital Memory and the Archive*, ed. Jussi Parikka. Minneapolis: University of Minnesota Press, 2013.

Fuller, Matthew. *Media Ecologies: Materialist Energies in Art and Technology*. Cambridge, Mass.: MIT Press, 2005.

Gifford, Terry. *Green Voices: Understanding Contemporary Nature Poetry*. Manchester: Manchester University Press, 1995

Gitelman, Lisa, and Virginia Jackson. *"Raw Data" Is an Oxymoron*. Cambridge, Mass.: MIT Press, 2013.

Gitelman, Lisa, and Geoffrey G. Pingree. "Introduction: What's New about New Media?" In *New Media, 1740–1915*, eds. Lisa Gitelman and Geoffrey B. Pingree, xi–xxxiv. Cambridge, Mass.: MIT Press, 2003.

Gold, Matthew. "Facts, Patterns, Methods, Meaning: Public Knowledge Building in the Digital Humanities." *The Lapland Chronicles* (blog), April 20, 1015. http://blog.mkgold.net/2015/04/20/facts-patterns-methods-meaning-public-knowledge-building-in-the-digital-humanities/.

Hall, Dewey W. *Romantic Naturalists, Early Environmentalists: An Ecocritical Study, 1789–1912*. Burlington, Vt.: Ashgate, 2014.

Hall, Gary. "Has Critical Theory Run Out of Time for Data-Driven Scholarship?" In *Debates in the Digital Humanities*, ed. Matthew K. Gold, 127–32. Minneapolis: University of Minnesota Press, 2012. http://dhdebates.gc.cuny.edu/debates/text/14.

Halpern, Orit. *Beautiful Data: A History of Vision and Reason since 1945*. Durham, N.C.: Duke University Press, 2014.

Hayles, N. Katherine. *Electronic Literature: New Horizons for the Literary*. Notre Dame, Ind.: University of Notre Dame Press, 2008.

———. *How We Became Posthuman: Virtual Bodies in Cybernetics, Literature, and Informatics*. Chicago: University of Chicago Press, 1999.

Hayles, N. Katherine, and Jessica Pressman, eds. *Comparative Textual Media: Transforming the Humanities in the Postprint Era*. Minneapolis: University of Minnesota Press, 2013.

Heise, Ursula K. *Sense of Place and Sense of Plant: The Environmental Imagination of the Global*. Oxford: Oxford University Press, 2008.

———. "Unnatural Ecologies: The Metaphor of the Environment in Media Theory." *Configurations* 10, no. 1 (Winter 2002): 149–68. http://muse.jhu.edu/journals/con/summary/v010/10.1heise.html.

Higgin, Tanner. "Cultural Politics, Critique, and the Digital Humanities." *Media Commons*, May 25, 2010. http://mediacommons.futureofthebook.org/content/cultural-politics-critique-and-digital-humanities.

Hockey, Susan. "The History of Humanities Computing. In *A Companion to Digital Humanities,* ed. Susan Schreibman, Ray Siemens, and John Unsworth, 3–19. Oxford: Blackwell, 2004. http://digitalhumanities.org:3030/companion/view?docId=blackwell/9781405103213/9781405103213.xml&chunk.id=ss1-2-1&toc.depth=1&toc.id=ss1-2-1&brand=9781405103213_brand.

Huggan, Graham, and Helen Tiffan. *Postcolonial Ecocriticism: Literature, Animals, Environment.* New York: Routledge, 2010.

Jasanoff, Sheila. "Image and Imagination: The Formation of Global Environmental Consciousness." In *Changing the Atmosphere: Expert Knowledge and Environmental Governance,* ed. Clark A. Miller and Paul N. Edwards, 309–37. Cambridge, Mass.: MIT Press, 2001.

Jockers, Matthew L. *Macroanalysis: Digital Methods and Literary History.* Urbana: University of Illinois Press, 2013.

Johnston, John. *The Allure of Machinic Life: Cybernetics, Artificial Life, and the New AI.* Cambridge, Mass.: MIT Press, 2008.

Jones, Steven E. *The Emergence of Digital Humanities.* New York: Routledge, 2014.

Kaizen, William. "Steps to an Ecology of Communication: *Radical Software,* Dan Graham, and the Legacy of Gregory Bateson." *Art Journal* 67, no. 3 (2008): 87–107.

Kirschenbaum, Matthew G. " 'So the Colors Cover the Wires': Interface, Aesthetics, and Usability. In *A Companion to Digital Humanities*, eds. Susan Schreibman, Ray Siemens, and John Unsworth, 523–42. Oxford: Blackwell, 2004. http://www.digitalhumanities.org/companion/view?docId=blackwell/9781405103213/9781405103213.xml&chunk.id=ss1-5-4&toc.depth=1&toc.id=ss1-5-4&brand=default.

———. "What Is Digital Humanities and What's It Doing in English Departments?" In *Debates in the Digital Humanities,* ed. Matthew K. Gold, 3–11. Minneapolis: University of Minnesota Press, 2012. http://dhdebates.gc.cuny.edu/debates/text/38.

Latour, Bruno. "Love Your Monsters: Why We Must Care for Our Technologies as We Do Our Children." *The Breakthrough Journal,* Winter 2012. http://thebreakthrough.org/index.php/journal/past-issues/issue-2/love-your-monsters.

Laue, Andrea. "How the Computer Works." In *A Companion to Digital Humanities,* ed. Susan Schreibman, Ray Siemens, and John Unsworth, 145–60. Oxford: Blackwell, 2004. http://digitalhumanities.org:3030/companion/view?docId=blackwell/9781405103213/9781405103213.xml&chunk.id=ss1-3-1&toc.depth=1&toc.id=ss1-3-1&brand=9781405103213_brand.

Liu, Alan. "Imagining the New Media Encounter." In *A Companion to Digital Literary Studies,* ed. Susan Schreibman and Ray Siemens. Oxford: Blackwell, 2008. http://www.digitalhumanities.org/companion/view?docId=blackwell/9781405148641/9781405148641.xml&chunk.id=ss1-3-1&toc.depth=1&toc.id=ss1-3-1&brand=9781405148641_brand.

———. "The Meaning of the Digital Humanities." *PMLA* 128, no. 2 (March 2013): 409–23.

———. "The State of the Digital Humanities: A Report and a Critique." *Arts and Humanities in Higher Education* 11, no. 8 (2012): 8–41.

———. *Wordsworth: The Sense of History.* Stanford: Stanford University Press, 1989.

Liu, Lydia. *The Freudian Robot: Digital Media and the Future of the Unconscious.* Chicago: University of Chicago Press, 2010.

Lum, Casey Man Kong. "Notes Toward an Intellectual History of Media Ecology." In *Perspectives on Culture, Technology and Communication: The Ecology Tradition,* ed. Casey Man Kong Lum, 1–60. Cresskill, N.J.: Hampton, 2006.

Manovich, Lev. *Software Takes Command.* London: Bloomsbury, 2013.

Marciano, Richard. "Big Humanities Data Space." October 21, 2013. http://bighumanities.net/.

Maturana, Humberto R., and Francisco J. Varela. *Autopoiesis and Cognition: The Realization of the Living.* London: D. Reidel, 1972.

McGann, Jerome. "Marking Texts of Many Dimensions." In *A Companion to Digital Humanities,* ed. Susan Schreibman, Ray Siemens, and John Unsworth, 198–217. Oxford: Blackwell, 2004. http://digitalhumanities.org:3030/companion/view?docId=blackwell/9781405103213/9781405103213.xml&chunk.id=ss1-3-4&toc.depth=1&toc.id=ss1-3-4&brand=9781405103213_brand.

———. *A New Republic of Letters: Memory and Scholarship in the Age of Digital Reproduction.* Cambridge, Mass.: Harvard University Press, 2014.

McIntosh, Robert P. *The Background of Ecology: Concept and Theory.* New York: Cambridge University Press, 1985.

McKusick, James. *Green Writing: Romanticism and Ecology.* New York: St. Martin's, 2000.

McLuhan, Marshall. "At the Moment of Sputnik the Planet Became a Global Theater in which There Are No Spectators but Only Actors." *Journal of Communication* 24, no. 1 (March 1974): 48–58.

———. *Understanding Media: The Extensions of Man.* Cambridge, Mass.: MIT Press, 1994.

Michel, Jean-Baptiste, Yuan Kui Shen, Aviva Presser Aiden, Adrian Veres, Matthew K. Gray, The Google Books Team, and Joseph P. Pickett. "Quantitative Analysis of Culture Using Millions of Digitized Books." *Science* 331 (January 2011): 176–82. http://www.sciencemag.org/content/331/6014/176.

Moretti, Franco. *Distant Reading.* New York: Verso, 2013.

———. *Graphs, Maps, Trees: Abstract Models for Literary History.* London: Verso, 2005.

Morton, Timothy. *The Ecological Thought.* Cambridge, Mass.: Harvard University Press, 2010.

Muir, John. *My First Summer in the Sierra.* Boston and New York: Houghton Mifflin, 1911. http://vault.sierraclub.org/john_muir_exhibit/writings/my_first_summer_in_the_sierra/.

Nardi, Bonnie A., and Vicki O'Day. *Information Ecologies: Using Technology with Heart.* Cambridge, Mass.: MIT Press, 1999.

Nowviskie, Bethany. "Digital Humanities in the Anthropocene," Author's blog, July 10, 2014. http://nowviskie.org/2014/anthropocene/.

Ong, Walter J. *Rhetoric, Romance, and Technology: Studies in the Interaction of Expression and Culture.* Ithaca, N.Y.: Cornell University Press, 1971.

Parikka, Jussi. *Geology of Media.* Minneapolis: University of Minnesota Press, 2015.

———. "The Universal Viral Machine: Bits, Parasites, and the Media Ecology of Network Culture." *CTheory,* December 2005. http://vxheaven.org/lib/mjp02.html.

———. *What Is Media Archaeology?* Cambridge: Polity, 2012.

Piper, Andrew. "Reading's Refrain: From Bibliography to Topology." *ELH* 80, no. 2 (2013): 373–99.

Piper, Andrew, and Mark Algee-Hewitt. "The Werther Effect 1: Goethe, Objecthood, and the Handling of Knowledge." In *Distant Readings: Topologies of German Culture in the Long Nineteenth Century,* ed. Matt Erlin and Lynn Tatlock, 155–84. Rochester, N.Y.: Camden House, 2014.

Postman, Neil. "The Day Our Children Disappear: Predications of a Media Ecologist." *The Phi Delta Kappan* 62, no. 5 (January 1981): 382–86.

———. *Technopoloy: The Surrender of Culture to Technology.* New York: Vintage, 1993.

Ramsay, Stephen. "On Building." Author's blog, January 11, 2011. http://stephenramsay .us/text/2011/01/11/on-building/.

Ramsay, Stephen, and Geoffrey Rockwell, "Developing Things: Notes Toward an Epistemology of Building in the Digital Humanities. In *Debates in the Digital Humanities,* ed. Matthew K. Gold, 75–84. Minneapolis: University of Minnesota Press, 2012. http:// dhdebates.gc.cuny.edu/debates/text/11.

Schreibman, Susan, Ray Siemens, and John Unsworth. "The Digital Humanities and Humanities Computing: An Introduction." In *A Companion to Digital Humanities,* eds. Susan Schreibman, Ray Siemens, and John Unsworth, xxiii–xxvii. Oxford: Blackwell, 2004. http://digitalhumanities.org:3030/companion/view?docId=blackwell /9781405103213/9781405103213.xml&chunk.id=ss1-1-3&toc.depth=1&toc.id=ss1 -1-3&brand=9781405103213_brand.

Schulz, Kathryn. "What Is Distant Reading?" *New York Times Book Review,* June 24, 2011. http://www.nytimes.com/2011/06/26/books/review/the-mechanic-muse-what-is-distant-reading.html?_r=0.

Scolari, Carlos A. "Media Ecology: Exploring the Metaphor to Expand the Theory." *Communication Theory* 22 (2012): 204–25.

Serlen, Rachel. "The Distant Future? Reading Franco Moretti." *Literature Compass* 7, no. 3 (2010): 214–25.

Sloterdijk, Peter. *In the World of Interior Capital: For a Philosophical Theory of Globalization,* trans. Wieland Hoban. Cambridge: Polity, 2013.

Smith, Martha Nell. "Electronic Scholarly Editing." In *A Companion to Digital Humanities,* ed. Susan Schreibman, Ray Siemens, and John Unsworth, 306–22. Oxford: Blackwell, 2004. http://digitalhumanities.org:3030/companion/view?docId=black well/9781405103213/9781405103213.xml&chunk.id=ss1-4-3&toc.depth=1&toc. id=ss1-4-3&brand=9781405103213_brand.

Strate, Lance. "Studying Media *as* Media: McLuhan and the Media Ecology Approach." *MediaTropes* 1 (2008): 127–42. http://www.mediatropes.com/index.php/Mediatropes /article/view/3344/1488.

Svensson, Patrik. "Beyond the Big Tent." In *Debates in the Digital Humanities,* ed. Matthew K. Gold, 36–49. Minneapolis: University of Minnesota Press, 2012. http://dhdebates.gc .cuny.edu/debates/text/22.

Thacker, Eugene. *Biomedia.* Minneapolis: University of Minnesota Press, 2004.

———. "Networks, Swarms, Multitudes: Part One." *CTheory,* May 18, 2004. http://www .ctheory.net/articles.aspx?id=422.

———. "Networks, Swarms, Multitudes: Part Two." *CTheory,* May 18, 2004. http://www .ctheory.net/articles.aspx?id=423.

Thill, Scott. "July 21, 1911: Media Messenger McLuhan Born." *Wired,* July 21, 2010. http:// www.wired.com/2010/07/0721marshall-mcluhan-born/.

Weingart, Scott. "Liveblogged Review of *Macroanalysis* by Matthew L. Jockers, Part 1." *The Scottbot Irregular* (blog), April 14, 2013. http://www.scottbot.net/HIAL/?p=34566.

Westling, Louise, ed. *The Cambridge Companion to Literature and the Environment.* Cambridge: Cambridge University Press, 2014.

Worster, Donald. *Nature's Economy: A History of Ecological Ideas.* Cambridge: Cambridge University Press, 1994.

Zielinski, Siegfried. *Deep Time of the Media: Toward an Archaeology of Hearing and Seeing by Technical Means,* trans. Gloria Custance. Cambridge, Mass.: MIT Press, 2006.

Toward a Cultural Critique of Digital Humanities

DOMENICO FIORMONTE

The English texts of non-native writers cannot be assumed to reflect their vernacular discourses.

—A. Suresh Canagarajah, *Geopolitics of Academic Writing*

[Nisargadatta] Maharaj said quite often that books get written; they are never written by authors. Only a little thought is necessary to see the truth of what he meant. He was NOT referring only to books on spiritual matters; he was referring to all *books. In the overall functioning of the manifested universe, whatever was necessary as written or spoken words appeared spontaneously. . . . No credit or blame could attach to any individual writer for the simple reason that the individual is a mere illusion and has not autonomous existence.*

—Ramesh S. Balsekar, *Experience of Immortality*

The Last Dinosaurs

Is there a non-Anglo-American digital humanities (DH), and if so, what are its characteristics? A number of eminent European scholars, especially Dino Buzzetti, Tito Orlandi, and Manfred Thaller, identify differences in methodology as the key criterion distinguishing several DH approaches (i.e., continental versus Anglo-American DH). I agree that methodological issues are very important, but I do not see our two opinions (i.e., methodological versus cultural monopolization) in strong conflict. Of course, much depends on what we mean by "culture" and "methodology." There has always been an attempt in Anglo-American DH/Humanities Computing to maintain a methodological dominion (and dominance) in terms of applications, standards, and protocols. This is natural in any situation of competition. Besides, to assume that the root of this dominion is cultural does not mean to deny that a methodological monopolization exists. But where do the "monopolies" come from? Methodologies are sets of interconnected discourses about procedures and rules that arise from dominant cultural visions. Any distinction or genealogic attempt reminds me of the obstinate persistence of the Aristotelian form/content dichotomy, and this simple dualistic approach does not reflect the multilayered nature of cultural objects. One of the core assumptions of my own approach to DH is that any human-born knowledge (including computer science) is subject to the *cultural law of the artifact* (Vygotsky, *Mind in Society*; *Thought and Language*). This law affirms that both material and cognitive artifacts produced by humans are subject to the influence of the environment, culture, and social habits of the individual and groups that devise and make use of them. The artifact influences and at the same time is influenced by its context; in other words, technology is always a part of culture, not a cause or an effect of it (Slack and Wise, 4, 112).

Given this perspective, it is clear that answering our opening question (is there a non-Anglo-American DH?) is far less simple than one could expect. From the historical point of view, it would be easy to answer "yes" since, for example, Italian "Informatica Umanistica" has a strong tradition and a long history.[1] But from the point of view of the scientific results, research projects, and institutional presence, Informatica Umanistica, like most of the "other" DH practiced in the world, practically does not exist. The reason for such a partial or total invisibility (depending, of course, on the countries and the observer) is no mystery: the indisputable Anglo-American hegemony in the academic research field. This phenomenon, certainly complex and debated, is perfectly summarized by Suresh Canagarajah (*Geopolitics of Academic Writing*) in the famous story of Chinese dinosaurs. In April 1997, the *New York Times* published an article titled "In China, a Spectacular Trove of Dinosaurs Fossils Is Found." Although the discovery had been made around one year earlier, the American newspaper reported the news in that moment (April 25, 1997) because it was publicly announced by Western scientists the day before, during a conference at the Academy of Natural Sciences at Philadelphia:

> The discovery had been made by a Chinese farmer. The date he discovered the site is not given anywhere in the report. His name is also not given. The name of the international team and their university affiliations are, on the other hand, cited very prominently. . . . When the newspaper claims that "the spectacular trove was not announced until today" there are many questions that arise in our minds. Announced *by* whom? *To* whom? . . . The whole world, it is claimed, knows about the fossils after the announcement at the Philadelphia conference. It is as if the finding is real only when the West gets to know about it. It is at that point that the discovery is recognized as a "fact" and constitutes legitimate knowledge. Whatever preceded that point is pushed into oblivion. (Canagarajah, 1–2)

Having said that, the aim of this paper is not to question the prestige of Anglo-American colleagues, reverse the current hierarchies, or propose new and more objective rankings of DH work and geopolitical presence. Peripheral cultures do not need any revenge or, worse, any seat at the winner's table, and that is why the aim of this paper is simply to acknowledge a situation, evaluating it for itself and perhaps suggesting that a different model is possible.

Forms of the Crisis

In the last ten years, the extended colonization, both material and symbolical, of digital technologies has completely overwhelmed the research and educational world. Digitalization has become not only a vogue or an imperative, but a normality. In this sort of digital "gold rush," the digital humanities perhaps have been losing their original openness and revolutionary potential. If we want to win them back and, at the same time, move forward, it is important to start from the analysis of the most relevant DH bottlenecks.

The first identifiable gap has to do with the slight tendency of DH to develop what French sociologist Pierre Bourdieu has called "a theoretical model for reflecting critically on the instruments through which we think of reality" (Bourdieu and Chartier, 47). Or rather, when new tools are created, one reflects on their use or their impact, but what is most important, namely their cultural foundation, is only rarely considered. In other words, it is as if DH has always started from the "results" without considering the entire process that led to them. Alan Liu in the previous volume of *Debates* expressed concerns about the "lack of cultural criticism" (Liu, 492) of DH, and with a very appropriate image (in complete contrast to mainstream tendencies), calling for the foundation of an "intellectual infrastructure" for the digital humanities. By underlining, among other things, the "political" limits of the instrumentalist approach, Liu's article was a breath of fresh air in the Anglo-American context, even though it did not address the geopolitical unbalance and the economic interests that operate at the heart of the DH system.

The reluctance of DH to reflect on the origins of its objectives has various causes, but there is no doubt that the historical character of the humanities disciplines has contributed to an excessive concentration on conservation, management, and data analysis, while neglecting the more revolutionary contribution (in both a positive and a negative sense) of computing and its capacity to affect research processes even before they produce anything.[2]

Another, more concrete, limitation concerns the geopolitical and the cultural-linguistic composition of the discipline, and hence the tools used (Fiormonte, "Il dibattito"). The problems here, although deeply entangled, are of two types:

a) The composition of the government organs, institutions, etc., inspiring and managing the processes, strategies, and ultimately the research methodologies (thus affecting also the visibility of the results).

b) The cultural-linguistic nuances and features of the tools (see Fiormonte, "Il testo digitale"; "Chi l'ha visto?").

Within this second category one can also identify:

b1) The cultural and political problem of software and platform (e.g., social networks) almost exclusively produced in the Anglo-American environment.

b2) The cultural-semiotic problem of the different tools of representation from the icons of the graphical interfaces to the Unicode standards, from the proxemics of *Second Life* to the universal concept of usability, etc.

The following section will focus primarily on the DH governance and the cultural-semiotic problems, sacrificing for reasons of space the other important issues. But proceeding in order, we start with the institutional and organizational structures.

Geopolitics of DH (and Beyond)

The influences of the coding system are in general pervasive, because they are usually accepted as the unquestioned standard. Each medium and its corresponding technical realization, as Harold Innis explained, implies a *bias* of communication, and is subject to the "cultural law" mentioned previously. A banal example is the long dominion of the 7 bit ASCII code (American Standard Code for Information Interchange), which has been the character set used by most computing platforms—the Web included—for more than forty years. The same technocultural bias also affects most of the services and instruments of the network (e.g., the domain name system). For the last forty years, it has not been possible to use accented vowels in a URL address, and in spite of IETF and ICANN efforts[3] the new *Internationalizing Domain Names in Applications* (IDNA) system can be implemented only in applications that are specifically designed for it, and is hardly used in Latin alphabet-based URLs. Some of the original top-level domains can be used only by U.S. institutions. For example, a European university cannot use the top-level domain .edu, which was and is still reserved only for U.S. academic institutions. The domain .eu could not be used as a top-level domain until 2006, and applications for top-level domains using characters outside of ISO-Latin were invited only more recently (requests were open from January 12 to April 12, 2012). The Internet Corporation for Assigned Names and Numbers (ICANN) finally allowed the opening up of top-level domains to Arabic or Chinese characters, included in Unicode, but every decision seems in the hands of an organization under the clear control of Western (and especially U.S.) industries and governments. We see evidence of this control in many ways. For example, the request procedure is very complicated, many of the rules are described only in English, the cost of the application is $185,000, and the application does not guarantee that the request will be accepted. The applying institution needs to show a clear technical and financial capability that must be certified discretionally by ICANN itself. The problem is that ICANN, although it has always taken decisions of global relevance, still lacks clear institutional and multi-stakeholder accountability.[4]

ICANN was founded in Marina del Rey, California, in September 1998, and up to 2009 was controlled by the U.S. Department of Commerce.[5] Until 2012 the CEO of ICANN was Rod Beckstrom, past president of the National Cybersecurity Center (NCSC) for the Department of Homeland Security—an impeccable pedigree for a cybercop but a less-than-desirable qualification for a manager of a shared resource such as the Internet.[6]

And in areas closest to the hearts of humanists, the power structures do not appear to be any less discouraging. Unicode is a case in point. By its own definition the Unicode Consortium is, at least in theory, a nonprofit organization "devoted to developing, maintaining, and promoting software internationalization standards and data, particularly the Unicode Standard, which specifies the representation of text in all modern software products and standards."[7] Its board of directors is currently composed of representatives from Google (one member), Microsoft (two members), Apple (one member), Intel (one member), IBM (one member), and IMS/Appature (one member). President of the Executive Office is Mark Davies, founder of Unicode and Google engineer since 2006. UC Berkley is the only educational organization represented (one of several Technical officers),[8] and no public institution appears to be represented either on a technical or managing level. Seen realistically, Unicode is an industrial standard controlled by the industry. And claims about the neutrality or impartiality of this organization appear to be at least questionable.

If this can be taken as a credible example of the global situation, it is clear that digital humanities must also be affected, as most of us are paid by public institutions that have educational aims but are forced to work with protocols, standards, and tools originally designed for the commercial interests of (mostly Anglophone) private companies.

Compared to a survey carried out in 2001 (Fiormonte, "Il dibattito"), even though so much effort has been expended in making existing DH associations and organizations more international, the impression remains the same: a solid Anglo-American stem onto which several individuals of mostly European countries are grafted. Figure 35.1 shows how boards and committees of the eight top DH international organizations (four associations, one network, one consortium, and two journals) are composed.[9] The data are organized by country of institutional affiliation—that is, what is shown is not the country of origin of the member, but the place where the individual appears to work. Figure 35.2 aggregates data from the same organizations and shows the effect of multiple appointments; namely, how committees and boards tend to replicate themselves, sometimes appointing the same people for up to five different organizations. These roughly collected data may be insufficient to demonstrate that current top DH organizations suffer from ethnocentrism, but they certainly point out a geopolitical and linguistic unbalance.

Of course, initiatives such as CenterNet, ADHO (Alliance of Digital Humanities Organizations[10]), and CHAIN (Coalition of Humanities and Arts Infrastructures and Networks) have the merit of gathering and registering the major realities of the

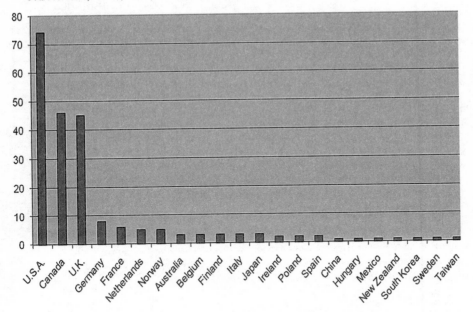

Figure 35.1. DH organizations: presence of individuals by country of institutional affiliation.

Anglophone axis (USA–Canada–U.K.–Australia), but this is just a self-strengthening operation of existing identities rather than actual knowledge sharing or exploration of other cultures, methodologies, or practices.

Consider also the monolingualism of the aforementioned sites and organizations. Their rhetorical structure does not leave space for anything but the "inner" Anglo-American rhetoric and academic narrative (Canagarajah, 109–127). Furthermore, the self-report of some initiatives, such as Melissa Terras's *flatland*, contributed to presenting the digital humanities as an empire made of two macro-kingdoms, the United States and the United Kingdom, about which orbit a few satellites.

These sort of universalistic representations (or self-representations) appear only to reveal the actual state of subordination from which non-English-speaking digital humanists suffer; a situation that is triggered the very moment we use the label "digital humanities."

One exception to this scenario is the THATCamp[11] un-conference series, which is becoming a good opportunity for peripheral communities to share alternative views of what the digital humanities are or could be.[12] This seemed to be the case of the Humanistica.eu initiative, a project launched at THATCamp Florence in 2011[13] for creating a European Association of DH: a "new common space for nurturing and practicing this discipline from a genuine multi-cultural and multi-lingual perspective," as can be read on the website.

	ACH	ADHO	ALLC	CNet	DHQ	LLC	SDH-SEMI	TEI
John Unsworth (5)		///		///	///	///		///
Melissa Terras (5)		///	///	///	///	///		
Geoffrey Rockwell (4)	⋮⋮			⋮⋮	⋮⋮		⋮⋮	
Michael Eberle-Sinatra (4)		⋮⋮		⋮⋮		⋮⋮	⋮⋮	
Ray Siemens (4)		⋮⋮		⋮⋮		⋮⋮	⋮⋮	
Stéfan Sinclair (4)	⋮⋮			⋮⋮	⋮⋮	⋮⋮		
Susan Brown (4)	⋮⋮			⋮⋮		⋮⋮	⋮⋮	
Bethany Nowviskie (3)	★★	★★		★★				
Daniel O'Donnell (3)		★★				★★	★★	
Jan Christoph Meister (3)			★★	★★	★★			
Lisa Lena Opas-Hänninen (3)		★★	★★			★★		
Lorna Hughes (3)		★★		★★		★★		
Neil Fraistat (3)	★★	★★		★★				
Susan Hockey (3)					★★	★★	★★	
Willard McCarty (3)	★★				★★	★★		

Figure 35.2. Multiple or cross-appointments top-list. In cross-hatching are shown people who appear in five organizations; those in four organizations are shown with dots; and those with stars are in three organizations.

In this perspective, I could go on with further considerations regarding the cultural and epistemic bias implied in the markup languages as well as in the solutions proposed by TEI.[14] However, I would rather focus on relaunching the fundamental question of the importance, especially in the humanities and social sciences, of the *residual categories.*

> Any attempt to create an obligatory system of classification, rigid and universal, will result in residual categories. . . . It is necessary to root the awareness of what happens every time one tries to standardize. In other words, that in this creation there is someone who wins and someone who loses. This not a simple question, nor a matter easy to analyze. (Bowker and Star, "Intervista su società," 13)

The problem of the crisis (which is also one of self-esteem) in the humanities[15] could be summarized as the constitutive necessity to continue to exist, to be always on the margins, to be a hybrid, a variant of the system. And it is here that the first obstacle arises: the potential friction between the role of DH and that of the humanities, because it is clear that a revival or at least a revitalization, which is not a simple defense of what already exists, cannot be realized without a critique of the economical and geopolitical interests that lie beyond the universe of the Internet and its applications. It appears that digital humanities is the victim of a continuous paradox: demonstrating an ability to keep up with technologies (and with their owners and gatekeepers) and, at the same time, not to become subject to them.

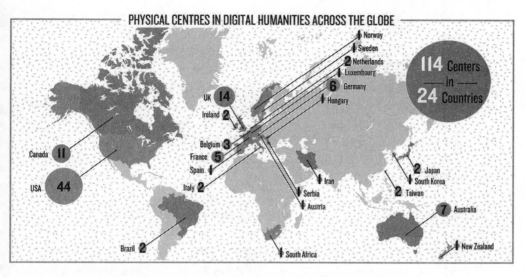

Figure 35.3. M. Terras's DH Graph. The complete graph is available online: http://
melissaterras.blogspot.in/2012/01/infographic-quanitifying-digital.html.

Standards and Cultural Hegemonies

According to G. Bowker and S. Leigh Star, "classifications and standards are material, as well as symbolic," and their control "is a central, often underanalyzed feature
of economic life" (Bowker and Star, *Sorting Things Out*, 15, 39). In their studies the
two sociologists show how classification techniques (and the standards generated
from them) have always played a fundamental economic and sociocultural role.
Current digital technologies standards appear to be the result of a double bias: the
technical one and the cultural one (geopolitical). These two biases are entangled and
it is almost impossible to discern where the technological choice begins and where
the cultural prejudice ends.

As the lexicographer and blogger José Antonio Millán noticed more than fifteen
years ago, "while networks are the highways of digital goods and service flows, technologies linked to the user's language are their compulsory tolls" (Millán, 140). Thus,
at the roots of economic, social, and political primacy we do not find "just" technology, but rather the mix of copyrighted algorithms and protocols that manipulate and
control languages. In this perspective, standards are the result of a balance of powers.[16]
Presiding over linguistic technologies has thus become both a profitable business
and a geopolitical matter. As Millán states, for many countries, not investing in this
sector presently means being forced to pay to be able to use one's own language.

"Localization still matters," and the researchers of the Language Observatory
Project (http://gii2.nagaokaut.ac.jp/gii/blog/lopdiary.php) have noted that although
Unicode is recognized as a step forward for multilingualism, "many problems in
language processing remain":

> The Mongolian language, for example, is written either in Cyrillic script or in its own historical and traditional script, for which at least eight different codes and fonts have been identified. No standardisation of typed fonts exists, causing inconsistency, even textual mistranslation, from one computer to another. As a result, some Mongolian web pages are made up of image files, which take much longer to load. Indian web pages face the same challenge. On Indian newspaper sites proprietary fonts for Hindi scripts are often used and some sites provide their news with image files. These technological limitations prevent information from being interchangeable, and lead to a digital language divide. (Yoshiki and Kodama, 122–23)

The Italian semiologist Antonio Perri has offered convincing examples of the cultural bias of the Unicode characters representational system, showing the concrete risks of oversimplifying and drying up of the "phenomenological richness of human writing practices" (Perri, 747). Perri analyzed a number of encoding solutions proposed by the Unicode consortium for different problems related to Indian subcontinental scripts and Chinese, Arabic, and Hangul (Korean writing). In all these cases, in addition to being excessively dependent on visualization software, which raises problems of portability, he showed that the Unicode solutions were based on a "hypertypographic" concept of writing—that is, Western writing embodied in its print form and logical sequencing. By neglecting the visual features of many writing systems, this view overlooks their important functional aspects. Perri gives a striking example of this bias when discussing Unicode treatment of ligatures and the position of vowel characters in the Devanagari Indic script. Often in Indian systems aspects of a graphic nature prevail over the reading order of the graphemes. As shown in Figure 35.4, in the second glyph the order pronunciation/graphic sequence is reversed. Unicode experts, however, argue that Indic scripts are represented in its system according to a "logical scheme" that ignores "typographic" details. Perri concludes:

> But why on earth should the order of characters corresponding to the phonetic segment be considered logical by an Indian literate? Who says that the linearity of Saussure's alphabetic signifier should play a role in his writing practices? . . . It is therefore all too evident that the alphabetic filter, the rendering software and the automatic process of normalization of Indic scripts are the result of a choice that reflects the need for structural uniformity as opposed to the *emic* cultural practices of the real user. (Perri, 736; our translation)

Unfortunately, the problem of cultural primacy overflows linguistic boundaries. The pervasiveness of cultural representations and metaphors belonging to the Anglo-American context in all technological appliances and computing tools is a well-known tendency since at least the 1960s. Many familiar elements borrowed from

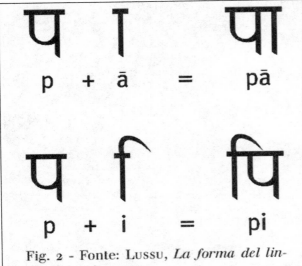

Fig. 2 - Fonte: Lussu, *La forma del linguaggio*, cit., p. 41.

Figure 35.4. Two graphemes of Devanagari Indic script as shown in Perri, 735.

everyday U.S. life were exported to the computer world. We are not speaking here of programming languages or algorithms, where the deep semiotic bias is intrinsically evident (Andersen), but of the "superficial" (and not less subtle) world of icons and graphic user interfaces (GUIs). One example is the manila folder, an ubiquitous object used in all American offices that owes its name to a fiber (manila hemp) commonly used in the Philippines for making ropes, paper products, and coarse fabrics. An object coming from a removed colonial past suddenly, thanks to the Xerox Star desktop,[17] later became the metaphor for any computing content: a symbol that conceals the bureaucratic origins of the desktop computer and its unique ties to the cultural imagination of the average U.S. customer. Examples of symbolic cyber-colonization are Second Life facial expressions and user-playable animations, where we find body language gestures that can be only deciphered by expert American native speakers.[18] Take, for example, the famous "kiss my butt" animation (see Figure 35.5), where both the verbal expression and the body posture are linked to North American culture and would suggest (at best) deceptive meanings to other cultures.

Language Differences and Global Inequalities

Our last example is not a real example, but a comparative experiment based on two graphic representations. The first image (Figure 35.6) is a map of world income inequalities from the University of California Atlas of Global Inequality database. The second world map (Figure 35.7) is a Wikipedia image based on Ethnologue. com sources, representing linguistic diversity in the world: in dark gray (red in the original map) are shown the eight megadiverse countries that together represent

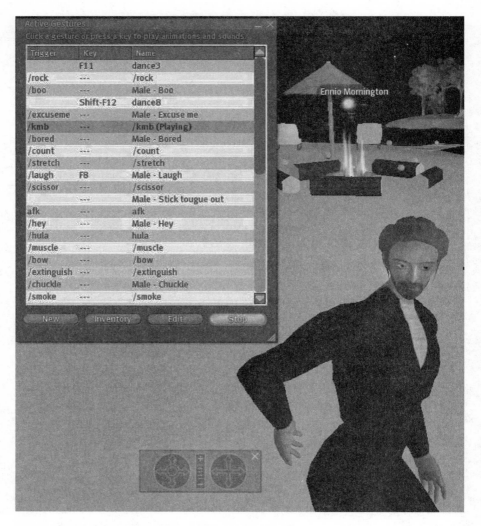

Figure 35.5. The "kiss my butt" gesture in Second Life.

more than 50 percent of the world's languages, and in lighter gray (blue in the orig-inal), areas of great diversity.

If we overlap these two maps, we can notice that—excluding Australia, where linguistic diversity is due to the enormous number of immigrants from all continents[19]—the lower income countries of the first map in many cases fit the areas of greater linguistic diversity. In other words: cultural richness does not neces-sarily match material wealth.[20]

The comparison between the two maps we have proposed does not seek to sug-gest superficial and easy conclusions; however, it is legitimate to believe that in some of the poorest areas of the world, in deserts, jungles, and mountains at the margins

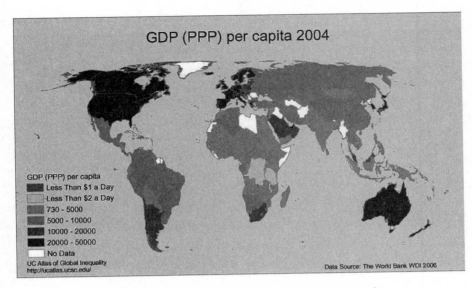

Figure 35.6. World Gross Domestic Product in 2004. Source: https://ccrec.ucsc.edu
/news_item/uc-atlas-global-inequality-0.

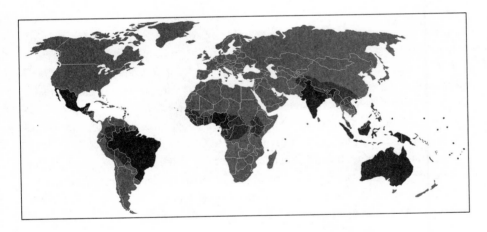

Figure 35.7. Linguistic diversity in the world. Source: http://en.wikipedia.org/wiki
/Linguistic_diversity#Linguistic_diversity.

of our globalized society, a handful of communities continue to cultivate the last
resource still entirely in their own hands: language.

Finally, it is not surprising that the world income map overlaps also with the
"Quantifying Digital Humanities" infographic produced by the University College
London Centre for Digital Humanities: two visual representations of a high-income
Western sphere (mostly Anglophone) leading the planet. This seems to confirm Mil-
lán's hypothesis on the strict relation between economic hegemony, technological

concentration, and linguistic impoverishment, raising the unapproached question of the internal and external *digital humanities divide* in Western countries.

Beyond the Alphabetic Machine?

What is the role and the position of DH in the geopolitical scenery presented so far? Notwithstanding the unquestionable expansion of the discipline (Gold), I have the impression that DH has been particularly slow in subsuming the social and political impact of its choices and discourses (the "dark sides" of DH; see Chun and Rhody). Maybe this has also to do with the inevitable repression of a too-bitter truth—that is to say, so far the digital humanities have not succeeded in either strengthening the field of humanities or putting some balance into the power relationships between humanities and computer science.

If, on one hand, the perspective of the "formal methods"[21] did not manage to establish an equal dialogue between humanities and computer science, on the other hand it made computer science too shortsighted and even hostile to the so-called digital cultures, relegating the latter to a mere "sociological" question. As pointed out by research done by the ACO*HUM[22] (De Smedt et al.) in the nineties, a computer is a "universal machine" and the application of formal methods is the lowest common denominator of DH. However, all forms of oral or written discourses are not reducible or ascribable to a logical structure or the "model" (Buzzetti), but reflect and imply a dynamic interaction between producers, codes, material supports, and audiences. The meaning does not simply emerge from the two processes of analysis and modeling but from cooperation (Halliday). In other words, a discourse is a cultural artifact made of syntax, semantics, and above all, pragmatics, and that is why all the data of human culture are so hard to formalize.

On the other hand, the dependence between the machine and the alphabet goes beyond the mere difficulty or impossibility to be independent from the print model. In fact, according to Giuseppe Longo, such dependence seems to be inscribed in the very DNA of the machine:

> So I would like to readdress the fact that the roots of this machine are very old and can be found in the alphabet. First of all, 5,000–6,000 years ago, the alphabet was, for different reasons, an invention comparable to the computer-mediated discretization of knowledge we have now performed. Think of the originality of these first social groups from Mesopotamia who fractioned the linguistic flux, a continuous spoken song, marking certain pitches as the first consonants (C. Herrenschmidt et al. 1996). It was the onset of development and a culture which were quite different to those inherent in the hieroglyphic writing of ideograms which proposed concepts or evoked whole images, situations, or feelings, by means of drawings. Conversely, the alphabet discretizes, subdivides continuous language into insignificant atoms, into the bits which are letters. (Longo, 58)[23]

As Longo reminds us, the present computational dimension is not the manifest destiny of humankind. Humanists can join other pioneering scientists around the globe who are starting to think "of the next machine: history is not over, with digital computability" (Longo, 60). The implicit flattening of the technological, commercial, and industrial policies, as well as the essentially monocultural origins of the logical and symbolical representations, are obstacles to the expansion of DH beyond the simply instrumental function. I agree with Alan Liu ("Where Is Cultural Criticism") who says that in order to extend its range of action and be legitimated as an actual discipline, DH needs to contaminate with other disciplines,[24] such as social sciences (from Science and Technology studies to Mediology[25]) and cultural anthropology (especially the variant dealing with the cultural artifacts from André Leroi-Gourhan to Jack Goody, from the ethnography of James Clifford and George E. Marcus to the *digital ethnography* of Michael Wesch[26]).

But perhaps the most urgent issue is to stop regarding the methodological and the sociocultural questions as separate. In other words, to stop thinking, paraphrasing Harold Innis, that the digital humanities were born in a *vacuum*:

> Innis happily accepted as a starting point the inevitably ethnocentric bias of social science. . . . He recognized that scholarship was not produced in a historical and cultural vacuum but reflected the hopes, aspirations, and heresies of national cultures. American and British scholarship was based, he thought, on a conceit: it pretended to discover Universal Truth, to proclaim Universal Laws, and to describe a Universal Man. Upon inspection it appeared, however, that its Universal Man resembled a type found around Cambridge, Massachusetts, or Cambridge, England: its Universal Laws resembled those felt to be useful by Congress and Parliament; and its Universal Truth bore English and American accents. Imperial powers, so it seems, seek to create not only economic and political clients but intellectual clients as well. (Carey, 149)

So, are we digital humanist intellectual clients, dinosaurs, or "the next big thing"?[27] Personally, I would rather prefer not to choose among these options. Instead, I would like to think of DH as a cultural *and* political project. We could start with three basic steps: (a) stop being obsessed with large-scale digitization projects and "archiving fever" (Derrida), which will only increase our dependency on private industry standards, products, and of course, funding; (b) *improve and cultivate the margins*—that is, give more attention to our variegated cultural and linguistic local diversity; (c) help to elaborate a new concept of *knowledge as commons*. As for (c), Hess and Ostrom provide a set of design principles for common-pool resource institutions:

- Clearly defined boundaries should be in place.
- Rules in use are well matched to local needs and conditions.
- Individuals affected by these rules can participate in modifying the rules.

- The right of community members to devise their own rules is respected by external authorities.
- A system for self-monitoring member's behavior has been established.
- A graduated system of sanctions is available.
- Community members have access to low-cost conflict resolution mechanisms.
- Nested enterprises—that is, appropriation, provision, monitoring, and sanctioning, conflict resolution, and other governance activities—are organized in a nested structure with multiple layers of activities. (Hess and Ostrom, 7)

Some of these rules could translate, for example, into a completely different governance system, negotiated and monitored dynamically by the linguistic and culturally diverse communities, rather than by a particularly powerful or successful academic group (today the Anglophone countries dominate ADHO, but tomorrow it could be China or other emerging global players). It is not acceptable that one organization functions as a private club that decides who can become a member and who cannot. This is an old-fashioned notion of academic community that does not reflect the present complexity of DH (Fiormonte, "Dreaming of Multiculturalism"). But it is also a matter of democracy, as the global scenario does not justify the existence of groups working as a legitimacy dispenser or "brand" guardians. In fact, knowledge commons does not only mean that knowledge (from both an abstract and practical point of view) should be treated as a common resource, but that each time communities need to sit down and redefine collectively and dynamically what knowledge(s) is (are) and how each piece of knowledge could be digitally represented. This does not mean, for example, refusing standards, but avoiding standards that take over objects, practices, and processes that they should serve.

So digital humanists are not only responsible for taking care of digital representations of cultural objects, but should engage in reducing the political, economic, and social unbalances produced by those (always partial) representations. If the DH community would start to discuss the possibility of applying some of these principles to its own organizations, projects, and products, a completely new way of thinking and researching would emerge—more respectful of our mutual cultures, more democratic, and more powerful.

Postscriptum

"Did we tell our stories faithfully?" This is a question raised (and tentatively answered) by Lisa Marie Rhody when she wrote on "digital humanities as chiaroscuro" (Chun and Rhody, 16), and it was perhaps with a similar question in mind that I started to work on this material in 2012, following the invitation of Manfred Thaller at the "Cologne Controversies around the Digital Humanities" in the same year. I am

grateful to Matt Gold for asking me, three years ago, if I was interested in repub-
lishing it, and I am proud to see it now anthologized in this new edition of *Debates
in the Digital Humanities*. For a number of reasons I decided to make only minor
revisions to the original text.[28] I am aware that some of the key figures provided
in this chapters have changed and that the present scenario is moving (hopefully)
toward organizations that are more culturally inclusive. However, the reason this
article became "infamous" in several DH "inner circles" is precisely that three years
ago those figures were real. I could not update or delete them without changing the
whole sense of the piece. Perhaps in my defense I can quote Daniel O' Donnell, present GO::DH chair, who wrote on Humanist: "Domenico's work has in fact greatly
influenced our thinking, his challenges are extremely useful in helping as part of
the ongoing process of defining the [GO::DH] project."[29]

But if "Toward a Cultural Critique" has somehow influenced the choices made
by ADHO, much still need to be changed. All efforts should be recognized and
encouraged, but I think we should remember that ADHO is not a democratic
organization with elected members, as are most of the academic organizations in
the world (including members associations of ADHO). It is still a strange hybrid
between an invitation-based private club and a corporate consortium. As I said in
various occasions, I would much prefer to see a "federation of diverse associations"
instead of applying the "unity in diversity" model. That is why I am suspicious of
any "global leadership."

But above all, I think it would be strategic to support and promote South–South
dialogue. I would like to remember here the observations of Octavio Kulesz, author
of an important survey of digital publishing in developing countries:

> Likewise, the electronic solutions that certain countries of the South have
> implemented to overcome their problems of content distribution can also serve
> as a model for others, thus facilitating South–South knowledge and technol-
> ogy transfer. . . . Sooner or later, these countries will have to ask themselves
> what kind of digital publishing highways they must build and they will be
> faced with two very different options: a) financing the installation of platforms
> designed in the North; b) investing according to the concrete needs, expecta-
> tions and potentialities of local authors, readers and entrepreneurs. Whatever
> the decision of each country may be, the long term impact will be immense.
> (Kulesz, 16–17)

I think that similar questions can be applied to the DH world.
So, what kind of DH do we want to build?

NOTES

Translated from the Italian by Federica Perazzini and Desmond Schmidt.

1. There is not much information in English available on the history of *Informatica Umanistica,* but Geoffrey Rockwell has effectively outlined the Italian scenario on a recent post on the Tito Orlandi *festschrift:* http://www.theoreti.ca/?p=4333.

2. Initiatives like the ADHO Special Interest Group GO::DH (http://www.globalout lookdh.org) and the DH Awards (http://dhawards.org) show that a sensitivity to cultural and linguistic diversity is growing within the DH international community.

3. "ICANN Bringing the Languages of the World to the Global Internet; Fast Track Process for Internationalized Domain Names Launches Nov 16," news release, October 30, 2009. http://www.icann.org/en/news/announcements/announcement-30oct09-en.htm.

4. This situation has started to change since the 2013 ICANN reform. There was an evident restyling of the image and a new mission statement was provided: "To broaden the range of stakeholders involved in Internet governance. . . ." The present CEO of ICANN is Fadi Chehadé, a Stanford-educated engineer who has been employed by a number of major IT industries throughout his career. According to Richard Hill, president of the Association for Proper Internet Governance and former ITU senior officer, "for the most part the narratives used to defend the current governance arrangements are about main-taining the geo-political and geo-economic dominance of the present incumbents, that is, of the [United States] and its powerful private companies" (Hill, 35).

5. Frederic Lardinois, "U.S. Department of Commerce Loosens Grip on ICANN," *ReadWrite,* September 30, 2009, http://www.readwriteweb.com/archives/commerce _department_loosens_grip_on_icann.php.

6. While Western governments and companies try to preserve their primacy on the Internet, data show a different scenario. In terms of access to the Internet, as of early 2015, Western countries (Europe and USA) represent only 35.7 percent out of the total of the users whereas Asia records 44 percent. (Source: http://www.internetworldstats. com/stats.htm.)

7. Unicode Consortium, http://www.unicode.org/consortium/consort.html.

8. Unicode Consortium, "Directors, Officers, and Staff," http://www.unicode.org /consortium/directors.html.

9. Association for Computers and the Humanities (ACH), Alliance of Digital Human-ities Organizations (ADHO), Association for Literary and Linguistic Computing (ALLC), CenterNet (International Networks of Digital Humanities Centers), Digital Humanities Quarterly, Literary and Linguistic Computing, Society for Digital Humanities/Société pour l'étude des médias interactifs (SDH-SEMI), Text Encoding Initiative (TEI).

10. Since July 2014 ADHO's Steering Committee has seen a substantial change of its composition. Although Anglo-Americans are still dominant, there was a clear effort toward the inclusion of non-Anglophone voices: http://digitalhumanities.org/administration /steering.

11. http://thatcamp.org.

12. At this writing a quick look at upcoming THATCamps shows that out of thirty-five THATCamps listed on the website on September 2015, twenty-four will take place in the United States.

13. See the relative Manifesto proposed in Paris: http://tcp.hypotheses.org/411. A group of scholars who signed the Manifesto in 2013 tried to map out the geographical composition and linguistic diversity of the field. The results were summarized and commented by Pierre Mounier, one of the main organizers of the survey: http://bn.hypotheses.org/11179.

14. To deepen this issue, see Schmidt ("Inadequacy of Embedded Markup"); Fiormonte and Schmidt ("La rappresentazione digitale"); Fiormonte, Martiradonna, and Schmidt ("Digital Encoding").

15. The link between the crisis of the humanities and the role of the DH is the central theme of 4Humanities, an *advocacy* initiative carried out by a group of universities, associations, as well as British, American, Canadian, and Australian research centers: http://4humanities.org/.

16. "On the other hand, our new global information structure is based on classification schemes elaborated within developed countries in order to solve problems particularly connected with the educated élite" (Bowker and Star, "Intervista su società," 15).

17. "By far its most striking feature was its graphical user interface.... The arrangement of folders and icons built around what the Star engineers called the 'desktop metaphor' is so familiar today that it seems to have been part of computing forever" (Hilzik 1999, 364).

18. A complete list of such animations can be found in: http://wiki.secondlife.com/wiki/Internal_Animations#User-playable_animations.

19. According to the Australian Bureau of Statistics, the European invasion during the nineteenth and twentieth centuries eradicated both languages and cultures from the aboriginal populations: "Today, there are approximately 22 million Australians, speaking almost 400 languages, including Indigenous languages"; see http://www.abs.gov.au/ausstats/abs@.nsf/Latestproducts/1301.0Feature%20Article32009%E2%80%9310?opendocument&tabname=Summary&prodno=1301.0&issue=2009%9610&num=&view=.

20. This observation seems now confirmed by a study on language extinction drivers: "By contrast, the dominating effect of a single socioeconomic factor, GDP per capita, on speaker growth rate suggests that economic growth and globalization . . . are primary drivers of recent language speaker declines (mainly since the 1970s onwards), for instance, via associated political and educational developments and globalized socioeconomic dynamics" (Amano et al., 8).

21. For a discussion on the formalization of humanities disciplines, see Van Zundert et al.

22. The website is still active and available on online: http://www.hd.uib.no/AcoHum/ /.

23. It is important to notice that the author of this *J'accuse* is a computer scientist and mathematician currently engaged into biology researching. A specular historical-technical support to Longo's thesis is to be found in the studies on the numerical origins of the cuneiform writing (see also Schmandt-Besserat, 1996).

24. I pointed out a list of possible intersections in Numerico, Fiormonte, and Tomasi, 102–3.

25. A loan from the French *médiologie* (http://www.mediologie.org/), this term spread also in Italy, see Pireddu and Serra, 2012. According to Régis Debray, mediology "deals with the analysis of the 'superior social function' (religion, ideology, art, politics) in their relationships with the transmission means and environments" (Debray).

26. Michael Wesch, Digital Ethnography at Kansas State University, http://mediated cultures.net.

27. This expression, referred to DH, became immediately famous after W. Panna-packer used it to describe the 2009 Modern Language Association (MLA) Convention.

28. However, in the following years I continued to investigate many of the issues raised in this article. See, for example, my work from 2013–15: Fiormonte, "Seven Points on DH and Multiculturalism," "Dreaming of Multiculturalism," and "Towards Monoculturalism."

29. Humanist Discussion Group, http://www.dhhumanist.org/cgi-bin/archive/archive _msg.cgi?file=/Humanist.vol26.txt&msgnum=696&start=98646&end=98998.

BIBLIOGRAPHY

Amano, Tatsuya, Brody Sandel, Heidi Eager, Edouard Bulteau, Jens-Christian Sven-ning, Bo Dalsgaard, Carsten Rahbek, Richard G. Davies, and William J. Sutherland. "Global Distribution and Drivers of Language Extinction Risk." *Proceedings of the Royal Society* B281 (September 3, 2014): 20141574: 1–10. http://dx.doi.org/10.1098 /rspb.2014.1574.

Andersen, Peter Bøgh. *A Theory of Computer Semiotics: Semiotic Approaches to Con-struction and Assessment of Computer Systems.* Cambridge: Cambridge University Press, 1997.

Bottéro, Jean, Clarisse Herrenschmidt, and Jean-Pierre Vernant, eds. *L'Orient et nous. L'écriture, la raison, les dieux.* Paris: Albin-Michel, 1996.

Bourdieu, Pierre, and Roger Chartier. *Le sociologue et l'historien.* Paris: Editions Agone et Raison D'Agir, 2010. Italian trans. *Il sociologo e lo storico. Dialogo sull'uomo e la società.* Bari: Dedalo, 2011.

Bowker, Geoffrey, and Susan Leigh Star. "Intervista su società dell'informazione e disugua-glianze." *Daedalus* 19 (2006): 13–20. http://www.ics.uci.edu/~gbowker/interview.pdf.
———. *Sorting Things Out: Classification and Its Consequences.* Cambridge, Mass.: MIT Press, 1999.

Buzzetti, Dino. "Digital Representation and the Text Model." *New Literary History* 33 (2002): 61–88.

Canagarajah, Suresh A. *A Geopolitics of Academic Writing.* Pittsburgh: University of Pitts-burgh Press, 2002.

Carey, James W. *Communication as Culture: Essays on Media and Society.* New York-London: Routledge, 1992.

Chun, Wendy H. K., and Lisa Marie Rhody. "Working the Digital Humanities: Uncovering Shadows between the Dark and the Light." *Differences: A Journal of Feminist Cultural Studies* 25, no. 1 (2014): 1–26.

Debray, Régis. "Qu'est-ce que la médiologie?" *Le Monde Diplomatique,* August 1999. http://www.monde-diplomatique.fr/1999/08/DEBRAY/12314.

Derrida, Jacques. *Archive Fever. A Freudian Impression.* Chicago: University of Chicago Press, 1996.

De Smedt, Koenraad, Hazel Gardiner, Espen Ore, Tito Orlandi, Harold Short, Jacques Souillot, and William Vaughan, eds. *Computing in Humanities Education: A European Perspective.* Bergen: University of Bergen, HIT Centre, 1999. http://www.hd.uib.no/AcoHum/book/.

Fiormonte, Domenico. "Chi l'ha visto? Testo digitale, semiotica, rappresentazione. In margine a un trittico di Dino Buzzetti." *Informatica Umanistica* 2 (2009): 21–46.

———. "Dreaming of Multiculturalism at DH2014." *InfoLet* (blog), July 7, 2014. http://infolet.it/2014/07/07/dreaming-of-multiculturalism-at-dh2014/.

———. "Il dibattito internazionale sull'informatica umanistica: formazione, tecnologia e primato delle lingua." *Testo e Senso* 4–5 (2002): 145–56. http://testoesenso.it/article/view/214.

———. "Il testo digitale: traduzione, codifica, modelli culturali." In *Italianisti in Spagna, ispanisti in Italia: la traduzione. Atti del Convegno Internazionale,* ed. P. R. Piras, A. Alessandro, and D. Fiormonte, 271–84. Roma: Edizioni Q, 2008.

———. "Seven Points on DH and Multiculturalism." *InfoLet* (blog), May 5, 2015. http://infolet.it/2013/05/05/seven-points-on-dh-and-multiculturalism/.

———. "Towards Monoculturalism in (digital) Humanities?" *InfoLet* (blog), July 12, 2015. http://infolet.it/2015/07/12/monocultural-humanities/.

Fiormonte, Domenico, Valentina Martiradonna, and Desmond Schmidt. "Digital Encoding as a Hermeneutic and Semiotic Act: The Case of Valerio Magrelli." *Digital Humanities Quarterly* 4, no. 1 (2010). http://digitalhumanities.org/dhq/vol/4/1/000082/000082.html.

Fiormonte, Domenico, and Desmond Schmidt. "La rappresentazione digitale della varianza testuale." In *Canoni liquidi,* ed. D. Fiormonte, 161–80. Napoli: ScriptaWeb, 2011.

Gold, Matthew K. "The Digital Humanities Moment." In *Debates in the Digital Humanities,* ed. M. K. Gold, 9–16. Minneapolis: University of Minnesota Press, 2012. http://dhdebates.gc.cuny.edu/debates/text/2.

Halliday, Michael A. K. "Text as semantic choice in social contexts." In *Grammars and Descriptions,* eds. Teun A. Van Dijk and János S. Petöfi, 176–226. Berlin: Walter De Gruyter, 1977. Reprinted in M. A. K. Halliday. *Linguistic Studies of Text and Discourse: The Collected Works of M. A. K. Halliday.* Vol. 2, 23–81. London; New York: Continuum, 2001.

Hess, Charlotte, and Elinor Ostrom. *Understanding Knowledge as a Commons: From Theory to Practice.* Cambridge, Mass.: MIT Press, 2011.

Hill, Richard. "The True Stakes of Internet Governance." In *State of Power 2015: An Annual Anthology on Global Power and Resistance,* ed. N. Buxton and M. Bélanger Dumontier, 28–37. Amsterdam: Transnational Institute, 2015. http://www.tni.org /stateofpower2015.

Hilzik, Michael A. *Dealers of Lightning.* New York: HarperCollins, 1999.

Innis, Harold A. *The Bias of Communication.* Toronto: University of Toronto Press, 1951.

Kulesz, Octavio. *Digital Publishing in Developing Countries.* Paris: International Alliance of Independent Publishers/Prince Claus Fund for Culture and Development, 2011. http://alliance-lab.org/etude/?lang=en.

Liu, Alan. "Where Is Cultural Criticism in the Digital Humanities?" In *Debates in the Digital Humanities,* ed. Matthew K. Gold, 490–509. Minneapolis: University of Minnesota Press, 2012. http://dhdebates.gc.cuny.edu/debates/text/20.

Longo, Giuseppe. "Critique of Computational Reason in the Natural Sciences." In *Fundamental Concepts in Computer Science,* eds. E. Gelenbe and J. P. Kahane, 43–69. London: Imperial College Press/World Scientific, 2009. ftp://ftp.di.ens.fr/pub/users /longo/PhilosophyAndCognition/CritiqCompReason-engl.pdf.

Millán, José Antonio. *Internet y el español.* Madrid: Retevision, 2001.

Numerico, Teresa, Domenico Fiormonte, and Francesca Tomasi. *L'umanista digitale.* Bologna: Il Mulino, 2010.

Perri, Antonio. "Al di là della tecnologia, la scrittura. Il caso Unicode." *Annali dell'Università degli Studi Suor Orsola Benincasa* II (2009): 725–48.

Pireddu, Mario, and Marcello Serra, eds. *Mediologia. Una disciplina attraverso i suoi classici.* Napoli: Liguori, 2012.

Schmandt-Besserat, Denise. *How Writing Came About.* Austin: University of Texas Press, 1996.

Schmidt, Desmond. "The Inadequacy of Embedded Markup for Cultural Heritage Texts." *Literary and Linguistic Computing* 25, no. 3 (2010): 337–56.

Slack, Jennifer Daryl, and John Macgregor Wise. *Culture and Technology: A Primer.* New York: Peter Lang, 2005.

Vygotsky, Lev Semënovič. *Mind in Society: Development of Higher Psychological Processes.* Cambridge, Mass.: Harvard University Press, 1978.

———. *Thought and Language.* Cambridge, Mass.: MIT Press, 1986.

Yoshiki, Mikami, and Shigeaki Kodama. "Measuring Linguistic Diversity on the Web." In *Net.Lang. Towards the Multilingual Cyberspace,* ed. L. Vannini and H. Le Crosnier, 121–39. Caen: C&F Éditions, 2012.

Zundert, Joris Van, Smiljana Antonijevic, Anne Beaulieu, Karina Van Dalen-Oskam, Douwe Zeldenrust, and Tara Andrews. "Cultures of Formalisation: Towards an Encounter between Humanities and Computing." In *Understanding Digital Humanities,* ed. D. M. Berry, 279–94. Basingstoke, Hampshire; New York: Palgrave Macmillan, 2012.

How Not to Teach Digital Humanities

RYAN CORDELL

In late summer of 2010, I arrived on the campus of St. Norbert College in De Pere, Wisconsin. I was a newly minted assistant professor, brimming with optimism, and the field with which I increasingly identified my work—this "digital humanities"—had just been declared "the first 'next big thing' in a long time" by William Pannapacker in his *Chronicle of Higher Education* column.[1] "We are now realizing," Pannapacker had written of the professors gathered at the Modern Language Association's annual convention, "that resistance is futile" ("MLA and the Digital Humanities"). So of course I immediately proposed a new "Introduction to Digital Humanities" course for upper-level undergraduates at St. Norbert. My syllabus was, perhaps, hastily constructed—patched together from "Intro to DH" syllabi in a Zotero group—but surely it would pass muster. They had hired me, after all; surely they were keen to see digital humanities in the curriculum. In any case, how could the curricular committee reject "the next big thing," particularly when resistance was futile?

But reject it they did. They wrote back with concerns about the "student constituency" for the course, its overall theme, my expected learning outcomes, the projected enrollment, the course texts, and the balance between theoretical and practical instruction in the day-to-day operations of the class.

1. What would be the student constituency for this course? It looks like it will be somewhat specialized and several topics seem to suggest graduate student level work. Perhaps you could spell out the learning objectives and say more about the targeted students. There is a concern about the course having sufficient enrollment.
2. The course itself could be fleshed out more. Is there an implied overall theme relating to digital technology other than "the impact of technology on humanities research and pedagogy"? Are there other texts and readings

other than "A Companion to Digital Studies"? How much of the course will be "learning about" as distinct from "learning how to"?

My initial reaction was umbrage; I was certain my colleagues' technological reticence was clouding their judgment. But upon further reflection—which came through developing, revising, and re-revising this course from their feedback, and learning from students who have taken each version of the course—I believe they were almost entirely right to reject that first proposal.

As a result of these experiences, I have been thinking more and more about the problem of "digital humanities *qua* digital humanities," particularly amidst the accelerated growth of undergraduate classes that explicitly engage with digital humanities methods. I want to outline three challenges I see hampering truly innovative digital pedagogy in humanities classrooms. To do so, I will draw on my experiences at two very different campuses: the first a small, relatively isolated liberal arts college (St. Norbert College) and the second a medium-size research university (Northeastern University). I will draw also on the experiences of colleagues in a variety of institutions around the country.

As an opening gambit, I want to suggest that undergraduate students do not care about digital humanities. I want to suggest further that their disinterest is right and even salutary, because what I *really* mean is that undergrads do not care about DH *qua* DH. In DH classes, meta-discussions about the field too often preclude engagement with its projects and theoretical engagements. In other words, we lead students brand-new to DH immediately into straw-man arguments about its broadest characterizations, whether good or bad, rather than substantive investigations of specific projects, thinkers, methods, books, or articles.

In addition, I would argue that most graduate students in literature, history, or other humanities fields do not come to graduate school primarily invested in becoming "digital humanists," though there are of course exceptions. Indeed, we are now well into a backlash against DH, particularly among graduate students who feel the priorities, required skills, and reward structures of their disciplines have shifted under their feet in ways they cannot account or adjust for. While I argue that the perception of wholesale DH transformation is largely wrong, I also contend that graduate students' skepticism of the rhetoric around DH—whether it stems from the field itself or from outside—is neither misguided nor inconsequential. Very broadly, then, I will argue that we must work to take both undergraduate disinterest and graduate resistance as instructive for the future of DH in the classroom. I make this argument not from a place of despair, but because I believe DH pedagogy at the undergraduate and graduate levels is essential to the futures of our fields. We need students and colleagues who are adept and thoughtful about the tools, platforms, and media of our day, and we should be wary of stifling their curiosity in our very attempts to kindle it. To that end, here are the major challenges I identify for effective integration of DH into curricula.

"What Is DH?" Always Excludes

Let us begin, then, with rhetoric—specifically, the rhetoric with which we often frame the DH field. The rejected course I proposed at St. Norbert revolved around DH itself, and it began with a bevy of articles grappling with the question, "What is digital humanities?" "What is DH?" has become a prolific genre in its own right; there are no shortage of such pieces making all sorts of claims about what the field is or should be. (If you want a primer, the Digital Humanities Department at University College London has published a book, *Defining Digital Humanities,* and their director Melissa Terras maintains a regularly updated bibliography of the genre).[2] What better way to outline the field we would study in this new class, I reasoned, than with such definitional pieces?

Except that it's not. "What is DH?"—or "Who is in/out of DH?" or another variation thereupon—are very "inside baseball" genres, by which I mean they are meta-academic genres. "Digital" humanities is often defined in these pieces by contrast to "traditional" humanities. DH is collaborative rather than solitary, DH is interdisciplinary, DH is interested in new scales of analysis, et cetera, et cetera, et cetera. This is because DH practitioners understand from hard-won experience how entrenched fields such as history and literature can be, how suspicious of computationally informed methods and tools. If you review the DH literature from just before the field's "next big thing" apotheosis, you will find a deep undercurrent of anxiety: will our work ever be understood, valued, or recognized by our disciplinary colleagues? Our undergraduates, however, are blissfully unaware of the disciplinary reticences that underlie that term, digital humanities, and are not eager for academic courses in which the primary conversation is about the mechanics and politics of the academy itself.

"What is DH?" pieces can be valuable to folks invested in conversations about the humanities, about the future of the academy, and so forth. They help articulate the value of digital scholarship to colleagues unaware or unsure about the work we do. But even here these pieces often fall short. They speak of "DH" as an identifiable and singular thing, even if that thing contains multitudes, when in fact DH is often local and peculiar: a specific configuration of those multitudes that makes sense for a given institution, given its faculty, staff, and students, and given its unique mission and areas of strength. Of more concern to me, pieces in this genre often begin and end at the institutional level, puzzling over definitions of "digital humanities" but not enacting the transformations they proclaim.

In one oft-cited "What is DH?" piece (which appeared in the first *Debates in the Digital Humanities* volume), Matthew Kirschenbaum calls digital humanities a "tactical term" that can help practitioners position themselves for institutional authorization of various sorts:

> On the one hand, then, digital humanities is a term possessed of enough currency and escape velocity to penetrate layers of administrative strata to get funds allocated, initiatives under way, and plans set in motion. On the other hand, it is a populist term, self-identified and self-perpetuating through the algorithmic structures of contemporary social media . . .
>
> Digital humanities, which began as a term of consensus among a relatively small group of researchers, is now backed on a growing number of campuses by a level of funding, infrastructure, and administrative commitments that would have been unthinkable even a decade ago. Even more recently, I would argue, the network effects of blogs and Twitter at a moment when the academy itself is facing massive and often wrenching changes linked both to new technologies and the changing political and economic landscape has led to the construction of "digital humanities" as a free-floating signifier, one that increasingly serves to focus the anxiety and even outrage of individual scholars over their own lack of agency amid the turmoil in their institutions and profession. (Kirschenbaum)

For Kirschenbaum, the "'tactical' coinage" of "digital humanities" can be "unabashedly deployed to get things done." As true as this can be, particularly at the administrative level, DH remains a murky term for our colleagues, our students, and, if we were being honest, for those administrators. What is more, the many options offered in "What is DH?" pieces rarely clarify the question for newcomers, except to erect ideas of barriers more rigid in prose than in practice. In particular, few "What is DH?" pieces apply digital methods to a humanities topic, demonstrating how DH methods might lead to new insight. In other words, we too often fail to produce evidence in support of our transformational claims, which is why "What is DH?" literature reads to so many of our colleagues as instrumental, administrative, even neoliberal.

For our undergraduate students such pieces simply fall flat. Shockingly, the language of "disciplinary landscapes" and "infrastructure" and "free-floating signifiers" does not set the average undergraduate's pulse a-twittering. Indeed, to assign such a piece to a class of undergraduates is to forget our audience entirely. Our students are just learning the rules of the humanities game. As Adeline Koh commented on the original version of this post, "to introduce DH discussions on the level that we're used to may alienate undergraduates, who are only starting to learn the conventions of disciplines that a lot of DH debates are critiquing at meta-levels."[3]

I would distinguish here between definitional pieces such as Kirschenbaum's—what I have been calling "What is DH?" literature—and theorizations of the field (or aspects thereof) that can serve similar framing purposes as foundational works of feminist or queer theory might in a literary methods class. While "What is DH?"

meditations tend to hover around the academy itself, more theoretical introductions to the field demonstrate how its approaches lead to new thinking. For instance, Alan Liu's remarkable "Imagining the New Media Encounter" introduces Blackwell's *Companion to Digital Literary Studies* by situating the field within a long history of media revolution and recursion. It is a piece not about the twenty-first-century academy, but about humanity's complex relationship with media and its technologies. "Imagining the New Media Encounter" demonstrates the necessity of new methods and pedagogies from a theoretical rather than instrumental perspective (Liu). As a consequence, it is an article that resonates loudly in the undergraduate and graduate classroom, framing a semester's discussions and laboratory experiments.

In the first version of this chapter, I posited that using the term "digital humanities" is often a tactical error, particularly when trying to introduce digital humanities into the undergraduate curriculum. In this version, however, I want to take this point one step further and suggest that our concern with defining and propagating the field writ large can interfere with innovative but necessarily local thinking about digital skills, curriculum, and research at both the undergraduate and graduate level. In the fall of 2014, I structured even my graduate DH course to avoid the "What is DH?" genre entirely, and I think the course was better for that decision.[4] Rather than beginning with interminable discussions of what counts or does not count, or who is in or who is out, we worked toward an understanding of the field's contours by studying the theories and methods that undergird it, focusing on projects and critical publications rather than the field's attempts at self-definition. This still is not a perfect model. For instance, I have realized from students' evaluations that in future iterations we need to spend more time analyzing "case study" projects in depth. But I have found "Texts, Maps, Networks: Digital Literary Studies" a more productive and stimulating class than its immediate predecessor, "Doing Digital Humanities."

"Humanities" Is a Vague and Often Local Configuration

Indeed, a course once called "Doing Digital Humanities" has become, in its subtitle, "Digital Methods for Literary Study." This is not because the course is no longer a DH course, or no longer interdisciplinary. In fact, more history students took the course on "Texts, Maps, Networks" than took previous iterations. But I have realized that while my teaching and scholarship benefit enormously from interdisciplinarity, that interdisciplinarity is grounded in my training in textual studies, the history of the book, and critical editing. In my teaching and my scholarship, I have become increasingly convinced that DH will only be a revolutionary interdisciplinary movement if its various practitioners bring to it the methods of distinct disciplines and take insights from it back to those disciplines.

We should not forget, of course, that "humanities" is not itself a self-evident signifier. What "humanities" does and does not comprise differs from definition to definition and from institution to institution. For our students, as for many of us, the word "humanities" is opaque, vaguely signaling fields that are not the sciences. Even that broad definition is hazy. Consider anthropology, which is in some institutional structures a humanities field and in others a social science; the same sometimes goes for history. To talk about "digital humanities," then, is not to talk to our students but to talk to each other. I write this not to disavow that important conversation, but to suggest that it need not interfere with our teaching.

Attempts have been made to revise the terms we use. Bill Pannapacker recently proposed "Digital Liberal Arts" as a replacement for DH, particularly at small liberal arts colleges in which a wider range of fields might be wanted to rally under the banner:

> Stop calling it "digital humanities." Or worse, "DH," with a knowing air. The backlash against the field has already arrived. The DH'ers have always known that their work is interdisciplinary (or metadisciplinary), but many academics who are not humanists think they're excluded from it.
>
> As an umbrella term for many kinds of technologically enhanced scholarly work, DH has built up a lot of brand visibility, especially at research universities. But in the context in which I work, it seems more inclusive to call it digital liberal arts (DLA) with the assumption that we'll lose the "digital" within a few years, once practices that seem innovative today become the ordinary methods of scholarship. (Pannapacker, "Stop Calling It 'Digital Humanities'")

It seems DLA has gotten some traction at several institutions. But for undergraduates, I would argue "digital liberal arts" misses the mark just as badly as "digital humanities." For many undergraduate students, "liberal arts" signifies no more than "humanities," and I actually suspect "digital" signifies in ways quite opposite to our intentions.

Undergraduates Are Scared by Digitality

We pair "digital" with "humanities" and feel we have something revolutionary, but for our undergraduate students the word "digital" is profoundly unimpressive. Their music is digital. Their television is digital. Many of their books and school materials are and have always been digital. To brag that *our* humanities (or our liberal arts) are digital is to proclaim that we have met a base requirement for modern communication. It would be like your bank crowing that you can check your account online. Of course you can. At this point, you would only notice if you could not do so.

Far from signaling our cutting-edge research and teaching, I suspect that the phrase "digital humanities" often raises perfectly valid worries with our students, many of whom have spent their entire educational careers sleepwalking through ed tech nightmares. The point I want to make here is exactly opposite familiar refrains about "digital natives." That our students have spent their educational lives using digital tools—researching online, using applications to learn math or spelling, listening to PowerPoint lectures and then downloading the slides, or even drawing boxes around the Mona Lisa's face on a Smartboard—does not mean that they have learned all that much about or from those digital tools.

These same students then came to universities being "disrupted" by the MOOC evangelists, though these students' very presence in our universities perhaps signals that they realized before many faculty and administrators that self-guided higher education from recorded lectures is not the newest thing in the world; lectures on tape and then CD have been around for decades. Of course, MOOCs are hardly synonymous with digital humanities, and indeed, DH practitioners have been among the most critical of the MOOC movement, which largely transplants a lecture-based model of education online. But our students' perceptions of educational technology are bound to shade their readings of tech in humanities classrooms.

In short, I worry that we dismiss our students' reservations about DH too blithely. Our students' technological skepticism—which is often expressed through the language of "I'm not very good at computer stuff"—is not the same as our colleagues' technological skepticism. Many of our students choose literature or history or art history or religious studies because they wanted to read and think deeply rather than follow what they perceive as a more instrumentalist education in business or technical fields. To do so they often resist substantial pressure from family and friends pushing them toward "more practical" majors, which are often (though incorrectly) perceived to be more technical majors. Of course, DH can help students read and think deeply, but we would do well to try and see this exchange from our students' perspective.

In many ways, I think the way we often frame DH tries a bit too hard to achieve a *Dead Poets Society* moment: "your other teachers taught you literature with close reading and literary criticism, but in my class we're going to disrupt that stale paradigm using *computers*. Now rip up your books and pull out your laptop!" But those attempts fall flat, for all the reasons I have tried to articulate thus far. Indeed, a growing body of evidence from students correlates at least two of the points I have made here. A 2011 survey by EDUCAUSE, for instance, found that only one in four students believe strongly that "their institution uses the technology it has effectively." The survey tells us also a good deal about what students (or perhaps more to the point, what EDUCAUSE) believe "technology" entails—namely, hardware and commercial software. Few students surveyed believe their instructors use technology effectively, and many more students (a majority) believe they understand technology better than their teachers.[5] For such a student, imagine how it must sound to hear her teacher talking up "computers" and "digital tools."

But Don't Panic

Because students do love doing DH things, when those DH things are framed around particular skills, often within disciplinary structures. I would argue more and more that the way we should integrate DH into the undergraduate curriculum is as a naturalized part of what literary scholars or historians or other humanists do. Teach distant reading alongside close reading and do not worry about proving how revolutionary the former is. Such an approach also lowers the barrier for "doing DH" in the undergraduate classroom. You do not have to be a DH expert to create—or better yet borrow—a few exciting DH assignments.

I find it helpful to look back at that EDUCAUSE report and infographic again, this time focused on what students reported wanting to learn more about. When asked what skills they wished they knew better, students responded programming language (48 percent), audio creation (41 percent), e-portfolios (40 percent), geo-tagging (40 percent), and speech recognition (38 percent). These skills have little to do with particular hardware or commercial software. Indeed, the skills students want are those that would allow them to create their own digital work and perhaps even their own tools—in other words, they want to learn to engage with, and not simply use, technology in the classroom.

So how do we do this in the humanities? In the remainder of this chapter I want to offer four principles for curricular incursion that have worked well in my own classes at both the undergraduate and graduate levels. I will use examples from a few of my courses, but I will draw most heavily on "Technologies of Text," the course I revised based on the curricular committee rejection that I described at the start of the chapter.[6] Where "Introduction to Digital Humanities" failed, "Technologies of Text" succeeded, and I think after teaching it (and thus revising it) four times I am beginning to understand why.

1. START SMALL

My first principle is simply to start small. You do not need an entire DH curriculum, or even a designated DH course, to introduce substantial digital pedagogy into your classes. In departments with a single faculty member interested in digital humanities—and this describes a *significant proportion* of humanities departments—small beginnings help instructors focus on what DH they can teach effectively. To be frank, I was not prepared to teach *all of DH* in that "Intro to Digital Humanities" course I proposed. By contrast, my "Technologies of Text" class is in essence a book history class with a strong DH undercurrent. Maintaining such disciplinary focus perhaps limits my students' sense of the wider DH field, but it allows me to teach a few things well rather than teaching everything poorly. And indeed, my graduate course has moved in the same direction. Over the years my syllabus has shifted from a rapid introduction to as many methods and tools as possible to a more focused introduction to a few tools, methods, and theoretical conversations I know very well. In the older version of my graduate course, in which I did try to survey *all of the DH* field, I felt students left with only a glancing understanding of any aspect of the field. In the current version, students leave with fewer but more well-developed skills from which they can build.

My courses aptly illustrate the challenges that Rafael Alvarado suggests the larger field faces in defining itself. Alvarado claims[7] that "there is simply no way to describe the digital humanities as anything like a discipline" in large part because of the sheer amount of skill and knowledge such a claim would require of DH scholars and teachers structures. If coverage is the aim of our "Introduction to DH" courses, only polymaths, as Alvarado names the occasional scholar who could master all facets of DH, could effectively teach those courses ("The Digital Humanities Situation").

In many of my courses, one way students start small with DH skills is through closer considerations of digital media for scholarly and popular communication. One of my students, for instance, used a Tumblr blog to analyze fandom communities on Tumblr. By working in the platform she was analyzing, she was able to directly interact with the communities under study, which enriched her argument significantly. In a course most broadly about book history, students can directly contrast the affordances and limitations of digital and print technologies, as in another student's remediation of Montaigne's essays into blog form (and be sure to read the FAQ).[8] Neither of these examples required extensive technical expertise from students or instructor, but such projects cultivate media thinking that could inform a deeper engagement with DH methods later in this class or in another. Indeed, the Tumblr project on fandom did blossom into a wider interest in digital humanities for the student who produced it and later expanded it as part of her thesis.

2. INTEGRATE WHEN POSSIBLE

My second principle builds on the first: integrate when possible. "Technologies of Text" teaches many DH ideas and skills: in our labs we edit Wikipedia, encode documents in TEI, learn the basics of computational text analysis, or program chatbots using the Python programming language. These labs, however, are framed not within a narrative of recent scholarly revolution, but instead within a sweeping discussion of book and media history. Before students learn to operate a 3D printer, then, they have transcribed manuscripts by candlelight in a simulation of the medieval scriptorium, made rag paper, set type and printed on a letterpress, visited the National Braille Press, and spent significant time with rare books in the university and local public libraries.

Each of these labs helps students understand technology not as something we invented ten years ago (give or take), but as a long continuum of human activity. As I write in the course description:

> Our primary objective in this course will be to develop ideas about the ways that such innovations shape our understanding of texts (both classic and contemporary) and the human beings that write, read, and interpret them. We will compare our historical moment with previous periods of textual and

Figure 36.1. "Technologies of Text" students transcribe manuscripts by candlelight.

technological upheaval. Many debates that seem unique to the twenty-first century—over privacy, intellectual property, information overload, and textual authority—are but new iterations of familiar battles in the histories of technology, new media, and literature. Through the semester we will get hands-on experience with textual technologies new and old through labs in paper making, letterpress printing, data analysis, and 3D printing. The class will also include field trips to museums, libraries, and archives in the Boston area.

By contextualizing our moment of digital remediation historically, as but the latest phase in a long history of textual reinvention, I help students understand why my assignments ask them to experiment across modalities. Those assignments push students beyond their comfort zone—for English students, their comfort zone is writing a seven-page paper—asking them to consider the medium as well as the message of their own research and arguments.

These labs prepare students to develop their own "unessays" as midterm and final assignments.[9] I am hoping to develop another piece about these unessays, and so won't belabor a discussion of them here, but I do want to highlight the broad range of engagements students choose in the model unessays linked from the assignment, which include theoretical engagements with media, personal TEI encoding projects, video essays, argumentative listicles, altered books, built Morse code devices, and even physical "twitter poetry bot" generators. These disparate assignments allowed

Figure 36.2. "Technologies of Text" students set type and print at the Museum of Printing in North Andover, Massachusetts.

students to grapple with those aspects of the course they found most compelling, both in terms of content and in terms of technology and method. In an "Introduction to DH" course these engagements might not all make sense, but under the rubric of book and communications history they certainly do. For several of these students, working on such assignments did generate a broader DH interest, and they have developed personal DH projects or gone on to work for other DH projects ongoing at Northeastern.

3. SCAFFOLD *EVERYTHING*

In order to move our students toward this kind of engagement, however, we must scaffold *everything*, from the introduction of new skills into particular classes to the progression of skills through a curriculum. The necessity of such scaffolding brings us back to the mistaken notion of the "digital native"—a notion, I would argue, that leads to frustration for both students and teachers. The idea that our students *must have* innate technological skills because they have grown up in a computer-saturated world is equal, to my mind, with assuming all drivers must be excellent mechanics or auto designers because they have spent so much time behind the wheel or, perhaps more germanely, assuming all students *must be* innately gifted writers because they have grown up around books and paper. We know the latter is not true—indeed, the very existence of college writing programs belies the idea—but we somehow persist in the former delusion when the fact is that our students need

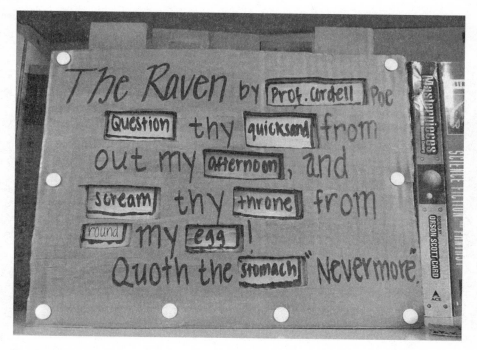

Figure 36.3. Part of a "Technologies of Texts" student's "unessay" assignment, in which she created a physical "twitter poetry bot" along the model of those we had programmed in Python for one of the course labs.

as much guidance thinking about and working with technologies of all kinds as they do writing a cogent argument. Indeed, these two tasks can be wonderfully coupled, as some of my classroom examples illustrate.

In making these points, I mean not to impugn our students' abilities. Decades of scholarship in rhetoric and composition have shown two very interesting things: first, at least since the late nineteenth century, each generation of college students has been writing at about the same relative ability level as the previous generation, though our demands of college writers have steadily increased over time. And second, at least since the late nineteenth century, each generation of college professors has been certain that "kids today" write far worse than their own generation did. Taking these historical studies as instructive, then, I mean only to suggest that so-called digital natives are neither more nor less innately adept at computational work than "digital immigrants." When introducing digital humanities into our classrooms, we must structure those introductions for students with a wide range of technical backgrounds and aptitudes.

Certainly technological imagination is not now nor has it ever been innate. Yes, our students have grown up with apps and iTunes and YouTube—but it is one thing to be able to use a particular piece of hardware or software and another thing altogether to imagine what it might do or mean if pushed beyond its typical use, or even more again to imagine what might be created in its stead. It is these latter skills that good digital humanities pedagogy must inculcate: not "how to use x tool," though that is likely part of it, but more "understanding how x functions, delineating its affordances and limitations, and then imagining y or z."

In an interdisciplinary course I taught on "Mapping Boston," for instance, students used Neatline in their final projects to build "deep maps" of particular neighborhoods or landmarks in the city, layering historical photographs, maps, geospatial data, literary texts, and other elements to build arguments about their city. These final projects grew out of a semester of labs in which students learned to work with geospatial data in GIS, georectify historical maps in Map Warper, and manage digital archival objects in Omeka. I was particularly struck by those students who worked to push Neatline to its limits. Consider one student's project on the 1919 Molasses Flood in Boston's North End, or another student's project on the history of Boston's Harbor Islands.[10] Both are messy in their way—we did not have time to revise these projects for usability as I would wish—but I was impressed by how these projects in particular integrated so many of our course methods and theoretical conversations and the creativity with which they approached the idea of "mapping" as interpretation. Both of these students brought to our seminar interests from their majors and previous courses, and both continued to think about mapping in subsequent classes in their majors.

4. THINK LOCALLY

In order to scaffold across classes, of course, we must have a clear sense of where DH skills and courses fit into our institutions. We must think locally and create versions of DH that make sense not at some ideal, universal level but at specific schools, in specific curricula, and with specific institutional partners. One major objection to my rejected "Introduction to Digital Humanities" course was that I wanted to offer it at the junior or senior level. Introductory courses, the curricular committee noted, are offered at the 100 level. Courses at the 300 and 400 level should build on those introductory courses.

I was at first perturbed by what I saw as semantic pedantry, but as a new professor I had little sense of how such committees operate and how they work to structure students' experiences through their time at a given institution. Since then I have worked on such committees and largely come to understand their perspective. I was tacitly assuming that my course would build on skills that students picked up in their lower-division courses. I expected my students to be competent researchers and independent workers. I planned to build on their work in lower-division literature and history courses. I was in essence proposing a digital capstone to the traditional humanities skills they had picked up elsewhere in the curriculum, and my colleagues were right to worry that branding it an "intro" would confuse students and advisers about the aims and activities of the course.

This is a very specific example, but there are broader implications. Thinking locally can help you connect DH classes and projects to collections, colleagues, and your institution's mission—all things more likely to generate student enthusiasm and buy-in, and perhaps also cooperation from colleagues and administrators. By thinking locally you can link your courses to libraries, museums, research centers, or other campus-level initiatives. Students love to build projects that make use of their institutions' collections and contribute to their institutions' legacy, and these often public projects can energize them to work that much harder, as they can create materials with a chance of life beyond the classroom itself. Such projects also give faculty the chance to work closely with librarians and other colleagues we might otherwise see only for short information sessions.

When I taught at St. Norbert College, for instance, our collections were very specialized, relating primarily to the holdings or records of the Norbertine Order that founded and supported the college. For their class projects, then, my "Technologies of Text" students worked with the materials we had, primarily through the Center for Norbertine Studies. One team created an exhibit of *Canon Missae* in the center's collections, for instance, while a biology student delved into the papers of a prominent Norbertine biologist who had worked at the college. Working with these materials benefited the students, who felt they were contributing to their institution, and the college as well, giving a public face to its hidden collections.

Whither "Digital Humanities"?

All of these reflections bring me—as always, it seems—to the term digital humanities itself.[11] I wrote in the earlier version of this chapter that "digital humanities will only remain a vital interdisciplinary movement" if it speaks self-consciously back to the legacy fields to which its practitioners also belong. In *Digital_Humanities*, the authors argue that humanities disciplines need to each establish agendas for computational practices—not as a way to assimilate, per say, but instead as a way to generate vital, critical, experimental questions that will keep the field moving forward. In particular, they assert in capital letters that "THE HUMANITIES NEED TO ESTABLISH DISCIPLINE-SPECIFIC AGENDAS FOR COMPUTATIONAL PRACTICE" (Burdick et al.). But if "digital humanities" is not a meaningful term in undergraduate classrooms, and graduate students and faculty are charged with developing discipline-specific computational approaches, then why use DH at all?

Perhaps "digital humanities" will one day fall away, as some have predicted. If it falls away because DH methodologies have become widely accepted as possible ways (among many) to study literature, history, and other humanities subjects, this seems to me a fine outcome. But that is not the DH situation right now. Despite the attention the field has received over the past few years, it remains a very small cohort.

There has certainly been a slight uptick in DH hiring over the past few years, but as a result we often forget that the vast majority of humanities departments include no digital humanities scholars. Indeed, as Roopika Risam showed in 2013,[12] rumors about the DH job market greatly outpace the actual numbers of DH jobs or hires ("Where Have All the DH Jobs Gone?"). We forget also that junior faculty hired to "do DH" for their institution face a steep challenge actually doing that work and making it legible to their colleagues at tenure time. Many colleges eager to "get a DH person"—and as a subtext, often, to begin getting grant money—have not well considered the infrastructure required to do DH well—and, as a corollary, to do DH in a way that will attract grant money. And certainly the vast majority of schools, including those actively working to build DH, have not actively reshaped their tenure and promotion guidelines to reward the kinds of knowledge that DH projects often produce. In such an environment, digital humanities remains a useful banner for gathering a community of scholars doing weird humanities work with computers. And I suspect it will continue to be useful for a while yet, long after the current wave of DH mania subsides, I hope, into a more productive rapprochement with the larger humanities fields.

NOTES

1. http://chronicle.com/blogPost/The-MLAthe-Digital/19468.

2. See Terras, Nyhan, and Vanhoutte, with further reading and updates at http://blogs.ucl.ac.uk/definingdh/further-reading/.

3. Adeline Koh, comment of February 21, 2012, at this author's blog: http://ryancordell.org/teaching/dh-interdisciplinarity-and-curricular-incursion/#comment-31.

4. Course details at http://f14tmn.ryancordell.org.

5. ECAR National Study of Undergraduate Students and Information Technology, 2011 Report, http://www.educause.edu/library/resources/ecar-national-study-undergraduate-students-and-information-technology-2011-report.

6. Course details at http://f14tot.ryancordell.org.

7. http://transducer.ontoligent.com/?p=717.

8. Two examples of student projects are available at http://operation-critique.tumblr.com and https://essais1580.wordpress.com.

9. The unessay assignment (with links to sample student work) can be found at http://f14tot.ryancordell.org/assignments/unessays/.

10. These student assignments are available at http://omekasites.northeastern.edu/DeepMap/neatline/fullscreen/1919-molasses-flood and http://omekasites.northeastern.edu/DeepMap/neatline/fullscreen/boston-harbor-islands.

11. This phrase I use echoes the title of a talk given by Lee Skallerup Bessette at the University of Cincinnati Libraries, November 17, 2014, https://storify.com/readywriting/wither-dh-new-tension-directions-evolutions-in-the.

12. http://roopikarisam.com/2013/09/15/where-have-all-the-dh-jobs-gone.

BIBLIOGRAPHY

Alvarado, Rafael. "The Digital Humanities Situation." *The Transducer* (blog), May 11, 2011. http://transducer.ontoligent.com/?p=717.

Burdick, Anne, Johanna Drucker, Peter Lunenfeld, Todd Presner, and Jeffrey Schnapp. *Digital_Humanities.* Cambridge, Mass.: MIT Press, 2012.

Kirschenbaum, Matthew. "What Is Digital Humanities and What's It Doing in English Departments?" In *Debates in the Digital Humanities,* ed. Matthew K. Gold. Minneapolis: University of Minnesota Press, 2012. http://dhdebates.gc.cuny.edu/debates/part/2.

Liu, Alan. "Imagining the New Media Encounter." In *A Companion to Digital Literary Studies,* ed. Susan Schreibman and Ray Siemens. Oxford: Blackwell, 2008. http://www.digitalhumanities.org/companionDLS/.

Pannapacker, William. "The MLA and the Digital Humanities." *Chronicle of Higher Education Brainstorm Blog,* December 28, 2009. http://chronicle.com/blogPost/The-MLAthe-Digital/19468/.

———. "Stop Calling It 'Digital Humanities.'" *Chronicle of Higher Education,* February 18, 2013. http://chronicle.com/article/Stop-Calling-It-Digital/137325/.

Risam, Roopika. "Where Have All the DH Jobs Gone?" Research blog, September 15, 2013. http://roopikarisam.com/2013/09/15/where-have-all-the-dh-jobs-gone/.

Terras, Melissa, Julianne Nyhan, and Edward Vanhoutte, eds. *Defining Digital Humanities: A Reader.* Burlington, Vt.: Ashgate, 2013. http://blogs.ucl.ac.uk/definingdh/further-reading/.

Dropping the Digital

JENTERY SAYERS

<script type="text/ruination"> // begin argument

VAR STR="DIGITAL HUMANITIES"; VAR STR="DIGITAL HUMANISTS";
// DEFINE VARIABLES

In the following paragraphs, I "ruin" digital humanities in order to isolate what makes them distinct or compelling in the first place. Ruination is a technique whereby a text is procedurally manipulated to render it less persuasive.[1] The manipulated text is interpreted alongside the original, and key differences between the two versions are analyzed. Informed by a long legacy of text manipulation, including work by OuLiPo, Brion Gysin, Kathy Acker, Tom Phillips, Lisa Samuels, Jerome McGann, Mark Sample, Stephen Ramsay, and—most relevant here—Kari Kraus, I consider ruination's conjectural exercises.[2] Borrowing from Kraus's "Conjectural Criticism," we might say ruinations are "concerned with issues of transmission, transformation, and prediction (as well as retrodiction)" (Kraus, ¶4).[3] They facilitate "knowledge about what might have been or could be or almost was," with a bias toward possibility rather than demonstrability or empiricism (¶5). Ruinations point to possible trajectories without fully illuminating them, and they insinuate that the stuff of digital humanities has been insufficiently identified and described. They also underscore how digital humanities may differ from other strains of humanities and—most important—ask what else digital humanities could be, or should do, or might at least consider.

For the purposes of this argument, my particular ruination technique is "dropping the digital," where I remove the word "digital" from a sentence in order to examine how its absence shapes meaning and interpretation.[4] My source material for ruination is the 2012 edition of *Debates in the Digital Humanities* (edited by Matthew K. Gold). Not only is this collection of essays rife with persuasive writing and argumentation, it also begs for additional attention to how the word "digital" is used to qualify humanities research.

document.write(str.replace("digital", " . . . ")); // commence ruinations

Here, then, is the first in a series of ruinations, where each use of ellipses marks the removal of the word "digital" from *Debates in Digital Humanities*:

And the field of digital humanities does move quickly. (Gold, xii)[5]

This first selection is found in Gold's introduction to the volume. It is compelling because it succinctly highlights the everyday information inundation that—for better or worse—subtends digital humanities. Consider how project developments are routinely announced via Twitter, or the rate at which short-form scholarship is published online, or the fact that a majority of the 2012 *Debates* volume is anchored in discussions about the future. As Ian Bogost suggests by way of Alex Reid: "The digital humanities are just the humanities of the present moment."[6] In practice, a digital humanities of the present moment entails studying and using emerging technologies, however alpha they may be. It also entails reconfiguring how humanities practitioners communicate and through what channels, reimagining the peer-review process, and keeping up with a high frequency of software updates, bug fixes, standards versioning, and hardware mods.

Appropriately enough, when I ruin Gold's sentence, we get what most would consider a contradiction in terms:

And the field of . . . humanities does move quickly. (Gold, xii)

Historically, the humanities have not been known for their speedy pace, but rather for the glacial temporality of archival research and print communications.[7] However, my intent here is not to ask how we can rev up the humanities, or how we can coax humanities faculty into running with new technologies. Instead I am interested in how this ruination raises questions about achieving a self-reflexive digital humanities, especially as scholarly labor comes face-to-face with the alienating instruments that organize and measure networked communications.[8] Kathleen Fitzpatrick's work on metrics as well as Matthew Kirschenbaum's insights about Twitter—both in the 2012 *Debates* volume—are a fantastic start here. On the topic of web traffic and usage statistics, Fitzpatrick observes: "Digital scholarly publishing will require rethinking the ways that such traffic is measured and assessed, moving from a focus on conversion to a focus on engagement—and engagement can be quite difficult to measure" ("Beyond Metrics," 457).[9] On the role of Twitter in digital humanities, Kirschenbaum remarks: "the fact is that Twitter more than any other technology or platform is—at the very moment when digital humanities is achieving its institutional apotheosis—the backchannel and professional grapevine for hundreds of people who self-identify as digital humanists" ("Digital Humanities As/Is," 416–17).[10] Both comments prompt us to seriously consider how digital scholarly communications are tied to productivity, the quantified self, social analytics, attention accumulation, and online reputation management.[11]

While analytics may help us study the nodes and edges of social networks, they also favor reification and individuation.[12] Many important questions emerge from this tension: what are the practical implications of keeping one foot in, say, hermeneutics, and the other in the immersive use of gadgets? What are the ethical implications of relying on backchannels and algorithms for sorting and circulating scholarship? What are the structural implications of usage statistics playing a prevalent role in the shelf lives of digital projects? What are the long-term implications of ripping a journal article from its binding and individually assessing its impact factor? How, if at all, can we actually measure an audience's engagement with digital projects? And what would it mean for digital humanities to establish their own metrics for scholarly communications, or to resist such metrics altogether?[13] These issues surely have complex histories—in the humanities as well as in the arts and sciences—and we need to spend some significant time assessing their potential consequences as we participate in networked scholarly communication.

Echoing the attention to attention running throughout this chapter thus far, my second selection for ruination stresses the public dimensions of digital humanities:

> The digital humanities amply demonstrates that there is no one size fits all. The heterogeneity of the field is in many ways an asset, and the current external interest and attraction presents a significant opportunity for expansion. (Svensson, 47)[14]

From "Beyond the Big Tent," Patrik Svensson's comment about external interest and attraction is telling, especially when we consider the ways in which digital humanities have garnered support from agencies such as the Social Sciences and Humanities Research Council of Canada (SSHRC) and the U.S. National Endowment for the Humanities (NEH). The passage is even more telling when it is ruined:

> The . . . humanities amply demonstrates that there is no one size that fits all. The heterogeneity of the field is in many ways an asset, and the current external interest and attraction presents a significant opportunity for expansion. (Svensson, 47)

Most people will likely agree with the first sentence. Arguing for a coherent or homogenous identity for the humanities is probably a stretch, and very few (if any) people would pursue such a unifying vision today. Still, the second half of the second sentence raises a brow. Many readers may wonder whether—especially since the mid-1990s (when, for example, the NEH budget was dramatically cut)—the humanities have managed to gain external interest and attraction. As goes the stereotype, most humanities researchers work alone in their contiguous-but-not-connected offices, generating scholarship intended for a small group of like-minded experts who are also in academe. In response to such stereotypes, the issue of external interest and attraction is central to ongoing initiatives such as 4Humanities as well as Alan Liu's arguments in "Where Is Cultural Criticism in the Digital Humanities?"[15] There, Liu claims cultural criticism has not played a prominent role in digital humanities thus far. In fact, he provocatively declares: "The digital humanities have been oblivious to cultural criticism" (491). Later, he adds that, if invested in cultural criticism (e.g., critical approaches to metadata), digital humanities would be poised to strategically direct eyes toward humanities research. And in the final paragraph of his essay, he asserts: "the greatest service that the digital humanities can contribute to the humanities is to practice instrumentalism in a way . . . to show that the humanities are needed alongside the sciences to solve the intricately interwoven natural, technological, economic, social, political, *and* cultural problems of the global age" (502).

The key word in that sentence—and perhaps in the entire piece—is "instrumentalism," a contentious term in technology studies, to say the least. It is contentious because (to polarize a debate for the sake of illustration) on the one hand instrumentality suggests either a purposeful or unconscious lack of attention to the value-laden character of technologies.[16] In this sense, an instrument is treated naively or enthusiastically, as a mere vehicle for unambiguously converting input into output. By extension, the instrument determines cultural change. It is a positivist agent of progress that gains authority over time. On the other hand, instrumentality is neatly imbricated with building infrastructure, developing projects, creating resources, and articulating action items.[17] It allows people to work within institutions and transform them. It is arguably essential to making a difference in the academy, and it is vital to laboratory research, for example. That said, balancing this impulse for institutional change with a critical awareness of how technologies proliferate worldviews is no doubt difficult; some would say impossible. Even if that balance is achieved, it inevitably produces contradictions and ironies. It is also new ground for most humanities practitioners, which is perhaps one reason why Svensson's ruined passage is not persuasive.[18]

That is, people in the humanities are rarely trained to conduct research and compose in ways that gain large-scale interest and external attraction. And the sorts of humanities Liu and Svensson imagine are public humanities that demand both rhetorical savvy and capacities for code-switching (e.g., switching between subject positions, languages, and rhetorical conventions), not to mention technical and theoretical competencies.[19] Presumably they also necessitate a distribution of expertise and communication across media types, disciplines, and communities of practice across sectors. Since such a knowledge base exceeds the time and labor of a single person, collaboration would seem essential to this work.

Consequently, we might follow Svensson's and Liu's gestures with two sets of questions: first, in what ways, exactly, are digital humanities public humanities? Is gaining external attraction and publicly communicating humanities research online a matter of access alone (e.g., the switch from pay-walled articles to open-access communications and open-source projects)? Is it primarily a matter of the medium (e.g., shifting from PDFs and DOCs to videos, blogs, and graphs)? Or is it a more fundamental transition toward participatory action research? Of intimately involving publics in the scholarly production process, much in the way many science studies practitioners and policy experts have advocated for at least the last decade?[20] For example, when working with culturally sensitive materials, who should oversee, moderate, and maintain digital collections? Where should they be stored? Through what kinds of institutional and community support? Whatever the answers here, one thing is certain: a mistake is made when public research is equated with a reduction of academic complexity (e.g., a "dumbing down" of research for "nonexpert" audiences). Code-switching and juggling instrumentalism's multiple valences are no simple tasks, and a digital public humanities requires a strategic-yet-flexible, multimodal-yet-medium-aware approach earnestly invested in the democratization of knowledge.[21]

The second set of questions takes another turn, away from method and toward the actual content of digital projects: To what will—or should—digital humanities attract attention? How can they balance their long-standing investments in pre-twentieth-century materials with cultural studies of the present? With inquiries into contemporary art, literature, and politics? Initiatives such as *Vectors* journal, Media Commons, HASTAC, 4Humanities, and many Omeka projects are already pushing the envelope in these directions, and more cultural work is going live by the day. Still, one tangible challenge for many humanities practitioners is learning how to unpack the present with the future in mind. Methods such as Kraus's conjectural criticism move in that direction.[22] Kraus argues: "We might, for starters, imagine conjecture as a knowledge toolkit designed to perform 'what if' analyses across a range of texts" (¶15). Another direction is the recent work of #transformDH, particularly the ways in which its participants occupy digital humanities, reimagine it, and directly address issues of equity and social justice.[23] For instance, in the "Periscope" section of *Social Text,* Alexis Lothian and Jayna Brown write: "speculation means something else for those who refuse to give its logic over to power and profit. To speculate, the act of speculation, is also to play, to invent, to engage in the practice of imagining." Words such as "speculation," "play," and "imagining" are growing increasingly familiar to digital humanities as of late, and the authors give such terms a tangible context when they remark: "At a moment when so many have been struggling to enact alternatives to the depressing world produced by Wall Street's speculative failures, we need to practice imagining now more than ever" (Lothian and Brown). Which is to say, both conjectural criticism and #transformDH exhibit how serious speculation about possible futures is irreducible to *Minority Report*-esque fetishes for gadgets. In this particular case, it is about arguing for what the cultural climate of digital humanities (as a set of social relations) should be, and—as the 2012 *Debates* volume demonstrates—such arguments are rife with productive anxieties and differences of opinion.[24]

Of course, the notion of difference is itself a line of inquiry in *Debates*. Not only does Svensson's 2012 essay explore the possibilities for a heterogeneous digital humanities involving multiple, perhaps incongruous traditions; in the volume, digital humanities also confront a prevailing ideology of niceness and its concomitant politics of inclusion, which risks eliding or foreclosing important cultural differences. Jamie "Skye" Bianco contends: "we must ask ourselves what sort of social narrative is [niceness]—one that smoothes out potential social differences before conflict sets in? Is this the substrate for our ethics and for a theorization of the social? Who does it include and what (self- and other-) disciplines must we practice and propagate?" (99). These questions are addressed to practitioners as well as projects.

Bianco's concerns about difference, narrative, and ethics bring me to my third selection for ruination:

> We need to examine the canon that we, as digital humanists, are constructing, a canon that skews toward traditional texts and excludes crucial work by women, people of color, and the GLBTQ community. (Earhart, 316)

This passage, from Amy Earhart's "Can Information Be Unfettered? Race and the New Digital Humanities Canon," is compelling because it identifies a tendency in digital humanities to construct and maintain a very skewed canon—a re-presentation of a normative past. Earhart contextualizes this observation, providing a number of telling examples from existing projects and initiatives. She writes: "A quick perusal of 'The Minority Studies' section [of *Voice of the Shuttle*] . . . reveals that a tremendous number of the projects have become lost. For example, of the six sites listed in 'General Resources in Minority Literature,' half cannot be located, suggesting that they have been removed or lost" (313). She adds: "The National Endowment of [*sic*] Humanities awarded 141 Digital Humanities Start-Up Grants from 2007 through 2010. Of those grants, only twenty-nine were focused on diverse communities and sixteen on the preservation or recovery of diverse community texts" (314). Earhart then caps off her remarks with a reference to her own work, particularly the ways in which it blends critical race theory with competencies in metadata and classification:[25] "My digital project, *The Nineteenth-Century Digital Concord Archive*, is . . . invested in exploring how to appropriately apply technological standards to shifting constructions of race represented in textual materials. Our current challenge is how we represent varying representations of blackness found in the census in a database" (316). These are only a few of the many examples referenced throughout Earhart's essay, and through a web ethnography of sorts, she convincingly shows how the vexed relations between race, representation, and digital technologies must be addressed through multiple layers of project development, from support (e.g., grants), digitization (e.g., encoding manuscripts), and metadata (e.g., Dublin Core descriptions) to expression (e.g., visualizing data), narrative (e.g., in online scholarly exhibits), discovery (e.g., through search engines), and storage (e.g., sustaining the shelf life of web-based resources). In short, project creation is important, but so, too, is caring for those projects over time.

And when the digital is dropped from her sentence—

> We need to examine the canon that we, as . . . humanists, are constructing, a canon that skews toward traditional texts and excludes crucial work by women, people of color, and the GLBTQ community. (Earhart, 316)

Now we are faced with an obvious yet necessary question: How did these exclusions happen, especially when, for decades now, humanities scholars have been demystifying and transforming canons? How and why has humanities work in cultural studies not more visibly—and "visibly" is a key word here—influenced the methods of many digital humanities projects? What are the histories that enabled such a bias in the creation and care of digital collections? And what other humanities approaches are necessary to not only revise skewed canons but also speak more directly to the contemporary intersections of computation and culture? This last question is vital, since it implies that biases are not simply glitches to be "remedied" or "fixed" through new, inclusionary collections of historical materials. They are symptomatic of worldviews warranting acknowledgment and sustained interrogation. In other words, much like the color-coded residential security maps exhibited via the *Testbed for the Redlining Archives of California's Exclusionary Spaces* (T-RACES), they are the stuff of material culture that can become our very objects of inquiry—the willfully ignored inscriptions of racism and sexism in national records, the discarded documents of local histories, the dusty artifacts in and outside our archives.[26] Through transformative methods across media cultures, these neglected objects should be encountered anew, interpreted, rendered discoverable, and maintained (with infrastructural and personnel support), not conveniently forgotten, corrected, or erased.

In other words, in tandem with recovery work, digital humanities need more projects accounting for how skews are produced in computational culture. Tara McPherson's "Why Are the Digital Humanities So White?" provides such an account, unfolding digital humanities' tendency to avoid topics like race, immigration, and neoliberalism through an intricate history of UNIX and color-blindness since World War II (140). Resonating with Wendy Chun's research on interface design and source code, McPherson interrogates the instrumental character of computational technologies and how they actively shape information (often beyond the perceptions and consciousness of their developers or users).[27] Importantly, this approach assumes neither a hermeneutics of suspicion nor a deliberate injection of discriminatory politics into technologies.[28] Resisting such reductive readings, McPherson makes two crucial moves in her essay. First, she writes: "I am highlighting the ways in which the organization and capital in the 1960s powerfully responds—across many registers—to the struggles for racial justice and democracy that so categorized the United States at the time" (149). She then adds: "The emergence of covert racism and its rhetoric of color blindness are not so much intentional as systemic. Computation is a primary delivery method of these new systems, and it seems at best naive to imagine that cultural and computational operating systems don't mutually infect one another" (149). For McPherson, digital humanities are so white because—for one reason among many—they are steeped in a longer legacy of bracketing off race from computational techniques, of justifying the reduction of cultural ambivalence for the sake of intuitive designs, neat ontologies, simple expressions, and clean interfaces (140, 145–48). Instead of identifying this legacy and stopping there, however, McPherson gestures toward some possible interventions: "In extending our critical methodologies, we must have at least a passing familiarity with code languages, operating systems, algorithmic thinking, and systems design. . . . We need new hybrid practitioners: artist-theorists, programming humanists, activist-scholars; theoretical archivists, critical race coders" (154). Comparable to Earhart's line of inquiry, this hybrid work necessarily resists any divide between critical theory and technical competencies, thinking and doing, or yacking and hacking. As it conjectures about possible futures (e.g., where canons are not skewed), it is also extremely aware of the frameworks it mobilizes for historical inquiry.

Of course, the history of digital humanities tends to be a very particular one, generally situated in humanities computing and differing just a touch from McPherson's articulation. For example, my last selection for ruination—from Johanna Drucker's "Humanistic Theory and Digital Scholarship"—states:

> As the first phase of digital humanities reveals, the exigencies of computational method reflect its origins in the automation of calculation. (87)

This first phase is anchored in Father Busa's concordance and corpus linguistics, including the discreteness, persistence, and general lack of ambiguity ostensibly afforded by midcentury computation (Drucker, 87).[29] Drucker then proceeds to highlight other phases, such as repository building and critical editing in the 1990s and, more recently, data mining, graphical expression, and geospatial representation (87–89). Ultimately, she argues that digital humanities need to extend humanities interpretations beyond the "effects of computational methods" and into the models, process, and warrants of those methods, including how data is taken, not given (89, 94). She compellingly concludes with this statement: "The question is not, Does digital humanities need theory? but rather, How will digital scholarship be humanistic without it?" (94).

When Drucker's sentence—and thus a portion of the history on which it relies—is ruined, we get a rather amusing statement:

> As the first phase of . . . humanities reveals, the exigencies of computational
> method reflect its origins in the automation of calculation. (87)

The exigencies of computational methods remain rooted in the automation of calculation, yet the humanities become a constellation of disciplines fundamentally about that method. That is, from their start the humanities reveal an interest in automation and computation. This scenario is difficult to imagine, indeed. Nevertheless, the ruination prompts us to speculate: What are the stakes of unpacking the humanities through the ways in which—returning for a moment to McPherson's arguments—they have historically infected computation and vice versa? How would such projects allow us to imagine the investments and methods of digital humanities as part and parcel of the humanities more generally, and to account for humanities computing as an important pressure point in a broad and no doubt conflicted genealogy of the field?

None of these questions invalidates corpus linguistics, critical editing, data visualization, or the construction of concordances and repositories. None of them denies histories articulated by scholars such as Kirschenbaum, who underscores "the institutional, material, and social contexts in which the term digital humanities has already been taken up and operationally embedded" ("Digital Humanities As/Is," 426). Yet most important, none of them tacitly or overtly advocates for abandoning digital humanities as a name, label, tradition, or set of social relations. On the contrary, these questions push the field to conjecture toward a big tent history for big tent humanities—to recognize how the array of practices falling under the digital humanities umbrella corresponds with an array of historical conditions and worldviews, many of which we may not classify as humanities computing or digital humanities. Here, Elizabeth Losh's "Hacktivism and the Humanities" is particularly relevant, as it carves out a space for digital dissent and electronic civil disobedience within digital humanities. Participants in these histories will probably not be found frequently on the pages of, say, *Literary and Linguistic Computing* or *Digital Humanities Quarterly*. And, as Losh acknowledges, some digital humanities practitioners may not deem hacktivism at all relevant to the field (178–79). Yet if critics actually attend to the history she provides, then they will learn that hacktivism tells us a lot about why "both the hacktivist and the more mainstream digital humanist must be sensitive to the vulnerability and imperfection of digital knowledge systems to pursue their avocations on a day-to-day basis," reminding us of the often overlooked, material roles that surprises play in our quotidian contributions to digital projects (181).

While Losh's account of hacktivism is more or less contemporary in character, we can easily reference others like it that precede World War II, personal computing, the Internet, or the terms "humanities computing" and "digital humanities." Consider the technology and media history work of Wendy Chun, Mary Ann Doane, Matthew

Fuller, Lisa Gitelman, Sadie Plant, Jonathan Sterne, and Cornelia Vismann, among many others. While these scholars' methods are not always (if ever) computational, their research gives audiences a robust sense of the humanities' long legacy of engaging technologies on issues such as instrumentalism, labor, power, positivism, exclusion, exploitation, and metrics. They also allow us to wrangle with current digital humanities topics without falling back on "digital" as our keyword—without assuming that the impulses of our work are unique to life after the Internet, the ENIAC, or the personal computer. Sure, emerging technologies included, much about life today is extraordinarily new. To acknowledge as much is pivotal to—recalling Bogost by way of Reid—a humanities of the present moment. Nevertheless, a big tent history of digital humanities (i.e., relying on material traditions of the term as well as material traditions of the practices informing it) provides us with some rich case studies for better understanding the technocultural complexity of the 2010s. For instance, what might data visualization and geospatial representation learn from a humanities history of graphic design and graphical expression?[30] What might encoding and metadata learn from a material history of classification and information organization?[31] What might interaction and user experience design learn from a literary history of experimental poetry? These kinds of questions respond directly, or so it seems, to Drucker's injunction: to practice digital humanities, from start to finish, with the humanities in mind. Of course, one possible consequence is that the boundaries between humanities and critical theory (on the one hand) and computation and technical competencies (on the other) are blurred. But that is precisely the point. After all, blurring is a likely outcome of a field that moves quickly. Yet we need not stop there. We can also learn a lot from how and why we blur lines *and* make boundaries in digital humanities.

</script> // *end ruinations*

In keeping with the routines of procedural manipulation, I now repeat myself: *Debates in the Digital Humanities* is rife with persuasive writing and argumentation; it also begs for additional attention to how the word "digital" is used to qualify humanities research. By dropping the digital, my intent was not only to—example after example after example—demonstrate how the volume is compelling. It was also to call more attention to the general economy of digital humanities: their evolving metrics, including means of quantification and accumulation; their perceptions of what it means to do public work, including external relations and instrumentalism; their canons and resources, including skews and exclusions; and their histories of particular terms and practices. Appeals to economy frequently entail speculation, generally so that people can anticipate the course of things and later confirm (or, better yet, reward) their suspicions. However, as we probably well know, another approach stresses complicity—not what we will risk, gain, or prove but what we can no longer ignore and what we must work to change. Although I can only conjecture, I hope the latter is the trajectory of digital humanities.

NOTES

This chapter is based on a paper I gave during the Debates in the Digital Humanities symposium at the University of Pittsburgh on April 6, 2012. I would like to thank Jamie "Skye" Bianco, Johanna Drucker, Matthew K. Gold, Lauren Klein, Richard Lane, Elizabeth Losh, Mark Marino, Tara McPherson, Amanda Phillips, and the UVic-VIU Digital Humanities-Theory Discussion Group (supported by the Electronic Textual Cultures Lab) for their generous and tremendously informative feedback on earlier versions of this chapter.

1. For an example of ruination, see Harman's "Lingis's Best Latour Litany." Harman ruins the fourth page of Alphonso Lingis's *Abuses*. While his aim is to show why Lingis's writing is compelling, his ruination also demonstrates how aesthetic exercises are value-laden and thus political. For instance, in a move subtended by orientalism, Harman suggests that the procedural removal of the "exotic" from Lingis's prose (e.g., replacing "the port of Balik-papan in Kalimantan" with "the port of Galveston in Texas") renders it banal. Harman does not engage questions about for whom, by whom, and under what assumptions the "exotic" becomes banal. Here, a lesson for ruination exercises is to avoid reducing them to harmless or purely aesthetic play, as if textual experimentation is somehow outside ideology.

2. For more on procedural approaches to writing and composition, see Motte on OuLiPo. As a group of writers and mathematicians, OuLiPo (Ouvroir de litterature poten-tiale) is—or has been—invested in creative production by means of generative constraints and procedures (as opposed to, say, romantic notions of inspiration). For more on "defor-mative" manipulations of texts, see Samuels and McGann, who suggest: "Deformance does want to show the poem's intelligibility is not a function of the interpretation, but that all interpretation is a function of the poem's systemic intelligibility. Interpreting a poem after it has been deformed clarifies the secondary status of the interpretation. Perhaps even more crucially, deformance reveals the special inner resources that texts have when they are con-stituted poetically. Nor do judgments about the putative quality of the poem matter" (Sam-uels and McGann, 40). They demonstrate two kinds of deformance: reading backward and "isolating deformation," or "eliminating everything from a poem except certain words, to see what happens when they are alone on the page" (40). Since this essay is not especially concerned with form or the "special inner resources that texts have," I prefer ruination to deformance. For more on hacking as a form of procedural text manipulation, see Sample's *Hacking the Accident,* which is an algorithmically altered version of *Hacking the Acad-emy* (Cohen and Scheinfeldt). According to Sample: "*Hacking the Accident* replaces every person, place, or thing in *Hacking the Academy* with the person, place, or thing—mostly things—that comes seven nouns later in the dictionary." For more on algorithmic criticism as text manipulation, see Ramsay, *Reading Machines*: "For while it is possible, and in some cases useful, to confine algorithmic procedures to the scientific realm, such procedures can

be made to conform to the methodological project of invention without transforming the nature of computation or limiting the rhetorical range of critical inquiry. This is possible because critical reading practices already contain elements of the algorithmic. Any reading of a text that is not a recapitulation of that text relies on a heuristic of radical transformation. The critic who endeavors to put forth a 'reading' puts forth not the text, but a new text in which the data has been paraphrased, elaborated, selected, truncated, and transduced" (*Reading Machines,* 16). The notion that critical reading practices already contain elements of the algorithmic is central to the gestures and warrants of this chapter, especially as they concern the ruination technique.

3. In that article, Kraus claims: "Not least, we would need to work decisively to bring conjectural criticism into the 21st century. Because it has traditionally been described as a balm to help heal a maimed or corrupted text, conjecture is in desperate need of a facelift; the washed-up pathological metaphors long ago ceased to strike a chord in editorial theory" ("Conjectural Criticism," ¶13). Although this chapter does not engage editorial theory, it nevertheless takes seriously Kraus's claim to reinvigorate conjectural criticism. Ruination is one technique for making claims not intended for testing. It also follows in the what-if, conjectural legacy of wordplay.

4. This gesture is not identical to the suggestion that, in the future, all humanities will become digital humanities, or the digital humanities will eventually be the humanities. Among other things, I am particularly interested in distinguishing digital humanities from other humanities fields, even if I am sympathetic to the growing use of digital methods across those fields.

5. This selection begins an important paragraph in Gold's introduction. Here is how the sentence proceeds: "And the field of digital humanities does move quickly; the speed of discourse in DH is often noted with surprise by newcomers, especially at conferences, when Twitter feeds buzz with links to announcements, papers, prototypes, slides, white papers, photos, data visualizations, and collaborative documents" (Gold, xii).

6. Bogost elaborates: "Everyone who does humanities today can't avoid immersion in digital stuff. We read and write with computers, we communicate with them, we administer our lives and our programs with them. That said, humanists have been among the least willing to admit that fact. Whether through age, ignorance, truculence, or idiocy, the humanities have tried desperately to pretend that the material world is the same as ever" ("Getting Real"). In "Digital Humanities: Two Venn Diagrams," to which Bogost refers, Reid writes: "For centuries (if not always), the humanities have dealt with objects: books, historical artificats [sic], works of art, performances, films, etc. But I think the Latourian-correlationist observation is insightful here. We have largely dealt with these objects in two ways. 1) We have addressed our human response, our ability to represent these objects to ourselves. 2) We have spoken of 'culture' and 'materiality' but in a vague, abstract way. As such, when we speak of the digital we have focused on the digital as a mode of representation and we have considered 'digital culture' in broad and abstract terms. A realist ontology allows us to investigate objects in new ways. It makes the laptop, the mobile phone, the AR network, the procedurality of the video game all sites for humanistic investigation in new ways."

7. One exception here is the very print volume under discussion. From writing to publication, the 2012 edition of *Debates in the Digital Humanities* was finished in roughly a year's time.

8. Here, I cannot help but refer to Benjamin on Klee's "Angelus Novus": "The angel would like to say, awaken the dead, and make whole what has been smashed. But a storm is blowing from Paradise; it has got caught in his wings with such violence that the angel can no longer close them. This storm irresistibly propels him into the future to which his back is turned, while the pile of debris before him grows skyward. This storm is what we call progress" (Benjamin, 257–58). If for only one reason, here Benjamin informs the current pace of digital humanities by drawing correlations between the storm of progress and universal (or self-fulfilling) history. To be self-reflexive (e.g., through a materialist historiography) is to arrest and interrupt time in the face of productivity, accumulation, and progress (262–64). Recalling this claim resists tendencies to speak about digital technologies in revolutionary terms, which are often temporal in character (e.g., more than ever before, digital technologies speed up the acquisition, exchange, and dissemination of information).

9. Fitzpatrick elaborates with an example: "A visitor to a substantive scholarly blog post, for instance, who simply snagged the post in Instapaper and moved on but then later sat and read the article at leisure would not appear to have had a significant engagement with the text when in fact that engagement could well have been far more in depth than the average. We need far better markers for that kind of engagement in order for basic traffic to become legible" ("Beyond Metrics," 457).

10. Elsewhere, Kirschenbaum writes: "Whatever else it might be, then, the digital humanities today is about a scholarship (and a pedagogy) that is publicly visible in ways to which we are generally unaccustomed, a scholarship and pedagogy that are bound up with infrastructure in ways that are deeper and more explicit than we are generally accustomed to, a scholarship and pedagogy that are collaborative and depend on networks of people and that live an active 24/7 life online" ("What Is Digital Humanities," 9). Of course, Twitter enables that 24/7 online presence.

11. For more on the Quantified Self movement, visit http://quantifiedself.com/about. There, Quantified Self is described as "a collaboration of users and tool makers who share an interest in self-knowledge through self-tracking. We exchange information about our personal projects, the tools we use, tips we've gleaned, lessons we've learned. We blog, meet face to face, and collaborate online. There are three main 'branches' to our work." According to the Quantified Self website, those branches are: "The Quantified Self blog and community site," "Quantified Self Show & Tell meetings," and the "Quantified Self conference."

12. For more, see Cohen. He writes: "There has been much talk recently of the social graph, the network of human connections that sites like Facebook bring to light and take advantage of. If widely adopted, ORE could help create the scholarly graph, the networked relations of scholars, publications, and resources" ("The Vision of ORE").

13. Of course, projects such as *Digital Humanities Now* (http://digitalhumanitiesnow .org/) and the "Badges for Lifelong Learning" Digital Media and Learning Competition

are already unpacking the question of metrics and related algorithms. An ongoing issue is whether digital mechanisms substantially differ from previous approaches—whether they are not simply more refined (rather than radically new) approaches to gathering, analyzing, and expressing data.

14. In a gesture central to his conclusion, Svensson elaborates: "At the same time, we need to acknowledge that there is a core community associated with the digital humanities and that the all-encompassing, inclusive digital humanities may not always seem an attractive option to it. Multitude and variation may be seen as diluting the field and taking away from a number of epistemic commitments. This is a very valid concern, and various initiatives are bound to tackle this challenge in different ways. It would seem, however, that a big-tent digital humanities should not be predominantly anchored in one tradition" ("Beyond the Big Tent," 47).

15. According to its website (http://humanistica.ualberta.ca/about/), "4Humanities is a platform and resource for advocacy of the humanities, drawing on the technologies, new-media expertise, and ideas of the international digital humanities community. The humanities are in trouble today, and digital methods have an important role to play in effectively showing the public why the humanities need to be part of any vision of a future society."

16. For a critique of this form of instrumentalism, see Bianco. She writes: "Tools don't reflect upon their own making, use, or circulation or upon the constraints under which their constitution becomes legible, much less attractive to funding. They certainly cannot account for their circulations and relations, the discourses and epistemic constellations in which they resonate. They cannot take responsibility for the social relations they inflect or control. Nor do they explain why 10 percent of today's computer science majors are women, a huge drop from 39 percent in 1984 (Stross), and 87 percent of Wikipedia editors—that would be the first-tier online resource for information after a Google search—are men (Wikimedia)" ("This Digital Humanities," 99).

17. This form of building and resource creation is more or less what Tom Scheinfeldt seems to have in mind when he argues: "At the very least, we need to make room for both kinds of digital humanities, the kind that seeks to make arguments and answer questions and the kind that builds tools and resources with questions in mind, but only in the back of its mind and only for later. We need time to experiment and even, as Bill Turkel and Kevin Kee have argued, time to play" ("Where's the Beef?" 57–58).

18. Of course, there are exceptions here. In the humanities, fields such as media studies and science and technology studies have engaged instrumentalism for some time. Liu highlights both fields as domains and practices that could inform digital humanities' otherwise oblivious relationship with cultural criticism (501).

19. Of note, Svensson's emphasis on a heterogeneous digital humanities (including his point that the "big tent" should not be predominantly anchored in a single tradition) echoes some of Jamie "Skye" Bianco's concerns in Debates: "What quick, concatenating, and centrifugal forces have so quickly rendered the many under the name of one, the digital humanities?" (97). Bianco's essay is also one reason why, throughout most of this chapter,

"the" does not preface "digital humanities." For an explanation of the "big tent" concept, see Fitzpatrick, "Reporting from the Digital Humanities 2010 Conference," where she uses the term to describe digital humanities as "a nexus of fields within which scholars use computing technologies to investigate the kinds of questions that are traditional to the humanities, or, as is more true of my own work, who ask traditional kinds of humanities-oriented questions about computing technologies." Later, Fitzpatrick adds: "By bringing together such a wide range of interests, affiliations, and perspectives to the connections between computing and the humanities, the [Digital Humanities annual] conference can give one a snapshot of the state of things, a broad sense of what scholars who work within those connections are concerned about."

20. For some responses to these questions, see "Democratizing Knowledge." Also see the *Mukurtu* project directed by Kim Christen as well as *Public Secrets* by Sharon Daniel. For example work from science studies, see the Science Studies Network at the University of Washington.

21. For more on this topic, see "Digital Humanities, Public Humanities," a special issue of *New American Notes Online* (http://nanocrit.com/issues/5/introduction-digital-humanities-public-humanities).

22. Kraus elaborates: "In this view, the text is a semiotic system whose discrete units of information can be artfully manipulated into alternate configurations that may represent past or future states. Of course the computing metaphors alone are not enough; they must be balanced by, among other things, an appreciation of the imponderable and distinctly human qualities that contribute to conjectural knowledge. But formalized and integrated into a curriculum, the various suggestions outlined here have the potential to give conjecture a new lease on life and incumbent editorial practices—much too conservative for a new generation of textual critics—a run for their money" (¶15).

23. For more on #transformDH, see http://www.transformdh.org.

24. On the social relations of digital humanities and the 2012 *Debates* volume in particular, see Ramsay, "The Hot Thing," where he argues: "The fundamental posture of a benevolent community is that it wishes its own members—and, more importantly, the people who are not members—well. It doesn't unduly concern itself with its own survival, or even its precise definition. And it doesn't concern itself at all with the idea that it will one day be supplanted by something else. It wishes the people it is 'supplanting' well; it wishes the people that will supplant it well."

25. For more on the topic of classification and cultural formations, see Brown, Clements, and Grundy. On the development of the *Orlando Project,* they write: "It is a challenge to represent diversity in an encoding scheme, because the tags assign material to categories, and so contain it. Some readers will come to Orlando to seek out writers associated with particular cultural identities and positions: Jewish, working-class, lesbian, or immigrant writers, for instance. But on the other hand such categories are discursive rather than ontological. Heritage is mixed, and allegiances and practices shift. And precisely because such identity labels are constituted through linguistic and social practices, vocabularies associated with them change over time. A history grounded largely in the careers of individual

writers must take account of the fact that cultural identities shift within the wider society, as well as within an individual's self-conception or lifetime."

26. Visit T-RACES at http://salt.umd.edu/T-RACES. The project visualizes the practice of redlining (i.e., when banks and other groups draw red lines around areas in which they will not invest) while also offering access to digitized documents from the National Home Owners' Loan Corporation (HOLC) archive. Ultimately, T-RACES exhibits the entanglement of white supremacy with banking practices and real estate development in the United States, specifically during the mid-twentieth century.

27. For instance, in *Programmed Visions,* Chun writes: "This book, therefore, links computers to governmentality neither at the level of content nor in terms of the many governmental projects that they have enabled, but rather at the level of their architecture and their instrumentality. Computers embody a certain logic of governing or steering through the increasingly complex world around us" (9).

28. For a particular history of this debate, see Winner, "Do Artifacts Have Politics?"

29. For more on Father Busa and the history of humanities computing, see Hockey.

30. For one such history of graphic design, see Drucker and McVarish. Here, I am also indebted to the Victorian studies work of Alison Hedley. For instance, see Hedley's contributions to Arbuckle et al., "Teaching and Learning Multimodal Communications."

31. For instance, see Bowker and Star.

BIBLIOGRAPHY

"About the Quantified Self." *Quantified Self: Knowledge through Numbers.* http://quanti-fiedself.com/about/.

Arbuckle, Alyssa, Alison Hedley, Shaun Macpherson, Alyssa McLeod, Jana Millar Usis-kin, Daniel Powell, Jentery Sayers, Emily Smith, and Michael Stevens. "Teaching and Learning Multimodal Communications." *International Journal of Learning and Media* 4, no. 1 (2013). http://ijlm.net/node/13300.

"Badges Competition: Call for Proposals." *Digital Media and Learning Competition 4: Badges for Lifelong Learning. http://dmlcompetition.net.*

Benjamin, Walter. "Theses on the Philosophy of History." In *Illuminations: Essays and Reflections,* ed. Hannah Arendt, 253–64. New York: Schocken, 1969.

Bianco, Jamie "Skye." "This Digital Humanities Which Is Not One." In *Debates in the Digital Humanities,* ed. Matthew K. Gold, 96–112. Minneapolis: University of Minnesota Press, 2012.

Bogost, Ian. "Getting Real." *Ian Bogost: Videogame Theory, Criticism, Design,* March 9, 2011. http://www.bogost.com/blog/getting_real.shtml.

Bowker, Geoffrey C., and Susan Leigh Star. *Sorting Things Out: Classification and Its Consequences.* Cambridge, Mass.: MIT Press, 1999.

Brown, Susan, Patricia Clements, and Isobel Grundy, eds. "Scholarly Introduction: Going Electronic." In *Orlando Help.* Cambridge: Cambridge University Press, 2006. http://orlando.cambridge.org/public/svDocumentation?formname=t&d_id=GOINGELECTRONIC.

Cohen, Dan. "The Vision of ORE." *Dan Cohen* (blog), March 3, 2008. http://www.dancohen
.org/2008/03/03/the-vision-of-ore/.

Cohen, Dan, and Tom Scheinfeldt, eds. *Hacking the Academy: A Book Crowdsourced in
One Week,* May 28, 2010. http://hackingtheacademy.org/.

Chun, Wendy H. K. *Programmed Visions: Software and Memory.* Cambridge, Mass.: MIT
Press, 2011.

Daniel, Sharon. "Public Secrets." *Vectors* 2, no. 2 (2007). http://vectors.usc.edu/projects
/index.php?project=57.

"Democratizing Knowledge." *HASTAC: Humanities, Arts, Science and Technology Advanced
Collaboratory,* September 21, 2009. http://hastac.org/forums/hastac-scholars
-discussions/democratizing-knowledge-digital-humanities.

Digital Humanities Now: Discover the Best of Digital Humanities Scholarship. http://digital
humanitiesnow.org/about/.

Drucker, Johanna. "Humanistic Theory and Digital Scholarship." In *Debates in the Digital Humanities,* ed. Matthew K. Gold, 85–95. Minneapolis: University of Minnesota
Press, 2012.

Drucker, Johanna, and Emily McVarish. *Graphic Design History: A Critical Guide.* New
York: Pearson, 2008.

Earhart, Amy. "Can Information Be Unfettered? Race and the New Digital Humanities
Canon." In *Debates in the Digital Humanities,* ed. by Matthew K. Gold, 309–18. Minneapolis: University of Minnesota Press, 2012.

Fitzpatrick, Kathleen. "Beyond Metrics: Community Authorization and Open Peer
Review." In *Debates in the Digital Humanities,* ed. Matthew K. Gold, 452–59. Minneapolis: University of Minnesota Press, 2012.

———. "Reporting from the Digital Humanities 2010 Conference." *Chronicle of Higher
Education ProfHacker* (blog), July 13, 2010. http://chronicle.com/blogs/profhacker
/reporting-from-the-digital-humanities-2010-conference/25473.

4Humanities: Advocating for the Humanities. http://4humanities.org/.

Gold, Matthew K. "Introduction." In *Debates in the Digital Humanities,* ed. by Matthew
K. Gold, Minneapolis: University of Minnesota Press, 2012.

Harman, Graham. "Lingis's Best Latour Litany." *Object-Oriented Philosophy,* December
10, 2010. http://doctorzamalek2.wordpress.com/2010/12/10/lingiss-best-latour
-litany/.

Hockey, Susan. "The History of Humanities Computing." In *A Companion to Digital
Humanities,* ed. Susan Schreibman, Ray Siemens, John Unsworth. Oxford: Blackwell, 2004. http://www.digitalhumanities.org/companion/.

Kirschenbaum, Matthew. "Digital Humanities As/Is a Tactical Term." In *Debates in the
Digital Humanities,* ed. Matthew K. Gold, 415–28. Minneapolis: University of Minnesota Press, 2012.

———. "What Is Digital Humanities and What's It Doing in English Departments?" In
Debates in the Digital Humanities, ed. by Matthew K. Gold, 3–11. Minneapolis: University of Minnesota Press, 2012.

Kraus, Kari. "Conjectural Criticism: Computing Past and Future Texts." *Digital Humanities Quarterly* 3, no. 4 (2009). http://www.digitalhumanities.org/dhq/vol/3/4/000069/000069.html.

Liu, Alan. "Where Is Cultural Criticism in the Digital Humanities?" In *Debates in the Digital Humanities*, ed. Matthew K. Gold, 490–509. Minneapolis: University of Minnesota Press, 2012.

Losh, Elizabeth. "Hacktivism and the Humanities: Programming Protest in the Era of the Digital University." In *Debates in the Digital Humanities*, ed. Matthew K. Gold, 161–86. Minneapolis: University of Minnesota Press, 2012.

Lothian, Alexis, and Jayna Brown. "Speculative Life: An Introduction." *Social Text: Periscope*, January 4, 2012. http://www.socialtextjournal.org/periscope/2012/01/speculative-life-introduction.php.

McPherson, Tara. "Why Are the Digital Humanities So White?" In *Debates in the Digital Humanities*, ed. Matthew K. Gold, 139–60. Minneapolis: University of Minnesota Press, 2012.

Motte, Warren F., ed. *Oulipo: A Primer of Potential Literature*. London: Dalkey Archive Press, 2008.

"Mukurtu Project History." *Murkurtu*. http://www.mukurtu.org/about.

Ramsay, Stephen. "The Hot Thing." *Stephen Ramsay* (blog), April 9, 2012. http://stephenramsay.us/text/2012/04/09/hot-thing/.

———. *Reading Machines: Toward an Algorithmic Criticism*. Champaign, Ill.: University of Illinois Press, 2011.

Reid, Alex. "Digital Humanities: Two Venn Diagrams." *Digital Digs*, March 9, 2011. http://www.alex-reid.net/2011/03/digital-humanities-two-venn-diagrams.html.

Sample, Mark. *Hacking the Accident*. http://hacking.fugitivetexts.net/.

Samuels, Lisa, and Jerome McGann. "Deformance and Interpretation." *New Literary History* 30, no. 1 (1999): 25–56.

Scheinfeldt, Tom. "Where's the Beef? Does Digital Humanities Have to Answer Questions?" In *Debates in the Digital Humanities*, ed. Matthew K. Gold, 56–58. Minneapolis: University of Minnesota Press, 2012.

"Science Studies Network (SSNet) at the University of Washington." *Science Studies Network*. http://depts.washington.edu/ssnet/about.php.

Svensson, Patrik. "Beyond the Big Tent." In *Debates in the Digital Humanities*, ed. by Matthew K. Gold, 36–49. Minneapolis: University of Minnesota Press, 2012.

"Testbed for the Redlining Archives of California's Exclusionary Spaces." *T-RACES*. http://salt.unc. edu/T-RACES/collaborate.html.

"Transformative Digital Humanities: Doing Race, Ethnicity, Gender, Sexuality, and Class in DH." *#tranformDH*. http://transformdh.org/.

Winner, Langdon. "Do Artifacts Have Politics?" *Daedalus* 109, no. 1 (1980): 121–36.

The Dark Side of the Digital Humanities

WENDY HUI KYONG CHUN, RICHARD GRUSIN,
PATRICK JAGODA, AND RITA RALEY

These four papers were presented at the 2013 MLA Convention in Boston, at a roundtable called "The Dark Side of Digital Humanities." Held in a large packed room, the session provoked a great deal of often-heated commentary—in the Twitter feed during and after the roundtable, in the discussion following the presentations, and in several blog posts and articles in the days following the convention. To get a sense of the aim of the roundtable, here is a selection from the roundtable proposal made to the MLA selection committee:

> The same neoliberal logic that informs the ongoing destruction of the mainstream humanities has encouraged foundations, corporations, and university administrations to devote new resources to the digital humanities. Indeed it is largely due to the apparently instrumental or utilitarian value of the digital humanities that university administrators, foundation officers, and government agencies are so eager to fund DH projects, create DH undergraduate and graduate programs, and hire DH faculty. And because there is no sign that these funding streams are going to dry up any time soon, and no sign on the horizon of an increase in funding for the "crisis humanities," there is great potential for increased tension between the "haves" of digital humanities and the "have-nots" of mainstream humanities.
>
> As a result of this tension, DH finds itself faced with a choice between what this roundtable playfully refers to as the "dark side" and "the light side" of the force. From the rise of for-profit universities to the push to develop online "content modules" branded with the names of established universities, it is clear that the 21st century university is fundamentally networked, nearly impossible to envisage without the objects and methodological practices of the computational sciences. What are the relations, then, between DH as a strict tool- and interface-based practice and the institutional logics of the new neoliberal networked universities? What can we make, further, of the links between the

claims made on behalf of both online learning initiatives and the new tools for digital humanities research: that they each have a radical, open, democratic aspect that is linked to mass literacy movements, making scholarly materials widely available to populations that had not previously had such access? What are the relations between new reading techniques (text mining, distant reading) and new modes of content delivery? Is it even possible to have "distant reading" without somehow also contributing to the project of distant education? Part of the work of this panel will be to envisage a model of digital humanities that is not rooted in technocratic rationality or neoliberal economic calculus but rather that emerges from as well as informs traditional practices of human-ist inquiry.

Our interest in this roundtable is on the impact of digital humanities on research and teaching in the humanities in higher education—the question of how digital humanities will impact the future of the humanities in general. Composed of entry-level, mid-career, and senior scholars with a history of curricular, scholarly, and hands-on engagement with digital media, this round-table will pose several questions and challenges to the digital humanities. Tak-ing neoliberalism as the economic framework within which we are reluctantly operating, we want to explore alternative paths on which digital humanists might travel to ameliorate, rather than exacerbate, some of the internecine divi-sions that this economic crisis has precipitated and intensified.

In order to preserve the flavor of the roundtable itself, the panelists have chosen to present their contributions in virtually unrevised form. Fuller versions, with appro-priate scholarly apparatus, can be found in a special issue of *Differences* (vol. 25, no. 1) 2014.

Wendy Hui Kyong Chun

This talk was given on January 4, 2013 at the Modern Language Association (MLA) convention. It focuses on a paradox surrounding DH: the disparity between the hype surrounding DH and the material work conditions surrounding much DH (adjunct/soft money positions, the constant drive to raise funds, the lack of scholarly recognition of DH work for promotions). In it, I call for us to work together—across the various fields and divisions—to create a university that is fair and just for all (teachers, students, researchers). I also call for us to find value in what is often dis-carded as "useless" in order to take on the really hard problems that face us.

We have been asked to be provocative, so I will use my eight minutes to provoke: to agitate and perhaps aggravate, excite, and perhaps incite. I want to propose that the dark side of the digital humanities is its bright side, its alleged promise: its alleged promise to save the humanities by making them and their graduates relevant, by giving their graduates technical skills that will allow them to thrive in a difficult and precarious job market. Speaking partly as a former engineer, this promise strikes me as bull: knowing GIS or basic statistics or basic scripting (or even server-side scripting) is not going to make English majors competitive with engineers or CS geeks trained here or increasingly abroad (****straight up programming jobs are becoming increasingly less lucrative***).[1]

But let me be clear. My critique is not directed at DH per se. DH projects have extended and renewed the humanities and revealed that the kind of critical thinking (close textual analysis) that the humanities have always been engaged in is and has always been central to crafting technology and society. DH projects such as "Feminist Dialogues in Technology," a distributed online cooperative course that will be taught in fifteen universities across the globe—courses that use technology not simply to disseminate but also to rethink and regenerate cooperatively education at a global scale—these projects are central. As well, the humanities should play a big role in "big data" not simply because we are good at pattern recognition (because we can read narratives embedded in data), but also and more importantly because can see what big data ignores. We can see the ways in which so many big data projects, by restricting themselves to certain databases and terms, shine a flashlight under a streetlamp.

I also want to stress that my sympathetic critique is not aimed at the humanities, but at the general euphoria surrounding technology and education. That is, it takes aim at the larger project of rewriting political and pedagogical problems into technological ones, into problems that technology can fix. This rewriting ranges from the idea that MOOCs, rather than a serious public commitment to education, can solve the problem of the spiraling cost of education (MOOCs that enroll, but do not graduate; MOOCs that miss the point of what we do, for when lectures work, they work because they create communities, because they are, to use Benedict Anderson's phrase, "extraordinary mass ceremonies") to the blind embrace of technical skills. To put it as plainly as possible: there are a lot of unemployed engineers out there, from forty-something assembly programmers in Silicon Valley to young kids graduating from community colleges with CS degrees and no jobs. Also, there is a huge gap between industrial skills and university training. Every good engineer has to be retaught how to program; every film graduate retaught how to make films.

My main argument is this: the vapid embrace of the digital is a form of what Lauren Berlant has called "cruel optimism." Berlant argues, "[A] relation of cruel optimism exists when something you desire is actually an obstacle to your flourishing" (1). She emphasizes that optimistic relations are not inherently cruel, but become so when "the object that draws your attachment actively impedes the aim that brought you to it initially." Crucially, this attachment is doubly cruel "insofar as the very pleasures of being inside a relation have become sustaining regardless of the content of the relation, such that a person or world finds itself bound to a situation of profound threat that is, at the same time, profoundly confirming" (2).

So, the blind embrace of DH (***think here of "The Old Order Changeth***)
allows us to believe that this time (once again) graduate students will get jobs.
It allows us to believe that the problem facing our students and our profession is a
lack of technical savvy rather than an economic system that undermines the future
of our students.

As Lauren Berlant points out, the hardest thing about cruel optimism is that,
even as it destroys us in the long term, it sustains us in the short term. DH allows
us to tread water: to survive, if not thrive (***think here of the ways in which so
many DH projects and jobs depend on soft money and the ways in which DH projects are often—and very unfairly—not counted towards tenure or promotion***).
It allows us to sustain ourselves and to justify our existence in an academy that is
increasingly a sinking ship.

The humanities are sinking—if they are—not because of their earlier embrace
of theory or multiculturalism, but because they have capitulated to a bureaucratic
technocratic logic. They have conceded to a logic, an enframing (***to use Heidegger's term***) that has made publishing a question of quantity rather than quality,
so that we spew forth MPUs or minimum publishable units. A logic, an enframing
that can make teaching a burden rather than a mission, so that professors and students are increasingly at odds. A logic, an enframing that has divided the profession
and made us our own worst enemies so that those who have jobs for life, deny jobs
to others—others who have often accomplished more than they (than we)—have.

The academy is a sinking ship—if it is—because it sinks our students into debt,
and this debt, generated by this optimistic belief that a university degree automatically guarantees a job, is what both sustains and kills us. This residual belief/hope
stems from another time when most of us could not go to university—another time
when young adults with degrees received good jobs, not necessarily because of what
they learned, but because of the society in which they lived.

Now, if the bright side of the digital humanities is the dark side, let me suggest
that the dark side—what is now considered to be the dark side—may be where we
need to be. The dark side, after all, is the side of passion. The dark side, or what has
been made dark, is what all that bright talk has been turning away from (critical
theory, critical race studies—all that fabulous work that #transformDH is doing).

This dark side also entails taking on our fears and biases to create deeper
collaborations with the sciences and engineering. It entails forging joint (frictional and sometimes fractious) coalitions to take on problems such as education, global change, etc. It means realizing that the humanities do not have a lock
on creative or critical thinking and realizing that research in the sciences can be
as useless as research in the humanities—and that this is a good thing. It is called
basic research.

It also entails realizing that what is most interesting about the digital in general is perhaps not what has been touted as its promise, but rather what is been dis-
carded or decried as its trash (***think here of all those failed DH tools, which have

still opened up new directions***). It entails realizing that what is most interesting is what has been discarded or decried as inhuman: rampant publicity, anonymity, the ways in which the Internet vexes the relationship between public and private, the ways it compromises our autonomy and involves us with others and other machines in ways we do not entirely know and control *(***think here of the constant and promiscuous exchange of information that drives the Internet, something that is usually hidden from us***).*

As Natalia Cecire has argued DH is best when it takes on the humanities, as well as the digital. Maybe, just maybe, by taking on the inhumanities, we will transform the digital as well.

Richard Grusin

The proposal I submitted for the 2013 roundtable opened with the following questions: "Is it only an accident that the emergence of digital humanities has coincided with the intensification of the economic crisis in the humanities in higher education? Or is there a connection between these two developments?" I began with these questions to help make sense of a feeling that has bothered me since MLA 2011—the incommensurate affective moods between panels on "digital" humanities and those on what might be understood as "crisis" humanities. This mood did not appear suddenly in 2011 but has been emerging, largely unspoken or ignored, at least since the financial meltdown of 2008. Nor has it gone away, as demonstrated by the current MOOC bubble, which generates digital utopian arguments about the remaking of higher education while intensifying the sense of precarity that has come to replace the security of tenure as the predominant affective mood of the academy. (See Figure 38.1.)

The first convention held on the new January schedule, MLA11 had been premediated as something of a new start for the Modern Language Association. This sense of a new beginning was accompanied in Los Angeles by a sense of loss evident in panels devoted to the crisis in the humanities that had been produced by radical funding cuts in public support for education in Europe, Australia, and the United States. These cuts, and the concomitant transformation of the professoriate, have been under way for several decades now (particularly in the United States), but in the recessionary aftermath of the financial crisis of 2008, they reached a level unimaginable to most academics. Panels on the immediacy of the crisis in the humanities were accompanied by widespread historical critique of the devastating effects of the neoliberal university and its catastrophic legacy for the future. The urgency of this new "critical university studies" was especially palpable in California, where the UC and CSU systems have only intensified their corporatism under continued funding cutbacks from the state.

Yet MLA11 was not all doom and gloom. The sessions I attended on the digital humanities were marked by an affectivity of vitality and growth, of optimism

Figure 38.1. "MOOC" search term trending for 2012.

and new beginnings. A comparatively prosperous IT funding climate created a set of issues and concerns for DH scholars very different from the economic crisis so palpable elsewhere. Packed panels on the future of digital humanities or the role of social media in fostering public intellectuals were filled with laughter, hope, and a sense of empowerment coming partly from the growing investment of human and economic capital in digital humanities projects by university administrators and partly from the financial resources available to DH teachers, scholars, and developers from corporate, nonprofit, and governmental foundations. DH panels, too, addressed challenges produced by the changing climate in the humanities. Of most concern among DHers was the difficulty in getting departmental and university tenure committees to provide appropriate credit to digital work that does not end up as refereed articles or scholarly monographs and the lack of professional recognition for technical labor, which was too often performed by nontenure track members of the academic precariate. For the purposes of this roundtable I would characterize the problem of reforming criteria for tenure and promotion a "first world problem" and note instead the way in which the institutional structure of digital humanities threatens to intensify (both within DH itself and among the humanities more broadly) the proliferation of temporary, insecure labor that is rampant not only in the academy but throughout twenty-first-century capitalism.

Paradoxically, the key to this dual intensification of academic precarity is the very act that digital humanists often use to distinguish themselves from the traditional humanities: "making things." At MLA11, DH panels devoted a good deal of energy to boundary drawing, which often depended on the distinction between making or producing things and critiquing them. In the panel on "The History and Future of Digital Humanities," for example, I learned that I was not a digital humanist because I did not code ("Keeping a blog does not make you a digital humanist") or because I did not "make things" (tell that to anyone who has labored for an hour or more over a single sentence). In the aftermath of MLA11, this invidious distinction between making things and merely critiquing them has come to be one of the generally accepted differences that marks DH off from the humanities in general. One could see the distinction at play in the brief Twitter exchange between HASTAC co-founder Cathy Davidson and *Vectors* founding editor Tara McPherson (see Figure 38.2). To McPherson's boundary-drawing "I worry that much of theory/cult studies tends toward critique as an end in itself," Davidson quickly replies: "Could not agree more. Critique hard. New ideas much harder. Making stuff work really, really hard!"

Put most starkly, academics on the left (which is pretty much everyone doing theory and cultural studies) blame the crisis in the humanities on the corporatization of the academy and the neoliberal insistence that the value of higher education must be understood instrumentally in economic terms. Thus the shrinking of the tenured and tenure-track professoriate, which has resulted in the sharp growth of temporary and part-time labor in the academy, has been justified by university administrators and state legislatures in terms of bottom-line economics and the need for higher education to train students for jobs not to read literature or study culture. Consciously or not, McPherson and Davidson echo the instrumentalism of neoliberal administrators and politicians in devaluing critique (or by extension any other humanistic inquiry that does not make things) for being an end in itself as opposed to the more valuable and useful acts "of making stuff work." But perhaps even more interestingly, as movements such as #transformDH have been articulating, it is the distinction between making things and doing more traditional scholarly work that perpetuates a class system *within* DH that generates an almost unbridgeable divide between those on the tenure-track, those in what have come to be called "alt-ac" positions, and those in even more precarious and temporary positions.

Sadly this pattern continues to reproduce itself in the current explosion of MOOC mania in print and online media, where much of the burgeoning interest in MOOCs has come from liberal administrators caught up in the convergence of neoliberal calculus and digital utopianism. At the same time that the market logic of neoliberalism has been used to decimate the mainstream humanities from within and without, this same logic has encouraged foundations, corporations, and university administrations to devote new resources to the digital humanities and to the development of MOOCs and other online forms of "content delivery." If it is largely due to their instrumental or utilitarian value that university administrators,

Figure 38.2. Cathy Davidson Twitter feed, September 9, 2012.

foundation officers, and government agencies are eager to fund DH projects, create DH undergraduate and graduate programs, and hire DH faculty, it is also the case that this neoliberal instrumentalism reproduces within the academy (both in traditional humanities and in digital humanities alike) the precaritization of labor that marks the dark side of information capitalism in the twenty-first century.

Patrick Jagoda

My remarks at the "Dark Side of the Digital Humanities" MLA roundtable on January 4, 2013, represent some preliminary thoughts and questions about games that I explore in greater detail in two essays that appeared in *boundary 2* and *Differences*.[2] My decision to include digital games in this conversation was not an attempt to claim the absolute centrality of games for the digital humanities. Additionally, my topic selection did not carry with it a necessary insistence upon a conflation between the "digital humanities" and "new media studies." Since 2013, and for the foreseeable future, these disciplinary categories, and the boundaries between them, are porous. They continue to be debated and renegotiated by scholars.

For the purpose of the broad and inclusive conversation that Richard Grusin organized for MLA, I decided to work within a broad rubric of "Comparative Media Studies," especially as it has been developed by N. Katherine Hayles in 2012 in *How We Think*. This inclusive category encourages conversations among scholars working in areas that include the materiality of print and digital productions (John Cayley, Matthew Kirschenbaum, and Jerome McGann); critical code studies (Wendy Chun, Matthew Fuller, and Lev Manovich); platform studies (Ian Bogost and Nick Montfort); technologically mediated forms of social interaction (Jodi Dean and Geert Lovink), information networks (Tiziana Terranova and Eugene Thacker) and electronic literature and digital art forms (N. Katherine Hayles, Henry Jenkins, Mark Marino, and Stephanie Strickland); the philosophical dimensions of digital media (Alexander Galloway, Richard Grusin, Mark Hansen, Friedrich Kittler, and McKenzie Wark); the cultural implications of digital technologies (Lisa Nakamura, Tara McPherson, and Rita Raley); the educational affordances of digital technologies (Cathy Davidson, Nichole Pinkard, and Katie Salen); and so on. This category also allows us to discuss a number of projects that include data mining, social network analysis, digital editions of print works, historical simulations, electronic literature, digital art, game design, and much more.

During our MLA roundtable, I was interested in producing a provocation and, briefly, introducing what is likely to remain one major problem of and for the digital humanities: the problem of games and gamification. The text that follows is meant as a starting point for a continued exchange. Perhaps, like the beginning of a game, it can be conceived as an invitation to play.

In recent years, games have touched practically every aspect of contemporary life. This certainly has something to do with a colossal video game industry that saw about $25 billion of revenue in 2011 in the United States alone with approximately 183 million American "active gamers" (that is, people who claim to play digital games an average of thirteen hours a week). Mobile gaming revenues rose to $1.2 billion in 2012 from $462 million just five years earlier.[3] Even with some stagnation in U.S. console sales, global digital game markets have also seen significant growth.

The expanding centrality of games, however, has also in many ways exceeded the realm of "gamers" through what is often called "gamification." Gamification, a term that derives from behavioral economics, refers to the use of game mechanics in traditionally nongame activities. This buzzword emerged only in the twenty-first century but has already found its way into writing on business, marketing, psychology, and design. We have seen the structure and logic of games creep into consumerism, crowdsourcing, and social media applications. For example, the *Chore*

Wars website, whose celebratory tagline claims that "finally, you can claim experience points for housework," converts undesirable chores into a game complete with superheroic role-playing and points that spur competition among housemates. *Nike+* shoes use sensors to transform a tedious running routine into a daily contest by tracking statistics, assigning achievement points, and allowing users to interface with cute avatars. *TaskRabbit* provides an online space for outsourcing minor jobs such as grocery delivery to other users while motivating contributors through a leaderboard and a statistics tracker that resembles a video game progress bar. *Phylo,* a game released by Jérôme Waldispühl's team at McGill University, invites players to help researchers with a common problem in comparative genomics—Multiple Sequence Alignments—by participating in pattern recognition challenges. All of these sites and apps (of which there are many others) suggest that life in the early twenty-first century is becoming permeated by games. Especially throughout the overdeveloped world in which digital media, smartphones, and high-speed Internet access have achieved a ubiquitous status for many people, games have become an exemplary cultural form that serves as a prominent metaphor of success.

Gamification is increasingly becoming a problem *of* and, in some ways, a problem *for* the digital humanities. This is especially noticeable in the realm of education. Over the last two years, we have seen numerous instances of game-based learning, including how-to guides (*Education Gamification Survival Kit*) and charter schools with gameplay curricula (Katie Salen's *Quest to Learn* and *ChicagoQuest* schools). Another ongoing initiative that has received a great deal of attention is the MacArthur Foundation's "Badges for Lifelong Learning" that began as a Digital Media and Learning competition. Subsequently, the badges concept was adopted by organizations such as the Digital Youth Network: a Chicago-based "digital literacy program that creates opportunities for youth to engage in learning environments that span both in-school and out-of-school contexts."[4] The Digital Youth Network awards badges to youth who develop skills in technology, new media art, and social media participation. The gamelike impulse to collect badges serves as motivation for continued learning and produces a "visual portfolio of competencies" for participating youth and mentors.

Adopters of gamification across different fields, including education, regularly proclaim it to be an unparalleled organizational technique. One leading proponent, Jane McGonigal, suggests that "reality is broken" and can only be saved through games that turn "a real problem into a voluntary obstacle" and activate "genuine interest, curiosity, motivation, effort, and optimism" among their players (*Reality Is Broken,* 311). Alongside beaming support for gamification as a cutting-edge panacea, however, there has been some resistance to this concept and its widespread application. Curiously, much of the criticism has come from game designers. Gamification has been condemned in these circles for adopting only the least artistic aspects of contemporary digital games—namely, their repetitive grinding and achievement-oriented operant conditioning. In a brief, polemical position paper published in *The Atlantic,* Ian Bogost contends that, above all, gamification is, in a philosophical sense, "bullshit." Drawing from moral philosopher Harry Frankfurt, he explains that "bullshit is used to conceal, to impress or to coerce." Gamification, for Bogost, engages in precisely this form of obfuscation insofar as it "takes games—a mysterious, magical, powerful medium that has captured the attention of millions of people—and makes them accessible in the context of contemporary business." Condemning the rhetorical deceptiveness of the term, Bogost suggests the alternative term "exploitationware," which decouples "gamification" from "games" ("Gamification is Bullshit").

As one starting point to this roundtable discussion, I hope this brief introduction to what we might call the problematic of gamification will suffice. As teachers, researchers, and university administrators, we are bound to see many more instances of gamification in the coming years. Digital games will remain a major topic of both the digital humanities and new media studies. So they are worth discussing. My own visceral reaction to the phenomenon has often been one of skepticism—or at least critical reflectiveness. Game-based badges or experience points motivate people to perform repetitive tasks but not necessarily to engage closely with texts or to undertake projects at a more complex level. At the same time, I am also a game designer and a scholar of digital games. In 2011, I co-founded an organization called Game Changer Chicago (GCC) with Melissa Gilliam, a professor of Obstetrics, Gynecology, and Pediatrics and Chief of Family Planning at the University of Chicago. GCC uses digital storytelling and game-oriented methods to teach disadvantaged youth on the South Side of Chicago about sexual and reproductive health.[5] We have focused on topics that include teen pregnancy, sexual violence, and socioeconomic health disparities. At GCC, our team produces interactive graphic novels, card games, and Alternate Reality Games projects with youth and for other youth to play. Through this new media production work and the research associated with it, I have found that when games are well designed, they entail many benefits. Such games offer players interactive contexts for thinking through and experimenting with complex problems in a hands-on fashion. Digital games enable multiple learning styles and engage players at several levels simultaneously through text, graphics, animation, audio, algorithms, haptic feedback, and different forms of interactivity. They spur decision making, enable role-playing, encourage play and discussion, and do many other things that exceed the addictiveness of point accumulation and victory that characterizes gamification.

So, then, despite the use of gamification for questionable ends (e.g., slot machines in Las Vegas), games are not, for me, a categorical evil but rather a rich problematic through which we might think, feel, and process our historical present. For this reason, I include games under Richard Grusin's heading of the "Dark Side of the Digital Humanities." I finish with three sets of questions that seek to navigate that darkness—a darkness that is, at different moments, terrifying and thrilling:

1. How should we think about games at a historical moment when gamification is arguably not merely a local phenomenon (for instance, in business, marketing, or education) but increasingly the form that economic and social reality takes in our world? Does it make sense to "game" an educational system that is founded on inequalities in a world that already uses games as a dominant metaphor and method?

2. Do the benefits of "badges" and other techniques of gamification outweigh their potential to operate as a reductive form of behaviorism? What are the benefits and limitations of incorporating badges into our pedagogy? Can we imagine (as many educators, theorists, and organizers are already attempting to do) badges that move beyond the superficial level of short-term behavioral modification? Can we instead create an infrastructure that builds a desire for lifelong learning and material skills into narratives, journeys, and games that youth (especially those youth coming from flailing or failing school systems) find compelling?

3. How might we imagine what are called "serious games" or "countergames" as complicating gamification? I am not necessarily advocating for either of these terms. However, along with scholar-designers such as Ian Bogost, Mary Flanagan, and Tracy Fullerton, I am committed to creating games that do not simply condition behaviors but encourage more complex forms of thought, speculation, practice, and action. For example, in 2012, along with my co-directors Katherine Hayles and Patrick LeMieux, I created an Alternate Reality Game called *Speculation* that explored the greed-driven culture of Wall Street investment banks and the 2008 economic crisis through a number of mini-games, collaborative narratives, and online forums.[6] This game experimented with a design that was more speculative (in a number of senses) than didactic. This final question, then, is one that I ask myself on a weekly basis. Within a period of gamification, how might we think, play, and act critically through games?

Rita Raley

For "The Dark Side of Digital Humanities" (tweeted at #s07), we were charged with producing eight-minute statements designed to provoke a wide-ranging discussion of the unsaid, understated, or under-theorized economic and political issues that are associated with, attend upon, or otherwise follow from the digital humanities as an institutional entity. In our respective prefatory statements we noted that we had been asked to provoke, but stimulate is closer to the thinking behind the roundtable. The formulation of the title of the roundtable was itself a provocation, however, and an exemplary instance of "behavioral priming," to borrow a phrase from N. Katherine Hayles's paper delivered the following day. One imagines that even the addition of a question mark in the program copy might have produced a different affective response in the audience, among which there still seems to be a fair bit of indignation, at least insofar as one can glean the mood from Twitter and blog postings. That the indignant audience should now include many who were not even at the conference, much less at the session, can only confirm Teresa Brennan's thesis on the "transmission of affect"—it was not simply biochemical response but also suggestion that produced the (contagious) affects of #s07.[7]

The upset seems in part to derive from a misunderstanding about our critical object: though our roundtable referred in passing to existing projects, collectives, and games that we take to be affirmative and inspiring, the "digital humanities" under analysis was a discursive construction and, I should add, clearly noted as such throughout. That audience members should have professed not to recognize themselves in our presentations is thus to my mind all to the good, even if it somewhat misses the mark. Indeed I would say that humanists above all else need continually to work to perceive and negotiate the institutional imaginary of informational technology so as not to fall into the trap of unconsciously adopting its optics. (My own cynicism about that institutional imaginary deepens with every administrative inquiry: I teach and write about digital media, so clearly I should want to participate in working groups and pilot programs for online education.)

Our topic is the dark side of the digital humanities. Not quite the evil side, as Matthew Fuller and Andrew Goffey term it, but, one hopes, not entirely unrelated. Evil media studies pursues "practices of trickery, deception, and manipulation"—one might even say tactics here—practices or tactics that endeavor "to escape [both] the order of critique" with all of its melancholic negativity, as well as "the postulates of representation," with their moralizing insistence on substance, essence, truth.[8] The dark side might on the face of it seem to suggest precisely that "order of critique," but our objective today is not to diagnose so as to circumscribe and pronounce upon the truth of things—not to uniformly fix what is after all a diverse set of techniques and activities within a singular frame and to seek out the hidden ideological core buried deep within it; not then to bring to light "the" dark side of "the" digital humanities. But it is to suggest that there are critical blind spots and assumptions that ought to be discussed before we triumphantly embrace the notion that the digital humanities is the only game in town worth playing or, even, the only conference sessions worth attending, not simply the "next big thing" but the only thing. If, as sometimes seems to be the case, the digital humanities is the hill on which the humanities has chosen to stake its last claim for relevance, to fight its last battle for recognition, then we would do well to examine the field and identify not just the exploits but perhaps also the lines of escape.

This is not new thinking of course, and indeed the cultural politics of the digital humanities—its lacunae, protocols, and technocratic function—are central research problems for many of my colleagues in the Transcriptions Center at UC Santa Barbara. For example, two of our graduate students, Amanda Phillips and Anne Cong-Huyen, have been active in a #transformDH initiative that explores the intersections of the digital humanities and race, gender, and sexuality.[9] And at the MLA convention in 2011, Alan Liu succinctly formulated the as-yet unanswered question that continues to serve as a critical challenge for all of us today: How, he asked, do "the digital humanities advance, channel, or resist the great postindustrial, neoliberal, corporatist, and globalist flows of information-cum-capital"?[10] To answer the question of how the digital humanities "advance and channel" such flows, one simply needs to track monetary circulation and study the attendant promotional materials. In our current mercantile knowledge regime, with its rational calculus of academic value—seats occupied, publications counted, funds procured—the digital humanities are particularly well positioned to answer administrative and public demands to make knowledge useful: after all, research based on quantification is itself readily available to quantification. Cynically, in an institutional context in which a corporate administrative class is already mystified by humanities research that it cannot assess in terms of the amorphous metrics of "excellence" and "innovation," one might say that the digital humanities are also particularly well positioned to exploit the expectation that we should be affectively awed by instrumentation ("oh my god, this lab, this application, is so cool"). In the "new world of brain-currency" shaped by engineers and economists, as Richard Hoggart once described it, it is the digital humanists who serve as cashiers, no longer ordinary schoolmasters peddling language as symbolic capital but academic service staff providing skills-based training—visual literacies, communicative competence, technological proficiency, data management—reinstantiating in the process the very categorical distinctions between theory and practice that DIY and maker culture have long sought to challenge (Hoggart, 229).

Advancing and channeling the great flows of information-cum-capital requires a certain elasticity, more specifically, the capacity to become more agile so as to achieve operability and move to market more quickly. Agility is more easily attained without the practical and financial burdens of infrastructure; if networking, storage, and computing are automated, if they are virtualized, redundancy is eliminated and companies (universities, labs, centers) are left with legacy hardware that can only be repurposed as art and furniture. Why invest in servers, then, if Amazon, Microsoft, and Google can offer IT as a service? Contemporary doxa holds that treating infrastructure and platform as services makes it possible to free up resources for innovation and experimentation, for the symbolic work claimed as the particular province of the human: architecture and design. But accepting IT as a service also means accepting terms of use, and if the digital humanities has had very little to say about protocols of finance and governance, it has arguably had even less to say about the very protocols that govern our everyday use of university Gmail accounts (or indeed the whole of Google Education).[11] As many have suggested but fewer have done, we ought to be marshaling the full critical, philosophical, and rhetorical resources at our disposal in order to think about all of the criteria that structure our communicative acts, from RFC standards and interface design, to privacy policies and terms of service.

The lesson one would like to think that the UC Office of the President had to learn, with its attempt to modernize its logo, is that interfaces and corporations alike have short life spans. Perhaps we too have to be jolted out of the cycle of innovating for the next grant cycle so that we might collaboratively speculate on a less-instrumental future for the humanities as a whole, one that brings into play the affordances of digital media but does so with a measured skepticism that might serve as a buffer against the irrational exuberance that too often characterizes the framing of our projects, initiatives, and entrepreneurial efforts.

To conclude, here are the questions I offer for discussion.

(1) Daniel Bell argued in *The Intellectual and the University* that the principle task of *humanitas* was to defend against the "increasingly powerful armory of intellectual techniques" (game theory, cybernetics, simulation) at the disposal of technocracy (Bell, 4–6). How are we now to regard the embrace of these very techniques, particularly when the actual work is outsourced to technical staff or when putatively interdisciplinary collaborations between humanists and computer scientists rely on a textbook division of labor? How, moreover, are we to regard the schism between high-end tool development as research and undergraduate pedagogy that maintains traditional disciplinary structures?

(2) What are the connections between the production of the aesthetic as techne in digital humanities research and contemporary courseware initiatives, and in what sense is each oriented toward technocratic knowledge production? What are the relations between new reading techniques (text mining, distant reading) and new modes of content delivery? We might also ask what we can make of the links between the political claims made for online learning platforms and the digital humanities: each is said to be radical, open, and democratic because of the varying efforts to make scholarly materials available to populations that have not previously had such access. Put another way, is it possible to have "distant reading" without somehow also contributing to the project of distant education?

(3) It is universally acknowledged that the digital humanities have made important contributions to traditional scholarship in literary studies, in particular introducing provocative questions about scale, multimodal scholarship, and changing reading and writing practices. Still one might ask why and how it is that it has come to function as the solution to every

crisis of disciplinary legitimacy and every methodological impasse. For example, the project of symptomatic reading is said to be exhausted, thus necessitating the turn toward surface reading, of which "digital modes" of reading serve as the preferred instance (Best and Marcus). But we might also ask if is there a sense in which our institutions have been caught flat-footed by the forces of disruptive innovation and by the disaggregation of higher education: university education conceived as piecework is apportioned to tutors and lecturers; tutoring centers develop on the model of the call center; online study groups develop and gradually morph into online universities such as P2P.[12] Can we then understand the exuberance that surrounds the digital humanities to be less of an attempt to shape a future than a salvific attempt to develop a sustainable organizational model for our profession that would include evaluative criteria and pedagogical practices particular to our current sociotechnological milieu? Are we still playing catch-up, and is the enthusiastic, transmedial promotion cover for our belatedness?[13] (Administrator: you can have any faculty position you like, as long as it is digital.)

NOTES

1. ***The sections in asterisks were either points implied in my visuals or in my 2013 MLA talk, which I have elaborated on in this written version. For an almost word-for-word transcription, see Alexis Lothian's excellent notes: http://www.queergeektheory .org/2013/01/mla13-the-dark-side-of-digital-humanities/.

2. This chapter appears essentially in its original form, with minor revisions and additions that gesture toward related and future work. For the essays I mention in the text, see Jagoda, "Gamification," and Jagoda, "Gaming the Humanities."

3. For updated numbers, see, for instance, Newzoo, "2015 Global Games Market Report," http://www.newzoo.com/product/2015-global-games-market-report/. These earlier numbers about mobile gaming are drawn from Jason Ankeny, "Independent Video Game Companies Gain Market Share," *NBC News,* http://www.nbcnews.com/id/50046922/ ns/business-small_business/t/independent-video-game-companies-gain-market-share/#. VZboEPlVhBc.

4. Digital Youth Network, http://www.digitalyouthnetwork.org.

5. Game Changer Chicago, http://gamechanger.uchicago.edu/.

6. *Speculation,* http://speculat1on.net/.

7. Steven Pile succinctly outlines the spatial transfer of affect. See Pile, "Distant Feelings."

8. See Matthew Fuller and Andrew Goffey, "Towards an Evil Media Studies," March 2007, http://www.spc.org/fuller/texts/towardsevil/.

9. See Amanda Phillips, #transformDH—A Call to Action Following ASA 2011," *HASTAC,* October 26, 2011, http://hastac.org/blogs/amanda-phillips/2011/10/26/transformdh -call-action-following-asa-2011.

10. See Liu. His January 7, 2011, conference presentation was revised and expanded for *Debates in the Digital Humanities*. Conference version available from http://liu.english .ucsb.edu/where-is-cultural-criticism-in-the-digital-humanities.

11. Google for Education, http://www.google.com/edu/.

12. "P2PU helps you navigate the wealth of open education materials that are out there, creates small groups of motivated learners, and supports the design and facilitation of courses." See https://www.p2pu.org/en/.

13. Strenuous individual efforts aside, such as Katherine Hayles's showcasing media studies at the MLA during her tenure as chair of the Division on Literary Criticism (Washington, D.C., 2005), it is, I hope, not controversial to suggest that the MLA as an organization was slow to make structural adjustments that would reflect the profound transformations in our medial environments and practices and that, from one angle, it is possible to read the exuberant embrace of social media platforms such as Twitter as compensatory.

BIBLIOGRAPHY

Bell, Daniel. *The Intellectual and the University.* New York: City College, 1966.

Berlant, Lauren. *Cruel Optimism.* Durham, N.C.: Duke University Press, 2011.

Best, Stephen, and Sharon Marcus. "Surface Reading: An Introduction." *Representations* 108, no. 1 (Fall 2009): 1–21.

Bogost, Ian. "Gamification Is Bullshit." *The Atlantic,* August 9, 2011. www.theatlantic.com /technology/archive/2011/08/gamification-is-bullshit/243338/.

Hayles, N. Katherine. "Contemporary Technogenesis: Implications for the New Materialism." Annual Convention, Modern Language Association. Boston, Massachusetts. January 5, 2013.

Hoggart, Richard. *The Uses of Literacy.* New Brunswick, N.J.: Transaction Publishers, 1998.

Jagoda, Patrick. "Gamification and Other Forms of Play." *boundary 2* 40, no. 2 (Summer 2013): 113–44.

———. "Gaming the Humanities." *Differences: A Journal of Feminist Cultural Studies* 25, no. 1 (2014): 189–215.

Liu, Alan. "Where Is Cultural Criticism in the Digital Humanities." In *Debates in the Digital Humanities,* ed. Matthew K. Gold, 490–509. Minneapolis: University of Minnesota Press, 2012.

McGonigal, Jane. *Reality Is Broken: Why Games Make Us Better and How They Can Change the World.* New York: Penguin Press, 2011.

Pile, Steven. "Distant Feelings." *Transactions of the Institute of British Geographers* 37, no. 1 (January 2012): 44–59.

Difficult Thinking about the Digital Humanities

MARK SAMPLE

Five years ago I attempted what I saw as a meaningful formulation of critical thinking—as opposed to the more vapid definitions you tend to come across in higher education. Critical thinking, I wrote, "stands in opposition to facile thinking. Critical thinking is difficult thinking. Critical thinking is being comfortable with difficulty."[1]

Two hallmarks of difficult thinking are imagining the world from multiple perspectives and wrestling with conflicting evidence about the world. Difficult thinking faces these ambiguities head-on and even preserves them, while facile thinking strives to eliminate complexity—both the complexity of different points of view and the complexity of inconvenient facts.

Adam Kirsch's infamous *New Republic* rejoinder to the digital humanities[2] pivots on a follow-up essay of mine, also about critical thinking (Kirsch). In my essay—which later appeared in the 2012 edition of *Debates in the Digital Humanities*[3]—I argue that most of the work we ask our students to produce is designed to eliminate ambiguity and complexity (Sample, "What's Wrong with Writing Essays").[4] It is ironic that Kirsch concludes that my vision of difficult thinking represents nothing less than "the obsequies of humanism"—ironic because Kirsch's piece is itself a remarkable example of facile thinking.

Others have already underscored the paranoid logic (Glen Worthey), glaring omissions[5] (Ryan Cordell), and poor history (Tim Hitchcock) in Kirsch's piece.[6] You might also read Wendy Hui Kyong Chun's and Lisa Rhody's essay in *Differences* as a preemptive commentary on Kirsch (Chun and Rhody). And finally, the *New Republic* has published a letter from the authors of *Digital_Humanities,* disputing Kirsch's claims.[7] I do not have much more to add about the particulars of Kirsch's essay, other than to say that I already wrote a response to it—back in 1998, in an issue of *Works and Days*[8] focused on the scholarship of teaching with technology (Sample, "Resisting Technology"). Even then there was concern about technology "taking over" English departments—inasmuch as faculty were using word processors instead of typewriters.

I do have something to say about the broader context of Kirsch's essay. It is part of a growing body of work committed to approaching the intersection of technology and the humanities with purely facile thinking. This facile thinking ignores contradictory evidence, dismisses alternative ways of seeing, and generally places its critiques of the digital humanities in the service of some other goal having little to do with either technology or the humanities. It might be clickbait for page views, it might be purely self-promotional, it might be crisis opportunism, and occasionally it is even a sincere but misdirected criticism. For example, in the case I explored in 1998, anxieties about teaching with technology were really anxieties about teaching, full stop.

The facile thinking about the digital humanities comes from both within and without the academy. It appears on blogs and social media. It is printed in *The Chronicle of Education* and *Inside Higher Ed, The New York Times,* and *Slate.* It is in scholarly journals, wrapped in the emperor's new clothes of jargon and theory. It comes from accomplished scholars, librarians, graduate students, journalists and interns, former academics, and university administrators. In nearly every case, the accounts eliminate complexity by leaving out history, ignoring counterexamples, and—in extreme examples—insisting that any other discourse about the digital humanities is invalid because it fails to take into consideration that particular account's perspective. Here facile thinking masterfully (yes, facile thinking can be masterful) twists the greatest strength of difficult thinking—appreciating multiple perspectives, but inevitably not *all* perspectives—into its fatal weakness.

In one sensible comment about Kirsch's account of the digital humanities, Ted Underwood reminds us that we cannot govern reception of our work.[9] We cannot control how others think or talk or write about our work. I agree, but the problem—diagnosed by Matt Kirschenbaum, again in *Differences*[10]—is that so often the facile thinking about the digital humanities is not focused on our actual work, but rather on some abstract "construct" called the digital humanities ("What Is 'Digital Humanities'"). Kirschenbaum thoroughly (and with humor) dismantles this construct. But more to my observation about facile thinking here, let me add a corollary to Underwood's point about reception. And this has to do with audience. We often mistake ourselves as the audience for other people's work. However, the intended audience for facile thinking about the digital humanities is rarely people who work at the intersection of technology and the humanities. Very often there is a third (or fourth or fifth) party involved. *Whomever you think a critic of the digital humanities is addressing, there is always someone else being addressed.* This does not just happen in the discussions outside of the academy, like Kirsch's essay in the *New Republic.* It happens when academics appear to be talking only to each other. Let us say one digital humanist levels an inflammatory charge against another.

The charge is not really directed toward the second digital humanist; it is a charge meant to resound among another audience entirely. Facile thinking about the digital humanities is a performance, not scholarship.

What we need, obviously, is more difficult thinking about the digital humanities. I am hardly the first to call for such a thing. Alan Liu is looking for more cultural criticism[11] in the digital humanities, while Fred Gibbs wants critical discourse[12] in the digital humanities (Liu; Gibbs). I am dissatisfied with that word "critical" and all its variations—that is why my formulation emphasizes difficult thinking over facile thinking. In other words, I do not care whether you are critical or not about the digital humanities—either the construct or its actual pedagogical and scholarly work. I simply want you to practice difficult thinking. That means evidentiary-based reasoning. That means perspectives not your own. That means welcoming unresolvable dilemmas. Taken together, these add up to a kind of rational empathy—the antidote to facile thinking. Show me how rational empathy means the death knell of the humanities and I will gladly take over the obsequies myself.

NOTES

1. Mark Sample, "What Is Critical Thinking?" blog post, March 10, 2009, http://www.samplereality.com/2009/03/10/what-is-critical-thinking/.

2. http://www.newrepublic.com/article/117428/limits-digital-humanities-adam-kirsch.

3. http://dhdebates.gc.cuny.edu/debates/text/42.

4. The original text for this piece was posted on March 12, 2009 at http://www.sample reality.com/2009/03/12/whats-wrong-with-writing-essays/.

5. http://ryan.cordells.us/blog/2014/05/08/on-ignoring-encoding.

6. See Glen Worthey, Glen, "Why Are Such Terrible Things Written about DH? Kirsch v. Kirschenbaum," *Stanford Digital Humanities,* May 7, 2014, https://digitalhumanities. stanford.edu/why-are-such-terrible-things-written-about-dh-kirsch-v-kirschenbaum; Ryan Cordell, "On Ignoring Encoding," May 8, 2014, http://ryancordell.org/research/dh /on-ignoring-encoding/; and Tim Hitchcock, "All These Rec. Critiques of DH Forget That History, Art, Museums, Archives and Geography Are There Too. This Is Not Just about Literature," Twitter post, *@TimHitchcock,* May 5, 2014, https://twitter.com/TimHitchcock /status/463223818912563200.

7. Jeffrey Schnapp et al., "The Immense Promise of the Digital Humanities: The Book as Technology," *The New Republic,* May 12, 2014, http://www.newrepublic.com/article /117711/digital-humanities-have-immense-promise-response-adam-kirsh. Schnapp's piece was written in collaboration with Anne Burdick, Johanna Drucker, Peter Lunenfeld, and Todd Presner.

8. http://www.worksanddays.net/1998/File22.Samp_File22.Samp.pdf.

9. Ted Underwood, "You Can't Govern Reception," *The Stone and the Shell,* May 3, 2014, http://tedunderwood.com/2014/05/03/you-cant-govern-reception/.

10. http://mkirschenbaum.files.wordpress.com/2014/04/dhterriblethingskirschen baum.pdf.

11. http://liu.english.ucsb.edu/where-is-cultural-criticism-in-the-digital-humanities.

12. http://journalofdigitalhumanities.org/1-1/critical-discourse-in-digital -humanities-by-fred-gibbs.

BIBLIOGRAPHY

Chun, Wendy Hui Kyong, and Lisa Marie Rhody. "Working the Digital Humanities: Uncovering Shadows between the Dark and the Light." *Differences* 25, no. 1 (2014): 1–25. doi:10.1215/10407391-2419985.

Gibbs, Fred. "Critical Discourse in Digital Humanities." *Journal of Digital Humanities* 1, no. 1 (Winter 2011). http://journalofdigitalhumanities.org/1-1/critical-discourse -in-digital-humanities-by-fred-gibbs/.

Kirsch, Adam. "Technology Is Taking over English Departments: The False Promise of the Digital Humanities." *New Republic,* May 2, 2014. http://www.newrepublic.com/article /117428/limits-digital-humanities-adam-kirsch.

Kirschenbaum, Matthew. "What Is 'Digital Humanities,' and Why Are They Saying Such Terrible Things about It?" *Differences* 25, no. 1 (2014): 46–63. doi:10.1215/10407391-2419997.

Liu, Alan. "Where Is Cultural Criticism in the Digital Humanities?" In *Debates in the Digital Humanities,* ed. Matthew K. Gold, 490–510. Minneapolis: University of Minnesota Press, 2012.

Sample, Mark. "Resisting Technology: The Right Idea for All the Wrong Reasons." *Works and Days* 16, no. 1–2 (1998): 423–26.

———. "What's Wrong with Writing Essays." In *Debates in the Digital Humanities,* ed. Matthew K. Gold, 404–5. Minneapolis: University of Minnesota Press, 2012.

The Humane Digital

TIMOTHY BURKE

As a way of tackling the question "Whither the humanities?" and the thorny issue of defining "digital humanities" in relationship to that question, I offer this: maybe one strategy is to talk about what can make intellectual work humane.

First, let us leave aside the rhetoric of "crisis." Yes, if we are talking about the humanities in academia, there are changes that might be called a crisis: fewer majors, fewer resources, and a variety of vigorous attacks on humanistic practice from inside and outside the academy. Are the subjects of the humanities—expressive culture, everyday practices, meaning and interpretation, philosophy and theory of human life, etc.—going to end? No. Will there be study and commentary on those subjects in the near-term future? Yes. There will be a humanities, even if its location, authority, and character will be much more unstable than they were in the last century.

If we want to speak about and defend the future of the humanities with confidence, it is important to concede that a highly specific organizational structuring of the highly specific institution of American higher education is not synonymous with humane inquiry as a whole. Humane ways of knowing and interpreting the world have had a lively, forceful existence in other kinds of institutions and social lives in the past and could again in the future. To some extent, we should defend the importance of humane thinking without specific regard for the manner of its institutionalization, in part to make clear just how important we think it is (i.e., so that our defense is not predicated on self-interest). We should do so even if we think (as I do) that the academic humanities are the best show in town when it comes to thinking humanely.

I keep going back to something that Louis Menand said during a 2013 talk at Swarthmore College, where I teach. The problem of humanistic thought in contemporary American life is not with a lack of clarity in writing and speaking, and it is not with a lack of "public intellectuals." The problem, he said, is simply that many other influential voices in the public sphere do not agree with humanists and the kind of knowledge and interpretation they have to offer.

With what do they disagree? (And thus, who are they that disagree?) Let us first bracket off the specifically aggrieved kind of highly politicized complaint that came out of the culture wars of the 1980s and 1990s and is still kicking around. I do not think that is the disagreement that matters, except when it is motivated by still deeper opposition to humanistic inquiry.

What matters more is the loose agglomeration of practices, institutions, and perspectives that view human experience and human subjectivity as a managerial problem, a cost burden, and an intellectual disruption. I would not call such views inhumane; they are more anti-humane. Proponents of such views do not believe that a humane approach to the problems of a technologically advanced global society is effective or fair; they believe that we need rules and instruments and systems of knowing that overrule intersubjective, experiential perspectives, and slippery rhetorical and cultural ways of communicating what we know about the world.

The anti-humane is in play:

- When someone works to make an algorithm to grade essays.
- When an IRB adopts inflexible rules derived from the governance of biomedical research and applies them to cultural anthropology.
- When law enforcement and public culture work together to create a highly typified, abstracted profile of a psychological type prone to commit certain crimes and then attempt to surveil or control everyone falling within that parameter.
- When quantitative social science pursues elaborate methodologies to isolate a single causal variable as having slightly more statistically significant weight than thousands of other variables, rather than just crafting a rhetorically persuasive interpretation of the importance of that factor.
- When public officials build testing and evaluation systems intended to automate and massify the work of assessing the performance of employees or students.

At these and many other moments across a wide scale of contemporary societies we set out to bracket off or excise the human element, to eliminate our reliance on intersubjective judgment. We are, in these moments, as James Scott has said of "high modernism," working to make human beings legible and fixed for the sake of systems that require them to be so.

Many of these moments are well-intentioned or rest on reliable and legitimate methodologies and technologies. As witnesses, evaluators, and interpreters, human beings are unreliable, biased, inscrutable, ambiguous, and irresolvably open to interpretation. Making sense of them can often be inefficient and time-consuming, without hope of resolution, and sometimes that is legitimately intolerable.

Accepting that this is the irreducible character of the human subject (the one universal that we might permit ourselves to accept without apology) should be the defining characteristic of the humanities. The humanities should be, across a variety of disciplines and subjects, committed to humane ways of knowing.

So what does that mean? To be humane should be:

Incomplete. The sociobiologist E. O. Wilson has complained that the humanities offer an "incomplete" account of culture, ethics, and consciousness (and has kindly offered to complete the account by removing the humanities from the picture completely). What Wilson sees as a bug is in fact a feature. The humanities are and should be incomplete by design—that is, there should be no technology or methodology we might imagine as a future possibility that would permit complete knowledge to be achieved via humane inquiry, nor should we ever want such a thing to begin with. A humane knowledge accepts that human beings and their works are contingent on interpretation, meaning that much—if not absolutely anything—can be said about their meaning and character. And they are contingent in action, meaning that knowledge about the relatively fixed or patterned dimensions of human nature and life is a very poor predictor of the future possibilities of culture, social life, and the intersubjective experience of selfhood.

Slow. As in "slow food," artisanal. Humane insights require human processes and habits of thought, observation, and interpretation, and even those processes augmented by or merged into algorithms and cybernetics should be in some sense mediated by or limited to a handcrafted pace. At the very bottom of most of our algorithmic culture now is hand-produced content, slow-culture interpretation: the fast streams of curation and assemblage that are visible at the top level of our searching and reading and linking rest on that foundation. This is not a weakness or a limitation to be transcended through singularity, but rather a source of the singular strength of humane thought. We use slow thought to make and manipulate algorithmic culture. Social media users understand very quickly how to "read" its infrastructures, but it is slow thought, gradual accumulations of experience, discrete moments of insight, that permit its speed. There is no algorithmic shortcut to making cultural life, just shortcuts that allow us to hack and reassemble and curate what has been and is made slowly.

Illegible. By this I do not mean "jargon-filled prose" in the sense that has inspired so much debate within and about the humanities. By illegible, I mean that humanistic thinking and expression should exhibit a permanent, necessary skepticism about all political and social projects that require human subjects and societies to remain firmly legible and transparent to authority. Often the political commitments of humanists settle down well above this foundational level, where they are perfectly fine as the choices of individual intellectuals and may derive from (but are not synonymous with) humane commitments. That is to say, our political and social projects should arise out of deeply vested humane skepticism about legibility and governability, but as a general rule many humanists truncate or limit their skepticism to a particular subset of derived views.

Is this a riff on Isaiah Berlin's liberal suspicions of the utopian? Yes, I suppose, when it is about configuring the human subject so that it is readily understandable by systems of power and amenable to their workings. But this is also a riff on "question authority": the point is that if power can be in many places, from a protest march to a drone strike, the humane thinker has to be a skeptic about its operations. Humane practice should always be about monkey-wrenching, always be the fly in the ointment, even (or perhaps especially) when the systems and legibility being made suit the political preferences of a humane thinker.

Playful, pleasurable, and extravagant. My colleague in a class I co-taught last semester made me feel much more comfortable with my long-felt wariness about influence of Bourdieu-inspired accounts of institutions and culture, and how in particular they have had a troubling effect on humanistic inquiry that often amounts to functionalism by another name. My colleague's reading of Michele Lamont's *How Professors Think* was to read it as calling attention to how often academics do not simply make judgments as an act of capital-d Distinction, as bagmen for habitus. Instead, she argued that this tendency was evidence for the persistence of an attention to aesthetics, meaning, and pleasure that is not tethered to the sociological (without arguing that this requires depoliticizing the humanities)—evidence that our intellectual lives not only should be humane but that they are already.

This is very much what I mean by saying that humane knowledge should be playful and even extravagant: that every humanistic work or analysis should produce an excess of perspectives, a variety of interpretations, that it should dance away from pinning culture to the social, to the functional, to the concrete. Humane work is excess: we should not apologize meekly for that or try to recuperate a sense of the dutifully instrumental things we can do, even as we *also* insist that excess, play, and pleasure are essential and generative to any humane society—that their programmatic absence is the signature diagnostic of cruelty, oppression, and injustice. This is what I think Albie Sachs was getting at in 1990 when he said that, with the beginnings of negotiations for the end of apartheid, South African artists and critics should thus "be banned from saying culture is a weapon of the struggle." Whatever fits the humane to a narrow instrumentality, whatever yokes it to efficiency, is ultimately anti-humane.

So what of the digital? Many defenders of the humane identify the digital as the quintessence of the anti-humane, recalling the earlier advent of computational or cliometric inquiry in the 1970s and 1980s. Should we prefer a John Henry narrative? Holding on to the last gasp of the humane under the assault of the machine?

Please, please no. Digital methods, digital technologies, and digital culture are already a good habitus of humane practice and the best opportunity to strengthen the human temperament in humanistic inquiry.

Again and again, algorithmic culture has confronted the inevitable need for humane understanding, often turning away both because of its costs (when the logic of such culture is to reduce costs by eliminating skilled human labor) and because of a lack of skill or expertise in humane understanding among the producers and owners of such culture. I have long observed, for example, that the live management teams for massively multiplayer online games frequently try to deal with the inevitable slippages and problems of human beings in digital environments by truncating the possibilities of human agency down to code, by making people as much like a codeable entity as possible, by engineering a reverse Turing test. And they always fail, both because they must fail and because they do not understand human beings very well.

This is an opportunity for humane knowledge (We can help! Give us jobs!) and also evidence of the vigor of humane understandings and expertise, of how the human subject as we understand it recurs and reinvents so insistently, even in expressive and everyday environments that see a humane sensibility as an inconvenience or obstacle.

But this is not just an extension of the old; it is sometimes a very exciting way to be genuinely new. "Big data" and data analytics are seen by some intellectuals as an example of opposition to the humane. But in the hands of many digital humanists or practitioners of "distant reading," the humane can become strange in very good ways. Thomas Schelling's "segregation model" is not an explanation of segregation but a demonstration that there are interpretations and analyses that we would not think of out of ourselves, a reworking without mastery. The extension and transformation of the humane self through algorithmic processing is not its extinction; approached in the right spirit, it is the magnification of the humane spirit as I have described it.

This is not a C. P. Snow "two cultures" picture, either. Being humane is not limited to the disciplines conventionally described as the humanities. Natural science that is centrally interested in phenomena described as emergent or complex adaptive systems, for example, is in many ways quite close to what I have described as humane.

We might, in fact, begin to argue that most academic disciplines need to move toward what I have described as humane because all of the problems and phenomena best described or managed in other approaches have already been understood and managed. The twentieth century picked all the low-hanging fruit. All the problems that could be solved by anti-humane thinking, all the solutions that could be achieved through technocratic management, are complete. What we need to know next, how we need to know it, and what we need to do falls much more into the domains—in and outside of the academy—where humane thinking has always excelled.

BIBLIOGRAPHY

Scott, James. *Seeing Like a State: How Certain Schemes to Improve the Human Condition Have Failed.* New Haven, Conn.: Yale University Press, 1999.

Hold on Loosely, or *Gemeinschaft* and *Gesellschaft* on the Web

TED UNDERWOOD

I want to try a quick experiment.

The digital humanities community must . . .

If that sounds like a plausible beginning to a sentence, what about this one?

The literary studies community must . . .

Does that sound as odd to you as it does to me? No one pretends literary studies is a community. In North America, the discipline becomes visible to itself mainly at the famously alienating yearly ritual of the Modern Language Association convention. A hotel that contains disputatious full professors and underemployed job-seekers may be many interesting things, but "community" is not the first word that comes to mind.

"Digital humanities," on the other hand, frequently invokes itself as a "community." The reasons may stretch back into the 1990s and to the early beleaguered history of humanities computing. But the contemporary logic of the term is probably captured by Matt Kirschenbaum, who stresses that the intellectually disparate projects now characterized as DH are unified above all by reliance on social media,[1] especially Twitter.

In many ways that's a wonderful thing. Twitter is not a perfectly open form, and it's certainly not an egalitarian one; it has a one-to-many logic. But you don't have to be a digital utopian to recognize that academic fields benefit from frequent informal contact among their members—what Dan Cohen has described as "the sidewalk life of successful communities."[2] Twitter is especially useful for establishing networks that cross disciplinary (and professional) boundaries; I've learned a lot from those connections.

On the other hand, the illusion of a perfectly open, intimate community created by Twitter has some downsides. The sociologist Ferdinand Tönnies's distinction between Gemeinschaft and Gesellschaft may be useful here as a set of ideal types. A Gemeinschaft (community) is bound together by personal contact among members and by shared values. It may lack formal institutions, so its members have to be restrained by moral suasion and peer pressure. A Gesellschaft (society) doesn't expect all its members to share the same values; it expects them to be guided mostly by individual aims, restrained and organized by formal institutions.

Given that choice, wouldn't everyone prefer to live in cozy Gemeinschaft? Well, sure, except . . . remember, you're going to have to agree on a set of values! Digital humanists have spent a lot of time discussing values, but it's always been a difficult conversation. "Digital humanities" is after all a broad phrase; Matt Kirschenbaum is probably right that it took shape less as a description of a specific research program than as a "tactical term."[3] I would add that the term was tactically successful precisely because it lumped together a diverse group of projects that might individually have been seen as outliers. Humanities computing and the study of new media appeared, separately, marginal to most humanities disciplines. But together, and allied with distant reading and with the open-access movement (among other things), they began to add up to a trend.

I don't mean to imply that the notion of a digital humanities "community" was purely a tactical ruse. There were of course real human connections involved, emerging in some cases from specific physical campuses. Social media has also fostered networking practices that are more expansive and informal than would have been typical for academics even ten or fifteen years ago. And those networks, also, are real.

But none of these things add up to a movement or community in the strong Gemeinschaft-y sense that would imply shared aims and values. Instead we have an expansive social network that feels like community, since it's bound together by personal connections through social media—but that in fact has always covered different projects, in different disciplines and professions, with different intellectual goals.

That, at any rate, is the short history of "digital humanities" I would offer, in an effort to explain why the phrase seems to evoke, and then immediately disappoint, expectations of intellectual community. Looking at the history of the term, I see little reason to expect digital humanists to be unified by shared aims and values at all (at least, not by values that are meaningfully different from the values held by intellectuals more generally).

That may sound like a melancholy admission, since "community" is generally held to be a good thing, and since many of us would like to affirm shared values—at least of the kind that Lisa Spiro affirms in her 2012 essay "This Is Why We Fight,"[4] broad ideals like "connection" or "openness." But here's where I circle back to the song in my title. If you're organizing an intellectual endeavor where debate about values is part of the point, there's a lot to be said for Gesellschaft. Academic communication doesn't have to be impersonal, but in the words of 38 Special, we need to give each other "a whole lot of space to breathe in."

For instance, "connection" is good. But there is probably such a thing as too much connection. Attempting to resolve academic debates through moral suasion on Twitter is not just a bad idea because it produces flame wars. It would be an even worse idea if it *worked*—because we don't really want intellectual projects to have that kind of consensus, enforced by personal ties and displays of collective solidarity. The value of "openness" may be equally problematic on the Web, which facilitates it all too well. In principle, one wants to engage all points of view, but no one can engage them all at one-hour intervals. Filter bubbles have their uses.

The original (2013) version of this piece closed with foreboding reflections on the future of academic Twitter, which I worried might lure "humanists into attempting a more cohesive, coercive kind of Gemeinschaft than academic social networks can (or should) sustain." But here I think the passage of time is tending to support a more optimistic view. At any rate, in my experience, Twitter is still a useful place for scholars to share links and leads.

Perhaps my anxieties were misplaced because the simulacrum of Gemeinschaft produced by social media simply doesn't run deep enough, in the end, to exert a problematically coercive power. Social media certainly tempt us to imagine loose academic networks as normative communities, but that may be an illusion even for networks within a single discipline, let alone for networks linked by a term as broad and abstract as "digital humanities."

NOTES

This chapter was originally published on September 11, 2013 on tedunderwood.com, and revised in January 2015.

1. http://dhdebates.gc.cuny.edu/debates/text/48.

2. http://mediacommons.futureofthebook.org/question/how-do-we-build-digital -cohorts-and-academic-communities/response/sidewalk-life-successfu-0.

3. http://dhdebates.gc.cuny.edu/debates/text/48.

4. http://dhdebates.gc.cuny.edu/debates/text/13.

BIBLIOGRAPHY

Cohen, Dan. "The Sidewalk Life of Successful Communities," *Media Commons,* January 30, 2013. http://mediacommons.futureofthebook.org/question/how-do-we-build -digital-cohorts-and-academic-communities/response/sidewalk-life-successfu-0.

Kirschenbaum, Matthew. "Digital Humanities As/Is a Tactical Term." In *Debates in the Digital Humanities,* ed. Matthew K. Gold, 415–28. Minneapolis: University of Minnesota Press, 2012. http://dhdebates.gc.cuny.edu/debates/text/48.

Spiro, Lisa. " 'This Is Why We Fight': Defining the Values of the Digital Humanities." In *Debates in the Digital Humanities,* ed. Matthew K. Gold, 16–37. Minneapolis: University of Minnesota Press, 2012. http://dhdebates.gc.cuny.edu/debates/text/13.

38 Special. "Hold on Loosely." *Wild-Eyed Southern Boys.* A&M, 1981.

Tönnies, Ferdinand. *Community and Society* (1887). Translated by Charles P. Loomis. East Lansing: Michigan University Press, 1957.

PART VI

FORUM:
TEXT ANALYSIS
AT SCALE

Introduction

MATTHEW K. GOLD AND LAUREN F. KLEIN

This forum marks the first instance of a new feature for the *Debates in the Digital Humanities* annual volumes, one that brings together position statements from a range of scholars who have contributed to the discussion around a topic of pressing import to the field. These statements are intended to serve as short provocations and declarations of values; in collecting them here, we aim to create a record of the key ideas animating current conversations in the field and to document the full extent—and the full intensity—of the surrounding debate.

The theme of this year's forum, "Text Analysis at Scale," takes its cue from the multiple conversations about "distant reading" that took place in the spring of 2015, ranging from lectures by Franco Moretti and his colleagues at the Stanford Literary Lab to multiple conferences exploring large-scale text analysis—the symposium on "Scale and Value" held at the University of Washington and a conference on cultural analytics held at the University of Chicago.[1] We were also inspired and provoked by the debate that accompanied the release of Syuzhet, Matthew Jockers's software package for automated plot analysis.[2] That discussion, initiated by Joanna Swafford, whose statement we include in this forum, was sustained through the input of scholars from a range of disciplines, including literature as well as computational linguistics, sociology, and information science.[3] More than the affordances of the algorithms it employed, Syuzhet came to stand for the potential of DH work to reach across multiple fields, introducing crucial issues in the digital humanities to interdisciplinary conversation.

The range of perspectives assembled here, while not exhaustive, nevertheless provides a basis to further explore the challenges associated with using digital tools to "read" large swaths of text. Indeed, if "distant reading" often serves in the public imagination as a synecdoche for the field itself, we hope that these statements offer a window into the future possibilities for the digital humanities, as well as a probing look at the limitations of the field, and its methods, that we must always keep in sight.

NOTES

1. For more information about the symposium on "Scale and Value," see http://scale andvalue.tumblr.com/; for more information on the conference on cultural analytics, see http://neubauercollegium.uchicago.edu/events/uc/cultural_analytics/.

2. For more information and to download the Syuzhet package, see: https://github .com/mjockers/syuzhet.

3. For a record of this conversation on Twitter, see https://storify.com/clancynew york/contretemps-a-syuzhet; for Swafford's original blog post, see https://annieswafford .wordpress.com/2015/03/02/syuzhet/.

Humane Computation

STEPHEN RAMSAY

A nyone who does text analysis in the humanities—or indeed, any kind of computational work in the humanities—has committed themselves to two kinds of conversations, two kinds of ethical frameworks, and two kinds of pedagogies.

The first kind of conversation is technical, and it involves something like the process of "getting it right." There are good ways to write software and bad ways. There are algorithms that work in a given situation and those that do not. There are best practices, design patterns, measures of statistical significance, and concerns about extensibility, reproducibility, fault-tolerance, and design that anyone working with digital materials needs to know and heed. It requires conversation, because the best way to be heedless and unknowing is to ignore the advice of others. It is an ethical commitment, because software needs to do what it says on the tin and behave as transparently as possible. It is a pedagogical commitment, because we have to pass these skills and habits of mind on to our students.

The second kind of conversation arises—or should arise—from the fact that we undertake these activities not at a corporation, or in a scientific laboratory, or as part of the (entirely distinct) research agendas of computer science and engineering, but within the context of humanistic inquiry. Here, the conversation is about the nature of the human condition and its artistic and historical artifacts. The ethics of humanistic inquiry demands that we treat our questions as always being fundamentally rhetorical in nature, if only as a way to respect the complexity of human culture. The pedagogy of the humanities follows on the heels of this ethic. We try to teach our students to think deeply, to think of things as being this *and* this, to be comfortable with the open-ended and the unresolved. Where the technologist speaks of progress, the humanist might speak (with like enthusiasm) of modulation and change.

There are many who think scatter plots filled with data points drawn from, say, English novels, are already a crime against the humanities—the death of all that is good and pure about humanistic study. For them, the problem is positivism in its properly technical sense. They fear an epistemology that does not merely value empirical data, but which (in its extreme philosophical forms) considers empirical data to be the *only* valid form of evidence. They imagine a computationally driven history or French literature curriculum that forsakes the ancient circle of the seminar for the modern angles of the server room. They imagine humanistic conversation debasing itself in the form of technical cavils, humanistic ethics becoming nothing more than "practical business ethics," and teaching degenerating into mere training.[1]

I believe these fears are not so much unwarranted as they are grossly overblown. They succumb to a shrill rhetoric that presupposes a forking path between one activity and another—as if the use of computers automatically entailed the foreclosure of humanistic discussion and summary commitment to a set of exaggerated epistemologies (chiefly scientism, and again, positivism).

Certainly, it is possible to regard text analysis as a way to settle humanistic questions once and for all. It is likewise possible to substitute those ethical frameworks that have traditionally been regarded as more congenial to humanistic discourse with a barren form of utilitarianism. And while training is simply necessary for computational work, one can easily imagine that training proceeding without any consideration of the humanistic concerns for which that training is intended. What is more, we all operate under the weight of computation as a powerful cultural force. It is not merely Google that is trying to convince us that an understanding of data is "more valid" than other kinds of knowing; the cultural processes that led us to such thinking began with the Enlightenment and, despite numerous countermovements, continue to exert a kind of Pavlovian response from us when data confronts speculative inquiry.

Digital humanities is at its strongest, though, when it is oriented toward resisting this response. We are aided in that project by our training in the humanities, which serves, above all, to reinforce those conversations, ethical commitments, and pedagogies proper to the nature of humanistic discourse. Our students may find it easy to think of software as somehow "culturally neutral" or scatter plots as inherently "more valid," but we, simply by virtue of being members of humanistic disciplinary communities, find it almost impossible to do so. The choice we face is therefore not between scientism and humanism, but between a willingness to allow digital objects—including those that deal with empirical data—to participate fully in humanistic discussions according to the terms of those discussions, and a dismissal of digital work as inherently incompatible with those discussions.

I have always lobbied for a "ludic" approach to text analysis—one that, following the work of Jerome McGann and others, seeks to twist and deform data in order to provoke discussion.[2] But at heart, this is not so much a methodology as a way for us to frame the nature of less extreme provocations (including traditional literary study). When Matthew Jockers tells us that there are "six, or possibly seven, archetypal plot shapes" in the English novel,[3] he is doing something that from a technical standpoint may be right or wrong. From a humanistic standpoint, he can only be doing something right by asking us to consider a new object, a new provocation, a new arrangement, a new thing to interrogate. The real failure would not be a result that is deemed incorrect, or not interesting, or theoretically flawed. The real failure would be the decision to banish this kind of work from all consideration as humanistic scholarship. To do so would be to *succumb* to what David Golumbia has called, with opprobrium, the "cultural logic of computation" (*Cultural Logic*). It would amount to an admission that data trumps story, logic is more useful than the human experience, and that the server room can exist without the seminar room.

NOTES

1. For a useful précis of various objections within the academy (as well as a pointed counterargument), see Kirschenbaum. For objections from without, see, for example, Adam Kirsch, "Technology Is Taking over English Departments: The False Promise of the Digital Humanities." *The New Republic*, May 2, 2014, http://www.newrepublic.com/article/117428/limits-digital-humanities-adam-kirsch/.

2. See especially McGann, *Radiant Textuality*. My own work on the subject appears mainly in *Reading Machines* (Ramsay).

3. Matthew L. Jockers, "The Rest of the Story," author's blog, February 25, 2015. http://www.matthewjockers.net/2015/02/25/the-rest-of-the-story/. Jockers's blog contains numerous posts about Syuzhet—the R package he developed for conducting sentiment analysis.

BIBLIOGRAPHY

Golumbia, David. *The Cultural Logic of Computation*. Cambridge, Mass.: Harvard University Press, 2009.

Kirschenbaum, Matthew. "What Is 'Digital Humanities,' and Why Are They Saying Such Terrible Things about It?" *Difference* 24, no. 1 (2014): 46–63. https://mkirschenbaum.files.wordpress.com/2014/04/dhterriblethingskirschenbaum.pdf.

McGann, Jerome. *Radiant Textuality: Literature after the World Wide Web*. New York: Palgrave, 2004.

Ramsay, Stephen. *Reading Machines: Toward an Algorithmic Criticism*. Urbana-Champaign: University of Illinois Press, 2011.

Distant Reading and Recent Intellectual History

TED UNDERWOOD

I love the phrase "distant reading." It's vivid, it doesn't overemphasize technology, and it candidly admits that new methods are mainly useful at larger scales of analysis. It's how I describe what I do. But the phrase does have two disadvantages.

First, since "distant reading" was coined by Franco Moretti on or around the year 2000, the phrase may seem to name a completely new project.[1] In fact, as Katherine Bode has noted, the questions posed by distant readers are often continuous with the older tradition of book history (*Reading*); as Jim English has noted, they are also continuous with the sociology of literature ("Everywhere").

The second disadvantage of the phrase "distant reading" is more serious. By defining a new mode of "reading," the phrase suggests to some that this project is still contained in literary studies—just another stage of our debate about the right way to interpret literature. That assumption has made conversation on the topic needlessly parochial and polemical. We have spent too much time on inward-looking debates that pit distant against close reading, and not enough time understanding connections to other disciplines.

Distant reading is better understood as part of a broad intellectual shift that has also been transforming the social sciences. The best-publicized part of this shared story is an increase in the sheer availability of data, mediated by the Internet and digital libraries. Because changes of scale are easy to describe, journalists often stop here—reducing recent intellectual history to the buzzword "big data." The more interesting part of the story is philosophical rather than technical, and involves what Leo Breiman, fifteen years ago, called a new "culture" of statistical modeling (Breiman). The conceptual premises informing models may at first seem arcane, but they're playing a crucial role behind the scenes: this is the fundamental reason why disciplines that used to seem remote from humanists are now working with us on shared problems.

In the twentieth century, the difficulty of representing unstructured text divided the quantitative social sciences from the humanities. Sociologists could use numbers to understand social mobility or inequality, but they had a hard time connecting those equations to the larger and richer domain of human discourse. Over the last twenty years, that barrier has fallen. A theory of learning that emphasizes generalization has shown researchers how to train models that have thousands of variables without creating the false precision called "overfitting."[2] That conceptual advance would be interesting in itself. But it also allows researchers to include qualitative evidence like text in a quantitative model by the simple expedient of using lots of variables (say, one for each word). Social scientists can now connect structured social evidence to loosely structured texts or images or sounds, and they're discovering that this connection opens up fascinating questions.[3]

Humanists are discovering the same thing. Distant reading may have begun with familiar forms of counting akin to book history. (How many novels were published in 1850?) But much of the momentum it acquired over the last decade came from the same representational strategies that are transforming social science. Instead of simply counting words or volumes, distant readers increasingly treat writing as a field of relations to be modeled, using equations that connect linguistic variables to social ones.[4] Once we grasp how this story fits into the larger intellectual history of our time, it no longer makes much sense to frame it as a debate *within* literary studies. The change we are experiencing is precisely that quantitative and qualitative evidence are becoming easier to combine, blurring disciplinary boundaries. We're working on a methodological continuum now that extends from history and literature through linguistics and sociology. Scholars are still free to specialize in parts of the continuum, of course, and specialization is still valuable. But nothing prevents us from ranging more widely. Since human affairs are also a continuum, we should feel free to use whatever mixture of methods gives us leverage on a particular problem.

Although distant readers are still a tiny minority in literary studies, they receive admonitions from all corners of the field (Spivak, 107–9; Marche). Much of this boils down to gatekeeping, and it is rarely informed by a clear understanding of the thing that is to be kept out. We are often warned about "big data," for instance, because the term is new, terrifying, and so poorly defined that it can signify a wide range of threats. But the substantive methodological changes that have actually created new disciplinary connections are rarely mentioned. Conversation of this kind amounts to an empty contest of slogans between the humanities and social sciences, and I think Thomas Piketty spends the right amount of time on those contests: "Disciplinary disputes and turf wars are of little or no importance" (*Capital*, 33).

Recent debates may also tend to overstate the technical challenges of interdisciplinarity. Distant readers admittedly enjoy discussing new unsupervised algorithms that are hard to interpret.[5] But many useful methods are supervised, comparatively straightforward, and have been in social-science courses for decades. A grad student could do a lot of damage to received ideas with a thousand novels, manually gathered metadata, and logistic regression.

What really matter, I think, are not new tools but three general principles. First, a negative principle: there's simply a lot we don't know about literary history above the scale of (say) a hundred volumes. We've become so used to ignorance at this scale, and so good at bluffing our way around it, that we tend to overestimate our actual knowledge.[6] Second, the theoretical foundation for macroscopic research isn't something we have to invent from scratch; we can learn a lot from computational social science. (The notion of a statistical model, for instance, is a good place to start.) The third thing that matters, of course, is getting at the texts themselves, on a scale that can generate new perspectives. This is probably where our collaborative energies could most fruitfully be focused. The tools we're going to need are not usually specific to the humanities. But the corpora often are.

NOTES

1. See Moretti's reflection on the origin of the term in *Distant Reading*, 43–44.

2. The field of machine learning is actually founded on a theory of learning. Specific new algorithms have mattered less than the general implications of this theory—for instance, that there is a tradeoff between bias and variance, and that models should ideally be tested on out-of-sample evidence (Breiman).

3. A brief survey of computational social science can be found in O'Connor, Bamman, and Smith; see also Wallach.

4. Supervised models often use linguistic evidence to predict a social variable. For differences of literary prestige, see Underwood and Sellers. For genre, gender, and nationality, see Jockers.

5. Although topic modeling is slippery in a way humanists find fun to argue about, I don't believe it's actually paradigmatic of new methods. If you like fun arguments, however, compare Liu ("Meaning of the Digital Humanities") to Goldstone and Underwood ("Quiet Transformations").

6. For an illuminating parable about this problem, see Lincoln, "Confabulation in the Humanities."

BIBLIOGRAPHY

Bode, Katherine. *Reading by Numbers*. London: Anthem, 2014.
Breiman, Leo. "Statistical Modeling: The Two Cultures." *Statistical Science* 16, no. 3 (2001): 199–231.
English, James F. "Everywhere and Nowhere: The Sociology of Literature after 'The Sociology of Literature.'" *New Literary History* 41, no. 2 (2010): v–xxiii.
Goldstone, Andrew, and Ted Underwood. "The Quiet Transformations of Literary Study: What Thirteen Thousand Scholars Could Tell Us." *New Literary History* 45, no. 3 (2014): 359–84.
Jockers, Matthew L. *Macroanalysis: Digital Methods and Literary History*. Urbana: University of Illinois Press, 2013.

Lincoln, Matthew. "Confabulation in the Humanities." Author's blog, March 21 2015. http://matthewlincoln.net/2015/03/21/confabulation-in-the-humanities.html.

Liu, Alan. "The Meaning of the Digital Humanities." *PMLA* 128 (2013): 409–23.

Marche, Stephen. "Literature Is Not Data: Against Digital Humanities." *Los Angeles Review of Books*. October 28, 2012. https://lareviewofbooks.org/essay/literature-is-not-data -against-digital-humanities.

Moretti, Franco. *Distant Reading*. London: Verso, 2013.

O'Connor, Brendan, David Bamman, and Noah Smith. "Computational Text Analysis for Social Science: Model Assumptions and Complexity." *Second Workshop on Computational Social Science and Wisdom of the Crowds (NIPS 2011)*, December 2011. http:// brenocon.com/oconnor+bamman+smith.nips2011css.text_analysis.pdf.

Piketty, Thomas. *Capital in the Twenty-First Century*. Translated by Arthur Goldhammer. Cambridge, Mass.: Harvard University Press, 2014.

Spivak, Gayatri C. *Death of a Discipline*. New York: Columbia University Press, 2003.

Underwood, Ted, and Jordan Sellers. "How Quickly Do Literary Standards Change?" Figshare. http://dx.doi.org/10.6084/m9.figshare.1418394.

Wallach, Hanna. "Computational Social Science: Toward a Collaborative Future." *Data Science for Politics, Policy, and Government*. Cambridge: Cambridge University Press, 2015. http://dirichlet.net/pdf/wallach15computational.pdf.

The Ground Truth of DH Text Mining

TANYA E. CLEMENT

In the digital humanities, text mining is a *logocentric* practice. That is, text mining in digital humanities usually begins with The Word. We extract The Word; we count The Word; we stem The Word to its root; we parse The Word; we name The Word; we disambiguate The Word; we collocate The Word; we count The Word again; we apply an algorithm that allows us to reconstruct the world of The Word as one we can visualize as a list, as a line graph, as a histogram in small multiples, or on big screens. We use the view this new world provides us to interpret The Word.

This practice of text mining presupposes a binary logic; there is meaning in the results or there is not. It begins with a "ground truth," or labels that signify the presence of meaning. Sometimes we determine ground truth through annotations for machine classification: "Here, machine, are the love letters that Susan Dickinson wrote to Emily Dickinson. Please, find more like these." Sometimes we determine ground truth after we receive clustering results: "Ah, machine, I see you have done your stemming and your parsing and your counting and you have given me a pile of words. I read them and will label them 'whaling'" (though someone else might have said "indigenous economy"). "Ah, machine, I see you have clustered novels written by 'women' here and novels written by 'men' there. You are very clever. You must understand gender, just as I do."

When engaged in this kind of text mining, we are reinscribing the simplest meaning of The Word. The authors of a text-mining textbook write that the results of text mining are easier to understand than numerical results because analysts "all have some expertise. The document is text." (Weiss et al., 51–52). Likewise, even when we are humanists and feminists and should know better, we think we understand the machine's results when they are words or when they cluster books according to an author of an "always already" gender. We see a pattern we think we can interpret, because we think we know what The Word means, and gender, which we have worked so hard to complicate, is suddenly reduced to "female author" or "male author." The Word has been proved to serve as ground truth. The Word is apodictic.

Sound, by comparison, is aporetic. Mining audio spoken word collections means extracting acoustic features for classification, clustering, and visualization. Choosing features is complicated. The Word seems to be interpretable at a determined length. What length of a sound is meaningful? The Word seems to have typical patterns of characters, seems to perform regularly as a part of speech even in the context of complex sentences, seems to have a root that grows, more usually than not, in prescribed ways. Hearing sound as digital audio means listening through filter banks, sampling rates, and compression scenarios that are meant to mimic the human ear (Salthouse and Sarpeshkar). To mine these acoustic features is to understand that ground truth must always be indeterminate. Which features you choose and how you label that cluster of acoustic features that is sound will often be different from the features and labels I might choose. We must ask: Whose ear are we mimicking? What is audible, and to whom? Playback means choosing the damping ratios and frequency ranges that include overlapping and audible signals. We must ask: What signal is noise? What signal is meaningful, and to whom? Extracting meaningful features for mining sound always means interpreting not only what sound means, but how sound creates meaning. Mining sound reminds us that we have constructed an analysis according to our own experiences with how sound is meaningful.

As humanists, we seek questions, not solutions. Practicing sound mining alerts us to the fact that in text mining, The Word should also be aporetic. Instead of The Word, we are working with *a* word that is always indeterminate—meaning is both present and absent at once. We construct text-mining analyses according to our own experiences with how words make meaning. We must use text mining as a hermeneutic of The Word or as a hermeneutic of text mining or as a hermeneutic of hermeneutics. The Word does not provide evidence of meaning, of identity. A word in text mining is a foil to ground truth, not its proof.

BIBLIOGRAPHY

Salthouse, Christopher D., and Rahul Sarpeshkar. "A Practical Micropower Programmable Bandpass Filter for Use in Bionic Ears." *IEEE Journal of Solid-State Circuits* 38, no. 1 (January 2003): 63–70.

Weiss, Sholom M., Nitin Indurkhya, Tong Zhang, and Fred J. Damerau. *Text Mining: Predictive Methods for Analyzing Unstructured Information.* New York: Springer, 2005.

Why I Dig: Feminist Approaches to Text Analysis

LISA MARIE RHODY

*I feel like I'm writing as part of a group of poets—historically—who are
potentially looking at the end of the medium itself as a vital part of their
culture—unless they do something to help it reconnect itself to mystery. . . .
We need to recover a high level of ambition, a rage if you will—the big hunger."*

—Jorie Graham (Gardner, 84)

In an oft-quoted interview for *Denver Quarterly* in 1997, Jorie Graham, who had
just received a Pulitzer Prize, offered a blistering critique of the state of contemporary American poetry. Lamenting the field's lack of ambition, she proposed
her own poetic experiments as a model for how contemporary poetry could pursue
"the big hunger." Graham employs postmodern and feminist strategies—syntactic
complexity, narrative gaps, and vertigo-inducing alterations in perspective—to
pose expansive, metaphysical questions that demand equal parts patience, participation, and restraint from her readers in the midst of uncomfortable textual
circumstances.

It is Graham's "big hunger"—the desire to ask sweeping metaphysical questions
that speak directly to a contemporary moment—that has inspired my own work,
where I have similarly sought to pose ambitious large-scale questions about literary tradition and genre convention. My "big hunger" compels me to consider what
literary studies can bring to bear on the text mining of big data, a practice similarly
steeped in the masculinized rhetoric of scale and ambition. Does the rhetoric of text
analysis or its assumed empiricism dissuade feminist scholars from using it to pose
questions about difference, erasure, and absence? How might the feminist literary
critic approach text analysis without succumbing to the positivistic claims of objectivity that such methods so often encourage? What happens when we introduce
diverse practitioners into text analysis, as Audre Lorde suggests, "as a fund of necessary polarities between which our creativity can spark like a dialectic?" (Lorde, 112).

In 2012, Bethany Nowviskie responded to discussions about a "Digging into Data" grant competition by asking "what do girls dig?" and wondering whether data mining had become "a gentleman's sport." Three years later, the question seems to have changed to "should women dig?" or, perhaps more fundamentally, should *anyone* dig? My own sense is that not only *should* women dig, but that it is necessary that we do so. Just as Lorde's dialectic and Graham's poetics activate feminist strategies of discomfort to unsettle deep-seated ideologies, so can feminist approaches to text analysis in literary studies. Feminist theory and methodology has already addressed research practices in the natural and physical sciences and social sciences; similar engagement is necessary in literary studies with respect to text analysis. "Big data" and computational text analysis, in fact, give feminist literary critics opportunities to embrace grand technical and social challenges through theorization and praxis, incorporating moments of productive discomfort into four stages of the research process: the assembling of text corpora; the translation of methodologies across disciplines; the gauging of interpretive value; and the selection of appropriate modes of scholarly expression. The language of feminist analysis, which challenges traditional modes of knowledge production, is well aligned with the practice of defamiliarizing a textual corpora in order to ask "new" questions at different scales.

While there is no single "feminist epistemology" or "feminist method," feminist approaches to text mining might begin by exposing implicit and explicit choices that influence the construction of textual corpora, articulating the rationale for their selection, and carefully scoping the claims they make in deference to the representative limitations of their datasets. For example, by calling attention to androcentric biases, feminist empiricist approaches to text mining might deconstruct perceived errors in datasets or correct biases through activist interventions with the corpora that make gender a category of analysis (Scott). When topic modeling poetic corpora in my own research, for example, I have included detailed descriptions of my dataset, which was scraped from the American Academy of Poets (poets.org) website in 2012 and includes a disappointing ratio of three poems by male poets to every one by a woman. Productive discomfort rendered through the assembly of my dataset means balancing recuperative strategies for including much higher representations of poetry by women with a competing acknowledgment that the representation of work by women in the collection remains unsatisfactory.

Since most text-mining methods used in literary study have been forged in linguistics or computer sciences, the algorithms we use for literary text analysis projects, such as topic modeling or sentiment analysis, potentially demonstrate an intrinsic bias toward the source texts used during development. Though the difference may be negligible, feminist approaches might lay bare differences in disciplinary values embedded within an algorithm's formal logic to expose moments of productive discomfort among transdisciplinary engagements, an approach akin to feminist calls for the integration of quantitative and qualitative research (Sprague and Zimmerman). For example, when beginning to work with topic modeling, my training as a scholar of poetry contrasted with the method's tacit expectation that "small" words, including pronouns, articles, and prepositions, should be removed from the text. For literary critics of poetry, the position and selection of articles and pronouns signals an interpretive significance that is disregarded in the usual preparation of texts for computational analysis. To account for this difference in disciplinary practice, I performed extensive preliminary studies to measure the degree to which the extraction of small words interfered with values in literary criticism, and in doing so sought to assure my literary studies audiences that I had met their disciplinary, methodological expectations.[1]

Algorithms do precisely as they are told, enacting a carefully articulated and rigid logic; in text analysis, that logic is based on assumptions about how language operates. Algorithms do not interpret their own failures, but their errors generate moments of rupture for the feminist literary scholar, in whose hands error and marginality expose the fault lines encoded in predictive methods such as classifying and organizing text. Consequently, my approach to text-mining methods such as topic modeling differs from others. I use large poetic corpora to interrogate the assumptions of topic modeling—that documents sharing similar words likewise share thematic coherence. Where most topic-modeling results demonstrate thematic coherence, mine represent discourse coherence; subsequently, the model points to ekphrastic poems by women who share similar discourses as their male counterparts, but do so ironically. By challenging accepted research practices and testing the assumed logic of algorithms rather than using it to classify texts into settled categories, feminist interventions into topic modeling effectively resist the positivistic paradigms.

New forms of knowledge sharing that are familiar to practitioners in text analysis may elicit frustration or even confusion from colleagues in literary studies, exposing a fourth site of productive discomfort: scholarly communication. Unfamiliar forms of social scholarly exchange, such as R and Python vignettes in GitHub,[2] blog posts (Swafford), or datasets on Figshare (Rand, Kraft-Todd, and Gruber), can unsettle deeply held expectations for sharing academic work. Here, feminist epistemologies of knowledge production afford scholarly debate in text analysis a language to begin engaging and responding to the collective unease of readers and authors. The formation of democratic communities of knowledge production requires mutual respect for the epistemic contributions of participants and care that their work is given credibility regardless of their academic status, identity, or mode of discourse (Grasswick).

So why do I dig? I dig as an act of re-vision. I dig to raise more questions than I can answer. I dig because—much like Jorie Graham's poetic "big hunger"—it affords one *more* way "to wrest beauty and meaning—however tentative and qualified—from the abyss of language and randomness of experience" (Costello). I dig because I believe that feminist literary studies can offer a necessary corrective to the androcentric tendencies of "big data," one that, in its unsettling, directly addresses the technological and epistemological challenges of our age.

NOTES

1. I discuss this approach at length in "The Story of Stopwords: Topic Modeling an Ekphrastic Tradition," http://www.lisarhody.com/the-story-of-stopwords/.

2. Vignettes are detailed, academic walk-throughs of code packages for programming language. For an example, see Jockers, "Mjockers/syuzhet."

BIBLIOGRAPHY

Costello, Bonnie. " 'The Big Hunger': Review of *Region of Unlikeness,* by Jorie Graham." *New Republic* (January 1992): 36–39. http://www.joriegraham.com/costello_1992.

Gardner, Thomas. *Jorie Graham: Essays on the Poetry.* Madison: University of Wisconsin Press, 2005.

Grasswick, Heidi. "Feminist Social Epistemology." In *The Stanford Encyclopedia of Philosophy* (spring edition), ed. by Edward N. Zalta, 2013. http://plato.stanford.edu/archives /spr2013/entries/feminist-social-epistemology/.

Jockers, Matthew. "Mjockers/syuzhet." *GitHub.* Accessed May 6, 2015. https://github.com /mjockers/syuzhet.

Lorde, Audre. *Sister Outsider: Essays and Speeches.* New York: Potter/TenSpeed/Harmony, 2012.

Nowviskie, Bethany. "What Do Girls Dig?" In *Debates in Digital Humanities,* ed. Matthew K. Gold. Minneapolis: University of Minnesota Press, 2012. http://dhdebates.gc.cuny .edu/static/debates/text/3.

Rand, David G., Gordon Kraft-Todd, and June Gruber. "Example Texts That Received High LIWC Scores for Positive Emotion, Negative Emotion, and Inhibition," *Figshare,* June 2015. http://figshare.com/articles/_Example_texts_that_received_high_LIWC_ scores_for_positive_emotion_negative_emotion_and_inhibition_/1295881.

Scott, Joan. "The Evidence of Experience." In *Feminist Approaches to Theory and Methodology,* ed. Christine Gilmartin and Robin Lydenberg, 79–99. New York: Oxford University Press, 1999.

Sprague, Joey, and Mark Zimmerman. "Overcoming Dualisms: A Feminist Agenda for Sociological Methodology." In *Theory on Gender: Feminism on Theory,* ed. Paula England, 2–24. New York: Aldine DeGruyter, 1993.

Swafford, Annie. "Problems with the Syuzhet Package." *Anglophile in Academia: Annie Swafford's Blog,* March 2, 2015. https://annieswafford.wordpress.com/2015/03/02 /syuzhet/.

More Scale, More Questions: Observations from Sociology

TRESSIE MCMILLAN COTTOM

Much of the debate about the whys and what-fors of textual analysis in the age of massive data is about scale. Take, for example, the current gold rush known as "big data." On its face, big data merely refers to bits and bytes of data that are too large to be stored or processed using traditional means. Discursively, big data has come to mean much more. More than just taxonomy of size, big data is notable "because of its relationality to other data" (boyd and Crawford, 2). The scale of large quantities of data portends analytical possibilities for uncovering fundamental social facts. In this context, scale is about a grand theory of human nature and human systems. For many actors, large-scale data is valuable simply because it is big and "now."[1] Franco Moretti's "distant reading" (Moretti; Schulz) is embedded in this larger political economy of what some sociologists have called the "datalogical turn" (Clough et al.) of quantification and digitization. This argument unfolds against a backdrop of sociopolitical processes that favor market relationships over social ties, individuals over collectivities. It also unfolds within the academic industrial complex, itself a microcosm of the larger sociopolitical context. In this context, scale is an end unto itself. Data-tizing literature at large scale becomes meaningful not because of its ontological superiority per se but because it rationalizes the hegemonic cultural imperative that all things (and beings) be data-tized. With scale come questions that are important for how we identify, understand, and analyze textual data.

One of boyd and Crawford's provocations for the big data moment ("Critical Questions") is that claims of objectivity and accuracy are misleading. What does the "mistaken belief that qualitative researchers are in the business of interpreting stories and quantitative researchers are in the business of producing facts" mean for textual analysis in the humanities given the discipline's emphasis on interpretation as opposed to production? Moretti seems excited by a digital humanities project that creates a "unified theory of plot and style" (Schulz). If plot and style can be attributed to a single unifying theory, a discernible objective pattern of words across context, plot and style risk losing their salience as analytical concepts. To put it more simply, plot and style are meaningful ways of thinking about text because they capture difference and not because they approach the singularity.

The tensions I describe are not unique to digital humanities or humanities writ large. The social and natural sciences are casting about the same waters of shifting university priorities, declining financial support, and academic entrepreneurship.[2] For sociology, the quantitative or datalogical turn as hegemonic has been a long, strange trip indeed. Latour writes that "sociology has been obsessed by the goal of becoming a quantitative science" ("Tarde's Idea"). In the 1970s sociologists Jerome Karabel and Albert Henry Halsey worried that changing political economies (e.g., state patronage) were legitimizing quantitative methodologies over qualitative sensemaking and empiricism over theory. It "would be naive not to recognize that state patronage has contributed to promoting atheoretical forms of methodological empiricism and has given less encouragement to other approaches" (17). Karabel and Halsey are talking about the normative and economic power that state-funded and controlled access to national datasets, the "big data" of the time, exerts over the questions scholars ask and how they set out to answer them. Miriam Posner provides an analogous discourse for digital humanities when she says that "most of the data and data models we've inherited [from business applications] deal with structures of power, like gender and race, with a crudeness that would never pass muster in a peer-reviewed humanities publication" ("What's Next"). Business applications exert influence over the data being produced, and the scale of which is being produced, and constrains how that data can be accessed, analyzed, and politicized. Like state patronage, business applications (or market actors in my parlance) give scale the relationality that boyd and Crawford critique and the taken-for-grantedness of Moretti's enthusiasm for distant reading. We do distant reading because we can. But that we can do it—these data, these methods—is inherently political.

Moretti would seem to agree that textual data are political (if I am not entirely sure that he would agree that our conceptualization of literature as textual data is also political). He has taken great pains to link distant reading and quantitative textual analysis to Immanuel Wallerstein's influential world-systems theory (WST). WST is Marxist in tradition and contemporary in its focus on nation-states as the primary unit of analysis, one of its primary contributions to contemporary social theory. Moretti proposes to "borrow this initial hypothesis from the world-system school of economic history, for which international capitalism is a system that is simultaneously one, and unequal: with a core, and a periphery (and a semiperiphery) that are bound together in a relationship of growing inequality" (Moretti, 55). It is an interesting theoretical treatment with important empirical considerations. WST has a particular emphasis on how powerful core nations manipulate the terms of a global economic system to extract resources from (semi-) peripheral nations to expand profit-taking in various forms of trade. The unit of analysis in WST is nation-state but its mechanisms are about resources, geopolitics, and capital. It is difficult to see how this translates to the methodological choice of some national texts to "uncover the true scope and nature of literature" (Schulz).

This application of quantitative textual analysis brings up several questions. One question is what constitutes a dataset when it is broadly defined as "literature"? In sociology, scholars have argued that there is not a significantly large enough corpus of textual data to substitute for qualitative inquiry of sociopolitical conditions that produce text. For instance, Moretti has made choices about language and time period. Roberto Franzosi and others (Franzosi, De Fazio, and Vicari) have applied quantitative methods to newspaper data on enslaved people in the U.S. South during a period of frequent public lynchings. There is a theoretical framework guiding these choices. In methodological terms from content analysis, something bounds these texts, making them a "dataset." Wallerstein is not much use here and it is where Moretti's theoretical choice of WST to ground quantitative textual analysis becomes difficult to grasp. Another question is what constitutes a form under the current conditions of prosumption, or "situations in which consumers collaborate with companies or with other consumers to produce things of value" (Humphreys and Grayson, 964). An example would be the production of long-form texts, produced over time by an individual or collective of authors on a digital publishing platform. The platform may be privately owned, as in the case of Blogger. The context produced by users of the platform can generate revenue for the private company, which operates under the logics of financialized capital. But the platform users are also producers. They conceive and author the content and can still own legal rights to that content. The content producers can be in one nation-state and the company that owns the publishing platform can be in another. The content producers can call their content a digital magazine but platform owners can call the same content a blog while readers can call it a book. The content is searchable in another corporate-owned platform (i.e., a search engine like Google). But it may not be classified in an academic library database using any hegemonic taxonomy for knowledge classification. Are these texts part of the literature on which quantitative textual analysis is refining its hypotheses and running experiments? Whether it is or not, a set of assumptions is embedded in the data on which models about the inherent nature of literature are based.

Sociology has developed a diverse toolkit to identify, measure, and analyze various forms of text with an attention to political economy. This includes content analysis (e.g., newspaper content), organizational analysis (e.g., texts produced by institutions or organizations), and quantitative narrative analysis or QNA (e.g., a sociological complement to distant reading). I will provide two examples of how political economies informed the theory that guided my methodological analysis of various texts. These examples are not meant to be instructive of best practices and certainly not across disciplinary borders. Instead, I aim to show the role theory has played in what I consider "text" as illustrative of how robust a unified theory would need to be in our contemporary research milieu.

The research project had a deceptively simple question: Are there more interracial couples on television today than some unspecified past? The question emerged from debates on social media about the hit network television show *How to Get Away with Murder*. The show has a black female protagonist who is married to a white male. Memes circulated on social media about the show seemed to focus heavily on the novelty of the pairing, if not outright claiming it as evidence of a new vanguard for the acceptability of black women as desirable sexual partners. To explore the question of the trope's significance via its novelty, I had to translate a type of text into a dataset. I needed a body of data about television programming. I ended up with a guidebook, "The Complete Directory to Prime Time Network and Cable TV Shows, 1946–Present." The encyclopedic text "cover[s] the entire history of network TV in the United States, from its inception on a regular basis in 1994 through April 15, 2007." I also used Wikipedia entries for television show descriptions and the International Movie Database for audience interpretation. When I chose these texts I incorporated the logics embedded in the making of the text. I adopted the epistemology of an English-language text. I adopted the history of network television and its concomitant market relationships with advertisers. I adopted the textual constraints of various platform architectures. I adopted the cultural logic of "race" and "gender" and "sex" and heteronormativity that would be reflected in a mass-produced genre that has been indexed for textual analysis. Even after accepting all of the constraints I inherited in the data, I had to deal with the complexity of categories that are at odds with critical theory. For example, is a character on *Grey's Anatomy* "black" because I interpret him as black, or because the show's writers write the character as black, or because the actor playing the character identifies as black? My analysis relied in great part on ascribing race to visual data that had been captured as text without any consideration of what constitutes race. Miriam Posner explores other examples of how our classification systems are produced within a political economy and how we inherit them through our tools. She wonders, "What would maps and data visualizations look like if they were built to show us categories like race as they have been experienced, not as they have been captured and advanced by businesses and governments?" (Posner). In my read of the current landscape of textual data in sociology, I extrapolate from Posner that it is important to ask what it means when distant reading or quantitative textual analysis does not theorize the power relations of financial actors or the social construction of race in computational models or analytical frameworks.

Without that lens I suspect that we get a quantitative textual analysis that is very popular with powerful actors precisely because it does not theorize power relations. Given our current political economy, especially in the rapidly corporatized academy, one should expect great enthusiasm for distant reading and acritical theorizing. We should not be distracted by the appeal to WST, a critical theory of global power relations. The devil, when it comes to analysis, is in the details of mechanisms. WST as currently applied to textual analysis does not go so far as to explicate *how* global systems of capital, geopolitics, and power define what is literature, the ways we produce various texts in new digital mediums, or to what ends we analyze them out of their given contexts. Sociologists who use QNA approach the challenge of the context of textual data by focusing on the qualitative decisions in quantitative text analysis. I could not find an analog among distant reading approaches as currently used by Moretti, but Roel Popping argues that mechanized and manual "coding is based on a qualitative decision that everybody should understand" (89). Coding schemas emerge from political contexts. Those political contexts have historical decisions embedded in contemporary categories. These contexts may not be of primary interest to humanities' traditional scope of inquiry, but when one adopts computational tools (and the political and market systems embedded in them) it is a good moment to reflect on what those tools mean. Big data does not solve the human conundrum of power of which every text—every kind of every epoch of every culture—engages. Big data can obscure that power, but then any inferences based on the unexamined assumptions and theoretical mechanisms cannot be said to be true of literature writ large but only of literature bound by the market's invisible hand.

NOTES

1. See Bady on temporality and technological moments.

2. See Slaughter for an excellent work on the macro context of these changes that I cannot treat fully in this essay. I suspect every academic (and academic-in-training) is familiar with the effects of that macro context (i.e., increased competition for limited funds, etc.). See also Tuchman, as well as Cottom and Tuchman, for an institutional-level analysis of the market's effect on college processes, policies, and various actors. Finally, Berman provides an important historical analysis of contemporary macro and meso (institutional) realities of the academic complex.

BIBLIOGRAPHY

Bady, Aaron. "The MOOC Moment and the End of Reform." *The New Inquiry,* May 15, 2013. http://thenewinquiry.com/blogs/zunguzungu/the-mooc-moment-and-the-end -of-reform/.

Berman, Elizabeth Popp. *Creating the Market University: How Academic Science Became an Economic Engine.* Princeton, N.J.: Princeton University Press, 2012.

boyd, danah, and Kate Crawford. "Critical Questions for Big Data: Provocations for a Cultural, Technological, and Scholarly Phenomenon." *Information, Communication & Society* 15, no. 5 (2012): 662–79.

Clough, Patricia Ticineto, Karen Gregory, Benjamin Haber, and R. Joshua Scannell. "The Datalogical Turn." In *Non-Representational Methodologies: Re-Envisioning Research,* ed. Phillip Vannini, 146–64. Oxford: Taylor & Francis, 2015.

Cottom, Tressie McMillan. "When White Men Love Black Women on TV." *tressiemc* (blog), December 22, 2014. http://tressiemc.com/2014/12/22/when-white-men-love -black-women-on-tv/.

Cottom, Tressie McMillan, and Gaye Tuchman. "Rationalization of Higher Education." In *Emerging Trends in the Social and Behavioral Sciences: An Interdisciplinary, Searchable, and Linkable Resource,* ed. Robert A. Scott and Stephen M. Kosslyn, 1–17. New York: John Wiley, 2015.

Franzosi, Roberto, Gianluca De Fazio, and Stefania Vicari. "Ways of Measuring Agency: An Application of Quantitative Narrative Analysis to Lynchings in Georgia (1875–1930)." *Sociological Methodology* 42, no. 1 (2012): 1–42.

Humphreys, Ashlee, and Kent Grayson. "The Intersecting Roles of Consumer and Producer: A Critical Perspective on Co-Production, Co-Creation, and Prosumption." *Sociology Compass* 2, no. 3 (2008): 963–80.

Karabel, Jerome, and Albert Henry Halsey. *Power and Ideology in Education.* Oxford: Oxford University Press, 1977.

Latour, Bruno. "Tarde's Idea of Quantification." In *The Social after Gabriel Tarde: Debates and Assessments,* ed. Matei Candea, 145–62. Oxfordshire: Routledge, 2010.

Moretti, Franco. "Conjectures on World Literature." *New Left Review* 1 (January–February 2000): 54–68.

Popping, Roel. "Qualitative Decisions in Quantitative Text Analysis Research." *Sociological Methodology* 42, no. 1 (2012): 88–90.

Posner, Miriam. "What's Next: The Radical, Unrealized Potential of Digital Humanities." *Miriam Posner's Blog,* July 27, 2015. http://miriamposner.com/blog/whats-next-the-radical -unrealized-potential-of-digital-humanities/.

Schulz, Kathryn. "What Is Distant Reading?" *New York Times Sunday Book Review,* June 24, 2011. http://www.nytimes.com/2011/06/26/books/review/the-mechanic-muse- what-is-distant-reading.html?_r=0.

Slaughter, Sheila. *Academic Capitalism and the New Economy: Markets, State, and Higher Education.* Baltimore: Johns Hopkins University Press, 2004.

Suchman, Mark C. "Managing Legitimacy: Strategic and Institutional Approaches." *Academy of Management Review* 20, no. 3 (1995): 571–610.

Tuchman, Gaye. *Wannabe U: Inside the Corporate University.* Chicago: University of Chicago Press, 2009.

Do Digital Humanists Need to Understand Algorithms?

BENJAMIN M. SCHMIDT

Algorithms and Transforms

Ian Bogost recently published an essay[1] arguing that fetishizing algorithms can pollute our ability to accurately describe the world we live in. "Concepts like 'algorithm,'" he writes, "have become sloppy shorthands, slang terms for the act of mistaking multipart complex systems for simple, singular ones" (Bogost). Even critics of computational culture succumb to the temptation to describe algorithms as though they operate with a single incontrovertible beauty, he argues; this leaves them with a "distorted, theological view of computational action" that ignores human agency.

As one of the few sites in the humanities where algorithms are created and deployed, the digital humanities are ideally positioned to help humanists better understand the operations of algorithms rather than blindly venerate or condemn them. But too often, we deliberately occlude understanding and meaning in favor of an instrumental approach that simply treats algorithms as tools whose efficacy can be judged intuitively. The underlying complexity of computers makes some degree of ignorance unavoidable. Past a certain point, humanists certainly do *not* need to understand the algorithms that produce results they use; given the complexity of modern software, it is unlikely that they could.

But although there are elements to software we can safely ignore, some basic standards of understanding remain necessary to practicing humanities data analysis as a scholarly activity and not merely a technical one. While some algorithms are indeed byzantine procedures without much coherence or purpose, others are laden with assumptions that we are perfectly well equipped to understand. What an algorithm does is distinct from, and more important to understand, than how it does it. I want to argue here that a fully realized field of humanities data analysis can do better than to test the validity of algorithms from the outside; instead, it will explore the implications of the assumptions underlying the processes described in software. Put simply: digital humanists do not need to understand algorithms *at all*.

They do need, however, to understand the transformations that algorithms attempt to bring about. If we do so, our practice will be more effective and more likely to be truly original.

The core of this argument lies in a distinction between *algorithms* and *transformations*. An algorithm is a set of precisely specifiable steps that produce an output. "Algorithms" are central objects of study in computer science; the primary intellectual questions about an algorithm involve the resources necessary for those steps to run (particularly in terms of time and memory). "Transformations," on the other hand, are the reconfigurations that an algorithm might effect. The term is less strongly linked to computer science: its strongest disciplinary ties are to mathematics (for example, in geometry, to describe the operations that can be taken on a shape) and linguistics (where it forms the heart of Noam Chomsky's theory of "transformational grammar").

Computationally, algorithms create transformations. Intellectually, however, people design algorithms in order to automatically perform a given transformation. That is to say: a transformation expresses a coherent goal that can be understood independently of the algorithm that produces it. Perhaps the simplest example is the transformation of sorting. "Sortedness" is a general property that any person can understand independently of the operations that produce it. The uses that one can make of alphabetical sorting in humanities research—such as producing a concordance to a text or arranging an index of names—are independent of the particular algorithm used to sort. There are, in fact, a multitude of particular algorithms that enable computers to sort a list. Certain canonical sorting algorithms, such as quicksort, are fundamental to the pedagogy in computer science. (The canonical collection and explanation of sorting algorithms is the first half of Knuth's canonical computer science text.) It would be ludicrous to suggest humanists need to understand an algorithm like quicksort to use a sorted list. But we *do* need to understand sortedness itself in order to make use of the distinctive properties of a sorted list.

The alternative to understanding the meaning of transformations is to use algorithms instrumentally; to hope, for example, that an algorithm like Latent Dirichlet Allocation will approximate existing objects like "topics," "discourses," or "themes" and explore the fissures where it fails to do so. (See, for example, Rhody; Goldstone and Underwood; Schmidt, "Words Alone.") This instrumental approach to software, however, promises us little in the way of understanding; in hoping that algorithms will approximate existing meanings, it in many ways precludes them from creating new ones. The signal criticism of large-scale textual analysis by traditional humanists is that it tells scholars nothing they did not know before. This critique is frequently misguided; but it does touch on a frustrating failure, which is that distant reading as commonly practiced frequently fails to offer any new ways of understanding texts.

Far more interesting, if less immediately useful, will be to marry large-scale analysis to what Stephen Ramsay calls "algorithmic criticism": the process of using algorithmic transformations as ways to open texts for new readings (Ramsay). This is true even when, as in some of the algorithms Ramsay describes, the transformation is inherently meaningless. But transformations that embody a purpose themselves can help us to create new versions of text that offer fresh or useful perspectives. Seeking out and describing how those transformations function is a type of work we can do more to recognize and promote.

The Fourier Transform and Literary Time

A debate between Annie Swafford and Matt Jockers over Jockers's "Syuzhet" package[2] for exploring the shape of plots through sentiment analysis offers a useful case study of how further exploring a transformation's purpose can enrich our vocabulary for describing texts. Although Swafford's initial critique raised several issues with the package, the bulk of her continuing conversation with Jockers centered on the appropriateness of his use of a low-pass filter from signal processing as a "smoothing function." Jockers argued it provided an excellent way to "filter out the extremes in the sentiment trajectories." Swafford, on the other hand, argued that it was often dominated by "ringing artifacts" which, in practice, means the curves produced place almost all their emphasis "at the lowest point only and consider rises or falls on either side irrelevant" (Jockers, "Revealing Sentiment"; Swafford "Problems"; Swafford, "Why Syuzhet Doesn't Work").

The Swafford and Jockers debate hinged over not just an algorithm, but a concretely defined transformation. The discrete Fourier transform undergirds the low-pass filters that Jockers uses to analyze plot. The thought that the Fourier transform might make sense as a formation for plot is an intriguing one; it is also, as Swafford argues, quite likely wrong. The ringing artifacts that Swafford describes are effects of a larger issue: the basic understanding of time embodied in the transformation itself.

The purpose of the Fourier transform is to represent cyclical events as *frequencies* by breaking complex signals into their component parts. Some of the most basic elements of human experience—most notably, light and sound—physically exist as repeating waves. The Fourier transform offers an easy way to describe these infinitely long waves as a short series of frequencies, constantly repeating. The pure musical note "A," for example, is a constant pulsation at 440 cycles per second; as actually produced by a clarinet, it has (among other components) a large number of regular "overtones," less powerful component notes that occur at a higher frequency and enrich the sound beyond a simple tone. A filter like the one Jockers uses strips away these regularities; it is typically used in processes like MP3 compression to strip out notes too high for the human ear to hear. When applied even more aggressively to such a clarinet tone, it would remove the higher frequencies, preserving the note "A" but attenuating the distinctive tone of the instrument.[3]

The idea that plots might be represented in the frequency domain is fascinating, but makes some highly questionable assumptions. Perhaps the most striking assumption is that plots, like sound or light, are composed of endlessly repeating signals. A low-pass filter like the one Jockers employs ignores any elements that seem to be regularly repeating in the text and instead focuses on the longest-term motions; those that take place over periods of time greater than a quarter or a third the length of the text. The process is analogous to predicting the continuing sound of the clarinet based on a sound clip of the note "A" just 1/440th of a second long, a single beat of the base frequency. This, remarkably, is feasible for the musical note, but only because the tone repeats endlessly. The default smoothing in the Syuzhet package assumes that books do the same; among other things, this means the smoothed versions assume the start of every book has an emotional valence that continues the trajectory of its final sentence. (I have explained this at slightly greater length in Schmidt, "Commodius Vici.")

For some plots, including Jockers's primary example, *Portrait of the Artist as a Young Man,* this assumption is not noticeably false. But for other plots, it causes great problems. Figure 48.1 shows the plot of *Portrait* and four other novels, with text taken from Project Gutenberg. William Dean Howell's *The Rise of Silas Lapham* is a story of ruination; *Ragged Dick,* by Horatio Alger, is the archetypal "Rags to Riches" novel of the nineteenth century; *Madame Bovary* is a classically tragic tale of decline. Three different smoothing functions are shown: a weighted moving average, among the simplest possible functions; a loess moving average, which is one of the most basic and least assumption-laden algorithms used in exploratory data analysis; and the low-pass filter included with Syuzhet.[4]

The problems with the Fourier transform here are obvious. A periodic function forces Madame Bovary to be "as well off" after her death as before her infidelity. The less assumption-laden methods, on the other hand, allow her fate to collapse at the end and for *Ragged Dick*'s trajectory to move upward instead of ending on the downslope. Andrew Piper suggests[5] that it may be quite difficult to answer the question, "How do we know when a curve is 'wrong'?" (Piper, "Validation"). But in this case, the wrongness is actually quite apparent; only the attempt to close the circle can justify the downturn in Ragged Dick's fate at the end of the novel.

What sort of evidence is this? By Jockers's account,[6] the Bovary example is simply a negative "validation" of the method, by which I believe he means a sort of empirical falsification of the claim that this is the best method in all cases (Jockers, "Requiem"). Swafford's posts imply similarly that case-by-case validation and falsification are the gold standard. In her words, the package (and perhaps the digital humanities as a whole) need "more peer review and rigorous testing—designed to confirm or refute hypotheses" (Swafford, "Continuing").

Seen in these terms, the algorithm is a process whose operations are fundamentally opaque; we can poke or prod to see if it matches our hopes, but we can never truly *know* it. But when the algorithm is a means of realizing a meaningful transformation, as in the case of the Fourier transform, we can do better than this kind of quality assurance testing; we can interpretively *know* in advance where a

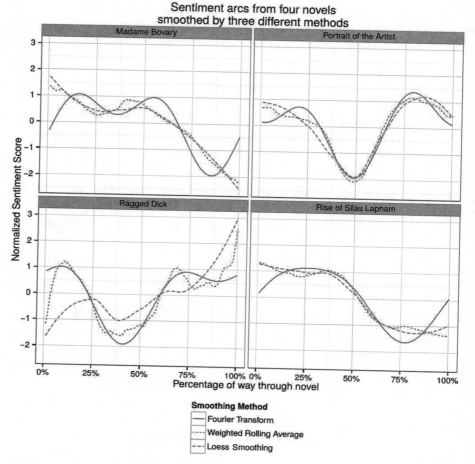

Figure 48.1. Four plot trajectories.

transformation will fail. I did not choose *Madame Bovary* at random to see if it looked good enough; instead, the implications of the smoothing method made it obvious that the tragedy, in general, was a *type* of novel that this conception of sentiment that Syuzhet's smoothing could not comprehend. I will admit, with some trepidation, that I have never actually read either *Madame Bovary* or *Ragged Dick*; but each is the archetype of a plot wholly incompatible with low-pass filter smoothing. Any other novel that ends in death and despair or extraordinary good fortune would fail in the same way.

These problems carry through to Jockers's set of fundamental plots: all begin and end at exactly the same sentiment. But the obvious problems with this assumption were not noted in the first two months of the package's existence (which surely included far more intensive scrutiny than any peer-review process might have). One particularly interesting reason that these failings were not immediately obvious is

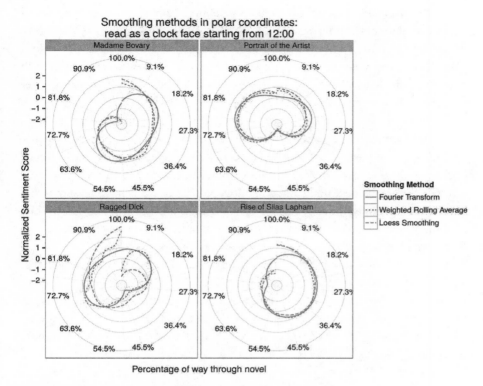

Figure 48.2. Four plot trajectories plotted in polar coordinates.

that line charts, like Figure 48.1, do not fully embody the assumptions of the Fourier transform. The statistical graphics we use to represent results can *themselves* be thought of as meaningful transformations into a new domain of analysis. And in this case, the geometries and coordinate systems we use to chart plots are themselves emblazoned with a particular model. Such line charts assume that time is linear and infinite. In general, this is far and away the easiest and most accurate way to represent time on paper. It is not, though, true to the frequency domain that the Fourier transform takes for granted. If the Fourier transform is the right way to look at plots, we should be plotting in polar coordinates, which wrap around to their beginning. I have replotted the same data in Figure 48.2, with percentage represented as an angle starting from 12:00 on a clock face and the sentiment defined not by height but by distance from the center.

Here, the assumptions of the Fourier transform are much more clear. For all of the novels here, time forms a closed loop; the ending points distort themselves to line up with the beginning, and vice versa. The other algorithms, on the other hand, allow great gaps: the *Madame Bovary* arc circles inward as if descending down a drain, and *Ragged Dick* propels outward into orbit.

These circular plots are more than falsifications. Fully embracing the underlying assumptions of the transform in this way does not only highlight problems with the model; it suggests a new perspective for thinking about plots. This view highlights the gap between the beginning and end as a central feature of the novel; in doing so, it challenges us to think of the time that plots occupy as something other than straightforwardly linear.

This is a conversation worth having, in part because it reminds us to question our other assumptions about plots and time. The infinite time that the Cartesian plot implies is, in some ways, just as false as the radial one. Many smoothing methods (including the one I would like to see used in Syuzhet, loess regression), can easily extrapolate past the beginning and end of the plot. That this is possible shows that they are, in some ways, equally unsuitable for the task at hand. The heart of the distinction between *fabula* and *syuzhet,* in fact, is that there is no way to speak about "before the beginning" of a novel, or what words Shakespeare might have written if he had spent a few more hours working past the end of *Hamlet*. Any model that implies such phrases exist is obviously incorrect.

But even when arguably false, these transformations may yet be productive of new understandings and forms of analysis. While this cyclical return is manifestly inappropriate to the novel, it has significant implications for the study of plot more generally. By asking what sorts of plots of the frequency domain might be useful for, we can abstractly identify whole domains where new applications may be more appropriate.

For example: the ideal form of the three-camera situation comedy is written so that episodes can air in any arbitrary order in syndication. That is to say, along some dimensions they *should* be cyclical. For sitcom episodes, cyclicality is a useful framework to keep in mind. The cleanness of the fit of sentiment, theme, or other attributes may be an incredibly useful tool both to understand how commercial implications intertwine with authorial independence, or for understanding the transformation of a genre over time. Techniques of signal processing could be invaluable in identifying, for example, when and where networks allow writers to spin out multi-episode plot lines.[7]

Though the bulk of the Swafford and Jockers conversation centered on the issue of smoothing, many digital humanists seem to have found a second critique Swafford offered far more interesting. She argued that the sentiment analysis algorithms provided by Jockers's package, most of which were based on dictionaries of words with assigned sentiment scores, produced results that frequently violated "common sense." While the first issue seems blandly technical, the second offers a platform for digital humanists to talk through how we might better understand the black boxes of algorithms we run. What does it mean for an algorithm to accord to common sense? For it to be useful, does it need to be right 100 percent of the time? 95 percent? 50.1 percent? If the digital humanities are to be a field that appropriates tools created by others, these are precisely the questions it needs to practice answering.

To phrase the question this way, though, is once again to consider the algorithm itself as unknowable. Just as with the Fourier transform, it is better to ask consciously what the transformation of sentiment analysis does. Rather than thinking of the sentiment analysis portion of Syuzhet as a set of word lists to be tested against anonymous human subjects, for example, we should be thinking about the best way to implement the underlying algorithms behind sentiment analysis—logistic regression, perhaps—to distinguish between things other than the binary of "positive" and "negative." Jockers's inspiration, Kurt Vonnegut, for example, believed that the central binary of plot was fortune and misfortune, not happiness and sadness; while sentiment analysis provides a useful shortcut, any large-scale platforms might do better to create a classifier that actually distinguishes within that desired binary itself. Andrew Piper's work on plot structure involves internal comparisons within the novel itself (Piper, "Novel Devotions"). Work like this can help us to better understand plot by placing it into conversation with itself *and* by finding useful new applications for transformations from other fields.

Doing so means that digital humanists can help to dispel the myths of algorithmic domination that Bogost unpacks, rather than participating in their creation. When historians applied psychoanalysis to historical subjects, we did not suggest they "collaborate" with psychoanalysts and then test their statements against the historical record to see how much they held true; instead, historians themselves worked to deploy concepts that were seen as themselves meaningful. It is good and useful for humanists to be able to push and prod at algorithmic black boxes when the underlying algorithms are inaccessible or overly complex. But when they are reduced to doing so, the first job of digital humanists should be to understand the goals and agendas of the transformations and systems that algorithms serve so that we can be creative users of new ideas, rather than users of tools the purposes of which we decline to know.

NOTES

1. http://www.theatlantic.com/technology/archive/2015/01/the-cathedral-of-com putation/384300.

2. http://www.matthewjockers.net/%202015/02/02/syuzhet.

3. It may be worth emphasizing that a low-pass filter removes all elements above a certain frequency; it does not reduce to its top five or ten frequencies, which is a different, equally sensible compression scheme.

4. For all three filters, I have used a span approximating a third of the novel. The loess span is one-third; the moving average uses a third of the novel at a time; and the cutoff for the low-pass filter is three. To avoid jagged breaks at outlying points, I use a sine-shaped

kernel to weight the moving average so that each point weights far-away points for its average less than the point itself.

5. http://txtlab.org/?p=470.

6. http://www.matthewjockers.net/2015/04/06/epilogue.

7. This does not necessarily mean that Fourier transform is the best way to think of plots as radial. Trying to pour plot time into the bottle of periodic functions, as we are seeing, produces extremely odd results. As Scott Enderle points out, even if a function is completely and obviously cyclical, it may not be regular enough for the Fourier transform to accurately translate it to the frequency domain (Enderle).

BIBLIOGRAPHY

Bogost, Ian. "The Cathedral of Computation." *The Atlantic*, January 15, 2015. http://www.the atlantic.com/technology/archive/2015/01/the-cathedral-of-computation/384300/.

Enderle, Scott. "What's a Sine Wave of Sentiment?" *The Frame of Lagado* (blog), April 2, 2015. http://www.lagado.name/blog/?p=78.

Goldstone, Andrew, and Ted Underwood. "The Quiet Transformations of Literary Studies: What Thirteen Thousand Scholars Could Tell Us." *New Literary History* 45, no. 3 (2014): 359–84. doi:10.1353/nlh.2014.0025.

Jockers, Matthew. "Requiem for a Low Pass Filter." *Matthewjockers.net*, April 6, 2015. http://www.matthewjockers.net/2015/04/06/epilogue/.

———. "Revealing Sentiment and Plot Arcs with the Syuzhet Package." *Matthewjockers. net*, February 2, 2015. http://www.matthewjockers.net/2015/02/02/syuzhet/.

Knuth, Donald E. *The Art of Computer Programming: Volume 3: Sorting and Searching.* Reading, Mass.: Addison-Wesley Professional, 1998.

Piper, Andrew. "Novel Devotions: Conversional Reading, Computational Modeling, and the Modern Novel." *New Literary History* 46, no. 1 (2015): 63–98. doi:10.1353/nlh .2015.0008.

———. "Validation and Subjective Computing." *txtLAB@Mcgill*, March 25, 2015. http:// txtlab.org/?p=470.

Ramsay, Stephen. *Reading Machines: Toward an Algorithmic Criticism.* Urbana: University of Illinois Press, 2011.

Rhody, Lisa M. "Topic Modeling and Figurative Language." *Journal of Digital Humanities* 2, no. 1 (2013). http://journalofdigitalhumanities.org/2–1/topic-modeling-and-figu rative-language-by-lisa-m-rhody/.

Schmidt, Benjamin. "Commodius Vici of Recirculation: The Real Problem with Syuzhet." Author's blog, April 13, 2015. http://benschmidt.org/2015/04/03/commodius -vici-of-recirculation-the-real-problem-with-syuzhet/.

———. "Words Alone: Dismantling Topic Models in the Humanities." *Journal of Digital Humanities* 2, no. 1 (2013). http://journalofdigitalhumanities.org/2-1/words-alone-by -benjamin-m-schmidt/.

Swafford, Annie. "Problems with the Syuzhet Package." *Anglophile in Academia: Annie Swafford's Blog,* March 2, 2015. https://annieswafford.wordpress.com/2015/03/02/syuzhet/.

———. "Continuing the Syuzhet Discussion." *Anglophile in Academia: Annie Swafford's Blog,* March 7, 2015. https://annieswafford.wordpress.com/2015/03/07/continuingsyuzhet/.

———. "Why Syuzhet Doesn't Work and How We Know." *Anglophile in Academia: Annie Swafford's Blog,* March 30, 2015. https://annieswafford.wordpress.com/2015/03/30/why-syuzhet-doesnt-work-and-how-we-know/.

Messy Data and Faulty Tools

JOANNA SWAFFORD

With our newfound access to unprecedented levels of data, we can ask questions we could not have dreamed of twenty years ago and better answer questions that would previously have taken scholars a lifetime to address: by examining thousands or millions of texts, we can learn about the Great Unread (Cohen, 23), look for changes in periodicals through topic modeling (Nelson), and examine changes in poetic meter over the centuries (Algee-Hewitt et al.). However, unless we focus more on creating quality-control systems for our work, we run the risk of drawing erroneous conclusions based on messy data and faulty tools.

Humanities scholars are used to knowing the details about their data: in literature, for example, we work with poems, essays, plays, and periodicals as well as publishing records, census data, and other number-driven documents. We often gather the information ourselves, so we usually know the origin and quality of our materials. This is not always true for large-scale text analysis projects: HathiTrust, Project Gutenberg, and the Internet Archive have a plethora of works in plain-text format, but the quality of the optical character recognition (OCR) can be unreliable.[1] No individual scholar can read and proofread each text, so the texts we use will have errors, from small typos to missing chapters, which may cause problems in the aggregate.[2] Ideally, to address this issue, scholars could create a large, collaboratively edited collection of plain-text versions of literary works that would be open access. The Eighteenth-Century Collections Online Text Creation Partnership,[3] the Early Modern OCR Project,[4] and the Corpus of Historical American English[5] have helpfully created repositories of texts, through both manual entry and automated OCR correction, but they still represent a comparatively small portion of all texts online.

In addition to clean data, we also need robust, well-tested tools. Traditional scholarship relies on peer review as a means of quality control, and groups like the Advanced Research Consortium[6] do peer-review digital archives. Unfortunately, digital humanities does not currently have a system for peer-reviewing tools. Although digital humanities scholars occasionally post their code online, members of our field are still learning to embrace the open-source philosophy of reviewing each other's code and making suggestions for improvement.[7] As a result, scholars either consult the DiRT directory[8] or informally recommend tools on Twitter.[9] As useful as these systems are, they do not have the rigor that peer review should provide. Certainly a peer-review system for tools presents serious challenges: we may not have enough scholars with programming expertise in the field that the tool supports to comprise a peer-review board; the variety of programming languages and documentation styles people use may also present a problem; and we lack a model for peer-reviewing projects that change. Nevertheless, we need to address these challenges if our data and tools are to meet the quality standards necessary to ensure the continued strength of digital humanities research.[10]

The software package Syuzhet demonstrates this necessity. Syuzhet uses sentiment analysis to graph the emotional trajectory of novels. It was released on GitHub to instant acclaim, both in digital humanities circles and the popular press (Clancy). Unfortunately, the package incorporated an overly simplified version of sentiment analysis and a poorly chosen signal processing filter; the latter problem in particular led to distortions that, in extreme cases, could actually invert the results such that the tool reported emotional highs at the novel's emotional lows (Swafford). These errors initially escaped the notice of those doing a more informal peer-review process over Twitter, as they accepted the maker's claims without interrogating the tool's methodology or code, and the errors were only acknowledged after a drawn-out blog exchange, the public nature of which encouraged the tool's supporters to double-down on their claims. If the tool had been peer-reviewed by experts in the field of sentiment analysis, signal processing, and English literature, it would have been altered at an earlier stage, producing a more reliable tool and, ultimately, better scholarship.

In the interim, we can make our tools for large-scale text analysis more accurate by collaborating with programmers and experts in other fields. For example, when using sentiment analysis, we could work with specialists in natural language processing and in marketing to create a human-annotated corpora of texts, from which we could estimate how an "average" reader evaluates documents and measure how well their algorithms approximate that "average" reader to make sure our tools work. Ultimately, then, while conceptions of words and analytical goals may differ between programmers, humanists, and marketing executives, our scholarship would benefit from a closer partnership.

NOTES

1. For information on the challenges of using OCR to study nineteenth-century newspapers, see Strange et al.

2. Tesseract is the most prominent open-source OCR option, and Ted Underwood has written some enhancements to improve OCR quality of eighteenth-century texts in HathiTrust, but both of these projects, by their own admission, still require human corrections.

3. http://www.textcreationpartnership.org/tcp-ecco.

4. http://emop.tamu.edu.

5. http://corpus.byu.edu/coha.

6. http://idhmc.tamu.edu/arcgrant/nodes.

7. According to Peter Rigby, peer-reviewing open-source software "involves . . . early, frequent reviews . . . of small, independent, complete contributions . . . that are broadcast to a large group of stakeholders, but only reviewed by a small set of self-selected experts" (26).

8. http://dirtdirectory.org.

9. The *Journal of Digital Humanities* has a handful of tool reviews, but these reviews, although helpful, do not actually address the code itself.

10. As an added bonus, having a tool peer-reviewed would help programmer-scholars count their project as scholarship rather than service for tenure and promotion.

BIBLIOGRAPHY

Algee-Hewitt, Mark, Ryan Heuser, Maria Kraxenberger, J. D. Porter, Jonny Sensenbaugh, and Justin Tackett. "The Stanford Literary Lab Transhistorical Poetry Project Phase II: Metrical Form." Paper prepared for the Digital Humanities Conference, Lausanne, Switzerland, July 11, 2014. http://dharchive.org/paper/DH2014/Paper-788.xml.

Clancy, Eileen. "A Fabula of Syuzhet: A Contretemps of Digital Humanities (with Tweets)." *Storify*. Accessed July 17, 2015. https://storify.com/clancynewyork/contretemps-a-syuzhet.

Cohen, Margaret. *The Sentimental Education of the Novel.* Princeton, N.J.: Princeton University Press. 1999.

Nelson, Robert K. "Mining the Dispatch." Digital Scholarship Lab, University of Richmond. Accessed April 30, 2015. http://dsl.richmond.edu/dispatch/.

Rigby, Peter. "Peer Review on Open-Source Software Projects: Parameters, Statistical Models, and Theory." *ACM Transactions on Software Engineering and Methodology* 23, no. 4 (August 2014): 1–33.

Strange, Carolyn, Daniel McNamara, Josh Wodak, and Ian Wood. "Mining for the Meanings of a Murder: The Impact of OCR Quality on the Use of Digitized Historical Newspapers." *Digital Humanities Quarterly* 8, no.1 (2014). http://www.digitalhumanities.org/dhq/vol/8/1/000168/000168.html.

Swafford, Joanna. "Problems with the Syuzhet Package." *Anglophile in Academia: Annie Swafford's Blog,* March 2, 2015. https://annieswafford.wordpress.com/2015/03/02/syuzhet/.

N + 1: A Plea for Cross-Domain Data
in the Digital Humanities

ALAN LIU

S ubtract the unique from the multiplicity," Deleuze and Guattari write. That is one of their programs for remaking modernity's repressive psychic and political-economic state into rhizomes and bodies-without-organs. Emancipate ourselves from totalizing forces, in other words, and see what happens. Their algorithm for that: "write at n – 1 dimensions" (6).

"Forms are the abstract of social relationships," Franco Moretti writes in "Conjectures on World Literature," introducing his program of distant reading (66). Later, in *Graphs, Maps, Trees,* he adds, "form [is revealed] as a diagram of forces; or perhaps, even, as nothing but force" (64). Expose the historical forces underlying the shapes of sociocultural experience, in other words, and conjecture what else might have happened. Moretti's algorithm for that is *forms* (plural) or, put another way, *n + 1.*

Though opposite in expression, Moretti's *n + 1* abstract diagram and Deleuze and Guattari's *n – 1* abstract machine (another of their neonisms) compile to the same criticism of the modern state of being. Both are in form and at root a critique—including but not limited to socioeconomic and political critique—of the notion of *one* form stemming from *one* root. Both are analyses of modernity's paradoxical power at once to compress people into apparently unitary forms (*the* state, *the* masses, *the* market, *the* zeitgeist) and to reveal—through the very transformations of modernity—the radical principle of the multiplicity of forms (Marx: modes of production; Bakhtin: heteroglossia; Williams: structures of feeling; Foucault: epistemes; Derrida: différance; Barthes: galaxy of signifiers; Cixous: woman's body; McGann: radiant textuality; Schumpeter: creative destruction).

Among the forms at stake are discursive ones of the kind that Moretti and the Stanford Literary Lab so brilliantly study. A compact example is the "Maps" chapter in Moretti's *Graphs, Maps, Trees,* which shows how the modern state distorted the form of spatial imagination in nineteenth-century "village stories" from circular, local idylls into ever more attenuated, transected geonetworks reoriented toward state power over the horizon. Moretti's point is not just to add more points on the map. It is to discern the plural, and differential, patterns bracketing the epistemological *before* and *after* of historical change. *Before* manifests in patterns knowable in stabilized forms of human expression, especially middle-level forms such as discursive genres, narrative plots, and geospatial maps mediating between macro-social and individual experience. *After* emerges in new patterns whose understanding requires new forms. At the moving terminator between epistemological day and night hides the grail of Moretti's distant-reading quest: the social, political, economic, and cultural forces that compel the churn of forms.

In the digital humanities, $n - 1$ is sometimes called *deformance* (in new media studies, *glitch*): a deliberate subtraction in unity of form designed to surface differences and rifts of force in known forms.

$N + 1$, by contrast, is *scale, big data,* etc. Typically, big data is understood to mean addition in units of form—for example, more documents or images in a corpus. Tacitly, though, incrementing units is acknowledged to corrode unity of form. Big data is messy, requiring *cleaning, scrubbing, wrangling, munging,* etc. In other words, it's glitchy. At a low level, noise from problems in OCR, character encoding, formatting, and extraneous material is often uninteresting. But the picture is different at the higher level of the analytics brought to bear on big data, which draw on the mathematics of informational "noise" (stochastic process, statistical variance, and probability theory). It is thus profoundly interesting what human observers find meaningful versus noisy, for example, in topic models, cluster analyses, data visualizations, and so on. Some patterns of noisy interference between correlation and difference (e.g., a topic in a topic model that only partly seems to make sense) come to attention as dramatic, meaning that we feel there is some humanly significant force behind the interference.

$N - 1$ and $n + 1$ are thus a circuit: $n \pm 1$. Really, anything to escape regimes of unity and their "monotonous nights" (one of Foucault's favorite zingers).[1]

Let me focus here on $n + 1$, which in my view is not yet robust enough in the digital humanities. How big is digital humanities data anyway, where the crucial measure is not just terabytes or unit-items but, to begin with, *facets* (as in the information-studies sense of "faceted search")?[2] Let's count:

One: My guess is that among branches of the digital humanities, unifacial corpora (e.g., collections of just one kind of material such as novels) occur most regularly in digital literary studies.[3] After the great formalist intervention of the twentieth century, literary scholars still largely focus on the *differentia specifica* of the authors, works, genres (in Russian Formalism, also system of genres), styles, movements, and so on of *literature* in its modern rather than historically more catholic sense. Even when adventuring outside literature, digital literary scholars often like single-malt brews—for instance, a corpus just of specific kinds of journalistic, historical, popular culture, and other sources.

Couplethree: Unifacial corpora, of course, are a Platonic ideal. In reality, two or three other facets are needed. For example, a corpus can be a genre of documents (first facet) in a chronological period (second facet) and nation (third facet). However, added facets are often unifacial in spirit because, whether due to focus or missing data, they narrow inquiry—just to the intersection of a genre, century, and nation, for example.

Further facets could be instanced, but they are not typical. Digital history has a broader remit because its materials are often (though they need not be) more diverse in genre and provenance. Consider, for instance, the amplitude of *The Old Bailey Proceedings Online* (Hitchcock et al.), whose corpus includes the Old Bailey *Proceedings* from 1674 to 1913, the *Ordinary of Newgate's Accounts,* advertisements in the *Proceedings* (brought forward for attention rather than filtered out), and guides and links to "Associated Records" (one descriptive section of which ventures into the literary and artistic realm of "Novels and Satirical Prints").[4] Of course, projects like *The Old Bailey* are relatively big, well-funded, or old enough to have extended their coverage over the years. But there is no necessary relation between being big-$-old and multifaceted. A solo digital humanist with little or no funding, for instance, could assemble a corpus of a few hundred literary works plus a few hundred sermons, ballads, political speeches, legislative acts, or newspaper articles from the same era. The crucial multiplier is not big-$-old, but number of facets.[5]

In this regard, it can be predicted that an important next-generation step for the digital humanities will be to scrape and aggregate content from the many smaller digital humanities projects whose mixed-media or multifaceted materials were conceived first of all as collections, editions, exhibitions, teaching materials, single-author or single-artist corpora, timelines, Neatline maps, story maps, and so on. Beyond their original missions, these can be tributaries into large-scale, multifaceted corpora designed for text analysis, visual analysis, social-network and prosopographical study, and other data mining at scale. An example is the Social Networks and Archival Contexts project (SNAC), which repurposes archival and other collection finding aids to release their prosopographical data for multifaceted views of relations between collections, persons, families, organizations, and so on. Or consider what might be done in the future with the proliferating story maps created in such platforms as ArcGIS, Odyssey.js, and StoryMapJS by instructors and students (and professionals in other fields such as journalism). The mixed texts, images, links, and so on in story maps might be scraped and aggregated so that their original narrative form is opened up to big-data analytics and other follow-on forms of understanding—for example, cluster analyses and topic models that, as in Benjamin M. Schmidt's innovative work on historical ship logs, include map coordinates.

The goal of multiplying facets in digital humanities corpora, whether by designing projects for the purpose or aggregating existing projects, is to bring such corpora (not the same as corpus linguistics corpora[6]) closer to what may well be their implicit, if rarely attainable *n + 1* ideal: *archives.* Pushing back against the loose appropriation of the term, research archivists have recently reminded digital humanists what the concept actually means. In an article in *Journal of Digital Humanities,* for example, Kate Theimer quotes the first definition of *archives* endorsed by the Society of American Archivists:

> Materials created or received by a person, family, or organization, public or private, in the conduct of their affairs and preserved because of the enduring value contained in the information they contain or as evidence of the functions and responsibilities of their creator, especially those materials maintained using the principles of provenance, original order, and collective control.

Then, repudiating the premise of many putative archives in the digital humanities, she comments: "There is nothing in this meaning of 'archives' that references a selection activity on the part of the archivist" (Theimer). In other words, while archives are indeed rigorous about the materials they ingest over their "archival threshold" (as Luciana Duranti calls it, with allusion to the architecture of the Roman Tabularium), their selection rigor is not keyed to purity of materials for a researcher's purpose. Archives are instead often *n + 1* mixes of materials witnessing the identity (and other needs) of the persons, organizations, cities, states, etc. that is their *raison d'être.*

Sparseness of facets, however, only gets us to the threshold of the more general lack in the digital humanities. That lack is data domains, a term I use here to mean the ontological, epistemological, formal, and social-political-economic provenances—put more generally, contexts—in which datasets arise no matter how richly or poorly faceted. Most digital humanities projects do not work with enough such domains at any one time. That means that they do not functionally encounter enough exogamous *otherness*. After all, corpora from exogamous domains challenge scholars' assumed or trained "feel" for their data, including not just for their dataset's explicit metadata but, more challenging, for the implicit assumptions governing how their dataset was originally constituted—what was not collected, what was overrepresented, what was ingested only as ephemera in bins labeled something like "materials from the Seattle 1962 World's Fair," etc. On this point, Noortje Marres and Esther Weltevrede's "Scraping the Social?" is insightful. There is never any scraping of unstructured data, they observe. (As Lisa Gitelman puts it in the title of her edited volume, "'raw data' is an oxymoron.") Instead, there is only the scraping of "*already formatted* data" whose pre-encoded structures, even when seemingly unstructured, inject "'alien' assumptions" (Marres and Weltevrede, 315).

For me, *alien assumptions* are what it's all about. That is the big promise of big data. I think playing it safe in endogamous domains will always get the digital humanities just to the point of producing interesting *demos*. Few game-changing discoveries will arise to satisfy the Idiot Questioners, as William Blake might have called them (*Milton a Poem,* object 43),[7] who keep asking doggedly: *do the digital humanities really discover anything new?* That is a rigged question because it is implicitly completed, for example, *about literature or history.* Domains of knowledge such as *literature* and *history* are pretuned to the predigital scholarly methods that arose over the past two-plus centuries (roughly since Blake's time, in fact) to define those domains as objects of inquiry. In such a feedback loop, other kinds of questions premised on other definitions of the object of inquiry are ruled out of scope—elided, marginalized, or at best, as in the case of the New Historicism's attempt at cross-domain inquiry without adequate technical means, "anecdotalized."[8]

But the etymological root of *demo—monstrāre* (to show, point out)—forks off rhizomatically to suggest something else corpora can demonstrate: *monsters.* The monsters of the digital humanities are the alien assumptions living in the cracks between familiar and unfamiliar domains of big data. A data domain is like a house in a gothic novel or film. It is haunted by something as near, yet far, as the attic. Who lives in the attic? Messy archives of ancestors, yesteryears, and other ghostly revenants of what today's domains try to unknow. Really, the digital humanities should go bump in the night. The field is currently not scary enough.

N + 1 should be the equation for transacting between a scholar's familiar domain and scary alien ontologies, epistemologies, forms, sociologies, economics, politics, and (perhaps scariest for humanists) sciences, including information science. Such a transaction would not just demonstrate but "operationalize" the *messiness* of humanities data as something more than accident or inconvenience (borrowing the powerful "operationalizing" concept from Moretti). After all, data mess witnesses fundamental collisions of logic and sociologic occurring in the background—for example, between different media, classificatory ontologies, and social-political-economic views of what should be recorded, how, and with what openness to other communities. Messiness is thus too valuable just to be "cleaned" from the corpus (scrubbed or filtered) in the interest of pure gene lines of genres, periods, nations, and languages.

So here is my program for the digital humanities. I hope digital humanists can build more experimental, cross-domain corpora designed on purpose to be *other* than tidy. Digital humanists should make corpora that mix disciplines, provenances, formats, metadata structures, and so on to remix the evidence of the human.

This need not mean a "culturomics" surfacing apparent trends from googols of documents with uncontrolled metadata and provenances.[9] It can, and should, mean highly controlled experiments with precisely defined cross-domain corpora—for example, novels plus just one or two of the following at a time gathered from controlled provenances: newspapers, advertisements, song lyrics, legal papers, political speeches, architectural documents, etc. A fascinating attempt at something like such an experiment is Tim Hitchcock's *Voices of Authority* project, using materials from the *Old Bailey Proceedings* mixed with other sources (Hitchcock).

Exploring cross-domains of data in this way would advance the digital humanities both technically and on a broader methodological front. Technically, cross-domain corpora pose intriguing next-frontier challenges. For instance, how do we use computation to negotiate between the metadata ontologies of one knowledge domain and another along the lines of the "fluid ontologies" theorized by Ramesh Srinivasan and his collaborators? Their work focuses on combined ethnographical and computational ways to bridge the knowledge protocols of indigenous peoples and the museums that collect their artifacts (Srinivasan and Huang; Srinivasan, Pepe, and Rodriguez; Srinivasan et al.).

But it is the broader methodological (and cultural-critical) challenge of cross-domain corpora—motivating Srinivasan and his collaborators as well—that is the research sweet spot. Sorting through facets of genre, period, and nation in a single domain, digital humanists hunt for the unknown in such evidence as frequencies of collocated words that reveal collective, larger, and to some degree, alien mentalities. Such mentalities are like what Timothy Morton calls *hyperobjects* exceeding the established interpretive lens frames of the *author, work, generation, movement,* etc. We think our diagrams, topic models, social network graphs, maps, and so on are the grainy photographs of those great aliens among us—a scholarly version of a Yeti or UFO or, perhaps better, an ant's guess at a "human" walking on its nest.

But that is just a 2D silhouette or at best 3D maquette. What if we could collaborate across fields to create other views from multiple disciplinary, generic, period, national, and other domain angles—like an MRI resonating not just in the single torpedo tube down which a patient today is inserted for data slicing, but in some fantastic multi-axial scanning array showing the human body, the literal corpus, from multiple simultaneous unexpected angles?[10] And what if those multi-angled slices revealed in composite the true many-splendored profile of the alien: the forms of ourselves caught in, but shaking against, the nets of modernity, neoliberalism, and everything else trying to aggregate capital out of $n = 1$ profiles of our selves, our precious $n \pm 1$ human selves?

What if the digital humanities did text analysis, which would also be cultural criticism, like that?

NOTES

My thanks to Lisa Marie Rhody for her astute, extremely helpful open peer review of this essay. I have added ideas and examples, and altered others, in response to her suggestions.

1. For example, "Not so long ago, [madness] had floundered about in broad daylight. . . . But in less than a half-century, it had been sequestered and, in the fortress

of confinement, bound to Reason, to the rules of morality and to their monotonous nights" (Foucault, *Madness*, 64); and "But twilight soon fell upon this bright day, followed by the monotonous nights of the Victorian bourgeoisie" (Foucault, *History of Sexuality*, 3).

2. "Faceted classification decomposes compound subjects into foci in component facets, offering expressive power and flexibility through the independence of the facets" (Tunkelang, 9).

3. Some points about my nomenclature: *digital humanities* here means primarily digital work created by or in relation to fields traditionally recognized as "the humanities," especially such older disciplines as history, literature, classics, the languages, corpus linguistics, etc. that were associated with so-called humanities computing before it evolved and widened into the now self-aware and professionalized field of "digital humanities." I thus do not encompass work in "new media studies and arts" or digital work in the social sciences and information science. The conversation is ongoing about how the digital humanities narrowly defined should engage more fully with other areas of the digital research space. After all, there are overlaps of interests, people, and projects among all these areas even if their convergence has not yet been realized at the programmatic and institutional level. But my intervention in this essay is addressed to the digital humanities in its present, institutionally recognized compass.

In regard to *corpus* and *corpora*: I use these terms in the vernacular digital-humanities sense of a focused collection of materials—for example, nineteenth-century British novels, historical newspaper articles, etc.—assembled for the study of a particular subject area using digital methods. Except as indicated in note 6, I thus do not mean corpora created in the corpus linguistics field—for example, samples of texts from a nation and era chosen to be broadly representative of language usage (e.g., Davies, *Corpus of Historical American English*).

4. I omit here consideration of digital work in near-humanities fields such as archaeology, which may be multifaceted by definition because the organizing principle for data collection and analysis (for example) is what is found at a site as opposed to any isolated kind of artifact or document.

5. Katie Trumpener's criticism of the digital humanities for lacking a robust comparative literature viewpoint and Domenico Fiormonte's parallel criticism of the field's Anglophone-centrism suggest that even the minimal threshold of a cross-national or cross-language *n + 1* is difficult to achieve for a variety of reasons.

6. I focus here on the contrast between digital humanities corpora and archives. But there is at least one other important contrast to be considered: between digital humanities corpora and corpora created for corpus linguistics research. Putting corpus linguistics in the picture opens up a fascinating triangular conceptual space. Corpora in corpus linguistics (e.g., Davies, *Corpus of Historical American English*) are unlike the usual digital humanities corpora; they include more than a particular author, genre, etc. But they are also unlike archives; they select representative language from multiple, mixed provenances. Nevertheless, like digital humanities corpora, they do focus on facets (e.g., linguistic

usage of a particular nation in a specific period). And, like archives, they do mix materials, albeit for the nonarchival purpose of representing broad linguistic usage. The triangulation between the digital humanities, corpus linguistics, and archival notions of *corpus* seems not well understood at present and may be a fertile zone for future theoretical and practical research.

7. See Blake, http://www.blakearchive.org/exist/blake/archive/object.xq?objectid= milton.a.illbk.43&java=no.

8. My mention of the New Historicism's method of "anecdotes" is not pejorative. See my *Local Transcendence* for fuller discussion, and appreciation, of anecdotes and the New Historicism. Having migrated from the New Historicism in my early career to the digital humanities now, I am highly aware of convergences and divergences between the approaches. The New Historicist anecdote is in some ways the missing link between the New Critical *verbal icon* and the digital humanist *model* (e.g., a diagram or graph). It was close reading's attempt to do distant reading.

9. See Reece Samuels for a cautionary critique of using Google Ngram Viewer to study "culturomics." Samuels's post includes summaries of earlier critiques of the metadata problems and other issues afflicting the Google Books corpora underlying the Ngram Viewer. For the concept of *culturomics* as it was introduced by the researchers behind the Google Ngram Viewer, see Michel et al.

10. While the usual perception of MRI (magnetic resonance imaging) is that it requires human bodies to be constrained for scanning in a single-axis tube and creates image slices on one plane at a time, in fact MRI technology is capable of simultaneous multiplane ("multi-angle oblique") imaging and also Position Imaging™ (scanning in several bodily positions and configurations, including standing). The Fonar company, which originated commercial MRI, holds the patents for these techniques. See Fonar, "Our History."

BIBLIOGRAPHY

Blake, William. *Milton a Poem*. Copy A (c. 1811). *The William Blake Archive*, ed. Morris Eaves, Robert Essick, and Joseph Viscomi. http://www.blakearchive.org/.

Davies, Mark. *The Corpus of Historical American English: 400 million words, 1810–2009*. Brigham Young University, 2010. http://corpus.byu.edu/coha/.

Deleuze, Gilles, and Félix Guattari. *A Thousand Plateaus: Capitalism and Schizophrenia*. Translated by Brian Massumi. Minneapolis: University of Minnesota Press, 1987.

Duranti, Luciana. "Archives as a Place." *Archives and Manuscripts* 24, no. 2 (1996): 242–55.

Fiormonte, Domenico. "Towards a Cultural Critique of the Digital Humanities." *Historical Social Research* 37, no. 3 (2012): 59–76.

Fonar, Inc. "Our History." n.d. http://fonar.com/history.htm.

Foucault, Michel. *The History of Sexuality—Volume 1: An Introduction*. Translated by Robert Hurley. New York: Vintage, 1980.

———. *Madness and Civilization: A History of Insanity in the Age of Reason*. Translated by Richard Howard. New York: Vintage, 1965.

Gitelman, Lisa, ed. *"Raw Data" Is an Oxymoron*. Cambridge, Mass.: MIT Press, 2013.

Hitchcock, Tim. "Voices of Authority: Towards a History from Below in Patchwork." *Historyonics* (blog), April 27, 2015. http://historyonics.blogspot.com/2015/04/voices-of -authority-towards-history.html.

Hitchcock, Tim, Robert Shoemaker, Clive Emsley, Sharon Howard, and Jamie McLaughlin et al. *The Old Bailey Proceedings Online, 1674–1913*. Version 7.2, March 2015. http:// www.oldbaileyonline.org/.

Liu, Alan. *Local Transcendence: Essays on Postmodern Historicism and the Database*. Chicago: University of Chicago Press, 2008.

Marres, Noortje, and Esther Weltevrede. "Scraping the Social? Issues in Live Social Research." *Journal of Cultural Economy* 6, no. 3 (2013): 313–35. http://research.gold .ac.uk/6768/.

Michel, Jean-Baptiste, Yuan Kui Shen, Aviva Presser Aiden, Adrian Veres, Matthew K. Gray, The Google Books Team, Joseph P. Pickett, et al. "Quantitative Analysis of Culture Using Millions of Digitized Books." *Science* 331, no. 6014 (2011): 176–82.

Moretti, Franco. "Conjectures on World Literature." *New Left Review* 1 (2000): 54–68.

———. *Graphs, Maps, Trees: Abstract Models for a Literary History*. London; New York: Verso, 2005.

———. "'Operationalizing': or, the Function of Measurement in Modern Literary Theory." Stanford Literary Lab, Pamphlet 6, December 2013. http://litlab.stanford.edu/Literary LabPamphlet6.pdf.

Morton. Timothy. *Hyperobjects: Philosophy and Ecology after the End of the World*. Minneapolis: University of Minnesota Press, 2013.

Samuels, Reece. "A Critique of Google NGram Viewer." *Reece_Digital_History* (blog), March 4, 2014. https://reecesamuels7.wordpress.com/2014/03/04/a-critique-of-google-ngram- viewer/.

Schmidt, Benjamin M. "When You Have a MALLET, Everything Looks Like a Nail." *Sapping Attention* (blog), November 2, 2012. http://sappingattention.blogspot.com/2012/11 /when-you-have-mallet-everything-looks.html.

Social Networks and Archival Context Project (SNAC). Institute for Advanced Technology in the Humanities. University of Virginia, 2013. http://socialarchive.iath.virginia. edu/.

Srinivasan, Ramesh, Katherine M. Becvar, Robin Boast, and Jim Enote. "Diverse Knowledges and Contact Zones within the Digital Museum." *Science, Technology, and Human Values* 35, no. 5 (2010): 735–68.

Srinivasan, Ramesh, and Jeffrey Huang. "Fluid Ontologies for Digital Museums." *International Journal on Digital Libraries* 5, no. 3 (2005): 193–204.

Srinivasan, Ramesh, Alberto Pepe, and Marko A. Rodriguez. "A Clustering-based Semi- automated Technique to Build Cultural Ontologies." *Journal of the American Society of Information Science and Technology* 60, no. 3 (2009): 608–20.

Stanford Literary Lab. Stanford University. http://litlab.stanford.edu/.

Theimer, Kate. "Archives in Context and as Context." *Journal of Digital Humanities* 1, no. 2 (Spring 2012). http://journalofdigitalhumanities.org/1–2/archives-in-context-and-as -context-by-kate-theimer/.

Trumpener, Katie. "Paratext and Genre System: A Response to Franco Moretti." *Critical Inquiry* 36, no. 1 (2009): 159–71.

Tunkelang, Daniel. *Faceted Search.* San Rafael, Calif.: Morgan & Claypool, 2009.

Series Introduction and Editors' Note

MATTHEW K. GOLD AND LAUREN F. KLEIN

Debates in the Digital Humanities 2016 marks the start of a new book series from the University of Minnesota Press. Building on the first edition of *Debates in the Digital Humanities* (2012), the series will explore the most compelling debates in the field as they emerge. As digital humanities (DH) scholars and practitioners, along with their critics, continue to articulate the field, *Debates in the Digital Humanities* will track the issues and tensions at stake in their discussions of methods, practices, theories, controversies, projects, and politics.

Central to the vision of the series is the DH annual, a book-length publication highlighting the particular debates that have shaped the field in a given year, to be published in both interactive online and traditional print forms. The annual publication cycle will ensure time for review, reflection, and revision, while also allowing authors and readers to see the release of publications along a more rapid scholarly timeline. By identifying key issues as they unfold and by offering a hybrid model of open-access publication, the series will articulate the present contours of the field and help to shape its future.

Debates in and around the digital humanities often take place across multiple networks and platforms; in a matter of days, or even hours, initial provocations can transform into deep discussions that engage a substantial portion of the DH community. An idea presented as a blog post or published in a journal article might be challenged on Twitter or Facebook—or, as is often the case, the other way around. Indeed, the field has long defined itself by the strength of its social media presence and by the intensity of its engagement with emerging issues and ideas. But to those outside of DH, or even to those offline for a single day, the full scope of any particular discussion can be difficult to determine after the fact.

For these reasons, the annual volumes will follow the model established by the first *Debates* book, pairing full-length scholarly essays with shorter pieces drawn from DH blogs and conference presentations, as well as commissioned interviews and position statements. We view this "gray literature," as it is termed, as central to the articulation of the field. Highlighting the range of work that has influenced the field during that calendar year, the annual volume will document both the work itself and its position within the larger constellation of field-level debates.

This attention to conversations across networked spaces is reflected in our publishing model, as the volumes will be published simultaneously in print, ebook, and interactive webtext formats. This last format is of particular note, since the creation of the first interactive open-access webtext version of *Debates in the Digital Humanities* has led the University of Minnesota Press, in partnership with the CUNY Graduate Center and through the sponsorship of the Andrew W. Mellon Foundation, to develop a new platform and mode of publishing called Manifold Scholarship. Focusing on "iterative editions," the platform will, like *Debates in the Digital Humanities,* seek to trace ideas as they evolve across the varied networked environments of scholarly communication.

As in the first volume of *Debates in the Digital Humanities*, the 2016 edition underwent a composite process of peer and editorial review. In an initial phase of peer-to-peer review, contributors to the volume reviewed one another's work on a private WordPress/CommentPress website, garnering 651 substantive comments. While this process was not fully public, it nevertheless brought together the work of all contributors in a single space, allowing them to view and review the contents of the collection at an early phase. First-pass revisions were then put through extensive editorial review and revised again. As noted in the introduction to the first volume of *Debates,* this public/private peer-to-peer review process knit together the many contributions to the volume, creating intersecting lines of inquiry and citation.

In addition to the DH annual, the *Debates in the Digital Humanities* series will include special volumes on topics that warrant extended treatment. Projects in progress include volumes on critical making in the humanities; feminist debates in the digital humanities; and global digital humanities, with others to follow. Readers interested in contributing to these collections or to the annual volumes of *Debates in the Digital Humanities* should consult the CFP section of the project website, viewable at: http://dhdebates.gc.cuny.edu/.

The editors wish to thank the authors of the essays included in this book for contributing their work to the collection. Operating under extremely tight deadlines, and responding with remarkable patience, industry, and care to a demanding editorial review process, they have exemplified the best qualities of the academy in their collegiality, rigor, and goodwill. We are grateful to them for entrusting us with their scholarship, the excellence of which is on display throughout this volume.

We also thank our colleagues at the University of Minnesota Press for making this series possible and for partnering with us on a project that has tested the limits of every editorial and production mechanism in the building. Special thanks are due to Doug Armato, Director of the Press, whose crystalline editorial vision has been central to the creation and development of the series since its inception, and to Danielle Kasprzak, Humanities Editor, who has guided this volume to completion. We thank the Production Department at the Press, including Daniel Ochsner and Mike Stoffel, for making this publication possible on an accelerated schedule.

Our institutions, The Graduate Center, CUNY and the Georgia Institute of Technology, supported our work on this project in numerous and indispensible ways; in particular, we wish to thank Chase F. Robinson, Louise Lennihan, Don

Robotham, Mario DiGangi, Jacqueline Jones Royster, and Richard Utz for their support. At the Graduate Center, CUNY, we wish to thank Andrew T. Dunn, a doctoral candidate in English, for his exemplary work as our editorial assistant. But our deepest thanks go to our partners, Liza and Greg, and to our children, Felix, Oliver, and Loie, who supported us through every stage of this process. We are so glad to be able to spend time with you again . . . until the preparations for *Debates in the Digital Humanities* 2017 begin in a few months.

Contributors

MOYA BAILEY is a postdoctoral scholar of women's studies and digital humanities at Northeastern University. Her work focuses on marginalized groups' use of digital media to promote social justice as acts of self-affirmation and health promotion.

FIONA BARNETT is completing her PhD at Duke University in the Literature and Women's Studies Program. Her dissertation is *Bodies of Evidence: Postmortem Technologies of Race and Gender,* and her work is grounded in feminist theory, visual studies, and the digital humanities. She is also the director of HASTAC Scholars, an annual fellowship program for innovative students engaged in interdisciplinary projects, and is an active member of FemTechNet.

MATTHEW BATTLES is associate director of metaLAB at Harvard, a research group at the Berkman Center for Internet and Society. His books include *Library: An Unquiet History* and *Palimpsest: A History of the Written Word.*

JEFFREY M. BINDER is a PhD student in the English department at the Graduate Center, City University of New York. He teaches literature at Hunter College.

ZACH BLAS is an artist and writer whose work engages technology, queerness, and politics. He is lecturer in Visual Cultures at Goldsmiths, University of London.

CAMERON BLEVINS is an Andrew Mellon Postdoctoral Fellow at Rutgers University and received his PhD from Stanford University in 2015.

SHEILA A. BRENNAN is director of strategic initiatives at the Roy Rosenzweig Center for History and New Media and research associate professor in the Department of History and Art History at George Mason University. She is codirector of *Histories of the National Mall.*

TIMOTHY BURKE is a professor of history at Swarthmore College. His specialty is modern African history. He is author of *Lifebuoy Men, Lux Women: Commodification, Consumption, and Cleanliness in Modern Zimbabwe* and the coauthor of *Saturday Morning Fever: Growing Up with Cartoon Culture.*

RACHEL SAGNER BUURMA is associate professor of English literature at Swarthmore College, where she works on Victorian literature and culture, the history of the novel, and the relation between literature and information science. Along with Jon Shaw, she codirects the Early Novels Database.

MICHA CÁRDENAS is an artist/theorist who creates and studies trans of color movement in digital media, where movement includes migration, performance, and mobility. cárdenas is assistant professor of interactive media design at the University of Washington, Bothell.

WENDY HUI KYONG CHUN is professor and chair of Modern Culture and Media at Brown University. She has studied both systems design engineering and English literature, which she combines and mutates in her current work on digital media. She is author of *Control and Freedom: Power and Paranoia in the Age of Fiber Optics* and *Programmed Visions: Software and Memory.*

TANYA E. CLEMENT is assistant professor in the School of Information at the University of Texas at Austin. She has a PhD in English literature and language and an MFA in fiction. She has published on sound studies and DH, digital literacies and pedagogy in DH, and text mining and DH as well as feminist inquiry in information studies, data mining, and modernist literature in *Digital Humanities Quarterly, Information & Culture, Journal of the Text Encoding Initiative, Literary and Linguistic Computing,* and *Texas Studies in Literature and Language.*

ANNE CONG-HUYEN is digital scholar at Whittier College's Digital Liberal Arts Center and a former Mellon Postdoctoral Fellow in the Humanities and visiting assistant professor of Asian American studies at the University of California, Los Angeles. Her research interests include the literature and media of migration and labor, Asian American studies, globalization and neoliberalism, postcolonial studies, and transnationalism.

RYAN CORDELL is assistant professor of English at Northeastern University and a founding core faculty member of NULab for Texts, Maps, and Networks.

TRESSIE McMILLAN COTTOM is assistant professor of sociology at Virginia Commonwealth University. She is a faculty associate at the Berkman Center for Internet and Society at Harvard University and the author of *Lower Ed: How For-Profit Colleges Deepen Inequality.* She is a contributing editor at *Dissent.*

AMY E. EARHART is associate professor of English at Texas A&M University. She is the author of *Traces of the Old, Uses of the New: The Emergence of Digital Literary Studies* and coeditor of *The American Literature Scholar in the Digital Age.*

DOMENICO FIORMONTE is lecturer in sociology of communication and culture at the Department of Political Sciences, University of Roma Tre (Italy), where he has taught courses on communication theory, composition, new media, humanities computing, and digital philology. He is the author of *Scrittura e filologia nell'era digitale.*

PAUL FYFE is associate professor at North Carolina State University in the English department and the Communication, Rhetoric, and Digital Media Program. He is also an Andrew W. Mellon Fellow in Critical Bibliography at Rare Book School. He is the author of *By Accident or Design: Writing the Victorian Metropolis.*

JACOB GABOURY is assistant professor of digital media and visual culture in the Department of Cultural Analysis and Theory at Stony Brook University.

KIM GALLON is assistant professor of history at Purdue University. She is director of the Black Press Research Collective and the Black Press Born-Digital Project.

ALEX GIL is digital scholarship coordinator for the Humanities and History Division at Columbia University and one of the founders of the Studio@Butler, a technology atelier for faculty, students, and librarians.

MATTHEW K. GOLD is associate professor of English and digital humanities at the Graduate Center of the City University of New York. His collaborative digital humanities projects include the CUNY Academic Commons, Looking for Whitman, Commons In A Box, Social Paper, DH Box, and Manifold Scholarship. He edited *Debates in the Digital Humanities* (Minnesota, 2012) and, with Lauren F. Klein, coedits the Debates in the Digital Humanities book series.

BRIAN GREENSPAN is associate professor in the Department of English and the doctoral program in Cultural Mediations at Carleton University. He is founding director of the Hyperlab, Carleton's first digital humanities research center, cofounder of the Digital Rhetorics and Ethics Lab, and champion of Carleton's Collaborative MA and BA (minor) programs in digital humanities.

RICHARD GRUSIN is a professor of English and director of the Center for 21st Century Studies at the University of Wisconsin, Milwaukee. He is the author of *Culture, Technology, and the Creation of America's National Parks* and editor of *The Nonhuman Turn* (Minnesota, 2015).

MICHAEL HANCHER, professor of English at the University of Minnesota, has written on Victorian writers and artists; intention and interpretation, speech-act theory, pragmatics, and the law; and the history and rationale of pictorial illustration in dictionaries.

MOLLY O'HAGAN HARDY received her PhD in English from the University of Texas at Austin. She is the digital humanities curator at the American Antiquarian Society in Worcester, Massachusetts. Her research examines debates around literary property and race in the eighteenth-century transatlantic world.

DAVID L. HOOVER is professor of English at New York University. His publications include *Digital Literary Studies: Corpus Approaches to Poetry, Prose, and Drama*, with Jonathan Culpeper and Kieran O'Halloran, and "Text Analysis," in Ken Price and Ray Siemens, editors, *Literary Studies in the Digital Age: An Anthology*.

WENDY F. HSU is a researcher, strategist, and educator who engages with hybrid research and organizing agendas to examine the cultural dimensions of arts, technology, and civic experience. She has published on digital ethnography, sound-based pedagogy, Asian American indie rock, Yoko Ono, Taqwacore, and Bollywood.

PATRICK JAGODA is assistant professor of English and an affiliate of cinema and media studies at the University of Chicago. He is coeditor of *Critical Inquiry* and cofounder of the Game Changer Chicago Design Lab. His first monograph, *Network Aesthetics,* is forthcoming.

JESSICA MARIE JOHNSON is assistant professor of history at Michigan State University. In 2008 she founded African Diaspora, PhD, a blog highlighting scholarship of Atlantic African diaspora history.

STEVEN E. JONES is professor of English and director of the Center for Textual Studies and Digital Humanities at Loyola University, Chicago. He is the author of a number of books, including *The Emergence of the Digital Humanities.*

LAUREN F. KLEIN is assistant professor in the School of Literature, Media, and Communication at Georgia Tech, where she also directs the Digital Humanities Lab. With Matthew K. Gold, she coedits the Debates in the Digital Humanities book series.

ANNA TIONE LEVINE is media associate at the Folger Shakespeare Library, where she works on Folger-supported digital humanities projects.

MARGARET LINLEY is associate professor of English at Simon Fraser University. She has published on Victorian poetry, literary annuals, and Victorian print culture and media history. She is coeditor of *Media, Technology, and Literature in the Nineteenth Century: Image, Sound, Touch.*

ALAN LIU is a professor of English at the University of California, Santa Barbara. His books include *Wordsworth: The Sense of History*; *The Laws of Cool: Knowledge Work and the Culture of Information*; and *Local Transcendence: Essays on Postmodern Historicism and the Database.*

ELIZABETH LOSH is associate professor of English and American studies at the College of William and Mary. She is author of *The War on Learning: Gaining Ground in the Digital University* and *Virtualpolitik.*

ALEXIS LOTHIAN is assistant professor of women's studies and member of the core faculty in the interdisciplinary Design | Cultures & Creativity Honors Program at University of Maryland College Park. Her work focuses on the intersections of digital media, speculative fiction, and social justice movements and has been published in *International Journal of Cultural Studies, Cinema Journal, Camera Obscura, Social Text Periscope, Journal of Digital Humanities, Extrapolation,* and by the feminist science fiction publisher Aqueduct Press.

MICHAEL MAIZELS is the Mellon Curator of New Media Art at the Davis Museum at Wellesley College and a fellow at Harvard University's metaLAB. He is author of *Barry Le Va: The Aesthetic Aftermath* (Minnesota, 2015).

MARK C. MARINO is an author and scholar of digital literature. His works include "Marginalia in the Library of Babel," "a show of hands," "Living Will," and a collection of interactive children's stories called "Mrs. Wobbles and the Tangerine House." He is associate professor (teaching) of writing at the University of Southern California, where he directs the Humanities and Critical Code Studies (HaCCS) Lab.

ANNE B. MCGRAIL teaches writing and literature at Lane Community College. In 2013 she was project director for an NEH Digital Humanities Start-Up Grant for "Bringing Digital Humanities to the Community College and Vice Versa." In summer 2015 she was project director for an NEH Advanced Topics in Digital Humanities Summer Institute for community college faculty.

BETHANY NOWVISKIE directs the nonprofit Digital Library Federation at CLIR, the Council on Library and Information Resources, and is research associate professor of digital humanities in the Department of English at the University of Virginia.

JULIANNE NYHAN is senior lecturer (associate professor) in digital information studies in the Department of Information Studies, University College London. Her research interests are the history of computing in the humanities and digital humanities. Her publications include the coedited *Digital Humanities in Practice*; *Digital Humanities: A Reader*; and *Clerics, Kings, and Vikings: Essays on Medieval Ireland*.

AMANDA PHILLIPS is the IMMERSE Postdoctoral Fellow at the University of California, Davis. Her research unites platform and software studies approaches with feminist, queer, and critical race theory, investigating specific video game design practices to understand how difference is produced and policed in gaming communities.

MIRIAM POSNER is the digital humanities program coordinator and a member of the core DH faculty at the University of California, Los Angeles. A film and media scholar by training, she frequently writes on the history of science and technology. She is a member of the executive council of the Association for Computers and the Humanities.

RITA RALEY is associate professor of English at the University of California, Santa Barbara. She is author of *Tactical Media* (Minnesota, 2009) and coeditor of the *Electronics Literature Collection,* Volume 2.

STEPHEN RAMSAY is Susan J. Rosowski Associate University Professor of English at the University of Nebraska–Lincoln and a fellow at the Center for Digital Research in the Humanities. He is the author of *Reading Machines: Toward an Algorithmic Criticism*.

MARGARET RHEE received her PhD from the University of California, Berkeley in ethnic studies with a designated emphasis in new media studies. She is visiting assistant professor in women's and gender studies at the University of Oregon. She lives in Eugene and Los Angeles.

LISA MARIE RHODY, previously associate director of research projects at the Roy Rosenzweig Center for History and New Media at George Mason University, is now at the CUNY Graduate Center as deputy director of Digital Initiatives. Her scholarly interests span contemporary poetry, topic modeling, data visualization, and scholarly communication.

ROOPIKA RISAM is assistant professor of English and English education at Salem State University. Her research examines the intersections of postcolonial, African American, and U.S. ethnic literatures and the role of digital humanities in mediating between them.

STEPHEN ROBERTSON is director of the Roy Rosenzweig Center for History and New Media and professor in the Department of History and Art History at George Mason University. He is one of the creators of the site Digital Harlem: Everyday Life, 1915–1930 (digitalharlem.org).

MARK SAMPLE is associate professor of digital studies at Davidson College. His teaching and research focuses on contemporary literature, new media, and video games. His examination of the representation of torture in video games appeared in *Game Studies*.

JENTERY SAYERS is assistant professor of English and cultural, social, and political thought, as well as director of the Maker Lab in the Humanities, at the University of Victoria. He works at the intersections of comparative media studies and digital humanities.

BENJAMIN M. SCHMIDT is assistant professor of history at Northeastern University and a member of the core faculty at the NULab for Texts, Maps, and Networks. His research interests are in the digital humanities and the intellectual and cultural history of the United States in the nineteenth and twentieth centuries.

SCOTT SELISKER is assistant professor of English at the University of Arizona. He is author of *Human Programming: Brainwashing, Automatons, and American Unfreedom* (Minnesota, 2016).

JONATHAN SENCHYNE is assistant professor of library and information studies and associate director of the Center for the History of Print and Digital Culture at the University of Wisconsin, Madison. His essays on the materiality of early American print culture appear in *Early African American Print Culture* and *Book History*. His research has been supported by fellowships from the National Endowment for the Humanities, the American Antiquarian Society, and the New York Public Library.

ANDREW STAUFFER is associate professor of English at the University of Virginia, where he directs the digital scholarly initiative NINES (http://nines.org), teaches in the Rare Book School, and directs the Book Traces project (http://booktraces.org). He is the author of *Anger, Revolution, and Romanticism* and the editor of works by H. Rider Haggard and Robert Browning.

JOANNA SWAFFORD is assistant professor of English at SUNY New Paltz, specializing in Victorian literature and culture, digital humanities, sound, and gender studies. Her book project, "Transgressive Tunes and the Gendered Music of Victorian Poetry," traces the gendered intermediations of poetry and music.

TONIESHA L. TAYLOR is associate professor in the Department of Languages and Communication at Prairie View A&M University. Her research focuses on African American, religious, intercultural, gender, and popular culture communications.

DENNIS TENEN pursues research at the intersection of people, texts, and technology. His recent work appears in *Computational Culture, boundary 2*, and *Modernism/Modernity* on topics that range from book piracy to algorithmic composition, unintelligent design, and the history of data visualization.

MELISSA TERRAS is director of the University College London Centre for Digital Humanities, a professor of digital humanities in UCL's Department of Information Studies, and vice dean of research in UCL's Faculty of Arts and Humanities. Her research focuses on computational techniques to enable research in the arts and humanities that would otherwise be impossible.

TED UNDERWOOD is a professor of English at the University of Illinois, Urbana-Champaign, and the author of *Why Literary Periods Mattered*.

ETHAN WATRALL is assistant professor in the Department of Anthropology and associate director of MATRIX: The Center for Digital Humanities & Social Sciences at Michigan State University. His primary research interests are publicly engaged digital archaeology and digital heritage.

JACQUELINE WERNIMONT is assistant professor of English at Arizona State University, specializing in literary history, feminist digital media, histories of quantification, and technologies of commemoration. She is a fellow of the Lincoln Center for Applied Ethics and an active part of the FemTechNet collective.

LAURA WEXLER is professor of American studies and women's, gender, and sexuality studies at Yale University, where she is cochair of the Public Humanities Program, director of the Photographic Memory Workshop, and principal investigator of the Photogrammar Project.

HONG-AN WU is a Taiwanese doctoral student in art education at the University of Illinois, Urbana-Champaign. Wu's research investigates the intersection of art education and new media, with an emphasis on video gaming, through the lens of cultural studies, feminist studies, and critical Internet studies.